# MACMILLAN ANTHOLOGIES OF ENGLISH LITERATURE



*General Editors:*

A. Norman Jeffares, formerly Professor of English, University of Stirling

Michael Alexander, Berry Professor of English Literature, University of St Andrews

MACMILLAN ANTHOLOGIES
OF ENGLISH LITERATURE

Volume 1 THE MIDDLE AGES (700–1550)
Michael Alexander and Felicity Riddy

Volume 2 THE RENAISSANCE (1550–1660)
Gordon Campbell

Volume 3 THE RESTORATION AND
EIGHTEENTH CENTURY (1660–1798)
Ian McGowan

Volume 4 THE NINETEENTH CENTURY (1798–1900)
Brian Martin

Volume 5 THE TWENTIETH CENTURY (1900–present)
Neil McEwan

MACMILLAN ANTHOLOGIES
OF ENGLISH LITERATURE

# THE RESTORATION AND EIGHTEENTH CENTURY

*Edited by*
*Ian McGowan*

MACMILLAN

First published 1989

Published by
MACMILLAN EDUCATION LTD
Houndmills, Basingstoke, Hampshire RG21 2XS
and London
Companies and representatives
throughout the world

Typeset by Wessex Typesetters
(Division of The Eastern Press Ltd)
Frome, Somerset

Printed in Hong Kong

British Library Cataloguing in Publication Data
Macmillan anthologies of English literature
Vol. 3: The Restoration and eighteenth century
1. English literature—Anthologies
I. McGowan, Ian
820.8
ISBN 0–333–39271–X
ISBN 0–333–46478–8 Pbk

# Contents

# Acknowledgements

For support and encouragement I owe thanks to my mother, Helena Burgoyne, Felicity Riddy and Felicity McGowan; and for typing to Mamie Prentice and Yvonne McClymont.

IMcG

The author and publishers wish to thank the following publishers for permission to use copyright material: **John Aubrey**, for an extract from *Brief Lives*, ed. A. Powell (Cresset Press, 1949), pp. 52–3, by permission of Century Hutchinson; **James Boswell**, for an extract from *Boswell's London Journal 1762–1763*, ed. F. A. Pottle (1950), pp. 135–41, *The Yale Editions of the Private Papers of James Boswell*, by permission of William Heinemann and Yale University; **William Congreve**, for an extract from *The Way of the World*, ed. Gibbons (1971), pp. 72–82, New Mermaid Edition. Copyright © Ernest Benn Ltd, by permission of A. & C. Black; **William Dampier**, for an extract from *The Scientific Background*, eds A. N. Jeffares and M. B. Davies (1958), pp. 194–6, by permission of Pitman Publishing; **Edward Gibbon**, for extracts from Edward Gibbon manuscripts included in *Memoirs of My Life*, ed. G. A. Bonnard (Nelson, 1966), by permission of John Murray; **Samuel Johnson**, for extracts from *Diaries, Prayers, and Annuals*, ed. W. L. McAdam, Jr, with Donald and Mary Hyde (1958), 1967, pp. 81–2, 264, by permission of Yale University Press; **Samuel Pepys**, for extracts from *The Diary of Samuel Pepys Vol. VII*, eds R. Latham and W. Matthews (G. Bell, 1972), pp. 267–72, 276–7, by permission of Unwin Hyman; **Alexander Pope**, for extracts from *The Poems of Alexander Pope*, ed. J. Butt (1963), by permission of Methuen & Co.; **Joshua Reynolds**, for extracts from *Discourses on Art*, ed. R. R. Wark (1959, 1975), pp. 42–5, 123–5, 191–3, by permission of Yale University Press; **Adam Smith**, for an extract from *The Scientific Background*, eds A. N. Jeffares and M. B. Davies (1958), pp. 130–1, by permission of Pitman Publishing; **Thomas Sprat**, for an extract from *The Scientific Background*, eds A. N. Jeffares and M. B. Davies (1958), p. 22, by permission of Pitman Publishing.

Every effort has been made to trace all the copyright holders, but if any have been inadvertently overlooked the publisher will be pleased to make the necessary arrangement at the first opportunity.

# General Introduction

There can often be a gulf between the restricted reading required by a school, college or university syllabus and the great expanse of English literature which is there to be explored and enjoyed. There are two effective ways of bridging that gulf. One is to be aware of how authors relate or have related to their contemporary situations and their contemporaries, how they accept, develop or react against what has been written by their predecessors or older contemporaries, how, in short, they fit into the long history of English literature. Good histories of literature – and there is a welcome increase of interest in them – serve to place authors in their contexts, as well as giving a panoptic view of their careers.

The second way is to sample their work, to discover the kind or kinds of writing they have produced. Here is where the anthology contributes to an enjoyment of reading. It conveys the flavour of an author as nothing but reading that author can. And when an author is compared to his or her fellow writers – a thing a good anthology facilitates – the reader gains several extra dimensions, not least an insight into what thoughts, what fears, what delights have occupied writers at different times. To gain such insights is to see, among other things, the relevance of past authors to the present, to the reader. Reading an anthology shows something of the vast range of our literature, its variety of form and outlook, of mood and expression, from black despair to ecstatic happiness; it is an expansive experience widening our horizons, enhancing specialised study, but also conveying its own particular pleasures, the joy of finding familiar pieces among unfamiliar, of reacting to fresh stimuli, of reaching new conclusions about authors, in short, of making literature a part of oneself.

Anthologies also play a large part in the life of a literature. If we are the beneficiaries of our literary inheritance, we are also trustees for it, and the maintenance of the inheritance for future generations requires new selections of properly edited texts. The Macmillan Literary Anthologies, which have followed on from the Macmillan Histories of Literature, are designed to present these texts with the essential pertinent information. The selection made of poetry, prose and plays has been wide and inclusive, authors appear in the order of their dates of birth, texts – with the exception of the Middle English section – are modernised and footnotes are kept to a minimum. A broadly representative policy has been the aim of the general editors, who have maintained a similar format and proportion in each volume, though the medieval volume has required more annotation.

MJA
ANJ

# Introduction: The Restoration and Eighteenth Century

Literary and political histories traditionally take the Restoration of the Stuart monarchy in 1660 as a convenient starting point; but that event marked neither a turning-back of the clock nor an abrupt break with the nation's past, as elements of the old coexisted with the new in the social and intellectual spheres. In 1798 Britain remained a mainly agricultural society. Its population had, however, doubled during the previous 150 years to about 9 million; London, always the largest and most influential concentration, was nearing 1 million, ten times the size of any rival city. But shifts in the economic life of the country, partly brought about by foreign trade, economic 'improvements' and growing industrialisation, had led to five English cities having populations over 50,000. These were Manchester, Liverpool, Birmingham, Bristol and Leeds – trading ports of the West, and manufacturing towns of the Midlands and North, which had outstripped traditional centres such as Norwich, York or Oxford.

The Restoration of Charles II was hailed as bringing stability after the political, economic and religious tensions of the earlier seventeenth century, which had led to the Civil War (1642–8), the execution of Charles I, and the Cromwellian Protectorate. Within three decades, however, renewed struggles had forced the flight of the Catholic James II, in 1688, ahead of the accession of the Dutchman William of Orange. Following the death of Queen Anne, the last Stuart monarch, in 1714, the introduction of the continental Protestant Hanoverians proved ultimately to have established the succession, which survived the challenges of Jacobite rebellions in 1715 and 1745; three Georges reigned from 1714 to 1820. The king continued to govern through his ministers, whose success from the age of Walpole onwards (1721–42) greatly relied on management of the House of Commons, which represented primarily the interests of the landed and moneyed minorities of the population. If, by the end of the period, American independence and the Revolution of 1789 in France were symptoms of widespread demands for the extension of influence in a nation's affairs and a wider sharing of its prosperity among the population, in Britain one immediate consequence of the wars against Revolutionary France, which only ended in 1815 at Waterloo, was domestic political repression.

By the end of the period covered by this anthology, Britain had clearly grown through military conquest and commerce to the status of a major power, with interests in North America, the West Indies, the Indian subcontinent, and Australia. If these depended in part on exploitation of natural resources and indigenous populations, on force, importation of slaves or transportation of convicts, the moral implications seem to have had less effect than the sense of Britain's growing standing in the world. This, together with the comparative political and religious order of the eighteenth century which was partly its cause, contributed to a cultural self-confidence which allowed native writers to see themselves as extending traditional forms and creating new. A theoretical respect for the conventions of continental neo-classicism was rarely allowed to stand in the way of innovation.

## *Religion and Ideas*

Especially in the first half of our period, many tensions sprang from differences in religious belief and external form. The established Church of England attempted in the later seventeenth century to steer its way between the alleged superstition, authoritarianism and foreign sympathies of Roman Catholics, and the anti-social individualism and republicanism charged against dissenters, both groups being effectively excluded from aspects of public life and subjected to penalties by the Anglican Test Act of 1673. The strength of the religio-political issues is easily identified here in the writings, from different points of view, of Bunyan, Butler, Dryden and Swift. Although there were no political parties in the modern sense, the century's closing decades saw the groupings of Tories – supporters of the king and established church, landed gentlemen, conservative clergy – and Whigs – rich aristocrats, the rising city middle class of traders and money-men, individual Anglicans and dissenters. (The significance of the church as a career, and the importance of political influence in the distribution of offices, should never be forgotten: the lives of Swift, Sterne and Crabbe emphasise literature's debt to the established church.) Even when the fury of the seventeenth-century religious debate had cooled, the legal position of Alexander Pope as a Catholic 'outsider', and the intensity of emotion in Johnson, Smart or Cowper remind us of the different effects religion continued to have in people's lives: in practice, the disabilities of various groups were somewhat moderated, while the real threat to true religion came to be seen in the indifference of the masses, or the intellectual challenges of the philosophers.

Partly in reaction against the hair-splitting religious controversies, there was by the end of the seventeenth century a recoil from fanatical 'enthusiasm' in favour of a more sober, rational and socially agreed attitude to religion, with a sense of its practical human value. Eighteenth-century philosophers such as Berkeley and Hume continued the process of investigating the limits of human knowledge reported by our senses, and the consequences for religious faith. Locke had said in his *Essay Concerning Human Understanding* (1690) that 'Our business here is not to know all things, but those which concern our conduct'. By the middle of the following century we find in the heroes of Fielding or the sentimental novel exemplars of natural benevolence in which charitable conduct to one's neighbour is not only morally right but a source of pleasure to the self. This increasing emphasis on feeling, paralleled in poetry and drama, also found expression in the Methodist revival, initially within the Anglican church, in which, to the delight of the satirists (see Smollett), much stress was laid on awakening the heart in even the lowest classes. Concurrent with the development of philosophical scepticism was the rise of physical science, encouraged by the Royal Society, to which Charles II gave a charter in 1662 and which included such poets as Cowley and Dryden among its numbers. The rise of the scientific method of investigation actually strengthened certain kinds of religious belief, as it revealed a universe operating to the Newtonian laws of physics, which implied the benevolent harmony of a Creator: this unmysterious attitude, with few specific doctrines and a lowered valuation of God's revelation to man in the Bible, was known as Deism. Such works as Pope's *Essay on Man* show the influence of the new science and philosophy.

Some awareness of the religious and political background is necessary in this period not merely because the imaginative writing reflected live issues as it will in any age, but also because the writers themselves were not for the most part men in retirement from the world, or yet fully professional authors. A glance at the headnotes will show how many had careers in the church or in politics: among later MPs were Horace Walpole, Gibbon and Burke. In the period from the Restoration to the fall of Robert Walpole in 1742, the partisan activity of writers was intense: their imaginative independence does not negate the political engagement of Dryden's *Absalom and Achitophel*, Swift's *Gulliver's Travels*, Pope's *Imitations of Horace*, Gay's *Beggar's Opera* and Fielding's satirical plays. (Despite the Whig sympathies of Addison and Steele, the association of Swift, Pope, Arbuthnot and other wits of the Scriblerus Club with the ruling Tory Party until the death of Queen Anne in 1714, and their opposition to the long domination of Walpole, ensured that the Tories had most of the best tunes.)

Indeed, much of the finest literature of this period owes its strength to this aspect of its engagement: the writer is not in retreat, but participating in or actively criticising the public life of his society, whose tensions he dramatises imaginatively; he knows the ways of the world (or that part of it which interests the limited reading public) and embodies them in forms which are publicly accessible. In the period before 1700, the witty, cynical Restoration comedies of Etherege, Wycherley and Congreve hold the mirror to the amorality of the tiny fashionable world while exploiting the shared nature of the drama: their comedy is a public act in which deviations from agreed social and moral standards are identified. The great satires of Dryden, Swift and Pope appeal to public scrutiny of public behaviour, whether in religion, politics, 'society', or the arts: it is appropriate that this is the great age of satire, which takes its stand not on the assertion of private emotion, but on the appeal to an argued case and the test of traditional, socially-tempered standards. It is entirely characteristic that the form which is the age's lasting contribution – the novel – though often concerned with the fate of the individual, regularly places him in a solidly realised social environment. (Compare the social reconciliations implicit in the Spectator's Club created by Addison and Steele after the previous century's divisions.) There is no contradiction between an author's awareness of this role and his personal commitment or individual voice.

## *'Augustanism'*

The return of the Court from France in 1660 reinforced changes in literature which were already under way in England: as in religion and politics, there was a reaction against the more extravagant heights of metaphysical wit (to which Dryden gave the name), against quaint images and rugged rhythms, while the spacious and figurative prose of the great preachers such as Donne, and learned authors such as Burton (*Anatomy of Melancholy*, 1621), was held insufficiently functional for the communication of new facts and ideas: the Royal Society commended a compact, unadorned style. This, with altered emphasis, also suited the desire for a style for gentlemanly intercourse, whether in essays, letters or discursive writing: Dryden's criticism and the *Spectator* essays are models of what poise and restraint could achieve; the comedies of the period were natural vehicles of well-bred wit; and the style extends, though often with ironic sharpness, into Swift and Fielding. By the later eighteenth century, both the expansion of the audience and some shifts in sensibility are reflected in the grander elaborations of Burke's oratory, Gibbon's history, and Johnson's Latinate style, in which the formal rhetoric has moved well away from the needs of one gentleman addressing another.

In poetry, the Restoration reforms were perhaps more easily identified: Johnson's 'Life of Cowley' lays the charges against the metaphysicals; in Dryden and Pope he traces the triumph of the new manner. 'Augustan', like 'Romantic', is a term now used with suspicion, but it draws attention to the awareness of at least some Restoration men of the parallels between their own situation, writing for a restored court after decades of turmoil, and that of the great Roman poets Virgil and Horace, encouraged in the flowering of the arts under the Emperor Augustus after the Roman civil war of the first century BC: the elegant, allusive craftsmanship seemed to offer stylistic as well as political pointers. In an essay of 1759, 'An Account of the Augustan Age in England', Goldsmith placed it as culminating in the reign of Queen Anne. Reinforced by French influence, the creative and critical ambition was for clearly-moulded and accessible forms, for an inventiveness whose imaginative expression was disciplined by judgement, and by decorum – language appropriate to the form and to the nature of the communication. Thus, in the hierarchy of genres inherited from classical literature, epic ranked highest among the poetic forms, being a long narrative of heroic deeds, often military, related in an elevated diction with elaborate figures of speech; satire, by contrast, dealt with less salubrious characters, and might require more colloquial language. In drama the ancient distinction between the action of tragedy (the province of leaders) and comedy was reinforced by linguistic differentiation. The writer's craft therefore consisted partly in the adaptation of style to subject-matter to produce a congruous effect unless, as in the 'mock' forms of Pope or Gay, an ironic effect was sought. When Johnson in his 'Life of Cowley' discusses Pope's famous definition of wit – 'nature to advantage dressed, / What oft was thought, but ne'er so well expressed' (*Essay on Criticism* 297–8) – he is insisting on the testing of literature by one of the period's crucial but difficult words – 'nature', which normally refers not so much to the external physical world (of whose beauties people were well aware) as to human nature, and particularly the permanent aspects of human experience: the neo-classical thinker believed these underpinned the view that, despite local diversities of time, place and custom, human nature was, in essence, always and everywhere the same. This being so, it is neither the business of the poet, as Johnson's Imlac says, to 'number the streaks of the tulip', nor, as his condemnation of the metaphysicals implies, to strive for originality of experience and perverse individuality of expression: 'originality' will not necessarily be a term of praise. The poet's (and by extension the artist's) business is to give expression to those permanent and fundamental truths long discovered; hence the stress on the past, on translation and 'imitation': Pope's *Essay on Criticism* reminds us that Nature and Homer are the same, and that the 'rules' of classical genres are not arbitrary, but grew from the poets' experience. The best literature is therefore usually that which does not shock or startle the reader by its astounding diction or imagery, but seems simultaneously both new and natural: see Johnson's comments on Gray's *Elegy*. (By the later eighteenth century, the old theories were severely weakened: it would be worth examining in the light of this debate Gray's Odes, or Smart, or Macpherson, or Burns; though Crabbe shows the survival of older attitudes.)

## *Writers and Readers*

Who were the writers in this period, and who bought their works? In this context, we are not directly concerned with the kind of writing which was published in ephemeral pamphlets, ballad collections or chapbooks, which have rarely survived: these might sell in tens of thousands at 6d. each. In the mid-eighteenth century, probably less than half of working men (and a smaller proportion of women) could read; their modest purchases would have to be met from a family income of perhaps £1 per week. For this reading public, even novels in two or three volumes at 2s. 6d. or 3s. per volume were likely to be prohibitive in their demands on cash and time: novels by Defoe and

Fielding were thought great successes in selling 4000–6000 copies; poetry and less popular subjects tended to be proportionately more expensive, and to sell perhaps in hundreds. The traditional court and aristocratic patronage of serious literature gradually gave way to a system whereby authors might solicit subscriptions for a forthcoming book from friends and the public or, more commonly, sell their copyrights to bookseller-publishers: although there are examples of substantial earnings – Pope's thousands from his Homers, the hundreds for Fielding's novels, the thousands made in the lucrative field of history by Smollett, Hume, Gibbon and Robertson – these are the exceptions: by the end of the eighteenth century, even with an increased reading public and more accessible forms, very few authors made a good regular living from writing. Few indeed of the major figures would have regarded themselves purely as professional writers; those who were not in politics or the church might have a background of medicine or the law: significant exceptions are Defoe's connections with trade, Richardson's printing business, and Burns's backbreaking acquaintance with a kind of agriculture remote from the great landscape gardeners. By the end of the eighteenth century, the reading public had widened from the few hundreds or thousands able to understand intimately the social allusions of Restoration comedy or the literary ancestry of Pope's Horace; but the average reader of the literature in this volume was still likely to be a relatively prosperous and educated male member of at least the middle class; the average writer here had probably attended one of the great English public schools, or Oxford or Cambridge, or a Scottish university, or Trinity College, Dublin. (Large contributions were made by the Scots – Arbuthnot, Thomson, Smollett, Boswell, Macpherson, Burns, Mackenzie, and the philosophers Smith and Hume – and the Anglo-Irish – Swift, Congreve, Burke, Goldsmith, Sheridan – most of whom had to come to London to make their names. Who but a Scot – Thomson – would have written 'Rule Britannia'?)

## *Drama*

The reopening of the theatres after the Restoration heralded a long period in which drama was regularly performed and enjoyed, whether as the wit of fashionable comedy or the rhymed heroic plays and more compassionate blank-verse tragedies of Dryden. The interest in feeling flowered in the earlier eighteenth century in the sentimental comedies of Cibber and Steele, whose morality came to have a stultifying effect only partly countered by the later 'laughing comedy' of Goldsmith and Sheridan. The drama was also the vehicle for the political comments of Fielding and others until subjected to censorship after the Licensing Act of 1737. It was a period of star actors – dominated after 1741 by the new naturalistic style of Garrick, actor–author–producer – and star actresses, permitted on stage after the Restoration. Shakespeare was frequently performed, though usually in versions that were cut or 'adapted', often in ways quite false to the originals. Through the period, then, theatre and acting may fairly be said to have flourished, with many major figures such as Pope and Johnson trying their hands at plays. Yet no tragedy from the entire period has held its place in the repertoire; and, apart from the cluster of Restoration works, only a handful of eighteenth-century comedies: *The Beggar's Opera*; Goldsmith's *The Good-Natur'd Man* and *She Stoops to Conquer*; Sheridan's *The Rivals*, *The Critic* and *The School for Scandal*. The diversion of talent into novel-writing after the Licensing Act is at best a partial explanation of this curious thinness of achievement. The extracts here from Congreve and Sheridan show something of the comic complexity of plot, the repartee, and the changing explorations of personal values; Gay's multi-layered *Beggar's Opera* is *sui generis*; its topsy-turvy world can be enjoyed without any knowledge of the music or the political context.

## *Fiction*

Most readers will come to eighteenth-century fiction having already encountered Jane Austen and the Victorian classics such as Dickens, the Brontës, George Eliot; for them there is the double pleasure of witnessing the infancy of the genre, and recognising in the early masters the origins of many familiar techniques of narration and characterisation, unencumbered by Victorian 'good taste'.

Given the long dominance of the novel among non-dramatic forms, we may easily forget that the form as we understand it has existed for only some two and a half centuries. Although there had been prose fiction since antiquity, it is clear that the eighteenth century saw the rise of new kinds of subject-matter and style, even though these were not uniform. In *Rambler*, 4 (1750) Johnson distinguished between the traditional romance – associated with remote settings, lofty characters, extravagant adventures – and modern 'familiar histories', in which the appeal is rather to the reader's recognition of the contemporary world. Although Robinson Crusoe on his desert island might seem an exception, his extraordinary adventure is not conducted by Defoe in terms of fantastic monsters or remote impossibilities: the core of the book relies on Crusoe's detailed descriptions of the practical efforts by which he comes to terms with his situation. The kind of novel of which Defoe was master – the retrospective first-person narration – no doubt owed much to existing non-fictional forms such as histories, travels, personal memoirs. Richardson, his successor in the depiction from inside of the struggles of the isolated individual, composed his narratives from his protagonists' letters and journals, again adapting existing forms. This line in the early novel has the capacity to draw us into the characters' dilemmas, to see the world from their points of view and, particularly in Richardson, to live through the instalments of their experiences without knowing the results: the comic possibilities arising from the first-person narrator's struggle with his material were soon richly explored by Sterne in *Tristram Shandy*. That the early novelists did not tamely adopt a uniform manner is easily seen in the contrast between Richardson and Fielding, who in *Joseph Andrews* and *Tom Jones* took the role of informed ironic commentator on the fortunes of his created world. But despite the varieties of technique and the establishment of new conventions, Johnson was right in discerning a common interest in the contemporary world, in people from the middle and lower ranks of life, and in situations which, if not commonplace, were at least plausible. The best explanation for the rise of the novel in this period is that it fulfilled the need of the growing middle class, with increasing education, money and leisure for books, but unwilling to be satisfied with the absurdities of romance or the values of an inherited classical culture, to articulate its own self-assurance and identify its own heroes. (The capacity of the form to explore sympathetically the economic role of women (*Moll Flanders*), their domestic role (Fielding's *Amelia*), and their struggles to choose their own lives (Richardson) made possible the rise of the female novelist, such as Sarah Fielding, Charlotte Lennox and Fanny Burney.) It is perhaps typical that in contrast to the sailor and servant offered by Defoe and Richardson, Fielding should contrive that his protagonists emerge as well-born heirs from their obscure social origins. In Fielding and Smollett, plotting and characterisation from the drama are recognisably transmitted to the nineteenth century: there is much evil and violence, but the prevailing mood is of comedy;

only in Richardson does the novel reach the intensity of tragedy. In the closing decades of the century, changes in taste and in readers' emotional response encourage the minor subgenres of the sentimental novel, as in Mackenzie, and its fellow-traveller in frissons, the gothic novel, from Walpole on, which in period, setting and extravagance of incident returns to the fancy-liberating remoteness foresworn by the major figures earlier: not until Jane Austen returned to the central interests of the novel was their achievement paralleled.

## *Poetry*

If poetry from Dryden to Crabbe seems puzzling, this is often because readers approach it expecting the dramatic flashes of the metaphysicals or the confessional intimacy of the post-Wordsworthians. For the second group in particular, the favoured poetry will be that which seems most to anticipate the Romantics' response to nature, their characteristic isolated introspection: the blank-verse descriptions of Thomson and Cowper, the melancholy of Gray's *Elegy*, seem closer to the heart of the matter than the intensely contemporary reference of the satirists and the snip-snap of the heroic couplet. But this view, though it reflects an eighteenth-century argument conducted by Johnson and the Warton brothers amongst others about the true tradition and future of English poetry, applies false assumptions and blocks off sources of pleasure. It may be salutary to remember that not all was satire, that the topographical blank verse of *The Seasons* is contemporary with *The Dunciad*, *The Castle of Indolence* with *The Vanity of Human Wishes*. There was always a concern to preserve earlier achievements, to keep open the springs of fancy and imagination associated in the minds of the Wartons with the descriptive properties of Milton's minor poems – *Il Penseroso* was influential – with the freer movement of blank verse, with the quaint diction, imagery and complex stanza of Spenser's *Faerie Queene*. This interest in the poetical possibilities of the past is further seen in Addison's *Spectator* essays on ballads, in Gray's interest in Old Norse and Welsh poetry, in Chatterton's medieval fabrications and Macpherson's Gaelic 'translations', and in Percy's collection of old ballads and romances in *Reliques of Ancient English Poetry* (1765). If there are antiquarian curiosities at play, there is also an attraction to the literature of simpler, more primitive societies, less trammelled by the conventions of urban neo-classicism and the traditions of Latin literature, more liberating to the poet's imagination. The argument about the nature and role of poetry and the position of the moderns is implicitly carried on both in the imaginative writing – Pope's Horatian Imitations, Gray's *Bard*, Beattie's *Minstrel*, Collins's *Ode on the Popular Superstitions of the Highlands* – and in the criticism: Burke's *Enquiry* applies the new interest in the sublime to *Paradise Lost*, and is contemporary with Gray's lofty, obscure Pindaric Odes; Thomas Warton's *History* (1774–81) revalued poetry from Chaucer to Spenser, while his brother Joseph's *Essay on Pope* (two volumes, 1756, 1782) placed him in a lower division than the truly sublime and pathetic Shakespeare, Spenser, Milton; Johnson's criticism over forty years applied more conservative standards. (Some aspects of the interest in poetry remote in time or place may be paralleled in the settings of gothic novels, the gothic houses created by Walpole and Beckford, the artificial ruins in landscape gardens, the exoticism of *Vathek*, Percy's first English translation of a Chinese novel, in 1761, and in the vogue for chinoiserie.)

The public nature of much writing in this period has already been discussed: it follows that the best poetry is often concerned with man in his social aspects, in his relationship with political or economic groups; but to take the rarity of the confessional note as a sign of weak emotions is a serious error – it is rather a source of strength for Dryden and Pope to be able to address publicly and urgently themes of shared significance for their readership; passion, albeit highly wrought, is there in plenty. Johnson, whose private papers show amply the personal relevance of hope and disillusion, chose to articulate those themes in the grand manner in *The Vanity of Human Wishes*, speaking partly in the voice of Juvenal to examine them in a series of externalised historical examples. For delicate handlings of the personal in the social, one need only look at Dryden's *To Mr Driden* or Pope's *Epistle to Miss Blount*: grasp of their themes and tones is a fair test of sympathy for the poetry of this period.

Objection is sometimes made to the 'poetic diction' used in certain contexts such as epic or pastoral poetry to extend the suggestiveness of the language by reference to the original Latin sense of words, or by elaborate phrases avoiding everyday diction (Johnson censured 'dun', 'knife', 'peeping through a blanket', in *Macbeth*, I.5.48–52). Thus in Pope's *Windsor Forest*, 139–43 'the scaly breed' are fish, and the eel's 'volumes' are not books but coils. The extent of this diction as compared with other literary periods is often exaggerated. More characteristic is the preference in narrative and satiric verse from Dryden to Crabbe for the heroic couplet (though there are numerous significant uses of blank verse, ballad stanzas, Spenserian stanzas, and the elaborate forms of Pindaric odes). The heroic couplet rhymes iambic pentameters (i.e. ten-syllabled lines) in pairs, each pair often marking a complete unit of thought, within which individual lines or half-lines can parallel each other; the poet can also exploit the 'caesura', or pause in mid-line, and can link words for intensification, by such sound affects as assonance or alliteration: in the *Epistle to Arbuthnot*, Pope imagines Atticus as

> Willing to wound, / and yet afraid to strike,
> Just hint a fault, / and hesitate dislike

where the opposing meanings of the first two half-lines are reinforced by parallel structures; in the first line, the alliteration of 'w' is confined to the first half; in the second line, the 'h' links the two halves. This is part of the traditional craftsmanship expected of the poet, who at best uses it as a means of organising and intensifying his thought. Compare the very different effects encouraged by the blank-verse flow in Milton or Wordsworth.

## *Other Forms*

Our understanding of the social, intellectual and literary background is greatly strengthened by reading in those other forms which flourished in our period. It was an age of great prose-writing, as styles of varying formality and flexibility evolved to meet different needs. In the criticism from Dryden to Johnson, we can trace the development of Shakespeare's reputation and the interest in the true poetic tradition; the periodical essay (*Spectator*, *Rambler*) was the vehicle of literary criticism as well as social and moral instruction. Letter-writing (often with an eye on publication) was a cultivated art: Walpole's great series is a major source. In the hands of Robertson or Gibbon, history was not fact-grubbing but art and elegant discipline. The vivid personal writing of journals (Pepys, Boswell) overlaps with more formal memoir, travels, autobiography and life (Cibber, Gibbon, Johnson, Boswell): these are amongst the most attractive ways of learning about the flesh and blood that gave the imaginative literature its context. In reading Johnson's diaries or Boswell's analysis of his conflicts, we see the tensions of the isolated individual at war with his own melancholy doubts: the headnotes to selections indicate how many writers suffered from mental instability. Yet the case of Johnson also suggests the positive aspect of the writer's position, as spokesman for a tradition, and as part of a social network of culture and public life, of which the famous Club is a symbol. Many of the age's achievements in other arts – painting, music, architecture from the modest villa to Palladian mansion or the large-scale urban developments of Bath and the New Town in Edinburgh – might be examined in this light.

## *This Anthology*

This selection can only begin to point the reader in certain directions by offering either short complete works or extracts from longer prose works in particular. In addition to the pleasure of individual works, he may use them as guides for the volumes of collected poems, other novels or plays by the same authors, and for more extensive collections of the poets. The charms of the miscellaneous, less formal writing also contribute to our understanding of the major authors, who did not work in a vacuum. By setting different kinds of poetry or fiction from the same period against each other, we clarify the choices of technique which authors were making, while a chronological reading reminds us of debts to the Renaissance and earlier seventeenth century, as well as the powerful inheritance transmitted to the nineteenth. A chronological sense also sharpens our awareness of the development of particular kinds of subject-matter (the rise of the middle classes, the presence of landscape) and of attitude (satire, sentimentalism).

Books for most of this period were originally printed with variations in spelling and punctuation from modern norms, and with much greater use of italics and initial capital letters: in this anthology the texts are usually modernised versions of reliable editions. However, the Scots poets Fergusson and Burns, the idiosyncratic Sterne, and the youthful Jane Austen have been allowed in part to retain their distinctive characters.

IMcG

# Note on Annotation and Glossing

An asterisk * at the end of a word indicates that such words are glossed in the margin.

A dagger † at the end of a word or phrase indicates that the word or phrase is annotated, or given a longer gloss, at the foot of the page.

# Note on Dates

Where dates appear at the end of extracts, that on the left denotes the date of composition, that on the right, the date of publication.

# Samuel Butler

## 1613–80

Having been a Justice of the Peace's clerk, and an officer in aristocratic households, Butler won rapid fame with *Hudibras* (1662), which examined some of the attitudes underlying the Civil War and Commonwealth. Further parts followed in 1663 and 1678; Butler also wrote shorter satires and prose *Characters*. Charles II rewarded him financially.

*Hudibras* aims at grotesque satiric effects undercutting the story of the chivalric hero (whose name comes from Spenser's *Faerie Queene*) by the semi-doggerel verse, forced rhymes and mean characters: the knight is a narrow-minded Presbyterian. The hard-hitting satire of religious self-deception was much admired by Swift.

## *From* HUDIBRAS

### *From* The First Part *Canto I*

### *[The Character of the Hero]*

THE ARGUMENT
Sir Hudibras his passing worth,
The manner how he sallied forth;
His arms and equipage are shown;
His horse's virtues and his own.
Th' adventure of the bear and fiddle
Is sung, but breaks off in the middle.

When civil fury first grew high,
And men fell out they knew not why;
When hard words, jealousies, and fears
Set folks together by the ears,
And made them fight, like mad or drunk,
For Dame Religion as for punk,* whore
Whose honesty they all durst swear for,
Though not a man of them knew wherefore;

When gospel-trumpeter, surrounded
With long-eared† rout, to battle sounded;
And pulpit, drum ecclesiastic,
Was beat with fist instead of a stick;
Then did Sir Knight abandon dwelling,
And out he rode a-colonelling.
  A wight* he was, whose very sight would                man
Entitle him Mirror of Knighthood,
That never bowed his stubborn knee
To anything but chivalry,
Nor put up blow† but that which laid
Right Worshipful on shoulder-blade;
Chief of domestic† knights and errant,
Either for chartel† or for warrant:
Great on the bench, great in the saddle,
That could as well bind o'er as swaddle;†
Mighty he was at both of these,
And styled of war as well as peace.
(So some rats, of amphibious nature,
Are either for the land or water.)
But here our authors make a doubt
Whether he were more wise or stout.†
Some hold the one, and some the other;
But howsoe'er they make a pother,
The difference was so small, his brain
Outweighed his rage but half a grain;
Which made some take him for a tool
That knaves do work with, called a fool;
And offer to lay wagers that,
As Montaigne,† playing with his cat,
Complains she thought him but an ass,
Much more she would Sir Hudibras.
(For that's the name our valiant knight
To all his challenges did write.)
But they're mistaken very much;
'Tis plain enough he was no such.
We grant, although he had much wit,
He was very shy of using it,

*long-eared* asses, but also short-haired Puritans
*blow* knighthood is conferred by a sword tap on shoulder
*domestic* as JP, on the bench
*chartel* written challenge (of knight errant)
*swaddle* beat; and bind up (hence play on legal 'bind o'er')
*stout* stout-hearted, brave
*Montaigne* (1533–92), sceptical French essayist

As being loath to wear it out,
And therefore bore it not about,
Unless on holidays or so,
As men their best apparel do.
Beside, 'tis known he could speak Greek
As naturally as pigs squeak;
That Latin was no more difficile,
Than to a blackbird 'tis to whistle.
Being rich in both, he never scanted
His bounty unto such as wanted;
But much of either would afford
To many that had not one word.
For Hebrew roots,† although they're found
To flourish most in barren ground,
He had such plenty as sufficed
To make some think him circumcised.†
And truly so he was perhaps,
Not as a proselyte, but for claps.†
  He was in logic a great critic,
Profoundly skilled in analytic.
He could distinguish and divide
A hair 'twixt south and south-west side;
On either which he would dispute,
Confute, change hands, and still confute.
He'd undertake to prove by force
Of argument, a man's no horse;
He'd prove a buzzard is no fowl,
And that a lord may be an owl,†
A calf* an alderman, a goose a justice, fool
And rooks* committee-men and trustees. cheats
He'd run in debt by disputation,
And pay with ratiocination.
All this by syllogism,† true
In mood and figure, he would do.
  For rhetoric, he could not ope
His mouth but out there flew a trope;†
And when he happened to break off
In the middle of his speech, or cough,
He had hard words ready to show why,
And tell what rules he did it by.

*Hebrew roots* elements of man's basic original language
*circumcised* as if a Hebrew
*claps* venereal diseases
*owl* symbolically, wise-seeming fool
*syllogism* logical form of argument
*trope* figure of speech

Else when with greatest art he spoke,
You'd think he talked like other folk;
For all a rhetorician's rules
Teach nothing but to name his tools.
His ordinary rate of speech
In loftiness of sound was rich,
A Babylonish[†] dialect
Which learned pedants much affect.
It was a parti-coloured dress
Of patched and piebald languages;
'Twas English cut on Greek and Latin,
Like fustian heretofore on satin.[†]
It had an odd promiscuous tone,
As if he had talked three parts in one;
Which made some think, when he did gabble,
They'd heard three labourers of Babel;
Or Cerberus[†] himself pronounce
A leash of languages at once.
This he as volubly would vent,
As if his stock would ne'er be spent;
And truly to support that charge
He had supplies as vast and large;
For he could coin or counterfeit
New words with little or no wit,
Words so debased and hard, no stone
Was hard enough to touch[†] them on;
And when with hasty noise he spoke 'em,
The ignorant for current took 'em;
That, had the orator[†] who once
Did fill his mouth with pebble stones
When he harangued, but known his phrase,
He would have used no other ways.
  In mathematics he was greater
Then Tycho Brahe[†] or Erra Pater;[†]
For he by geometric scale
Could take the size of pots of ale;
Resolve by sines and tangents[†] straight
If bread or butter wanted weight;

*Babylonish* mixture of languages (Genesis 11)
*fustian . . . satin* coarse cloth, cut to show satin lining
*Cerberus* in classical legend, three-headed dog at entry to Hades
*touch* test their quality
*orator* Demosthenes, Athenian of the fourth century BC
*Brahe* (1546–1601), Danish astronomer
*Pater* pseudonym of sixteenth-century astrologer
*sines . . . tangents* mathematical terms

And wisely tell what hour o' the day
The clock does strike, by algebra.
  Besides he was a shrewd philosopher,
And had read every text and gloss over:
Whate'er the crabbedest author hath,
He understood by implicit faith;
Whatever sceptic could inquire for,
For every why he had a wherefore;
Knew more than forty of them do,
As far as words and terms could go.
All which he understood by rote,
And, as occasion served, would quote;
No matter whether right or wrong,
They might be either said or sung.
His notions fitted things so well,
That which was which he could not tell;
But oftentimes mistook the one
For th' other, as great clerks* have done. scholars
He could reduce all things to acts,
And knew their natures by abstracts,
Where entity and quiddity,†
The ghosts of defunct bodies, fly;
Where Truth in person does appear,
Like words congealed in northern air.
He knew what's what, and that's as high
As metaphysic wit can fly.
  In school-divinity as able
As he that hight Irrefragable;
A second Thomas, or, at once
To name them all, another Duns,†
Profound in all the nominal†
And real ways beyond them all;†
For he a rope of sand could twist
As tough as learned Sorbonist;†
And weave fine cobwebs, fit for skull
That's empty when the moon is full;
Such as take lodgings in a head
That's to be let unfurnishèd.

*entity . . . quiddity* being and essence (in philosophy)

*hight Irrefragable . . . Duns* called Unanswerable: Alexander of Hales (?1175–1245); St Thomas Aquinas (1225–74); Duns Scotus (*c.* 1266–1308), origin of 'dunce'; all theologians

*nominal . . . them all* argument about reality of mental objects

*Sorbonist* scholar from Sorbonne, the University of Paris

He could raise scruples dark and nice,* precise
And after solve 'em in a trice;
As if divinity had catched
The itch of purpose to be scratched;
Or, like a mountebank,† did wound
And stab herself with doubts profound,
Only to show with how small pain
The sores of faith are cured again;
Although by woeful proof we find
They always leave a scar behind.
He knew the seat of Paradise,†
Could tell in what degree it lies,
And, as he was disposed, could prove it
Below the moon, or else above it;
What Adam dreamt of when his bride
Came from her closet in his side;
Whether the devil tempted her
By a High Dutch interpreter;
If either of them had a navel;
Who first made music malleable;†
Whether the Serpent at the Fall
Had cloven feet, or none at all.
All this, without a gloss or comment,
He would unriddle in a moment
In proper terms, such as men smatter
When they throw out and miss the matter.
  For his religion, it was fit
To match his learning and his wit:
'Twas Presbyterian true blue,†
For he was of that stubborn crew
Of errant† saints whom all men grant
To be the true church militant;
Such as do build their faith upon
The holy text of pike and gun;
Decide all controversies by
Infallible artillery;
And prove their doctrine orthodox
By apostolic blows and knocks;

*mountebank* performer, medicine-seller
*He knew . . . Paradise* all actual topics of historic speculation
*malleable* Pythagoras allegedly studied hammer notes
*true blue* colour of religious loyalty and therefore anti-royalism
*errant* wandering, but also notorious (arrant)

Call fire and sword and desolation
A godly, thorough Reformation,
Which always must be carried on,
And still be doing, never done;
As if religion were intended
For nothing else but to be mended:
A sect whose chief devotion lies
In odd perverse antipathies,
In falling out with that or this,
And finding somewhat still amiss;
More peevish, cross, and splenetic,
Than dog distract or monkey sick;
That with more care keep holy-day
The wrong,† than others the right way;
Compound for sins they are inclined to,
By damning those they have no mind to;
Still so perverse and opposite,
As if they worshipped God for spite.
The self-same thing they will abhor
One way,† and long another† for.
Free will they one way disavow,
Another, nothing else allow.
All piety consists therein
In them, in other men all sin.
Rather than fail, they will defy
That which they love most tenderly:
Quarrel with minced-pies, and disparage
Their best and dearest friend, plum-porridge;
Fat pig and goose itself oppose,
And blaspheme custard through the nose.† . . .

1658–60 1662

*The wrong* excessively severe
*one way* by predestination
*another* by private inspiration
*nose* puritan preacher's nasal whine

# John Aubrey

1626–97

Aubrey was an antiquarian who unsystematically collected information about archaeological sites and about interesting figures of the present and recent past. Educated at Trinity College, Oxford, he later became a fellow of the Royal Society. He is now best known for the *Brief Lives* published after his death from the collection of his manuscripts in Oxford's Ashmolean Museum, although another Oxford antiquarian, Antony Wood, had made some unfair use of his material. Aubrey's *Lives*, not always reliable, combine revealing anecdotes, accurate fact, tradition and gossip.

## *From* BRIEF LIVES

### *William Shakespeare*

Mr William Shakespeare was born at Stratford upon Avon in the county of Warwick. His father was a butcher, and I have been told heretofore by some of the neighbours, that when he was a boy he exercised his father's trade, but when he killed a calf he would do it in a high style, and make a speech. There was at that time another butcher's son in this town that was held not at all inferior to him for a natural wit, his acquaintance and coetanean†, but died young.

This William being inclined naturally to poetry and acting, came to London, I guess, about eighteen, and was an actor at one of the playhouses, and did act exceedingly well (now B. Jonson† was never a good actor, but an excellent instructor). He began early to make essays at dramatic poetry, which at that time was very low; and his plays took well. He was a handsome, well shaped man: very good company, and of a very ready and pleasant smooth wit.

The humour† of the constable, in *Midsummer Night's Dream*, he happened to take at Grendon in Bucks – I think it was midsummer night that he happened to lie there – which is the road from London to

*coetanean* person of same age
*Ben Jonson* (1572–1637) poet, dramatist and friend of Shakespeare
*humour* dominant mood

Stratford, and there was living that constable about 1642, when I first came to Oxon: Mr Josias Howe is of that parish, and knew him. Ben Jonson and he did gather humours of men daily wherever they came. One time as he was at the tavern at Stratford super Avon, one Combes, an old rich usurer, was to be buried, he makes there this extemporary epitaph,

Ten in the hundred the Devill allowes,
But Combes will have twelve, he sweares and vowes:
If any one askes who lies in this tombe,
'Hoh!' quoth the Devill, 'Tis my John o Combe.'

He was wont to go to his native country once a year. I think I have been told that he left 2 or 300 £ *per annum* there and thereabout to a sister.

I have heard Sir William Davenant[†] and Mr Thomas Shadwell[†] (who is counted the best comedian we have now) say that he had a most prodigious wit, and did admire his natural parts[†] beyond all other dramatical writers. He was wont to say (B. Jonson's *Underwoods*[†]) that he 'never blotted out a line in his life'; said Ben Jonson, 'I wish he had blotted-out a thousand.'

His comedies will remain wit as long as the English tongue is understood, for that he handles *mores hominum* [the customs of men]. Now our present writers reflect so much upon particular persons and coxcombeities, that twenty years hence they will not be understood.

Though, as Ben Jonson says[†] of him, that he had but little Latin and less Greek, he understood Latin pretty well, for he had been in his younger years a schoolmaster in the country.

1813

*Davenant* (1606–68) dramatist and Poet Laureate, alleged son of Shakespeare
*Shadwell* (?1642–92) comic dramatist and Poet Laureate
*parts* talents
*Underwoods* verse collection (actually said in his prose *Discoveries*, 1641)
*says* 'To the Memory of . . . Shakespeare' (1618), misquoted

# John Bunyan
## 1628–88

Bunyan was born near Bedford, the son of a metal-worker, and had a local education. He served in the parliamentary army in the Civil War. His early reading was in the Bible and in works of piety and Protestant history. After joining a nonconformist church in 1653, he took to preaching in Bedford; arrested for this in 1660, since he was unlicensed, he spent almost all of a twelve-year period in jail: on his release he became pastor at the church, but was reimprisoned in 1676. During the first period in prison, he wrote several books, notably *Grace abounding to the Chief of Sinners* (1666), the record of his progress from sin to religion. During the second, he completed the first part of *The Pilgrim's Progress* (published 1678; second part, 1684). *The Life and Death of Mr. Badman* (1680) is an allegory of crime and punishment; *The Holy War* (1682) an allegory of spiritual struggle. In the allegory of his most famous work, the author dreams of Christian's journey from the City of Destruction, through areas of test and temptation, to the Celestial City. Its style blends the imagery of the Bible with the vivid simplicity of a realistic novel.

## *From* THE PILGRIM'S PROGRESS

### *[Christian in Vanity Fair]*[†]

Then I saw in my dream that when they were got out of the wilderness they presently saw a town before them, and the name of that town is Vanity;[†] and at the town there is a fair kept called Vanity Fair. It is kept all the year long; it beareth the name of Vanity Fair, because the town where 'tis kept is lighter than vanity; and also, because all that is there sold, or that cometh thither, is Vanity. As is the saying of the wise, *All that cometh is vanity.*

This Fair is no new erected business, but a thing of ancient standing; I will show you the original of it.

Christian and his companion Faithful have been warned by Evangelist that they face martyrdom in the next town

*Vanity* worthlessness

Almost five thousand years agone, there were pilgrims walking to the Celestial City, as these two honest persons are; and Beelzebub,[†] Apollyon, and Legion,[†] with their companions, perceiving by the path that the Pilgrims made that their way to the City lay through this town of Vanity, they contrived here to set up a fair; a fair wherein should be sold of all sorts of vanity, and that it should last all the year long. Therefore at this Fair are all such merchandise sold, as houses, lands, trades, places, honours, preferments,[†] titles, countries, kingdoms, lusts, pleasures, and delights of all sorts, as whores, bawds, wives, husbands, children, masters, servants, lives, blood, bodies, souls, silver, gold, pearls, precious stones, and what not.

And moreover, at this Fair there is at all times to be seen jugglings, cheats, games, plays, fools, apes, knaves, and rogues, and that of all sorts.

Here are to be seen too, and that for nothing, thefts, murders, adulteries, false-swearers, and that of a blood-red colour.

And as in other fairs of less moment there are the several rows and streets under their proper names, where such and such wares are vended: so here likewise, you have the proper places, rows, streets (*viz.*[†] countries and kingdoms), where the wares of this Fair are soonest to be found: here is the Britain Row, the French Row, the Italian Row, the Spanish Row, the German Row, where several sorts of vanities are to be sold. But as in other fairs, some one commodity is as the chief of all the fair, so the ware of Rome[†] and her merchandise is greatly promoted in this Fair: only our English nation, with some others, have taken a dislike thereat.

Now, as I said, the way to the Celestial City lies just through this town, where this lusty Fair is kept; and he that will go to the City, and yet not go through this town, must needs go out of the world. The Prince of Princes[†] himself, when here, went through this Town to his own country, and that upon a fair-day too. Yea, and as I think it was Beelzebub, the chief lord of this Fair, that invited him to buy of his vanities; yea, would have made him lord of the Fair, would he but have done him reverence as he went through the town. Yea, because he was such a person of honour, Beelzebub had him from street to street, and showed him all the kingdoms of the world in a little time, that he might if possible allure that Blessed One, to cheapen and buy some of his vanities. But he had no mind to the merchandise, and therefore left the town without laying out so much as one farthing upon these vanities.

*Beelzebub . . . Legion* biblical fiends; Christian has already defeated Apollyon in battle
*preferments* promotions to worldly 'places'
*viz.* (Latin) videlicet: namely
*Rome* the Roman Catholic Church
*Prince of Princes* Jesus, tempted to 'cheapen' (bargain) in Matthew 4

This Fair therefore is an ancient thing, of long standing, and a very great Fair.

Now these pilgrims, as I said, must needs go through this Fair: well, so they did; but behold, even as they entered into the Fair, all the people in the Fair were moved, and the town itself as it were in a hubbub about them; and that for several reasons: for,

First, the pilgrims were clothed with such kind of raiment as was diverse from the raiment of any that traded in that Fair. The people therefore of the Fair made a great gazing upon them: Some said they were fools, some they were bedlams,[†] and some 'They are outlandish-men.'

Secondly, and as they wondered at their apparel so they did likewise at their speech; for few could understand what they said; they naturally spoke the language of Canaan,[†] but they that kept the Fair, were the men of this world: so that from one end of the Fair to the other, they seemed barbarians[†] each to the other.

Thirdly, but that which did not a little amuse the merchandisers was that these pilgrims set very light by all their wares, they cared not so much as to look upon them; and if they called upon them to buy, they would put their fingers in their ears, and cry, *Turn away mine eyes from beholding vanity*; and look upwards, signifying that their trade and traffic was in Heaven.

One chanced mockingly, beholding the carriages[†] of the men, to say unto them, 'What will ye buy?' but they, looking gravely upon him, said, 'We buy the truth.' At that there was an occasion taken to despise the men the more; some mocking, some taunting, some speaking reproachfully, and some calling upon others to smite them. At last things came to an hubbub and great stir in the Fair; insomuch that all order was confounded. Now was word presently brought to the great one of the Fair, who quickly came down and deputed some of his most trusty friends to take these men into examination about whom the Fair was almost overturned. So the men were brought to examination; and they that sat upon them asked them whence they came, whither they went, and what they did there in such an unusual garb? The men told them that they were pilgrims and strangers in the world, and that they were going to their own country, which was the heavenly Jerusalem; and that they had given none occasion to the men of the town, nor yet to the merchandisers, thus to abuse them, and to let[†] them in their journey; except it was for that when one asked them what they would buy, they said they would buy the truth. But they that were appointed

*bedlams* insane (from Bethlehem Royal Hospital)
*Canaan* the biblical Promised Land
*barbarians* foreigners
*carriages* behaviour
*let* hinder

to examine them did not believe them to be any other than bedlams and mad, or else such as came to put all things into a confusion in the Fair. Therefore they took them, and beat them, and besmeared them with dirt, and then put them into the cage, that they might be made a spectacle to all the men of the Fair. There therefore they lay for some time, and were made the objects of any man's sport, or malice, or revenge, the great one of the Fair laughing still at all that befell them. But the men being patient, and not rendering railing for railing, but contrariwise blessing, and giving good words for bad, and kindness for injuries done, some men in the Fair that were more observing, and less prejudiced than the rest, began to check and blame the baser sort for their continual abuses done by them to the men. They therefore in angry manner let fly at them again, counting them as bad as the men in the cage, and telling them that they seemed confederates, and should be made partakers of their misfortunes. The other replied that for aught they could see, the men were quiet, and sober, and intended nobody any harm; and that there were many that traded in their Fair that were more worthy to be put into the cage, yea, and pillory too, than were the men that they had abused. Thus, after divers words had passed on both sides (the men behaving themselves all the while very wisely and soberly before them), they fell to some blows among themselves and did harm one to another. Then were these two poor men brought before their examiners again, and there charged as being guilty of the late hubbub that had been in the Fair. So they beat them pitifully, and hanged irons upon them, and led them in chains up and down the Fair, for an example and a terror to others, lest any should further speak in their behalf, or join themselves upon them. But Christian and Faithful behaved themselves yet more wisely, and received the ignominy and shame that was cast upon them with so much meekness and patience, that it won to their side (though but few in comparison of the rest) several of the men in the Fair. This put the other party yet into a greater rage, insomuch that they concluded the death of these two men. Wherefore they threatened that the cage, nor irons, should serve their turn, but that they should die for the abuse they had done and for deluding the men of the Fair.

Then were they remanded to the cage again, until further order should be taken with them. So they put them in, and made their feet fast in the stocks.

Here also they called again to mind what they had heard from their faithful friend Evangelist, and was the more confirmed in their way and sufferings by what he told them would happen to them. They also now comforted each other that whose lot it was to suffer, even he should have the best on't; therefore each man secretly wished that he might have that preferment; but committing themselves to the all-wise dispose of him that ruleth all things, with much content they abode in the condition in which they were, until they should be otherwise disposed of.

Then a convenient time being appointed, they brought them forth to their trial in order to their condemnation. When the time was come, they were brought before their enemies and arraigned; the Judge's name was Lord Hategood. Their indictment was one and the same in substance, though somewhat varying in form; the contents whereof was this:

*That they were enemies to, and disturbers of their trade; that they had made commotions and divisions in the town, and had won a party to their own most dangerous opinions, in contempt of the law of their prince.*

Then Faithful began to answer that he had only set himself against that which had set itself against him that is higher than the highest. 'And,' said he, 'as for disturbance, I make none, being myself a man of peace; the party that were won to us were won by beholding our truth and innocence, and they are only turned from the worse to the better. And as to the King you talk of; since he is Beelzebub, the enemy of our Lord, I defy him and all his angels.'

Then proclamation was made, that they that had aught to say for their lord the King against the prisoner at the bar, should forthwith appear, and give in their evidence. So there came in three witnesses, to wit, Envy, Superstition, and Pickthank. They was then asked if they knew the prisoner at the bar and what they had to say for the lord the King against him.

Then stood forth Envy, and said to this effect: 'My lord, I have known this man a long time, and will attest upon my oath before this honourable bench, that he is –'

*Judge*. 'Hold, give him his oath.' So they sware him. Then he said, 'My lord, this man, notwithstanding his plausible name, is one of the vilest men in our country; he neither regardeth prince nor people, law nor custom, but doth all that he can to possess all men with certain of his disloyal notions, which he in the general calls principles of faith and holiness. And in particular, I heard him once myself affirm that Christianity, and the customs of our town of Vanity were diametrically opposite, and could not be reconciled. By which saying, my Lord, he doth at once not only condemn all our laudable doings, but us in the doing of them.'

*Judge*. Then did the Judge say to him, 'Hast thou any more to say?'

*Envy*. 'My lord, I could say much more, only I would not be tedious to the court. Yet if need be, when the other gentlemen have given in their evidence, rather than anything shall be wanting that will dispatch him, I will enlarge my testimony against him.' So he was bid stand by.

Then they called Superstition, and bid him look upon the prisoner; they also asked what he could say for their lord the King against him. Then they sware him, so he began.

*Superstition.* 'My lord, I have no great acquaintance with this man, nor do I desire to have further knowledge of him; however this I know, that he is a very pestilent fellow, from some discourse that the other day I had with him in this town; for then talking with him, I heard him say that our religion was naught, and such by which a man could by no means please God: which sayings of his, my lord, your lordship very well knows what necessarily thence will follow, to wit, that we still do worship in vain, are yet in our sins, and finally shall be damned; and this is that which I have to say.'

Then was Pickthank sworn, and bid say what he knew, in behalf of their lord the King against the prisoner at the bar.

*Pickthank.* 'My lord, and you gentlemen all, this fellow I have known of a long time, and have heard him speak things that ought not to be spoke. For he hath railed on our noble Prince Beelzebub, and hath spoke contemptibly of his honourable friends, whose names are the Lord Old Man, the Lord Carnal Delight, the Lord Luxurious, the Lord Desire of Vain-glory, my old Lord Lechery, Sir Having Greedy, with all the rest of our nobility; and he hath said moreover, that if all men were of his mind, if possible, there is not one of these noblemen should have any longer a being in this town. Besides, he hath not been afraid to rail on you, my lord, who are now appointed to be his judge, calling you an ungodly villain, with many other such like vilifying terms, with which he hath bespattered most of the gentry of our town.' When this Pickthank had told his tale, the Judge directed his speech to the prisoner at the bar, saying, 'Thou runagate,† heretic, and traitor, hast thou heard what these honest gentlemen have witnessed against thee?'

*Faithful.* 'May I speak a few words in my own defence?'

*Judge.* 'Sirrah, sirrah, thou deservest to live no longer, but to be slain immediately upon the place; yet that all men may see our gentleness towards thee, let us hear what thou hast to say.'

*Faithful.* '1. I say then in answer to what Mr Envy hath spoken, I never said aught but this, that what rule, or laws, or custom, or people, were flat against the Word of God, are diametrically opposite to Christianity. If I have said amiss in this, convince me of my error, and I am ready here before you to make my recantation.

'2. As to the second, to wit, Mr Superstition, and his charge against me, I said only this, that in the worship of God there is required a divine faith; but there can be no divine faith without a divine revelation of the will of God: therefore whatever is thrust into the worship of

*runagate* vagabond

God that is not agreeable to divine revelation, cannot be done but by an human faith, which faith will not profit to eternal life.

'3. As to what Mr Pickthank hath said, I say (avoiding terms, as that I am said to rail,† and the like), that the Prince of this town, with all the rabblement his attendants by this gentleman named, are more fit for being in Hell than in this town and country; and so the Lord have mercy upon me.'

Then the Judge called to the jury (who all this while stood by, to hear and observe), 'Gentlemen of the jury, you see this man about whom so great an uproar hath been made in this town: you have also heard what these worthy gentlemen have witnessed against him; also you have heard his reply and confession: it lieth now in your breasts to hang him, or save his life. But yet I think meet to instruct you into our law.

'There was an act made in the days of Pharoah† the Great, servant to our prince, that lest those of a contrary religion should multiply and grow too strong for him, their males should be thrown into the river. There was also an act made in the days of Nebuchadnezzar the Great, another of his servants, that whoever would not fall down and worship his golden image, should be thrown into a fiery furnace. There was also an act made in the days of Darius, that who so, for some time, called upon any god but his, should be cast into the lions' den.† Now the substance of these laws this rebel has broken, not only in thought (which is not to be borne), but also in word and deed, which must therefore needs be intolerable.

'For that of Pharoah, his law was made upon a supposition, to prevent mischief, no crime being yet apparent; but here is a crime apparent. For the second and third, you see he disputeth against our religion; and for the treason he hath confessed he deserveth to die the death.'

Then went the jury out, whose names were Mr Blind-man, Mr No-good, Mr Malice, Mr Love-lust, Mr Live-loose, Mr Heady, Mr High-mind, Mr Enmity, Mr Liar, Mr Cruelty, Mr Hate-light, and Mr Implacable, who every one gave in his private verdict against him among themselves, and afterwards unanimously concluded to bring him in guilty before the Judge. And first Mr Blind-man, the foreman, said, 'I see clearly that this man is an heretic.' Then said Mr No-good, 'Away with such a fellow from the earth.' 'Ay,' said Mr Malice, 'for I hate the very looks of him.' Then said Mr Love-lust, 'I could never endure him.' 'Nor I,' said Mr Live-loose, 'for he would always be condemning my

*rail* reproach abusively
*Pharaoh . . . lions' den* biblical oppressors of the chosen people: Exodus 1; Daniel 3; Daniel 6

way.' 'Hang him, hang him,' said Mr Heady. 'A sorry scrub,'† said Mr High-mind. 'My heart riseth against him,' said Mr Enmity. 'He is a rogue,' said Mr Liar. 'Hanging is too good for him,' said Mr Cruelty. 'Let's dispatch him out of the way,' said Mr Hate-light. Then said Mr Implacable, 'Might I have all the world given me, I could not be reconciled to him, therefore let us forthwith bring him in guilty of death.' And so they did, therefore he was presently condemned to be had from the place where he was, to the place from whence he came, and there to be put to the most cruel death that could be invented.

They therefore brought him out to do with him according to their law; and first they scourged him, then they buffeted him, then they lanced his flesh with knives; after that they stoned him with stones, then pricked him with their swords; and last of all they burned him to ashes at the stake. Thus came Faithful to his end. Now, I saw that there stood behind the multitude a chariot and a couple of horses, waiting for Faithful, who (so soon as his adversaries had dispatched him) was taken up into it, and straightway was carried up through the clouds, with sound of trumpet, the nearest way to the Celestial Gate. But as for Christian, he had some respite, and was remanded back to prison; so he there remained for a space: but he that over-rules all things, having the power of their rage in his own hand, so wrought it about that Christian for that time escaped them, and went his way. . . .

1678

*scrub* inferior person

# John Dryden
## 1631–1700

Dryden was educated at Westminster School and at Trinity College, Cambridge. He produced much of his early work in dramatic form, including (tragi-)comedy (*Marriage à-la-Mode*, 1672) and heroic plays in rhyme (*The Conquest of Granada*, 1670), later turning to blank verse (*All for Love*, 1678): these are now rarely performed, but his prologues reveal his practical interest in literary questions, developed in his elegant critical prose (*An Essay of Dramatic Poesy*, 1668). He became Poet Laureate in 1668 and Historiographer Royal in 1670, under Charles II, but lost office under William and Mary: *The Hind and the Panther* (1687) had marked his conversion to Catholicism from the Anglicanism of *Religio Laici* (1682). In his later years he returned to drama, but found more congenial expression in translation, notably of Virgil (1697), Ovid and Chaucer (in *Fables Ancient and Modern*, 1700), together with his critical writing. Dryden's criticism is accessible and unpedantic, the fruit of his creative experience; his vigour, mastery of the heroic couplet, and refinement of poetic language gave him great influence on the verse of the next century.

*Mac Flecknoe* (1682) ridicules the rival dramatist Thomas Shadwell, and provided Pope with hints for *The Dunciad* (1728). In *Absalom and Achitophel* (1681), Dryden presents, in a brilliant reworking of the biblical story in II Samuel 13–19, the contemporary political drama of the potential succession to Charles II, whether by his Catholic brother, James Duke of York, or by his Protestant illegitimate son, James Duke of Monmouth, following the hysteria of the 'Popish Plot' (1678), which Titus Oates alleged was aimed at the king's life after Charles's dissolution of Parliament. England is represented as Israel, Charles as King David, Monmouth as Absalom, Oates as Corah, and the Earl of Shaftesbury, former royal counsellor and now opponent, as Achitophel. When the poem appeared, Shaftesbury was awaiting trial for high treason (the heroic style, with echoes of *Paradise Lost*, 1667, reflects the public issues at stake). Monmouth's later rebellion led to his execution in 1685.

# ABSALOM AND ACHITOPHEL

In pious times, ere priestcraft did begin,
Before polygamy was made a sin;
When man on many multiplied his kind,
Ere one to one was cursedly confined;
When nature prompted, and no law denied
Promiscuous use of concubine and bride;
Then Israel's monarch, after Heaven's own heart,
His vigorous warmth did, variously, impart
To wives and slaves; and, wide as his command,
Scattered his Maker's image through the land.
Michal,† of royal blood, the crown did wear,
A soil ungrateful to the tiller's care:
Not so the rest; for several mothers bore
To godlike David several sons before.
But since like slaves his bed they did ascend,
No true succession could their seed attend.
Of all this numerous progeny was none
So beautiful, so brave as Absalon:†
Whether, inspired by some diviner lust,
His father got him with a greater gust;
Or that his conscious destiny made way
By manly beauty to imperial sway.
Early in foreign fields he won renown,
With kings and states allied to Israel's crown:
In peace the thoughts of war he could remove
And seemed as he were only born for love.
Whate'er he did was done with so much ease,
In him alone 'twas natural to please.
His motions all accompanied with grace;
And Paradise was opened in his face.
With secret joy indulgent David viewed
His youthful image in his son renewed:
To all his wishes nothing he denied,
And made the charming Annabel his bride.
What faults he had (for who from faults is free?)
His father could not, or he would not see.

*Michal* Queen Catherine was childless, unlike Charles's mistresses

*Absalon* Monmouth (1649–85), son of Lucy Walters, had fought against the Dutch, French, and rebel Scots. He married the Countess of Buccleuch ('Annabel', l.34)

Some warm excesses, which the law forbore,
Were construed youth that purged by boiling o'er;
And Amnon's murder,† by a specious name,
Was called a just revenge for injured fame.
Thus praised and loved, the noble youth remained,
While David undisturbed in Sion reigned.
But life can never be sincerely blest:
Heaven punishes the bad, and proves* the best. tests
The Jews, a headstrong, moody, murmuring race,
As ever tried th' extent and stretch of grace;
God's pampered people whom, debauched with ease,
No king could govern, nor no God could please;
(Gods they had tried of every shape and size
That godsmiths could produce or priests devise)
These Adam-wits, too fortunately free,
Began to dream they wanted liberty;
And when no rule, no precedent was found
Of men by laws less circumscribed and bound,
They led their wild desires to woods and caves
And thought that all but savages were slaves.
They who, when Saul† was dead, without a blow
Made foolish Ishbosheth the crown forego;
Who banished David did from Hebron† bring,
And with a general shout proclaimed him King:
Those very Jews who, at their very best,
Their humour† more than loyalty exprest,
Now wondered why so long they had obeyed
An idol monarch which their hands had made;
Thought they might ruin him they could create;
Or melt him to that golden calf,† a State.
But these were random bolts: no formed design
Nor interest made the factious crowd to join.
The sober part of Israel, free from stain,
Well knew the value of a peaceful reign;
And, looking backward with a wise affright,
Saw seams of wounds, dishonest to the sight;
In contemplation of whose ugly scars
They cursed the memory of civil wars.

*Amnon's murder* Monmouth was involved in several acts of violence, though not murder
*Saul* Oliver Cromwell (d.1658) had been Lord Protector during Charles's exile. His son Richard ('Ishbosheth') briefly ruled; but the Restoration of the Stuarts followed in 1660
*Hebron* either Brussels, or Scotland, where Charles was crowned (1651)
*humour* mood, fickleness
*golden calf* false idol of the Israelites, here a 'state', republic

The moderate sort of men, thus qualified,
Inclined the balance to the better side;
And David's mildness managed it so well,
The bad found no occasion to rebel.
But when to sin our biassed nature leans,
The careful Devil is still at hand with means,
And providently pimps for ill desires:
The Good Old Cause,† revived, a plot requires.
Plots, true or false, are necessary things,
To raise up commonwealths, and ruin kings.
Th' inhabitants of old Jerusalem†
Were Jebusites; the town so called from them;
And theirs the native right –
But when the chosen people grew more strong,
The rightful cause at length became the wrong;
And every loss the men of Jebus bore,
They still were thought God's enemies the more.
Thus worn and weakened, well or ill content,
Submit they must to David's government:
Impoverished and deprived of all command,
Their taxes doubled as they lost their land;
And, what was harder yet to flesh and blood,
Their gods disgraced, and burnt like common wood.
This set the heathen priesthood in a flame,
For priests of all religions are the same:
Of whatsoe'er descent their godhead be,
Stock, stone, or other homely pedigree,
In his defence his servants are as bold
As if he had been born of beaten gold.
The Jewish Rabbins,† though their enemies,
In this conclude them honest men and wise:
For 'twas their duty, all the learned think,
T'espouse his cause by whom they eat and drink.
From hence began that Plot,† the nation's curse,
Bad in itself, but represented worse;
Raised in extremes, and in extremes decried;
With oaths affirmed, with dying vows denied;
Not weighed or winnowed by the multitude,

*Good Old Cause* the anti-monarchical struggle which led to the Civil War and deposition of the Stuarts

*Jerusalem* London; its ancient people, Roman Catholics, subject to penalties; the chosen people, Protestants

*Jewish Rabbins* Church of England clergymen

*that Plot* the 'Popish Plot' (see introductory note)

But swallowed in the mass, unchewed and crude.
Some truth there was, but dashed and brewed with lies,
To please the fools and puzzle all the wise.
Succeeding times did equal folly call
Believing nothing, or believing all.
Th' Egyptian rites† the Jebusites embraced,
Where gods were recommended by their taste.
Such savoury deities must needs be good,
As served at once for worship and for food.
By force they could not introduce these gods,
For ten to one in former days was odds;
So fraud was used (the sacrificer's trade):
Fools are more hard to conquer than persuade.
Their busy teachers mingled with the Jews,
And raked for converts even the court and stews;
Which Hebrew priests the more unkindly took,
Because the fleece accompanies the flock.
Some thought they God's anointed meant to slay
By guns, invented since full many a day:
Our author swears it not; but who can know
How far the Devil and Jebusites may go?
This plot, which failed for want of common sense,
Had yet a deep and dangerous consequence:
For, as when raging fevers boil the blood,
The standing lake soon floats into a flood,
And every hostile humour, which before
Slept quiet in its channels, bubbles o'er;
So several factions from this first ferment
Work up to foam, and threat the government.
Some by their friends, more by themselves thought wise,
Opposed the power to which they could not rise.
Some had in courts been great and, thrown from thence,
Like fiends were hardened in impenitence.
Some, by their Monarch's fatal mercy grown
From pardoned rebels kinsmen to the throne,
Were raised in power and public office high:
Strong bands, if bands ungrateful men could tie.
　Of these the false Achitophel† was first,
A name to all succeeding ages curst:

*Egyptian rites* French, hence Catholic (such as transubstantiation)

*Achitophel* Anthony Ashley Cooper (1621–83), 1st Earl of Shaftesbury, former Lord Chancellor, now active against royal and Catholic power; once a supporter of Cromwell

For close designs and crooked counsels fit,
Sagacious, bold, and turbulent of wit;
Restless, unfixed in principles and place,
In power unpleased, impatient of disgrace;
A fiery soul, which, working out its way,
Fretted the pigmy body to decay,
And o'er-informed the tenement of clay.
A daring pilot in extremity;
Pleased with the danger, when the waves went high
He sought the storms; but, for a calm unfit,
Would steer too nigh the sands, to boast his wit.
Great wits are sure to madness near allied,
And thin partitions do their bounds divide:
Else, why should he, with wealth and honour blest,
Refuse his age the needful hours of rest?
Punish a body which he could not please,
Bankrupt of life, yet prodigal of ease?
And all to leave what with his toil he won
To that unfeathered, two-legged thing, a son,
Got,[*] while his soul did huddled notions try, begotten
And born a shapeless lump, like anarchy.
In friendship false, implacable in hate,
Resolved to ruin or to rule the state.
To compass this the triple bond[†] he broke,
The pillars of the public safety shook,
And fitted Israel for a foreign yoke;
Then, seized with fear, yet still affecting fame,
Usurped a patriot's all-atoning name.
So easy still it proves in factious times
With public zeal to cancel private crimes;
How safe is treason, and how sacred ill,
Where none can sin against the people's will:
Where crowds can wink, and no offence be known,
Since in another's guilt they find their own.
Yet fame deserved no enemy can grudge;
The statesman we abhor, but praise the judge.
In Israel's courts ne'er sat an Abbethdin[†]
With more discerning eyes, or hands more clean;
Unbribed, unsought, the wretched to redress,
Swift of dispatch and easy of access.

*triple bond* 1668 Alliance of England, Sweden and Holland, against France

*Abbethdin* Judge in the Jewish high court (i.e. S. as Chancellor), hence his gown (l.193)

Oh, had he been content to serve the crown
With virtues only proper to the gown;
Or had the rankness of the soil been freed
From cockle that oppressed the noble seed;
David for him his tuneful harp had strung
And Heaven had wanted[†] one immortal song.
But wild ambition loves to slide, not stand,
And fortune's ice prefers to virtue's land.
Achitophel, grown weary to possess
A lawful fame, and lazy happiness,
Disdained the golden fruit to gather free,
And lent the crowd his arm to shake the tree.
Now, manifest of crimes contrived long since,
He stood at bold defiance with his Prince;
Held up the buckler of the people's cause
Against the crown, and skulked behind the laws.
The wished occasion of the Plot he takes;
Some circumstances finds, but more he makes;
By buzzing emissaries fills the ears
Of listening crowds with jealousies and fears
Of arbitrary counsels brought to light,
And proves the King himself a Jebusite.
Weak arguments! which yet he knew full well
Were strong with people easy to rebel.
For, governed by the moon, the giddy Jews
Tread the same track when she the prime[†] renews:
And once in twenty years, their scribes record,
By natural instinct they change their lord.
Achitophel still wants a chief, and none
Was found so fit as warlike Absalon:
Not that he wished his greatness to create,
(For politicians neither love nor hate)
But, for he knew his title not allowed,
Would keep him still depending on the crowd:
That kingly power, thus ebbing out, might be
Drawn to the dregs of a democracy.[†]
Him he attempts with studied arts to please,
And sheds his venom in such words as these:

*wanted* lacked (as often), because David the Psalmist praised Absalom instead
*prime* the moon's cycle, which would therefore refer to the roots of the Civil War under Charles I (*c.* 1640), and the Restoration of his son, 1660
*democracy* rule of the people, then rarely a term of praise

'Auspicious prince! at whose nativity
Some royal planet ruled the southern sky;
Thy longing country's darling and desire;
Their cloudy pillar and their guardian fire;
Their second Moses,† whose extended wand
Divides the seas and shows the promised land;
Whose dawning day in every distant age
Has exercised the sacred prophet's rage;
The people's prayer, the glad diviner's theme,
The young men's vision, and the old men's dream!
Thee, Saviour, thee, the nation's vows confess,
And, never satisfied with seeing, bless;
Swift, unbespoken pomps thy steps proclaim,
And stammering babes are taught to lisp thy name.
How long wilt thou the general joy detain,
Starve and defraud the people of thy reign?
Content ingloriously to pass thy days,
Like one of virtue's fools that feeds on praise;
Till thy fresh glories, which now shine so bright,
Grow stale and tarnish with our daily sight.
Believe me, royal youth, thy fruit must be
Or gathered ripe, or rot upon the tree.
Heaven has to all allotted, soon or late,
Some lucky revolution of their fate;
Whose motions if we watch and guide with skill,
(For human good depends on human will)
Our fortune rolls as from a smooth descent,
And from the first impression takes the bent;
But, if unseized, she glides away like wind,
And leaves repenting folly far behind.
Now, now she meets you with a glorious prize,
And spreads her locks before her† as she flies.
Had thus old David, from whose loins you spring,
Not dared, when fortune called him, to be King,
At Gath† an exile he might still remain,
And Heaven's anointing oil had been in vain.
Let his successful youth your hopes engage,
But shun th' example of declining age:
Behold him setting in his western skies,
The shadows lengthening as the vapours rise.

*Moses* Exodus 13–14 tells of the Israelites' flight from Egypt
*before her* fortune, like opportunity, is to be seized by the forelock
*Gath* Brussels, where David/Charles was in exile from Saul/Cromwell. He crossed the Jordan/English Channel in 1660

He is not now, as when on Jordan's sand
The joyful people thronged to see him land,
Covering the beach and blackening all the strand;
But, like the Prince of Angels, from his height
Comes tumbling downward with diminished light;
Betrayed by one poor plot to public scorn,
(Our only blessing since his curst return)
Those heaps of people, which one sheaf did bind,
Blown off and scattered by a puff of wind.
What strength can he to your designs oppose,
Naked of friends, and round beset with foes?
If Pharaoh's† doubtful succour he should use,
A foreign aid would more incense the Jews:
Proud Egypt would dissembled friendship bring,
Foment the war, but not support the King;
Nor would the royal party e'er unite
With Pharaoh's arms, t'assist the Jebusite;
Or, if they should, their interest soon would break,
And with such odious aid make David weak.
All sorts of men by my successful arts
Abhorring kings, estrange their altered hearts
From David's rule: and 'tis the general cry,
"Religion, commonwealth, and liberty."
If you, as champion of the public good,
Add to their arms a chief of royal blood,
What may not Israel hope, and what applause
Might such a general gain by such a cause?
Not barren praise alone, that gaudy flower,
Fair only to the sight, but solid power;
And nobler is a limited command,
Given by the love of all your native land,
Than a successive title, long and dark,
Drawn from the mouldy rolls of Noah's ark.†'
What cannot praise effect in mighty minds
When flattery soothes and when ambition blinds!
Desire of power, on earth a vicious weed,
Yet, sprung from high, is of celestial seed:
In God 'tis glory; and when men aspire,
'Tis but a spark too much of heavenly fire.

*Pharaoh* Ruler of Egypt, hence Louis XIV of France
*Noah's ark* kingship based on long descent is contrasted with that based on popular support

Th' ambitious youth, too covetous of fame,
Too full of angel's metal† in his frame,
Unwarily was led from virtue's ways,
Made drunk with honour, and debauched with praise.
Half loath, and half consenting to the ill,
(For loyal blood within him struggled still)
He thus replied: 'And what pretence have I
To take up arms for public liberty?
My father governs with unquestioned right,
The faith's defender,† and mankind's delight;
Good, gracious, just, observant of the laws;
And Heaven by wonders has espoused his cause.
Whom has he wronged in all his peaceful reign?
Who sues for justice to his throne in vain?
What millions has he pardoned of his foes,
Whom just revenge did to his wrath expose?
Mild, easy, humble, studious of our good,
Inclined to mercy and averse from blood.
If mildness ill with stubborn Israel suit,
His crime is God's beloved attribute.
What could he gain, his people to betray,
Or change his right for arbitrary sway?
Let haughty Pharaoh curse with such a reign
His fruitful Nile, and yoke a servile train.
If David's rule Jerusalem displease,
The dog-star† heats their brains to this disease.
Why then should I, encouraging the bad,
Turn rebel, and run popularly mad?
Were he a tyrant who, by lawless might,
Oppressed the Jews and raised the Jebusite,
Well might I mourn; but nature's holy bands
Would curb my spirits and restrain my hands:
The people might assert their liberty;
But what was right in them were crime in me.
His favour leaves me nothing to require,
Prevents* my wishes, and outruns desire. anticipates
What more can I expect while David lives?
All but his kingly diadem he gives;
And that' – But there he paused; then sighing, said –
'Is justly destined for a worthier head.

*angel's metal* puns on 'angel' (coin) and 'mettle' (spirit)
*faith's defender* monarchs from Henry VIII on held the title Defender of the Faith
*dog-star* Sirius, associated with summer heat and madness

For when my father from his toils shall rest,
And late augment the number of the blest,
His lawful issue shall the throne ascend,
Or the collateral line,† where that shall end.
His brother, though oppressed with vulgar spite,
Yet dauntless and secure of native right,
Of every royal virtue stands possest,
Still dear to all the bravest and the best.
His courage foes, his friends his truth proclaim;
His loyalty the King, the world his fame.
His mercy even th' offending crowd will find,
For sure he comes of a forgiving kind.
Why should I then repine at Heaven's decree,
Which gives me no pretence to royalty?
Yet Oh that Fate, propitiously inclined,
Had raised my birth, or had debased my mind;
To my large soul not all her treasure lent,
And then betrayed it to a mean descent!
I find, I find my mounting spirits bold,
And David's part disdains my mother's mould.
Why am I scanted by a niggard birth?
My soul disclaims the kindred of her earth,
And, made for empire, whispers me within,
Desire of greatness is a godlike sin.'
 Him staggering so when Hell's dire agent found,
While fainting virtue scarce maintained her ground,
He pours fresh forces in, and thus replies:
 'Th' eternal God, supremely good and wise,
Imparts not these prodigious gifts in vain;
What wonders are reserved to bless your reign!
Against your will your arguments have shown,
Such virtue's only given to guide a throne.
Not that your father's mildness I condemn;
But manly force becomes the diadem.
'Tis true, he grants the people all they crave,
And more perhaps than subjects ought to have:
For lavish grants suppose a monarch tame,
And more his goodness than his wit proclaim.
But when should people strive their bonds to break,
If not when kings are negligent or weak?

*collateral line* having no legitimate child, Charles would be succeeded by his brother James

Let him give on till he can give no more,
The thrifty Sanhedrin† shall keep him poor;
And every shekel which he can receive
Shall cost a limb of his prerogative.
To ply him with new plots shall be my care,
Or plunge him deep in some expensive war;
Which when his treasure can no more supply,
He must with the remains of kingship buy.
His faithful friends, our jealousies and fears
Call Jebusites, and Pharaoh's pensioners;
Whom when our fury from his aid has torn,
He shall be naked left to public scorn.
The next successor, whom I fear and hate,
My arts have made obnoxious to the State,
Turned all his virtues to his overthrow,
And gained our elders to pronounce a foe.
His right, for sums of necessary gold,
Shall first be pawned, and afterwards be sold;
Till time shall ever-wanting David draw
To pass your doubtful title into law.
If not, the people have a right supreme
To make their kings; for kings are made for them.
All empire is no more than power in trust,
Which, when resumed, can be no longer just.
Succession, for the general good designed,
In its own wrong a nation cannot bind:
If altering that the people can relieve,
Better one suffer than a nation grieve.
The Jews well know their power: ere Saul they chose,
God was their King, and God they durst depose.
Urge now your piety, your filial name,
A father's right, and fear of future fame;
The public good, that universal call,
To which even Heaven submitted, answers all.
Nor let his love enchant your generous mind;
'Tis Nature's trick to propagate her kind.
Our fond begetters, who would never die,
Love but themselves in their posterity.
Or let his kindness by th' effects be tried,
Or let him lay his vain pretence aside.

*Sanhedrin* Jewish council, hence Parliament, which tried to limit royal power by restricting votes of money. The 'elders' (404) were hostile to James

God said he loved your father; could he bring
A better proof than to anoint him King?
It surely showed he loved the shepherd well
Who gave so fair a flock as Israel.
Would David have you thought his darling son?
What means he then, to alienate[†] the crown?
The name of godly he may blush to bear:
'Tis after God's own heart to cheat his heir.
He to his brother gives supreme command,
To you a legacy of barren land;
Perhaps th' old harp[†] on which he thrums his lays,
Or some dull Hebrew ballad in your praise.
Then the next heir, a prince severe and wise,
Already looks on you with jealous eyes;
Sees through the thin disguises of your arts,
And marks your progress in the people's hearts.
Though now his mighty soul its grief contains,
He meditates revenge who least complains;
And like a lion, slumbering in the way,
Or sleep dissembling, while he waits his prey,
His fearless foes within his distance draws,
Constrains his roaring and contracts his paws;
Till at the last, his time for fury found,
He shoots with sudden vengeance from the ground,
The prostrate vulgar passes o'er and spares,
But with a lordly rage his hunters tears.
Your case no tame expedients will afford;
Resolve on death, or conquest by the sword,
Which for no less a stake than life you draw;
And self-defence is nature's eldest law.
Leave the warm people no considering time,
For then rebellion may be thought a crime.
Prevail yourself of what occasion gives,
But try your title while your father lives;
And that your arms may have a fair pretence,
Proclaim you take them in the King's defence;
Whose sacred life each minute would expose
To plots from seeming friends and secret foes.
And who can sound the depth of David's soul?
Perhaps his fear his kindness may control:
He fears his brother, though he loves his son,

*alienate* transfer the title in property to another (James)

*harp* refers to the Psalms of David

For plighted vows too late to be undone.
If so, by force he wishes to be gained,
Like women's lechery, to seem constrained.
Doubt not, but, when he most affects the frown,
Commit a pleasing rape upon the crown.
Secure his person to secure your cause;
They who possess the Prince, possess the laws.'
He said, and this advice above the rest
With Absalom's mild nature suited best;
Unblamed of life (ambition set aside),
Not stained with cruelty, nor puffed with pride,
How happy had he been, if Destiny
Had higher placed his birth, or not so high!
His kingly virtues might have claimed a throne,
And blessed all other countries but his own;
But charming greatness since so few refuse,
'Tis juster to lament him than accuse.
Strong were his hopes a rival to remove,
With blandishments to gain the public love;
To head the faction while their zeal was hot,
And popularly prosecute the plot.
To farther this, Achitophel unites
The malcontents of all the Israelites,
Whose differing parties he could wisely join,
For several ends, to serve the same design:
The best (and of the princes some were such),
Who thought the power of monarchy too much;
Mistaken men, and patriots in their hearts;
Not wicked, but seduced by impious arts.
By these the springs of property were bent,
And wound so high, they cracked the government.
The next for interest sought t'embroil the state,
To sell their duty at a dearer rate;
And make their Jewish markets of the throne,
Pretending public good to serve their own.
Others thought kings an useless heavy load,
Who cost too much, and did too little good.
These were for laying honest David by,
On principles of pure good husbandry.
With them joined all th' haranguers of the throng,
That thought to get preferment by the tongue.
Who follow next, a double danger bring,
Not only hating David, but the King:

The Solymaean rout,† well versed of old
In godly faction and in treason bold;
Cowering and quaking at a conqueror's sword,
But lofty to a lawful prince restored;
Saw with disdain an ethnic† plot begun,
And scorned by Jebusites to be outdone.
Hot Levites† headed these; who, pulled before
From th' ark, which in the Judges' days they bore,
Resumed their cant, and with a zealous cry
Pursued their old beloved theocracy,
Where Sanhedrin and priest enslaved the nation,
And justified their spoils by inspiration;
For who so fit for reign as Aaron's race,†
If once dominion they could found in grace?
These led the pack; though not of surest scent,
Yet deepest mouthed against the government.
A numerous host of dreaming saints† succeed
Of the true old enthusiastic† breed:
'Gainst form and order they their power employ,
Nothing to build and all things to destroy.
But far more numerous was the herd of such,
Who think too little and who talk too much.
These, out of mere instinct, they knew not why,
Adored their fathers' God and property;
And, by the same blind benefit of fate,
The Devil and the Jebusite did hate;
Born to be saved, even in their own despite,
Because they could not help believing right.
Such were the tools; but a whole Hydra† more
Remains, of sprouting heads too long to score.
    Some of their chiefs were princes of the land:
In the first rank of these did Zimri† stand:
A man so various that he seemed to be
Not one, but all mankind's epitome.
Stiff in opinions, always in the wrong,
Was everything by starts, and nothing long;

*Solymaean rout* the London mob (Solyma was Jerusalem)

*ethnic . . . Aaron's race* Gentile, heathen; hence, Catholic. The opposing party of *Levites* are Presbyterian clergy ejected by the Act of Uniformity (1662) from the privileges (ark) they enjoyed under the Commonwealth, when there was no monarch. In a theocracy, clergy (*Aaron's race*) rule in God's name

*saints* the elect, chosen for salvation (539)

*enthusiasm* self-deluded fanaticism

*Hydra* legendary monster which renewed its many heads when lopped

*Zimri* George Villiers (1628–87), 2nd Duke of Buckingham, wit, former minister, now in opposition. The Biblical Zimris are adulterous and rebellious (Numbers 25; I Kings 16)

But, in the course of one revolving moon,
Was chemist, fiddler, statesman, and buffoon;
Then all for women, painting, rhyming, drinking,
Besides ten thousand freaks that died in thinking.
Blest madman, who could every hour employ
With something new to wish or to enjoy!
Railing and praising were his usual themes,
And both (to show his judgment) in extremes:
So over violent, or over civil,
That every man with him was God or Devil.
In squandering wealth was his peculiar art:
Nothing went unrewarded but desert.
Beggared by fools, whom still he found too late;
He had his jest, and they had his estate.
He laughed himself from Court, then sought relief
By forming parties, but could ne'er be chief;
For, spite of him, the weight of business fell
On Absalom and wise Achitophel:
Thus, wicked but in will, of means bereft,
He left not faction, but of that was left.
  Titles and names 'twere tedious to rehearse
Of lords below the dignity of verse.
Wits, warriors, commonwealth's-men, were the best:
Kind husbands and mere nobles all the rest.
And therefore in the name of dullness be
The well-hung Balaam† and cold Caleb† free;
And canting Nadab† let oblivion damn,
Who made new porridge for the paschal lamb.
Let friendship's holy band some names assure;
Some their own worth, and some let scorn secure.
Nor shall the rascal rabble here have place,
Whom kings no titles gave, and God no grace:
Not bull-faced Jonas,† who could statutes draw
To mean rebellion, and make treason law.
But he, though bad, is followed by a worse,
The wretch who Heaven's anointed dared to curse:
Shimei,† whose youth did early promise bring
Of zeal to God, and hatred to his King,

*well-hung Balaam . . . Nadab* the lustful Earl of Huntingdon (Numbers 22–4); *Caleb*, the Earl of Essex (Numbers 13–14); *Nadab*, Lord Howard of Escrick, republican and dissenter (Leviticus 10) – l.576 refers to his travesty of an Anglican service

*Jonas* Sir William Jones as Attorney General prosecuted 'Popish Plotters'

*Shimei* Slingsby Bethel (1617–97), republican merchant, who as a sheriff of London packed juries with Whigs to acquit royal enemies, including Shaftesbury

Did wisely from expensive sins refrain,
And never broke the Sabbath, but for gain;
Nor ever was he known an oath to vent,
Or curse unless against the government.
Thus heaping wealth by the most ready way
Among the Jews, which was to cheat and pray,
The city, to reward his pious hate
Against his master, chose him magistrate:
His hand a vare[†] of justice did uphold;
His neck was loaded with a chain of gold.
During his office treason was no crime.
The sons of Belial[†] had a glorious time:
For Shimei, though not prodigal of pelf,
Yet loved his wicked neighbour as himself.
When two or three[†] were gathered to declaim
Against the monarch of Jerusalem,
Shimei was always in the midst of them;
And, if they cursed the King when he was by,
Would rather curse than break good company.
If any durst his factious friends accuse,
He packed a jury of dissenting Jews,
Whose fellow-feeling in the godly cause
Would free the suffering saint from human laws;
For laws are only made to punish those
Who serve the King, and to protect his foes.
If any leisure time he had from power,
(Because 'tis sin to misemploy an hour)
His business was by writing to persuade
That kings were useless, and a clog to trade;
And, that his noble style he might refine,
No Rechabite[†] more shunned the fumes of wine.
Chaste were his cellars, and his shrieval* board   sheriff's
The grossness of a city feast abhorred:
His cooks with long disuse their trade forgot;
Cool was his kitchen, though his brains were hot.
Such frugal virtue malice may accuse,
But sure 'twas necessary to the Jews:
For towns once burnt such magistrates require
As dare not tempt God's providence by fire.

*vare* wand of office
*sons of Belial* evil, rebellious men
*two or three* inverts the Biblical community of the faithful
*Rechabite* Rechab commanded his sons not to drink wine (Jeremiah 35)

With spiritual food he fed his servants well,
But free from flesh that made the Jews rebel;
And Moses' laws he held in more account
For forty days of fasting in the Mount.†
 To speak the rest, who better are forgot,
Would tire a well-breathed witness of the Plot.
Yet, Corah,† thou shalt from oblivion pass;
Erect thyself, thou monumental brass,
High as the serpent of thy metal made,
While nations stand secure beneath thy shade.
What though his birth were base, yet comets rise
From earthy vapours ere they shine in skies.
Prodigious actions may as well be done
By weaver's issue as by prince's son.
This arch-attester for the public good
By that one deed ennobles all his blood.
Who ever asked the witnesses' high race,
Whose oath with martyrdom did Stephen† grace?
Ours was a Levite, and as times went then,
His tribe were God Almighty's gentlemen.
Sunk were his eyes, his voice was harsh and loud,
Sure signs he neither choleric was nor proud;
His long chin proved his wit; his saintlike grace
A church vermilion, and a Moses' face.
His memory, miraculously great,
Could plots, exceeding man's belief, repeat;
Which therefore cannot be accounted lies,
For human wit could never such devise.
Some future truths are mingled in his book;
But where the witness failed, the prophet spoke:
Some things like visionary flights appear;
The spirit caught him up, the Lord knows where;
And gave him his rabbinical degree,
Unknown to foreign university.
His judgment yet his memory did excel;
Which pieced his wondrous evidence so well;
And suited to the temper of the times,
Then groaning under Jebusitic crimes.
Let Israel's foes suspect his heavenly call,
And rashly judge his writ apocryphal;

*Mount* Moses fasted forty days on Mount Sinai (Exodus 34)
*Corah* Titus Oates (1649–1705), chief witness against the 'Popish Plot'; son of a weaver, he falsely claimed a degree from Salamanca University
*Stephen* first Christian martyr, victim of false witness (Acts 6–7)

Our laws for such affronts have forfeits made:
He takes his life, who takes away his trade.
Were I myself in witness Corah's place,
The wretch who did me such a dire disgrace
Should whet my memory, though once forgot,
To make him an appendix of my plot.
His zeal to Heaven made him his Prince despise,
And load his person with indignities:
But zeal peculiar privilege affords,
Indulging latitude to deeds and words;
And Corah might for Agag's murder† call,
In terms as coarse as Samuel used to Saul.
What others in his evidence did join,
(The best that could be had for love or coin)
In Corah's own predicament will fall:
For *witness* is a common name to all.
  Surrounded thus with friends of every sort,
Deluded Absalom forsakes the court;
Impatient of high hopes, urged with renown,
And fired with near possession of a crown.
Th' admiring crowd are dazzled with surprise,
And on his goodly person feed their eyes.
His joy concealed, he sets himself to show,
On each side bowing popularly low:
His looks, his gestures, and his words he frames,
And with familiar ease repeats their names.
Thus, formed by nature, furnished out with arts,
He glides unfelt into their secret hearts;
Then with a kind compassionating look,
And sighs, bespeaking pity ere he spoke,
Few words he said, but easy those and fit,
More slow than Hybla drops,† and far more sweet.
  'I mourn, my countrymen, your lost estate,
Though far unable to prevent your fate:
Behold a banished man, for your dear cause
Exposed a prey to arbitrary laws!
Yet Oh! that I alone could be undone,
Cut off from empire, and no more a son!
Now all your liberties a spoil are made;
Egypt and Tyrus† intercept your trade,
And Jebusites your sacred rites invade.

*Agag's murder* uncertain: possibly Lord Stafford, an executed Catholic peer (I Samuel 15)

*Hybla drops* honey from Hybla in Sicily

*Egypt and Tyrus* France and Holland

My father, whom with reverence yet I name,
Charmed into ease, is careless of his fame;
And, bribed with petty sums of foreign gold,
Is grown in Bathsheba's[†] embraces old;
Exalts his enemies, his friends destroys,
And all his power against himself employs.
He gives, and let him give, my right away;
But why should he his own and yours betray?
He, only he, can make the nation bleed,
And he alone from my revenge is freed.
Take then my tears (with that he wiped his eyes),
'Tis all the aid my present power supplies:
No court informer can these arms accuse,
These arms may sons against their fathers use;
And 'tis my wish, the next successor's reign
May make no other Israelite complain.'
  Youth, beauty, graceful action, seldom fail,
But common interest always will prevail;
And pity never ceases to be shown
To him who makes the people's wrongs his own.
The crowd (that still believe their kings oppress)
With lifted hands their young Messiah bless,
Who now begins his progress[†] to ordain
With chariots, horsemen, and a numerous train;
From east to west his glories he displays,
And, like the sun, the promised land surveys.
Fame runs before him as the morning star,
And shouts of joy salute him from afar;
Each house receives him as a guardian god,
And consecrates the place of his abode;
But hospitable treats did most commend
Wise Issachar,[†] his wealthy western friend.
This moving court, that caught the people's eyes,
And seemed but pomp, did other ends disguise:
Achitophel had formed it, with intent
To sound the depths, and fathom, where it went,
The people's hearts, distinguish friends from foes,
And try their strength before they came to blows.
Yet all was coloured with a smooth pretence
Of specious love, and duty to their prince.

*Bathsheba* Duchess of Portsmouth, the king's mistress, possibly a French agent (II Samuel 11)

*progress . . . Issachar* a public journey in 1680 in the west of England, where he visited Thomas Thynne (*Issachar*) in Wiltshire

Religion, and redress of grievances,
Two names that always cheat and always please,
Are often urged; and good King David's life
Endangered by a brother† and a wife.
Thus, in a pageant show, a plot is made,
And peace itself is war in masquerade.
Oh foolish Israel! never warned by ill;
Still the same bait, and circumvented still!
Did ever men forsake their present ease,
In midst of health imagine a disease,
Take pains contingent mischiefs to foresee,
Make heirs for monarchs, and for God decree?
What shall we think? Can people give away,
Both for themselves and sons, their native sway?
Then they are left defenceless to the sword
Of each unbounded, arbitrary lord;
And laws are vain, by which we right enjoy,
If kings unquestioned can those laws destroy.
Yet, if the crowd be judge of fit and just,
And kings are only officers in trust,
Then this resuming covenant† was declared
When kings were made, or is for ever barred.
If those who gave the sceptre could not tie
By their own deed their own posterity,
How then could Adam bind his future race?
How could his forfeit† on mankind take place?
Or how could heavenly justice damn us all
Who ne'er consented to our father's fall?
Then kings are slaves to those whom they command,
And tenants to their people's pleasure stand.
Add, that the power for property allowed,
Is mischievously seated in the crowd;
For who can be secure of private right,
If sovereign sway may be dissolved by might?
Nor is the people's judgment always true:
The most may err as grossly as the few;
And faultless kings run down, by common cry,
For vice, oppression, and for tyranny.

*brother* James and the queen were both accused of plots against Charles
*resuming covenant* agreement that the people can take back the control of the succession
*forfeit* human inheritance of Adam's original sin

What standard is there in a fickle rout,
Which, flowing to the mark, runs faster out?
Nor only crowds, but Sanhedrins may be
Infected with this public lunacy;
And share the madness of rebellious times,
To murder monarchs for imagined crimes.
If they may give and take whene'er they please,
Not kings alone (the Godhead's images),
But government itself at length must fall
To nature's state, where all have right to all.
Yet, grant our lords the people kings can make,
What prudent men a settled throne would shake?
For whatsoe'er their sufferings were before,
That change they covet makes them suffer more.
All other errors but disturb a state,
But innovation is the blow of fate.
If ancient fabrics nod, and threat to fall,
To patch the flaws and buttress up the wall,
Thus far 'tis duty; but here fix the mark,
For all beyond it is to touch our ark.†
To change foundations, cast the frame anew,
Is work for rebels who base ends pursue;
At once divine and human laws control,
And mend the parts by ruin of the whole.
The tampering world is subject to this curse,
To physic their disease into a worse.
  Now what relief can righteous David bring?
How fatal 'tis to be too good a king!
Friends he has few, so high the madness grows;
Who dare be such must be the people's foes.
Yet some there were, even in the worst of days;
Some let me name, and naming is to praise.
  In this short file Barzillai† first appears;
Barzillai, crowned with honour and with years;
Long since, the rising rebels he withstood
In regions waste, beyond the Jordan's flood;
Unfortunately brave to buoy the state,
But sinking underneath his master's fate.
In exile with his godlike prince he mourned,

*touch our ark* commit sacrilege by touching the Ark of the Covenant

*Barzillai* James Butler, Duke of Ormonde (1610–88), loyal in Ireland to Charles I and II

For him he suffered, and with him returned.
The court he practised, not the courtier's art;
Large was his wealth, but larger was his heart,
Which well the noblest objects knew to choose,
The fighting warrior, and recording Muse.
His bed could once a fruitful issue boast;
Now more than half a father's name is lost.
His eldest hope, with every grace adorned,
By me (so Heaven will have it) always mourned,
And always honoured, snatched in manhood's prime
By'unequal fates, and Providence's crime:
Yet not before the goal of honour won,
All parts fulfilled of subject and of son;
Swift was the race, but short the time to run.
Oh narrow circle, but of power divine,
Scanted in space, but perfect in thy line!
By sea, by land, thy matchless worth was known;
Arms thy delight, and war was all thy own;
Thy force, infused, the fainting Tyrians† propped,
And haughty Pharaoh found his fortune stopped.
Oh ancient honour! oh unconquered hand,
Whom foes unpunished never could withstand!
But Israel was unworthy of thy name:
Short is the date of all immoderate fame.
It looks as Heaven our ruin had designed,
And durst not trust thy fortune and thy mind.
Now, free from earth, thy disencumbered soul
Mounts up, and leaves behind the clouds and starry pole:
From thence thy kindred legions mayest thou bring
To aid the guardian angel of thy King.
Here stop, my Muse, here cease thy painful flight;
No pinions can pursue immortal height:
Tell good Barzillai thou canst sing no more,
And tell thy soul she should have fled before;
Or fled she with his life, and left this verse
To hang on her departed patron's hearse?
Now take thy steepy flight from heaven, and see
If thou canst find on earth another *he*;
Another he would be too hard to find;
See then whom thou canst see not far behind.
Zadoc† the priest, whom, shunning power and place,

*Tyrians* the Dutch
*Zadoc* William Sancroft, Archbishop of Canterbury

His lowly mind advanced to David's grace;
With him the Sagan† of Jerusalem,
Of hospitable soul and noble stem;
Him of the western dome,† whose weighty sense
Flows in fit words and heavenly eloquence.
The Prophets' sons, by such example led,
To learning and to loyalty were bred:
For colleges on bounteous kings depend,
And never rebel was to arts a friend.
To these succeed the pillars of the laws,
Who best could plead, and best can judge a cause.
Next them a train of loyal peers ascend:
Sharp-judging Adriel,† the Muses' friend,
Himself a Muse – in Sanhedrin's debate
True to his Prince, but not a slave of state;
Whom David's love with honours did adorn,
That from his disobedient son were torn.
Jotham† of piercing wit and pregnant thought,
Endued by nature, and by learning taught
To move assemblies, who but only tried
The worse a while, then chose the better side;
Nor chose alone, but turned the balance too,
So much the weight of one brave man can do.
Hushai,† the friend of David in distress,
In public storms of manly steadfastness;
By foreign treaties he informed his youth,
And joined experience to his native truth.
His frugal care supplied the wanting throne,
Frugal for that, but bounteous of his own:
'Tis easy conduct when exchequers flow,
But hard the task to manage well the low;
For sovereign power is too depressed or high,
When kings are forced to sell or crowds to buy.
Indulge one labour more, my weary Muse,
For Amiel,† who can Amiel's praise refuse?
Of ancient race by birth, but nobler yet
In his own worth, and without title great:
The Sanhedrin long time as chief he ruled,

*Sagan* (priest) is Henry Compton, Bishop of London

*western dome* suggests John Dolben, Dean of Westminster (1662–6), where there was a school (l.870)

*Adriel* John Sheffield, Earl of Mulgrave, poet and patron of Dryden

*Jotham* George Savile, Marquess of Halifax, opposed Shaftesbury in the House of Lords

*Hushai* Laurence Hyde, Earl of Rochester

*Amiel* Edmond Seymour, Speaker of the House of Commons

Their reason guided, and their passion cooled;
So dexterous was he in the Crown's defence,
So formed to speak a loyal nation's sense,
That, as their band was Israel's tribes in small,
So fit was he to represent them all.
Now rasher charioteers the seat ascend,
Whose loose careers his steady skill commend:
They, like th' unequal ruler[†] of the day,
Misguide the seasons and mistake the way,
While he, withdrawn, at their mad labour smiles,
And safe enjoys the sabbath of his toils.
  These were the chief, a small but faithful band
Of worthies, in the breach who dared to stand
And tempt th' united fury of the land.
With grief they viewed such powerful engines bent
To batter down the lawful government:
A numerous faction, with pretended frights,
In Sanhedrins to plume the regal rights;
The true successor from the Court removed;
The plot by hireling witnesses improved.
These ills they saw, and, as their duty bound,
They showed the King the danger of the wound:
That no concessions from the throne would please,
But lenitives fomented[†] the disease;
That Absalom, ambitious of the crown,
Was made the lure to draw the people down;
That false Achitophel's pernicious hate
Had turned the plot to ruin Church and State;
The council violent, the rabble worse;
That Shimei taught Jerusalem to curse.
  With all these loads of injuries oppressed,
And long revolving in his careful breast
Th' event of things, at last his patience tired,
Thus from his royal throne, by Heaven inspired,
The godlike David spoke[†]: with awful fear
His train their Maker in their master hear.
  'Thus long have I, by native mercy swayed,
My wrongs dissembled, my revenge delayed:
So willing to forgive th' offending age,
So much the father did the king assuage.

---

*unequal ruler* Phaeton was unable to control the chariot of his father, the sun god, Apollo

*lenitives fomented* soothing medicines only increased the heat of

*David spoke* the speech stresses his divine attributes of justice, mercy, and ultimate power

But now so far my clemency they slight,
Th' offenders question my forgiving right.
That one was made for many, they contend;
But 'tis to rule, for that's a monarch's end.
They call my tenderness of blood my fear,
Though manly tempers can the longest bear.
Yet, since they will divert my native course,
'Tis time to show I am not good by force.
Those heaped affronts that haughty subjects bring
Are burdens for a camel, not a King.
Kings are the public pillars of the State,
Born to sustain and prop the nation's weight:
If my young Samson† will pretend a call
To shake the column, let him share the fall.
But Oh that yet he would repent and live!
How easy 'tis for parents to forgive!
With how few tears a pardon might be won
From nature, pleading for a darling son!
Poor pitied youth, by my paternal care
Raised up to all the height his frame could bear!
Had God ordained his fate for empire born,
He would have given his soul another turn:
Gulled with a patriot's name, whose modern sense
Is, one that would by law supplant his prince;
The people's brave, the politician's tool;
Never was patriot yet but was a fool.
Whence comes it that religion and the laws
Should more be Absalom's than David's cause?
His old instructor,† ere he lost his place,
Was never thought endued with so much grace.
Good heavens, how faction can a patriot paint!
My rebel ever proves my people's saint.
Would *they* impose an heir upon the throne?
Let Sanhedrins be taught to give their own.
A King's at least a part of government,
And mine as requisite as their consent:
Without my leave a future King to choose,
Infers a right the present to depose.
True, they petition me t'approve their choice;
But Esau's hands† suit ill with Jacob's voice.

*Samson* killed as he shook the pillars of the Philistine house (Judges 16)
*old instructor* Achitophel/Shaftesbury
*Esau's hands* Jacob attempted to deceive his blind father by simulating the hairy hands of his elder brother, Esau, with goatskin, to win his blessing (Genesis 27)

My pious subjects for my safety pray,
Which to secure they take my power away.
From plots and treasons Heaven preserve my years,
But save me most from my petitioners:
Unsatiate as the barren womb or grave;
God cannot grant so much as they can crave.
What then is left but with a jealous eye
To guard the small remains of royalty?
The law shall still direct my peaceful sway,
And the same law teach rebels to obey;
Votes shall no more established power control,
Such votes as make a part exceed the whole:
No groundless clamours shall my friends remove,
Nor crowds have power to punish ere they prove;
For gods and godlike kings their care express,
Still to defend their servants in distress.
Oh that my power to saving were confined!
Why am I forced, like Heaven, against my mind,
To make examples of another kind?
Must I at length the sword of justice draw?
Oh curst effects of necessary law!
How ill my fear they by my mercy scan:
Beware the fury of a patient man.
Law they require, let law then show her face:
They could not be content to look on grace,
Her hinder parts,† but with a daring eye
To tempt the terror of her front, and die.
By their own arts, 'tis righteously decreed,
Those dire artificers of death shall bleed.
Against themselves their witnesses will swear
Till, viper-like,† their mother plot they tear,
And suck for nutriment that bloody gore
Which was their principle of life before.
Their Belial† with their Belzebub will fight;
Thus on my foes, my foes shall do me right.
Nor doubt th' event; for factious crowds engage
In their first onset all their brutal rage.
Then let 'em take an unresisted course,
Retire and traverse, and delude their force:

*her hinder parts* as no man might safely see God's 'front', face (Exodus 33)
*viper-like* vipers traditionally devour their mother in the birth-process
*Belial* with Beelzebub, among the evil fallen angels in *Paradise Lost*, II

But when they stand all breathless, urge the fight,
And rise upon 'em with redoubled might:
For lawful power is still superior found;
When long driven back, at length it stands the ground.'
  He said. Th' Almighty, nodding, gave consent;
And peals of thunder shook the firmament.
Henceforth a series of new time[†] began,
The mighty years in long procession ran:
Once more the godlike David was restored,
And willing nations knew their lawful lord.

1681

# MAC FLECKNOE

All human things are subject to decay,
And when fate summons, monarchs must obey:
This Flecknoe[†] found, who, like Augustus,[†] young
Was called to empire, and had governed long;
In prose and verse was owned, without dispute,
Through all the realms of Nonsense, absolute.
This aged Prince, now flourishing in peace,
And blest with issue of a large increase,
Worn out with business, did at length debate
To settle the succession of the State;
And pondering which of all his sons was fit
To reign, and wage immortal war with wit,
Cried: ''Tis resolved! For nature pleads that he
Should only rule, who most resembles me.
Sh – – – alone my perfect image bears,
Mature in dullness from his tender years;
Sh – – – alone, of all my sons, is he
Who stands confirmed in full stupidity;

*new time* recalls a famous prophecy of renovation in the fourth *Eclogue* of the Roman poet Virgil (70–19 BC)

*Flecknoe* Richard Flecknoe, priest, minor poet and dramatist, died *c.* 1678. Dryden presents as his chosen successor ('Mac') to the throne of dullness Thomas Shadwell (1640–92). The allusive mock-heroic manner is an ironic comment on Shadwell's talents; a Whig, he succeeded Dryden as Poet Laureate in 1689. The poem is the seed of Pope's *Dunciad*

*Augustus* Octavius became the first Roman emperor aged 32, and ruled 45 years

The rest to some faint meaning make pretence,
But Sh – – – never deviates into sense.
Some beams of wit on other souls may fall,
Strike through and make a lucid interval;
But Sh – – – 's genuine night admits no ray,
His rising fogs prevail upon the day.
Besides, his goodly fabric fills the eye,
And seems designed for thoughtless majesty:
Thoughtless as monarch oaks that shade the plain,
And, spread in solemn state, supinely reign.
Heywood[†] and Shirley were but types of thee,
Thou last great prophet of tautology.
Even I, a dunce of more renown than they,
Was sent before but to prepare thy way;
And coarsely clad in Norwich drugget[†] came
To teach the nations in thy greater name.
My warbling lute, the lute I whilom strung
When to King John[†] of Portugal I sung,
Was but the prelude to that glorious day,
When thou on silver Thames didst cut thy way,
With well-timed oars before the royal barge,
Swelled with the pride of thy celestial charge;
And big with hymn, commander of an host,
The like was ne'er in Epsom blankets[†] tossed.
Methinks I see the new Arion[†] sail,
The lute still trembling underneath thy nail.
At thy well-sharpened thumb from shore to shore
The treble squeaks for fear, the basses roar:
Echoes from Pissing Alley[†] Sh – – – call,
And Sh – – – they resound from Aston Hall.
About thy boat the little fishes throng,
As at the morning toast* that floats along. sewage
Sometimes as prince of thy harmonious band
Thou wield'st thy papers in thy threshing hand.
St. André's[†] feet ne'er kept more equal time,
Not even the feet of thy own *Psyche*'s rhyme:

---

*Heywood* Thomas Heywood (*c.* 1574–1641) and James Shirley (1596–1666), old-fashioned dramatists, are precursors of Shadwell, as Flecknoe is John the Baptist to his Christ (l.32: see Matthew 3)

*drugget* coarse woollen cloth from Shadwell's native Norfolk

*King John* Flecknoe claimed the patronage of the Portuguese king

*Epsom blankets* refers to blanket-tossing in Shadwell's *The Virtuoso* and to his *Epsom Wells*

*Arion* legendary Greek, whose music charmed dolphins

*Pissing Alley* a real street near the river; Aston Hall is obscure

*St. André* French choreographer of Shadwell's opera *Psyche* (1675)

Though they in number as in sense excel,
So just, so like tautology, they fell,
That, pale with envy, Singleton† forswore
The lute and sword which he in triumph bore,
And vowed he ne'er would act Villerius† more.'
Here stopped the good old sire, and wept for joy
In silent raptures of the hopeful boy.
All arguments, but most his plays, persuade,
That for anointed dullness he was made.
  Close to the walls which fair Augusta bind,
(The fair Augusta† much to fears inclined)
An ancient fabric, raised t'inform the sight,
There stood of yore, and Barbican† it hight* : was called
A watchtower once; but now, so fate ordains,
Of all the pile an empty name remains.
From its old ruins brothel-houses rise,
Scenes of lewd loves, and of polluted joys;
Where their vast courts the mother-strumpets keep,
And, undisturbed by watch, in silence sleep.
Near these a nursery† erects its head,
Where queens are formed, and future heroes bred;
Where unfledged actors learn to laugh and cry,
Where infant punks* their tender voices try, whores
And little Maximins† the gods defy.
Great Fletcher† never treads in buskins† here,
Nor greater Jonson† dares in socks† appear.
But gentle Simkin† just reception finds
Amidst this monument of vanished minds:
Pure clinches* the suburbian Muse affords, puns
And Panton† waging harmless war with words.
Here Flecknoe, as a place to fame well known,
Ambitiously designed his Sh – – – 's throne;
For ancient Dekker† prophesied long since,
That in this pile should reign a mighty prince,
Born for a scourge of wit and flail of sense:

*Singleton* a royal musician
*Villerius* character in Davenant's *Siege of Rhodes* (1656)
*Augusta* ancient name for London
*Barbican* then a decayed area
*nursery* young actors' training ground
*Maximins* Maximin was a ranting character in Dryden's own *Tyrannic Love* (1669)
*Fletcher . . . socks* John Fletcher (1579–1625); Ben Jonson (1572–1637): dramatists. *Buskin* and *sock* are the traditional footwear in tragedy and comedy
*Simkin* a farcical character
*Panton* may be another farcical character
*Dekker* Thomas Dekker (*c.* 1570–1632), dramatist

To whom true dullness should some *Psyches* owe,
But worlds of *Misers*† from his pen should flow;
*Humorists* and *Hypocrites* it should produce,
Whole Raymond families, and tribes of Bruce.†
Now Empress Fame had published the renown
Of Sh – – – 's coronation through the town.
Roused by report of Fame, the nations meet,
From near Bunhill and distant Watling Street.
No Persian carpets spread th'imperial way,
But scattered limbs of mangled poets lay:
From dusty shops neglected authors come,
Martyrs of pies,† and relics of the bum.
Much Heywood, Shirley, Ogilby† there lay,
But loads of Sh – – – almost choked the way.
Bilked stationers* for yeomen stood prepared, booksellers
And H – – – was captain of the guard.
The hoary Prince in majesty appeared,
High on a throne of his own labours reared.
At his right hand our young Ascanius† sate,
Rome's other hope, and pillar of the State.
His brows thick fogs, instead of glories, grace,
And lambent dullness played around his face.
As Hannibal† did to the altars come,
Sworn by his sire a mortal foe to Rome;
So Sh – – – swore, nor should his vow be vain,
That he till death true dullness would maintain;
And in his father's right, and realm's defence,
Ne'er to have peace with wit, nor truce with sense.
The King himself the sacred unction† made,
As King by office, and as priest by trade:
In his sinister hand, instead of ball,†
He placed a mighty mug of potent ale;
*Love's Kingdom*† to his right he did convey,
At once his sceptre and his rule of sway;
Whose righteous lore the prince had practised young,
And from whose loins recorded *Psyche* sprung.

*Misers . . . Bruce* plays by Shadwell, and characters from them
*pies* waste paper lined baking dishes or served in privies
*Ogilby* John Ogilby (1600–76), in Dryden's view a bad poet and translator. Henry Herringman published plays by Shadwell and Dryden
*Ascanius* son of the hero of Virgil's epic *Aeneid*: Book II is parodied here
*Hannibal* Carthaginian hero, sworn to be a foe to Rome when aged nine
*unction* oil used at coronation ceremony, which is further parodied in *ball* (monarch's orb)
*Love's Kingdom* a play by Flecknoe

His temples last with poppies[†] were o'erspread,
That nodding seemed to consecrate his head.
Just at that point of time, if fame not lie,
On his left hand twelve reverend owls did fly.
So Romulus,[†] 'tis sung, by Tiber's brook,
Presage of sway from twice six vultures took.
Th' admiring throng loud acclamations make,
And omens of his future empire take.
The sire then shook the honours of his head,
And from his brows damps of oblivion shed
Full on the filial dullness: long he stood,
Repelling from his breast the raging god;[†]
At length burst out in this prophetic mood:
'Heavens bless my son, from Ireland let him reign
To far Barbados on the western main;
Of his dominion may no end be known,
And greater than his father's be his throne.
Beyond *Love's Kingdom* let him stretch his pen.'
He paused, and all the people cried, 'Amen.'
Then thus continued he: 'My son, advance
Still in new impudence, new ignorance.
Success let others teach, learn thou from me
Pangs without birth, and fruitless industry.
Let *Virtuosos* in five years be writ,
Yet not one thought accuse thy toil of wit.
Let gentle George[†] in triumph tread the stage,
Make Dorimant betray, and Loveit rage;
Let Cully, Cockwood, Fopling charm the pit,
And in their folly show the writer's wit.
Yet still thy fools shall stand in thy defence,
And justify their author's want of sense.
Let 'em be all by thy own model made
Of dullness, and desire no foreign aid:
That they to future ages may be known,
Not copies drawn, but issue of thy own.
Nay let thy men of wit too be the same,
All full of thee, and differing but in name;

*poppies* sleep-inducing; but Shadwell also used opium
*Romulus* founder of Rome; owls suggest unheroic darkness
*raging god* Flecknoe is possessed, in a parody of epic prophecy
*George* Sir George Etherege (*c.* 1635–91), a truly witty dramatist, creator of the characters listed

But let no alien S–dl–y† interpose
To lard with wit thy hungry *Epsom* prose.
And when false flowers of rhetoric thou wouldst cull,
Trust nature, do not labour to be dull;
But write thy best, and top; and in each line
Sir Formal's† oratory will be thine;
Sir Formal, though unsought, attends thy quill,
And does thy northern dedications fill.
Nor let false friends seduce thy mind to fame,
By arrogating Jonson's hostile name.
Let father Flecknoe fire thy mind with praise,
And uncle Ogilby thy envy raise.
Thou art my blood, where Jonson has no part;
What share have we in nature or in art?
Where did his wit on learning fix a brand,
And rail at arts he did not understand?
Where made he love in Prince Nicander's† vein,
Or swept the dust in *Psyche*'s humble strain?
Where sold he bargains, "whip-stitch, kiss my arse,"
Promised a play and dwindled to a farce?
When did his muse from Fletcher scenes purloin,
As thou whole Etherege dost transfuse to thine?
But so transfused as oil on water's flow,
His always floats above, thine sinks below.
This is thy province, this thy wondrous way,
New humours to invent for each new play:
This is that boasted bias of thy mind,
By which one way, to dullness, 'tis inclined,
Which makes thy writings lean on one side still,
And in all changes that way bends thy will.
Nor let thy mountain belly make pretence
Of likeness; thine's a tympany† of sense.
A tun of man in thy large bulk is writ,
But sure thou'rt but a kilderkin† of wit.
Like mine thy gentle numbers feebly creep,
Thy tragic muse gives smiles, thy comic sleep.
With whate'er gall thou settest thyself to write,
Thy inoffensive satires never bite.

*S–dl–y* Sir Charles Sedley (1638–1701), playwright, gave *Epsom Wells* at least its prologue
*Sir Formal* Sir Formal Trifle, a florid orator in *The Virtuoso*
*Nicander* Prince Nicander is in *Psyche*. The low language of l.181 is an example from Shadwell of 'selling a bargain' – giving an unexpected coarse reply
*tympany* Shadwell's large but empty belly
*kilderkin* small cask

In thy felonious heart though venom lies,
It does but touch thy Irish† pen and dies.
Thy genius calls thee not to purchase fame
In keen iambics,† but mild anagram:
Leave writing plays, and choose for thy command
Some peaceful province in acrostic land.
There thou may'st wings display† and altars raise,
And torture one poor word ten thousand ways.
Or if thou wouldst thy different talents suit,
Set thy own songs, and sing them to thy lute.'
He said; but his last words were scarcely heard,
For Bruce and Longvil† had a trap prepared,
And down they sent the yet declaiming bard.
Sinking he left his drugget robe behind,
Borne upwards by a subterranean wind.
The mantle† fell to the young prophet's part,
With double portion of his father's art.

*c.* 1678 1682

# TO THE MEMORY OF MR OLDHAM†

Farewell, too little and too lately known,
Whom I began to think and call my own;
For sure our souls were near allied, and thine
Cast in the same poetic mould with mine.
One common note on either lyre did strike,
And knaves and fools we both abhorred alike:
To the same goal did both our studies drive;
The last set out the soonest did arrive.
Thus Nisus† fell upon the slippery place,
While his young friend performed and won the race.

*Irish* neither poet was Irish, but it suggested barbarousness
*keen iambics* sharp satire
*display* George Herbert's *Easter Wings* and *The Altar* (1633) take the shape of their subjects
*Bruce and Longvil* characters who drop Sir Formal Trifle through a trapdoor
*mantle* parodies the succession of Elisha, as a whirlwind carries the prophet Elijah to heaven (II Kings 2)

*To the memory of Mr Oldham* John Oldham (1653–83), author of *Satires upon the Jesuits*, probably met Dryden within the two years before his early death. The allusions recall classical laments for promise cut short
*Nisus* Virgil tells in *Aeneid*, V. 315–19 how Nisus slipped in a pool of blood, and his friend Euryalus won

O early ripe! to thy abundant store
What could advancing age have added more?
It might (what nature never gives the young)
Have taught the numbers† of thy native tongue.
But satire needs not those, and wit will shine
Through the harsh cadence of a rugged line;
A noble error, and but seldom made,
When poets are by too much force betrayed.
Thy generous fruits, though gathered ere their prime,
Still showed a quickness; and maturing time
But mellows what we write to the dull sweets of rhyme.
Once more, hail and farewell;† farewell, thou young,
But ah too short, Marcellus† of our tongue;
Thy brows with ivy, and with laurels† bound;
But fate and gloomy night encompass thee around.

1684

# A SONG FOR ST CECILIA'S DAY, 1687†

I

From harmony, from heavenly harmony
This universal frame† began.
When Nature underneath a heap
Of jarring atoms lay,
And could not heave her head,
The tuneful voice was heard from high:
'Arise, ye more than dead.'
Then cold, and hot, and moist, and dry,
In order to their stations leap,
And music's power obey.
From harmony, from heavenly harmony

*numbers* versification (often 'harsh' in earlier satire)
*hail and farewell* translates a phrase, *ave atque vale*, from the elegy to his brother by the Roman poet, Catullus (*c.* 84–*c.* 54 BC)
*Marcellus* another Roman, prematurely dead; nephew of Augustus, commemorated in *Aeneid*, VI
*laurels* the traditional wreath of the poet
*A Song for St Cecilia's Day* The patroness of music was regularly commemorated by odes on 22 November. This was set to music by Draghi and later by Handel. It touches the traditional themes of the harmony of creation and the emotional power of music
*frame* the universe divinely created from the elements of chaos (l.8)

This universal frame began:
From harmony to harmony
Through all the compass* of the notes it ran, range
The diapason† closing full in man.

II

What passion cannot music raise and quell!
When Jubal† struck the corded shell,
His listening brethren stood around,
And wondering, on their faces fell
To worship that celestial sound.
Less than a god they thought there could not dwell
Within the hollow of that shell
That spoke so sweetly and so well.
What passion cannot music raise and quell!

III

The trumpet's loud clangour
Excites us to arms
With shrill notes of anger
And mortal alarms.
The double double double beat
Of the thundering drum
Cries: 'Hark! the foes come;
Charge, charge, 'tis too late to retreat.'

IV

The soft complaining flute
In dying notes discovers
The woes of hopeless lovers,
Whose dirge is whispered by the warbling lute.

V

Sharp violins proclaim
Their jealous pangs, and desperation,
Fury, frantic indignation,
Depth of pains, and height of passion,
For the fair, disdainful dame.

VI

But oh! what art can teach,
What human voice can reach,

*diapason* concord of an octave

*Jubal* father of music (Genesis 4), with a strung shell

The sacred organ's praise?
Notes inspiring holy love,
Notes that wing their heavenly ways
To mend the choirs above.

VII

Orpheus† could lead the savage race;
And trees unrooted left their place,
Sequacious* of the lyre; following
But bright Cecilia raised the wonder higher;
When to her organ vocal breath was given,
An angel heard, and straight appeared,
Mistaking earth for heaven.

GRAND CHORUS

*As from the power of sacred lays*
*The spheres† began to move,*
*And sung the great Creator's praise*
*To all the blest above;*
*So, when the last and dreadful hour*
*This crumbling pageant shall devour,*
*The trumpet† shall be heard on high,*
*The dead shall live, the living die,*
*And music shall untune the sky.*

1688

# LINES ON MILTON

Three poets,† in three distant ages born,
Greece, Italy, and England did adorn.
The first in loftiness of thought surpassed;
The next in majesty; in both the last.

*Orpheus* legendary for his musical power over nature; Cecilia's music can affect even angels
*spheres* traditionally, the spheres carrying the planets moved to music
*trumpet* the last trump will announce the end of the world
*Three poets* Homer, Virgil, Milton, masters respectively of Greek, Latin and modern (1608–74) English epic poetry

The force of Nature could no farther go:
To make a third she joined the former two.

1688

## TO MY HONOURED KINSMAN JOHN DRIDEN†

How blessed is he who leads a country life,
Unvexed with anxious cares, and void of strife!
Who, studying peace and shunning civil rage,
Enjoyed his youth, and now enjoys his age:
All who deserve his love, he makes his own;
And, to be loved himself, needs only to be known.
Just, good, and wise, contending neighbours come,
From your award to wait their final doom;* judgement
And, foes before, return in friendship home.
Without their cost, you terminate the cause,
And save th' expense of long litigious laws,
Where suits are traversed, and so little won,
That he who conquers is but last undone:
Such are not your decrees; but so designed,
The sanction leaves a lasting peace behind;
Like your own soul, serene: a pattern of your mind.
Promoting concord, and composing strife,
Lord of yourself, uncumbered with a wife;
Where, for a year, a month, perhaps a night,
Long penitence succeeds a short delight:
Minds are so hardly matched, that even the first,
Though paired by Heaven, in Paradise were cursed,
For man and woman, though in one they grow,
Yet, first or last, return again to two.
He to God's image, she to his was made;
So, farther from the fount, the stream at random strayed.
How could he stand, when, put to double pain,
He must a weaker than himself sustain?

*To my Honoured Kinsman John Driden* the poet's cousin (1635–1708) was an MP (l.121). The praise of rural independence owes much to the Roman poet Horace

Each might have stood perhaps, but each alone;
Two wrestlers help to pull each other down.
Not that my verse would blemish all the fair;
But yet if *some* be bad, 'tis wisdom to beware;
And better shun the bait, than struggle in the snare.
Thus have you shunned, and shun the married state,
Trusting as little as you can to fate.
No porter guards the passage of your door,
T'admit the wealthy, and exclude the poor;
For God, who gave the riches, gave the heart
To sanctify the whole, by giving part.
Heaven, who foresaw the will, the means has wrought,
And to the second son a blessing brought:
The first-begotten had his father's share;
But you, like Jacob,† are Rebecca's heir.
So may your stores and fruitful fields increase;
And ever be you blessed, who live to bless.
As Ceres† sowed, where'er her chariot flew;
As Heaven in deserts rained the bread of dew,
So free to many, to relations most,
You feed with manna† your own Israel host.
With crowds attended of your ancient race,
You seek the champaign† sports, or sylvan chase;
With well-breathed beagles you surround the wood,
Even then industrious of the common good;
And often have you brought the wily fox
To suffer for the firstlings of the flocks;
Chased even amid the folds, and made to bleed,
Like felons, where they did the murderous deed.
This fiery game your active youth maintained;
Not yet by years extinguished, though restrained:
You season still with sports your serious hours;
For age but tastes of pleasures, youth devours.
The hare in pastures or in plains is found,
Emblem of human life, who runs the round;
And after all his wandering ways are done,
His circle fills, and ends where he begun,
Just as the setting meets the rising sun.
Thus princes ease their cares; but happier he
Who seeks not pleasure through necessity,

*Jacob* John, the younger son, inherited an estate through his mother (see Genesis 27)
*Ceres* Roman goddess of corn
*manna* Israelites' food in wilderness (Exodus 16)
*champaign* open fields

Than such as once on slippery thrones were placed;
And chasing, sigh to think themselves are chased.
  So lived our sires, ere doctors learned to kill,
And multiplied with theirs the weekly bill,†
The first physicians by debauch were made;
Excess began and sloth sustains the trade.
Pity the generous kind their cares bestow
To search forbidden truths (a sin to know),
To which if human science could attain,
The doom of death, pronounced by God, were vain.
In vain the leech would interpose delay;
Fate fastens first, and vindicates† the prey.
What help from art's endeavours can we have?
Gibbons† but guesses, nor is sure to save;
But Maurus† sweeps whole parishes, and peoples every grave;
And no more mercy to mankind will use,
Than when he robbed and murdered Maro's† muse.
Would'st thou be soon dispatched, and perish whole?
Trust Maurus† with thy life, and M–lb—rne with thy soul.
  By chase our long-lived fathers earned their food;
Toil strung the nerves, and purified the blood:
But we their sons, a pampered race of men,
Are dwindled down to threescore years and ten.
Better to hunt in fields for health unbought
Than fee the doctor for a nauseous draught.
The wise, for cure, on exercise depend;
God never made his work for man to mend.
  The tree of knowledge, once in Eden placed,
Was easy found, but was forbid the taste:
O had our grandsire† walked without his wife,
He first had sought the better plant of life!
Now, both are lost: yet, wandering in the dark,
Physicians, for the tree, have found the bark.
They, labouring for relief of human kind,
With sharpened sight some remedies may find;
Th' apothecary-train is wholly blind.
From files a random recipe they take,
And many deaths of one prescription make.

---

*bill* of mortality: death statistics
*vindicates* takes vengeance on
*Gibbons* Dryden's doctor
*Maurus* Sir Richard Blackmore (1654–1729), doctor and dull epic poet (*Maro* – Virgil – represents true epic). He and Milbourne, a clergyman, had attacked Dryden
*grandsire* Adam (Genesis 2,3)

Garth,[†] generous as his Muse, prescribes and gives;
The shopman sells, and by destruction lives:
Ungrateful tribe! who, like the viper's brood,
From medicine issuing, suck their mother's blood!
Let these obey, and let the learned prescribe,
That men may die without a double bribe:
Let them but under their superiors kill,
When doctors first have signed the bloody bill:
He 'scapes the best who, nature to repair,
Draws physic from the fields, in draughts of vital air.
  You hoard not health for your own private use,
But on the public spend the rich produce;
When, often urged, unwilling to be great,
Your country calls you from your loved retreat,
And sends to senates, charged with common care,
Which none more shuns, and none can better bear.
Where could they find another formed so fit,
To poise with solid sense a sprightly wit?
Were these both wanting (as they both abound),
Where could so firm integrity be found?
  Well born, and wealthy, wanting no support,
You steer betwixt the country and the court;
Nor gratify whate'er the great desire,
Nor grudging give what public needs require.
Part must be left, a fund when foes invade,
And part employed to roll the watery trade:
Even Canaan's[†] happy land, when worn with toil,
Required a sabbath[†] year to mend the meagre soil.
  Good senators (and such are you) so give,
That kings may be supplied, the people thrive:
And he, when want requires, is truly wise,
Who slights not foreign aids, nor overbuys;
But on our native strength, in time of need, relies.
Munster was bought, we boast not the success;
Who fights for gain, for greater makes his peace.
  Our foes, compelled by need, have peace[†] embraced;
The peace both parties want is like to last:
Which if secure, securely we may trade;
Or, not secure, should never have been made.
Safe in ourselves, while on ourselves we stand,

*Garth* Sir Samuel Garth (1661–1719), doctor and burlesque poet (*The Dispensary*)
*Canaan* Jews' promised land
*sabbath* one rest period in seven (Leviticus 25)
*peace* a long war against France ended in the Peace of Ryswick (1697)

The sea is ours, and that defends the land.
Be, then, the naval stores the nation's care,
New ships to build, and battered to repair.
  Observe the war, in every annual course;
What has been done, was done with British force:
Namur subdued is England's palm alone;
The rest besieged, but we constrained the town:
We saw th' event that followed our success;
France, though pretending arms, pursued the peace,
Obliged, by one sole treaty, to restore
What twenty years of war had won before.
Enough for Europe has our Albion fought;
Let us enjoy the peace our blood has bought.
When once the Persian king was put to flight,
The weary Macedons refused to fight;
Themselves their own mortality confessed,
And left the son of Jove† to quarrel for the rest.
  Even victors are by victories undone;
Thus Hannibal,† with foreign laurels won,
To Carthage was recalled, too late to keep his own.
While sore of battle, while our wounds are green,
Why should we tempt the doubtful die again?
In wars renewed, uncertain of success;
Sure of a share, as umpires of the peace.
  A patriot both the king and country serves;
Prerogative and privilege preserves:
Of each our laws the certain limit show;
One must not ebb, nor t'other overflow.
Betwixt the prince and parliament we stand;
The barriers of the state on either hand:
May neither overflow, for then they drown the land.
When both are full, they feed our blessed abode;
Like those that watered once the paradise of God.
  Some overpoise of sway by turns they share;
In peace the people, and the prince in war;
Consuls† of moderate power in calms were made;
When the Gauls came, one sole dictator† swayed.
  Patriots, in peace, assert the people's right,
With noble stubbornness resisting might:
No lawless mandates from the court receive,

*son of Jove* Alexander the Great, of Macedon (356–323 BC)
*Hannibal* leading general against Rome
*consuls* appointed joint leaders of Rome; in crisis, replaced by a single *dictator*

Nor lend by force, but in a body give.
Such was your generous grandsire,[†] free to grant
In parliaments that weighed their prince's want:
But so tenacious of the common cause,
As not to lend the king against his laws;
And, in a loathsome dungeon doomed to lie,
In bonds retained his birthright liberty,
And shamed oppression, till it set him free.
O true descendant of a patriot line,
Who, while thou sharest their lustre, lendest 'em thine,
Vouchsafe this picture of thy soul to see;
'Tis so far good, as it resembles thee.
The beauties to th' original I owe,
Which when I miss, my own defects I show:
Nor think the kindred Muses thy disgrace;
A poet is not born in every race.
Two of a house few ages can afford;
One to perform, another to record.
Praiseworthy actions are by thee embraced,
And 'tis my praise to make thy praises last.
For even when death dissolves our human frame,
The soul returns to Heaven, from whence it came;
Earth keeps the body, verse preserves the fame.

1700

## *From* AN ESSAY OF DRAMATIC POESY

### *[Shakespeare and Ben Jonson Compared]*

To begin, then, with Shakespeare: he was the man who of all modern, and perhaps ancient poets, had the largest and most comprehensive soul. All the images of nature were still present to him, and he drew them not laboriously, but luckily; when he describes anything, you more than see it, you feel it too. Those who accuse him to have wanted learning give him the greater commendation: he was naturally learned; he needed not the spectacles of books to read nature; he looked inwards, and found her there. I cannot say he is everywhere alike; were he so, I

*grandsire* Sir Erasmus Dryden opposed illegal loans to Charles I, and was imprisoned

should do him injury to compare him with the greatest of mankind. He is many times flat, insipid; his comic wit degenerating into clenches,[†] his serious swelling into bombast. But he is always great when some great occasion is presented to him; no man can say he ever had a fit subject for his wit, and did not then raise himself as high above the rest of poets,

> quantum lenta solent inter viburna cupressi.[†]
> [as do cypresses among the bending osiers]

The consideration of this made Mr Hales[†] of Eton say that there was no subject of which any poet ever writ, but he would produce it much better treated of in Shakespeare; and however others are now generally preferred before him, yet the age wherein he lived, which had contemporaries with him Fletcher[†] and Jonson, never equalled them to him in their esteem. And in the last King's court, when Ben's reputation was at highest, Sir John Suckling,[†] and with him the greater part of the courtiers, set our Shakespeare far above him. . . .

As for Jonson, to whose character I am now arrived, if we look upon him while he was himself (for his last plays were but his dotages), I think him the most learned and judicious writer which any theatre ever had. He was a most severe judge of himself as well as others. One cannot say he wanted wit, but rather that he was frugal of it. In his works you find little to retrench or alter. Wit and language, and humour also in some measure, we had before him; but something of art was wanting to the drama till he came. He managed his strength to more advantage than any who preceded him. You seldom find him making love in any of his scenes, or endeavouring to move the passions; his genius was too sullen and saturnine to do it gracefully, especially when he knew he came after those who had performed both to such an height. Humour was his proper sphere, and in that he delighted most to represent mechanic people. He was deeply conversant in the Ancients, both Greek and Latin, and he borrowed boldly from them: there is scarce a poet or historian among the Roman authors of those times whom he has not translated in *Sejanus* and *Catiline*.[†] But he has done his robberies so openly that one may see he fears not to be taxed by any law. He invades authors like a monarch, and what would be theft in other poets is only victory in him. With the spoils of these writers he so represents old Rome to us, in its rites, ceremonies, and customs, that if one of their poets had written either of his tragedies, we had seen

*clenches* puns, mere word play
*quantum . . . cupressi* (Virgil, *Eclogues*, I)
*Hales* John Hales (1584–1656) of Eton College
*Fletcher* John Fletcher (1579–1625), dramatist
*Suckling* Sir John Suckling (1609–41), courtier-dramatist under Charles I
*Sejanus* and *Catiline* Roman tragedies (1603, 1611) by Ben Jonson (1572–1637)

less of it than in him. If there was any fault in his language, 'twas that he weaved it too closely and laboriously in his serious plays; perhaps, too, he did a little too much romanize our tongue, leaving the words which he translated almost as much Latin as he found them: wherein, though he learnedly followed the idiom of their language, he did not enough comply with ours. If I would compare him with Shakespeare, I must acknowledge him the more correct poet, but Shakespeare the greater wit. Shakespeare was the Homer, or father of our dramatic poets; Jonson was the Virgil, the pattern of elaborate writing; I admire him, but I love Shakespeare. To conclude of him, as he has given us the most correct plays, so in the precepts which he has laid down in his *Discoveries*,† we have as many and profitable rules for perfecting the stage as any wherewith the French can furnish us. . . .

1668, 1684

## *From* GROUNDS OF CRITICISM IN TRAGEDY

### *[Shakespeare's language]*

If Shakespeare be allowed, as I think he must, to have made his characters distinct, it will easily be inferred that he understood the nature of the passions: because it has been proved already that confused passions make undistinguishable characters: yet I cannot deny that he has his failings; but they are not so much in the passions themselves as in his manner of expression: he often obscures his meaning by his words, and sometimes makes it unintelligible. I will not say of so great a poet that he distinguished not the blown puffy style from true sublimity; but I may venture to maintain that the fury of his fancy often transported him beyond the bounds of judgment, either in coining of new words and phrases, or racking words which were in use into the violence of a catachresis.† 'Tis not that I would explode the use of metaphors from passions, for Longinus† thinks 'em necessary to raise it; but to use 'em at every word, to say nothing without a metaphor, a simile, an image, or description, is I doubt to smell a little too strongly of the buskin.† . . . [quotes from *Hamlet* and *Richard II*]

*Discoveries* or *Timber*, Jonson's notebooks (pub. 1640)
*catachresis* misapplication of a word
*Longinus* critic who wrote on the sublime (first century AD)
*buskin* literally, boot worn in classical tragedy

If Shakespeare were stripped of all the bombast† in his passions, and dressed in the most vulgar words, we should find the beauties of his thoughts remaining; if his embroideries were burnt down, there would still be silver at the bottom of the melting-pot: but I fear (at least let me fear it for myself) that we who ape his sounding words have nothing of his thought, but are all outside; there is not so much as a dwarf within our giant's clothes. Therefore, let not Shakespeare suffer for our sakes; 'tis our fault, who succeed him in an age which is more refined, if we imitate him so ill that we copy his failings only, and make a virtue of that in our writings which in his was an imperfection. . . .

1679

## *From the* PREFACE TO *OVID'S EPISTLES* *[Translation]*

All translation, I suppose, may be reduced to these three heads.

First, that of metaphrase, or turning an author word by word, and line by line, from one language into another. Thus, or near this manner, was Horace† his *Art of Poetry* translated by Ben Jonson. The second way is that of paraphrase, or translation with latitude, where the author is kept in view by the translator, so as never to be lost, but his words are not so strictly followed as his sense, and that too is admitted to be amplified, but not altered. Such is Mr Waller's† translation of Virgil's Fourth Aeneid. The third way is that of imitation, where the translator (if now he has not lost that name) assumes the liberty not only to vary from the words and sense, but to forsake them both as he sees occasion; and taking only some general hints from the original, to run division† on the ground-work, as he pleases. Such is Mr Cowley's† practice in turning two Odes of Pindar, and one of Horace, into English. . . .

1680

*bombast* inflated language
*Horace* Latin poet and critic (65–8 BC)
*Waller* Edmund Waller (1608–87), poetic father of 'Augustanism'
*run division* (musical) make variation on theme
*Cowley* Abraham Cowley (1618–67) imitated Greek odes of Pindar (522–443 BC)

# *From* DISCOURSE CONCERNING SATIRE

The nicest and most delicate touches of satire consist in fine raillery. . . . 'Tis not reading, 'tis not imitation of an author, which can produce this fineness: it must be inborn; it must proceed from a genius, and particular way of thinking, which is not to be taught; and therefore not to be imitated by him who has it not from nature. How easy it is to call rogue and villain, and that wittily! But how hard to make a man appear a fool, a blockhead, or a knave, without using any of those opprobrious terms! To spare the grossness of the names, and to do the thing yet more severely, is to draw a full face, and to make the nose and cheeks stand out, and yet not to employ any depth of shadowing. This is the mystery of that noble trade, which yet no master can teach to his apprentice: he may give the rules, but the scholar is never the nearer in his practice. Neither is it true that this fineness of raillery is offensive. A witty man is tickled while he is hurt in this manner, and a fool feels it not. The occasion of an offence may possibly be given, but he cannot take it. If it be granted that in effect this way does more mischief; that a man is secretly wounded, and though he be not sensible himself, yet the malicious world will find it for him: yet there is still a vast difference betwixt the slovenly butchering of a man, and the fineness of a stroke that separates the head from the body, and leaves it standing in its place. A man may be capable, as Jack Ketch's† wife said of his servant, of a plain piece of work, a bare hanging; but to make a malefactor die sweetly was only belonging to her husband. I wish I could apply it to myself, if the reader would be kind enough to think it belongs to me. The character of Zimri in my *Absalom* is, in my opinion, worth the whole poem: 'tis not bloody, but 'tis ridiculous enough. And he for whom it was intended was too witty to resent it as an injury. If I had railed, I might have suffered for it justly: but I managed my own work more happily, perhaps more dexterously. I avoided the mention of great crimes, and applied myself to the representing of blindsides,† and little extravagancies; to which, the wittier a man is, he is generally the more obnoxious†. It succeeded as I wished; the jest went round, and he was laughed at in his turn who began the frolic. . . .

1693

*Jack Ketch* public executioner (d.1686)
*blindsides* unseen foibles
*obnoxious* liable

# *From* PREFACE TO *FABLES ANCIENT AND MODERN*

## *[Chaucer]*

In the first place, as he is the father of English poetry, so I hold him in the same degree of veneration as the Grecians held Homer, or the Romans Virgil. He is a perpetual fountain of good sense; learned in all sciences; and therefore speaks properly on all subjects. As he knew what to say, so he knows also when to leave off; a continence which is practised by few writers, and scarcely by any of the Ancients, excepting Virgil and Horace. . . .

Chaucer followed nature everywhere, but was never so bold to go beyond her; and there is a great difference of being *poeta* and *nimis poeta*,† if we may believe Catullus, as much as betwixt a modest behaviour and affectation. The verse of Chaucer, I confess, is not harmonious to us; but 'tis like the eloquence of one whom Tacitus† commends, it was *auribus istius temporis accommodata* [suited to the ears of that time]. They who lived with him, and some time after him, thought it musical; and it continues so, even in our judgment, if compared with the numbers of Lydgate and Gower,† his contemporaries: there is the rude sweetness of a Scotch tune in it, which is natural and pleasing, though not perfect. 'Tis true, I cannot go so far as he who published the last edition of him; for he would make us believe the fault is in our ears, and that there were really ten syllables in a verse where we find but nine. But this opinion is not worth confuting; 'tis so gross and obvious an error that common sense (which is a rule in everything but matters of faith and revelation) must convince the reader that equality of numbers, in every verse which we call *heroic*, was either not known or not always practised, in Chaucer's age. It were an easy matter to produce some thousands of his verses which are lame† for want of half a foot, and sometimes a whole one, and which no pronunciation can make otherwise. We can only say that he lived in the infancy of our poetry, and that nothing is brought to perfection at the first. We must be children before we grow men. . . .

He must have been a man of a most wonderful comprehensive nature, because, as it has been truly observed of him, he has taken into the compass of his *Canterbury Tales* the various manners and humours (as

*nimis poeta* too much a poet (actually from Latin satirist Martial, 40–104)
*Tacitus* Roman historian (55–*c.* 115)
*Lydgate . . . Gower* John Lydgate (1370–1449); John Gower (1330–1408), poets
*lame* the true pronunciation of Chaucer's verse had been forgotten

we now call them) of the whole English nation in his age. Not a single character has escaped him. All his pilgrims are severally distinguished from each other; and not only in their inclinations, but in their very physiognomies and persons. Baptista Porta† could not have described their natures better than by the marks which the poet gives them. The matter and manner of their tales, and of their telling, are so suited to their different educations, humours, and callings, that each of them would be improper in any other mouth. Even the grave and serious characters are distinguished by their several sorts of gravity: their discourses are such as belong to their age, their calling, and their breeding; such as are becoming of them, and of them only. Some of his persons are vicious, and some virtuous; some are unlearned, or (as Chaucer calls them) *lewd*, and some are learned. Even the ribaldry of the low characters is different: the Reeve, the Miller, and the Cook, are several men, and distinguished from each other as much as the mincing Lady Prioress and the broad-speaking, gap-toothed Wife of Bath. But enough of this: there is such a variety of game springing up before me that I am distracted in my choice, and know not which to follow. 'Tis sufficient to say, according to the proverb, that here is God's plenty. We have our forefathers and great-grand-dames all before us, as they were in Chaucer's days; their general characters are still remaining in mankind, and even in England, though they are called by other names than those of Monks, and Friars, and Canons, and Lady Abbesses, and Nuns: for mankind is ever the same, and nothing lost out of nature, though everything is altered. . . .

1700

*Baptista Porta* Giambattista della Porta (1535–1615), Italian author on face and character

# Samuel Pepys

1633–1703

Pepys was educated at St Paul's School, and at Cambridge. He gradually rose in his career as a civil servant, which culminated in two periods as Secretary to the Admiralty, in which he worked hard to improve the navy. In 1660–9, he kept his famous shorthand *Diary* (pub. 1825), where observation of the Court and public life is combined with his personal interests in music, drama, science and women. The extracts are from the period of the Great Fire of London, which destroyed 13,000 houses and many public buildings, leaving 100,000 people homeless. Note the use of the river for everyday transport.

## *From* DIARY

### *[The Great Fire of London]*

September 1666

2d. *Lords day.* Some of our maids sitting up late last night to get things ready against our feast today, Jane called us up, about 3 in the morning, to tell us of a great fire they saw in the City. So I rose, and slipped on my nightgown and went to her window, and thought it to be on the back side of Mark Lane at the furthest; but being unused to such fires as followed, I thought it far enough off, and so went to bed again and to sleep. About 7 rose again to dress myself, and there looked out at the window and saw the fire not so much as it was, and further off. So to my closet to set things to rights after yesterday's cleaning. By and by Jane comes and tells me that she hears that above 300 houses have been burned down tonight by the fire we saw, and that it was now burning down all Fish Street by London Bridge. So I made myself ready presently, and walked to the Tower and there got up upon one of the high places, Sir J. Robinson's little son going up with me; and there I did see the houses at that end of the bridge[†] all on fire, and an infinite great fire on this and the other side the end of the bridge – which, among other people, did trouble me for poor little Michell and

*bridge* old London Bridge carried houses and shops

our Sarah on the bridge. So down, with my heart full of trouble, to the Lieutenant of the Tower, who tells me that it begun this morning in the King's baker's house in Pudding Lane, and that it hath burned down St Magnus Church and most part of Fish Street already. So I down to the water-side and there got a boat and through bridge, and there saw a lamentable fire. Poor Michell's house, as far as the Old Swan, already burned that way and the fire running further, that in a very little time it got as far as the Steelyard while I was there. Everybody endeavouring to remove their goods, and flinging into the river or bringing them into lighters[†] that lay off. Poor people staying in their houses as long as till the very fire touched them, and then running into boats or clambering from one pair of stair by the water-side to another. And among other things, the poor pigeons I perceive were loath to leave their houses, but hovered about the windows and balconies till they were some of them burned, their wings, and fell down.

Having stayed, and in an hour's time seen the fire rage every way, and nobody to my sight endeavouring to quench it, but to remove their goods and leave all to the fire, and having seen it get as far as the Steelyard, and the wind mighty high and driving it into the City, and everything, after so long a drought, proving combustible, even the very stones of churches, and among other things, the poor steeple by which pretty Mrs Horsley lives, and whereof my old school-fellow Elborough is parson, taken fire in the very top and there burned till it fall down – I to Whitehall with a gentleman with me who desired to go off from the Tower to see the fire in my boat – to Whitehall, and there up to the King's closet in the chapel, where people came about me and I did give them an account dismayed them all; and word was carried in to the King, so I was called for and did tell the King and Duke of York what I saw, and that unless his Majesty did command houses to be pulled down, nothing could stop the fire. They seemed much troubled, and the King commanded me to go to my Lord Mayor from him and command him to spare no houses but to pull down before the fire every way. The Duke of York bid me tell him that if he would have any more soldiers, he shall; and so did my Lord Arlington afterward, as a great secret. Here meeting with Captain Cocke, I in his coach, which he lent me, and Creed with me, to Paul's;[†] and there walked along Watling Street as well as I could, every creature coming away loaden with goods to save – and here and there sick people carried away in beds. Extraordinary good goods carried in carts and on backs. At last met my Lord Mayor in Canning Street, like a man spent, with a handkercher about his neck. To the King's message, he cried like a fainting woman, 'Lord, what can I do? I am spent. People will not obey me. I have been

*lighters* goods-barges

*Paul's* old St Paul's Cathedral

pulling down houses. But the fire overtakes us faster then we can do it.' That he needed no more soldiers; and that for himself, he must go and refresh himself, having been up all night. So he left me, and I him, and walked home – seeing people all almost distracted and no manner of means used to quench the fire. The houses too, so very thick thereabouts, and full of matter for burning, as pitch and tar, in Thames Street – and warehouses of oil and wines and brandy and other things. Here I saw Mr Isaac Houblon, that handsome man – prettily dressed and dirty at his door at Dowgate, receiving some of his brothers' things whose houses were on fire; and as he says, have been removed twice already, and he doubts (as it soon proved) that they must be in a little time removed from his house also – which was a sad consideration. And to see the churches all filling with goods, by people who themselves should have been quietly there at this time. . . .

As soon as dined, I and Moone away and walked through the City, the streets full of nothing but people and horses and carts loaden with goods, ready to run over one another, and removing goods from one burned house to another – they now removing out of Canning Street (which received goods in the morning) into Lombard Street and further; and among others, I now saw my little goldsmith Stokes receiving some friend's goods, whose house itself was burned the day after. We parted at Paul's, he home and I to Paul's Wharf, where I had appointed a boat to attend me; and took in Mr Carcasse and his brother, whom I met in the street, and carried them below and above bridge, to and again, to see the fire, which was now got further, both below and above, and no likelihood of stopping it. Met with the King and Duke of York in their barge, and with them to Queenhithe and there called Sir Rd. Browne to them. Their order was only to pull down houses apace, and so below bridge at the water-side; but little was or could be done, the fire coming upon them so fast. Good hopes there was of stopping it at the Three Cranes above, and at Botolphs Wharf below bridge, if care be used; but the wind carries it into the City, so as we know not by the water-side what it doth there. River full of lighters and boats taking in goods, and good goods swimming in the water; and only, I observed that hardly one lighter or boat in three that had the goods of a house in, but there was a pair of virginals† in it. Having seen as much as I could now, I away to Whitehall by appointment, and there walked to St James's Park, and there met my wife and Creed and Wood and his wife and walked to my boat, and there upon the water again, and to the fire up and down, it still increasing and the wind great. So near the fire as we could for smoke; and all over the Thames, with one's face in the

*virginals* keyboard musical instrument in a case

wind you were almost burned with a shower of firedrops – this is very true – so as houses were burned by these drops and flakes of fire, three or four, nay five or six houses, one from another. When we could endure no more upon the water, we to a little alehouse on the Bankside over against the Three Cranes, and there stayed till it was dark almost and saw the fire grow; and as it grew darker, appeared more and more, and in corners and upon steeples and between churches and houses, as far as we could see up the hill of the City, in a most horrid malicious bloody flame, not like the fine flame of an ordinary fire. Barbary and her husband away before us. We stayed till, it being darkish, we saw the fire as only one entire arch of fire from this to the other side the bridge, and in a bow up the hill, for an arch of above a mile long. It made me weep to see it. The churches, houses, and all on fire and flaming at once, and a horrid noise the flames made, and the cracking of houses at their ruin. So home with a sad heart, and there find everybody discoursing and lamenting the fire; and poor Tom Hater came with some few of his goods saved out of his house, which is burned upon Fish Street Hill. I invited him to lie at my house, and did receive his goods: but was deceived in his lying there, the noise coming every moment of the growth of the fire, so as we were forced to begin to pack up our own goods and prepare for their removal. And did by moonshine (it being brave, dry, and moonshine and warm weather) carry much of my goods into the garden, and Mr Hater and I did remove my money and iron chests into my cellar – as thinking that the safest place. And got my bags of gold into my office ready to carry away, and my chief papers of accounts also there, and my tallies† into a box by themselves. So great was our fear, as Sir W. Batten had carts come out of the country to fetch away his goods this night. We did put Mr Hater, poor man, to bed a little; but he got very little rest, so much noise being in my house, taking down of goods. . . .

5th. Home, and whereas I expected to have seen our house on fire, it being now about 7 a-clock, it was not. But to the fire, and there find greater hopes than I expected; for my confidence in finding our office† on fire was such, that I durst not ask anybody how it was with us, till I came and saw it not burned. But going to the fire, I find, by the blowing up of houses and the great help given by the workmen out of the King's yards, sent up by Sir W. Penn, there is a good stop given to it, as well at Mark Lane end as ours – it having only burned the dial of Barking Church, and part of the porch, and was there quenched. I up to the top of Barking steeple, and there saw the saddest sight of desolation that I

*tallies* notched accounting sticks
*office* the fire stopped just short of the Navy Office, north of the Tower

ever saw. Everywhere great fires. Oil-cellars and brimstone and other things burning. I became afeared to stay there long; and therefore down again as fast as I could, the fire being spread as far as I could see it, and to Sir W. Penn's and there eat a piece of cold meat, having eaten nothing since Sunday but the remains of Sunday's dinner.

Here I met with Mr Young and Whistler; and having removed all my things, and received good hopes that the fire at our end is stopped, they and I walked into the town and find Fenchurch Street, Gracious Street, and Lombard Street all in dust. The Exchange[†] a sad sight, nothing standing there of all the statues or pillars but Sir Tho. Gresham's picture[†] in the corner. Walked into Moorfields (our feet ready to burn, walking through the town among the hot coals) and find that full of people, and poor wretches carrying their goods there, and everybody keeping his goods together by themselves (and a great blessing it is to them that it is fair weather for them to keep abroad night and day); drank there, and paid twopence for a plain penny loaf.

Thence homeward, having passed through Cheapside and Newgate market, all burned – and seen Anthony Joyce's house in fire. And took up (which I keep by me) a piece of glass of Mercer's chapel in the street, where much more was, so melted and buckled with the heat of the fire, like parchment. I also did see a poor cat taken out of a hole in the chimney joining to the wall of the Exchange, with the hair all burned off the body and yet alive. So home at night, and find there good hopes of saving our office – but great endeavours of watching all night and having men ready; and so we lodged them in the office, and had drink and bread and cheese for them. And I lay down and slept a good night about midnight – though when I rose, I hear that there had been a great alarm of French and Duch being risen – which proved nothing. But it is a strange thing to see how long this time did look since Sunday, having been alway full of variety of actions, and little sleep, that it looked like a week or more. And I had forgot almost the day of the week.

1666

1825

*Exchange* the Royal Exchange, founded by Gresham (1519–79)

*picture* statue

# Thomas Sprat

1635–1713

Sprat became Bishop of Rochester, and published verse and a life of the poet Cowley; but he is best remembered for his *History of the Royal Society* (1667), the embodiment of modern experimental science, to which such writers as Aubrey, Cowley and Dryden also belonged. The first extract describes the Society's stylistic reforms; the second, the imaginative excitement of discovery.

## *From* THE HISTORY OF THE ROYAL SOCIETY

### *[The Prose Style Sought by the Royal Society]*

They have therefore been most rigorous in putting in execution the only remedy that can be found for this extravagance, i.e. this vicious abundance of phrase, the stricken metaphors, this volubility of tongue, which makes so great a noise in the world; and that has been, a constant resolution, to reject all the amplifications, digressions, and swellings of style; to return back to the primitive purity, and shortness, when men delivered so many things, almost in an equal number of words. They have exacted from all their members a close, naked, natural way of speaking; positive expressions; clear senses; a native easiness: bringing all things as near the mathematical plainness as they can; and preferring the language of artizans, countrymen, and merchants, before that of wits or scholars. . . .

1667

### *[Prospects of Scientific Discovery]*

This is the most natural method of the foundation and progress of manual arts. And they may still be advanced to a higher perfection, than they have yet obtained, either by the discovery of new matter, to employ men's hands, or by a new transplantation of the same matter, or by handling the old subjects of manufactures after a new way, in the same places.

And first, we have reason to expect that there may still arise new matter to be managed by human art and diligence; and that from the parts of the earth that are yet unknown, or from the new discovered America, or from our own seas and land, that have been long searched into, and inhabited.

If ever any more countries, which are now hidden from us, shall be revealed, it is not to be questioned, but there will be also opened to our observation, very many kinds of living creatures, of minerals, of plants, nay, of handicrafts, with which we have been hitherto unacquainted. This may well be expected, if we remember, that there was never yet any land discovered, which has not given us divers new sorts of animals, and fruits of different features and shapes, and virtues† from our own, or has not supplied us with some new artificial engine, and contrivance. And that our discoveries may still be enlarged to farther countries, it is a good proof, that so many spacious shores and mountains, and promontories, appear to our southern and northern sailors; of which we have yet no account, but only such as could be taken by a remote prospect at sea. From whence, and from the figure of the earth, it may be concluded, that almost as much space of ground remains still in the dark, as was fully known in the times of the Assyrian or Persian monarchy. So that without assuming the vain prophetic spirit, which I lately condemned, we may foretell, that the discovery of another new world is still behind.

To accomplish this, there is only wanting the invention of longitude,† which cannot now be far off, seeing it is generally allowed to be feasible, seeing so many rewards are ready to be heaped on the inventors; and (I will also add) seeing the Royal Society has taken it into its peculiar care. This, if it shall be once accomplished, will make well-nigh as much alteration in the world, as the invention of the needle† did before: and then our posterity may outgo us, as much as we can travel farther than the ancients; whose demigods and heroes did esteem it one of their chief exploits, to make a journey as far as the Pillars of Hercules.† Whoever shall think this to be a desperate business, they can only use the same arguments, wherewith Columbus† was at first made ridiculous, if he had been discouraged by the raillery of his adversaries, by the judgment of most astronomers of his time, and even by the entreaties of his own companions; but three days before he had a sight of land, we had lost the knowledge of half the world at once.

And as for the new discovered America, 'tis true, that has not been

*virtues* qualities
*longitude* map position east or west of a set line; the solution came in the later eighteenth century
*needle* magnetic compass
*Pillars of Hercules* limits of classical world, at Straits of Gibraltar
*Columbus* (1451–1506) 'discovered' America in 1492

altogether useless to the mechanic arts: but still we may guess, that much more of its bounty is to come, if we consider, that it has not yet been shown above two hundred years; which is scarce enough time to travel it over, describe, and measure it, much less to pierce into all its secrets. Beside this, a good part of this space was spent in the conquest and settling the Spanish government, which is a season improper for philosophical† discoveries. To this may be added, that the chief design of the Spaniards thither, has been the transportation of bullion; which being so profitable, they may well be thought to have overseen many other of its native riches. But above all, let us reflect on the temper of the Spaniards themselves: they suffer no strangers to arrive there; they permit not the natives to know more than becomes their slaves. And how unfit the Spanish humour is to improve manufactures, in a country so distant as the West Indies, we may learn by their practice in Spain itself, where they commonly disdain to exercise any manual crafts, and permit the profit of them to be carried away by strangers.

From all this we may make this conclusion, that if ever that vast tract of ground shall come to be more familiar to Europe, either by a free trade, or by conquest, or by any other revolution in its civil affairs, America will appear quite a new thing to us; and may furnish us with an abundance of rarities, both natural and artificial; of which we have been almost as much deprived by its present masters, as if it had still remained a part of the unknown world.

But lastly, to come nearer home, we have no ground to despair, but very much more matter, which has been yet unhandled, may still be brought to light, even in the most civil and most peopled countries; whose lands have been thoroughly measured by the hands of the most exact surveyors; whose underground riches have been accurately pried into; whose cities, islands, rivers, and provinces, have been described by the labours of geographers. It is not to be doubted, but still there may be an infinite number of creatures over our heads, round about us, and under our feet, in the large space of the air, in the caverns of the earth, in the bowels of mountains, in the bottom of seas, and in the shades of forests, which have hitherto escaped all mortal senses. In this the microscope alone is enough to silence all opposers. Before that was invented, the chief help that was given to the eyes by glasses, was only to strengthen the dim sight of old age; but now by the means of that excellent instrument, we have a far greater number of different kinds of things revealed to us, than were contained in the visible universe before; and even this is not yet brought to perfection: the chief labours that are published in this way, have been the observations of some Fellows of the Royal Society, nor have they as yet applied it to all

*philosophical* scientific, in natural philosophy

subjects, nor tried it in all materials and figures of glass.

To the eyes therefore there may still be given a vast addition of objects: and proportionably to all the other senses. . . .

1667

# John Wilmot, Earl of Rochester

1647–80

Rochester's short life had many sides. After Oxford and a continental tour, he abducted an heiress and fought the Dutch. He was famous at the court of Charles II as both rake and writer of lyric and satiric poetry: the frankness of his language and honesty of attitude led to a reputation as pornographer. He died a quiet religious death. Rochester's satires and classical imitations are early examples of the pointed, lucid 'Augustan' manner. His sceptical scrutiny of human behaviour has much in common with contemporary philosophy, or the cynicism of the comic drama patronised by the court.

## SATIRE

Were I (who to my cost already am
One of those strange prodigious* creatures, man) — monstrous
A spirit free to choose, for my own share,
What case* of flesh and blood I pleased to wear, — covering
I'd be a dog, a monkey, or a bear,
Or anything but that vain animal
Who is so proud of being rational.
The senses are too gross, and he'll contrive
A sixth to contradict the other five;
And before certain instinct will prefer
Reason, which fifty times for one does err;
Reason, an *ignis fatuus*† in the mind,
Which, leaving light of nature, sense, behind,
Pathless and dangerous wandering ways it takes
Through error's fenny bogs and thorny brakes;
Whilst the misguided follower climbs with pain
Mountains of whimseys, heaped in his own brain;
Stumbling from thought to thought falls headlong down
Into doubt's boundless sea, where, like to drown,

*ignis fatuus* deluding light

Books bear him up a while, and make him try
To swim with bladders[*] of philosophy; air-bags
In hopes still to o'ertake th' escaping light,
The vapour dances in his dazzling sight
Till spent, it leaves him to eternal night.
Then old age and experience, hand in hand,
Lead him to death and make him understand,
After a search so painful and so long,
That all his life he has been in the wrong;
Huddled in dirt the reasoning engine lies,
Who was so proud, so witty, and so wise.
Pride drew him in, as cheats their bubbles[†] catch,
And makes him venture to be made a wretch.
His wisdom did his happiness destroy,
Aiming to know that world he should enjoy;
And wit was his vain, frivolous pretence
Of pleasing others at his own expense;
For wits are treated just like common whores,
First they're enjoyed, and then kicked out of doors.
The pleasure past, a threatening doubt remains
That frights th' enjoyer with succeeding pains.[†]
Women and men of wit are dangerous tools,
And ever fatal to admiring fools;
Pleasure allures, and when the fops escape,
'Tis not that they're beloved, but fortunate,
And therefore what they fear, at heart they hate.
  But now methinks some formal band[†] and beard
Takes me to task. Come on, sir; I'm prepared.
  'Then, by your favour, anything that's writ
Against this gibing, jingling knack called wit
Likes[†] me abundantly, but[†] you take care
Upon this point, not to be too severe.
Perhaps my muse were fitter for this part,
For I profess I can be very smart
On wit, which I abhor with all my heart:
I long to lash it in some sharp essay,
But your grand indiscretion bids me stay
And turns my tide of ink another way.
What rage ferments in your degenerate mind
To make you rail at reason and mankind?

*bubbles* foolish victims
*pains* from disease
*band* clergymen's garment
*likes . . . but* pleases; *but*: provided that

Blest, glorious man! to whom alone kind heaven
An everlasting soul has freely given;
Whom his great Maker took such care to make
That from himself he did the image take;
And this fair frame in shining reason dressed
To dignify his nature above beast;
Reason, by whose aspiring influence
We take a flight beyond material sense,
Dive into mysteries, then soaring pierce
The flaming limits of the universe,
Search heaven and hell, find out what's acted there,
And give the world true grounds of hope and fear.'
  Hold, mighty man, I cry, all this we know
From the pathetic pen of Ingelo,
From Patrick's *Pilgrim*, Stillingfleet's[†] replies,
And 'tis this very reason I despise:
This supernatural gift that makes a mite[†]
Think he's the image of the infinite,
Comparing his short life, void of all rest,
To the eternal and the ever blest;
This busy, puzzling stirrer-up of doubt
That frames deep mysteries, then finds 'em out;
Filling with frantic crowds of thinking fools
Those reverend bedlams, colleges and schools;
Borne on whose wings, each heavy sot can pierce
The limits of the boundless universe;
So charming[†] ointments make an old witch fly
And bear a crippled carcass through the sky.
'Tis this exalted power, whose business lies
In nonsense and impossibilities,
This made a whimsical philosopher[†]
Before the spacious world, his tub prefer,
And we have modern cloistered coxcombs who
Retire to think, cause they have nought to do.
  But thoughts are given for action's government;
Where action ceases, thought's impertinent.* irrelevant
Our sphere of action is life's happiness,
And he who thinks beyond thinks like an ass.

*Ingelo . . . Stillingfleet* Nathaniel Ingelo (*c.* 1621–83); Bishop Patrick (*Parable of the Pilgrim*, 1664); Edward Stillingfleet (1635–99), critic of this poem: clerical writers

*mite* parasitic insect

*charming* with magic spells

*philosopher* Diogenes, fourth century BC Greek, went from dissolute life to the asceticism of a tub

Thus, whilst against false reasoning I inveigh,
I own† right reason, which I would obey:
That reason which distinguishes by sense,
And gives us rules of good and ill from thence;
That bounds desires with a reforming will
To keep 'em more in vigour, not to kill.
Your reason hinders, mine helps to enjoy,
Renewing appetites yours would destroy.
My reason is my friend, yours is a cheat;
Hunger calls out, my reason bids me eat;
Perversely yours your appetite does mock:
This asks for food, that answers, 'What's o'clock?'
This plain distinction, sir, your doubt secures:†
'Tis not true reason I despise, but yours.
  Thus I think reason righted; but for man,
I'll ne'er recant, defend him if you can.
For all his pride and his philosophy,
'Tis evident beasts are, in their degree,†
As wise at least and better far than he.
Those creatures are the wisest who attain
By surest means the ends at which they aim.
If therefore Jowler† finds and kills his hares
Better than Meres† supplies committee chairs,
Though one's a statesman, th' other but a hound,
Jowler, in justice, would be wiser found.
  You see how far man's wisdom here extends;
Look next if human nature makes amends:
Whose principles most generous are and just,
And to whose morals you would sooner trust.
Be judge yourself, I'll bring it to the test:
Which is the basest creature, man or beast?
Birds feed on birds, beasts on each other prey,
But savage man alone does man betray.
Pressed by necessity, they kill for food;
Man undoes man to do himself no good.
With teeth and claws by nature armed, they hunt
Nature's allowance, to supply their want.
But man, with smiles, embraces, friendships, praise,
Inhumanly his fellow's life betrays;

*own* admit (cf. l.189)
*secures* turns to certainty
*degree* relative position
*Jowler* heavy-jowled dog
*Meres* Sir Thomas Meres (1635–1715), parliamentary chairman

With voluntary pains works his distress,
Not through necessity, but wantonness.
For hunger or for love they fight or tear,
Whilst wretched man is still in arms for fear.
For fear he arms, and is of arms afraid,
By fear to fear successively betrayed;
Base fear, the source whence his best passions came:
His boasted honour, and his dear-bought fame;
That lust of power, to which he's such a slave,
And for the which alone he dares be brave;
To which his various projects are designed,
Which makes him generous, affable, and kind;
For which he takes such pains to be thought wise,
And screws his actions in a forced disguise;
Leading a tedious life in misery
Under laborious, mean hypocrisy.
Look to the bottom of his vast design,
Wherein man's wisdom, power, and glory join;
The good he acts, the ill he does endure,
'Tis all from fear, to make himself secure.
Merely for safety, after fame we thirst,
For all men would be cowards if they durst.
And honesty's against all common sense:
Men must be knaves, 'tis in their own defence.
Mankind's dishonest; if you think it fair
Amongst known cheats to play upon the square,
You'll be undone –
Nor can weak truth your reputation save;
The knaves will all agree to call you knave.
Wronged shall he live, insulted o'er, oppressed,
Who dares be less a villain than the rest.
Thus, sir, you see what human nature craves;
Most men are cowards, all men should be knaves:
The difference lies (as far I can see)
Not in the thing itself but the degree;
And all the subject matter of debate
Is only who's a knave of the first rate?
All this with indignation have I hurled
At the pretending part of the proud world,
Who, swollen with selfish vanity, devise
False freedoms, holy cheats, and formal lies
Over their fellow slaves to tyrannize.
But if in court so just a man there be
(In court a just man, yet unknown to me)

Who does his needful flattery direct
Not to opress and ruin, but protect;
Since flattery, which way soever laid,
Is still a tax on that unhappy trade;
If so upright a statesman you can find,
Whose passions bend to his unbiased mind,
Who does his arts and policies apply
To raise his country, not his family,
Nor, while his pride owned* avarice withstands, open
Receives close* bribes through friends' corrupted hands. secret
  Is there a churchman who on God relies;
Whose life his faith and doctrine justifies?
Not one blown up with vain prelatic† pride,
Who for reproof of sins does man deride;
Whose envious heart makes preaching a pretence,
With his obstreperous, saucy eloquence,
To chide at kings and rail at men of sense;
Who from his pulpit vents more peevish lies,
More bitter railings, scandals, calumnies,
Than at a gossiping are thrown about,
When the good wives get drunk, and then fall out;
None of that sensual tribe whose talents lie
In avarice, pride, sloth, and gluttony;
Who hunt good livings† but abhor good lives;
Whose lust exalted to that height arrives
They act adultery with their own wives,
And ere a score of years completed be,
Can from the lofty pulpit proudly see
Half a large parish their own progeny.
Nor doting bishop who would be adored
For domineering at the council board;
A greater fop in business at fourscore,
Fonder of serious toys, affected more,
Than the gay, glittering fool at twenty proves,
With all his noise, his tawdry clothes, and loves.
  But a meek, humble man of honest sense,
Who, preaching peace, does practice continence;
Whose pious life's a proof he does believe
Mysterious truths, which no man can conceive.
If upon earth there dwell such God-like men,
I'll here recant my paradox to them,
Adore those shrines of virtue, homage pay,

*prelatic* of major churchman    *livings* paid church offices

And, with the rabble world, their laws obey.
If such there are, yet grant me this at least:
Man differs more from man, than man from beast.

1674 1679

# William Dampier
## 1652–1715

Dampier wrote several accounts of his voyages as a buccaneering explorer, which took him to South America, the East Indies and Australia: *New Voyage Round the World* (1697); *Voyage to New Holland* (1703–9). He is a link between the adventurous narratives of the seventeenth century and the more scientifically documented explorations of the eighteenth. He features in the history of Alexander Selkirk, whose being marooned on Juan Fernandez gave Defoe the kernel of *Robinson Crusoe* (see p. 85); Swift's Gulliver refers to his 'cousin Dampier'.

## *From* A NEW VOYAGE ROUND THE WORLD

### *[Australian Natives]*

At last we went over to the islands, and there we found a great many of the natives: I do believe there were forty on one island, men, women, and children. The men, at our first coming ashore, threatened us with their lances and swords; but they were frighted by firing one gun, which we fired purposely to scare them. The island was so small that they could not hide themselves; but they were much disordered at our landing, especially the women and children, for we went directly to their camp. The lustiest of the women snatching up their infants ran away howling, and the little children ran after squeaking and bawling, but the men stood still. One of the women, and such people as could not go from us, lay still by a fire; making a doleful noise as if we had been coming to devour them; but when they saw that we did not intend to harm them they were pretty quiet, and the rest that fled from us at our first coming returned again. This, their place of dwelling, was only a fire, with a few boughs before it, set up on that side the wind was of.

After we had been here a little while the men began to be familiar, and we clothed some of them, designing to have some service of them for it; for we found some wells of water here, and intended to carry two or three barrels of it aboard. But being somewhat troublesome to carry to the canoes, we thought to have made these men to have carried it for us, and therefore we gave them some clothes; to one an old pair of breeches, to another a ragged shirt, to a third a jacket that was scarce worth owning, which yet would have been very acceptable at some places where we had been, and so we thought they might have been with these people. We put them on them, thinking that this finery would have brought them to work heartily for us; and our water being filled in small long barrels, about six gallons in each, which were made purposely to carry water in, we brought these our new servants to the wells, and put a barrel on each of their shoulders for them to carry to the canoe. But all the signs we could make were to no purpose, for they stood like statues, without motion, but grinned like so many monkeys, staring one upon another; for these poor creatures seem not accustomed to carry burdens, and I believe that one of our ship-boys of ten years old would carry as much as one of them. So we were forced to carry our water ourselves, and they very fairly put the clothes off again and laid them down, as if clothes were only to work in. I did not perceive that they had any great liking to them at first, neither did they seem to admire anything that we had.

At another time, our canoe being among these islands seeking for game, we espied a drove of these men swimming from an island to another; for they have no boats, canoes, or bark-logs. They took up four of them and brought them aboard; two of them were middle aged, the other two were young men about eighteen or twenty years old. To these we gave boiled rice, and with it turtle and manatee[†] boiled. They did greedily devour what we gave them, but took no notice of the ship or any thing in it, and when they were set on land again they ran away as fast as they could. At our first coming, before we were acquainted with them or they with us, a company of them who lived on the main came just against our ship, and standing on a pretty high bank, threatened us with their swords and lances by shaking them at us; at last the captain ordered the drum to be beaten, which was done of a sudden with much vigour, purposely to scare the poor creatures. They hearing the noise ran away as fast as they could drive, and when they ran away in haste they would cry, *Gurry Gurry*, speaking deep in the throat. Those inhabitants also that live on the main would always run away from us, yet we took several of them. For, as I have already observed, they had such bad eyes that they could not see us till we came close to them. We did always give them victuals and let them go again, but the islanders, after our first time of being among them, did not stir for us. . . .

1697

*manatee* sea-cow

# Daniel Defoe

1660–1731

The son of a London butcher of dissenting views called Foe, Defoe travelled widely on the Continent before becoming a hosiery merchant. He supported the accession of William III in verse (*The True-Born Englishman*, 1701) but suffered in prison and the pillory for the misreading of his ironic *The Shortest Way with the Dissenters* (1702). After the failure of several business ventures, he travelled the country as a Tory secret agent (1703–14), and later put his observations to good use in his *Tour through the Whole Island of Great Britain* (1724–6). He wrote and edited many hundreds of books and pamphlets on social, religious and economic questions (*The Complete English Tradesman*, 1726); these show more learning and a wider range of styles than might be suspected by casual readers of the novels on which his fame depends: *Robinson Crusoe* (1719); *Moll Flanders* (1722); *A Journal of the Plague Year* (1722); *Roxana* (1724). Often regarded as the first real novelist, he presents fictional material with the appearance of authenticity through his detailed, realistic style, which creates a solid world.

## *From* ROBINSON CRUSOE[†]

### *[Shipwreck]*

After we had rowed, or rather driven about a league[†] and a half, as we reckoned it, a raging wave, mountain-like, came rolling astern of us, and plainly bade us expect the *Coup de Grace*. In a word, it took us with such a fury, that it overset the boat at once; and separating us as well from the boat, as from one another, gave us not time hardly to say, O God! for we were all swallowed up in a moment.

Nothing can describe the confusion of thought which I felt when I sunk into the water; for though I swam very well, yet I could not deliver myself from the waves so as to draw breath, till that wave having

*Robinson Crusoe* Crusoe is shipwrecked on an island, where he remains twenty-eight years

*league* about three miles

driven me, or rather carried me a vast way on towards the shore, and having spent itself, went back, and left me upon the land almost dry, but half-dead with the water I took in. I had so much presence of mind as well as breath left, that seeing myself nearer the mainland than I expected, I got upon my feet, and endeavoured to make on towards the land as fast as I could, before another wave should return, and take me up again. But I soon found it was impossible to avoid it; for I saw the sea come after me as high as a great hill, and as furious as an enemy which I had no means or strength to contend with; my business was to hold my breath, and raise myself upon the water, if I could; and so by swimming to preserve my breathing, and pilot myself towards the shore, if possible; my greatest concern now being, that the sea, as it would carry me a great way towards the shore when it came on, might not carry me back again with it when it gave back towards the sea.

The wave that came upon me again, buried me at once 20 or 30 foot deep in its own body; and I could feel myself carried with a mighty force and swiftness towards the shore a very great way; but I held my breath, and assisted myself to swim still forward with all my might. I was ready to burst with holding my breath, when as I felt myself rising up, so to my immediate relief, I found my head and hands shoot out above the surface of the water; and though it was not two seconds of time that I could keep myself so, yet it relieved me greatly, gave me breath and new courage. I was covered again with water a good while, but not so long but I held it out; and finding the water had spent itself, and began to return, I struck forward against the return of the waves, and felt ground again with my feet. I stood still a few moments to recover breath, and till the water went from me, and then took to my heels, and ran with what strength I had farther towards the shore. But neither would this deliver me from the fury of the sea, which came pouring in after me again, and twice more I was lifted up by the waves, and carried forwards as before, the shore being very flat.

The last time of these two had well near been fatal to me; for the sea having hurried me along as before, landed me, or rather dashed me against a piece of a rock, and that with such force, as it left me senseless, and indeed helpless, as to my own deliverance; for the blow taking my side and breast, beat the breath as it were quite out of my body; and had it returned again immediately, I must have been strangled in the water; but I recovered a little before the return of the waves, and seeing I should be covered again with the water, I resolved to hold fast by a piece of the rock, and so to hold my breath, if possible, till the wave went back; now as the waves were not so high as at first, being nearer land, I held my hold till the wave abated, and then fetched another run, which brought me so near the shore, that the next wave, though it went over me, yet did not so swallow me up as to carry me away, and the next run I took, I got to the mainland, where, to my great comfort, I clambered up the cliffs of the shore, and sat me down upon the grass, free from danger, and quite out of the reach of the water.

I was now landed, and safe on shore, and began to look up and thank God that my life was saved in a case wherein there was some minutes before scarce any room to hope. I believe it is impossible to express to the life what the ecstasies and transports of the soul are, when it is so saved, as I may say, out of the very grave; and I do not wonder now at that custom, *viz.* that when a malefactor who has the halter about his neck, is tied up, and just going to be turned off,† and has a reprieve brought to him: I say, I do not wonder that they bring a surgeon with it, to let him blood that very moment they tell him of it, that the surprise may not drive the animal spirits from the heart, and overwhelm him:

*For sudden joys, like griefs, confound at first.*

I walked about on the shore, lifting up my hands, and my whole being, as I may say, wrapt up in the contemplation of my deliverance, making a thousand gestures and motions which I cannot describe, reflecting upon all my comrades that were drowned, and that there should not be one soul saved but myself; for, as for them, I never saw them afterwards, or any sign of them, except three of their hats, one cap, and two shoes that were not fellows.

I cast my eyes to the stranded vessel, when the breach and froth of the sea being so big, I could hardly see it, it lay so far off, and considered, Lord! how was it possible I could get on shore?

After I had solaced my mind with the comfortable part of my condition, I began to look round me to see what kind of place I was in, and what was next to be done, and I soon found my comforts abate, and that in a word I had a dreadful deliverance: For I was wet, had no clothes to shift† me, nor any thing either to eat or drink to comfort me, neither did I see any prospect before me, but that of perishing with hunger, or being devoured by wild beasts; and that which was particularly afflicting to me, was, that I had no weapon either to hunt and kill any creature for my sustenance, or to defend myself against any other creature that might desire to kill me for theirs: in a word, I had nothing about me but a knife, a tobacco-pipe, and a little tobacco in a box; this was all my provision, and this threw me into terrible agonies of mind, that for a while I ran about like a madman; night coming upon me, I began with a heavy heart to consider what would be my lot if there were any ravenous beasts in that country, seeing at night they always come abroad for their prey.

*turned off* hanged    *shift* change clothes

All the remedy that offered to my thoughts at that time, was, to get up into a thick bushy tree like a fir, but thorny, which grew near me, and where I resolved to set all night, and consider the next day what death I should die, for as yet I saw no prospect of life; I walked about a furlong from the shore, to see if I could find any fresh water to drink, which I did, to my great joy; and having drunk and put a little tobacco in my mouth to prevent hunger, I went to the tree, and getting up into it, endeavoured to place myself so, as that if I should sleep I might not fall; and having cut me a short stick, like a truncheon, for my defence, I took up my lodging, and having been excessively fatigued, I fell fast asleep, and slept as comfortably as, I believe, few could have done in my condition, and found myself the most refreshed with it, that I think I ever was on such an occasion.

When I waked it was broad day, the weather clear, and the storm abated, so that the sea did not rage and swell as before: but that which surprised me most, was, that the ship was lifted off in the night from the sand where she lay, by the swelling of the tide, and was driven up almost as far as the rock which I first mentioned, where I had been so bruised by the dashing me against it; this being within about a mile from the shore where I was, and the ship seeming to stand upright still, I wished myself on board, that, at least, I might save some necessary things for my use.

When I came down from my apartment in the tree, I looked about me again, and the first thing I found was the boat, which lay as the wind and the sea had tossed her up upon the land, about two miles on my right hand. I walked as far as I could upon the shore to have got to her, but found a neck or inlet of water between me and the boat, which was about half a mile broad, so I came back for the present, being more intent upon getting at the ship, where I hoped to find something for my present subsistence.

A little after noon I found the sea very calm, and the tide ebbed so far out, that I could come within a quarter of a mile of the ship; and here I found a fresh renewing of my grief, for I saw evidently, that if we had kept on board, we had been all safe, that is to say, we had all got safe on shore, and I had not been so miserable as to be left entirely destitute of all comfort and company, as I now was; this forced tears from my eyes again, but as there was little relief in that, I resolved, if possible, to get to the ship, so I pulled off my clothes, for the weather was hot to extremity, and took the water, but when I came to the ship, my difficulty was still greater to know how to get on board, for as she lay aground, and high out of the water, there was nothing within my reach to lay hold of; I swam round her twice, and the second time I spied a small piece of a rope, which I wondered I did not see at first, hang down by the fore-chains so low, as that with great difficulty I got hold of it, and by the help of that rope, got up into the forecastle of the ship; here I found that the ship was bulged,† and had a great deal of water in her hold, but that she lay so on the side of a bank of hard sand, or rather earth, that her stern lay lifted up upon the bank and her head low almost to the water; by this means all her quarter† was free, and all that was in that part was dry; for you may be sure my first work was to search and to see what was spoiled and what was free; and first I found that all the ship's provisions were dry and untouched by the water, and being very well disposed to eat, I went to the bread-room and filled my pockets with biscuit, and ate it as I went about other things, for I had no time to lose; I also found some rum in the great cabin, of which I took a large dram, and which I had indeed need enough of to spirit me for what was before me: Now I wanted nothing but a boat to furnish myself with many things which I foresaw would be very necessary to me.

It was in vain to sit still and wish for what was not to be had, and this extremity roused my application; we had several spare yards, and two or three large spars of wood, and a spare top-mast or two in the ship; I resolved to fall to work with these, and I flung as many of them overboard as I could manage for their weight, tieing every one with a rope that they might not drive away; when this was done I went down the ship's side, and pulling them to me, I tied four of them fast together at both ends as well as I could, in the form of a raft, and laying two or three short pieces of plank upon them cross-ways, I found I could walk upon it very well, but that it was not able to bear any great weight, the pieces being too light; so I went to work, and with the carpenter's saw I cut a spare top-mast into three lengths, and added them to my raft, with a great deal of labour and pains, but hope of furnishing myself with necessaries encouraged me to go beyond what I should have been able to have done upon another occasion. . . .

## *[Spiritual Awakening]*

I thought, that I was sitting on the ground on the outside of my wall, where I sat when the storm blew after the earthquake, and that I saw a man descend from a great black cloud, in a bright flame of fire, and light upon the ground: he was all over as bright as a flame, so that I could but just bear to look towards him; his countenance was most inexpressibly dreadful, impossible for words to describe; when he stepped upon the ground with his feet, I thought the earth trembled, just as it had done before in the earthquake, and all the air looked, to

*bulged* pierced at bottom *quarter* after part

my apprehension, as if it had been filled with flashes of fire.

He was no sooner landed upon the earth, but he moved forward towards me, with a long spear or weapon in his hand, to kill me; and when he came to a rising ground, at some distance, he spoke to me, or I heard a voice so terrible, that it is impossible to express the terror of it; all that I can say I understood, was this, *Seeing all these things have not brought thee to repentance, now thou shalt die*: at which words, I thought he lifted up the spear that was in his hand, to kill me.

No one that shall ever read this account will expect that I should be able to describe the horrors of my soul at this terrible vision, I mean, that even while it was a dream, I even dreamed of those horrors; nor is it any more possible to describe the impression that remained upon my mind when I awaked and found it was but a dream.

I had alas! no divine knowledge; what I had received by the good instruction of my father was then worn out by an uninterrupted series, for 8 years, of seafaring wickedness, and a constant conversation with nothing but such as were like my self, wicked and profane to the last degree: I do not remember that I had in all that time one thought that so much as tended either to looking upwards toward God, or inwards towards a reflection upon my own ways: but a certain stupidity of soul, without desire of good, or conscience[†] of evil, had entirely overwhelmed me, and I was all that the most hardened, unthinking, wicked creature among our common sailors, can be supposed to be, not having the least sense, either of the fear of God in danger, or of thankfulness to God in deliverances.

In the relating what is already past of my story, this will be the more easily believed, when I shall add that through all the variety of miseries that had to this day befallen me, I never had so much as one thought of it being the hand of God, or that it was a punishment for my sin; my rebellious behaviour against my father, or my present sins which were great; or so much as a punishment for the general course of my wicked life. When I was on the desperate expedition on the desert shores of Africa, I never had so much as one thought of what would become of me; or one wish to God to direct me whither I should go, or to keep me from the danger which apparently surrounded me, as well from voracious creatures as cruel savages: but I was merely[†] thoughtless of a God, or a Providence; acted like a mere brute from the principles of nature, and by the dictates of common sense only, and indeed hardly that.

When I was delivered and taken up at sea by the Portugal Captain, well used, and dealt justly and honourably with, as well as charitably,

*conscience* awareness *merely* entirely

I had not the least thankfulness in my thoughts: when again I was shipwrecked, ruined, and in danger of drowning on this island, I was as far from remorse, or looking on it as a judgment; I only said to myself often, that I was *an unfortunate dog*, and born to be always miserable.

It is true, when I got on shore first here, and found all my ship's crew drowned, and myself spared, I was surprised with a kind of ecstasy, and some transports of soul, which, had the grace of God assisted, might have come up to true thankfulness; but it ended where it began, in a mere common flight of joy, or as I may say, *being glad I was alive*, without the least reflection upon the distinguishing goodness of the hand which had preserved me, and had singled me out to be preserved, when all the rest were destroyed; or an enquiry why Providence had been thus merciful to me; even just the same common sort of joy which seamen generally have after they are got safe ashore from a shipwreck, which they drown all in the next bowl of punch, and forget almost as soon as it is over, and all the rest of my life was like it.

Even when I was afterwards, on due consideration, made sensible of my condition, how I was cast on this dreadful place, out of the reach of human kind, out of all hope of relief, of prospect of redemption, as soon as I saw but a prospect of living, and that I should not starve and perish for hunger, all the sense of my affliction wore off, and I began to be very easy, applied myself to the works proper for my preservation and supply, and was far enough from being afflicted at my condition, as a judgment from heaven, or as the hand of God against me; these were thoughts which very seldom entered into my head.

The growing up of the corn, as is hinted in my journal, had at first some little influence upon me, and began to affect me with seriousness, as long as I thought it had something miraculous in it; but as soon as ever that part of the thought was removed, all the impression which was raised from it, wore off also, as I have noted already.

Even the earthquake, though nothing could be more terrible in its nature, or more immediately directing to the invisible power which alone directs such things, yet no sooner was the first fright over, but the impression it had made went off also. I had no more sense of God or his judgments, much less of the present affliction of my circumstances being from his hand, than if I had been in the most prosperous condition of life.

But now when I began to be sick, and a leisurely view of the miseries of death came to place itself before me; when my spirits began to sink under the burden of a strong distemper, and nature was exhausted with the violence of the fever; conscience that had slept so long, began to awake, and I began to reproach myself with my past life, in which I had so evidently, by uncommon wickedness, provoked the justice of

God to lay me under uncommon strokes, and to deal with me in so vindictive a manner.

These reflections oppressed me for the second or third day of my distemper, and in the violence, as well of the fever, as of the dreadful reproaches of my conscience, extorted some words from me, like praying to God, though I cannot say they were either a prayer attended with desires or with hopes; it was rather the voice of mere fright and distress; my thoughts were confused, the convictions great upon my mind, and the horror of dying in such a miserable condition raised vapours into my head with the mere apprehensions; and in these hurries of my soul, I know not what my tongue might express; but it was rather exclamation, such as, Lord! what a miserable creature am I! If I should be sick, I shall certainly die for want of help, and what will become of me? then the tears burst out of my eyes, and I could say no more for a good while.

In this interval, the good advice of my father came to my mind, and presently his prediction which I mentioned at the beginning of this story, *viz. that if I did take this foolish step*,† *God would not bless me, and I would have leisure hereafter to reflect upon having neglected his counsel, when there might be none to assist in my recovery.* Now, said I aloud, my dear father's words are come to pass: God's justice has overtaken me, and I have none to help or hear me: I rejected the voice of Providence, which had mercifully put me in a posture or station of life, wherein I might have been happy and easy; but I would neither see it myself, or learn to know the blessing of it from my parents; I left them to mourn over my folly, and now I am left to mourn under the consequences of it: I refused their help and assistance who would have lifted me into the world, and would have made every thing easy to me, and now I have difficulties to struggle with, too great for even nature itself to support, and no assistance, no help, no comfort, no advice; then I cried out, *Lord be my help, for I am in great distress.*

This was the first prayer, if I may call it so, that I had made for many years . . .

1719

---

*foolish step* going to sea

## *From* MOLL FLANDERS†

## *[Temptation]*

In this distress I had no assistant, no friend to comfort or advise me, I sat and cried and tormented myself night and day; wringing my hands, and sometimes raving like a distracted woman; and indeed I have often wondered it had not affected my reason, for I had the vapours† to such a degree, that my understanding was sometimes quite lost in fancies and imaginations.

I lived two years in this dismal condition wasting that little I had, weeping continually over my dismal circumstances, and as it were only bleeding to death, without the least hope or prospect of help from God or man; and now I had cried so long, and so often, that tears were, as I might say, exhausted, and I began to be desperate, for I grew poor apace.

For a little relief I had put off my house and took lodgings, and as I was reducing my living so I sold off most of my goods, which put a little money in my pocket, and I lived near a year upon that, spending very sparingly, and eking things out to the utmost; but still when I looked before me, my very heart would sink within me at the inevitable approach of misery and want: O let none read this part without seriously reflecting on the circumstances of a desolate state, and how they would grapple with mere want of friends and want of bread; it will certainly make them think not of sparing what they have only, but of looking up to heaven for support, and of the wise man's prayer, *Give me not poverty lest I steal.*

Let 'em remember that a time of distress is a time of dreadful temptation, and all the strength to resist is taken away; poverty presses, the soul is made desperate by distress, and what can be done? It was one evening, when being brought, as I may say, to the last gasp, I think I may truly say I was distracted and raving, when prompted by I know not what spirit, and as it were, doing I did not know what, or why; I dressed me, for I had still pretty good clothes, and went out: I am very sure I had no manner of design in my head, when I went out, I neither knew or considered where to go, or on what business; but as the Devil carried me out and laid his bait for me, so he brought me to be sure to the place, for I knew not whither I was going or what I did.

Wandering thus about I knew not whither, I passed by an apothecary's shop in Leadenhall Street,† where I saw lie on a stool just before the

*Moll Flanders* Moll tells of her varying fortunes and marriages; her latest husband has been defrauded and dies

*vapours* hysterical fits

*Leadenhall Street . . . Billingsgate* in the mercantile City area

counter a little bundle wrapped in a white cloth; beyond it, stood a maid servant with her back to it, looking up towards the top of the shop, where the apothecary's apprentice, as I suppose, was standing up on the counter, with his back also to the door, and a candle in his hand, looking and reaching up to the upper shelf for something he wanted, so that both were engaged mighty earnestly and nobody else in the shop.

This was the bait; and the Devil who I said laid the snare as readily prompted me, as if he had spoke, for I remember, and shall never forget it, 'twas like a voice spoken to me over my shoulder, take the bundle; be quick; do it this moment; it was no sooner said but I stepped into the shop, and with my back to the wench, as if I had stood up for a cart that was going by, I put my hand behind me and took the bundle, and went off with it, the maid or the fellow not perceiving me, or any one else.

It is impossible to express the horror of my soul all the while I did it: when I went away I had no heart to run, or scarce to mend my pace; I crossed the street indeed, and went down the first turning I came to, and I think it was a street that went through into Fenchurch Street; from thence I crossed and turned through so many ways and turnings that I could never tell which way it was, nor where I went, for I felt not the ground, I stepped on, and the farther I was out of danger, the faster I went, till tired and out of breath, I was forced to sit down on a little bench at a door, and then I began to recover, and found I was got into Thames Street near Billingsgate. I rested me a little and went on, my blood was all in a fire, my heart beat as if I was in a sudden fright: in short, I was under such a surprise that I still knew not whither I was a going, or what to do.

After I had tired myself thus with walking a long way about, and so eagerly, I began to consider and make home to my lodging, where I came about nine a clock at night.

What the bundle was made up for, or on what occasion laid where I found it, I knew not, but when I came to open it I found there was a suit of child-bed linen in it, very good and almost new, the lace very fine; there was a silver porringer† of a pint, a small silver mug and six spoons, some other linen, a good smock, and three silk handkerchiefs, and in the mug wrapped up in a paper eighteen shillings and sixpence in money.

All the while I was opening these things I was under such dreadful impressions of fear, and in such terror of mind, though I was perfectly safe, that I cannot express the manner of it; I sat me down and cried most vehemently; 'Lord,' said I, 'what am I now? a thief! why I shall

*porringer* dish for soup

be taken next time and be carried to Newgate† and be tried for my life!' and with that I cried again a long time, and I am sure, as poor as I was, if I had durst for fear, I would certainly have carried the things back again; but that went off after a while: well, I went to bed for that night, but slept little, the horror of the fact was upon my mind, and I knew not what I said or did all night, and all the next day: then I was impatient to hear some news of the loss; and would fain know how it was, whether they were a poor body's goods, or a rich; 'perhaps,' said I, 'it may be some poor widow like me, that had packed up these goods to go and sell them for a little bread for herself and a poor child, and are now starving and breaking their hearts, for want of that little they would have fetched,' and this thought tormented me worse than all the rest, for three or four days time.

But my own distresses silenced all these reflections, and the prospect of my own starving, which grew every day more frightful to me, hardened my heart by degrees; it was then particularly heavy upon my mind, that I had been reformed, and had, as I hoped, repented of all my past wickednesses; that I had lived a sober, grave, retired life for several years, but now I should be driven by the dreadful necessity of my circumstances to the gates of destruction, soul and body; and two or three times I fell upon my knees, praying to God, as well as I could, for deliverance; but I cannot but say my prayers had no hope in them; I knew not what to do, it was all fear without, and dark within; and I reflected on my past life as not sincerely repented of, that heaven was now beginning to punish me on this side the grave, and would make me as miserable as I had been wicked.

Had I gone on here I had perhaps been a true penitent; but I had an evil counsellor within, and he was continually prompting me to relieve myself by the worst means; so one evening he tempted me again by the same wicked impulse that had said, *take that bundle*, to go out again and seek for what might happen.

I went out now by daylight, and wandered about I knew not whither, and in search of I knew not what, when the Devil put a snare in my way of a dreadful nature indeed, and such a one as I have never had before or since; going through Aldersgate Street there was a pretty little child had been at a dancing-school, and was going home, all alone, and my prompter, like a true Devil, set me upon this innocent creature, I talked to it, and it prattled to me again, and I took it by the hand and led it along till I came to a paved alley that goes into Bartholomew Close, and I led it in there; the child said that was not its way home; I said, 'yes, my dear it is, I'll show you the way home;' the child had a

*Newgate* prison (many minor offences carried the death penalty)

little necklace on of gold beads, and I had my eye upon that, and in the dark of the alley I stooped, pretending to mend the child's clog that was loose, and took off her necklace and the child never felt it, and so led the child on again: here, I say, the Devil put me upon killing the child in the dark alley, that it might not cry; but the very thought frighted me so that I was ready to drop down, but I turned the child about and bade it go back again, for that was not its way home; the child said so she would, and I went through into Bartholomew Close, and then turned round to another passage that goes into Long Lane, so away into Charterhouse Yard and out into St John's Street, then crossing into Smithfield, went down Chick Lane and into Field Lane to Holborn Bridge, when mixing with the crowd of people usually passing there, it was not possible to have been found out; and thus I enterprised my second sally into the world.

The thoughts of this booty put out all the thoughts of the first, and the reflections I had made wore quickly off; poverty, as I have said, hardened my heart, and my own necessities made me regardless of any thing: the last affair left no great concern upon me, for as I did the poor child no harm, I only said to myself, I had given the parents a just reproof for their negligence in leaving the poor little lamb to come home by itself, and it would teach them to take more care of it another time.

This string of beads was worth about twelve or fourteen pounds, I suppose it might have been formerly the mother's, for it was too big for the child's wear, but that, perhaps, the vanity of the mother to have her child look fine at the dancing-school, had made her let the child wear it, and no doubt the child had a maid sent to take care of it, but she, like a careless jade, was taken up perhaps with some fellow that had met her by the way, and so the poor baby wandered till it fell into my hands.

However, I did the child no harm, I did not so much as fright it, for I had a great many tender thoughts about me yet, and did nothing but what, as I may say, mere necessity drove me to.

I had a great many adventures after this, but I was young in the business, and did not know how to manage, otherwise than as the Devil put things into my head; and indeed he was seldom backward to me: one adventure I had which was very lucky to me; I was going through Lombard Street in the dusk of the evening, just by the end of Three King Court, when on a sudden comes a fellow running by me as swift as lightning, and throws a bundle that was in his hand just behind me, as I stood up against the corner of the house at the turning into the alley; just as he threw it in he said, 'God bless you Mistress let it lie there a little,' and away he runs swift as the wind; after him comes two more, and immediately a young fellow without his hat, crying 'stop thief,' and after him two or three more; they pursued the two last fellows so close, that they were forced to drop what they had got, and one of them was taken into the bargain, the other got off free.

I stood stock still all this while till they came back, dragging the poor fellow they had taken, and lugging the things they had found, extremely well satisfied that they had recovered the booty, and taken the thief; and thus they passed by me, for I looked only like one who stood up while the crowd was gone.

Once or twice I asked what was the matter, but the people neglected answering me, and I was not very importunate; but after the crowd was wholly passed, I took my opportunity to turn about and take up what was behind me and walk away: this indeed I did with less disturbance than I had done formerly, for these things I did not steal, but they were stolen to my hand: I got safe to my lodgings with this cargo, which was a piece of fine black lustring silk, and a piece of velvet; the latter was part of a piece of about a 11 yards; the former was a whole piece of near 50 yards; it seems it was a mercer's shop that they had rifled; I say rifled, because the goods were so considerable that they had lost; for the goods that they recovered were pretty many, and I believe came to about six or seven several pieces of silk: how they came to get so many I could not tell; but as I had only robbed the thief I made no scruple at taking these goods, and being very glad of them too. . . .

1722

# Jonathan Swift

## 1667–1745

Swift, a cousin of Dryden, was born in Dublin, and educated beside Congreve at Kilkenny School and Trinity College, Dublin. A period as secretary to the statesman-author Sir William Temple having failed to win him advancement, he was ordained in Ireland (1694). Back in Temple's household at Moor Park, he wrote *The Battle of the Books* (1697), part of the debate on the superiority of ancient or modern learning, and *A Tale of a Tub* (1696; both works published 1704), a combination of religious allegory and intellectual virtuosity. Here too he first met 'Stella', Esther Johnson, recipient of many of his writings, with whom his relationship remains unclear. After Temple's death, he returned to Ireland, receiving church offices, but visiting London often, and writing pamphlets of varying irony (*An Argument against Abolishing Christianity*, 1708). The Whigs' favouring dissenters led to his support of the Tories, on whose side he wrote political works (*The Conduct of the Allies*, 1711; *The Public Spirit of the Whigs*, 1714). He was a leading member of the Scriblerus Club with Pope (see p. 205).

After the death of Queen Anne and the fall of the Tory government, his hostility to the long Whig dominance left him for most of his life in Dublin, where he had become Dean of St Patrick's Cathedral. Despite his position as officer of the established (Anglican) church in a largely Catholic country, Swift devoted much of his income to practical charity, and his satiric power to attacking England's colonial exploitation of Ireland (*The Drapier's Letters*, 1724; *A Modest Proposal*, 1729). He normally issued his works anonymously or pseudonymously, often exploiting ironically the 'persona' of a supposed author whose ideas differ significantly from Swift's: *Travels into Several Remote Nations of the World* (1726) by 'Lemuel Gulliver' develops his political and moral satire.

In his Irish period, despite increasing illness which led many to think him insane, Swift had great public influence. Nineteenth-century critics often emphasised his ferocity and complexity as symptoms of a disturbed mind; but his ruthless economy is balanced by an exuberant revelation of human absurdity. His enormous versatility, partly masked by his use of unusual literary forms, has become recognised, as has the value of his large body of verse. Swift's great satires never rest on individual targets: they challenge the reader's response to complex problems, often in unpalatable terms (is man a 'Yahoo'?). St Patrick's Cathedral preserves his Latin epitaph on himself, at rest 'where savage indignation can no further tear his heart', a 'strenuous defender of liberty'.

## *From* A TALE OF A TUB[†]

### Sect. II *[History of Christianity]*

Once upon a time, there was a man who had three sons by one wife, and all at a birth, neither could the midwife tell certainly which was the eldest. Their father died while they were young, and upon his deathbed, calling the lads to him, spoke thus:

'Sons, because I have purchased no estate, nor was born to any, I have long considered of some good legacies to bequeath you; and at last, with much care as well as expense, have provided each of you (here they are) a new coat. Now, you are to understand that these coats have two virtues contained in them: one is, that with good wearing they will last you fresh and sound as long as you live; the other is that they will grow in the same proportion with your bodies, lengthening and widening of themselves so as to be always fit. Here; let me see them on you before I die. So; very well; pray, children, wear them clean and brush them often. You will find in my will (here it is) full instructions in every particular concerning the wearing and management of your coats, wherein you must be very exact to avoid the penalties I have appointed for every transgression or neglect, upon which your future fortunes will entirely depend. I have also commanded in my will that you should live together in one house like brethren and friends, for then you will be sure to thrive and not otherwise.'

*A Tale of a Tub* The title phrase suggests both something nonsensical and a distraction from external threats. The *Tale* has a complex form: a battery of introductory pieces leads into the allegory of the growth and perversion of the Christian sects; this in turn is gradually overwhelmed by digressions, the main one a celebration of madness. The alleged 'author' of the *Tale*, a 'modern' hack-writer, is undercut by Swift's deliberate disruption of its form, which itself illustrates the decay of learning and religion. The extract introduces the allegory: Peter represents the Pope and Roman Catholic Church; Martin: Luther and the moderate Church of England; Jack: Calvin and extreme, dissenting Protestantism. The coats are 'the doctrine and faith of Christianity'; the will, the New Testament

Here the story says this good father died, and the three sons went all together to seek their fortunes.

I shall not trouble you with recounting what adventures they met for the first seven years, any further than by taking notice that they carefully observed their father's will, and kept their coats in very good order, that they travelled through several countries, encountered a reasonable quantity of giants, and slew certain dragons.

Being now arrived at the proper age for producing themselves, they came up to town and fell in love with the ladies,† but especially three who about that time were in chief reputation, the Duchess d'Argent, Madame de Grands Titres, and the Countess d'Orgueil. On their first appearance our three adventurers met with a very bad reception, and soon with great sagacity guessing out the reason, they quickly began to improve in the good qualities of the town: they writ, and rallied, and rhymed, and sung, and said, and said nothing; they drank, and fought, and whored, and slept, and swore, and took snuff; they went to new plays on the first night, haunted the chocolate-houses, beat the watch, lay on bulks,† and got claps; they bilked† hackney-coachmen, ran in debt with shopkeepers, and lay with their wives; they killed bailiffs, kicked fiddlers down stairs, eat at Locket's, loitered at Will's,† they talked of the drawing-room and never came there; dined with lords they never saw; whispered a duchess, and spoke never a word; exposed the scrawls of their laundress for billets-doux of quality; came ever just from court and were never seen in it; attended the Levee† *sub dio* [outside]; got a list of the peers by heart in one company, and with great familiarity retailed them in another. Above all, they constantly attended those Committees of Senators who are silent in the House,† and loud in the Coffee-House, where they nightly adjourn to chew the cud of politics, and are encompassed with a ring of disciples who lie in wait to catch up their droppings. The three brothers had acquired forty other qualifications of the like stamp too tedious to recount, and by consequence were justly reckoned the most accomplished persons in town. But all would not suffice and the ladies aforesaid continued still inflexible. To clear up which difficulty I must, with the reader's good leave and patience, have recourse to some points of weight which the authors of that age have not sufficiently illustrated.

For about this time it happened a sect arose whose tenets obtained and spread very far, especially in the *grand monde* and among

*ladies* covetousness, social ambition, and pride
*bulks* shop stalls
*bilked* cheated
*Locket's . . . Will's* coffee-houses were fashionable places in London
*Levee* royal reception
*House* of Commons; the above references are all contemporary

everybody of good fashion. They worshipped a sort of idol† who, as their doctrine delivered, did daily create men by a kind of manufactory operation. This idol they placed in the highest parts of the house, on an altar erected about three foot. He was shewn in the posture of a Persian emperor, sitting on a superficies with his legs interwoven under him. This god had a goose† for his ensign, whence it is that some learned men pretend to deduce his original from Jupiter Capitolinus. At his left hand beneath the altar, Hell† seemed to open and catch at the animals the idol was creating; to prevent which, certain of his priests hourly flung in pieces of the uninformed mass or substance, and sometimes whole limbs already enlivened, which that horrid gulf insatiably swallowed, terrible to behold. The goose was also held a subaltern divinity or *deus minorum gentium* [god of lesser tribes], before whose shrine was sacrificed that creature† whose hourly food is human gore, and who is in so great renown abroad for being the delight and favourite of the Egyptian Cercopithecus. Millions of these animals were cruelly slaughtered every day to appease the hunger of that consuming deity. The chief idol was also worshipped as the inventor of the yard and needle, whether as the god of seamen† or on account of certain other mystical attributes, hath not been sufficiently cleared.

The worshippers of this deity had also a system of their belief which seemed to turn upon the following fundamentals. They held the universe to be a large suit of clothes, which invests† everything: that the earth is invested by the air; the air is invested by the stars; and the stars are invested by the *primum mobile* [outer sphere]. Look on this globe of earth, you will find it to be a very complete and fashionable dress.† What is that which some call land, but a fine coat faced with green? or the sea, but a waistcoat of water-tabby.† Proceed to the particular works of the creation, you will find how curious journeyman Nature hath been, to trim up the vegetable beaux; observe how sparkish a periwig adorns the head of a beech and what a fine doublet of white satin is worn by the birch. To conclude from all, what is man himself but a micro-coat,† or rather a complete suit of clothes with all its trimmings? As to his body, there can be no dispute; but examine even the acquirements of his mind, you will find them all contribute in their order towards furnishing out an exact dress. To instance no more: is not religion a cloak, honesty a pair of shoes worn out in the dirt, self-

*idol* a tailor
*goose* a tailor's iron is called a goose; the Roman temple of Jupiter was guarded by geese
*Hell* receptacle for scraps
*that creature* lice, food of the Egyptian monkey-god
*seamen* from puns on yard-arm and compass-needle (possibly also sexual puns – 'semen')
*invests* the planetary spheres enclose, hence:
*dress* others
*water-tabby* watered silk
*micro-coat* microcosm, little world

love a surtout,[†] vanity a shirt, and conscience a pair of breeches which, though a cover for lewdness as well as nastiness, is easily slipped down for the service of both?

These *postulata* [assumptions] being admitted it will follow in due course of reasoning that those beings which the world calls improperly suits of clothes are in reality the most refined species of animals; or to proceed higher, that they are rational creatures, or men. For is it not manifest that they live, and move, and talk, and perform all other offices of human life? Are not beauty, and wit, and mien, and breeding, their inseparable proprieties? In short, we see nothing but them, hear nothing but them. Is it not they who walk the streets, fill up parliament –, coffee –, play –, bawdy-houses? 'Tis true indeed, that these animals which are vulgarly called suits of clothes, or dresses, do, according to certain compositions, receive different appellations. If one of them be trimmed up with a gold chain, and a red gown, and a white rod, and a great horse it is called a Lord Mayor; if certain ermines and furs be placed in a certain position we style them a Judge; and so an apt conjunction of lawn[†] and black satin we entitle a Bishop.

Others of these professors,[†] though agreeing in the main system, were yet more refined upon certain branches of it, and held that man was an animal compounded of two dresses, the natural and the celestial suit, which were the body and the soul; that the soul was the outward, and the body the inward clothing; that the latter was *ex traduce* [begotten by parents], but the former of daily creation and circumfusion. This last they proved by scripture, because in them[†] we live, and move, and have our being; as likewise by philosophy because they are all in all,[†] and all in every part. Besides, said they, separate these two, and you will find the body to be only a senseless unsavoury carcase. By all which it is manifest that the outward dress must needs be the soul.

To this system of religion were tagged several subaltern doctrines which were entertained with great vogue; as particularly, the faculties of the mind were deduced by the learned among them in this manner: embroidery was sheer wit; gold fringe was agreeable conversation; gold lace was repartee; a huge long periwig was humour, and a coat full of powder was very good raillery; all which required abundance of finesse and delicatesse to manage with advantage, as well as a strict observance after times and fashions.

I have with much pains and reading collected out of ancient authors this short summary of a body of philosophy and divinity, which seems to have been composed by a vein and race of thinking very different

*surtout* coat
*lawn* linen
*professors* religious believers
*in them* Acts 17.28;
*all in all* I Corinthians 15.28

from any other systems either ancient or modern. And it was not merely to entertain or satisfy the reader's curiosity but rather to give him light into several circumstances of the following story; that knowing the state of dispositions and opinions in an age so remote, he may better comprehend those great events which were the issue of them. I advise therefore the courteous reader to peruse with a world of application, again and again, whatever I have written upon this matter. And so leaving these broken ends, I carefully gather up the chief thread of my story, and proceed.

These opinions therefore were so universal, as well as the practices of them, among the refined part of court and town, that our three brother-adventurers as their circumstances then stood were strangely at a loss. For, on the one side, the three ladies they addressed themselves to (whom we have named already) were ever at the very top of the fashion, and abhorred all that were below it but the breadth of a hair. On the other side, their father's will was very precise, and it was the main precept in it with the greatest penalties annexed, not to add to, or diminish from their coats one thread without a positive command in the will. Now the coats their father had left them were, 'tis true, of very good cloth and, besides, so neatly sewn you would swear they were all of a piece, but at the same time very plain, and with little or no ornament. And it happened that before they were a month in town, great shoulder-knots† came up. Straight, all the world was shoulder-knots; no approaching the ladies' *ruelles*† without the quota of shoulder-knots. 'That fellow,' cries one, 'has no soul; where is his shoulder-knot?' Our three brethren soon discovered their want by sad experience, meeting in their walks with forty mortifications and indignities. If they went to the playhouse, the door-keeper showed them into the twelve-penny gallery. If they called a boat, says a waterman, 'I am first sculler'.† If they stepped to the Rose† to take a bottle, the drawer would cry, 'Friend, we sell no ale.' If they went to visit a lady, a footman met them at the door with, 'Pray send up your message.' In this unhappy case they went immediately to consult their father's Will, read it over and over, but not a word of the shoulder-knot. What should they do? What temper† should they find? Obedience was absolutely necessary, and yet shoulder-knots appeared extremely requisite. After much thought one of the brothers who happened to be more book-learned than the other two, said he had found an expedient. ''Tis true,' said he, 'there is nothing here in this Will, *totidem verbis* [in so many

*shoulder-knots* decorative ribbons, *c.* 1670 (here, Church pageantry and ornament)
*ruelles* bedroom areas
*sculler* a sculler rowed a cheap boat (all their experiences indicate social exclusion)
*Rose* a tavern
*temper* way of moderating

words], making mention of shoulder-knots, but I dare conjecture we may find them inclusive, or *totidem syllabis* [in so many syllables].' This distinction was immediately approved by all, and so they fell again to examine the will. But their evil star had so directed the matter that the first syllable was not to be found in the whole writing. Upon which disappointment, he who found the former evasion took heart and said, 'Brothers, there is yet hopes; for though we cannot find them *totidem verbis*, nor *totidem syllabis*, I dare engage we shall make them out *tertio modo*, or *totidem literis* [a third way, in so many letters].' This discovery was also highly commended, upon which they fell once more to the scrutiny, and soon picked out *S,H,O,U,L,D,E,R,* when the same planet, enemy to their repose, had wonderfully contrived that a K was not to be found. Here was a weighty difficulty! But the distinguishing brother (for whom we shall hereafter find a name) now his hand was in, proved by a very good argument that K was a modern, illegitimate letter, unknown to the learned ages nor anywhere to be found in ancient manuscripts. ''Tis true,' said he, 'the word *Calendæ* hath in Q.V.C. [some ancient manuscripts] been sometimes writ with a K, but erroneously, for in the best copies, it is ever spelt with a C. And by consequence it was a gross mistake in our language to spell "knot" with a K'; but that from henceforward he would take care it should be writ with a C. Upon this all further difficulty vanished; shoulder-knots were made clearly out to be *jure paterno* [by fatherly law], and our three gentlemen swaggered with as large and as flaunting ones as the best.

But as human happiness is of a very short duration, so in those days were human fashions upon which it entirely depends. Shoulder-knots had their time, and we must now imagine them in their decline; for a certain lord came just from Paris with fifty yards of gold lace upon his coat, exactly trimmed after the court fashion of that month. In two days all mankind appeared closed up in bars of gold lace: whoever durst peep abroad without his complement of gold lace, was as scandalous as a [eunuch], and as ill received among the women. What should our three knights do in this momentous affair? They had sufficiently strained a point already in the affair of shoulder-knots. Upon recourse to the Will nothing appeared there but *altum silentium* [deep silence]. That of the shoulder-knots was a loose, flying, circumstantial point; but this of gold lace seemed too considerable an alteration without better warrant. It did *aliquo modo essentiæ adhærere* [somehow belong to the essence], and therefore required a positive precept. But about this time it fell out that the learned brother aforesaid had read *Aristotelis Dialectica*, and especially that wonderful piece *de Interpretatione* [Aristotle on Interpretation] which has the faculty of teaching its readers to find out a meaning in everything but itself, like commentators on the Revelations who proceed prophets without understanding a syllable of the text.

'Brothers,' said he, 'you are to be informed that of wills *duo sunt genera*, nuncupatory and scriptory [there are two kinds, oral and written]; that in the scriptory will here before us, there is no precept or mention about gold lace, *conceditur* but, *si idem affirmetur de nuncupatorio, negatur* [I agree; but I deny the same of the oral]. For brothers, if you remember, we heard[†] a fellow say when we were boys, that he heard my father's man say, that he heard my father say, that he would advise his sons to get gold lace on their coats, as soon as ever they could procure money to buy it.' 'By G—! that is very true,' cries the other. 'I remember it perfectly well,' said the third. And so without more ado they got the largest gold lace in the parish, and walked about as fine as lords.

A while after there came up all in fashion a pretty sort of flame-coloured[†] satin for linings, and the mercer brought a pattern of it immediately to our three gentlemen. 'An please your worships,' said he, 'my Lord C[lifford] and Sir J[ohn] W[alters] had linings out of this very piece last night; it takes wonderfully, and I shall not have a remnant left enough to make my wife a pin-cushion, by tomorrow morning at ten o'clock.' Upon this, they fell again to rummage the Will, because the present case also required a positive precept, the lining being held by orthodox writers to be of the essence of the coat. After long search they could fix upon nothing to the matter in hand except a short advice of their father's in the Will to take care of fire[†] and put out their candles[†] before they went to sleep. This, though a good deal for the purpose and helping very far towards self-conviction, yet not seeming wholly of force to establish a command; and being resolved to avoid farther scruple, as well as future occasion for scandal, says he that was the scholar, 'I remember to have read in wills of a codicil[†] annexed, which is indeed a part of the will, and what it contains hath equal authority with the rest. Now, I have been considering of this same will here before us, and I cannot reckon it to be complete, for want of such a codicil. I will therefore fasten one in its proper place very dexterously. I have had it by me some time; it was written by a dog-keeper of my grandfather's, and talks a great deal (as good luck would have it) of this very flame-coloured satin.' The project was immediately approved by the other two; an old parchment scroll was tagged on according to art, in the form of a codicil annexed, and the satin bought and worn.

Next winter a player, hired for the purpose by the corporation of

*we heard* church traditions which went beyond the scripture texts
*flame-coloured* the doctrine of Purgatory
*fire* Hell
*candles* passions
*codicil* appendix to a will, here the biblical Apocrypha (not in the Protestant Old Testament) where a dog appears in the Book of Tobit

fringe-makers, acted his part in a new comedy all covered with silver fringe,[†] and according to the laudable custom, gave rise to that fashion. Upon which the brothers consulting their father's Will, to their great astonishment found these words, 'Item, I charge and command my said three sons to wear no sort of silver fringe upon or about their said coats,' etc., with a penalty in case of disobedience, too long here to insert. However after some pause, the brother so often mentioned for his erudition, who was well skilled in criticisms, had found in a certain author which he said should be nameless, that the same word which in the will is called fringe, does also signify a broomstick, and doubtless ought to have the same interpretation in this paragraph. This, another of the brothers disliked because of that epithet silver, which could not, be humbly conceived, in propriety of speech be reasonably applied to a broomstick; but it was replied upon him that this epithet was understood in a mythological and allegorical sense. However, he objected again why their father should forbid them to wear a broomstick on their coats, a caution that seemed unnatural and impertinent; upon which he was taken up short, as one who spoke irreverently of a mystery which doubtless was very useful and significant, but ought not to be over-curiously pried into or nicely reasoned upon. And in short, their father's authority being now considerably sunk, this expedient was allowed to serve as a lawful dispensation for wearing their full proportion of silver fringe.

A while after was revived an old fashion, long antiquated, of embroidery with Indian figures[†] of men, women, and children. Here they had no occasion to examine the Will. They remembered but too well how their father had always abhorred this fashion; that he made several paragraphs on purpose importing his utter detestation of it, and bestowing his everlasting curse to his sons, whenever they should wear it. For all this, in a few days they appeared higher in the fashion than anybody else in town. But they solved the matter by saying that these figures were not at all the same with those that were formerly worn and were meant in the will. Besides, they did not wear them in that sense as forbidden by their father, but as they were a commendable custom, and of great use to the public. That these rigorous clauses in the will did therefore require some allowance, and a favourable intepretation, and ought to be understood *cum grano salis* [with a grain of salt].

But fashions perpetually altering in that age, the scholastic brother grew weary of searching further evasions and solving everlasting

*fringe* religious ornamentation
*Indian figures* images of saints. Swift parodies allegorical interpretation of scripture

contradictions. Resolved, therefore, at all hazards to comply with the modes of the world, they concerted matters together and agreed unanimously to lock up their father's Will in a strong box,† brought out of Greece or Italy (I have forgot which) and trouble themselves no further to examine it, but only refer to its authority whenever they thought fit. In consequence whereof, a while after it grew a general mode to wear an infinite number of points,† most of them tagged with silver: upon which, the scholar pronounced *ex cathedra*† [by (papal) authority] that points were absolutely *jure paterno*, as they might very well remember. 'Tis true indeed, the fashion prescribed somewhat more than were directly named in the Will; however, that they as heirs general of their father had power to make and add certain clauses for public emolument, though not deducible *totidem verbis* from the letter of the Will, or else, *multa absurda sequerentur* [many absurdities would follow]. This was understood for canonical,† and therefore on the following Sunday they came to church all covered with points.

The learned brother, so often mentioned, was reckoned the best scholar in all that or the next street to it; insomuch as, having run something behind-hand with the world, he obtained the favour from a certain lord,† to receive him into his house and to teach his children. A while after the lord died, and he, by long practice upon his father's Will, found the way of contriving a deed of conveyance of that house to himself and his heirs; upon which he took possession, turned the young squires out, and received his brothers in their stead.

*c.* 1697 1704

*strong box* restriction of the New Testament to Greek and Latin texts
*points* laces on clothing
*ex cathedra* reflects the Pope's claim of doctrinal authority
*canonical* in the biblical text, authorised
*certain lord* Constantine the Great, a Christian Roman Emperor (AD 306–37), who was claimed to have conveyed secular power and property to the Popes

# A DESCRIPTION OF THE MORNING[†]

APRIL 1709

Now hardly here and there an hackney-coach
Appearing, showed the ruddy morn's approach.
Now Betty[†] from her master's bed had flown,
And softly stole to discompose her own.
The slip-shod 'prentice from his master's door
Had pared the street, and sprinkled round the floor.
Now Moll had whirled her mop with dexterous airs,
Prepared to scrub the entry and the stairs.
The youth with broomy stumps began to trace
The kennel edge, where wheels had worn the place.
The small-coal[†] man was heard with cadence[†] deep,
Till drowned in shriller notes of chimney-sweep.
Duns[†] at his lordship's gate began to meet;
And brickdust[†] Moll had screamed through half a street.
The turnkey[†] now his flock returning sees,
Duly let out a-nights to steal for fees.
The watchful bailiffs take their silent stands;
And schoolboys lag with satchels in their hands.

1709 1709

# A DESCRIPTION OF A CITY SHOWER[†]

OCTOBER 1710

Careful observers may foretell the hour
(By sure prognostics) when to dread a shower:
While rain depends,* the pensive cat gives o'er — impends
Her frolics, and pursues her tail no more.
Returning home at night, you'll find the sink
Strike your offended sense with double stink.

---

*A Description of the morning* Ironically presented in contrast to the sights and sounds of pastoral
*Betty* conventional maid's name
*small-coal* charcoal
*cadence* his street cry;
*Duns* bill collectors
*brickdust* an abrasive cleanser
*turnkey* gaoler, reliant on prisoners' fees
*A Description of a City Shower* *City*: the traditional commercial area. The mock-heroic diction contrasts with the mundane scene

If you be wise, then go not far to dine:
You'll spend in coach-hire more than save in wine.
A coming shower your shooting corns presage,
Old achès† throb, your hollow tooth will rage.
Sauntering in coffeehouse is Dulman seen;
He damns the climate, and complains of spleen.* melancholy
  Meanwhile the South, rising with dabbled† wings,
A sable cloud athwart the welkin* flings sky
That swilled more liquor that it could contain,
And, like a drunkard, gives it up again.
Brisk Susan whips her linen from the rope,
While the first drizzling shower is borne aslope;
Such is that sprinkling which some careless quean* wench
Flirts on you from her mop, but not so clean:
You fly, invoke the gods; then turning, stop
To rail; she singing, still whirls on her mop.
Not yet the dust had shunned th'unequal strife,
But, aided by the wind, fought still for life,
And wafted with its foe by violent gust,
'Twas doubtful which was rain, and which was dust.
Ah! where must needy poet seek for aid,
When dust and rain at once his coat invade?
His only coat, where dust confused with rain
Roughen the nap, and leave a mingled stain.
  Now in contiguous drops the flood comes down,
Threatening with deluge this devoted* town. doomed
To shops in crowds the daggled females fly,
Pretend to cheapen† goods, but nothing buy.
The Templar† spruce, while every spout's abroach,
Stays till 'tis fair, yet seems to call a coach.
The tucked-up sempstress walks with hasty strides,
While streams run down her oiled umbrella's sides.
Here various kinds, by various fortunes led,
Commence acquaintance underneath a shed:
Triumphant Tories,† and desponding Whigs,
Forget their feuds, and join to save their wigs.
Boxed in a chair† the beau impatient sits,
While spouts run clattering o'er the roof by fits,

*achès* pronounced 'aitches' (2 syllables)
*dabbled* (also 'daggled'): splashed
*cheapen* haggle over
*Templar* lawyer from the Temple, an Inn of Court
*Tories* their party had recently taken power after the Whigs
*chair* leather-roofed sedan chair, for carrying passengers

And ever and anon with frightful din
The leather sounds; he trembles from within.
So when Troy† chairmen bore the wooden steed,
Pregnant with Greeks impatient to be freed
(Those bully Greeks, who, as the moderns do,
Instead of paying chairmen, run them through),
Laocoon struck the outside with his spear,
And each imprisoned hero quaked for fear,
Now from all parts the swelling kennels† flow,
And bear their trophies with them, as they go;
Filth of all hues and odours seem to tell
What street they sailed from, by their sight and smell.
They, as each torrent drives with rapid force,
From Smithfield,† or St. 'Pulchre's† shape their course,
And in huge confluent joined at Snow Hill ridge,
Fall from the Conduit* prone to Holborn-bridge. channel
Sweepings from butchers' stalls, dung, guts, and blood,
Drowned puppies, stinking sprats, all drenched in mud,
Dead cats, and turnip-tops, come tumbling down the flood.

1710

1710

## *From* GULLIVER'S TRAVELS†

### *[Gulliver arrives in Lilliput]*

I was surgeon successively in two ships, and made several voyages, for six years, to the East and West Indies, by which I got some addition to my fortune. My hours of leisure I spent in reading the best authors ancient and modern, being always provided with a good number of books; and when I was ashore, in observing the manners and dispositions of the people, as well as learning their language, wherein I had a great facility by the strength of my memory.

*Troy* the hidden Greeks entered the city in the wooden horse (*Aeneid*, II.50)
*kennels* mid-street gutters
*Smithfield* meat market
*St 'Pulchre's* St Sepulchre's Church, up Snow Hill; the details are accurate. 11.61–3 parody Dryden's triplets; 1.63 his Alexandrine (six feet)
*Gulliver's Travels* Exploiting contemporary interest in travels such as Dampier's voyages (p. 83), Swift has his narrator Lemuel Gulliver, ship's surgeon and then captain, describe his experiences in hitherto unknown lands, whose history, social organisation and morality reflect on those of Western Europe. The meaning of the satire, especially in Part IV, has been controversial; but the narrative skill has always been recognised

The last of these voyages not proving very fortunate I grew weary of the sea, and intended to stay at home with my wife and family. I removed from the Old Jury to Fetter Lane, and from thence to Wapping,† hoping to get business among the sailors; but it would not turn to account. After three years expectation that things would mend, I accepted an advantageous offer from Captain William Prichard, master of the *Antelope*, who was making a voyage to the South Sea. We set sail from Bristol May 4th, 1699, and our voyage at first was very prosperous.

It would not be proper, for some reasons, to trouble the reader with the particulars of our adventures in those seas: Let it suffice to inform him, that in our passage from thence to the East Indies, we were driven by a violent storm to the north-west of Van Diemen's Land.† By an observation, we found ourselves in the latitude of 30 degrees 2 minutes south. Twelve of our crew were dead by immoderate labour, and ill food, the rest were in a very weak condition. On the fifth of November, which was the beginning of summer in those parts, the weather being very hazy, the seamen spied a rock, within half a cable's length of the ship; but the wind was so strong, that we were driven directly upon it, and immediately split. Six of the crew, of whom I was one, having let down the boat into the sea, made a shift to get clear of the ship, and the rock. We rowed by my computation about three leagues,† till we were able to work no longer, being already spent with labour while we were in the ship. We therefore trusted ourselves to the mercy of the waves, and in about half an hour the boat was overset by a sudden flurry from the north. What became of my companions in the boat, as well as of those who escaped on the rock, or were left in the vessel, I cannot tell; but conclude they were all lost. For my own part, I swam as fortune directed me, and was pushed forward by wind and tide. I often let my legs drop, and could feel no bottom: but when I was almost gone, and able to struggle no longer, I found myself within my depth; and by this time the storm was much abated. The declivity was so small, that I walked near a mile before I got to the shore, which I conjectured was about eight a-clock in the evening. I then advanced forward near half a mile, but could not discover any sign of houses or inhabitants; at least I was in so weak a condition, that I did not observe them. I was extremely tired, and with that, and the heat of the weather, and about half a pint of brandy that I drank as I left the ship, I found myself much inclined to sleep. I lay down on the grass, which was very

*Wapping* Gulliver moves from the City to the dock area

*Van Diemen's Land* Tasmania, south of Australian mainland

*three leagues* about 9 miles

short and soft, where I slept sounder than ever I remember to have done in my life, and as I reckoned, above nine hours; for when I awaked, it was just daylight. I attempted to rise, but was not able to stir: for as I happened to lie on my back, I found my arms and legs were strongly fastened on each side to the ground; and my hair, which was long and thick, tied down in the same manner. I likewise felt several slender ligatures across my body, from my armpits to my thighs. I could only look upwards, the sun began to grow hot, and the light offended my eyes. I heard a confused noise about me, but in the posture I lay, could see nothing except the sky. In a little time I felt something alive moving on my left leg, which advancing gently forward over my breast, came almost up to my chin; when bending my eyes downwards as much as I could, I perceived it to be a human creature not six inches high, with a bow and arrow in his hands, and a quiver at his back. In the mean time, I felt at least forty more of the same kind (as I conjectured) following the first. I was in the utmost astonishment, and roared so loud, that they all ran back in a fright; and some of them, as I was afterwards told, were hurt with the falls they got by leaping from my sides upon the ground. However, they soon returned, and one of them, who ventured so far as to get a full sight of my face, lifting up his hands and eyes by way of admiration, cried out in a shrill, but distinct voice, *Hekinah Degul*: the others repeated the same words several times, but I then knew not what they meant. I lay all this while, as the reader may believe, in great uneasiness: at length, struggling to get loose, I had the fortune to break the strings, and wrench out the pegs that fastened my left arm to the ground; for, by lifting it up to my face I discovered the methods they had taken to bind me; and, at the same time, with a violent pull, which gave me excessive pain, I a little loosened the strings that tied down my hair on the left side, so that I was just able to turn my head about two inches. But the creatures ran off a second time, before I could seize them; whereupon there was a great shout in a very shrill accent, and after it ceased, I heard one of them cry aloud, *Tolgo Phonac*; when in an instant I felt above an hundred arrows discharged on my left hand, which pricked me like so many needles; and besides they shot another flight into the air, as we do bombs in Europe, whereof many, I suppose, fell on my body (though I felt them not), and some on my face, which I immediately covered with my left hand. When this shower of arrows was over, I fell a groaning with grief and pain; and then striving again to get loose, they discharged another volley larger than the first, and some of them attempted with spears to stick me in the sides; but, by good luck, I had on me a buff† jerkin, which they

*buff* yellow leather

could not pierce. I thought it the most prudent method to lie still, and my design was to continue so till night, when, my left hand being already loose, I could easily free myself: and as for the inhabitants, I had reason to believe I might be a match for the greatest armies they could bring against me, if they were all of the same size with him that I saw. But fortune disposed otherwise of me. When the people observed I was quiet, they discharged no more arrows: but by the noise I heard, I knew their numbers increased; and about four yards from me, over-against my right ear, I heard a knocking for above an hour, like that of people at work; when turning my head that way, as well as the pegs and strings would permit me, I saw a stage erected about a foot and a half from the ground, capable of holding four of the inhabitants, with two or three ladders to mount it: from whence one of them, who seemed to be a person of quality, made me a long speech, whereof I understood not one syllable. But I should have mentioned, that before the principal person began his oration, he cried out three times *Langro Dehul san* (these words and the former were afterwards repeated and explained to me). Whereupon immediately about fifty of the inhabitants came, and cut the strings that fastened the left side of my head, which gave me the liberty of turning it to the right, and of observing the person and gesture of him that was to speak. He appeared to be of a middle age, and taller than any of the other three who attended him, whereof one was a page that held up his train, and seemed to be somewhat longer than my middle finger; the other two stood one on each side to support him. He acted every part of an orator, and I could observe many periods of threatenings, and others of promises, pity and kindness. I answered in a few words, but in the most submissive manner, lifting up my left hand and both my eyes to the sun, as calling him for a witness; and being almost famished with hunger, having not eaten a morsel for some hours before I left the ship, I found the demands of nature so strong upon me, that I could not forbear showing my impatience (perhaps against the strict rules of decency) by putting my finger frequently on my mouth, to signify that I wanted food. The *Hurgo* (for so they call a great lord, as I afterwards learnt) understood me very well. He descended from the stage, and commanded that several ladders should be applied to my sides, on which above an hundred of the inhabitants mounted and walked towards my mouth, laden with baskets full of meat,† which had been provided, and sent thither by the King's orders upon the first intelligence he received of me. I observed there was the flesh of several animals, but could not distinguish them by the taste. There were shoulders, legs and loins shaped like those of

*meat* food in general

mutton, and very well dressed,[†] but smaller than the wings of a lark. I eat[†] them by two or three at a mouthful, and took three loaves at a time, about the bigness of musket bullets. They supplied me as fast as they could, showing a thousand marks of wonder and astonishment at my bulk and appetite. I then made another sign that I wanted drink. They found by my eating that a small quantity would not suffice me, and being a most ingenious people, they slung up with great dexterity one of their largest hogsheads, then rolled it towards my hand, and beat out the top; I drank it off at a draught, which I might well do, for it did not hold half a pint, and tasted like a small wine of Burgundy, but much more delicious. They brought me a second hogshead, which I drank in the same manner, and made signs for more, but they had none to give me. When I had performed these wonders, they shouted for joy, and danced upon my breast, repeating several times as they did at first, *Hekinah Degul*. They made me a sign that I should throw down the two hogsheads, but first warned the people below to stand out of the way, crying aloud, *Borach Mivola*, and when they saw the vessels in the air, there was an universal shout of *Hekinah Degul*. I confess I was often tempted while they were passing backwards and forwards on my body to seize forty or fifty of the first that came in my reach, and dash them against the ground. But the remembrance of what I had felt, which probably might not be the worst they could do, and the promise of honour I made them, for so I interpreted my submissive behaviour, soon drove out these imaginations. Besides, I now considered myself as bound by the laws of hospitality to a people who had treated me with so much expense and magnificence. However in my thoughts I could not sufficiently wonder at the intrepidity of these diminutive mortals, who durst venture to mount and walk upon my body, while one of my hands was at liberty, without trembling at the very sight of so prodigious a creature as I must appear to them. After some time, when they observed that I made no more demands for meat, there appeared before me a person of high rank from his Imperial Majesty. His Excellency having mounted on the small of my right leg, advanced forwards up to my face, with about a dozen of his retinue. And producing his credentials under the signet royal, which he applied close to my eyes, spoke about ten minutes without any signs of anger, but with a kind of determinate resolution; often pointing forwards, which, as I afterwards found, was towards the capital city, about half a mile distant, whither it was agreed by his Majesty in council that I must be conveyed. I answered in few words, but to no purpose, and made a sign with my hand that was loose, putting it to the other (but over his Excellency's head, for fear of hurting him or his train) and then to my

*dressed* prepared　　*eat* ate

own head and body, to signify that I desired my liberty. It appeared that he understood me well enough, for he shook his head by way of disapprobation, and held his hand in a posture to show that I must be carried as a prisoner. However, he made other signs to let me understand that I should have meat and drink enough, and very good treatment. Whereupon I once more thought of attempting to break my bonds, but again, when I felt the smart of their arrows upon my face and hands, which were all in blisters, and many of the darts still sticking in them, and observing likewise that the number of my enemies increased, I gave tokens to let them know that they might do with me what they pleased. Upon this the *Hurgo* and his train withdrew with much civility and cheerful countenances. Soon after I heard a general shout, with frequent repetitions of the words, *Peplom Selan*, and I felt great numbers of the people on my left side relaxing the cords to such a degree that I was able to turn upon my right, and to ease myself with making water; which I very plentifully did, to the great astonishment of the people, who conjecturing by my motions what I was going to do, immediately opened to the right and left on that side to avoid the torrent which fell with such noise and violence from me. But before this, they had daubed my face and both my hands with a sort of ointment very pleasant to the smell, which in a few minutes removed all the smart of their arrows. These circumstances, added to the refreshment I had received by their victuals and drink, which were very nourishing, disposed me to sleep. I slept about eight hours, as I was afterwards assured; and it was no wonder, for the physicians, by the Emperor's order, had mingled a sleepy potion in the hogsheads of wine.

It seems that upon the first moment I was discovered sleeping on the ground after my landing, the Emperor had early notice of it by an express,† and determined in council that I should be tied in the manner I have related (which was done in the night while I slept) that plenty of meat and drink should be sent me, and a machine prepared to carry me to the capital city.

This resolution perhaps may appear very bold and dangerous, and I am confident would not be imitated by any prince in Europe on the like occasion; however, in my opinion it was extremely prudent as well as generous. For supposing these people had endeavoured to kill me with their spears and arrows while I was asleep, I should certainly have awaked with the first sense of smart, which might so far have roused my rage and strength, as to have enabled me to break the strings wherewith I was tied; after which, as they were not able to make resistance, so they could expect no mercy.

*express* messenger

## *[Gulliver in Brobdingnag]*†

It is the custom that every Wednesday (which as I have before observed, was their sabbath) the King and Queen, with the royal issue of both sexes, dine together in the apartment of his Majesty, to whom I was now become a great favourite; and at these times my little chair and table were placed at his left hand before one of the saltcellars. This prince took a pleasure in conversing with me, enquiring into the manners, religion, laws, government, and learning of Europe, wherein I gave him the best account I was able. His apprehension was so clear, and his judgment so exact, that he made very wise reflections and observations upon all I said. But, I confess, that after I had been a little too copious in talking of my own beloved country, of our trade, and wars by sea and land, of our schisms† in religion, and parties in the state, the prejudices of his education prevailed so far, that he could not forbear taking me up in his right hand, and stroking me gently with the other, after an hearty fit of laughing, asked me whether I were a Whig or a Tory. Then turning to his first minister, who waited behind him with a white staff, near as tall as the mainmast of the *Royal Sovereign*, he observed how contemptible a thing was human grandeur, which could be mimicked by such diminutive insects as I: 'And yet,' said he, 'I dare engage, these creatures have their titles and distinctions of honour, they contrive little nests and burrows, that they call houses and cities; they make a figure in dress and equipage,† they love, they fight, they dispute, they cheat, they betray.' And thus he continued on, while my colour came and went several times, with indignation to hear our noble country, the mistress of arts and arms, the scourge of France, the arbitress of Europe, the seat of virtue, piety, honour and truth, the pride and envy of the world, so contemptuously treated.

But, as I was not in a condition to resent injuries, so, upon mature thoughts, I began to doubt whether I were injured or no. For, after having been accustomed several months to the sight and converse of this people, and observed every object upon which I cast my eyes to be of proportionable magnitude, the horror I had first conceived from their bulk and aspect was so far worn off, that if I had then beheld a company of English lords and ladies in their finery and birthday† clothes, acting their several parts in the most courtly manner of strutting, and bowing and prating; to say the truth, I should have been strongly tempted to laugh as much at them as this King and his grandees did at me. Neither indeed could I forbear smiling at myself, when the Queen used to place me upon her hand towards a looking-glass, by which both our persons

*[Gulliver in Brobdingnag]* Gulliver's second voyage takes him to the land of giants, where he becomes a kind of pet to the royal family

*schisms* divisions

*equipage* carriage and servants

*birthday* fine, for king's birthday

appeared before me in full view together; and there could nothing be more ridiculous than the comparison: so that I really began to imagine myself dwindled many degrees below my usual size.

Nothing angered and mortified me so much as the Queen's dwarf, who being of the lowest stature that was ever in that country (for I verily think he was not full thirty foot high) became so insolent at seeing a creature so much beneath him, that he would always affect to swagger and look big as he passed by me in the Queen's antechamber, while I was standing on some table talking with the lords or ladies of the court, and he seldom failed of a smart word or two upon my littleness; against which I could only revenge myself by calling him brother, challenging him to wrestle, and such repartees as are usual in the mouths of court pages. One day at dinner this malicious little cub was so nettled with something I had said to him, that raising himself upon the frame of her Majesty's chair, he took me up by the middle, as I was sitting down, not thinking any harm, and let me drop into a large silver bowl of cream, and then ran away as fast as he could. I fell over head and ears, and if I had not been a good swimmer, it might have gone very hard with me; for *Glumdalclitch* in that instant happened to be at the other end of the room, and the Queen was in such a fright that she wanted† presence of mind to assist me. But my little nurse ran to my relief, and took me out, after I had swallowed above a quart of cream. I was put to bed; however I received no other damage than the loss of a suit of clothes, which was utterly spoiled. The dwarf was soundly whipped and as a further punishment, forced to drink up the bowl of cream, into which he had thrown me; neither was he ever restored to favour: for, soon after, the Queen bestowed him to a lady of high quality, so that I saw him no more, to my very great satisfaction; for I could not tell to what extremities such a malicious urchin might have carried his resentment.

He had before served me a scurvy trick, which set the Queen a laughing, although at the same time she were heartily vexed, and would have immediately cashiered† him, if I had not been so generous as to intercede. Her Majesty had taken a marrow-bone upon her plate, and after knocking out the marrow, placed the bone again in the dish erect as it stood before; the dwarf watching his opportunity, while *Glumdalclitch* was gone to the sideboard, mounted upon the stool she stood on to take care of me at meals, took me up in both hands, and squeezing my legs together, wedged them into the marrow-bone above my waist, where I stuck for some time, and made a very ridiculous figure. I believe it was near a minute before any one knew what was become of me, for I thought it below me to cry out. But, as princes

*wanted* lacked

*cashiered* dismissed

seldom get their meat hot, my legs were not scalded, only my stockings and breeches in a sad condition. The dwarf at my entreaty had no other punishment than a sound whipping.

I was frequently rallied† by the Queen upon account of my fearfulness, and she used to ask me whether the people of my country were as great cowards as myself. The occasion was this. The kingdom is much pestered with flies in summer, and these odious insects, each of them as big as a Dunstable Lark, hardly gave me any rest while I sat at dinner, with their continual humming and buzzing about my ears. They would sometimes alight upon my victuals, and leave their loathsome excrement or spawn behind, which to me was very visible though not to the natives of that country, whose large optics were not so acute as mine in viewing smaller objects. Sometimes they would fix upon my nose or forehead, where they stung me to the quick, smelling very offensively, and I could easily trace that viscous matter, which our naturalists tell us enables those creatures to walk with their feet upwards upon a ceiling. I had much ado to defend myself against these detestable animals, and could not forbear starting when they came on my face. It was the common practice of the dwarf to catch a number of these insects in his hand as schoolboys do among us, and let them out suddenly under my nose on purpose to frighten me, and divert the Queen. My remedy was to cut them in pieces with my knife as they flew in the air, wherein my dexterity was much admired.

I remember one morning when *Glumdalclitch* had set me in my box† upon a window, as she usually did in fair days to give me air (for I durst not venture to let the box be hung on a nail out of the window, as we do with cages in England) after I had lifted up one of my sashes, and sat down at my table to eat a piece of sweet cake for my breakfast, above twenty wasps, allured by the smell, came flying into the room, humming louder than the drones of as many bagpipes. Some of them seized my cake, and carried it piecemeal away, others flew about my head and face, confounding me with the noise, and putting me in the utmost terror of their stings. However I had the courage to rise and draw my hanger,† and attack them in the air. I dispatched four of them, but the rest got away, and I presently shut my window. These insects were as large as partridges, I took out their stings, found them an inch and a half long, and as sharp as needles. I carefully preserved them all, and having since shown them with some other curiosities in several parts of Europe, upon my return to England I gave three of them to Gresham College,† and kept the fourth for myself.

*rallied* teased
*box* like a doll's house, with sash-windows
*hanger* short sword
*Gresham College* early home of the Royal Society, and of a curio collection

## *[Gulliver praises England to the King]*

He was perfectly astonished with the historical account I gave him of our affairs during the last century, protesting it was only an heap of conspiracies, rebellions, murders, massacres, revolutions, banishments, the very worst effects that avarice, faction, hypocrisy, perfidiousness, cruelty, rage, madness, hatred, envy, lust, malice, or ambition could produce.

His Majesty in another audience was at the pains to recapitulate the sum of all I had spoken, compared the questions he made with the answers I had given; then taking me into his hands, and stroking me gently, delivered himself in these words, which I shall never forget, nor the manner he spoke them in. 'My little friend *Grildrig*; you have made a most admirable panegyric upon your country. You have clearly proved that ignorance, idleness and vice are the proper ingredients for qualifying a legislator; that laws are best explained, interpreted, and applied by those whose interest and abilities lie in perverting, confounding, and eluding them. I observe among you some lines of an institution, which in its original might have been tolerable, but these half erased, and the rest wholly blurred and blotted by corruptions. It doth not appear from all you have said, how any one virtue is required towards the procurement of any one station among you, much less that men are ennobled on account of their virtue, that priests are advanced for their piety or learning, soldiers for their conduct or valour, judges for their integrity, senators[†] for the love of their country, or counsellors for their wisdom. As for yourself (continued the King) who have spent the greatest part of your life in travelling, I am well disposed to hope you may hitherto have escaped many vices of your country. But, by what I have gathered from your own relation, and the answers I have with much pains wringed and extorted from you, I cannot but conclude the bulk of your natives, to be the most pernicious race of little odious vermin that nature ever suffered to crawl upon the surface of the earth.'

Nothing but an extreme love of truth could have hindered me from concealing this part of my story. It was in vain to discover[†] my resentments, which were always turned into ridicule; and I was forced to rest with patience while my noble and most beloved country was so injuriously treated. I am heartily sorry as any of my readers can possibly be, that such an occasion was given: but this prince happened to be so curious and inquisitive upon every particular, that it could not consist either with gratitude or good manners to refuse giving him what satisfaction I was able. Yet thus much I may be allowed to say in my

*senators* MPs

*discover* reveal

own vindication, that I artfully eluded many of his questions, and gave to every point a more favourable turn by many degrees tan the strictness of truth would allow. For, I have always borne that laudable partiality to my own country, which Dionysius† Halicarnassensis with so much justice recommends to an historian. I would hide the frailties and deformities of my political mother, and place her virtues and beauties in the most advantageous light. This was my sincere endeavour in those many discourses I had with that mighty monarch, although it unfortunately failed of success.

But, great allowances should be given to a King who lives wholly secluded from the rest of the world, and must therefore be altogether unacquainted with the manners and customs that most prevail in other nations: the want of which knowledge will ever produce many prejudices, and a certain narrowness of thinking, from which we and the politer countries of Europe are wholly exempted. And it would be hard indeed, if so remote a prince's notions of virtue and vice were to be offered as a standard for all mankind.

To confirm what I have now said, and further to show the miserable effects of a confined education, I shall here insert a passage which will hardly obtain belief. In hopes to ingratiate myself farther into his Majesty's favour, I told him of an invention discovered between three and four hundred years ago, to make a certain powder, into an heap of which the smallest spark of fire falling, would kindle the whole in a moment, although it were as big as a mountain, and make it all fly up in the air together, with a noise and agitation greater than thunder. That a proper quantity of this powder rammed into an hollow tube of brass or iron, according to its bigness, would drive a ball of iron or lead with such violence and speed as nothing was able to sustain its force. That the largest balls thus discharged would not only destroy whole ranks of an army at once, but batter the strongest walls to the ground, sink down ships with a thousand men in each, to the bottom of the sea; and when linked together by a chain, would cut through masts and rigging, divide hundreds of bodies in the middle, and lay all waste before them. That we often put this powder into large hollow balls of iron, and discharged them by an engine into some city we were besieging, which would rip up the pavements, tear the houses to pieces, burst and throw splinters on every side, dashing out the brains of all who came near. That I knew the ingredients very well, which were cheap, and common; I understood the manner of compounding them, and could direct his workmen how to make those tubes of a size proportionable to all other things in his Majesty's kingdom, and the

*Dionysius* Greek historian in first century BC Rome

largest need not be above an hundred foot long; twenty or thirty of which tubes, charged with the proper quantity of powder and balls, would batter down the walls of the strongest town in his dominions in a few hours, or destroy the whole metropolis, if ever it should pretend† to dispute his absolute commands. This I humbly offered to his Majesty as a small tribute of acknowledgment in return of so many marks that I had received of his royal favour and protection.

The King was struck with horror at the description I had given of those terrible engines, and the proposal I had made. He was amazed how so impotent and grovelling an insect as I (these were his expressions) could entertain such inhuman ideas, and in so familiar a manner as to appear wholly unmoved at all the scenes of blood and desolation, which I had painted as the common effects of those destructive machines, whereof, he said, some evil genius, enemy to mankind, must have been the first contriver. As for himself, he protested, that although few things delighted him so much as new discoveries in art or in nature, yet he would rather lose half his kingdom than be privy to such a secret, which he commanded me, as I valued my life, never to mention any more.

A strange effect of narrow principles and short views! that a prince possessed of every quality which procures veneration, love and esteem; of strong parts,† great wisdom and profound learning, endued with admirable talents for government, and almost adored by his subjects, should from a nice† unnecessary scruple, whereof in Europe we can have no conception, let slip an opportunity put into his hands, that would have made him absolute master of the lives, the liberties, and the fortunes of his people. Neither do I say this with the least intention to detract from the many virtues of that excellent King, whose character I am sensible will on this account be very much lessened in the opinion of an English reader: but, I take this defect among them to have risen from their ignorance, they not having hitherto reduced politics into a science, as the more acute wits of Europe have done. For, I remember very well, in a discourse one day with the King, when I happened to say there were several thousand books among us written upon the art of government, it gave him (directly contrary to my intention) a very mean opinion of our understandings. He professed both to abominate and despise all mystery, refinement, and intrigue, either in a prince or a minister. He could not tell what I meant by secrets of state, where an enemy or some rival nation were not in the case. He confined the knowledge of governing within very narrow bounds; to common sense and reason, to justice and lenity, to the speedy determination of civil and criminal causes; with some other obvious topics which are not

*pretend* attempt
*parts* talents
*nice* fastidious

worth considering. And, he gave it for his opinion, that whoever could make two ears of corn, or two blades of grass to grow upon a spot of ground where only one grew before, would deserve better of mankind, and do more essential service to his country than the whole race of politicians put together.

The learning of this people is very defective, consisting only in morality, history, poetry and mathematics, wherein they must be allowed to excel. But, the last of these is wholly applied to what may be useful in life, to the improvement of agriculture and all mechanical arts; so that among us it would be little esteemed. And as to ideas, entities, abstractions and transcendentals,[†] I could never drive the least conception into their heads. . . .

## *[The Immortals of Luggnagg]*[†]

One day in much good company I was asked by a person of quality, whether I had seen any of their *Struldbruggs* or immortals. I said I had not, and desired he would explain to me what he meant by such an appellation applied to a mortal creature. He told me that sometimes, though very rarely, a child happened to be born in a family with a red circular spot in the forehead, directly over the left eyebrow, which was an infallible mark that it should never die. The spot, as he described it, was about the compass of a silver threepence, but in the course of time grew larger, and changed its colour; for at twelve years old it became green, so continued till five and twenty, then turned to a deep blue; at five and forty it grew coal black, and as large as an English shilling, but never admitted any farther alteration. He said these births were so rare, that he did not believe there could be above eleven hundred *Struldbruggs* of both sexes in the whole kingdom, of which he computed about fifty in the metropolis, and among the rest a young girl born about three years ago. That these productions were not peculiar to any family but a mere effect of chance, and the children of the *Struldbruggs* themselves were equally mortal with the rest of the people.

I freely own myself to have been struck with inexpressible delight upon hearing this account: and the person who gave it me happening to understand the *Balnibarbian*[†] language, which I spoke very well, I could not forbear breaking out into expressions perhaps a little too extravagant. I cried out as in a rapture: 'Happy nation where every child hath at least a chance for being immortal! Happy people who

*ideas . . . transcendentals* all unpractical

*The Immortals of Luggnagg* In the third voyage, Gulliver has arrived in the kingdom of Luggnagg

*Balnibarbi* recently visited by G.

enjoy so many living examples of ancient virtue, and have masters ready to instruct them in the wisdom of all former ages! But, happiest beyond all comparison are those excellent *Struldbruggs*, who, born exempt from that universal calamity of human nature, have their minds free and disengaged, without the weight and depression of spirits caused by the continual apprehension of death.' I discovered my admiration† that I had not observed any of these illustrious persons at court: the black spot on the forehead being so remarkable a distinction that I could not have easily overlooked it; and it was impossible that his Majesty, a most judicious prince, should not provide himself with a good number of such wise and able counsellors. Yet perhaps the virtue of those reverend sages was too strict for the corrupt and libertine manners of a court. And we often find by experience that young men are too opinionative and volatile to be guided by the sober dictates of their seniors. However, since the King was pleased to allow me access to his royal person, I was resolved upon the very first occasion to deliver my opinion to him on this matter freely and at large by the help of my interpreter; and whether he would please to take my advice or no, yet in one thing I was determined, that his Majesty having frequently offered me an establishment in this country, I would with great thankfulness accept the favour, and pass my life here in the conversation of those superior beings the *Struldbruggs*, if they would please to admit me.

The gentleman to whom I addressed my discourse, because (as I have already observed) he spoke the language of *Balnibarbi*, said to me with a sort of a smile, which usually ariseth from pity to the ignorant, that he was glad of any occasion to keep me among them, and desired my permission to explain to the company what I had spoke. He did so, and they talked together for some time in their own language, whereof I understood not a syllable, neither could I observe by their countenances what impression my discourse had made on them. After a short silence the same person told me that his friends and mine (so he thought fit to express himself) were very much pleased with the judicious remarks I had made on the great happiness and advantages of immortal life, and they were desirous to know in a particular manner, what scheme of living I should have formed to myself, if it had fallen to my lot to have been born a *Struldbrugg*.

I answered, it was easy to be eloquent on so copious and delightful a subject, especially to me who have been often apt to amuse myself with visions of what I should do if I were a king, a general, or a great lord; and upon this very case I had frequently run over the whole system

*admiration* wonder

how I should employ myself, and pass the time if I were sure to live for ever.

That, if it had been my good fortune to come into the world a *Struldbrugg*, as soon as I could discover my own happiness by understanding the difference between life and death, I would first resolve by all arts and methods whatsoever to procure myself riches; in the pursuit of which by thrift and management, I might reasonably expect in about two hundred years to be the wealthiest man in the kingdom. In the second place, I would from my earliest youth apply myself to the study of arts and sciences, by which I should arrive in time to excel all others in learning. Lastly I would carefully record every action and event of consequence that happened in the public, impartially draw the characters of the several successions of princes, and great ministers of state, with my own observations on every point. I would exactly set down the several changes in customs, language, fashions of dress, diet and diversions. By all which acquirements, I should be a living treasury of knowledge and wisdom, and certainly become the oracle of the nation.

I would never marry after threescore, but live in an hospitable manner, yet still on the saving side. I would entertain myself in forming and directing the minds of hopeful young men, by convincing them from my own remembrance, experience and observation, fortified by numerous examples, of the usefulness of virtue in public and private life. But, my choice and constant companions should be a set of my own immortal brotherhood, among whom I would elect a dozen from the most ancient down to my own contemporaries. Where any of these wanted fortunes, I would provide them with convenient lodges round my own estate, and have some of them always at my table, only mingling a few of the most valuable among you mortals, whom length of time would harden me to lose with little or no reluctance, and treat your posterity after the same manner, just as a man diverts himself with the annual succession of pinks and tulips in his garden, without regretting the loss of those which withered the preceding year.

These *Struldbruggs* and I would mutually communicate our observations and memorials through the course of time, remark the several gradations by which corruption steals into the world, and oppose it in every step, by giving perpetual warning and instruction to mankind; which, added to the strong influence of our own example, would probably prevent that continual degeneracy of human nature so justly complained of in all ages.

Add to all this, the pleasure of seeing the various revolutions of states and empires, the changes in the lower and upper world, ancient cities in ruins, and obscure villages become the seats of kings; famous rivers lessening into shallow brooks, the ocean leaving one coast dry, and overwhelming another; the discovery of many countries yet unknown;

barbarity over-running the politest nations, and the most barbarous become civilised. I should then see the discovery of the longitude, the perpetual motion, the universal medicine, and many other great inventions brought to the utmost perfection.

What wonderful discoveries should we make in astronomy, by outliving and confirming our own predictions, by observing the progress and returns of comets, with the changes of motion in the sun, moon and stars.

I enlarged upon many other topics which the natural desire of endless life and sublunary happiness could easily furnish me with. When I had ended, and the sum of my discourse had been interpreted as before to the rest of the company, there was a good deal of talk among them in the language of the country, not without some laughter at my expense. At last the same gentleman who had been my interpreter said he was desired by the rest to set me right in a few mistakes which I had fallen into through the common imbecility of human nature, and upon that allowance was less answerable for them. That, this breed of *Struldbruggs* was peculiar to their country, for there were no such people either in *Balnibarbi* or Japan, where he had the honour to be ambassador from his Majesty, and found the natives in both those kingdoms very hard to believe that the fact was possible, and it appeared from my astonishment when he first mentioned the matter to me, that I received it as a thing wholly new, and scarcely to be credited. That in the two kingdoms above mentioned, where during his residence he had conversed very much, he observed long life to be the universal desire and wish of mankind. That whoever had one foot in the grave, was sure to hold back the other as strongly as he could. That the oldest had still hopes of living one day longer, and looked on death as the greatest evil, from which nature always prompted him to retreat; only in this island of *Luggnagg* the appetite for living was not so eager, from the continual example of the *Struldbruggs* before their eyes.

That the system of living contrived by me was unreasonable and unjust, because it supposed a perpetuity of youth, health, and vigour, which no man could be so foolish to hope, however extravagant he may be in his wishes. That the question therefore was not whether a man would choose to be always in the prime of youth, attended with prosperity and health, but how he would pass a perpetual life under all the usual disadvantages which old age brings along with it. For although few men will avow their desires of being immortal upon such hard conditions, yet in the two kingdoms before-mentioned of *Balnibarbi* and Japan, he observed that every man desired to put off death for sometime longer, let it approach ever so late, and he rarely heard of any man who died willingly, except he were incited by the extremity of grief or torture. And he appealed to me whether in those countries I had travelled as well as my own, I had not observed the same general disposition.

After this preface he gave me a particular account of the *Struldbruggs* among them. He said they commonly acted like mortals, till about thirty years old, after which by degrees they grew melancholy and dejected, increasing in both till they came to four-score. This he learned from their own confession; for otherwise, there not being above two or three of that species born in an age, they were too few to form a general observation by. When they came to four-score years, which is reckoned the extremity of living in this country, they had not only all the follies and infirmities of other old men, but many more which arose from the dreadful prospects of never dying. They were not only opinionative, peevish, covetous, morose, vain, talkative, but uncapable of friendship, and dead to all natural affection, which never descended below their grandchildren. Envy and impotent desires are their prevailing passions. But those objects against which their envy seems principally directed, are the vices of the younger sort, and the deaths of the old. By reflecting on the former they find themselves cut off from all possibility of pleasure; and whenever they see a funeral, they lament and repine that others are gone to an harbour of rest, to which they themselves never can hope to arrive. They have no remembrance of any thing but what they learned and observed in their youth and middle age, and even that is very imperfect. And for the truth or particulars of any fact it is safer to depend on common traditions than upon their best recollections. The least miserable among them appear to be those who turn to dotage, and entirely lose their understandings; these meet with more pity and assistance, because they want many bad qualities which abound in others.

If a *Struldbrugg* happen to marry one of his own kind, the marriage is dissolved of course by the courtesy of the kingdom, as soon as the younger of the two comes to be four-score. For the law thinks it a reasonable indulgence, that those who are condemned without any fault of their own to a perpetual continuance in the world, should not have their misery doubled by the load of a wife.

As soon as they have completed the term of eighty years, they are looked on as dead in law; their heirs immediately succeed to their estates, only a small pittance is reserved for their support, and the poor ones are maintained at the public charge. After that period they are held incapable of any employment of trust or profit, they cannot purchase lands or take leases, neither are they allowed to be witnesses in any cause, either civil or criminal, not even for the decision of meres† and bounds.

*meres* landmarks

At ninety they lose their teeth and hair, they have at that age no distinction of taste, but eat and drink whatever they can get, without relish or appetite. The diseases they were subject to still continue without increasing or diminishing. In talking they forget the common appellation of things, and the names of persons, even of those who are their nearest friends and relations. For the same reason they never can amuse themselves with reading, because their memory will not serve to carry them from the beginning of a sentence to the end; and by this defect they are deprived of the only entertainment whereof they might otherwise be capable.

The language of this country being always upon the flux, the *Struldbruggs* of one age do not understand those of another, neither are they able after two hundred years to hold any conversation (farther than by a few general words) with their neighbours the mortals, and thus they lie under the disadvantage of living like foreigners in their own country.

This was the account given me of the *Struldbruggs*, as near as I can remember. I afterwards saw five or six of different ages, the youngest not above two hundred years old, who were brought to me at several times by some of my friends; but although they were told that I was a great traveller, and had seen all the world, they had not the least curiosity to ask me a question; only desired I would give them *Slumskudask*, or a token of remembrance, which is a modest way of begging, to avoid the law that strictly forbids it, because they are provided for by the public, although indeed with a very scanty allowance.

They are despised and hated by all sorts of people; when one of them is born, it is reckoned ominous, and their birth is recorded very particularly; so that you may know their age by consulting the registry, which however hath not been kept above a thousand years past, or at least hath been destroyed by time or public disturbances. But the usual way of computing how old they are, is by asking them what kings or great persons they can remember, and then consulting history, for infallibly the last prince in their mind did not begin his reign after they were four-score years old.

They were the most mortifying sight I ever beheld, and the women more horrible than the men. Besides the usual deformities in extreme old age, they acquired an additional ghastliness in proportion to their number of years, which is not to be described, and among half a dozen I soon distinguished which was the eldest, although there was not above a century or two between them.

The reader will easily believe, that from what I had heard and seen, my keen appetite for perpetuity of life was much abated. I grew heartily ashamed of the pleasing visions I had formed, and thought no tyrant could invent a death into which I would not run with pleasure from such a life. The King heard of all that had passed between me and my friends upon this occasion, and rallied me very pleasantly, wishing I would send a couple of *Struldbruggs* to my own country, to arm our people against the fear of death; but this it seems is forbidden by the fundamental laws of the kingdom, or else I should have been well content with the trouble and expense of transporting them.

I could not but agree that the laws of this kingdom relating to the *Struldbruggs* were founded upon the strongest reasons, and such as any other country would be under the necessity of enacting in the like circumstances. Otherwise, as avarice is the necessary consequent of old age, those immortals would in time become proprietors of the whole nation, and engross the civil power, which, for want of abilities to manage, must end in the ruin of the public.

## *[Houyhnhnms and Yahoos]*†

As I ought to have understood human nature much better than I supposed it possible for my master to do, so it was easy to apply the character he gave of the *Yahoos* to myself and my countrymen, and I believed I could yet make farther discoveries from my own observation. I therefore often begged his favour to let me go among the herds of *Yahoos* in the neighbourhood, to which he always very graciously consented, being perfectly convinced that the hatred I bore those brutes would never suffer me to be corrupted by them; and his honour ordered one of his servants, a strong sorrel nag,† very honest and goodnatured, to be my guard, without whose protection I durst not undertake such adventures. For I have already told the reader how much I was pestered by those odious animals upon my first arrival. And I afterwards failed very narrowly three or four times of falling into their clutches, when I happened to stray at any distance without my hanger. And I have reason to believe they had some imagination that I was of their own species, which I often assisted myself, by stripping up my sleeves, and showing my naked arms and breast in their sight, when my protector was with me. At which times they would approach as near as they durst, and imitate my actions after the manner of monkeys, but ever with great signs of hatred, as a tame jackdaw with cap and stockings is always persecuted by the wild ones, when he happens to be got among them.

---

*[Houyhnhnms and Yahoos]* In his final voyage Gulliver is marooned by his men in the land of the houyhnhnms (pronounced 'hwee-nim', as neighing). These horse-like creatures are instinctively rational, and rule over humanoid naked creatures, Yahoos, whose savagery, greed, lust and corruption Gulliver's 'Master' describes

*sorrel nag* reddish-brown horse

They are prodigiously nimble from their infancy; however, I once caught a young male of three years old, and endeavoured by all marks of tenderness to make it quiet; but the little imp fell a squalling and scratching, and biting with such violence, that I was forced to let it go, and it was high time, for a whole troop of old ones came about us at the noise, but finding the cub was safe (for away it ran) and my sorrel nag being by, they durst not venture near us. I observed the young animal's flesh to smell very rank, and the stink was somewhat between a weasel and a fox, but much more disagreeable. I forgot another circumstance (and perhaps I might have the reader's pardon, if it were wholly omitted) that while I held the odious vermin in my hands, it voided its filthy excrements of a yellow liquid substance, all over my clothes; but by good fortune there was a small brook hard by, where I washed myself as clean as I could, although I durst not come into my master's presence, until I were sufficiently aired.

By what I could discover, the *Yahoos* appear to be the most unteachable of all animals, their capacities never reaching higher than to draw or carry burthens. Yet I am of opinion this defect ariseth chiefly from a perverse, restive disposition. For they are cunning, malicious, treacherous and revengeful. They are strong and hardy, but of a cowardly spirit, and by consequence, insolent, abject, and cruel. It is observed, that the red-haired of both sexes are more libidinous and mischievous than the rest, whom yet they much exceed in strength and activity.

The *Houyhnhnms* keep the *Yahoos* for present use in huts not far from the house; but the rest are sent abroad to certain fields, where they dig up roots, eat several kinds of herbs, and search about for carrion, or sometimes catch weasels and *Luhimuhs* (a sort of wild rat) which they greedily devour. Nature hath taught them to dig deep holes with their nails on the side of a rising ground, wherein they lie by themselves, only the kennels of the females are larger, sufficient to hold two or three cubs.

They swim from their infancy like frogs, and are able to continue long under water, where they often take fish, which the females carry home to their young. And upon this occasion, I hope the reader will pardon my relating an odd adventure.

Being one day abroad with my protector the sorrel nag, and the weather exceeding hot, I entreated him to let me bathe in a river that was near. He consented, and I immediately stripped myself stark naked, and went down softly into the stream. It happened that a young female *Yahoo* standing behind a bank saw the whole proceeding, and enflamed by desire, as the nag and I conjectured, came running with all speed, and leaped into the water within five yards of the place where I bathed. I was never in my life so terribly frighted; the nag was grazing at some distance, not suspecting any harm. She embraced me after a most fulsome manner; I roared as loud as I could, and the nag came galloping towards me, whereupon she quitted her grasp with the utmost reluctancy, and leaped upon the opposite bank, where she stood gazing and howling all the time I was putting on my clothes.

This was matter of diversion to my master and his family, as well as of mortification to myself. For now I could no longer deny that I was a real *Yahoo*, in every limb and feature, since the females had a natural propensity to me as one of their own species: neither was the hair of this brute of a red colour, (which might have been some excuse for an appetite a little irregular) but black as a sloe, and her countenance did not make an appearance altogether so hideous as the rest of the kind; for, I think, she could not be above eleven years old.

Having lived three years in this country, the reader I suppose will expect that I should, like other travellers, give him some account of the manners and customs of its inhabitants, which it was indeed my principal study to learn.

As these noble *Houyhnhnms* are endowed by nature with a general disposition to all virtues, and have no conceptions or ideas of what is evil in a rational creature, so their grand maxim is, to cultivate reason, and to be wholly governed by it. Neither is reason among them a point problematical as with us, where men can argue with plausibility on both sides of a question; but strikes you with immediate conviction; as it must needs do where it is not mingled, obscured or discoloured by passion and interest. I remember it was with extreme difficulty that I could bring my master to understand the meaning of the word opinion, or how a point could be disputable; because reason taught us to affirm or deny only where we are certain; and beyond our knowledge we cannot do either. So that controversies, wranglings, disputes, and positiveness in false or dubious propositions are evils unknown among the *Houyhnhnms*. In the like manner when I used to explain to him our several systems of natural philosophy,† he would laugh that a creature pretending to reason, should value itself upon the knowledge of other people's conjectures, and in things where that knowledge, if it were certain, could be of no use. Wherein he agreed entirely with the sentiments of Socrates,† as Plato delivers them; which I mention as the highest honour I can do that prince of philosophers. I have often since reflected what destruction such a doctrine would make in the libraries of Europe, and how many paths to fame would be then shut up in the learned world.

*natural philosophy* scientific thought
Socrates (469–399 BC) Greek philosopher, reported in Plato's Dialogues

Friendship and benevolence are the two principal virtues among the *Houyhnhnms*, and these not confined to particular objects, but universal to the whole race. For a stranger from the remotest part is equally treated with the nearest neighbour, and wherever he goes, looks upon himself as at home. They preserve decency and civility in the highest degrees, but are altogether ignorant of ceremony. They have no fondness† for their colts or foals, but the care they take in educating them proceeds entirely from the dictates of reason. And I observed my master to show the same affection to his neighbour's issue that he had for his own. They will have it that nature teaches them to love the whole species, and it is reason only that maketh a distinction of persons, where there is a superior degree of virtue.

When the matron *Houyhnhnms* have produced one of each sex, they no longer accompany with their consorts, except they lose one of their issue by some casualty, which very seldom happens: but in such a case they meet again. Or when the like accident befalls a person whose wife is past bearing, some other couple bestow him one of their own colts, and then go together again till the mother is pregnant. This caution is necessary to prevent the country from being overburdened with numbers. But the race of inferior *Houyhnhnms* bred up to be servants is not so strictly limited upon this article. These are allowed to produce three of each sex, to be domestics in the noble families.

In their marriages they are exactly careful to choose such colours as will not make any disagreeable mixture in the breed. Strength is chiefly valued in the male, and comeliness in the female, not upon the account of love, but to preserve the race from degenerating; for where a female happens to excel in strength, a consort is chosen with regard to comeliness. Courtship, love, presents, jointures,† settlements, have no place in their thoughts; or terms whereby to express them in their language. The young couple meet and are joined, merely because it is the determination of their parents and friends: it is what they see done every day, and they look upon it as one of the necessary actions of a rational being. But the violation of marriage, or any other unchastity, was never heard of: and the married pair pass their lives with the same friendship and mutual benevolence that they bear to all others of the same species, who come in their way; without jealousy, fondness, quarrelling, or discontent.

In educating the youth of both sexes, their method is admirable, and highly deserves our imitation. These are not suffered to taste a grain of oats, except upon certain days, till eighteen years old; nor milk, but very rarely; and in summer they graze two hours in the morning, and as long in the evening, which their parents likewise observe, but the

*fondness* foolish indulgence

*jointures* property settled in marriage

servants are not allowed above half that time, and a great part of their grass is brought home which they eat at the most convenient hours, when they can be best spared from work.

Temperance, industry, exercise and cleanliness are the lessons equally enjoined to the young ones of both sexes; and my master thought it monstrous in us to give the females a different kind of education from the males, except in some articles of domestic management; whereby, as he truly observed, one half of our natives were good for nothing but bringing children into the world; and to trust the care of our children to such useless animals, he said, was yet a greater instance of brutality. . . .

## *[Return to Civilisation?]*†

The ship came within half a league of this creek, and sent out her longboat with vessels to take in fresh water (for the place it seems was very well known) but I did not observe it till the boat was almost on shore, and it was too late to seek another hiding-place. The seamen at their landing observed my canoe, and rummaging it all over, easily conjectured that the owner could not be far off. Four of them, well-armed, searched every cranny and lurking-hole, till at last they found me flat on my face behind the stone. They gazed a while in admiration at my strange uncouth dress, my coat made of skins, my wooden-soled shoes, and my furred stockings; from whence, however, they concluded I was not a native of the place, who all go naked. One of the seamen in Portuguese bid me rise, and asked who I was. I understood that language very well, and getting upon my feet, said, I was a poor *Yahoo*, banished from the *Houyhnhnms*, and desired they would please to let me depart. They admired to hear me answer them in their own tongue, and saw by my complexion I must be an European; but were at a loss to know what I meant by *Yahoos* and *Houyhnhnms*, and at the same time fell a laughing at my strange tone in speaking, which resembled the neighing of a horse. I trembled all the while betwixt fear and hatred: I again desired leave to depart, and was gently moving to my canoe; but they laid hold on me, desiring to know what country I was of? whence I came? with many other questions. I told them, I was born in England, from whence I came about five years ago, and then their country and ours were at peace. I therefore hoped they would not treat me as an enemy, since I meant them no harm, but was a poor *Yahoo*, seeking some desolate place where to pass the remainder of his unfortunate life.

When they began to talk, I thought I never heard or saw anything so

[*Return to Civilisation?*] Despite adopting their values, Gulliver is expelled by the houyhnhnms as a threat to society. He is horrified to see 'European Yahoos' approach

unnatural; for it appeared to me as monstrous as if a dog or a cow should speak in England, or a *Yahoo* in *Houyhnhnm-Land*. The honest Portuguese were equally amazed at my strange dress, and the odd manner of delivering my words, which however they understood very well. They spoke to me with great humanity, and said they were sure their captain would carry me gratis to Lisbon, from whence I might return to my own country; that two of the seamen would go back to the ship, inform the captain of what they had seen, and receive his orders; in the meantime, unless I would give my solemn oath not to fly, they would secure me by force. I thought it best to comply with their proposal. They were very curious to know my story, but I gave them very little satisfaction; and they all conjectured, that my misfortunes had impaired my reason. In two hours the boat, which went loaden with vessels of water, returned with the captain's commands to fetch me on board. I fell on my knees to preserve my liberty; but all was in vain, and the men, having tied me with cords, heaved me into the boat, from whence I was taken into the ship and from thence into the captain's cabin.

His name was Pedro de Mendez, he was a very courteous and generous person; he entreated me to give some account of myself, and desired to know what I would eat or drink; said I should be used as well as himself, and spoke so many obliging things, that I wondered to find such civilities from a *Yahoo*. However, I remained silent and sullen; I was ready to faint at the very smell of him and his men. At last I desired something to eat out of my own canoe; but he ordered me a chicken and some excellent wine, and then directed that I should be put to bed in a very clean cabin. I would not undress myself, but lay on the bedclothes, and in half an hour stole out, when I thought the crew was at dinner, and getting to the side of the ship was going to leap into the sea, and swim for my life, rather than continue among *Yahoos*. But one of the seamen prevented me, and having informed the captain, I was chained to my cabin.

After dinner Don Pedro came to me, and desired to know my reason for so desperate an attempt; assured me he only meant to do me all the service he was able, and spoke so very movingly, that at last I descended to treat him like an animal which had some little portion of reason. I gave him a very short relation of my voyage, of the conspiracy against me by my own men, of the country where they set me on shore, and of my three years residence there. All which he looked upon as if it were a dream or a vision; whereat I took great offence; for I had quite forgot the faculty of lying, so peculiar to *Yahoos* in all countries where they preside, and consequently the disposition of suspecting truth in others of their own species. I asked him, whether it were the custom in his country to *say the thing that was not?* I assured him I had almost forgot what he meant by falsehood, and if I had lived a thousand years in *Houyhnhnm-Land*, I should never have heard a lie from the meanest servant; that I was altogether indifferent whether he believed me or no; but however, in return for his favours, I would give so much allowance to the corruption of his nature, as to answer any objection he would please to make, and then he might easily discover the truth.

The captain, a wise man, after many endeavours to catch me tripping in some part of my story, at last began to have a better opinion of my veracity, and the rather because he confessed, he met with a Dutch skipper, who pretended to have landed with five others of his crew upon a certain island or continent south of New Holland,† where they went for fresh water, and observed a horse driving before him several animals exactly resembling those I described under the name of *Yahoos*, with some other particulars, which the captain said he had forgot; because he then concluded them all to be lies. But he added, that since I professed so inviolable an attachment to truth, I must give him my word of honour to bear him company in this voyage without attempting anything against my life, or else he would continue me a prisoner till we arrived at Lisbon. I gave him the promise he required; but at the same time protested that I would suffer the greatest hardships rather than return to live among *Yahoos*.

Our voyage passed without any considerable accident. In gratitude to the captain I sometimes sat with him at his earnest request, and strove to conceal my antipathy to human kind, although it often broke out, which he suffered to pass without observation. But the greatest part of the day, I confined myself to my cabin, to avoid seeing any of the crew. The captain had often entreated me to strip myself of my savage dress, and offered to lend me the best suit of clothes he had. This I would not be prevailed on to accept, abhorring to cover myself with anything that had been on the back of a *Yahoo*. I only desired he would lend me two clean shirts, which having been washed since he wore them, I believed would not so much defile me. These I changed every second day, and washed them myself.

We arrived at Lisbon, Nov. 5. 1715. At our landing the captain forced me to cover myself with his cloak, to prevent the rabble from crowding about me. I was conveyed to his own house, and at my earnest request, he led me up to the highest room backwards.† I conjured him to conceal from all persons what I had told him of the *Houyhnhnms*, because the least hint of such a story would not only draw numbers of people to see me, but probably put me in danger of being imprisoned, or burnt by the Inquisition. The captain persuaded me to accept a suit of clothes newly made, but I would not suffer the tailor to take my

*New Holland* Australia *backwards* at the back

measure; however Don Pedro being almost of my size, they fitted me well enough. He accoutred me with other necessaries all new, which I aired for twenty-four hours before I would use them.

The captain had no wife, nor above three servants, none of which were suffered to attend at meals, and his whole deportment was so obliging, added to very good human understanding, that I really began to tolerate his company. He gained so far upon me, that I ventured to look out of the back window. By degrees I was brought into another room, from whence I peeped into the street, but drew my head back in a fright. In a week's time he seduced me down to the door. I found my terror gradually lessened, but my hatred and contempt seemed to increase. I was at last bold enough to walk the street in his company, but kept my nose well stopped with rue, or sometimes with tobacco.

In ten days Don Pedro, to whom I had given some account of my domestic affairs, put it upon me as a matter of honour and conscience, that I ought to return to my native country, and live at home with my wife and children. He told me there was an English ship in the port just ready to sail, and he would furnish me with all things necessary. It would be tedious to repeat his arguments and my contradictions. He said it was altogether impossible to find such a solitary island as I had desired to live in; but I might command in my own house, and pass my time in a manner as recluse as I pleased.

I complied at last, finding I could not do better. I left Lisbon the 24th day of November in an English merchant man, but who was the master I never enquired. Don Pedro accompanied me to the ship, and lent me twenty pounds. He took kind leave of me, and embraced me at parting, which I bore as well as I could. During the last voyage I had no commerce with the master or any of his men, but pretending I was sick kept close in my cabin. On the fifth of December 1715, we cast anchor in the Downs[†] about nine in the morning, and at three in the afternoon I got safe to my house at Rotherhithe.[†]

My wife and family received me with great surprise and joy, because they concluded me certainly dead; but I must freely confess the sight of them filled me only with hatred, disgust and contempt, and the more by reflecting on the near alliance I had to them. For, although since my unfortunate exile from the *Houyhnhnm* country I had compelled myself to tolerate the sight of *Yahoos*, and to converse with Don Pedro de Mendez, yet my memory and imaginations were perpetually filled with the virtues and ideas of those exalted *Houyhnhnms*. And when I began to consider, that by copulating with one of the *Yahoo*-species I had become a parent of more, it struck me with the utmost shame, confusion and horror.

*Downs* in English Channel

*Rotherhithe* East London dock area

As soon as I entered the house, my wife took me in her arms, and kissed me, at which, having not been used to the touch of that odious animal for so many years, I fell in a swoon for almost an hour. At the time I am writing it is five years since my last return to England: during the first year I could not endure my wife or children in my presence, the very smell of them was intolerable, much less could I suffer them to eat in the same room. To this hour they dare not presume to touch my bread, or drink out of the same cup, neither was I ever able to let one of them take me by the hand. The first money I laid out was to buy two young stone-horses† which I keep in a good stable, and next to them the groom is my greatest favourite; for I feel my spirits revived by the smell he contracts in the stable. My horses understand me tolerably well; I converse with them at least four hours every day. They are strangers to bridle or saddle, they live in great amity with me, and friendship to each other.

## *[Gulliver's Doubts]*†

I do in the next place complain of my own great want of judgment, in being prevailed upon by the entreaties and false reasonings of you and some others, very much against mine own opinion, to suffer my travels to be published. Pray bring to your mind how often I desired you to consider, when you insisted on the motive of public good, that the *Yahoos* were a species of animals utterly incapable of amendment by precepts or examples. And so it hath proved; for instead of seeing a full stop put to all abuses and corruptions, at least in this little island, as I had reason to expect: behold, after above six months warning, I cannot learn that my book hath produced one single effect according to mine intentions. I desired you would let me know by a letter, when party and faction were extinguished; judges learned and upright; pleaders† honest and modest, with some tincture of common sense; and Smithfield† blazing with pyramids of law books; the young nobility's education entirely changed; the physicians banished; the female *Yahoos* abounding in virtue, honour, truth and good sense: courts and levees† of great ministers thoroughly weeded and swept; wit, merit and learning rewarded; all disgracers of the press in prose and verse, condemned to eat nothing but their own cotton† and quench their thirst with their own ink. These, and a thousand other reformations, I firmly counted

*stone-horses* stallions
*[Gulliver's Doubts]* The 1735 edition has a 'Letter from Captain Gulliver to his Cousin', about the publication of the original edition
*pleaders* barristers
*Smithfield* space where heretics had been burned
*levees* morning receptions
*cotton* paper

upon by your encouragement; as indeed they were plainly deducible from the precepts delivered in my book. And, it must be owned, that seven months were a sufficient time to correct every vice and folly to which *Yahoos* are subject; if their natures had been capable of the least disposition to virtue or wisdom: yet so far have you been from answering mine expectation in any of your letters, that on the contrary, you are loading our carrier every week with libels, and keys, and reflections, and memoirs, and second parts; wherein I see myself accused of reflecting upon great statesfolk; of degrading human nature (for so they have still the confidence to style it) and of abusing the female sex. I find likewise, that the writers of those bundles are not agreed among themselves; for some of them will not allow me to be author of mine own travels; and others make me author of books to which I am wholly a stranger. . . .

1726, 1735

# A MODEST PROPOSAL

## FOR PREVENTING THE CHILDREN OF POOR PEOPLE FROM BEING A BURDEN TO THEIR PARENTS OR THE COUNTRY, AND FOR MAKING THEM BENEFICIAL TO THE PUBLIC.†

It is a melancholy object to those who walk through this great town,† or travel in the country, when they see the streets, the roads, and cabin-doors crowded with beggars of the female sex, followed by three, four, or six children, all in rags, and importuning every passenger for an alms. These mothers, instead of being able to work for their honest livelihood, are forced to employ all their time in strolling† to beg sustenance for their helpless infants who, as they grow up, either turn thieves for want of work, or leave their dear Native Country to fight for the Pretender† in Spain, or sell themselves to the Barbadoes.†

*A Modest Proposal* Ironically using the voice of a naïve, humane, economic calculator, who accepts people as 'the wealth of the nation', Swift explores the moral and practical problems underlying the plight of Ireland; the argument is not merely anti-colonialist: the degeneracy of the natives, the callousness of the higher orders, and the complacency of the reader all come under fire

*great town* Dublin; 'this kingdom' is Ireland alone

*strolling* wandering without fixed homes

*Pretender* James Stuart, son of James II, was supported by France and Spain in his claim to the British throne

*Barbadoes* West Indian colonies

I think it is agreed by all parties that this prodigious number of children, in the arms, or on the backs, or at the heels of their mothers, and frequently of their fathers, is in the present deplorable state of the kingdom, a very great additional grievance; and therefore whoever could find out a fair, cheap and easy method of making these children sound useful members of the commonwealth would deserve so well of the public, as to have his statue set up for a preserver of the nation.

But my intention is very far from being confined to provide only for the children of professed beggars, it is of a much greater extent, and shall take in the whole number of infants at a certain age, who are born of parents in effect as little able to support them as those who demand our charity in the streets.

As to my own part, having turned my thoughts for many years upon this important subject, and maturely weighed the several schemes of other projectors,† I have always found them grossly mistaken in their computation. It is true a child just dropped from its dam may be supported by her milk for a solar year with little other nourishment, at most not above the value of two shillings, which the mother may certainly get, or the value in scraps, by her lawful occupation of begging. And it is exactly at one year old that I propose to provide for them in such a manner as, instead of being a charge upon their parents, or the parish, or wanting food and raiment for the rest of their lives, they shall, on the contrary, contribute to the feeding and partly to the clothing of many thousands.

There is likewise another great advantage in my scheme, that it will prevent those voluntary abortions, and that horrid practice of women murdering their bastard children, alas! too frequent among us, sacrificing the poor innocent babes, I doubt, more to avoid the expense than the shame, which would move tears and pity in the most savage and inhuman breast.

The number of souls in this kingdom being usually reckoned one million and a half, of these I calculate there may be about two hundred thousand couple whose wives are breeders, from which number I subtract thirty thousand couples who are able to maintain their own children, although I apprehend there cannot be so many under the present distresses of the kingdom, but this being granted, there will remain an hundred and seventy thousand breeders. I again subtract fifty thousand for those women who miscarry, or whose children die by accident, or disease within the year. There only remain an hundred and twenty thousand children of poor parents annually born. The question therefore is, how this number shall be reared and provided for, which,

---

*projectors* devisers of schemes, often financial or scientific

as I have already said, under the present situation of affairs is utterly impossible by all the methods hitherto proposed: for we can neither employ them in handicraft, or agriculture; we neither build houses (I mean in the country) nor cultivate land; they can very seldom pick up a livelihood by stealing till they arrive at six years old, except where they are of towardly parts, although I confess they learn the rudiments much earlier, during which time they can however be properly looked upon only as probationers, as I have been informed by a principal gentleman in the County of Cavan, who protested to me that he never knew above one or two instances under the age of six, even in a part of the kingdom so renowned for the quickest proficiency in that art.

I am assured by our merchants that a boy or a girl, before twelve years old, is no saleable commodity, and even when they come to this age, they will not yield above three pounds, or three pounds and half-a-crown at most on the Exchange, which cannot turn to account either to the parents or the kingdom, the charge of nutriment and rags having been at least four times that value.

I shall now therefore humbly propose my own thoughts, which I hope will not be liable to the least objection.

I have been assured by a very knowing American of my acquaintance in London, that a young healthy child, well nursed, is at a year old a most delicious, nourishing, and wholesome food, whether stewed, roasted, baked, or boiled, and I make no doubt that it will equally serve in a fricassee, or a ragout.†

I do therefore humbly offer it to public consideration, that of the hundred and twenty thousand children, already computed, twenty thousand may be reserved for breed, whereof only one fourth part to be males, which is more than we allow to sheep, black-cattle, or swine; and my reason is that these children are seldom the fruits of marriage, a circumstance not much regarded by our savages; therefore one male will be sufficient to serve four females. That the remaining hundred thousand may at a year old be offered in sale to the persons of quality and fortune, through the kingdom, always advising the mother to let them suck plentifully of the last month, so as to render them plump and fat for a good table. A child will make two dishes at an entertainment for friends, and when the family dines alone the fore or hind quarter will make a reasonable dish, and seasoned with a little pepper or salt will be very good boiled on the fourth day, especially in winter.

I have reckoned upon a medium,† that a child just born will weigh 12 pounds, and in a solar year if tolerably nursed increaseth to 28 pounds.

*ragout* stew

*upon a medium* on average

I grant this food will be somewhat dear, and therefore very proper for landlords, who, as they have already devoured most of the parents, seem to have the best title to the children.

Infants' flesh will be in season throughout the year, but more plentiful in March, and a little before and after, for we are told by a grave author,† an eminent French physician, that fish being a prolific diet, there are more children born in Roman Catholic countries about nine months after Lent, than at any other season; therefore reckoning a year after Lent,† the markets will be more glutted than usual, because the number of Popish infants is at least three to one in this kingdom, and therefore it will have one other collateral advantage by lessening the number of Papists among us.

I have already computed the charge of nursing a beggar's child (in which list I reckon all cottagers, labourers, and four fifths of the farmers) to be about two shillings per annum, rags included, and I believe no gentleman would repine to give ten shillings for the carcass of a good fat child, which, as I have said, will make four dishes of excellent nutritive meat, when he hath only some particular friend, or his own family to dine with him. Thus the Squire will learn to be a good landlord, and grow popular among his tenants, the mother will have eight shillings net profit, and be fit for work till she produces another child.

Those who are more thrifty (as I must confess the times require) may flay the carcass; the skin of which, artificially† dressed, will make admirable gloves for ladies, and summer boots for fine gentlemen.

As to our City of Dublin, shambles† may be appointed for this purpose in the most convenient parts of it, and butchers we may be assured will not be wanting, although I rather recommend buying the children alive, and dressing them hot from the knife, as we do roasting pigs.

A very worthy person, a true lover of his country, and whose virtues I highly esteem, was lately pleased in discoursing on this matter, to offer a refinement upon my scheme. He said that many gentlemen of this kingdom having of late destroyed their deer, he conceived that the want of venison might be well supplied by the bodies of young lads and maidens not exceeding fourteen years of age, nor under twelve, so great a number of both sexes in every country being now ready to starve for want of work and service; and these to be disposed of by their parents if alive, or otherwise by their nearest relations. But with due deference to so excellent a friend and so deserving a patriot, I

*grave author* François Rabelais (*c.* 1494–1553), a comic influence on Swift
*Lent* the penitential season before Easter
*artificially* done skilfully
*shambles* slaughter-houses

cannot be altogether in his sentiments; for as to the males, my American acquaintance assured me from frequent experience that their flesh was generally tough and lean, like that of our schoolboys, by continual exercise, and their taste disagreeable, and to fatten them would not answer the charge. Then as to the females, it would, I think with humble submission, be a loss to the public, because they soon would become breeders themselves. And besides, it is not improbable that some scrupulous people might be apt to censure such a practice (although indeed very unjustly) as a little bordering upon cruelty, which, I confess, hath always been with me the strongest objection against any project, however so well intended.

But in order to justify my friend, he confessed that this expedient was put into his head by the famous Psalmanazar,[†] a native of the island Formosa, who came from thence to London above twenty years ago, and in conversation told my friend that in his country when any young person happened to be put to death, the executioner sold the carcass to persons of quality, as a prime dainty, and that in his time, the body of a plump girl of fifteen, who was crucified for an attempt to poison the emperor, was sold to his Imperial Majesty's Prime Minister of State, and other great mandarins of the Court, in joints from the gibbet, at four hundred crowns. Neither indeed can I deny, that if the same use were made of several plump young girls in this town, who, without one single groat to their fortunes, cannot stir abroad without a chair, and appear at the playhouse and assemblies in foreign fineries which they never will pay for, the kingdom would not be the worse.

Some persons of a desponding spirit are in great concern about that vast number of poor people who are aged, diseased, or maimed, and I have been desired to employ my thoughts what course may be taken to ease the nation of so grievous an encumbrance. But I am not in the least pain upon that matter because it is very well known that they are every day dying, and rotting, by cold and famine, and filth, and vermin, as fast as can be reasonably expected. And as to the younger labourers, they are now in almost as hopeful a condition. They cannot get work, and consequently pine away for want of nourishment, to a degree that if at any time they are accidentally hired to common labour, they have not strength to perform it; and thus the country and themselves are happily delivered from the evils to come.

I have too long digressed, and therefore shall return to my subject. I think the advantages by the proposal which I have made are obvious and many, as well as of the highest importance.

*Psalmanazar* George Psalmanazar, a Frenchman, published a fraudulent account of Formosa (1704)

For first, as I have already observed, it would greatly lessen the number of Papists, with whom we are yearly over-run, being the principal breeders of the nation as well as our most dangerous enemies, and who stay at home on purpose with a design to deliver the kingdom to the Pretender, hoping to take their advantage by the absence of so many good Protestants,[†] who have chosen rather to leave their country than stay at home and pay tithes against their conscience to an Episcopal curate.

Secondly, the poorer tenants will have something valuable of their own, which by law may be made liable to distress,[†] and help to pay their landlord's rent, their corn and cattle being already seized and money a thing unknown.

Thirdly, whereas the maintenance of an hundred thousand children, from two years old and upwards, cannot be computed at less than ten shillings a piece per annum, the nation's stock will be thereby increased fifty thousand pounds per annum, besides the profit of a new dish introduced to the tables of all gentlemen of fortune in the kingdom who have any refinement in taste; and the money will circulate among ourselves, the goods being entirely of our own growth and manufacture.

Fourthly, the constant breeders, besides the gain of eight shillings sterling per annum by the sale of their children, will be rid of the charge of maintaining them after the first year.

Fifthly, this food would likewise bring great custom to taverns, where the vintners will certainly be so prudent as to procure the best receipts for dressing it to perfection, and consequently have their houses frequented by all the fine gentlemen, who justly value themselves upon their knowledge in good eating; and a skilful cook, who understands how to oblige his guests, will contrive to make it as expensive as they please.

Sixthly, this would be a great inducement to marriage, which all wise nations have either encouraged by rewards, or enforced by laws and penalties. It would increase the care and tenderness of mothers toward their children, when they were sure of a settlement for life to the poor babes, provided in some sort by the public to their annual profit instead of expense. We should see an honest emulation among the married women, which of them could bring the fattest child to the market. Men would become as fond of their wives, during the time of their pregnancy, as they are now of their mares in foal, their cows in calf, or sows when they are ready to farrow; nor offer to beat or kick them (as it is too frequent a practice) for fear of a miscarriage.

*Protestants* here, dissenters, who resented paying taxes to the established Episcopal church

*distress* legal seizure

Many other advantages might be enumerated. For instance, the addition of some thousand carcasses in our exportation of barrelled beef; the propagation of swine's flesh and improvement in the art of making good bacon, so much wanted among us by the great destruction of pigs, too frequent at our tables, which are no way comparable in taste, or magnificence to a well-grown, fat yearling child, which roasted whole will make a considerable figure at a Lord Mayor's feast, or any other public entertainment. But this and many others I omit, being studious of brevity.

Supposing that one thousand families in this city would be constant customers for infants' flesh, besides others who might have it at merry-meetings, particularly weddings and christenings, I compute that Dublin would take off annually about twenty thousand carcasses, and the rest of the kingdom (where probably they will be sold somewhat cheaper) the remaining eighty thousand.

I can think of no one objection that will possibly be raised against this proposal, unless it should be urged that the number of people will be thereby much lessened in the kingdom. This I freely own, and it was indeed one principal design in offering it to the world. I desire the reader will observe, that I calculate my remedy for this one individual Kingdom of Ireland, and for no other that ever was, is, or, I think, ever can be upon earth. Therefore let no man talk to me of other expedients;† of taxing our absentees† at five shillings a pound; of using neither clothes, nor household furniture, except what is of our own growth and manufacture; of utterly rejecting the materials and instruments that promote foreign luxury; of curing the expensiveness of pride, vanity, idleness, and gaming in our women; of introducing a vein of parsimony, prudence and temperance; of learning to love our Country, wherein we differ even from Laplanders, and the inhabitants of Topinamboo;† of quitting our animosities and factions, nor act any longer like the Jews, who were murdering one another at the very moment their city† was taken; of being a little cautious not to sell our country and consciences for nothing; of teaching landlords to have at least one degree of mercy toward their tenants; lastly of putting a spirit of honesty, industry and skill into our shopkeepers, who, if a resolution could now be taken to buy only our native goods, would immediately unite to cheat and exact upon us in the price, the measure, and the goodness, nor could ever yet be brought to make one fair proposal of just dealing, though often and earnestly invited to it.

Therefore I repeat, let no man talk to me of these and the like

*other expedients* all seriously proposed elsewhere by Swift

*absentees* landlords and officials who remained in England

*Topinamboo* savage region of Brazil

*city* the Emperor Titus captured Jerusalem in AD 70, during civil strife

expedients, till he hath at least some glimpse of hope that there will ever be some hearty and sincere attempt to put them in practice.

But as to myself, having been wearied out for many years with offering vain, idle, visionary thoughts, and at length utterly despairing of success, I fortunately fell upon this proposal, which as it is wholly new, so it hath something solid and real, of no expense and little trouble, full in our own power, and whereby we can incur no danger in disobliging England. For this kind of commodity will not bear exportation, the flesh being of too tender a consistence to admit a long continuance in salt, although perhaps I could name a country which would be glad to eat up our whole nation without it.

After all, I am not so violently bent upon my own opinion as to reject any offer proposed by wise men, which shall be found equally innocent, cheap, easy and effectual. But before something of that kind shall be advanced in contradiction to my scheme, and offering a better, I desire the author, or authors, will be pleased maturely to consider two points. First, as things now stand, how they will be able to find food and raiment for an hundred thousand useless mouths and backs. And secondly, there being a round million of creatures in human figure throughout this kingdom, whose whole subsistence put into a common stock would leave them in debt two millions of pounds sterling, adding those who are beggars by profession, to the bulk of farmers, cottagers and labourers with their wives and children, who are beggars in effect; I desire those politicians who dislike my overture and may perhaps be so bold to attempt an answer, that they will first ask the parents of these mortals, whether they would not at this day think it a great happiness to have been sold for food at a year old, in the manner I prescribe; and thereby have avoided such a perpetual scene of misfortunes as they have since gone through, by the oppression of landlords, the impossibility of paying rent without money or trade, the want of common sustenance, with neither house nor clothes to cover them from the inclemencies of the weather, and the most inevitable prospect of entailing the like, or greater miseries upon their breed for ever.

I profess in the sincerity of my heart that I have not the least personal interest in endeavouring to promote this necessary work, having no other motive than the public good of my country, by advancing our trade, providing for infants, relieving the poor, and giving some pleasure to the rich. I have no children, by which I can propose to get a single penny; the youngest being nine years old, and my wife past child-bearing.

1729 1729

# A BEAUTIFUL YOUNG NYMPH GOING TO BED†

## *Written for the Honour of the* Fair Sex

*Pars minima est ipsa Puella sui.* Ovid
[The actual girl is the smallest part of herself]

Corinna, pride of Drury Lane,†
For whom no shepherd sighs in vain;
Never did Covent Garden boast
So bright a battered, strolling toast!
No drunken rake to pick her up,
No cellar where on tick to sup;
Returning at the midnight hour,
Four stories climbing to her bower;
Then, seated on a three-legged chair,
Takes off her artificial hair;
Now picking out a crystal eye,
She wipes it clean, and lays it by.
Her eyebrows from a mouse's hide,
Stuck on with art on either side,
Pulls off with care, and first displays 'em,
Then in a play-book smoothly lays 'em,
Now dexterously her plumpers draws,
That serve to fill her hollow jaws,
Untwists a wire, and from her gums
A set of teeth completely comes;
Pulls out the rags contrived to prop
Her flabby dugs, and down they drop.
Proceeding on, the lovely goddess
Unlaces next her steel-ribbed bodice,
Which, by the operator's skill,
Press down the lumps, the hollows fill.
Up goes her hand, and off she slips
The bolsters that supply her hips;
With gentlest touch, she next explores

*A Beautiful Young Nymph Going to Bed* The Roman poet Ovid had celebrated in *Amores* I.5 the modesty and naked perfection of his mistress Corinna. Swift deflates romantic images by showing the 'reality' of the prostitute

*Drury Lane* with Covent Garden, an area of theatres and brothels

Her chancres,† issues, running sores,
Effects of many a sad disaster;
And then to each applies a plaster:
But must, before she goes to bed,
Rub off the daubs of white and red,
And smooth the furrows in her front
With greasy paper stuck upon't.
She takes a *bolus*† ere she sleeps,
And then between two blankets creeps.
With pains of love tormented lies;
Or, if she chance to close her eyes,
Of Bridewell and the Compter† dreams,
And feels the lash, and faintly screams;
Or, by a faithless bully drawn,
At some hedge-tavern lies in pawn;
Or to Jamaica seems transported,
Alone, and by no planter courted;
Or, near Fleet-ditch's† oozy brinks,
Surrounded with a hundred stinks;
Belated, seems on watch to lie,
And snap some cully* passing by; fool
Or, struck with fear, her fancy runs
On watchmen, constables and duns,
From whom she meets with frequent rubs;
But never from religious clubs;†
Whose favour she is sure to find
Because she pays 'em all in kind.
Corinna wakes. A dreadful sight!
Behold the ruins of the night!
A wicked rat her plaster stole,
Half eat, and dragged it to his hole.
The crystal eye, alas, was missed;
And puss had on her plumpers p—ssed,
A pigeon picked her issue-peas:†
And Shock* her tresses filled with fleas. dog
The nymph, though in this mangled plight,
Must every morn her limbs unite.
But how shall I describe her arts
To re-collect the scattered parts?
Or show the anguish, toil, and pain,

*chancres* ulcers from venereal disease
*bolus* large pill
*Bridewell . . . Compter* both prisons
*Fleet-ditch* an open sewer
*clubs* moral vigilantes (seen as hypocrites)
*issue-peas* peas keeping open discharging sores

Of gathering up herself again?
The bashful Muse will never bear
In such a scene to interfere.
Corinna, in the morning dizened,[†]
Who sees, will spew; who smells, be poisoned.

1731 1734

# *From* VERSES ON THE DEATH OF DR SWIFT, D.S.P.D.

## Occasioned by reading a Maxim in Rochefoucault[†]

As Rochefoucault his maxims drew
From nature, I believe 'em true:
They argue no corrupted mind
In him; the fault is in mankind.
This maxim more than all the rest
Is thought too base for human breast:
'In all distresses of our friends
We first consult our private ends,
While nature, kindly bent to ease us,
Points out some circumstance to please us.'
If this perhaps your patience move,
Let reason and experience prove. . . .

Vain human kind! fantastic race!
Thy various follies, who can trace?
Self-love, ambition, envy, pride,
Their empire in our hearts divide:
Give others riches, power, and station,
'Tis all on me an usurpation.
I have no title to aspire;
Yet when you sink, I seem the higher.
In Pope, I cannot read a line
But with a sigh, I wish it mine:

---

*dizened* gaudily dressed

*Verses on the Death of Dr Swift* Written some fourteen years before Swift's actual death, this poem combines genial knowledge of self and the world with a defence of his public and satiric roles. It shows his mastery of the eight-syllable line. Swift found congenial the cynicism of the French moralist, François de la Rochefoucauld (1613–18). The 'Maxim' is paraphrased in ll.7–10

When he can in one couplet fix
More sense, than I can do in six,
It gives me such a jealous fit,
I cry, 'pox take him and his wit.'
   I grieve to be outdone by Gay
In my own humorous, biting way.
   Arbuthnot is no more my friend,
Who dares to irony pretend;
Which I was born to introduce,
Refined it first, and showed its use.
   St John, as well as Pulteney,† knows
That I had some repute for prose;
And, till they drove me out of date,
Could maul a minister of state.
If they have mortified my pride.
And made me throw my pen aside,
If with such talents Heav'n hath blest 'em,
Have I not reason to detest 'em?
   To all my foes, dear Fortune, send
Thy gifts, but never to my friend:
I tamely can endure the first,
But, this with envy makes me burst.
   Thus much may serve by way of proem;
Proceed we therefore to our poem.
   The time is not remote, when I
Must by the course of nature die:
When I foresee, my special friends
Will try to find their private ends.
And though 'tis hardly understood
Which way my death can do them good,
Yet thus, methinks, I hear 'em speak:
'See, how the Dean begins to break!
Poor gentleman, he droops apace,
You plainly find it in his face:
That old vertigo† in his head
Will never leave him, till he's dead:
Besides, his memory decays,
He recollects not what he says;
He cannot call his friends to mind;
Forgets the place where last he dined:

*St John . . . Pulteney* Viscount Bolingbroke (see l.366 n.), with William Pulteney, wrote in a periodical *The Craftsman* against Sir Robert Walpole, already Swift's victim

*vertigo* (stress on second syllable) probably Ménière's disease, causing dizziness

Plies you with stories o'er and o'er,
He told them fifty times before.
How does he fancy, we can sit
To hear his out-of-fashioned wit?
But he takes up with younger folks,
Who, for his wine, will bear his jokes.
Faith, he must make his stories shorter,
Or change his comrades once a quarter.
In half the time, he talks them round;
There must another set be found.
'For poetry, he's past his prime,
He takes an hour to find a rhyme:
His fire is out, his wit decayed,
His fancy sunk, his muse a jade.
I'd have him throw away his pen;
But there's no talking to some men.'
And then, their tenderness appears
By adding largely to my years:
'He's older than he would be reckoned,
And well remembers Charles the Second.
'He hardly drinks a pint of wine;
And that, I doubt, is no good sign.
His stomach too begins to fail:
Last year we thought him strong and hale,
But now, he's quite another thing;
I wish he may hold out till spring.'
Then hug themselves, and reason thus:
'It is not yet so bad with us.'. . .
Behold the fatal day arrive!
'How is the Dean?' – 'He's just alive.'
Now the departing prayer is read.
He hardly breathes. The Dean is dead.
Before the passing-bell† begun,
The news through half the town has run.
'O, may we all for death prepare!
What has he left? And who's his heir?
I know no more than what the news is,
'Tis all bequeathed to public uses.
To public uses! There's a whim!
What had the public done for him?
Mere envy, avarice, and pride!
He gave it all – but first he died.

*passing-bell* tolled immediately after death

And had the Dean, in all the nation,
No worthy friend, no poor relation?
So ready to do strangers good,
Forgetting his own flesh and blood?'. . .

From Dublin soon to London spread,
'Tis told at Court, the Dean is dead.
And Lady Suffolk[†] in the spleen
Runs laughing up to tell the Queen.
The Queen so gracious, mild, and good,
Cries, 'Is he gone? 'Tis time he should.
He's dead you say? Why, let him rot;
I'm glad the medals were forgot.
I promised him, I own, but when?
I only was the Princess then;
But now as consort of a king,
You know 'tis quite a different thing.'. . .
Here shift the scene, to represent
How those I love, my death lament.
Poor Pope will grieve a month; and Gay
A week, and Arbuthnot a day.
St John himself will scarce forbear
To bite his pen, and drop a tear.
The rest will give a shrug, and cry
'I'm sorry; but we all must die!'. . .
My female friends, whose tender hearts
Have better learned to act their parts,
Receive the news in doleful dumps,[*] gloom
'The Dean is dead, (pray what is trumps?)
Then Lord have mercy on his soul.
(Ladies, I'll venture for the vole.)
Six deans, they say, must bear the pall.[†]
(I wish I knew what king to call.)'
'Madam, your husband will attend
The funeral of so good a friend?'
'No, madam, 'tis a shocking sight,
And he's engaged tomorrow night!
My Lady Club would take it ill,
If he should fail her at quadrille.
He loved the Dean – (I lead a heart)
But dearest friends, they say, must part.

*Lady Suffolk* Mistress of George II, and friend of Swift. Queen Caroline, when Princess of Wales, had promised him some medals

*pall* coffin-cloth; the ladies are playing the card game of quadrille, in which the *vole* is a bold bid

His time was come, he ran his race;
We hope he's in a better place.'
  Why do we grieve that friends should die?
No loss more easy to supply.
One year is past; a different scene;
No further mention of the Dean;
Who now, alas, no more is missed
Than if he never did exist.
Where's now the favourite of Apollo?†
Departed; and his works must follow: . . .
  Suppose me dead; and then suppose
A club assembled at the Rose:†
Where, from discourse of this and that,
I grow the subject of their chat:
And while they toss my name about,
With favour some, and some without –
One quite indifferent in the cause,
My character impartial draws:
  'The Dean, if we believe report,
Was never ill received at Court.
As for his Works in Verse or Prose,
I own myself no judge of those:
Nor can I tell what critics thought 'em;
But this I know, all people bought 'em,
As with a moral view designed
To cure the vices of mankind.
Although ironically grave,
He shamed the fool, and lashed the knave.
To steal a hint was never known,
But what he writ, was all his own.
  'He never thought an honour done him
Because a peer was proud to own* him: acknowledge
Would rather slip aside, and choose
To talk with wits in dirty shoes:
And scorn the fools with Stars and Garters,†
So often seen caressing Chartres.†
He never courted men in station,
Nor persons had in admiration;
Of no man's greatness was afraid,
Because he sought for no man's aid.

*Apollo* god of poetry
*the Rose* a tavern (clubs often met in such places)
*Garters* indicates the highest British order of knighthood
*Chartres* usurer and rapist

Though trusted long in great affairs,
He gave himself no haughty airs:
Without regarding private ends,
Spent all his credit for his friends:
And only chose the wise and good,
No flatterers, no allies in blood;
But succoured virtue in distress,
And seldom failed of good success;
As numbers in their hearts must own,
Who, but for him, had been unknown.
'He kept with princes due decorum,
Yet never stood in awe before 'em:
He followed David's lesson† just,
In princes never put his trust.
And, would you make him truly sour,
Provoke him with a slave in power:
The Irish Senate if you named,
With what impatience he declaimed!
Fair LIBERTY was all his cry;
For her he stood prepared to die;
For her he boldly stood alone;
For her he oft exposed his own.
Two kingdoms,† just as faction led,
Had set a price upon his head;
But not a traitor could be found,
To sell him for six hundred pound.
'Had he but spared his tongue and pen,
He might have rose like other men:
But, power was never in his thought,
And wealth he valued not a groat.
Ingratitude he often found,
And pitied those who meant the wound:
But kept the tenor of his mind,
To merit well of human kind;
Nor made a sacrifice of those
Who still were true, to please his foes.
He laboured many a fruitless hour
To reconcile his friends† in power;

*David's lesson* in Psalm 146.3
*two kingdoms* in 1714, the government in London offered £300 for information of the author of *The Public Spirit of the Whigs*; in 1724, the Irish government offered £300 after 'the Drapier's' *Letter to the Whole People*
*his friends* the Tory leaders, St John, Viscount Bolingbroke; Harley, Earl of Oxford; Butler, Duke of Ormonde

Saw mischief by a faction brewing,
While they pursued each other's ruin.
But, finding vain was all his care,
He left the court in mere despair.
'And, O! how short are human schemes!
Here ended all our golden dreams.
What St John's skill in state affairs,
What Ormonde's valour, Oxford's cares,
To save their sinking country lent,
Was all destroyed by one event.
Too soon that precious life was ended,
On which alone, our weal depended.
When up a dangerous faction† starts,
With wrath and vengeance in their hearts;
By solemn League and Covenant† bound,
To ruin, slaughter, and confound;
To turn religion to a fable,
And make the Government a Babel:* confusion
Pervert the law, disgrace the gown,
Corrupt the senate, rob the crown;
To sacrifice old England's glory,
And make her infamous in story.
When such a tempest shook the land,
How could unguarded virtue stand?
'With horror, grief, despair, the Dean
Beheld the dire destructive scene:
His friends in exile,† or the Tower,†
Himself within the frown of power;
Pursued by base envenomed pens,
Far to the land of slaves† and fens;
A servile race in folly nursed,
Who truckle most, when treated worst. . . .

'The Dean did by his pen defeat
An infamous destructive cheat;†
Taught fools their interest how to know;
And gave them arms to ward the blow.

*faction* The death of Queen Anne in 1714 (l.376) let in the Whig *faction*, allegedly hostile to traditional order
*Covenant* suggests Presbyterianism
*in exile* Bolingbroke; Oxford was imprisoned in the *Tower* of London
*land of slaves* Ireland, where Ormonde had got him the Deanery of St Patrick's
*cheat* the attempt to impose Wood's debased coinage in Ireland, attacked in his *Drapier's Letters*

Envy hath owned it was his doing,
To save that helpless land from ruin;
While they who at the steerage stood
And reaped the profit, sought his blood. . . .

But Heaven his innocence defends,
The grateful people stand his friends:
Not strains of law, nor judge's frown,
Nor topics brought to please the crown,
Nor witness hired, nor jury picked,
Prevail to bring him in convict.
'In exile with a steady heart,
He spent his life's declining part;
Where folly, pride, and faction sway,
Remote from St John, Pope, and Gay. . . .

'Perhaps I may allow, the Dean
Had too much satire in his vein,
And seemed determined not to starve it,
Because no age could more deserve it.
Yet, malice never was his aim;
He lashed the vice, but spared the name.†
No individual could resent
Where thousands equally were meant.
His satire points at no defect,
But what all mortals may correct;
For he abhorred that senseless tribe
Who call it humour when they jibe:
He spared a hump, or crooked nose,
Whose owners set not up for beaux,
True genuine dullness moved his pity,
Unless it offered to be witty.
Those who their ignorance confessed
He ne'er offended with a jest;
But laughed to hear an idiot quote
A verse from Horace, learned by rote.
'He knew an hundred pleasant stories,
With all the turns of Whigs and Tories:
Was cheerful to his dying day,
And* friends would let him have his way.
'He gave the little wealth he had,

If

---

*spared the name* despite occasional personal hits, his satire is more general than Dryden's or Pope's

To build a house[†] for fools and mad:
To show, by one satiric touch,
No nation wanted it so much:
That kingdom he hath left his debtor,
I wish it soon may have a better.'

1731 1739

*a house* St Patrick's Hospital for the mentally ill opened in 1757

# William Congreve

## 1670–1729

Born in Yorkshire, Congreve went to school in Kilkenny and to Trinity College, Dublin, beside Swift. After a brief period studying law in London, he turned to writing: a novel *Incognita* appeared in 1691. His fame was achieved with four comedies: *The Old Bachelor* (1693); *The Double Dealer* (1694); *Love for Love* (1695); *The Way of the World* (1700). To his mastery of the Restoration comedy of manners, with its wit and sexual intrigue, he added a delicacy of investigating the underlying emotions; the plays are regularly revived. Johnson praised the poetry of his tragedy *The Mourning Bride* (1697). In the second half of his life, he wrote little, holding official posts and moving in fashionable and literary circles.

In the complex plot of *The Way of the World*, Mirabell, a former rake, loves Millamant, but has pretended to love her aunt, Lady Wishfort, who controls half her fortune. To prevent Lady Wishfort's revenge, he hopes to trap her in a false marriage to his servant, impersonating Mirabell's uncle, Sir Rowland. The aunt's daughter, Mrs Fainall, is Mirabell's former mistress; Sir Wilfull Witwoud, Lady Wishfort's rustic nephew; Foible, her servant. (Fainall and Mrs Marwood, hostile to the lovers, do not appear in the extract.) The scene contrasts motivation, self-awareness, and sophistication of behaviour, wittily dramatising the serious issue of survival in a highly-mannered society (where the names suggest character or situation). The plot ends happily for the lovers.

## *From* THE WAY OF THE WORLD

### *From* Act IV, Scene i *[Marriage Conditions]*

*Lady Wishfort's house*

*Enter* LADY WISHFORT *and* FOIBLE

LADY WISHFORT

Is Sir Rowland coming, sayest thou, Foible? And are things in order?

FOIBLE

Yes madam. I have put wax lights in the sconces, and placed the footmen in a row in the hall in their best liveries, with the coachman and postilion to fill up the equipage.†

LADY WISHFORT

Have you pulvilled† the coachman and postilion, that they may not stink of the stable when Sir Rowland comes by?

FOIBLE

Yes madam.

LADY WISHFORT

And are the dancers and the music ready, that he may be entertained in all points with correspondence to his passion?

FOIBLE

All is ready, madam.

LADY WISHFORT

And – well – and how do I look, Foible?

FOIBLE

Most killing well, madam.

LADY WISHFORT

Well, and how shall I receive him? In what figure shall I give his heart the first impression? There is a great deal in the first impression. Shall I sit? No, I won't sit, I'll walk. Ay, I'll walk from the door upon his entrance, and then turn full upon him. No, that will be too sudden. I'll lie, ay, I'll lie down. I'll receive him in my little dressing-room, there's a couch – yes, yes, I'll give the first impression on a couch. I won't lie neither, but loll and lean upon one elbow, with one foot a little dangling off, jogging in a thoughtful way. Yes; and then as soon as he appears, start, ay, start and be surprised, and rise to meet him in a pretty disorder. Yes. Oh, nothing is more alluring than a levee† from a couch in some confusion; it shows the foot to advantage and furnishes with blushes and recomposing airs beyond comparison. Hark! There's a coach.

FOIBLE

'Tis he, madam.

LADY WISHFORT

Oh dear, has my nephew made his addresses to Millamant? I ordered him.

FOIBLE

Sir Wilfull is set in to drinking, madam, in the parlour.

LADY WISHFORT

Ods my life I'll send him to her. Call her down, Foible, bring her hither. I'll send him as I go. When they are together, then come to me Foible, that I may not be too long alone with Sir Rowland. *Exit*

*equipage* suite of servants
*pulvilled* perfumed with powder
*levee* rising, often royal

*Enter* MRS[†] MILLAMANT *and* MRS FAINALL

FOIBLE

Madam, I stayed here to tell your ladyship that Mr Mirabell has waited this half hour for an opportunity to talk with you, though my lady's orders were to leave you and Sir Wilfull together. Shall I tell Mr Mirabell that you are at leisure?

MILLAMANT

No. What would the dear man have? I am thoughtful and would amuse myself; bid him come another time.

'There never yet was woman made
Nor shall, but to be cursed.' (*repeating and walking about*)

That's hard.

MRS FAINALL

You are very fond of Sir John Suckling[†] today, Millamant, and the poets.

MILLAMANT

He? Ay, and filthy verses; so I am.

FOIBLE

Sir Wilfull is coming madam; shall I send Mr Mirabell away?

MILLAMANT

Ay, if you please Foible, send him away – or send him hither – just as you will dear Foible. I think I'll see him – shall I? Ay, let the wretch come. [*Exit* FOIBLE]

'Thyrsis a youth of the inspired train' – (*repeating*)

Dear Fainall, entertain Sir Wilfull; thou hast philosophy to undergo a fool, thou art married and hast patience. I would confer with my own thoughts.

MRS FAINALL

I am obliged to you, that you would make me your proxy in this affair, but I have business of my own.

*Enter* SIR WILFULL

Oh Sir Wilfull, you are come at the critical instant. There's your mistress up to the ears in love and contemplation; pursue your point, now or never.

SIR WILFULL

Yes, my aunt would have it so. I would gladly have been encouraged with a bottle or two, because I'm somewhat wary at first, before I am acquainted. (*this while* MILLAMANT *walks about repeating to herself*) But I hope after a time I shall break my mind – that is, upon further acquaintance – so, for the present, cousin, I'll take my leave. If so be

*Mrs* used of unmarried women
*Suckling* 1609–41: cavalier poet, whom, with Waller (1606–87), Millamant keeps quoting

you'll be so kind to make my excuse, I'll return to my company.

MRS FAINALL

Oh fie Sir Wilfull! What, you must not be daunted.

SIR WILFULL

Daunted? No, that's not it, it is not so much for that – for if so be that I set on't, I'll do't. But only for the present, 'tis sufficient till further acquaintance, that's all. Your servant.

MRS FAINALL

Nay, I'll swear you shall never lose so favourable an opportunity if I can help it. I'll leave you together and lock the door. *Exit*

SIR WILFULL

Nay nay cousin – I have forgot my gloves – what d'ye do? 'Sheart! 'A† has locked the door indeed, I think! Nay, cousin Fainall, open the door! Pshaw, what a vixen trick is this? Nay, now 'a has seen me too! Cousin, I made bold to pass through as it were – I think this door's enchanted!

MILLAMANT (*repeating*)

'I prithee spare me, gentle boy,
Press me no more for that slight toy.'

SIR WILFULL

Anan? Cousin your servant.

MILLAMANT

'That foolish trifle of a heart – '
Sir Wilfull!

SIR WILFULL

Yes – your servant. No offence I hope, cousin.

MILLAMANT (*repeating*)

'I swear it will not do its part
Though thou dost thine, employest thy power and art.'
Natural, easy Suckling!

SIR WILFULL

Anan? Suckling? No such suckling† neither, cousin, nor stripling; I thank heaven I'm no minor.

MILLAMANT

Ah rustic! Ruder than Gothic!†

SIR WILFULL

Well, well, I shall understand your lingo one of these days, cousin; in the meanwhile I must answer in plain English.

MILLAMANT

Have you any business with me, Sir Wilfull?

---

*'A* she
*suckling* young child

*Gothic* savage

SIR WILFULL

Not at present, cousin. Yes, I made bold to see, to come and know if that how you were disposed to fetch a walk this evening; if so be that I might not be troublesome, I would have sought a walk with you.

MILLAMANT

A walk? What then?

SIR WILFULL

Nay nothing – only for the walk's sake, that's all.

MILLAMANT

I nauseate walking, 'tis a country diversion. I loathe the country and everything that relates to it.

SIR WILFULL

Indeed? Hah! Look ye, look ye, you do? Nay, 'tis like you may. Here are choice of pastimes here in town, as plays and the like – that must be confessed indeed –

MILLAMANT

Ah, *l'étourdie* [the giddy thing]! I hate the town too.

SIR WILFULL

Dear heart, that's much – hah! – that you should hate 'em both! Hah! 'Tis like you may; there are some can't relish the town, and others can't away with the country – 'tis like you may be one of those, cousin.

MILLAMANT

Ha, ha, ha! Yes, 'tis like I may. You have nothing further to say to me?

SIR WILFULL

Not at present cousin; 'tis like, when I have an opportunity to be more private, I may break† my mind in some measure – I conjecture you partly guess – however that's as time shall try; but spare to speak and spare to speed, as they say.

MILLAMANT

If it is of no great importance, Sir Wilfull, you will oblige me to leave me; I have just now a little business.

SIR WILFULL

Enough, enough, cousin, yes, yes, all a case; when you're disposed, when you're disposed. Now's as well as another time, and another time as well as now. All's one for that. Yes, yes, if your concerns call you, there's no haste; it will keep cold, as they say. Cousin, your servant. I think this door's locked.

MILLAMANT

You may go this way sir.

---

*break* reveal

SIR WILFULL

Your servant; then with your leave I'll return to my company. *Exit*

MILLAMANT

Ay, ay, ha, ha, ha!
'Like Phoebus sung the no less amorous boy.'

*Enter* MIRABELL

MIRABELL

'Like Daphne[†] she, as lovely and as coy.'
Do you lock yourself up from me, to make my search more curious?[†] Or is this pretty artifice contrived, to signify that here the chase must end, and my pursuit be crowned, for you can fly no further?

MILLAMANT

Vanity! No. I'll fly and be followed to the last moment, though I am upon the very verge of matrimony; I expect you should solicit me as much as if I were wavering at the grate of a monastery, with one foot over the threshold. I'll be solicited to the very last, nay, and afterwards.

MIRABELL

What, after the last?

MILLAMANT

Oh, I should think I was poor and had nothing to bestow if I were reduced to an inglorious ease, and freed from the agreeable fatigues of solicitation.

MIRABELL

But do not you know that when favours are conferred upon instant and tedious solicitation that they diminish in their value, and that both the giver loses the grace and the receiver lessens his pleasure?

MILLAMANT

It may be in things of common application, but never sure in love. Oh, I hate a lover that can dare to think he draws a moment's air independent on the bounty of his mistress. There's not so impudent a thing in nature as the saucy look of an assured man, confident of success. The pedantic arrogance of a very husband has not so pragmatical an air. Ah, I'll never marry, unless I am first made sure of my will and pleasure.

MIRABELL

Would you have 'em both before marriage, or will you be contented with the first now, and stay for the other till after grace?

MILLAMANT

Ah don't be impertinent. My dear liberty, shall I leave thee? My faithful solitude, my darling contemplation, must I bid you then adieu?

---

*Daphne* pursued by Phoebus Apollo *curious* anxious

Ay-h, adieu; my morning thoughts, agreeable wakings, indolent slumbers, all ye *douceurs* [sweet things], ye *sommeils du matin* [morning slumbers], adieu? I can't do't, 'tis more than impossible. Positively, Mirabell, I'll lie a-bed in a morning as long as I please.

MIRABELL

Then I'll get up in a morning as early as I please.

MILLAMANT

Ah, idle creature, get up when you will – and, d'ye hear, I won't be called names after I'm married; positively, I won't be called names.

MIRABELL

Names!

MILLAMANT

Ay, as wife, spouse, my dear, joy, jewel, love, sweetheart, and the rest of that nauseous cant in which men and their wives are so fulsomely familiar. I shall never bear that. Good Mirabell, don't let us be familiar or fond, nor kiss before folks like my Lady Fadler† and Sir Francis, nor go to Hyde Park together the first Sunday in a new chariot, to provoke eyes and whispers, and then never be seen there together again; as if we were proud of one another the first week, and ashamed of one another for ever after. Let us never visit together, nor go to a play together, but let us be very strange† and well-bred; let us be as strange as if we had been married a great while, and as well-bred as if we were not married at all.

MIRABELL

Have you any more conditions to offer? Hitherto your demands are pretty reasonable.

MILLAMANT

Trifles – as, liberty to pay and receive visits to and from whom I please, to write and receive letters, without interrogatories or wry faces on your part; to wear what I please, and choose conversation with regard only to my own taste; to have no obligation upon me to converse with wits that I don't like, because they are your acquaintance, or to be intimate with fools, because they may be your relations. Come to dinner when I please, dine in my dressing-room when I'm out of humour, without giving a reason. To have my closet† inviolate, to be sole empress of my tea table, which you must never presume to approach without first asking leave; and lastly, wherever I am, you shall always knock at the door before you come in. These articles subscribed, if I continue to endure you a little longer, I may by degrees dwindle into a wife.

*Fadler* Fondler
*strange* distant
*closet* private room

MIRABELL

Your bill of fare is something advanced in this latter account. Well, have I liberty to offer conditions, that when you are dwindled into a wife, I may not be beyond measure enlarged into a husband?

MILLAMANT

You have free leave; propose your utmost, speak and spare not.

MIRABELL

I thank you. *Imprimis*[†] [first] then, I covenant that your acquaintance be general; that you admit no sworn confidante or intimate of your own sex, no she-friend to screen her affairs under your countenance and tempt you to make trial of a mutual secrecy; no decoy-duck to wheedle you a fop, scrambling to the play in a mask,[†] then bring you home in a pretended fright when you think you shall be found out, and rail at me for missing the play, and disappointing the frolic, which you had to pick me up and prove my constancy!

MILLAMANT

Detestable *imprimis*! I go to the play in a mask!

MIRABELL

*Item*, I article that you continue to like your own face as long as I shall, and while it passes current with me, that you endeavour not to new-coin it. To which end, together with all vizards[†] for the day, I prohibit all masks for the night made of oiled skins and I know not what – hog's bones, hare's gall, pig-water, and the marrow of a roasted cat. In short, I forbid all commerce with the gentlewoman in what-d'ye-call-it Court. *Item*, I shut my doors against all bawds with baskets, and pennyworths of muslin, china, fans, atlases, etc. *Item*, when you shall be breeding –

MILLAMANT

Ah! Name it not.

MIRABELL

Which may be presumed, with a blessing on your endeavours –

MILLAMANT

Odious endeavours!

MIRABELL

I denounce against all strait-lacing, squeezing, for a shape, till you mould my boy's head like a sugar-loaf,[†] and instead of a man-child make me the father to a crooked billet.[†] Lastly, to the dominion of the tea table I submit, but with proviso that you exceed not in your province, but restrain yourself to native and simple tea table drinks, as tea, chocolate and coffee; as, likewise, to genuine and authorised

*Imprimis* Mirabell uses legal terms
*in a mask* as ladies often did
*vizard* mask
*sugar-loaf* tall, moulded shape
*billet* log

tea table talk, such as mending of fashions, spoiling reputations, railing at absent friends, and so forth; but that on no account you encroach upon the men's prerogative and presume to drink healths or toast fellows; for prevention of which I banish all foreign forces,† all auxiliaries to the tea table, as orange brandy, all aniseed, cinnamon, citron and Barbadoes waters, together with ratafia and the most noble spirit of clary. But, for cowslip wine, poppy water and all dormitives,† those I allow. These provisos admitted, in other things I may prove a tractable and complying husband.

MILLAMANT

Oh horrid provisos! Filthy strong waters! I toast fellows, odious men! I hate your odious provisos!

MIRABELL

Then we're agreed. Shall I kiss your hand upon the contract? And here comes one to be a witness to the sealing of the deed.

*Enter* MRS FAINALL

MILLAMANT

Fainall, what shall I do? Shall I have him? I think I must have him.

MRS FAINALL

Ay, ay, take him, take him, what should you do?

MILLAMANT

Well then – I'll take my death I'm in a horrid fright – Fainall, I shall never say it – well – I think – I'll endure you.

MRS FAINALL

Fie, fie, have him, have him, and tell him so in plain terms; for I am sure you have a mind to him.

MILLAMANT

Are you? I think I have; and the horrid man looks as if he thought so too. Well, you ridiculous thing you, I'll have you – I won't be kissed, nor I won't be thanked – here, kiss my hand though – so, hold your tongue now, and don't say a word.

MRS FAINALL

Mirabell, there's a necessity for your obedience: you have neither time to talk nor stay. My mother is coming, and, in my conscience, if she should see you, would fall into fits and maybe not recover time enough to return to Sir Rowland, who as Foible tells me is in a fair way to succeed. Therefore, spare your ecstasies for another occasion and slip down the back stairs, where Foible waits to consult you.

MILLAMANT

Ay, go, go. In the mean time I suppose you have said something to please me.

*foreign forces* all pungent or alcoholic drinks *dormitives* sleeping draughts

MIRABELL

I am all obedience. *Exit*

MRS FAINALL

Yonder Sir Wilfull's drunk, and so noisy that my mother has been forced to leave Sir Rowland to appease him, but he answers her only with singing and drinking. What they have done by this time I know not, but Petulant and he were upon quarrelling as I came by.

MILLAMANT

Well, if Mirabell should not make a good husband, I am a lost thing, for I find I love him violently. . . .

1700

# Colley Cibber

## 1671–1757

The son of a well-known sculptor, Cibber (pronounced ‘K’) became an actor and dramatist, best known for genteel sentimental comedy and a popular adaptation of Shakespeare’s *Richard III*. He was made Poet Laureate in 1743, in preference to many better writers, and was duly satirised by Pope, his old antagonist, as the epitome of literary dullness in the revised *Dunciad* of 1743. Insensitive and egocentric though he was, his *Apology* for his life (1740), an autobiography, is a valuable document of theatrical history, and often reveals a pleasant, common-sensical personality.

## *From* AN APOLOGY FOR THE LIFE OF COLLEY CIBBER

### *[A Cheerful Dunce?]*

When I look into my present self, and afterwards cast my eye round all my hopes, I don’t see any one pursuit of them that should so reasonably rouse me out of a nod in my great chair, as a call to those agreeable parties I have sometimes the happiness to mix with, where I always assert the equal liberty of leaving them, when my spirits have done their best with them.

Now, Sir, as I have been making my way for above forty years through a crowd of cares (all which, by the favour of Providence, I have honestly got rid of), is it a time of day for me to leave off those fooleries, and to set up a new character? Can it be worth my while to waste my spirits, to bake my blood, with serious contemplations, and perhaps impair my health, in the fruitless study of advancing myself into the better opinion of those very – very few wise men that are as old as I am? No, the part I have acted in real life, shall be all of a piece.

*– – Servetur ad imum,*
*Qualis ab incepto processerit.* (Horace)
[Let it continue to the end as it has from the first]

I will not go out of my character, by straining to be wiser than I *can* be, or by being more affectedly pensive than I *need* be; whatever I am, men of sense will know me to be, put on what disguise I will; I can no more put off my follies, than my skin; I have often tried, but they stick too close to me; nor am I sure my friends are displeased with them; for, beside that in this light I afford them frequent matter of mirth, they may possibly be less uneasy at their *own* foibles, when they have so old a precedent to keep them in countenance: nay, there are some frank enough to confess, they envy what they laugh at; and when I have seen others, whose rank and fortune have laid a sort of restraint upon their liberty of pleasing their company, by pleasing themselves, I have said softly to myself – Well, there is some advantage in having neither rank nor fortune! Not but there are among them a third sort, who have the particular happiness of unbending into the very wantonness of good-humour, without depreciating their dignity: he that is not master of that freedom, let his condition be never so exalted, must still want something to come up to the happiness of his inferiors who enjoy it. If Socrates† could take pleasure in playing at Even or Odd with his children, or Agesilaus† divert himself in riding the hobby-horse with them, am I obliged to be as eminent as either of them before I am as frolicsome? If the Emperor Hadrian,† near his death, could play with his very soul, his Animula, &c. and regret that it could no longer be companionable; if greatness, at the same time, was not the delight he was so loath to part with, sure then these cheerful amusements I am contending for, must have no inconsiderable share in our happiness; he that does not choose to live his own way, suffers others to choose for him. Give me the joy I always took in the end of an old song,

*My Mind, my Mind is a Kingdom to me!*

If I can please myself with my own follies, have I not a plentiful provision for life? If the world thinks me a trifler, I don't desire to break in upon their wisdom; let them call me any fool, but an uncheerful one! I live as I write; while my way amuses me, it's as well as I with it; when another writes better, I can like him too, though he should not like me. Not our great Imitator† of Horace himself can have more pleasure in writing his verses, than I have in reading them, though I sometimes find myself there (as Shakespeare† terms it) *dispraisingly* spoken of: if he is a little fret with me, I am generally in good company, he is as blunt with my betters; so that even here I might laugh in my turn. My superiors, perhaps, may be mended by him; but, for my part, I own myself incorrigible: I look upon my follies as the best part of my fortune, and am more concerned to be a good husband of them, than of that; not do I believe I shall ever be rhymed out of them. . . .

*Socrates* (469–399 BC) Greek philosopher
*Agesilaus* (400–360 BC) Spartan king
*Hadrian* (AD 76–138) Roman emperor
*Imitator* Pope in the 1730s
*Shakespeare* *Othello*, III.3.73

## 60 *[The Status of Actors]*

The allurements of a theatre are still so strong in my memory, that perhaps few, except those who have felt them, can conceive: and I am yet so far willing to excuse my folly, that I am convinced, were it possible to take off that disgrace and prejudice, which custom has thrown upon the profession of an actor, many a well-born younger brother, and beauty of low fortune would gladly have adorned the theatre, who by their not being able to brook such dishonour to their birth, have passed away their lives decently unheeded and forgotten.

Many years ago, when I was first in the management of the theatre, I remember a strong instance, which will show you what degree of ignominy the profession of an actor was then held at – A lady, with a real title, whose female indiscretions had occasioned her family to abandon her, being willing in her distress to make an honest penny of what beauty she had left, desired to be admitted as an actress; when before she could receive our answer, a gentleman (probably by her relation's permission) advised us not to entertain her, for reasons easy to be guessed. You may imagine we could not be so blind to our interest as to make an honourable family our unnecessary enemies, by not taking his advice; which the lady too being sensible[†] of, saw the affair had its difficulties; and therefore pursued it no further. Now it is not hard that it should be a doubt, whether this lady's condition or ours were the more melancholy? For here, you find her honest endeavour, to get bread from the stage, was looked upon as an addition of new scandal to her former dishonour! So that I am afraid, according to this way of thinking, had the same lady stooped to have sold patches and pomatum, in a bandbox, from door to door, she might in that occupation have starved with less infamy than had she relieved her necessities by being famous on the theatre. Whether this prejudice may have arisen from the abuses that so often have crept in upon the stage, I am not clear in; though when that is grossly the case, I will allow there ought to be no limits set to the contempt of it; yet in its lowest condition, in my time, methinks there could have been no great pretence of preferring the bandbox to the buskin.[†] But this severe opinion, whether merited or not, is not the greatest distress that this profession is liable to.

I shall now give you another anecdote, quite the reverse of what I have instanced, wherein you will see an actress as hardly used for an act of modesty (which, without being a prude, a woman, even upon the stage, may sometimes think it necessary not to throw off). This too I am forced to premise, that the truth of what I am going to tell you may not be sneered at before it be known. About the year 1717, a

*sensible* aware

*buskin* actor's shoe

young actress, of a desirable person, sitting in an upper box at the opera, a military gentleman thought this a proper opportunity to secure a little conversation with her; the particulars of which were, probably, no more worth repeating than it seems the *Damoiselle* then thought them worth listening to; for, notwithstanding the fine things he said to her, she rather chose to give the music the preference of her attention. This indifference was so offensive to his high heart, that he began to change the tender into the terrible, and, in short, proceeded at last to treat her in a style too grossly insulting for the meanest female ear to endure unresented: upon which, being beaten too far out of her discretion, she turned hastily upon him with an angry look and a reply which seemed to set his mérit in so low a regard that he thought himself obliged in honour to take his time to resent it. This was the full extent of her crime, which his glory delayed no longer to punish, than till the next time she was to appear upon the stage. There, in one of her best parts, wherein she drew a favourable regard and approbation from the audience, he, dispensing with the respect which some people think due to a polite assembly, began to interrupt her performance with such loud and various notes of mockery as other young men of honour, in the same place, have sometimes made themselves undauntedly merry with: thus, deaf to all murmurs or entreaties of those about him, he pursued his point, even to throwing near her such trash as no person can be supposed to carry about him, unless to use on so particular an occasion.

A gentleman then behind the scenes, being shocked at his unmanly behaviour, was warm enough to say, that no man, but a fool, or a bully, could be capable of insulting an audience, or a woman, in so monstrous a manner. The former valiant gentleman, to whose ear the words were soon brought by his spies whom he had placed behind the scenes to observe how the action was taken there, came immediately from the pit in a heat and demanded to know of the author of those words, if he was the person that spoke them. To which he calmly replied, that though he had never seen him before, yet, since he seemed so earnest to be satisfied, he would do him the favour to own, that, indeed, the words were his, and that they would be the last words he should choose to deny, whoever they might fall upon. To conclude, their dispute was ended the next morning in Hyde Park, where the determined combatant, who first asked for satisfaction, was obliged afterwards to ask his life too; whether he mended it or not, I have not yet heard; but his antagonist, in a few years after, died in one of the principal posts of the Government.

Now though I have sometimes known these gallant insulters of audiences draw themselves into scrapes which they have less honourably got out of, yet, alas! what has that availed? This generous public-spirited method of silencing a few, was but repelling the disease in one part, to make it break out in another: all endeavours at protection are new provocations to those who pride themselves in pushing their courage to a defiance of humanity. Even when a Royal resentment has shown itself in the behalf of an injured actor, it has been unable to defend him from further insults! an instance of which happened in the late King James's time. Mr Smith (whose character as a gentleman could have been no way impeached, had he not degraded it by being a celebrated actor) had the misfortune, in a dispute with a gentleman behind the scenes, to receive a blow from him: the same night an account of this action was carried to the King, to whom the gentleman was represented so grossly in the wrong that, the next day, his Majesty sent to forbid him the Court upon it. This indignity cast upon a gentleman, only for having maltreated a player, was looked upon as the concern of every gentleman; and a party was soon formed to assert and vindicate their honour, by humbling this favoured actor, whose slight injury had been judged equal to so severe a notice. Accordingly, the next time Smith acted, he was received with a chorus of cat-calls, that soon convinced him he should not be suffered to proceed in his part; upon which, without the least discomposure, he ordered the curtain to be dropped; and, having a competent fortune of his own, thought the conditions of adding to it, by his remaining upon the stage, were too dear, and from that day entirely quitted it. I shall make no observation upon the King's resentment, or on that of his good subjects; how far either was or was not right, is not the point I dispute for: be that as it may, the unhappy condition of the actor was so far from being relieved by this Royal interposition in his favour, that it was the worse for it.

While these sort of real distresses on the stage are so unavoidable, it is no wonder that young people of sense (though of low fortune) should be so rarely found to supply a succession of good actors. Why then may we not, in some measure, impute the scarcity of them to the wanton inhumanity of those spectators who have made it so terribly mean to appear there? Were there no ground for this question, where could be the disgrace of entering into a society whose institution, when not abused, is a delightful school of morality; and where to excel, requires as ample endowments of nature, as any one profession (that of holy institution excepted) whatsoever? . . .

1740

# Joseph Addison
1672–1719
# Sir Richard Steele
1672–1729

Addison was educated at Charterhouse with his future colleague, Richard Steele, and at Oxford, where he became a fellow of Magdalen College. A classical scholar, he wrote Latin poetry and travelled on the Continent 1699–1703 (*Dialogues upon Ancient Medals*). A Whig supporter, he celebrated Marlborough's victories in verse (*The Campaign*, 1705), was an MP 1708–19, and held important offices (Under-Secretary of State; Chief Secretary for Ireland). With Congreve and Steele, he was a member of the Whig Kit-Cat Club. After contributing papers to Steele's tri-weekly *Tatler* (1709–11), Addison joined him as editor of the daily *Spectator* (March 1711–December 1712; tri-weekly, June–December 1714, by Addison). Their invention of the Club as a microcosm of English society (with Sir Roger de Coverley from the country gentry, Sir Andrew Freeport from business) allowed them agreeably to instruct the rising middle classes in questions of social behaviour and literary taste, with series of papers on imagination, ballads and *Paradise Lost*. Addison, whose prose Johnson praised as 'the model of the middle style', was one of the major influences on the middle classes for well over a century. A successful classical dramatist (*Cato*, 1713), husband of a countess, and centre of a literary clique, he was lukewarm about the rising talent of Pope, who sketched him as 'Atticus' in the *Epistle to Arbuthnot*.

Steele was born in Dublin, educated at Oxford, and became a captain in the Guards. Early comedies were followed by the periodicals with Addison and others. Having written in the Whig interest (an MP 1713–14 and later), he was knighted 1715. His moral concerns and his reaction against Restoration comedy's degeneracy are seen in his last play, *The Conscious Lovers* (1722), influential on domestic and sentimental literature.

# *The Spectator*

## No. 2 *[The Club] Friday March* 2 1711

[STEELE]

> ... *Ast Alii sex*
> *Et plures uno conclamant ore.*
> [Six and more cry out with one voice]
>
> Juvenal [*Satires*, 7.167–8]

The first of our society is a gentleman of Worcestershire, of ancient descent, a baronet, his name Sir Roger de Coverley. His great grandfather was inventor of that famous country dance[†] which is called after him. All who know that shire are very well acquainted with the parts and merits of Sir Roger. He is a gentleman that is very singular in his behaviour, but his singularities proceed from his good sense, and are contradictions to the manners of the world, only as he thinks the world is in the wrong. However, this humour creates him no enemies, for he does nothing with sourness or obstinacy; and his being unconfined to modes and forms, makes him but the readier and more capable to please and oblige all who know him. When he is in town he lives in Soho Square:[†] it is said he keeps himself a bachelor by reason he was crossed in love, by a perverse beautiful widow of the next county to him. Before this disappointment, Sir Roger was what you call a fine gentleman, had often supped with my Lord Rochester and Sir George Etherege, fought a duel upon his first coming to town, and kicked Bully Dawson[†] in a public coffee-house for calling him youngster. But being ill-used by the abovementioned widow, he was very serious for a year and a half; and though his temper being naturally jovial, he at last got over it, he grew careless of himself and never dressed afterwards; he continues to wear a coat and doublet of the same cut that were in fashion at the time of his repulse, which, in his merry humours, he tells us, has been in and out twelve times since he first wore it. 'Tis said Sir Roger grew humble in his desires after he had forgot this cruel beauty, insomuch that it is reported he has frequently offended in point of chastity with beggars and gypsies: but this is looked upon by his friends rather as matter of raillery than truth. He is now in his fifty-sixth year, cheerful, gay, and hearty, keeps a good house both in town and country; a great lover of mankind; but there is such a mirthful cast in his

*country dance* it dates from the 1680s
*Soho Square* then fashionable, far from commercial City
*Rochester ... Dawson* Rochester the poet; Etherege (?1635–91), the dramatist; Dawson, a sharper: notorious Restoration rakes

behaviour, that he is rather beloved than esteemed: his tenants grow rich, his servants look satisfied, all the young women profess love to him, and the young men are glad of his company; when he comes into a house he calls the servants by their names, and talks all the way up stairs to a visit. I must not omit that Sir Roger is a Justice† of the *Quorum*; that he fills the chair at a quarter session with great abilities, and three months ago gained universal applause by explaining a passage in the Game Act.

The gentleman next in esteem and authority among us, is another bachelor, who is a member of the Inner Temple,† a man of great probity, wit, and understanding; but he has chosen his place of residence rather to obey the direction of an old humoursome† father than in pursuit of his own inclinations. He was placed there to study the laws of the land, and is the most learned of any of the house in those of the stage. Aristotle and Longinus† are much better understood by him than Littleton or Coke. The father sends up every post questions relating to marriage articles, leases, and tenures, in the neighbourhood; all which questions he agrees with an attorney to answer and take care of in the lump: he is studying the passions themselves, when he should be inquiring into the debates among men which arise from them. He knows the argument of each of the Orations of Demosthenes and Tully,† but not one case in the reports of our own courts. No one ever took him for a fool, but none, except his intimate friends, know he has a great deal of wit. This turn makes him at once both disinterested and agreeable: as few of his thoughts are drawn from business, they are most of them fit for conversation. His taste of books is a little too just for the age he lives in; he has read all, but approves of very few. His familiarity with the customs, manners, actions, and writings of the ancients, makes him a very delicate observer of what occurs to him in the present world. He is an excellent critic, and the time of the play, is his hour of business; exactly at five he passes through New-Inn,† crosses through Russel Court, and takes a turn at Will's† till the play begins; he has his shoes rubbed and his perriwig powdered at the barber's as you go into the Rose.† It is for the good of the audience when he is at a play, for the actors have an ambition to please him.

The person of next consideration is Sir Andrew Freeport, a merchant

*Justice* a local magistrate
*Inner Temple* body of lawyers and students
*humoursome* capricious
*Aristotle . . . Longinus* Aristotle 384–322 BC) philosopher and, like Longinus (1st century AD), literary critic rather than legal commentator
*Demosthenes, Tully* Greek (383–322 BC) and Roman orators; Tully: M. Tullius Cicero (106–43 BC)
*New-Inn* he goes from the legal area to the literary world near Covent Garden
*Will's* Will's Coffee House
*Rose* the Rose Tavern

of great eminence in the City of London: a person of indefatigable industry, strong reason, and great experience. His notions of trade are noble and generous, and (as every rich man has usually some sly way of jesting, which would make no great figure were he not a rich man) he calls the sea the British Common. He is acquainted with commerce in all its parts, and will tell you that it is a stupid and barbarous way to extend dominion by arms; for true power is to be got by arts and industry. He will often argue, that if this part of our trade were well cultivated, we should gain from one nation; and if another, from another. I have heard him prove, that diligence makes more lasting acquisitions than valour, and that sloth has ruined more nations than the sword. He abounds in several frugal maxims, among which the greatest favourite is, 'A penny saved is a penny got.' A general trader of good sense is pleasanter company than a general scholar; and Sir Andrew having a natural unaffected eloquence, the perspicuity of his discourse gives the same pleasure that wit would in another man. He has made his fortunes himself; and says that England may be richer than other kingdoms, by as plain methods as he himself is richer than other men; though at the same time I can say this of him, that there is not a point in the compass but blows home a ship in which he is an owner.

Next to Sir Andrew in the Club-room sits Captain Sentry, a gentleman of great courage, good understanding, but invincible modesty. He is one of those that deserve very well, but are very awkward at putting their talents within the observation of such as should take notice of them. He was some years a captain, and behaved himself with great gallantry in several engagements and at several sieges; but having a small estate of his own, and being next heir to Sir Roger, he has quitted a way of life in which no man can rise suitably to his merit, who is not something of a courtier as well as a soldier. I have heard him often lament, that in a profession where merit is placed in so conspicuous a view, impudence should get the better of modesty. When he has talked to this purpose I never heard him make a sour expression, but frankly confess that he left the world because he was not fit for it. A strict honesty and an even regular behaviour are in themselves obstacles to him that must press through crowds who endeavour at the same end with himself, the favour of a commander. He will however in this way of talk excuse generals for not disposing according to men's desert, or inquiring into it: For, says he, that great man who has a mind to help me, has as many to break through to come at me, as I have to come at him; therefore he will conclude, that the man who would make a figure, especially in a military way, must get over all false modesty, and assist his patron against the importunity of other pretenders by a proper assurance in his own vindication. He says it is a civil cowardice to be backward in asserting what you ought to expect, as it is a military fear to be slow in attacking when it is your duty. With this candour does the gentleman speak of himself and others. The same frankness runs through all his conversation. The military part of his life has furnished him with many adventures, in the relation of which he is very agreeable to the company; for he is never over-bearing, though accustomed to command men in the utmost degree below him; nor ever too obsequious, from an habit of obeying men highly above him.

But that our society may not appear a set of humourists† unacquainted with the gallantries and pleasures of the age, we have among us the gallant Will. Honeycomb, a gentleman who according to his years should be in the decline of his life, but having ever been very careful of his person, and always had a very easy fortune, time has made but very little impression, either by wrinkles on his forehead, or traces in his brain. His person is well turned, of a good height. He is very ready at that sort of discourse with which men usually entertain women. He has all his life dressed very well, and remembers habits as others do men. He can smile when one speaks to him, and laughs easily. He knows the history of every mode, and can inform you from which of the French King's wenches our wives and daughters had this manner of curling their hair, that way of placing their hoods; whose frailty was covered by such a sort of petticoat, and whose vanity to show her foot made that part of the dress so short in such a year. In a word, all his conversation and knowledge has been in the female world: as other men of his age will take notice to you what such a minister said upon such and such an occasion, he will tell you when the Duke of Monmouth danced at Court such a woman was then smitten, another was taken with him at the head of his troop in the Park. In all these important relations, he has ever about the same time received a kind glance or a blow of a fan from some celebrated beauty, mother of the present Lord such-a-one. If you speak of a young Commoner† that said a lively thing in the House, he starts up, 'He has good blood in his veins, Tom Mirabell begot him, the rogue cheated me in that affair; that young fellow's mother used me more like a dog than any woman I ever made advances to.' This way of talking of his very much enlivens the conversation among us of a more sedate turn; and I find there is not one of the company but myself, who rarely speak at all, but speaks of him as of that sort of man who is usually called a well-bred fine gentleman. To conclude his character, where women are not concerned, he is an honest worthy man.

I cannot tell whether I am to account him whom I am next to speak of, as one of our company; for he visits us but seldom, but when he

*humourists* faddists, cranks

*Commoner* member of House of Commons

does it adds to every man else a new enjoyment of himself. He is a clergyman, a very philosophic man, of general learning, great sanctity of life, and the most exact good breeding. He has the misfortune to be of a very weak constitution, and consequently cannot accept of such cares and business as preferments† in his function would oblige him to: he is therefore among divines what a chamber-counsellor is among lawyers. The probity of his mind, and the integrity of his life, create him followers, as being eloquent or loud advances others. He seldom introduces the subject he speaks upon; but we are so far gone in years, that he observes, when he is among us, an earnestness to have him fall on some divine topic, which he always treats with much authority, as one who has no interests in this world, as one who is hastening to the object of all his wishes, and conceives hope from his decays and infirmities. These are my ordinary companions.

## No. 70 *[The Ballad]* *Monday May* 21 1711

[ADDISON]

*Interdum vulgus rectum videt.*
[Sometimes the public see things rightly.]
Horace [*Epistles*, 2.1.63]

When I travelled, I took a particular delight in hearing the songs and fables that are come from father to son, and are most in vogue among the common people of the countries through which I passed; for it is impossible that any thing should be universally tasted and approved by a multitude, though they are only the rabble of a nation, which hath not in it some peculiar aptness to please and gratify the mind of man. Human nature is the same in all reasonable creatures; and whatever falls in with it, will meet with admirers amongst readers of all qualities and conditions. Molière, as we are told by Monsieur Boileau,† used to read all his comedies to an old woman who was his housekeeper, as she sat with him at her work by the chimney-corner; and could foretell the success of his play in the theatre, from the reception it met at his fireside: for he tells us the audience always followed the old woman, and never failed to laugh in the same place.

I know nothing which more shows the essential and inherent perfection of simplicity of thought, above that which I call the Gothic manner in writing, than this, that the first pleases all kinds of palates,

*preferments* promotions
*Molière . . . Boileau* Molière (1622–73) French comic dramatist, friend of the poet and critic Boileau (1636–1711)

and the latter only such as have formed to themselves a wrong artificial taste, upon little fanciful authors and writers of epigram. Homer, Virgil, or Milton, so far as the language of their poems is understood, will please a reader of plain common sense, who would neither relish nor comprehend an epigram of Martial or a poem of Cowley:† so, on the contrary, an ordinary song or ballad that is the delight of the common people, cannot fail to please all such readers as are not unqualified for the entertainment by their affectation or ignorance; and the reason is plain, because the same paintings of nature which recommended it to the most ordinary reader, will appear beautiful to the most refined.

The old song of *Chevy Chase*† is the favourite ballad of the common people of England; and Ben Jonson used to say he had rather have been the author of it than of all his works. Sir Philip Sidney† in his discourse of poetry speaks of it in the following words: 'I never heard the old song of Percy and Douglas, that I found not my heart more moved than with a trumpet; and yet is it sung by some blind crowder† with no rougher voice than rude style; which being so evil apparelled in the dust and cobweb of that uncivil age, what would it work trimmed in the gorgeous eloquence of Pindar?'† For my own part, I am so professed an admirer of this antiquated song, that I shall give my reader a critique upon it, without any further apology for so doing.

The greatest modern critics have laid it down as a rule, that an heroic poem should be founded upon some important precept of morality, adapted to the constitution of the country in which the poet writes. Homer and Virgil have formed their plans in this view. As Greece was a collection of many governments, who suffered very much among themselves, and gave the Persian emperor, who was their common enemy, many advantages over them by their mutual jealousies and animosities, Homer, in order to establish among them an union, which was so necessary for their safety, grounds his poem upon the discords of the several Grecian princes who were engaged in a confederacy against an Asiatic prince, and the several advantages which the enemy gained by such their discords. At the time the poem we are now treating of was written, the dissensions of the barons, who were then so many petty princes, ran very high, whether they quarrelled among themselves or with their neighbours, and produced unspeakable calamities to the country: the poet, to deter men from such unnatural contentions, describes a bloody battle and dreadful scene of death, occasioned by

*Martial . . . Cowley* Martial, Latin epigrammatist (d.AD 104); influenced Abraham Cowley (1618–67) – see extract from Johnson's 'Life'

*Chevy Chase* Addison quotes one of the versions of an ancient border ballad

*Sidney* (1554–86) poet and soldier; *A Defence of Poetry*, publ. 1595

*crowder* fiddler

*Pindar* (d.443 BC) Greek lyric poet

the mutual feuds which reigned in the families† of an English and Scotch nobleman. That he designed this for the instruction of his poem, we may learn from his four last lines, in which, after the example of the modern tragedians, he draws from it a precept for the benefit of his readers.

God save the King and bless the land
  In plenty, joy, and peace;
And grant henceforth that foul debate
  'Twixt noblemen may cease.

The next point observed by the greatest heroic poets, hath been to celebrate persons and actions which do honour to their country: thus Virgil's hero was the founder of Rome, Homer's a prince of Greece; and for this reason Valerius Flaccus and Statius, who were both Romans, might be justly derided for having chosen the Expedition of the Golden Fleece and the Wars of Thebes, for the subjects of their epic writings.†

The poet before us, has not only found out an hero in his own country, but raises the reputation of it by several beautiful incidents. The English are the first who take the field, and the last who quit it. The English bring only fifteen hundred to the battle, the Scotch two thousand. The English keep the field with fifty-three: the Scotch retire with fifty-five: all the rest on each side being slain in battle. But the most remarkable circumstance of this kind, is the different manner in which the Scotch and English kings receive the news of this fight, and of the great men's deaths who commanded in it.

This news was brought to Edinburgh,
  Where Scotland's King did reign,
That brave Earl Douglas suddenly
  Was with an arrow slain.

O heavy news, King James did say,
  Scotland can witness be,
I have not any captain more
  Of such account as he.

Like tidings to King Henry came
  Within as short a space,
That Percy of Northumberland
  Was slain in Chevy-Chase.

Now God be with him, said our King,
  Sith 'twill no better be,
I trust I have within my realm
  Five hundred as good as he.

*families* Percy and Douglas

*writings* *Argonautica* and *Thebais* respectively

Yet shall not Scot nor Scotland say
But I will vengeance take,
And he revenged on them all
For brave Lord Percy's sake.

This vow full well the King performed
After on Humble-down,
In one day fifty knights were slain
With lords of great renown.

And of the rest of small account
Did many thousands die, etc.

At the same time that our poet shows a laudable partiality to his countrymen, he represents the Scots after a manner not unbecoming so bold and brave a people.

Earl Douglas on a milk-white steed,
Most like a baron bold,
Rode foremost of the company
Whose armour shone like gold.

His sentiments and actions are every way suitable to an hero. One of us two, says he, must die: I am an earl as well as yourself, so that you can have no pretence for refusing the combat: however, says he, 'tis pity, and indeed would be a sin, that so many innocent men should perish for our sakes; rather let you and I end our quarrel in single fight.

Ere thus I will out-braved be,
One of us two shall die;
I know thee well, an earl thou art,
Lord Percy, so am I.

But trust me, Percy, pity it were,
And great offence, to kill
Any of these our harmless men,
For they have done no ill.

Let thou and I the battle try,
And set our men aside;
Accurst be he, Lord Percy said,
By whom this is denied.

When these brave men had distinguished themselves in the battle and in single combat with each other, in the midst of a generous parley, full of heroic sentiments, the Scotch earl falls; and with his dying words encourages his men to revenge his death, representing to them, as the most bitter circumstances of it, that his rival saw him fall.

With that there came an arrow keen
  Out of an English bow,
Which struck Earl Douglas to the heart
  A deep and deadly blow.

Who never spoke more words than these,
  Fight on my merry men all;
For why, my life is at an end,
  Lord Percy sees my fall.

'Merry men', in the language of those times, is no more than a cheerful word for companions and fellow-soldiers. A passage in the eleventh book of Virgil's *Aeneid* is very much to be admired, where Camilla in her last agonies, instead of weeping over the wound she had received, as one might have expected from a warrior of her sex, considers only (like the hero of whom we are now speaking) how the battle should be continued after her death.

Tum sic exspirans, etc.
A gathering mist o'erclouds her cheerful eyes;
And from her cheeks the rosy colour flies.
Then, turns to her, whom, of her female train,
She trusted most, and thus she speaks with pain.
'Acca, 'tis past! He swims before my sight,
Inexorable death; and claims his right.
Bear my last words to Turnus, fly with speed,
And bid him timely to my charge succeed:
Repel the Trojans, and the town relieve:
Farewell. . . .' [transl. Dryden]

Turnus did not die in so heroic a manner; though our poet seems to have had his eye upon Turnus's speech in the last verse

Lord Percy sees my fall.
  . . . Vicisti, et victum tendere palmas
Ausonii videre. . . .
[You have conquered, and the Ausonians have seen me defeated stretch out my hands]

Earl Percy's lamentation over his enemy is generous, beautiful, and passionate; I must only caution the reader not to let the simplicity of the style, which one may well pardon in so old a poet, prejudice him against the greatness of the thought.

Then leaving life Earl Percy took
The dead man by the hand,
And said Earl Douglas for thy life
Would I had lost my land.

O Christ! my very heart doth bleed
With sorrow for thy sake;
For sure a more renowned knight
Mischance did never take.

That beautiful line *Taking the dead man by the hand*, will put the reader in mind of Aeneas's behaviour towards Lausus, whom he himself had slain as he came to the rescue of his aged father.

At vero ut vultum vidit morientis, et ora,
ora modis Anchisiades, pallentia miris:
ingemuit, miserans graviter, dextramque tetendit, etc.
The pious prince beheld young Lausus dead;
He grieved, he wept; then grasped his hand, and said,
'Poor hapless youth! What praises can be paid
To worth so great . . .!' [transl. Dryden]

I shall take another opportunity to consider the other parts of this old song.

## No. 74 *[The Ballad, continued]* Friday May 25 1711

[ADDISON]

. . . *Pendent opera interrupta*. . . .
[The works are suspended] Virgil [*Aeneid*, 4.88]

In my last Monday's paper I gave some general instances of those beautiful strokes which please the reader in the old song of *Chevy Chase*; I shall here, according to my promise, be more particular, and show that the sentiments in that ballad are extremely natural and poetical, and full of the majestic simplicity which we admire in the greatest of the ancient poets: for which reason I shall quote several passages of it, in which the thought is altogether the same with what we meet in several passages of the *Aeneid*; not that I would infer from thence that the poet (whoever he was) proposed to himself any imitation of those passages, but that he was directed to them in general by the same kind of poetical genius, and by the same copyings after nature.

Had this old song been filled with epigrammatical turns and points of wit, it might perhaps have pleased the wrong taste of some readers;

but it would never have become the delight of the common people, nor have warmed the heart of Sir Philip Sidney like the sound of a trumpet; it is only nature that can have this effect, and please those tastes which are the most unprejudiced or the most refined. I must however beg leave to dissent from so great an authority as that of Sir Philip Sidney, in the judgement which he has passed as to the rude style and evil apparel of this antiquated song; for there are several parts in it where not only the thought but the language is majestic, and the numbers sonorous; at least, the apparel is much more gorgeous than many of the poets made use of in Queen Elizabeth's time, as the reader will see in several of the following quotations.

What can be greater than either the thought or the expression in that stanza,

> To drive the deer with hound and horn
> Earl Percy took his way;
> The child may rue that was unborn
> The hunting of that day?

This way of considering the misfortunes which this battle would bring upon posterity, not only on those who were born immediately after the battle and lost their fathers in it, but on those also who perished in future battles which took their rise from this quarrel of the two earls, is wonderfully beautiful, and conformable to the way of thinking among the ancient poets.

> Audiet pugnas vitio parentum
> rara juventus. Horace
> [fewer by fatherly fault, the youth shall hear of battles]

What can be more sounding and poetical, or resemble more the majestic simplicity of the Ancients, than the following stanzas?

> The stout Earl of Northumberland
> A vow to God did make,
> His pleasure in the Scottish woods
> Three summer's days to take.
>
> With fifteen hundred bowmen bold,
> All chosen men of might,
> Who knew full well, in time of need,
> To aim their shafts aright.
>
> The hounds ran swiftly through the woods
> The nimble deer to take,
> And with their cries the hills and dales
> An echo shrill did make.
>
> . . . Vocat ingenti clamore Cithaeron

Taygetique canes, domitrixque Epidaurus equorum:
et vox assensu nemorum ingeminata remugit
[Virgil: *Georgics*, 3]

[Cithaeron calls loudly, and the hounds of Taygetus, and Epidaurus, tamer of horses: and the call re-echoes, doubled by the responding groves.]

Lo, yonder doth Earl Douglas come,
His men in armour bright;
Full twenty hundred Scottish spears,
All marching in our sight.

All men of pleasant Tividale,
Fast by the River Tweed, etc.

The country of the Scotch warriors described in these two last verses, has a fine romantic situation, and affords a couple of smooth words for verse. If the reader compares the foregoing six lines of the song with the following Latin verses, he will see how much they are written in the spirit of Virgil.

Adversi campo apparent . . . [quotes from *Aeneid*; transl. here by Dryden: 11, 605–6; 7. 682–4, 712–15:

Advancing in a line, they couch their spears;
And less and less the middle space appears.
His own Praeneste sends a chosen band,
With those who plough Saturnia's Gabine land:
Besides the succour which cold Anien yields,
The rocks of Hernicus, and dewy fields.
Besides a band
That followed from Velinum's dewy land:
And Amiternian troops, of mighty fame,
And mountaineers, that from Severus came.
And from the craggy cliffs of Tetrica,
And those where yellow Tiber takes his way,
And where Himella's wanton waters play.
Casperia sends her arms, with those that lie
By Fabaris, and fruitful Foruli.]

But to proceed.

Earl Douglas on a milk-white steed,
Most like a baron bold,
Rode foremost of the company,
Whose armour shone like gold.

Turnus ut antevolans tardum praecesserat agmen, etc
Vidisti, quo Turnus equo, quibus ibat in armis
aureus. . . .

[*Aeneid*, 9. 47, 269–70:
The fiery Turnus flew before the rest.
Thou saw'st the courser by proud Turnus pressed. Dryden]

Our English archers bent their bows,
  Their hearts were good and true;
At the first flight of arrows sent,
  Full threescore Scots they slew.

They closed full fast on every side,
  No slackness there was found;
And many a gallant gentleman
  Lay gasping on the ground.

With that there came an arrow keen
  Out of an English bow,
Which struck Earl Douglas to the heart
  A deep and deadly blow.

Aeneas was wounded after the same manner by an unknown hand in the midst of a parley.

Has inter voces, media inter talia verba,
ecce viro stridens alis allapsa sagitta est,
incertum qua pulsa manu. . . .

[*Aeneid*, 12, 318–20:
Thus while he spoke, unmindful of defence,
A winged arrow struck the pious prince.
But whether from some human hand it came,
Or hostile god, is left unknown by fame. Dryden]

But of all the descriptive parts of this song, there are none more beautiful than the four following stanzas, which have a great force and spirit in them, and are filled with very natural circumstances. The thought in the third stanza was never touched by any other poet, and is such an one as would have shined in Homer or in Virgil.

So thus did both these nobles die
  Whose courage none could stain;
An English archer then perceived
  The noble Earl was slain.

He had a bow bent in his hand,
  Made of a trusty tree,

An arrow of a cloth-yard long
  Unto the head drew he.

Against Sir Hugh Montgomery
  So right his shaft he set,
The grey-goose wing that was thereon
  In his heart-blood was wet.

This fight did last from break of day
  Till setting of the sun.
For when they rung the evening bell
  The battle scarce was done.

One may observe likewise, that in the catalogue of the slain the author has followed the example of the greatest ancient poets, not only in giving a long list of the dead, but by diversifying it with little characters of particular persons.

And with Earl Douglas there was slain
  Sir Hugh Montgomery,
Sir Charles Carrel, that from the field
  One foot would never fly:

Sir Charles Murrel of Ratcliff too,
  His sister's son was he,
Sir David Lamb, so well esteemed,
  Yet saved could not be.

The familiar sound in these names destroys the majesty of the description; for this reason I do not mention this part of the poem but to show the natural cast of thought which appears in it, as the two last verses look almost like a translation of Virgil.

. . . Cadit et Ripheus justissimus unus
qui fuit in Teucris et servantissimus aequi,
diis aliter visum est. . . .

[*Aeneid*, 2. 426–8:
Then Ripheus followed, in th' unequal fight;
Just of his word, observant of the right;
Heaven thought not so. Dryden]

In the catalogue of the English who fell, Witherington's behaviour is in the same manner particularised very artfully, as the reader is prepared for it by that account which is given of him in the beginning of the battle: though I am satisfied your little buffoon readers (who have seen that passage ridiculed in *Hudibras*)† will not be able to take the beauty

*Hudibras* I.3.94–6

of it: for which reason I dare not so much as quote it.

Then stepped a gallant squire forth,
 Witherington was his name,
Who said, I would not have it told
 To Henry our King for shame,

That e'er my Captain fought on foot
 And I stood looking on.

We meet with the same heroic sentiment in Virgil.

Non pudet, O Rutuli, cunctis pro talibus unam
objectare animam? numerone an viribus aequi
non sumus? . . .

[*Aeneid*. 12, 229–31:
For shame, Rutulians, can you bear the sight,
Of one exposed for all, in single fight?
Can we, before the face of Heaven, confess
Our courage colder, or our numbers less? Dryden]

What can be more natural or more moving, than the circumstances in which he describes the behaviour of those women who had lost their husbands on this fatal day?

Next day did many widows come
 Their husbands to bewail,
They washed their wounds in brinish tears,
 But all would not prevail.

Their bodies bathed in purple blood,
 They bore with them away;
They kissed them dead a thousand times,
 When they were clad in clay.

Thus we see how the thoughts of this poem, which naturally arise from the subject, are always simple, and sometimes exquisitely noble; that the language is often very sounding, and that the whole is written with a true poetical spirit.

If this song had been written in the Gothic manner, which is the delight of all our little wits, whether writers or readers, it would not have hit the taste of so many ages, and have pleased the readers of all ranks and conditions. I shall only beg pardon for such a profusion of Latin quotations; which I should not have made use of, but that I feared my own judgement would have looked too singular on such a subject, had not I supported it by the practice and authority of Virgil.

# John Gay
## 1685–1732

A native of Barnstaple, Gay first made his name as a poet: *The Shepherd's Week* (1714) is a series of modern pastorals ironically based on classical models; *Trivia* (1716) offers sketches of London street life. A member of the Scriblerus group of Tory satirists, he collaborated with Pope and Arbuthnot in the comedy *Three Hours after Marriage* (1717), and was dear to them and to Swift, who gave a hint for his 'Newgate pastoral' *The Beggar's Opera* (1728); this combines well-known tunes, literary parody, satire of Italian opera, and an ironic reflection of Walpole's political corruption in the world of thieves. A huge success, it is still performed, as is the Brecht–Weill modern adaptation, *The Threepenny Opera*. Performance of the sequel, *Polly*, was banned by the Lord Chamberlain. Gay also wrote librettos for musical works, notably Handel's *Acis and Galatea*. His lively verse *Fables* appeared in 1727 and 1738. His persistent financial difficulties were partly relieved by the Duke and Duchess of Queensberry. Much of Gay's best work depends on playing off varying levels of subject-matter and style: Polly's romantic notions are set in a thieves' world which yet parallels the 'normal'.

## THE BEGGAR'S OPERA

### *Act I*

*Scene, Peachum's house.*
Peachum *sitting at a table with a large book of accounts before him.*
AIR I, *An Old Woman Clothed in Gray, etc.*

PEACHUM.

Through all the employments of life
Each neighbour abuses his brother;
Whore and rogue they call husband and wife;
All professions be-rogue one another.
The priest calls the lawyer a cheat;
The lawyer be-knaves the divine;

And the statesman, because he's so great,
Thinks his trade as honest as mine.

A lawyer is an honest employment; so is mine. Like me too he acts in a double capacity,† both against rogues and for 'em; for 'tis but fitting that we should protect and encourage cheats, since we live by them.

*Enter* Filch.

FILCH.
Sir, Black Moll hath sent word her trial comes on in the afternoon, and she hopes you will order matters so as to bring her off.

PEACHUM.
Why, she may plead her belly† at worst; to my knowledge she hath taken care of that security. But as the wench is very active and industrious, you may satisfy her that I'll soften the evidence.

FILCH.
Tom Gagg, sir, is found guilty.

PEACHUM.
A lazy dog! When I took him the time before, I told him what he would come to if he did not mend his hand. This is death without reprieve. I may venture to book him. (*Writes.*) 'For Tom Gagg, forty pounds.' – Let Betty Sly know that I'll save her from transportation,† for I can get more by her staying in England.

FILCH.
Betty hath brought more goods into our lock to-year than any five of the gang; and in truth, 'tis a pity to lose so good a customer.

PEACHUM.
If none of the gang take her off, she may, in the common course of business, live a twelvemonth longer. I love to let women scape. A good sportsman always lets the hen partridges fly, because the breed of the game depends upon them. Besides, here the law allows us no reward; there is nothing to be got by the death of women, except our wives.

FILCH.
Without dispute, she is a fine woman. 'Twas to her I was obliged for my education, and (to say a bold word) she hath trained up more young fellows to the business than the gaming table.

PEACHUM.
Truly, Filch, thy observation is right. We and the surgeons are more beholden to women than all the professions besides.

---

*double capacity* Peachum receives stolen goods, but also betrays (impeaches) criminals for reward

*her belly* pregnant women were not hanged

*transportation* to the prison colonies

AIR II, *The Bonny Gray-Eyed Morn, etc.*

FILCH.

'Tis woman that seduces all mankind,
By her we first were taught the wheedling arts;
Her very eyes can cheat; when most she's kind,
She tricks us of our money with our hearts.
For her, like wolves by night, we roam for prey,
And practice every fraud to bribe her charms;
For suits of love, like law, are won by pay,
And beauty must be fee'd into our arms.

PEACHUM.

But make haste to Newgate,† boy, and let my friends know what I intend; for I love to make them easy one way or other.

FILCH.

When a gentleman is long kept in suspense, penitence may break his spirit ever after. Besides, certainty gives a man a good air upon his trial, and makes him risk another without fear or scruple. But I'll away, for 'tis a pleasure to be the messenger of comfort to friends in affliction. [*Exit*]

PEACHUM.

But 'tis now high time to look about me for a decent execution against next sessions. I hate a lazy rogue, by whom one can get nothing till he is hanged. A register of the gang. (*Reading.*) 'Crook-fingered Jack.' A year and a half in the service. Let me see how much the stock owes to his industry: one, two, three, four, five gold watches, and seven silver ones. A mighty clean-handed fellow! Sixteen snuffboxes, five of them of true gold. Six dozen of handkerchiefs, four silver-hilted swords, half a dozen of shirts, three tie-periwigs, and a piece of broadcloth. Considering these are only the fruits of his leisure hours, I don't know a prettier fellow, for no man alive hath a more engaging presence of mind upon the road. – 'Wat Dreary, alias Brown Will,' an irregular dog, who hath an underhand way of disposing of his goods. I'll try him only for a sessions or two longer upon his good behaviour. – 'Harry Paddington,' a poor petty-larceny rascal, without the least genius; that fellow, though he were to live these six months, will never come to the gallows with any credit. – 'Slippery Sam'; he goes off the next sessions,† for the villain hath the impudence to have views of following his trade as a tailor, which he calls an honest employment. – 'Matt of the Mint'; listed not above a month ago, a promising sturdy fellow, and diligent in his way; somewhat too bold and hasty, and may raise good contributions on the public, if he does not cut himself short by murder. – 'Tom

*Newgate* prison, where they await trial

*sessions* regular court sittings

Tipple', a guzzling, soaking sot, who is always too drunk to stand himself, or to make others stand. A cart† is absolutely necessary for him. – 'Robin of Bagshot, alias Gorgon, alias Bluff Bob, alias Carbuncle, alias Bob Booty.'†

*Enter* Mrs Peachum.

MRS PEACHUM.

What of Bob Booty, husband? I hope nothing bad hath betided him. You know, my dear, he's a favourite customer of mine. 'Twas he made me a present of this ring.

PEACHUM.

I have set his name down in the black-list, that's all, my dear; he spends his life among women, and as soon as his money is gone, one or other of the ladies will hang him for the reward, and there's forty pound lost to us forever.

MRS PEACHUM.

You know, my dear, I never meddle in matters of death; I always leave those affairs to you. Women indeed are bitter bad judges in these cases, for they are so partial to the brave that they think every man handsome who is going to the camp or the gallows.

AIR III, *Cold and Raw, etc.*

If any wench Venus's girdle wear,†
Though she be never so ugly,
Lilies and roses will quickly appear,
And her face look wondrous smugly.
Beneath the left ear so fit but a cord
(A rope so charming a zone† is!),
The youth in his cart hath the air of a lord,
And we cry, 'There dies an Adonis!'†

But really, husband, you should not be too hardhearted, for you never had a finer, braver set of men than at present. We have not had a murder among them all, these seven months. And truly, my dear, that is a great blessing.

PEACHUM.

What a dickens is the woman always a-whimpering about murder for? No gentleman is ever looked upon the worse for killing a man in his own defence; and if business cannot be carried on without it, what would you have a gentleman do?

---

*cart* to ride to hanging
*Robin of Bagshot . . . Bob Booty* recognisable allusions to Sir Robert Walpole, the Prime Minister
*Venus's Girdle wear* fall in love
*zone* is also a girdle
*Adonis* in classical mythology, fine youth loved by Venus, but killed

MRS PEACHUM.

If I am in the wrong, my dear, you must excuse me, for nobody can help the frailty of an overscrupulous conscience.

PEACHUM.

Murder is as fashionable a crime as a man can be guilty of. How many fine gentlemen have we in Newgate every year, purely upon that article? If they have wherewithal to persuade the jury to bring it in manslaughter, what are they the worse for it? So, my dear, have done upon this subject. Was Captain Macheath here this morning, for the bank notes he left with you last week?

MRS PEACHUM.

Yes, my dear; and though the bank hath stopped[†] payment, he was so cheerful and so agreeable! Sure there is not a finer gentleman upon the road than the Captain! If he comes from Bagshot at any reasonable hour he hath promised to make one this evening with Polly, and me, and Bob Booty, at a party of quadrille.[†] Pray, my dear, is the Captain rich?

PEACHUM.

The Captain keeps too good company ever to grow rich. Marybone and the chocolate houses are his undoing. The man that proposes to get money by play[†] should have the education of a fine gentleman, and be trained up to it from his youth.

MRS PEACHUM.

Really, I am sorry upon Polly's account the Captain hath not more discretion. What business hath he to keep company with lords and gentlemen? He should leave them to prey upon one another.

PEACHUM.

'Upon Polly's account!' What a plague does the woman mean? 'Upon Polly's account!'

MRS PEACHUM.

Captain Macheath is very fond of the girl.

PEACHUM.

And what then?

MRS PEACHUM.

If I have any skill in the ways of women, I am sure Polly thinks him a very pretty man.

PEACHUM.

And what then? You would not be so mad to have the wench marry him. Gamesters and highwaymen are generally very good to their whores, but they are very devils to their wives.

---

*stopped* bank 'notes' were receipts for cash deposits

*quadrille* fashionable card game

*play* gambling took place in chocolate houses and at Marylebone, several miles from the City

MRS PEACHUM.

But if Polly should be in love, how should we help her, or how can she help herself? Poor girl, I am in the utmost concern about her.

AIR IV, *Why is Your Faithful Slave Disdained? etc.*

If love the virgin's heart invade,
How, like a moth, the simple maid
Still plays about the flame!
If soon she be not made a wife,
Her honour's singed, and then for life,
She's – what I dare not name.

PEACHUM.

Look ye, wife. A handsome wench in our way of business is as profitable as at the bar of a Temple† coffeehouse, who looks upon it as her livelihood to grant every liberty but one. You see I would indulge the girl as far as prudently we can – in anything but marriage! After that, my dear, how shall we be safe? Are we not then in her husband's power? For a husband hath the absolute power over all a wife's secrets but her own. If the girl had the discretion of a court lady, who can have a dozen young fellows at her ear without complying with one, I should not matter it; but Polly is tinder, and a spark will at once set her on a flame. Married! If the wench does not know her own profit, sure she knows her own pleasure better than to make herself a property! My daughter to me should be, like a court lady to a minister of state, a key to the whole gang. Married! If the affair is not already done, I'll terrify her from it, by the example of our neighbours.

MRS PEACHUM.

Mayhap, my dear, you may injure the girl. She loves to imitate the fine ladies, and she may only allow the Captain liberties in the view of interest.

PEACHUM.

But 'tis your duty, my dear, to warn the girl against her ruin, and to instruct her how to make the most of her beauty. I'll go to her this moment, and sift† her. In the meantime, wife, rip out the coronets and marks of these dozen of cambric handkerchiefs, for I can dispose of them this afternoon to a chap† in the City. [*Exit.*]

MRS PEACHUM.

Never was a man more out of the way in an argument than my husband. Why must our Polly, forsooth, differ from her sex, and love only her husband? And why must Polly's marriage, contrary to

*Temple* at the heart of the legal area
*sift* examine closely
*chap* chapman, customer

all observation, make her the less followed by other men? All men are thieves in love, and like a woman the better for being another's property.

AIR V, *Of All the Simple Things We Do, etc.*

A maid is like the golden ore,
Which hath guineas intrinsical in't,
Whose worth is never known before
It is tried and impressed in the mint.
A wife's like a guinea in gold,
Stamped with the name of her spouse,
Now here, now there, is bought, or is sold,
And is current in every house.

*Enter* Filch.

MRS PEACHUM.

Come hither, Filch. I am as fond of this child as though my mind misgave me he were my own. He hath as fine a hand at picking a pocket as a woman, and is as nimble-fingered as a juggler. If an unlucky session does not cut the rope of thy life, I pronounce, boy, thou wilt be a great man in history. Where was your post last night, my boy?

FILCH.

I plied at the opera, madam; and considering 'twas neither dark nor rainy, so that there was no great hurry in getting chairs and coaches, made a tolerable hand on't. These seven handkerchiefs, madam.

MRS PEACHUM.

Coloured ones, I see. They are of sure sale from our warehouse at Redriff† among the seamen.

FILCH.

And this snuffbox.

MRS PEACHUM.

Set in gold! A pretty encouragement this to a young beginner.

FILCH.

I had a fair tug at a charming gold watch. Pox take the tailors for making the fobs† so deep and narrow! It stuck by the way, and I was forced to make my escape under a coach. Really, madam, I fear I shall be cut off in the flower of my youth, so that every now and then (since I was pumped)† I have thoughts of taking up and going to sea.

MRS PEACHUM.

You should go to Hockley† in the Hole, and to Marybone, child, to

*Redriff* Rotherhithe, dock area
*fobs* small pockets
*pumped* punished at a street water-pump
*Hockley* area of low, violent sports

learn valour. These are the schools that have bred so many brave men. I thought, boy, by this time, thou hadst lost fear as well as shame. Poor lad! How little does he know as yet of the Old Bailey. For the first fact I'll insure thee from being hanged; and going to sea, Filch, will come time enough upon a sentence of transportation. But now, since you have nothing better to do, even go to your book, and learn your catechism; for really a man makes but an ill figure in the Ordinary's† paper, who cannot give a satisfactory answer to his questions. But, hark you, my lad. Don't tell me a lie, for you know I hate a liar. Do you know of anything that hath passed between Captain Macheath and our Polly?

FILCH.

I beg you, madam, don't ask me; for I must either tell a lie to you or to Miss Polly; for I promised her I would not tell.

MRS PEACHUM.

But when the honour of our family is concerned –

FILCH.

I shall lead a sad life with Miss Polly if ever she come to know that I told you. Besides, I would not willingly forfeit my own honour by betraying anybody.

MRS PEACHUM.

Yonder comes my husband and Polly. Come, Filch, you shall go with me into my own room, and tell me the whole story. I'll give thee a glass of a most delicious cordial that I keep for my own drinking. [*They go out*]

*Enter* Peachum *and* Polly.

POLLY.

I know as well as any of the fine ladies how to make the most of myself and of my man too. A woman knows how to be mercenary, though she hath never been in a court or at an assembly. We have it in our natures, Papa. If I allow Captain Macheath some trifling liberties, I have this watch and other visible marks of his favour to show for it. A girl who cannot grant some things, and refuse what is most material, will make but a poor hand of her beauty, and soon be thrown upon the common.

AIR VI, *What Shall I Do to Show How Much I Love Her, etc.*

Virgins are like the fair flower in its lustre,
Which in the garden enamels the ground;
Near it the bees in play flutter and cluster,
And gaudy butterflies frolic around.

*Ordinary* prison chaplain; passing his reading test could mean a lighter sentence

But, when once plucked, 'tis no longer alluring,
To Covent Garden† 'tis sent (as yet sweet),
There fades, and shrinks, and grows past all enduring,
Rots, stinks, and dies, and is trod under feet.

PEACHUM.

You know, Polly, I am not against your toying and trifling with a customer in the way of business, or to get out a secret, or so. But if I find out that you have played the fool and are married, you jade you, I'll cut your throat, hussy. Now you know my mind.

*Enter* Mrs Peachum.

AIR VII, *Oh London Is a Fine Town*

MRS PEACHUM (*in a very great passion*).

Our Polly is a sad slut, nor heeds what we have taught her.
I wonder any man alive will ever rear a daughter!
For she must have both hoods and gowns, and hoops to swell her pride,
With scarfs and stays, and gloves and lace; and she will have men beside;
And when she's dressed with care and cost, all-tempting, fine and gay,
As men should serve a cowcumber,† she flings herself away.
Our Polly is a sad slut, etc.

You baggage! You hussy! You inconsiderate jade! Had you been hanged, it would not have vexed me, for that might have been your misfortune; but to do such a mad thing by choice! The wench is married, husband.

PEACHUM.

Married! The Captain is a bold man, and will risk anything for money; to be sure he believes her a fortune. Do you think your mother and I should have lived comfortably so long together, if ever we had been married? Baggage!

MRS PEACHUM.

I knew she was always a proud slut; and now the wench hath played the fool and married, because forsooth she would do like the gentry. Can you support the expense of a husband, hussy, in gaming, drinking, and whoring? Have you money enough to carry on the daily quarrels of man and wife about who shall squander most? There are not many husbands and wives who can bear the charges of plaguing one another in a handsome way. If you must be married, could you introduce nobody into our family but a highwayman? Why, thou foolish jade, thou wilt be as ill used, and as much neglected, as if thou hadst married a lord!

---

*Covent Garden* market place, used by whores *cowcumber* regarded as worthless

PEACHUM.

Let not your anger, my dear, break through the rules of decency, for the Captain looks upon himself in the military capacity, as a gentleman by his profession. Besides what he hath already, I know he is in a fair way of getting, or of dying; and both these ways, let me tell you, are most excellent chances for a wife. Tell me, hussy, are you ruined or no?

MRS PEACHUM.

With Polly's fortune, she might very well have gone off to a person of distinction. Yes, that you might, you pouting slut!

PEACHUM.

What, is the wench dumb? Speak, or I'll make you plead by squeezing out an answer from you. Are you really bound wife to him, or are you only upon liking? (*Pinches her.*)

POLLY (*screaming*).

Oh!

MRS PEACHUM.

How the mother is to be pitied who hath handsome daughters! Locks, bolts, bars, and lectures of morality are nothing to them; they break through them all. They have as much pleasure in cheating a father and mother as in cheating at cards.

PEACHUM.

Why, Polly, I shall soon know if you are married, by Macheath's keeping from our house.

AIR VIII, *Grim King of the Ghosts, etc.*

POLLY.

Can love be controlled by advice?
Will Cupid our mothers obey?
Though my heart were as frozen as ice,
At his flame 'twould have melted away.
When he kissed me so closely he pressed,
'Twas so sweet that I must have complied;
So I thought it both safest and best
To marry, for fear you should chide.

MRS PEACHUM.

Then all the hopes of our family are gone forever and ever.

PEACHUM.

And Macheath may hang his father and mother-in-law, in hope to get into their daughter's fortune.

POLLY.

I did not marry him (as 'tis the fashion) coolly and deliberately for honour or money. But I love him.

MRS PEACHUM.

Love him! Worse and worse! I thought the girl had been better bred. Oh husband, husband! Her folly makes me mad! My head swims!

I'm distracted! I can't support myself. – Oh! *Faints.*

PEACHUM.

See, wench, to what a condition you have reduced your poor mother. A glass of cordial, this instant. How the poor woman takes it to heart. Ah, hussy, now this is the only comfort your mother has left.

POLLY.

Give her another glass, sir; my mama drinks double the quantity whenever she is out of order. This, you see, fetches her.

MRS PEACHUM.

The girl shows such a readiness, and so much concern, that I could almost find in my heart to forgive her.

AIR IX, *Oh Jenny, Oh Jenny, Where Hast Thou Been*

Oh Polly, you might have toyed and kissed.
By keeping men off, you keep them on.

POLLY. But he so teased me,
And he so pleased me,
What I did, you must have done.

MRS PEACHUM.

Not with a highwayman. You sorry slut!

PEACHUM.

A word with you, wife. 'Tis no new thing for a wench to take man without consent of parents. You know 'tis the frailty of woman, my dear.

MRS PEACHUM.

Yes, indeed, the sex is frail. But the first time a woman is frail, she should be somewhat nice† methinks, for then or never is the time to make her fortune. After that, she hath nothing to do but to guard herself from being found out, and she may do what she pleases.

PEACHUM.

Make yourself a little easy; I have a thought shall soon set all matters again to rights. Why so melancholy, Polly? Since what is done cannot be undone, we must all endeavour to make the best of it.

MRS PEACHUM.

Well, Polly, as far as one woman can forgive another, I forgive thee. Your father is too fond of you, hussy.

POLLY.

Then all my sorrows are at an end.

MRS PEACHUM.

A mighty likely speech in troth, for a wench who is just married!

*nice* fastidious

AIR X, *Thomas, I Cannot, etc.*

POLLY.
I, like a ship in storms, was tossed;
Yet afraid to put in to land;
For seized in the port the vessel's lost
Whose treasure is contraband.
The waves are laid,
My duty's paid.
Oh joy beyond expression!
Thus, safe ashore,
I ask no more,
My all is in my possession.

PEACHUM.
I hear customers in t'other room. Go, talk with 'em, Polly, but come to us again as soon as they are gone. But hark ye, child: If 'tis the gentleman† who was here yesterday about the repeating watch, say you believe we can't get intelligence of it till tomorrow. For I lent it to Suky Straddle, to make a figure with it tonight at a tavern in Drury Lane. If t'other gentleman calls for the silver-hilted sword, you know Beetle-Browed Jemmy hath it on; and he doth not come from Tunbridge till Tuesday night, so that it cannot be had till then. [*Exit* Polly.]

PEACHUM.
Dear wife, be a little pacified. Don't let your passion run away with your senses. Polly, I grant you, hath done a rash thing.

MRS PEACHUM.
If she had had only an intrigue with the fellow, why the very best families have excused and huddled up a frailty of that sort. 'Tis marriage, husband, that makes it a blemish.

PEACHUM.
But money, wife, is the true fuller's earth for reputations; there is not a spot or a stain but what it can take out. A rich rogue nowadays is fit company for any gentleman; and the world, my dear, hath not such a contempt for roguery as you imagine. I tell you, wife, I can make this match turn to our advantage.

MRS PEACHUM.
I am very sensible, husband, that Captain Macheath is worth money, but I am in doubt whether he hath not two or three wives already, and then if he should die in a session or two, Polly's dower† would come into dispute.

---

*gentleman* who offers a reward for his stolen watch

*dower* a widow's material support (jointure)

PEACHUM.

That, indeed, is a point which ought to be considered.

AIR XI, *A Soldier and a Sailor*

A fox may steal your hens, sir,
A whore your health and pence, sir,
Your daughter rob your chest, sir,
Your wife may steal your rest, sir,
  A thief your goods and plate.
But this is all but picking,
With rest, pence, chest, and chicken;
It ever was decreed, sir,
If lawyer's hand is fee'd, sir,
  He steals your whole estate.

The lawyers are bitter enemies to those in our way. They don't care that anybody should get a clandestine livelihood but themselves.

*Enter* Polly.

POLLY.

'Twas only Nimming Ned. He brought in a damask window curtain, a hoop-petticoat, a pair of silver candlesticks, a periwig, and one silk stocking, from the fire that happened last night.

PEACHUM.

There is not a fellow that is cleverer in his way, and saves more goods out of the fire, than Ned. But now, Polly, to your affair; for matters must not be left as they are. You are married then, it seems?

POLLY.

Yes, sir.

PEACHUM.

And how do you propose to live, child?

POLLY.

Like other women, sir, upon the industry of my husband.

MRS PEACHUM.

What, is the wench turned fool? A highwayman's wife, like a soldier's, hath as little of his pay as of his company.

PEACHUM.

And had not you the common views of a gentlewoman in your marriage, Polly?

POLLY.

I don't know what you mean, sir.

PEACHUM.

Of a jointure, and of being a widow.

POLLY.

But I love him, sir. How then could I have thoughts of parting with him?

PEACHUM.

Parting with him! Why, that is the whole scheme and intention of all marriage articles. The comfortable estate of widowhood is the only hope that keeps up a wife's spirits. Where is the woman who would scruple to be a wife, if she had it in her power to be a widow whenever she pleased? If you have any views of this sort, Polly, I shall think the match not so very unreasonable.

POLLY.

How I dread to hear your advice! Yet I must beg you to explain yourself.

PEACHUM.

Secure what he hath got, have him peached† the next sessions, and then at once you are made a rich widow.

POLLY.

What, murder the man I love! The blood runs cold at my heart with the very thought of it.

PEACHUM.

Fie, Polly! What hath murder to do in the affair? Since the thing sooner or later must happen, I dare say, the Captain himself would like that we should get the reward for his death sooner than a stranger. Why, Polly, the Captain knows that as 'tis his employment to rob, so 'tis ours to take robbers. Every man in his business. So that there is no malice in the case.

MRS PEACHUM.

Ay, husband, now you have nicked† the matter. To have him peached is the only thing could ever make me forgive her.

AIR XII, *Now Ponder Well, Ye Parents Dear*

POLLY.

Oh, ponder well! Be not severe;
So save a wretched wife!
For on the rope that hangs my dear
Depends† poor Polly's life.

MRS PEACHUM.

But your duty to your parents, hussy, obliges you to hang him. What would many a wife give for such an opportunity.

POLLY.

What is a jointure, what is widowhood to me? I know my heart. I cannot survive him.

AIR XIII, *Le Printemps Rappelle aux Armes* [Spring Calls to Arms]

The turtle† thus with plaintive crying,
Her lover dying,

*peached* informed on
*nicked* hit exactly
*depends* (Latin) hangs
*turtle* dove

The turtle thus with plaintive crying
Laments her dove.
Down she drops quite spent with sighing
Paired in death, as paired in love.

Thus, sir, it will happen to your poor Polly.

MRS PEACHUM.

What, is the fool in love in earnest then? I hate thee for being particular. Why, wench, thou art a shame to thy very sex.

POLLY.

But hear me, mother. If you ever loved –

MRS PEACHUM.

Those cursed playbooks she reads have been her ruin. One word more, hussy, and I shall knock your brains out, if you have any.

PEACHUM.

Keep out of the way, Polly, for fear of mischief, and consider of what is proposed to you.

MRS PEACHUM.

Away, hussy. Hang your husband, and be dutiful.

[*Exit* Polly *to a hiding place listening*]

MRS PEACHUM.

The thing, husband, must and shall be done. For the sake of intelligence we must take other measures, and have him peached the next session without her consent. If she will not know her duty, we know ours.

PEACHUM.

But really, my dear, it grieves one's heart to take off a great man. When I consider his personal bravery, his fine stratagem, how much we have already got by him, and how much more we may get, methinks I can't find in my heart to have a hand in his death. I wish you could have made Polly undertake it.

MRS PEACHUM.

But in a case of necessity – our own lives are in danger.

PEACHUM.

Then, indeed, we must comply with the customs of the world, and make gratitude give way to interest. He shall be taken off.

MRS PEACHUM.

I'll undertake to manage Polly.

PEACHUM.

And I'll prepare matters for the Old Bailey. [*they go out*]

POLLY.

Now I'm a wretch, indeed. Methinks I see him already in the cart, sweeter and more lovely than the nosegay† in his hand. I hear the

*nosegay* bunch of flowers

crowd extolling his resolution and intrepidity. What volleys of sighs are sent from the windows of Holborn† that so comely a youth should be brought to disgrace. I see him at the tree! The whole circle are in tears! Even butchers weep! Jack Ketch himself hesitates to perform his duty, and would be glad to lose his fee by a reprieve. What then will become of Polly? – As yet I may inform him of their design, and aid him in his escape. It shall be so. But then he flies, absents himself, and I bar myself from his dear, dear conversation. That too will distract me. If he keep out of the way, my papa and mama may in time relent, and we may be happy. If he stays, he is hanged, and then he is lost forever! He intended to lie concealed in my room till the dusk of the evening. If they are abroad, I'll this instant let him out, lest some accident should prevent him.

*Exit, and returns with* Macheath.

AIR XIV, *Pretty Parrot, Say*

MACHEATH.
Pretty Polly, say,
When I was away,
Did your fancy never stray
To some newer lover?

POLLY.
Without disguise,
Heaving sighs,
Doting eyes,
My constant heart discover.
Fondly let me loll!

MACHEATH.
Oh pretty, pretty Poll.

POLLY.
And are you as fond as ever, my dear?

MACHEATH.
Suspect my honour, my courage, suspect anything but my love. May my pistols miss fire, and my mare slip her shoulder while I am pursued, if I ever forsake thee.

POLLY.
Nay, my dear, I have no reason to doubt you, for I find in the romance you lent me, none of the great heroes were ever false in love.

AIR XV, *Pray, Fair One, Be Kind*

MACHEATH.
My heart was so free,
It roved like the bee,
Till Polly my passion requited;

---

*Holborn* on the route from Newgate to Tyburn gallows

I sipped each flower,
I changed every hour,
But here every flower is united.

POLLY.

Were you sentenced to transportation, sure, my dear, you could not leave me behind you, could you?

MACHEATH.

Is there any power, any force that could tear me from thee? You might sooner tear a pension out of the hands of a courtier, a fee from a lawyer, a pretty woman from a looking glass, or any woman from quadrille. But to tear me from thee is impossible.

AIR XVI, *Over the Hills and Far Away*

Were I laid on Greenland's coast,
And in my arms embraced my lass:
Warm amidst eternal frost,
Too soon the half year's night would pass.
POLLY. Were I sold† on Indian soil
Soon as the burning day was closed,
I could mock the sultry toil,
When on my charmer's breast reposed.
MACHEATH. And I would love you all the day,
POLLY. Every night would kiss and play,
MACHEATH. If with me you'd fondly stray
POLLY. Over the hills and far away.

Yes, I would go with thee. But oh, how shall I speak it? I must be torn from thee. We must part.

MACHEATH.

How? Part?

POLLY.

We must, we must. My papa and mama are set against thy life. They now, even now, are in search after thee. They are preparing evidence against thee. Thy life depends upon a moment.

AIR XVII, *Gin Thou Wert Mine Awn Thing*

Oh what pain it is to part!
Can I leave thee, can I leave thee?
Oh what pain it is to part!
Can thy Polly ever leave thee?
But lest death my love should thwart,
And bring thee to the fatal cart,

*sold* as a slave

Thus I tear thee from my bleeding heart!
Fly hence, and let me leave thee.

One kiss and then – one kiss – begone – farewell.

MACHEATH.

My hand, my heart, my dear, is so riveted to thine, that I cannot unloose my hold.

POLLY.

But my papa may intercept thee, and then I should lose the very glimmering of hope. A few weeks, perhaps, may reconcile us all. Shall thy Polly hear from thee?

MACHEATH.

Must I then go?

POLLY.

And will not absence change your love?

MACHEATH.

If you doubt it, let me stay, and be hanged.

POLLY.

Oh how I fear! How I tremble! Go, but when safety will give you leave, you will be sure to see me again; for till then Polly is wretched.

[*Parting, and looking back at each other with fondness; he at one door, she at the other.*]

AIR XVIII, *Oh, the Broom, etc.*

MACHEATH. The miser thus a shilling sees,
Which he's obliged to pay,
With sighs resigns it by degrees,
And fears 'tis gone for aye.

POLLY. The boy thus, when his sparrow's flown,
The bird in silence eyes;
But soon as out of sight 'tis gone,
Whines, whimpers, sobs, and cries. [*both go out*]

[*End of the First Act.*]

1728

# Alexander Pope

## 1688–1744

After a retired childhood in Windsor Forest, under the double disability of retarded growth from chronic ill-health and of Catholic parentage in an age of civil penalties, Pope showed precocious talent in his *Pastorals* (1709) and *Essay on Criticism* (1711); *The Rape of the Lock* (1714, enlarged version) placed him at the forefront of contemporary poetry, while he became associated with the wits and satirists of the Scriblerus Club (Gay, Swift, Arbuthnot). His translation of Homer's *Iliad* (1715–20) established his financial security, permitting his long residence at Twickenham (then well outside London), where by the river he built up his famous garden and grotto, which show his interest in the visual arts. Despite his friendships with literary men, and with Martha Blount and Lady Mary Wortley Montagu (see p. 256), his growing fame and his collaboration in the Scriblerian ridicule of bad writing increasingly involved him in literary warfare: Theobald criticised his edition of Shakespeare and was enthroned in *The Dunciad* (1728; revised in four books with C. Cibber as hero, 1743). Partly under the influence of the former politician Henry St John, Viscount Bolingbroke, Pope produced *An Essay on Man* (1733–4); the four *Moral Essays* (1731–5) are epistles to friends on appropriate topics. Also in the 1730s, he cultivated *Imitations of Horace*, in which he fruitfully exploits the parallels between his situation and the Roman satirist's, to criticise the decay of morality and literature, opposing the life of retired contemplation and friendship to the money-grubbing and corruption of business and public life: the *Epistle to Dr. Arbuthnot* stands as the prologue to these satires.

Pope laboured to refine the verse techniques inherited from Dryden, and attempted the traditional genres from pastoral to epic (mock, in his case). His great satires transcend personal animosity in their traditional concern to expose deviation from sound social and moral values. The romantic reaction against the heroic couplet reached its apogee in Matthew Arnold's verdict (1880) that 'Dryden and Pope are not classics of our poetry, they are classics of our prose'.

# *From* AN ESSAY ON CRITICISM

## *[Poetic Technique]*[†]

But most by numbers* judge a poet's song, versification
And smooth or rough, with them, is right or wrong;
In the bright Muse though thousand charms conspire,
Her voice is all these tuneful fools admire,
Who haunt Parnassus[†] but to please their ear,
Not mend their minds; as some to church repair,
Not for the doctrine, but the music there.
These *equal syllables* alone require,
Though oft the ear the *open vowels*[†] tire,
While *expletives*[†] their feeble aid *do* join,
And ten low words oft creep in one dull line,
While they ring round the same unvaried chimes,
With sure returns of still expected rhymes.
Where'er you find *the cooling western breeze*,
In the next line, it *whispers through the trees*;
If *crystal streams with pleasing murmurs creep*,
The reader's threatened (not in vain) with *sleep*.
Then, at the last and only couplet fraught
With some unmeaning thing they call a thought,
A *needless Alexandrine*[†] ends the song,
That, like a wounded snake, drags its slow length along.
Leave such to tune their own dull rhymes, and know
What's *roundly smooth*, or *languishingly slow*;
And praise the *easy vigour* of a line,
Where Denham's strength and Waller's[†] sweetness join.
True ease in writing comes from art, not chance,
As those move easiest who have learned to dance.
'Tis not enough no harshness gives offence,
The sound must seem an echo to the sense.
*Soft* is the strain when *Zephyr*[†] gently blows,
And the *smooth stream* in *smoother numbers* flows;
But when loud surges lash the sounding shore,
The *hoarse, rough verse* should like the torrent roar.

[*Poetic Technique*] Pope here imitates tricks of feeble verse-writing and contrasts his own virtuoso repertoire. His original italics are partly retained to emphasise his effects

*Parnassus* Mount of the Muses in Greece

*open vowels* as the 'o' sounds here

*expletives* words merely padding out the line, as *do*

*Alexandrine* a line of six, not the usual five, iambic feet, e.g. l.357

*Denham's . . . Waller's* Sir John Denham (1615–69) and Edmund Waller (1606–87), praised by Dryden for their metrical reforms

*Zephyr* west wind; the easy movement of ll.366–7 contrasts with 368–71

When Ajax† strives, some rock's vast weight to throw,
The line too *labours*, and the words move *slow*:
Not so, when swift Camilla† scours the plain,
Flies o'er th' unbending corn, and skims along the main. . . .

*c.* 1709 1711

## *From* WINDSOR FOREST†

### *[Order in Variety]*

The groves of Eden, vanished now so long,
Live in description, and look green in song:
These, were my breast inspired with equal flame,
Like them in beauty, should be like in fame.
Here hills and vales, the woodland and the plain,
Here earth and water seem to strive again,
Not chaos-like together crushed and bruised,
But, as the world, harmoniously confused:
Where order in variety we see,
And where, though all things differ, all agree.
Here waving groves a chequered scene display,
And part admit and part exclude the day;
As some coy nymph her lover's warm address
Nor quite indulges, nor can quite repress.
There, interspersed in lawns and opening glades,
Thin trees arise that shun each other's shades.
Here in full light the russet plains extend;
There wrapped in clouds the bluish hills ascend:
Even the wild heath displays her purple dyes,
And midst the desert fruitful fields arise,
That, crowned with tufted trees and springing corn,
Like verdant isles the sable waste adorn.
Let India boast her plants, nor envy we
The weeping amber† or the balmy tree,

*Ajax* Greek hero in Trojan War
*Camilla* Princess in *Aeneid*, VII.808, light of foot
*Windsor Forest* Pope, brought up in the Forest, exploits its royal associations to chart the growth of harmony and prosperity, illustrating the aesthetic principle of 'order in variety'. His descriptions blend terms of nature and art ('dye', 'painted')
*amber* like balm, a valuable resin, imported in ships of English oak, on which colonial power depended

While by our oaks the precious loads are borne,
And realms commanded which those trees adorn.
Not proud Olympus[†] yields a nobler sight,
Though gods assembled grace his towering height,
Than what more humble mountains offer here,
Where, in their blessings, all those gods appear.
See Pan with flocks, with fruits Pomona crowned,
Here blushing Flora paints th' enamelled ground,[†]
Here Ceres'[†] gifts in waving prospect stand,
And nodding tempt the joyful reaper's hand;
Rich Industry sits smiling on the plains,
And peace and plenty tell, a Stuart[†] reigns. . . .

## *[Man's Victims]*

See! from the brake* the whirring pheasant springs, thicket
And mounts exulting on triumphant wings;
Short is his joy! he feels the fiery wound,
Flutters in blood, and panting beats the ground.
Ah! what avail his glossy, varying dyes,
His purple crest, and scarlet-circled eyes,
The vivid green his shining plumes unfold,
His painted wings, and breast that flames with gold?
Nor yet, when moist Arcturus[†] clouds the sky,
The woods and fields their pleasing toils deny.
To plains with well-breathed beagles we repair,
And trace the mazes of the circling hare.
(Beasts, urged by us, their fellow beasts pursue,
And learn of man each other to undo.)
With slaughtering guns th'unwearyed fowler roves,
When frosts have whitened all the naked groves;
Where doves in flocks the leafless trees o'ershade,
And lonely woodcocks haunt the watery glade.
He lifts the tube,[†] and levels with his eye;
Strait a short thunder breaks the frozen sky.
Oft as in airy rings they skim the heath,
The clamorous lapwings feel the leaden death:

*Olympus* Mount of the gods, in Greece
*Flora . . . ground* goddess of flowers, which adorn the 'ground', surface prepared for painting
*Ceres* goddess of corn
*a Stuart* Queen Anne (reigned 1702–14), the last Stuart monarch
*Arcturus* star in the constellation of the Great Bear
*tube* barrel of gun, firing lead shot

Oft as the mounting larks their notes prepare,
They fall, and leave their little lives in air.
  In genial† spring, beneath the quivering shade
Where cooling vapours breathe along the mead,
The patient fisher takes his silent stand
Intent, his angle trembling in his hand;
With looks unmoved, he hopes the scaly breed,†
And eyes the dancing cork and bending reed.
Our plenteous streams a various race supply:
The bright-eyed perch with fins of Tyrian† dye,
The silver eel, in shining volumes* rolled,    *coils*
The yellow carp, in scales bedropped with gold,
Swift trouts, diversified with crimson stains,
And pikes, the tyrants of the watery plains. . . .

1704      1713

# THE RAPE OF THE LOCK†

## *Canto I*

  What dire offence† from amorous causes springs,
What mighty contests rise from trivial things,
I sing – This verse to Caryll, Muse! is due;
This, even Belinda may vouchsafe to view:
Slight is the subject, but not so the praise,
If she inspire, and he approve my lays.
  Say what strange motive, Goddess! could compel
A well-bred lord t' assault a gentle belle?
Oh, say what stranger cause, yet unexplored,
Could make a gentle belle reject a lord?

---

*genial* pleasant, healthful
*scaly breed* poetic diction for fish
*Tyrian* a famous purple
*The Rape of the Lock* Pope's friend John Caryll (l.3) hoped he might laugh away the quarrel caused when Lord Petre cut a lock of hair from Arabella Fermor ('Belinda'). The two-canto version of 1712 was expanded by the 'machinery' and further incidents into five cantos in 1714; Clarissa's speech in Canto V was added in 1717. The poem continually juxtaposes the trivial modern action with the mock-heroic manner: the speeches, battles, descent to the underworld, are epic in origin, with many echoes of the *Iliad*, *Aeneid*, and *Paradise Lost*; but the comparison is not entirely to the discredit of the modern world
*dire offence* begins by traditional epic statement of the subject

In tasks so bold can little men engage,
And in soft bosoms dwells such mighty rage?
Sol through white curtains shot a timorous ray,
And oped those eyes that must eclipse the day;
Now lapdogs give themselves the rousing shake,
And sleepless lovers just at twelve awake:
Thrice rung the bell, the slipper knocked the ground,
And the pressed watch† returned a silver sound.
Belinda still her downy pillow pressed,
Her guardian Sylph† prolonged the balmy rest:
'Twas he had summoned to her silent bed
The morning dream that hovered o'er her head.
A youth more glittering than a birthnight beau†
(That even in slumber caused her cheek to glow)
Seemed to her ear his winning lips to lay,
And thus in whispers said, or seemed to say:
'Fairest of mortals, thou distinguished care
Of thousand bright inhabitants of air!
If e'er one vision touched thy infant thought,
Of all the nurse and all the priest have taught,
Of airy elves by moonlight shadows seen,
The silver token, and the circled green,†
Or virgins visited by angel powers,
With golden crowns and wreaths of heavenly flowers,
Hear and believe! thy own importance know,
Nor bound thy narrow views to things below.
Some secret truths, from learned pride concealed,
To maids alone and children are revealed:
What though no credit doubting wits may give?
The fair and innocent shall still believe.
Know then unnumbered spirits round thee fly,
The light militia of the lower sky;
These, though unseen, are ever on the wing,
Hang o'er the box,† and hover round the Ring.†
Think what an equipage thou hast in air,
And view with scorn two pages and a chair.†
As now your own, our beings were of old,
And once enclosed in woman's beauteous mould;

*pressed watch* it indicates each quarter-hour by chiming
*Sylph* a spirit of the air (as gnomes of earth, nymphs of water, salamanders of fire), with a hint of 'guardian angel'
*birthnight beau* Courtier in magnificent attire for the sovereign's birthday
*circled green* marks left on grass by fairies
*box* in theatre
*Ring* fashionable circular drive in Hyde Park
*chair* sedan chair, for carrying passengers

Thence, by a soft transition, we repair
From earthly vehicles to these of air.
Think not, when woman's transient breath is fled,
That all her vanities at once are dead:
Succeeding vanities she still regards,
And, though she plays no more, o'erlooks the cards.
Her joy in gilded chariots,† when alive,
And love of ombre,† after death survive.
For when the fair in all their pride expire,
To their first elements† their souls retire:
The sprites of fiery termagants in flame
Mount up, and take a Salamander's name.
Soft yielding minds to water glide away,
And sip with Nymphs their elemental tea.
The graver prude sinks downward to a Gnome,
In search of mischief still on earth to roam.
The light coquettes in Sylphs aloft repair,
And sport and flutter in the fields of air.
'Know further yet; whoever fair and chaste
Rejects mankind, is by some Sylph embraced:
For spirits, freed from mortal laws, with ease
Assume what sexes and what shapes they please.
What guards the purity of melting maids,
In courtly balls and midnight masquerades,
Safe from the treacherous friend, the daring spark,†
The glance by day, the whisper in the dark,
When kind occasion prompts their warm desires,
When music softens, and when dancing fires?
'Tis but their Sylph, the wise Celestials know,
Though Honour is the word with men below.
'Some nymphs there are, too conscious of their face,
For life predestined to the Gnomes' embrace.
These swell their prospects and exalt their pride,
When offers are disdained, and love denied.
Then gay ideas crowd the vacant brain,
While peers and dukes, and all their sweeping train,
And garters,† stars, and coronets† appear,
And in soft sounds, "your Grace" salutes their ear.
'Tis these that early taint the female soul,
Instruct the eyes of young coquettes to roll,

*chariot* pleasure carriage
*ombre* the card game played in Canto III
*elements* earth, air, fire, water: basic constituents of matter
*spark* a lively man, a lover
*garters . . . coronets* the externals of aristocratic rank

Teach infant cheeks a bidden blush to know,
And little hearts to flutter at a beau.
'Oft when the world imagine women stray,
The Sylphs through mystic mazes guide their way,
Through all the giddy circle they pursue,
And old impertinence expel by new.
What tender maid but must a victim fall
To one man's treat, but for another's ball?
When Florio speaks, what virgin could withstand,
If gentle Damon did not squeeze her hand?
With varying vanities, from every part,
They shift the moving toyshop of their heart;
Where wigs with wigs, with sword-knots† sword-knots strive,
Beaux banish beaux, and coaches coaches drive.
This erring mortals levity may call;
Oh blind to truth! the Sylphs contrive it all.
'Of these am I, who thy protection claim,
A watchful sprite, and Ariel is my name.
Late, as I ranged the crystal wilds of air,
In the clear mirror of thy ruling star
I saw, alas! some dread event impend,
Ere to the main this morning sun descend,
But Heaven reveals not what, or how, or where:
Warned by the Sylph, Oh pious maid, beware!
This to disclose is all thy guardian can:
Beware of all, but most beware of Man!'
He said; when Shock,† who thought she slept too long,
Leaped up, and waked his mistress with his tongue.
'Twas then, Belinda, if report say true,
Thy eyes first opened on a billet-doux;
Wounds, charms, and ardours were no sooner read,
But all the vision vanished from thy head.
And now, unveiled, the toilet† stands displayed,
Each silver vase in mystic order laid.
First, robed in white, the nymph intent adores,
With head uncovered, the cosmetic powers.
A heavenly image in the glass appears;
To that she bends, to that her eyes she rears;
Th' inferior priestess,† at her altar's side,
Trembling begins the sacred rites of pride.

*sword-knots* decorative ribbons on sword hilt
*Shock* a shough, rough-haired lap-dog
*toilet* the dressing-table, an altar at which Belinda worships her own image. After the epic dream-warning, Pope parodies religious ritual and the arming of the hero
*inferior priestess* the maid, commonly called Betty (l.148)

Unnumbered treasures ope at once, and here
The various offerings of the world appear;
From each she nicely culls with curious toil,
And decks the goddess with the glittering spoil.
This casket India's glowing gems unlocks,
And all Arabia† breathes from yonder box.
The tortoise here and elephant unite,
Transformed to combs, the speckled and the white.
Here files of pins extend their shining rows,
Puffs, powders, patches,† bibles, billet-doux.
Now awful beauty puts on all its arms;
The fair each moment rises in her charms,
Repairs her smiles, awakens every grace,
And calls forth all the wonders of her face;
Sees by degrees a purer blush arise,
And keener lightnings quicken in her eyes.
The busy Sylphs surround their darling care;
These set the head, and those divide the hair,
Some fold the sleeve, whilst others plait the gown;
And Betty's praised for labours not her own.

## *Canto II*

Not with more glories, in th' ethereal plain,
The sun first rises o'er the purpled main,
Than, issuing forth, the rival of his beams
Launched on the bosom of the silver Thames.
Fair nymphs and well-dressed youths around her shone,
But every eye was fixed on her alone.
On her white breast a sparkling cross she wore,
Which Jews might kiss, and infidels adore.
Her lively looks a sprightly mind disclose,
Quick as her eyes, and as unfixed as those:
Favours to none, to all she smiles extends;
Oft she rejects, but never once offends.
Bright as the sun, her eyes the gazers strike,
And, like the sun, they shine on all alike.
Yet graceful ease, and sweetness void of pride,
Might hide her faults, if belles had faults to hide:

*Arabia* eastern perfumes; the combs are of tortoise-shell and ivory

*patches* artificial beauty-spots

If to her share some female errors fall,
Look on her face, and you'll forget 'em all.
This nymph, to the destruction of mankind,
Nourished two locks, which graceful hung behind
In equal curls, and well conspired to deck
With shining ringlets the smooth ivory neck.
Love in these labyrinths his slaves detains,
And mighty hearts are held in slender chains.
With hairy springes† we the birds betray,
Slight lines of hair surprise the finny prey,
Fair tresses man's imperial race ensnare,
And beauty draws us with a single hair.
Th' adventurous Baron the bright locks admired,
He saw, he wished, and to the prize aspired:
Resolved to win, he meditates the way,
By force to ravish, or by fraud betray;
For when success a lover's toil attends,
Few ask if fraud or force attained his ends.
For this, ere Phoebus rose, he had implored
Propitious Heaven, and every power adored,
But chiefly Love – to Love an altar built,
Of twelve vast French romances,† neatly gilt.
There lay three garters, half a pair of gloves,
And all the trophies of his former loves.
With tender billet-doux he lights the pyre,
And breathes three amorous sighs to raise the fire.
Then prostrate falls, and begs with ardent eyes
Soon to obtain, and long possess the prize:
The powers gave ear, and granted half his prayer,
The rest, the winds dispersed in empty air.
But now secure the painted vessel glides,
The sunbeams trembling on the floating tides,
While melting music steals upon the sky,
And softened sounds along the waters die.
Smooth flow the waves, the zephyrs gently play,
Belinda smiled, and all the world was gay.
All but the Sylph – with careful thoughts oppressed,
Th' impending woe sat heavy on his breast.
He summons straight his denizens of air;
The lucid squadrons round the sails repair:

*springes* snares (two syllables)
*French romances* long love stories, bound in gold-stamped leather

Soft o'er the shrouds aërial whispers breathe,
That seemed but zephyrs to the train beneath.
Some to the sun their insect-wings unfold,
Waft on the breeze, or sink in clouds of gold.
Transparent forms too fine for mortal sight,
Their fluid bodies half dissolved in light.
Loose to the wind their airy garments flew,
Thin glittering textures of the filmy dew,
Dipped in the richest tincture of the skies,
Where light disports in ever-mingling dyes,
While every beam new transient colours flings,
Colours that change whene'er they wave their wings.
Amid the circle, on the gilded mast,
Superior† by the head was Ariel placed;
His purple pinions opening to the sun,
He raised his azure wand, and thus begun:
'Ye Sylphs and Sylphids, to your chief give ear!
Fays, Fairies, Genii, Elves, and Daemons, hear!
Ye know the spheres and various tasks assigned
By laws eternal to th' aërial kind.
Some in the fields of purest ether play,
And bask and whiten in the blaze of day.
Some guide the course of wandering orbs on high,
Or roll the planets through the boundless sky.
Some less refined, beneath the moon's pale light
Pursue the stars that shoot athwart the night,
Or suck the mists in grosser air below,
Or dip their pinions in the painted bow,
Or brew fierce tempests on the wintry main,
Or o'er the glebe† distill the kindly rain.
Others on earth o'er human race preside,
Watch all their ways, and all their actions guide:
Of these the chief the care of nations own,
And guard with arms divine the British Throne.
'Our humbler province is to tend the fair,
Not a less pleasing, though less glorious care:
To save the powder from too rude a gale,
Nor let th' imprisoned essences exhale;
To draw fresh colours from the vernal flowers,
To steal from rainbows e'er they drop in showers

*superior* taller: Ariel's attributes and speech again suggest the epic hero

*glebe* cultivated land

A brighter wash; to curl their waving hairs,
Assist their blushes, and inspire their airs;
Nay oft, in dreams invention we bestow,
To change a flounce, or add a furbelow.†
'This day, black omens threat the brightest fair
That e'er deserved a watchful spirit's care;
Some dire disaster, or by force or slight,
But what, or where, the Fates have wrapped in night:
Whether the nymph shall break Diana's law,†
Or some frail china jar receive a flaw,
Or stain her honour or her new brocade,
Forget her prayers, or miss a masquerade,
Or lose her heart, or necklace, at a ball;
Or whether Heaven has doomed that Shock must fall.
Haste then ye spirits! to your charge repair:
The fluttering fan be Zephyretta's care;
The drops† to thee, Brillante, we consign;
And, Momentilla, let the watch be thine;
Do thou, Crispissa, tend her favourite lock;
Ariel himself shall be the guard of Shock.
'To fifty chosen Sylphs, of special note,
We trust th' important charge, the petticoat;
Oft have we known that sevenfold fence to fail,
Though stiff with hoops, and armed with ribs of whale.†
Form a strong line about the silver bound,
And guard the wide circumference around.
'Whatever spirit, careless of his charge,
His post neglects, or leaves the fair at large,
Shall feel sharp vengeance soon o'ertake his sins,
Be stopped in vials, or transfixed with pins;
Or plunged in lakes of bitter washes lie,
Or wedged whole ages in a bodkin's* eye; needle
Gums and pomatums† shall his flight restrain,
While clogged he beats his silken wings in vain;
Or alum styptics† with contracting power
Shrink his thin essence like a rivelled flower:
Or, as Ixion† fixed, the wretch shall feel
The giddy motion of the whirling mill,

*furbelow* ruffle on a lady's gown
*Diana's law* Diana was goddess of chastity
*drops* diamond earrings
*whale* petticoats were elaborately constructed
*pomatums* hair ointments
*styptics* astringents; the domestic objects contrast with the epic threats
*Ixion* mythical Greek seducer, bound in hell to a moving wheel

In fumes of burning chocolate shall glow,
And tremble at the sea that froths below!'
  He spoke; the spirits from the sails descend;
Some, orb in orb, around the nymph extend;
Some thread the mazy ringlets of her hair,
Some hang upon the pendants of her ear;
With beating hearts the dire event they wait,
Anxious, and trembling for the birth of Fate.

## *Canto III*

  Close by those meads forever crowned with flowers,
Where Thames with pride surveys his rising towers,
There stands a structure† of majestic frame,
Which from the neighbouring Hampton takes its name.
Here Britain's statesmen oft the fall foredoom
Of foreign tyrants, and of nymphs at home;
Here thou, great Anna! whom three realms obey,
Dost sometimes counsel take – and sometimes tea.†
  Hither the heroes and the nymphs resort,
To taste awhile the pleasures of a court;
In various talk th' instructive hours they passed,
Who gave the ball, or paid the visit last;
One speaks the glory of the British Queen,
And one describes a charming Indian screen;
A third interprets motions, looks, and eyes;
At every word a reputation dies.
Snuff, or the fan, supply each pause of chat,
With singing, laughing, ogling, and all that.
  Meanwhile, declining from the noon of day,
The sun obliquely shoots his burning ray;
The hungry judges soon the sentence sign,
And wretches hang that jurymen may dine;
The merchant from th' Exchange returns in peace,
And the long labours of the toilet cease.
Belinda now, whom thirst of fame invites,
Burns to encounter two adventurous knights,
At ombre† singly to decide their doom,

*structure* Hampton Court Palace, upriver from London; Queen Anne ruled until 1714
*tea* pronounced 'tay'
*ombre . . . Codille* ombre, presented as an epic battle, a game for three players with nine cards each. The *Matadores* (highest cards) are *Spadillio* (ace of spades), *Manillio* (two of spades), *Basto* (ace of clubs); *Pam* (knave of clubs) is the highest in loo, another card game. The *amazon* is the warlike queen of spades; *Codille*: defeat

And swells her breast with conquests yet to come.
Straight the three bands prepare in arms to join,
Each band the number of the sacred nine.
Soon as she spreads her hand, th' aërial guard
Descend, and sit on each important card:
First Ariel perched upon a Matadore,†
Then each according to the rank they bore;
For Sylphs, yet mindful of their ancient race,
Are, as when women, wondrous fond of place.
  Behold, four Kings in majesty revered,
With hoary whiskers and a forky beard;
And four fair Queens whose hands sustain a flower,
Th' expressive emblem of their softer power;
Four Knaves in garbs succinct, a trusty band,
Caps on their heads, and halberds in their hand;
And particoloured troops, a shining train,
Draw forth to combat on the velvet plain.
  The skilful nymph reviews her force with care;
'Let Spades be trumps!' she said, and trumps they were.
  Now move to war her sable Matadores,
In show like leaders of the swarthy Moors.
Spadillio† first, unconquerable lord!
Led off two captive trumps, and swept the board.
As many more Manillio† forced to yield,
And marched a victor from the verdant field.
Him Basto† followed, but his fate more hard
Gained but one trump and one plebian card.
With his broad sabre next, a chief in years,
The hoary Majesty of Spades appears,
Puts forth one manly leg, to sight revealed,
The rest his many-coloured robe concealed.
The rebel Knave, who dares his prince engage,
Proves the just victim of his royal rage.
Even mighty Pam,† that kings and queens o'erthrew
And mowed down armies in the fights of loo,
Sad chance of war! now destitute of aid,
Falls undistinguished by the victor Spade.
  Thus far both armies to Belinda yield;
Now to the Baron fate inclines the field.
His warlike amazon† her host invades,
Th' imperial consort of the crown of Spades.
The Club's black tyrant first her victim died,
Spite of his haughty mien and barbarous pride:

What boots the regal circle on his head,
His giant limbs in state unwieldy spread?
That long behind he trails his pompous robe,
And of all monarchs only grasps the globe?
  The Baron now his Diamonds pours apace;
Th' embroidered King who shows but half his face,
And his refulgent Queen, with powers combined,
Of broken troops an easy conquest find.
Clubs, Diamonds, Hearts, in wild disorder seen,
With throngs promiscuous strew the level green.
Thus when dispersed a routed army runs,
Of Asia's troops, and Afric's sable sons,
With like confusion different nations fly,
Of various habit, and of various dye,
The pierced battalions disunited fall
In heaps on heaps; one fate o'erwhelms them all.
  The Knave of Diamonds tries his wily arts,
And wins (oh shameful chance!) the Queen of Hearts.
At this, the blood the virgin's cheek forsook,
A livid paleness spreads o'er all her look;
She sees, and trembles at th' approaching ill,
Just in the jaws of ruin, and Codille;†
And now (as oft in some distempered state)
On one nice trick depends the general fate.
An Ace of Hearts steps forth: the King unseen
Lurked in her hand, and mourned his captive Queen.
He springs to vengeance with an eager pace,
And falls like thunder on the prostrate Ace.
The nymph exulting fills with shouts the sky,
The walls, the woods, and long canals reply.
  Oh thoughtless mortals! ever blind to fate,
Too soon dejected, and too soon elate!
Sudden these honours shall be snatched away,
And cursed forever this victorious day.
  For lo! the board with cups and spoons is crowned,
The berries crackle, and the mill turns round.
On shining altars† of Japan they raise
The silver lamp; the fiery spirits blaze;
From silver spouts the grateful liquors glide,
While China's earth receives the smoking tide.

*altars* lacquered tables, on which coffee is ritually made

At once they gratify their scent and taste,
And frequent cups prolong the rich repast.
Straight hover round the fair her airy band;
Some, as she sipped, the fuming liquor fanned,
Some o'er her lap their careful plumes displayed,
Trembling, and conscious of the rich brocade.
Coffee (which makes the politician wise,
And see through all things with his half-shut eyes)
Sent up in vapours to the Baron's brain
New stratagems, the radiant lock to gain.
Ah cease, rash youth! desist ere 'tis too late,
Fear the just Gods, and think of Scylla's† fate!
Changed to a bird, and sent to flit in air,
She dearly pays for Nisus' injured hair!
But when to mischief mortals bend their will,
How soon they find fit instruments of ill!
Just then, Clarissa drew with tempting grace
A two-edged weapon from her shining case;
So ladies in romance assist their knight,
Present the spear, and arm him for the fight.
He takes the gift with reverence, and extends
The little engine on his fingers' ends;
This just behind Belinda's neck he spread,
As o'er the fragrant steams she bends her head:
Swift to the lock a thousand sprites repair,
A thousand wings, by turns, blow back the hair,
And thrice they twitched the diamond in her ear,
Thrice she looked back, and thrice the foe drew near.
Just in that instant, anxious Ariel sought
The close recesses of the virgin's thought;
As, on the nosegay in her breast reclined,
He watched th' ideas rising in her mind,
Sudden he viewed, in spite of all her art,
An earthly lover lurking at her heart.
Amazed, confused, he found his power expired,
Resigned to fate, and with a sigh retired.
The Peer now spreads the glittering forfex† wide,
T' enclose the lock; now joins it, to divide.
Even then, before the fatal engine closed,
A wretched Sylph too fondly interposed;

*Scylla* transformed after her theft of the purple lock which held her father Nisus's power

*forfex* scissors ('the fatal engine')

Fate urged the shears, and cut the Sylph in twain
(But airy substance soon unites again);
The meeting points the sacred hair dissever
From the fair head, for ever and for ever!
Then flashed the living lightning from her eyes,
And screams of horror rend th' affrighted skies.
Not louder shrieks to pitying heaven are cast,
When husbands or when lapdogs breathe their last;
Or when rich china vessels, fallen from high,
In glittering dust and painted fragments lie!
'Let wreaths of triumph now my temples twine,'
The victor cried, 'the glorious prize is mine!
While fish in streams, or birds delight in air,
Or in a coach and six the British fair,
As long as *Atalantis*† shall be read,
Or the small pillow grace a lady's bed,
While visits shall be paid on solemn days,
When numerous wax-lights in bright order blaze,
While nymphs take treats, or assignations give,
So long my honour, name, and praise shall live!'
What Time would spare, from Steel receives its date,
And monuments, like men, submit to fate!
Steel could the labour of the gods† destroy,
And strike to dust th' imperial towers of Troy;
Steel could the works of mortal pride confound,
And hew triumphal arches to the ground.
What wonder then, fair nymph! thy hairs should feel
The conquering force of unresisted steel?

## *Canto IV*

But anxious cares the pensive nymph oppressed,
And secret passions laboured in her breast.
Not youthful kings in battle seized alive,
Not scornful virgins who their charms survive,
Not ardent lovers robbed of all their bliss,
Not ancient ladies when refused a kiss,
Not tyrants fierce that unrepenting die,
Not Cynthia when her manteau's† pinned awry,

*Atalantis* A recent (1709) book of court scandal, by Mary Manley

*gods* Troy was built by Apollo and Poseidon

*manteau* loose robe

E'er felt such rage, resentment and despair,
As thou, sad virgin! for thy ravished hair.
For, that sad moment, when the Sylphs withdrew,
And Ariel weeping from Belinda flew,
Umbriel,† a dusky, melancholy sprite
As ever sullied the fair face of light,
Down to the central earth, his proper scene,
Repaired to search the gloomy Cave of Spleen.†
Swift on his sooty pinions flits the Gnome,
And in a vapour reached the dismal dome.
No cheerful breeze this sullen region knows,
The dreaded east is all the wind that blows.
Here in a grotto, sheltered close from air,
And screened in shades from day's detested glare,
She sighs forever on her pensive bed,
Pain at her side, and Megrim† at her head.
Two handmaids wait the throne: alike in place,
But differing far in figure and in face.
Here stood Ill-nature like an ancient maid,
Her wrinkled form in black and white arrayed;
With store of prayers for mornings, nights and noons,
Her hand is filled; her bosom with lampoons.
There Affectation with a sickly mien
Shows in her cheek the roses of eighteen,
Practised to lisp, and hang the head aside,
Faints into airs, and languishes with pride;
On the rich quilt sinks with becoming woe,
Wrapped in a gown, for sickness and for show.
The fair ones feel such maladies as these,
When each new nightdress gives a new disease.
A constant vapour o'er the palace flies,
Strange phantoms rising as the mists arise;
Dreadful as hermit's dreams in haunted shades,
Or bright as visions of expiring maids.
Now glaring fiends and snakes on rolling spires,
Pale spectres, gaping tombs, and purple fires;
Now lakes of liquid gold, Elysian scenes,
And crystal domes, and angels in machines.
Unnumbered throngs on every side are seen
Of bodies changed to various forms by Spleen.

*Umbriel* from Latin 'umbra' (shade); his visit to *Spleen* (fashionable melancholy) constitutes an epic descent

*Megrim* headache. The Cave combines pantomime effects with images of female hysteria

Here living teapots stand, one arm held out,
One bent; the handle this, and that the spout:
A pipkin[†] there like Homer's tripod walks;
Here sighs a jar, and there a goose pie talks;
Men prove with child as powerful fancy works,
And maids, turned bottles, call aloud for corks.
  Safe passed the Gnome through this fantastic band,
A branch of healing spleenwort[†] in his hand.
Then thus addressed the Power: 'Hail, wayward Queen!
Who rule the sex to fifty from fifteen;
Parent of vapours and of female wit,
Who give th' hysteric or poetic fit,
On various tempers act by various ways,
Make some take physic, others scribble plays;
Who cause the proud their visits to delay,
And send the godly in a pet to pray.
A nymph there is that all thy power disdains,
And thousands more in equal mirth maintains.
But oh! if e'er thy Gnome could spoil a grace,
Or raise a pimple on a beauteous face,
Like citron-waters[†] matrons' cheeks inflame,
Or change complexions at a losing game;
If e'er with airy horns[†] I planted heads,
Or rumpled petticoats or tumbled beds,
Or caused suspicion when no soul was rude,
Or discomposed the headdress of a prude,
Or e'er to costive lapdog gave disease,
Which not the tears of brightest eyes could ease;
Hear me, and touch Belinda with chagrin:
That single act gives half the world the spleen.'
  The Goddess with a discontented air
Seems to reject him, though she grants his prayer.
A wondrous bag with both her hands she binds,
Like that where once Ulysses[†] held the winds;
There she collects the force of female lungs,
Sighs, sobs and passions, and the war of tongues.
A vial next she fills with fainting fears,
Soft sorrows, melting griefs and flowing tears.

---

*pipkin* earthenware pot; the allusion is to *Iliad*, XVIII.439

*spleenwort* a plant which counteracts spleen's effects

*citron-waters* brandy flavoured with lemon-like fruit

*airy horns* groundless signs of a man cuckolded by his wife

*Ulysses* given a bag of winds by Aeolus (*Odyssey*, X)

The Gnome rejoicing bears her gifts away,
Spreads his black wings, and slowly mounts to day.
Sunk in Thalestris'† arms the nymph he found,
Her eyes dejected and her hair unbound.
Full o'er their heads the swelling bag he rent,
And all the Furies issued at the vent.
Belinda burns with more than mortal ire,
And fierce Thalestris fans the rising fire.
'O wretched maid!' she spread her hands, and cried
(While Hampton's echoes, 'Wretched maid!' replied),
'Was it for this you took such constant care
The bodkin, comb and essence to prepare;
For this your locks in paper durance bound,
For this with torturing irons† wreathed around?
For this with fillets† strained your tender head,
And bravely bore the double loads of lead?†
Gods! shall the ravisher display your hair,
While the fops envy, and the ladies stare!
Honour forbid! at whose unrivalled shrine
Ease, pleasure, virtue, all, our sex resign.
Methinks already I your tears survey,
Already hear the horrid things they say,
Already see you a degraded toast,
And all your honour in a whisper lost!
How shall I, then, your helpless fame defend?
'Twill then be infamy to seem your friend!
And shall this prize, th' inestimable prize,
Exposed through crystal to the gazing eyes,
And heightened by the diamond's circling rays,
On that rapacious hand forever blaze?
Sooner shall grass in Hyde Park Circus grow,
And wits take lodgings in the sound of Bow;†
Sooner let earth, air, sea, to chaos fall,
Men, monkeys, lapdogs, parrots, perish all!'
She said; then raging to Sir Plume† repairs,
And bids her beau demand the precious hairs
(Sir Plume, of amber snuffbox justly vain,
And the nice conduct of a clouded* cane); mottled
With earnest eyes, and round unthinking face,
He first the snuffbox opened, then the case,

*Thalestris* Queen of the Amazons, hence a fierce woman

*fillets* headbands, in epic; the references (*irons*, *lead*) are to hairdressing

*Circus* a busy fashionable place; by contrast, *Bow* was middle-class

*Sir Plume* a blustering, if gentlemanly, foil to the Baron

And thus broke out – 'My Lord, why, what the devil!
Zounds![†] damn the lock! 'fore Gad, you must be civil!
Plague on't! 'tis past a jest – nay prithee, pox!
Give her the hair' – he spoke, and rapped his box.
'It grieves me much,' replied the Peer again,
'Who speaks so well should ever speak in vain.
But by this lock, this sacred lock I swear
(Which never more shall join its parted hair,
Which never more its honours shall renew,
Clipped from the lovely head where late it grew),
That while my nostrils draw the vital air,
This hand, which won it, shall forever wear.'
He spoke, and speaking, in proud triumph spread
The long-contended honours of her head.
But Umbriel, hateful Gnome, forbears not so;
He breaks the vial whence the sorrows flow.
Then see! the nymph in beauteous grief appears,
Her eyes half languishing, half drowned in tears;
On her heaved bosom hung her drooping head,
Which with a sigh she raised; and thus she said:
'Forever cursed be this detested day,
Which snatched my best, my favourite curl away!
Happy! ah ten times happy had I been,
If Hampton Court these eyes had never seen!
Yet am not I the first mistaken maid,
By love of courts to numerous ills betrayed.
Oh had I rather unadmired remained
In some lone isle, or distant northern land;
Where the gilt chariot never marks the way,
Where none learn ombre, none e'er taste bohea![†]
There kept my charms concealed from mortal eye,
Like roses that in deserts bloom and die.
What moved my mind with youthful lords to roam?
Oh had I stayed, and said my prayers at home!
'Twas this the morning omens seemed to tell;
Thrice from my trembling hand the patch box fell;
The tottering china shook without a wind,
Nay, Poll sat mute, and Shock was most unkind!
A Sylph too warned me of the threats of fate,
In mystic visions, now believed too late!

*Zounds* a mild oath
*bohea* tea. This speech imitates Achilles' lament for Patroclus: *Iliad*, XVIII

See the poor remnants of these slighted hairs!
My hands shall rend what even thy rapine spares.
These, in two sable ringlets taught to break,
Once gave new beauties to the snowy neck;
The sister lock now sits uncouth, alone,
And in its fellow's fate foresees its own;
Uncurled it hangs, the fatal shears demands,
And tempts once more thy sacrilegious hands.
Oh hadst thou, cruel! been content to seize
Hairs less in sight, or any hairs but these!'

## *Canto V*

She said: the pitying audience melt in tears,
But Fate and Jove had stopped the Baron's ears.
In vain Thalestris with reproach assails,
For who can move when fair Belinda fails?
Not half so fixed the Trojan† could remain,
While Anna begged and Dido raged in vain.
Then grave Clarissa† graceful waved her fan;
Silence ensued, and thus the nymph began:
'Say why are beauties praised and honoured most,
The wise man's passion, and the vain man's toast?
Why decked with all that land and sea afford,
Why angels called, and angel-like adored?
Why round our coaches crowd the white-gloved beaux,
Why bows the side box from its inmost rows?
How vain are all these glories, all our pains,
Unless good sense preserve what beauty gains;
That men may say, when we the front box grace,
"Behold the first in virtue as in face!"
Oh if to dance all night, and dress all day,
Charmed the smallpox, or chased old age away,
Who would not scorn what housewife's cares produce,
Or who would learn one earthly thing of use?
To patch, nay ogle, might become a saint,
Nor could it sure be such a sin to paint.
But since, alas! frail beauty must decay,
Curled or uncurled, since locks will turn to grey,

*Trojan . . . Dido* Aeneas deserted Dido of Carthage, despite her sister Anna
*Clarissa* her speech, added in 1717, imitates that of Sarpedon to Glaucus, *Iliad*, XII.371–96

Since painted, or not painted, all shall fade,
And she who scorns a man must die a maid;
What then remains, but well our power to use,
And keep good humour still whate'er we lose?
And trust me, dear, good humour can prevail,
When airs, and flights, and screams, and scolding fail.
Beauties in vain their pretty eyes may roll;
Charms strike the sight, but merit wins the soul.'
So spoke the dame, but no applause ensued;
Belinda frowned, Thalestris called her prude.
'To arms, to arms!' the fierce virago cries,
And swift as lightning to the combat flies.
All side in parties, and begin th' attack;
Fans clap, silks rustle, and tough whalebones crack;
Heroes' and heroines' shouts confusedly rise,
And bass and treble voices strike the skies.
No common weapons in their hands are found,
Like gods they fight, nor dread a mortal wound.
So when bold Homer makes the gods engage,
And heavenly breasts with human passions rage;
'Gainst Pallas, Mars; Latona, Hermes arms;
And all Olympus† rings with loud alarms.
Jove's thunder roars, heaven trembles all around;
Blue Neptune storms, the bellowing deeps resound;
Earth shakes her nodding towers, the ground gives way;
And the pale ghosts start at the flash of day!
Triumphant Umbriel on a sconce's† height
Clapped his glad wings, and sat to view the fight:
Propped on their bodkin spears, the sprites survey
The growing combat, or assist the fray.
While through the press enraged Thalestris flies,
And scatters deaths around from both her eyes,
A beau and witling perished in the throng,
One died in metaphor, and one in song.
'O cruel nymph! a living death I bear,'
Cried Dapperwit,† and sunk beside his chair.
A mournful glance Sir Fopling† upwards cast,
'Those eyes are made so killing' – was his last:
Thus on Maeander's flowery margin† lies

---

*Olympus* mountain of the gods, who in Homer fight each other and humans
*sconce* candlestick fixed on a bracket
*Dapperwit* like *Sir Fopling*, a character in Restoration comedy
*Maeander's flowery margin* river banks

Th' expiring swan,† and as he sings he dies.
When bold Sir Plume had drawn Clarissa down,
Chloe stepped in, and killed him with a frown;
She smiled to see the doughty hero slain,
But at her smile the beau revived again.
Now Jove suspends his golden scales† in air,
Weighs the men's wits against the lady's hair;
The doubtful beam long nods from side to side;
At length the wits mount up, the hairs subside.
See, fierce Belinda on the Baron flies,
With more than usual lightning in her eyes;
Nor feared the chief th' unequal fight to try,
Who sought no more than on his foe to die.†
But this bold lord, with manly strength endued,
She with one finger and a thumb subdued:
Just where the breath of life his nostrils drew,
A charge of snuff the wily virgin threw;
The Gnomes direct, to every atom just,
The pungent grains of titillating dust.
Sudden, with starting tears each eye o'erflows,
And the high dome re-echoes to his nose.
'Now meet thy fate,' incensed Belinda cried,
And drew a deadly bodkin from her side.
(The same,† his ancient personage to deck,
Her great-great-grandsire wore about his neck
In three seal-rings; which after, melted down,
Formed a vast buckle for his widow's gown:
Her infant grandam's whistle next it grew,
The bells she jingled, and the whistle blew;
Then in a bodkin graced her mother's hairs,
Which long she wore, and now Belinda wears.)
'Boast not my fall,' he cried, 'insulting foe!
Thou by some other shalt be laid as low.
Nor think, to die dejects my lofty mind;
All that I dread is leaving you behind!
Rather than so, ah let me still survive,
And burn in Cupid's flames – but burn alive.'
'Restore the lock!' she cries; and all around
'Restore the lock!' the vaulted roofs rebound.

*swan* traditionally sings as it dies

*golden scales* used in epic by Jove to decide a battle's outcome

*die* the pun on sexual climax continues the poem's vein of innuendo (compare l.98)

*the same* parody of the descent of a heroic object

Not fierce Othello† in so loud a strain
Roared for the handkerchief that caused his pain.
But see how oft ambitious aims are crossed,
And chiefs contend till all the prize is lost!
The lock, obtained with guilt, and kept with pain,
In every place is sought, but sought in vain:
With such a prize no mortal must be blest,
So Heaven decrees! with Heaven who can contest?
  Some thought it mounted to the lunar sphere,
Since all things lost on earth are treasured there.
There heroes' wits are kept in ponderous vases,
And beaux' in snuffboxes and tweezer-cases.
There broken vows and deathbed alms are found,
And lovers' hearts with ends of riband bound;
The courtier's promises, and sick man's prayers,
The smiles of harlots, and the tears of heirs,
Cages for gnats, and chains to yoke a flea,
Dried butterflies, and tomes of casuistry†
  But trust the Muse – she saw it upward rise,
Though marked by none but quick poetic eyes
(So Rome's great founder to the heavens withdrew,
To Proculus† alone confessed in view):
A sudden star, it shot through liquid air,
And drew behind a radiant trail of hair.
Not Berenice's locks† first rose so bright,
The heavens bespangling with dishevelled light.
The Sylphs behold it kindling as it flies,
And pleased pursue its progress through the skies.
  This the beau monde shall from the Mall† survey,
And hail with music its propitious ray.
This the blest lover shall for Venus† take,
And send up vows from Rosamonda's Lake.
This Partridge† soon shall view in cloudless skies,
When next he looks through Galileo's† eyes;
And hence th' egregious wizard shall foredoom
The fate of Louis,† and the fall of Rome.

*Othello* in Shakespeare's play, III.4
*casuistry* quibbling about moral conduct
*Proculus* saw Romulus ascend to heaven in a storm
*Berenice's locks* offered to the gods for safe return of her husband Ptolemy III from war, they turned into a constellation
*Mall . . . Rosamonda's Lake* walk in St James's Park (where the Lake was associated with unhappy love)
*Venus* goddess of love
*Partridge* astrologer, satirised by Swift c. 1708
*Galileo* Italian astronomer (1564–1642), improved the telescope
*Louis* Louis XIV, King of France (d.1715); Rome, of course, was long fallen

Then cease, bright nymph! to mourn thy ravished hair,
Which adds new glory to the shining sphere!
Not all the tresses that fair head can boast
Shall draw such envy as the lock you lost.
For, after all the murders of your eye,
When, after millions slain, yourself shall die;
When those fair suns shall set, as set they must,
And all those tresses shall be laid in dust;
This lock the Muse shall consecrate to fame,
And 'midst the stars inscribe Belinda's name!

1712–14 1714, 1717

# EPISTLE TO MISS BLOUNT†

On her leaving the town, after the coronation

As some fond virgin, whom her mother's care
Drags from the town to wholesome country air,
Just when she learns to roll a melting eye,
And hear a spark,† yet think no danger nigh;
From the dear man unwilling she must sever,
Yet takes one kiss before she parts forever:
Thus from the world fair Zephalinda flew,
Saw others happy, and with sighs withdrew;
Not that their pleasures caused her discontent;
She sighed not that they stayed, but that she went.
She went to plain-work,† and to purling brooks,
Old-fashioned halls, dull aunts, and croaking rooks;
She went from opera, park, assembly, play,
To morning walks, and prayers three hours a day;
To pass her time 'twixt reading and bohea,
To muse, and spill her solitary tea,
Or o'er cold coffee trifle with the spoon,
Count the slow clock, and dine exact at noon;

*Epistle to Miss Blount* Probably addressed to Teresa ('Zephalinda') sister of his closer friend Martha Blount ('Parthenia'). George I succeeded Anne in 1714

*spark* lively man, lover

*plain-work* needlework, a lady's occupation. The poem stresses the gap between fashionable and rural life. London would mean late nights and dinner in mid-afternoon

Divert her eyes with pictures in the fire,
Hum half a tune, tell stories to the squire;
Up to her godly garret after seven,
There starve and pray, for that's the way to heaven.
  Some squire, perhaps, you take delight to rack,
Whose game is whist, whose treat a toast in sack,†
Who visits with a gun, presents you birds,
Then gives a smacking buss,* and cries – 'No words!' kiss
Or with his hound comes hollowing from the stable,
Makes love with nods and knees beneath a table;
Whose laughs are hearty, though his jests are coarse,
And loves you best of all things – but his horse.
  In some fair evening, on your elbow laid,
You dream of triumphs in the rural shade;
In pensive thought recall the fancied scene,
See coronations rise on every green:
Before you pass th' imaginary sights
Of lords and earls and dukes and gartered knights;
While the spread fan o'ershades your closing eyes,
Then gives one flirt,* and all the vision flies. jerk
Thus vanish sceptres, coronets, and balls,
And leave you in lone woods, or empty walls.
  So when your slave,† at some dear idle time
(Not plagued with headaches or the want of rhyme)
Stands in the streets, abstracted from the crew,
And while he seems to study, thinks of you;
Just when his fancy points your sprightly eyes,
Or sees the blush of soft Parthenia rise,
Gay† pats my shoulder, and you vanish quite;
Streets, chairs and coxcombs rush upon my sight;
Vexed to be still in town, I knit my brow,
Look sour, and hum a tune – as you may now.

1714 1717

*sack* Spanish wine; perhaps also a pun on 'lady's gown'

*your slave* Pope himself

*Gay* his friend, the poet

# *From* ELOISA TO ABELARD†

In these deep solitudes and awful cells,†
Where heavenly-pensive contemplation dwells,
And ever-musing melancholy reigns;
What means this tumult in a vestal's* veins? virgin
Why rove my thoughts beyond this last retreat?
Why feels my heart its long-forgotten heat?
Yet, yet I love! – From Abelard it came,
And Eloisa yet must kiss the name.
  Dear fatal name! rest ever unrevealed,
Nor pass these lips in holy silence sealed.
Hide it, my heart, within that close disguise,
Where, mixed with God's, his loved idea† lies.
Oh write it not, my hand – The name appears
Already written – wash it out, my tears!
In vain lost Eloisa weeps and prays,
Her heart still dictates, and her hand obeys.
  Relentless walls! whose darksome round contains
Repentant sighs, and voluntary pains;
Ye rugged rocks! which holy knees have worn;
Ye grots and caverns shagged with horrid† thorn!
Shrines! where their vigils pale-eyed virgins keep,
And pitying saints, whose statues learn to weep!
Though cold like you, unmoved, and silent grown,
I have not yet forgot my self to stone.
All is not Heaven's while Abelard has part,
Still rebel nature holds out half my heart;
Nor prayers nor fasts its stubborn pulse restrain,
Nor tears, for ages, taught to flow in vain. . . .

  Thou know'st how guiltless first I met thy flame,
When love approached me under friendship's name;
My fancy formed thee of angelic kind,
Some emanation of† th' all-beauteous Mind.
Those smiling eyes, attempering* every ray, moderating

*Eloisa to Abelard* In the twelfth century, the scholar Abelard was forcibly separated from his pupil and love, Eloisa; both entered religious houses. Pope presents Eloisa's passionate conflict, caught between heavenly and earthly love, responding, in a heroic epistle in the manner of Ovid, to a letter from Abelard (l.7). The abrupt changes of mood are appropriate to subject and genre

*cells* of nuns, in her convent

*idea* image ('mixed' in his religious and secular roles)

*horrid* bristling (Latin); her emotions and surroundings are closely linked

*some emanation of* something issuing from

Shone sweetly lambent[*] with celestial day: radiant
Guiltless I gazed; heaven listened while you sung;
And truths divine[†] came mended from that tongue.
From lips like those what precept failed to move?
Too soon they taught me 'twas no sin to love.
Back through the paths of pleasing sense[†] I ran,
Nor wished an angel whom I loved a man.
Dim and remote the joys of saints I see,
Nor envy them, that heaven I lose for thee. . . .

Alas how changed what sudden horrors rise!
A naked lover bound and bleeding lies!
Where, where was Eloise? her voice, her hand,
Her poniard, had opposed the dire command.
Barbarian stay! that bloody stroke[†] restrain;
The crime was common, common be the pain.
I can no more; by shame, by rage supprest,
Let tears, and burning blushes speak the rest.

Canst thou forget that sad, that solemn day,[†]
When victims at yon altar's foot we lay?
Canst thou forget what tears that moment fell,
When, warm in youth, I bade the world farewell?
As with cold lips I kissed the sacred veil,
The shrines all trembled, and the lamps grew pale:
Heaven scarce believed the conquest it surveyed,
And saints with wonder heard the vows I made.
Yet then, to those dread altars as I drew,
Not on the Cross my eyes were fixed, but you;
Not grace, or zeal, love only was my call,
And if I lose thy love, I lose my all.
Come! with thy looks, thy words, relieve my woe;
Those still at least are left thee to bestow.
Still on that breast enamoured let me lie,
Still drink delicious poison from thy eye,
Pant on thy lip, and to thy heart be prest;
Give all thou canst – and let me dream the rest.
Ah no! instruct me other joys to prize,
With other beauties charm my partial eyes,
Full in my view set all the bright abode,[†]
And make my soul quit Abelard for God.

*truths divine* Abelard was her tutor
*pleasing sense* indicates her response to his physical attraction as a man
*bloody stroke* the castration of Abelard by Eloisa's relatives
*solemn day* when Eloisa took the nun's veil
*bright abode* the spiritual goal of heaven (light/dark images recur)

Ah think at least thy flock deserves thy care,
Plants of thy hand, and children of thy prayer.
From the false world in early youth they fled,
By thee to mountains, wilds, and deserts led.
You raised† these hallowed walls; the desert smiled,
And Paradise was opened in the wild.
No weeping orphan saw his father's stores
Our shrines irradiate, or emblaze the floors;
No silver saints, by dying misers given,
Here bribed the rage of ill-requited heaven:
But such plain roofs as piety could raise,
And only vocal with the Maker's praise.
In these lone walls (their day's eternal bound)
These moss-grown domes† with spiry turrets crowned,
Where awful† arches make a noon-day night,
And the dim windows shed a solemn light;
Thy eyes diffused a reconciling ray,
And gleams of glory brightened all the day.
But now no face divine contentment wears,
'Tis all blank sadness, or continual tears.
See how the force of others' prayers I try,
(Oh pious fraud† of amorous charity!)
But why should I on others' prayers depend?
Come thou, my father, brother, husband, friend!
Ah let thy handmaid, sister, daughter, move,
And, all those tender names in one, thy love!
The darksome pines that o'er yon rocks reclined
Wave high, and murmur to the hollow wind,
The wandering streams that shine between the hills,
The grots that echo to the tinkling rills,
The dying gales that pant upon the trees,
The lakes that quiver to the curling breeze;
No more these scenes my meditation aid,
Or lull to rest the visionary maid:
But o'er the twilight groves, and dusky caves,
Long-sounding isles, and intermingled graves,
Black melancholy sits, and round her throws
A death-like silence, and a dread repose:
Her gloomy presence saddens all the scene,
Shades every flower, and darkens every green,

*you raised* Abelard had founded her convent, which is not expensively adorned (l.136)
*domes* solemn buildings (Latin)
*awful* inspiring dread
*pious fraud* in asking him to come for the consolation of others

Deepens the murmur of the falling floods,
And breathes a browner horror on the woods.
Yet here for ever, ever must I stay;
Sad proof how well a lover can obey!
Death, only death, can break the lasting chain;
And here, even then, shall my cold dust remain,
Here all its frailties, all its flames resign,
And wait, till 'tis no sin to mix with thine. . . .

What scenes appear where-e'er I turn my view!
The dear ideas,† where I fly, pursue,
Rise in the grove, before the altar rise,
Stain all my soul, and wanton in my eyes!
I waste the Matin† lamp in sighs for thee,
Thy image steals between my God and me,
Thy voice I seem in every hymn to hear,
With every bead† I drop too soft a tear.
When from the censer† clouds of fragrance roll,
And swelling organs lift the rising soul;
One thought of thee puts all the pomp to flight,
Priests, tapers, temples, swim before my sight:
In seas of flame my plunging soul is drowned,
While altars blaze, and angels tremble round.
While prostrate here in humble grief I lie,
Kind, virtuous drops just gathering in my eye,
While praying, trembling, in the dust I roll,
And dawning grace is opening on my soul:
Come, if thou darest, all charming as thou art!
Oppose thy self to heaven; dispute my heart;
Come, with one glance of those deluding† eyes,
Blot out each bright idea of the skies.
Take back that grace, those sorrows, and those tears,
Take back my fruitless penitence and prayers,
Snatch me, just mounting, from the blest abode,
Assist the fiends and tear me from my God!
No, fly me, fly me! far as Pole from Pole;
Rise Alps between us! and whole oceans roll!
Ah come not, write not, think not once of me,
Nor share one pang of all I felt for thee.

*ideas* Abelard's image has already appeared in her dreams
*Matin* first part of the religious day, the office recited before dawn
*bead* on the cord by which she counts her prayers
*censer* vessel in which incense is burned
*deluding* Abelard's presence would cause her to break her vow to heaven

Thy oaths I quit, thy memory resign,
Forget, renounce me, hate whate'er was mine. . .

1716 1717

# EPISTLE II. TO A LADY†

### Of the characters of women

Nothing so true as what you once let fall,
'Most women have no characters at all:'
Matter too soft a lasting mark to bear,
And best distinguished by black, brown, or fair.
How many pictures† of one nymph we view,
All how unlike each other, all how true!
Arcadia's countess, here, in ermined pride,
Is, there, Pastora by a fountain side;
Here Fannia, leering on her own good man,
Is there, a naked Leda† with a swan.
Let then the fair one beautifully cry,
In Magdalen's loose hair and lifted eye,
Or dressed in smiles of sweet Cecilia shine,
With simpering angels, palms, and harps divine;
Whether the charmer sinner it, or saint it,
If folly grows romantic, I must paint it.
Come then, the colours and the ground† prepare!
Dip in the rainbow, trick* her off in air; sketch
Choose a firm cloud, before it fall, and in it
Catch, ere she change, the Cynthia† of this minute.
Rufa, whose eye quick-glancing o'er the park,
Attracts each light gay meteor of a spark,
Agrees as ill with Rufa studying Locke,†
As Sappho's diamonds with her dirty smock;

[The closing paragraphs anticipate Abelard's religious attendance at Eloisa's death-bed; their eventual burials in the same grave; and their commemoration by a sympathetic poet]

*Epistle II. To a Lady* Addressed to his old friend, Martha Blount (1690–1763). The leading idea of the portraits is the inconsistency of women

*pictures . . . Leda* the examples show the variety of attitude in a single woman: sophisticated, pastoral, modest, wanton (Jupiter as a swan seduced Leda), fallen woman or patron saint

*ground* painting surface

*Cynthia* goddess of the changing moon

*Locke* John Locke (1632–1704), English philosopher

Or Sappho† at her toilet's greasy task,
With Sappho fragrant at an evening masque:
So morning insects that in muck begun,
Shine, buzz, and flyblow in the setting sun.
  How soft is Silia! fearful to offend,
The frail one's advocate, the weak one's friend:
To her, Calista proved her conduct nice,†
And good Simplicius asks of her advice.
Sudden, she storms! she raves! You tip the wink,
But spare your censure; Silia does not drink.
All eyes may see from what the change arose,
All eyes may see – a pimple on her nose.
  Papillia, wedded to her doting spark,
Sighs for the shades – 'How charming is a park!'
A park is purchased, but the fair he sees
All bathed in tears – 'Oh odious, odious trees!'
  Ladies, like variegated tulips, show,
'Tis to their changes half their charms we owe;
Their happy spots the nice admirer take,
Fine by defect, and delicately weak.
'Twas thus Calypso† once each heart alarmed,
Awed without virtue, without beauty charmed;
Her tongue bewitched as oddly as her eyes,
Less wit than mimic, more a wit than wise:
Strange graces still, and stranger flights she had,
Was just not ugly, and was just not mad;
Yet ne'er so sure our passion to create,
As when she touched the brink of all we hate.
  Narcissa's† nature, tolerably mild,
To make a wash, would hardly stew a child,
Has even been proved to grant a lover's prayer,
And paid a tradesman once to make him stare,
Gave alms at Easter, in a Christian trim,
And made a widow happy, for a whim.
Why then declare good nature is her scorn,
When 'tis by that alone she can be borne?
Why pique all mortals, yet affect a name?
A fool to pleasure, and a slave to fame;

*Sappho* originally, a Greek poetess; here, Lady Mary Wortley Montagu, friend then enemy of Pope (see p. 256); a notorious sloven
*nice* precise, punctilious
*Calypso* in Homer's *Odyssey*, the original detained Odysseus on her island for seven years
*Narcissa* from Narcissus, who fell in love with his own reflection, in Greek legend

Now deep in Taylor[†] and the *Book of Martyrs*,[†]
Now drinking citron with His Grace[†] and Chartres.[†]
Now conscience chills her, and now passion burns;
And atheism and religion take their turns;
A very heathen in the carnal part,
Yet still a sad, good Christian at her heart.
  See Sin in state, majestically drunk,
Proud as a peeress, prouder as a punk,[*] prostitute
Chaste to her husband, frank to all beside,
A teeming mistress, but a barren bride.
What then? let blood and body bear the fault,
Her head's untouched, that noble seat of thought:
Such this day's doctrine – in another fit
She sins with poets through pure love of wit.
What has not fired her bosom or her brain?
Caesar and Tallboy,[†] Charles[†] and Charlemagne.
As Helluo,[†] late dictator of the feast,
The nose of hautgout,[†] and the tip of taste,
Criticked your wine, and analyzed your meat,
Yet on plain pudding deigned at home to eat;
So Philomede, lecturing all mankind
On the soft passion, and the taste refined,
Th' address, the delicacy – stoops at once,
And makes her hearty meal upon a dunce.
  Flavia's a wit, has too much sense to pray;
To toast our wants and wishes, is her way;
Nor asks of God, but of her stars, to give
The mighty blessing, 'while we live, to live.'
Then all for death, that opiate of the soul!
Lucretia's[†] dagger, Rosamonda's[†] bowl.
Say, what can cause such impotence of mind?
A spark too fickle, or a spouse too kind.
Wise wretch! with pleasures too refined to please,
With too much spirit to be e'er at ease,
With too much quickness ever to be taught,
With too much thinking to have common thought:

*Taylor* John Taylor (1613–67), devotional writer
*Book of Martyrs* by John Foxe, 1563
*His Grace* a duke
*Chartres* Francis Chartres: usurer and rapist (d.1732), often attacked by Pope
*Tallboy* a stage booby
*Charles* a footman; contrasted with mighty rulers
*Helluo* glutton (Latin)
*hautgout* anything strong in taste or scent
*Lucretia* Roman who committed suicide after rape by Tarquin
*Rosamonda* mistress of Henry II, was forced by the queen to drink poison

Who purchase pain with all that joy can give,
And die of nothing but a rage to live.
Turn then from wits; and look on Simo's mate,
No ass so meek, no ass so obstinate;
Or her, that owns her faults, but never mends,
Because she's honest, and the best of friends;
Or her, whose life the Church and scandal share,
Forever in a passion, or a prayer;
Or her, who laughs at hell, but (like Her Grace)
Cries, 'Ah! how charming if there's no such place!'
Or who in sweet vicissitude appears
Of mirth and opium, ratafie[†] and tears,
The daily anodyne, and nightly draught,
To kill those foes to fair ones, time and thought.
Woman and fool are two hard things to hit,
For true no-meaning puzzles more than wit.
But what are these to great Atossa's[†] mind?
Scarce once herself, by turns all womankind!
Who, with herself, or others, from her birth
Finds all her life one warfare upon earth;
Shines in exposing knaves, and painting fools,
Yet is whate'er she hates and ridicules.
No thought advances, but her eddy brain
Whisks it about, and down it goes again.
Full sixty years the world has been her trade,
The wisest fool much time has ever made.
From loveless youth to unrespected age,
No passion gratified except her rage.
So much the fury still outran the wit,
The pleasure missed her, and the scandal hit.
Who breaks with her, provokes revenge from hell,
But he's a bolder man who dares be well:
Her every turn with violence pursued,
Nor more a storm her hate than gratitude.
To that each passion turns, or soon or late;
Love, if it makes her yield, must make her hate:
Superiors? death! and equals? what a curse!
But an inferior not dependent? worse.
Offend her, and she knows not to forgive;
Oblige her, and she'll hate you while you live:

*ratafie* ratafia, a fruit-flavoured brandy
*Atossa* historically, daughter of the Persian Emperor Cyrus; here, possibly the Duchess of Buckinghamshire (*c.* 1682–1743), daughter of James II; friend then enemy of Pope. Her children died before her (l.148)

But die, and she'll adore you – Then the bust
And temple rise – then fall again to dust.
Last night, her lord was all that's good and great;
A knave this morning, and his will a cheat.
Strange! by the means defeated of the ends,
By spirit robbed of power, by warmth of friends,
By wealth of followers! without one distress
Sick of herself through very selfishness!
Atossa, cursed with every granted prayer,
Childless with all her children, wants an heir.
To heirs unknown descends th' unguarded store,
Or wanders, Heaven-directed, to the poor.
   Pictures like these, dear Madam, to design,
Asks no firm hand, and no unerring line;
Some wandering touch, or some reflected light,
Some flying stroke alone can hit 'em right:
For how should equal colours do the knack?
Chameleons who can paint in white and black?
   'Yet Chloe sure was formed without a spot –'
Nature in her then erred not, but forgot.
'With every pleasing, every prudent part,
Say, what can Chloe want?' – She wants a heart.
She speaks, behaves, and acts just as she ought;
But never, never, reached one generous thought.
Virtue she finds too painful an endeavour,
Content to dwell in decencies for ever.
So very reasonable, so unmoved,
As never yet to love, or to be loved.
She, while her lover pants upon her breast,
Can mark the figures on an Indian chest;
And when she sees her friend in deep despair,
Observes how much a chintz exceeds mohair.
Forbid it Heaven, a favour or a debt
She e'er should cancel – but she may forget.
Safe is your secret still in Chloe's ear;
But none of Chloe's shall you ever hear.
Of all her dears she never slandered one,
But cares not if a thousand are undone.
Would Chloe know if you're alive or dead?
She bids her footman put it in her head.
Chloe is prudent – Would you too be wise?
Then never break your heart when Chloe dies.

One certain portrait may (I grant) be seen,
Which Heaven has varnished out, and made a Queen:†
The same for ever! and described by all
With truth and goodness, as with crown and ball.
Poets heap virtues, painters gems at will,
And show their zeal, and hide their want of skill.
'Tis well – but, artists! who can paint or write,
To draw the naked is your true delight.
That robe of quality so struts and swells,
None see what parts of Nature it conceals.
Th' exactest traits of body or of mind,
We owe to models of an humble kind.
If Queensberry to strip there's no compelling,
'Tis from a handmaid we must take a Helen.†
From peer or bishop 'tis no easy thing
To draw the man who loves his God, or king:
Alas! I copy (or my draft would fail)
From honest Mah'met† or plain Parson Hale.†
But grant, in public men sometimes are shown,
A woman's seen in private life alone:
Our bolder talents in full light displayed;
Your virtues open fairest in the shade.
Bred to disguise, in public 'tis you hide;
There, none distinguish 'twixt your shame or pride,
Weakness or delicacy; all so nice,
That each may seem a virtue, or a vice.
In men, we various ruling passions find,
In women, two almost divide the kind;
Those, only fixed, they first or last obey,
The love of pleasure, and the love of sway.
That, Nature gives; and where the lesson taught
Is but to please, can pleasure seem a fault?†
Experience, this; by man's oppression cursed,
They seek the second not to lose the first.
Men, some to business, some to pleasure take;
But every woman is at heart a rake;
Men, some to quiet, some to public strife;
But every lady would be queen for life.

---

*Queen* Queen Caroline (1683–1737). Pope disliked her association with Sir Robert Walpole, Whig Prime Minister and with Lord Hervey (*Ep. to Arbuthnot*, 319)

*Queensberry . . . Helen* the Duchess, a beauty (like Helen of Troy), had helped John Gay

*Mah'met* George I's Turkish servant

*Hale* Stephen Hales was a clerical friend of Pope

*fault* Pope often rhymes this with words containing no 'l'

Yet mark the fate of a whole sex of queens!
Power all their end, but beauty all the means.
In youth they conquer, with so wild a rage,
As leaves them scarce a subject in their age:
For foreign glory, foreign joy, they roam;
No thought of peace or happiness at home.
But wisdom's triumph is well-timed retreat,
As hard a science to the fair as great!
Beauties, like tyrants, old and friendless grown,
Yet hate to rest, and dread to be alone,
Worn out in public, weary every eye,
Nor leave one sigh behind them when they die.
Pleasures the sex, as children birds, pursue,
Still out of reach, yet never out of view,
Sure, if they catch, to spoil the toy at most,
To covet flying, and regret when lost:
At last, to follies youth could scarce defend,
'Tis half their age's prudence to pretend;
Ashamed to own they gave delight before,
Reduced to feign it, when they give no more:
As hags hold sabbaths, less for joy than spite,
So these their merry, miserable night;
Still round and round the ghosts of beauty glide,
And haunt the places where their honour died.
See how the world its veterans rewards!
A youth of frolics, an old age of cards;
Fair to no purpose, artful to no end,
Young without lovers, old without a friend;
A fop their passion, but their prize a sot;
Alive, ridiculous, and dead, forgot!
Ah friend! to dazzle let the vain design,
To raise the thought and touch the heart be thine!
That charm shall grow, while what fatigues the Ring†
Flaunts and goes down, an unregarded thing.
So when the sun's broad beam has tired the sight,
All mild ascends the moon's more sober light,
Serene in virgin† modesty she shines,
And unobserved the glaring orb declines.
Oh! blest with temper, whose unclouded ray
Can make tomorrow cheerful as today;

*Ring* fashionable drive
*virgin* Diana was Roman goddess of chastity and of the moon

She, who can love a sister's charms, or hear
Sighs for a daughter with unwounded ear;
She, who ne'er answers till a husband cools,
Or, if she rules him, never shows she rules;
Charms by accepting, by submitting sways,
Yet has her humour most, when she obeys;
Let fops or fortune fly which way they will;
Disdains all loss of tickets,† or codille;†
Spleen, vapours, or smallpox, above them all,
And mistress of herself, though China fall.
  And yet, believe me, good as well as ill,
Woman's at best a contradiction still.
Heaven, when it strives to polish all it can
Its last best work, but forms a softer man;
Picks from each sex, to make its favourite blest,
Your love of pleasure, our desire of rest;
Blends, in exception to all general rules,
Your taste of follies, with our scorn of fools;
Reserve with frankness, art with truth allied,
Courage with softness, modesty with pride,
Fixed principles, with fancy ever new;
Shakes all together, and produces – you.
  Be this a woman's fame: with this unblest,
Toasts live a scorn, and queens may die a jest.
This Phoebus promised (I forget the year)
When those blue eyes first opened on the sphere;
Ascendant Phoebus watched that hour with care,
Averted half your parents' simple prayer,
And gave you beauty, but denied the pelf
Which buys your sex a tyrant o'er itself.
The generous god, who wit and gold refines,†
And ripens spirits as he ripens mines,
Kept dross for duchesses, the world shall know it,
To you gave sense, good humour, and a poet.

1732–4 1735, 1744

*tickets* lottery tickets
*codille* defeat at cards

*refines* in Phoebus' double role, as god of poetry and of the sun

# EPISTLE TO DR ARBUTHNOT†

'Shut, shut the door, good John!'† fatigued, I said,
'Tie up the knocker, say I'm sick, I'm dead.'
The Dog Star† rages! nay 'tis past a doubt,
All Bedlam,† or Parnassus,† is let out:
Fire in each eye, and papers in each hand,
They rave, recite, and madden round the land.
What walls can guard me, or what shades can hide?
They pierce my thickets, through my grot† they glide,
By land, by water, they renew the charge,
They stop the chariot, and they board the barge.
No place is sacred, not the church is free,
Even Sunday shines no Sabbath day to me:
Then from the Mint† walks forth the man of rhyme,
Happy to catch me just at dinner time.
Is there a parson, much bemused in beer,
A maudlin poetess, a rhyming peer,
A clerk foredoomed his father's soul to cross,
Who pens a stanza when he should engross?†
Is there who, locked from ink and paper, scrawls
With desperate charcoal round his darkened walls?
All fly to Twit'nam, and in humble strain
Apply to me to keep them mad or vain.
Arthur,† whose giddy son neglects the laws,
Imputes to me and my damned works the cause:
Poor Cornus† sees his frantic wife elope,
And curses wit, and poetry, and Pope.
Friend to my life (which did not you prolong,
The world had wanted many an idle song),
What drop or nostrum† can this plague remove?
Or which must end me, a fool's wrath or love?
A dire dilemma! either way I'm sped,
If foes, they write, if friends, they read me dead.

*Epistle to Dr Arbuthnot* John Arbuthnot (1667–1735) had been physician to Queen Anne. Long associated with the wits of the Scriblerus group, he was the creator of John Bull. Pope's Epistle is an informal but impassioned Horatian defence of his own character and art against increasing attacks

*John* John Serle, Pope's servant

*Dog Star* Sirius, associated with heat and madness

*Bedlam* London lunatic asylum

*Parnassus* Mount of the Muses in Greece

*grot* Pope's famous shell-decorated grotto at Twickenham

*Mint* a sanctuary for debtors, who could escape all arrest on Sundays

*engross* write a legal document (as clerk)

*Arthur* father of James Moore Smythe, who plagiarised from Pope

*Cornus* a cuckold

*nostrum* medicine (appropriate to A's profession, and P's ill-health)

Seized and tied down to judge, how wretched I!
Who can't be silent, and who will not lie:
To laugh, were want of goodness and of grace,
And to be grave exceeds all power of face.
I sit with sad civility, I read
With honest anguish and an aching head,
And drop at last, but in unwilling ears,
This saving counsel, 'Keep your piece nine years.'[†]
'Nine years!' cries he, who high in Drury Lane,[†]
Lulled by soft zephyrs through the broken pane,
Rhymes ere he wakes, and prints before Term[†] ends,
Obliged by hunger and request of friends:
'The piece you think is incorrect: why, take it,
I'm all submission; what you'd have it, make it.'
Three things another's modest wishes bound,
My friendship, and a prologue, and ten pound.
Pitholeon[†] sends to me: 'You know His Grace,
I want a patron; ask him for a place.'
Pitholeon libelled me – 'but here's a letter
Informs you, sir, 'twas when he knew no better.
Dare you refuse him? Curll[†] invites to dine,
He'll write a *Journal*,[†] or he'll turn divine.'
Bless me! a packet. – ' 'Tis a stranger sues,
A virgin tragedy, an orphan Muse.'
If I dislike it, 'Furies, death, and rage!'
If I approve, 'Commend it to the stage.'
There (thank my stars) my whole commission ends,
The players and I are, luckily, no friends.
Fired that the house reject him, ' 'Sdeath, I'll print it,
And shame the fools – your interest, sir, with Lintot!'[†]
Lintot, dull rogue, will think your price too much.
'Not, sir, if you revise it, and retouch.'
All my demurs but double his attacks;
At last he whispers, 'Do, and we go snacks.'[†]
Glad of a quarrel, straight I clap the door,
'Sir, let me see your works and you no more.'

*nine years* as advised by Horace, *Ars Poetica*, 388
*Drury Lane* abode of whores and hack-writers
*Term* law and publishing season
*Pitholeon* historically, a foolish and libellous poet of Rhodes
*Curll* Edmund Curll, an old enemy, publisher of scandal, and of Pope's letters
*Journal* a periodical
*Lintot* Bernard Lintot published Pope
*go snacks* share the profits

'Tis sung, when Midas'[†] ears began to spring
(Midas, a sacred person and a king),
His very minister who spied them first,
(Some say his queen) was forced to speak, or burst.
And is not mine, my friend, a sorer case,
When every coxcomb perks them in my face?
'Good friend, forbear! you deal in dangerous things:
I'd never name queens, ministers, or kings;
Keep close to ears, and those let asses prick;
'Tis nothing' – Nothing? if they bite and kick?
Out with it, *Dunciad!*[†] let the secret pass,
That secret to each fool, that he's an ass:
The truth once told (and wherefore should we lie?),
The queen of Midas slept, and so may I.
You think this cruel? take it for a rule,
No creature smarts so little as a fool.
Let peals of laughter, Codrus![†] round thee break,
Thou unconcerned canst hear the mighty crack.
Pit, box and gallery in convulsions hurled,
Thou stand'st unshook amidst a bursting world.
Who shames a scribbler? break one cobweb through,
He spins the slight, self-pleasing thread anew;
Destroy his fib or sophistry; in vain,
The creature's at his dirty work again,
Throned in the centre of his thin designs,
Proud of a vast extent of flimsy lines.
Whom have I hurt? has poet yet, or peer,
Lost the arched eyebrow or Parnassian sneer?
And has not Colley[†] still his lord and whore?
His butchers Henley[†] his freemasons Moore?
Does not one table Bavius[†] still admit?
Still to one bishop Philips[†] seem a wit?
Still Sappho[†] – – 'Hold! for God's sake – you'll offend:
No names – be calm – learn prudence of a friend.
I too could write, and I am twice as tall;
But foes like these!' – – One flatterer's worse than all:

*Midas* legendary king, who could not conceal the secret of his ass's ears. Pope glances at the Queen and Walpole's manipulation of George II
*Dunciad* Pope's extended attack on literary dullness (1728), in the tradition of *Mac Flecknoe*
*Codrus* a ridiculed Roman poet
*Colley* Colley Cibber: Poet Laureate, hero of the revised *Dunciad* (1743)
*Henley* 'Orator' Henley: popular preacher
*Bavius* bad Roman poet
*Philips* Ambrose Philips (1674–1749), insipid poet, secretary to an Irish bishop
*Sappho* poetess (Lady Mary Wortley Montagu)

Of all mad creatures, if the learn'd are right,
It is the slaver* kills, and not the bite. saliva
A fool quite angry is quite innocent;
Alas! 'tis ten times worse when they repent.
One dedicates in high heroic prose,
And ridicules beyond a hundred foes;
One from all Grub Street will my fame defend,
And, more abusive, calls himself my friend.
This prints my letters, that expects a bribe,
And others roar aloud, 'Subscribe,† subscribe!'
There are, who to my person pay their court:
I cough like Horace;† and, though lean, am short;
Ammon's† great son, one shoulder had too high,
Such Ovid's† nose, and 'Sir! you have an eye –'
Go on, obliging creatures, make me see
All that disgraced my betters met in me:
Say for my comfort, languishing in bed,
'Just so immortal Maro† held his head';
And when I die, be sure you let me know
Great Homer died three thousand years ago.
Why did I write? what sin to me unknown
Dipped me in ink, my parents', or my own?
As yet a child, nor yet a fool to fame,
I lisped in numbers,† for the numbers came.
I left no calling for this idle trade,
No duty broke, no father disobeyed.
The Muse but served to ease some friend, not wife,
To help me through this long disease, my life,
To second, Arbuthnot! thy art and care,
And teach the being you preserved, to bear.
But why then publish? Granville† the polite,
And knowing Walsh,† would tell me I could write;
Well-natured Garth† inflamed with early praise,
And Congreve† loved, and Swift† endured my lays;

---

*subscribe* order copies of a book before publication
*Horace . . . Maro* Horace, Roman satirist (65–8 BC); *Ovid* the elegist and Virgil (*Maro*) were his contemporaries; *Ammon*: Jupiter, claimed ancestor of Alexander the Great. The references are to Pope's feebleness and deformity (cf.l.132)
*numbers* verse: Pope wrote poetry in his early teens
*Granville . . . Dryden's friends* Pope places himself socially and intellectually by the association with statesmen and writers: George *Granville*, Lord Lansdowne, dedicatee of *Windsor Forest*; William *Walsh*, Pope's early adviser; Sir Samuel *Garth*, poet; *Congreve*, the dramatist; *Swift* and his friend Lord *Somers*; Charles *Talbot*, Duke of Shrewsbury; Lord *Sheffield*; Francis Atterbury, Bishop of *Rochester*; Henry *St. John*, Viscount Bolingbroke, addressee of *An Essay on Man*

The courtly Talbot,† Somers,† Sheffield,† read;
Even mitred Rochester† would nod the head,
And St John's† self (great Dryden's friends† before)
With open arms received one poet more.
Happy my studies, when by these approved!
Happier their author, when by these beloved!
From these the world will judge of men and books,
Not from the Burnets, Oldmixons, and Cookes.†
  Soft were my numbers; who could take offence
While pure description held the place of sense?
Like gentle Fanny's† was my flowery theme,
A painted mistress, or a purling stream.
Yet then did Gildon† draw his venal quill;
I wished the man a dinner, and sat still.
Yet then did Dennis† rave in furious fret;
I never answered, I was not in debt.
If want provoked, or madness made them print,
I waged no war with Bedlam or the Mint.
  Did some more sober critic come abroad?
If wrong, I smiled; if right, I kissed the rod.
Pains, reading, study are their just pretence,
And all they want is spirit, taste, and sense.
Commas and points† they set exactly right,
And 'twere a sin to rob them of their mite.
Yet ne'er one sprig of laurel graced these ribalds,
From slashing Bentley† down to piddling Tibbalds.†
Each wight who reads not, and but scans and spells,
Each word-catcher that lives on syllables,
Even such small critics some regard may claim,
Preserved in Milton's or in Shakespeare's name.
Pretty! in amber to observe the forms
Of hairs, or straws, or dirt, or grubs, or worms;
The things, we know, are neither rich nor rare,
But wonder how the devil they got there.
  Were others angry? I excused them too;
Well might they rage; I gave them but their due.
A man's true merit 'tis not hard to find;
But each man's secret standard in his mind,

*Burnets . . . Cookes* called by P. 'authors of . . . scandalous history'
*Fanny* the effeminate Lord Hervey, the Sporus of l.305
*Gildon . . . Dennis* Charles Gildon and John Dennis were critics associated with Addison
*points . . . Tibbalds* full stops, the concern of textual critics like Richard Bentley, editor of *Paradise Lost*, and Lewis Theobald, critic of Pope's Shakespeare edition, and original hero of *The Dunciad*

That casting weight pride adds to emptiness,
This, who can gratify? for who can guess?
The bard† whom pilfered pastorals renown,
Who turns a Persian tale for half a crown,†
Just writes to make his barrenness appear,
And strains from hard-bound brains eight lines a year:
He who still wanting, though he lives on theft,
Steals much, spends little, yet has nothing left;
And he who now to sense, now nonsense leaning,
Means not, but blunders round about a meaning:
And he whose fustian's so sublimely bad,
It is not poetry, but prose run mad:
All these, my modest satire bade translate,
And owned that nine such poets made a Tate.†
How did they fume, and stamp, and roar, and chafe!
And swear, not Addison† himself was safe.
  Peace to all such! but were there one whose fires
True Genius kindles, and fair Fame inspires,
Blessed with each talent and each art to please,
And born to write, converse, and live with ease:
Should such a man, too fond to rule alone,
Bear, like the Turk,† no brother near the throne,
View him with scornful, yet with jealous eyes,
And hate for arts that caused himself to rise;
Damn with faint praise, assent with civil leer,
And without sneering, teach the rest to sneer;
Willing to wound, and yet afraid to strike,
Just hint a fault, and hesitate dislike;
Alike reserved to blame or to commend,
A timorous foe, and a suspicious friend,
Dreading even fools, by flatterers besieged,
And so obliging that he ne'er obliged;
Like Cato,† give his little senate laws,
And sit attentive to his own applause;
While wits and Templars† every sentence raise,
And wonder with a foolish face of praise.

*The bard* Ambrose Philips (l.99) wrote pastorals and translated Persian tales
*half a crown* a whore's charge
*Tate* Nahum Tate, Poet Laureate 1692–1715, had written Part II of Dryden's *Absalom*
*Addison* sketched as Atticus (originally a Roman man of letters): poet, essayist and statesman, he had seemed jealous of the rise of Pope; and in the coffee-house was like the hero of his own drama *Cato* (1713)
*the Turk* Turkish rulers murdered relatives as potential rivals
*Cato* see note on Addison, above
*Templars* lawyers: the Temple contained Inns of Court

Who but must laugh, if such a man there be?
Who would not weep, if Atticus[†] were he?
What though my name stood rubric[†] on the walls,
Or plastered posts, with claps[*] in capitals? posters
Or smoking forth, a hundred hawkers' load,
On wings of winds came flying all abroad?
I sought no homage from the race that write;
I kept, like Asian monarchs, from their sight:
Poems I heeded (now be-rhymed so long)
No more than thou, great George![†] a birthday song.
I ne'er with wits or witlings passed my days
To spread about the itch of verse and praise;
Nor like a puppy daggled through the town
To fetch and carry sing-song up and down;
Nor at rehearsals sweat, and mouthed, and cried,
With handkerchief and orange at my side:
But sick of fops, and poetry, and prate,
To Bufo[†] left the whole Castalian[†] state.
Proud as Apollo[†] on his forkèd hill,
Sat full-blown Bufo, puffed by every quill;
Fed with soft dedication all day long,
Horace and he went hand in hand in song.
His library (where busts of poets dead
And a true Pindar[†] stood without a head)
Received of wits an undistinguished race,
Who first his judgment asked, and then a place.[*] employment
Much they extolled his pictures, much his seat,[†]
And flattered every day, and some days eat:
Till grown more frugal in his riper days,
He paid some bards with port, and some with praise,
To some a dry rehearsal was assigned,
And others (harder still) he paid in kind.
Dryden alone (what wonder?) came not nigh,
Dryden alone escaped this judging eye:
But still the great have kindness in reserve;
He helped to bury whom he helped to starve.[†]
May some choice patron bless each gray goose quill!
May every Bavius have his Bufo still!

---

*Atticus* see note on Addison, above
*rubric* advertised in red
*George* George II, recipient of poems by the Laureate
*Bufo . . . Apollo* toad (Latin): a puffed-up patron; the *Castalian* spring on Mt Parnassus was sacred to *Apollo*, god of poetry, and the Muses
*Pindar* Greek lyric poet
*seat* (country) estate
*starve* Dryden, after a life of poverty, had a fine funeral

So when a statesman wants a day's defence,
Or envy holds a whole week's war with sense,
Or simple pride for flattery makes demands,
May dunce by dunce be whistled off my hands!
Blessed be the great! for those they take away,
And those they left me – for they left me Gay;
Left me to see neglected genius bloom,
Neglected die! and tell it on his tomb;†
Of all thy blameless life the sole return
My verse, and Queensberry weeping o'er thy urn!
Oh let me live my own, and die so too!
('To live and die is all I have to do'†)
Maintain a poet's dignity and ease,
And see what friends, and read what books I please.
Above a patron, though I condescend
Sometimes to call a minister my friend:
I was not born for courts or great affairs,
I pay my debts, believe, and say my prayers,
Can sleep without a poem in my head,
Nor know if Dennis be alive or dead.
  Why am I asked what next shall see the light?
Heavens! was I born for nothing but to write?
Has life no joys for me? or (to be grave)
Have I no friend to serve, no soul to save?
'I found him close with Swift' – 'Indeed? no doubt'
(Cries prating Balbus) 'something will come out.'
'Tis all in vain, deny it as I will.
'No, such a genius never can lie still,'
And then for mine obligingly mistakes
The first lampoon Sir Will† or Bubo† makes.
Poor guiltless I! and can I choose but smile,
When every coxcomb knows me by my style?
  Cursed be the verse, how well soe'er it flow,
That tends to make one worthy man my foe,
Give virtue scandal, innocence a fear,
Or from the soft-eyed virgin steal a tear!
But he who hurts a harmless neighbour's peace,
Insults fallen worth, or beauty in distress,

*tomb* Pope wrote his epitaph; Gay was helped by the Duke and Duchess of Queensberry, not the court

*'To live . . . to do'* from Sir John Denham (1615–69), *Of Prudence*

*Sir Will* Sir William Yonge

*Bubo* Bubb Dodington; both politicians of modest literary taste

Who loves a lie, lame slander helps about,
Who writes a libel, or who copies out:
That fop whose pride affects a patron's name,
Yet absent, wounds an author's honest fame;
Who can your merit selfishly approve,
And show the sense of it without the love;
Who has the vanity to call you friend,
Yet wants the honour, injured, to defend;
Who tells whate'er you think, whate'er you say,
And, if he lie not, must at least betray:
Who to the dean† and silver bell† can swear,
And sees at Cannons† what was never there;
Who reads but with a lust to misapply,
Make satire a lampoon, and fiction, lie:
A lash like mine no honest man shall dread,
But all such babbling blockheads in his stead.
    Let Sporus† tremble – 'What? that thing of silk,
Sporus, that mere white curd of ass's milk?
Satire or sense, alas! can Sporus feel?
Who breaks a butterfly upon a wheel?'†
Yet let me flap this bug with gilded wings,
This painted child of dirt, that stinks and stings;
Whose buzz the witty and the fair annoys,
Yet wit ne'er tastes, and beauty ne'er enjoys;
So well-bred spaniels civilly delight
In mumbling of the game they dare not bite.
Eternal smiles his emptiness betray,
As shallow streams run dimpling all the way.
Whether in florid impotence he speaks,
And, as the prompter breathes, the puppet squeaks;
Or at the ear of Eve, familiar toad,†
Half froth, half venom, spits himself abroad,
In puns, or politics, or tales, or lies,
Or spite, or smut, or rhymes, or blasphemies.
His wit all seesaw between that and this,
Now high, now low, now master up, now miss,
And he himself one vile antithesis.

*dean, bell, Cannons* details from Pope's *Epistle to Burlington* (1731), wrongly understood to refer to Cannons, estate of the Duke of Chandos

*Sporus* boy lover of the Roman Emperor Nero; here, Lord Hervey (1696–1743), who aided Lady Mary Wortley Montagu in the vicious attacks which provoked publication of this poem. An effeminate courtier, he is seen as Satan to Queen Caroline's Eve (l.319)

*wheel* an instrument of human torture

*toad* Pope's note refers us to *Paradise Lost*, IV.800

Amphibious† thing! that acting either part,
The trifling head or the corrupted heart,
Fop at the toilet, flatterer at the board,
Now trips a lady, and now struts a lord.
Eve's tempter thus the rabbins† have expressed,
A cherub's face, a reptile all the rest;
Beauty that shocks you, parts that none will trust,
Wit that can creep, and pride that licks the dust.
  Not fortune's worshipper, nor fashion's fool,
Not lucre's madman, nor ambition's tool,
Not proud, nor servile, be one poet's praise,
That, if he pleased, he pleased by manly ways;
That flattery, even to kings, he held a shame,
And thought a lie in verse or prose the same:
That not in fancy's maze he wandered long,
But stooped† to truth, and moralized his song;
That not for fame, but virtue's better end,
He stood the furious foe, the timid friend,
The damning critic, half-approving wit,
The coxcomb hit, or fearing to be hit;
Laughed at the loss of friends he never had,
The dull, the proud, the wicked, and the mad;
The distant threats of vengeance on his head,
The blow unfelt, the tear he never shed;
The tale revived, the lie so oft o'erthrown,
Th' imputed trash, and dullness not his own;
The morals blackened when the writings 'scape,
The libelled person, and the pictured† shape;
Abuse on all he loved, or loved him, spread,
A friend in exile,† or a father dead;
The whisper, that to greatness still too near,
Perhaps, yet vibrates on his Sovereign's ear –
Welcome for thee, fair virtue! all the past:
For thee, fair virtue! welcome even the last!
  'But why insult the poor, affront the great?'
A knave's a knave to me in every state;
Alike my scorn, if he succeed or fail,
Sporus at court, or Japhet† in a jail,

*Amphibious* like other detail, hints at bisexuality
*rabbins* Jewish scholars
*stooped* as a falcon swoops down on its prey
*pictured* his deformity had been drawn as that of a hunchbacked ape
*in exile* Atterbury (l.140: 1662–1732), who had first been imprisoned for Jacobite conspiracy
*Japhet* Japhet Crook, a forger, punished by ear-slitting

A hireling scribbler, or a hireling peer,
Knight of the post† corrupt, or of the shire,†
If on a pillory, or near a throne,
He gain his prince's ear, or lose his own.
  Yet soft by nature, more a dupe than wit,
Sappho† can tell you how this man was bit;†
This dreaded satirist Dennis will confess
Foe to his pride, but friend to his distress:
So humble, he has knocked at Tibbald's door,
Has drunk with Cibber, nay has rhymed for Moore.
Full ten years slandered, did he once reply?
Three thousand suns went down on Welsted's† lie;
To please a mistress, one aspersed his life;
He lashed him not, but let her be his wife.
Let Budgell† charge low Grub Street on his quill,
And write whate'er he pleased, except his will;
Let the two Curlls† of town and court abuse
His father, mother, body, soul, and muse.
Yet why? that father held it for a rule
It was a sin to call our neighbour fool;
That harmless mother thought no wife a whore:
Hear this, and spare his family, James Moore!
Unspotted names! and memorable long,
If there be force in virtue, or in song.
  Of gentle blood† (part shed in honour's cause,
While yet in Britain honour had applause)
Each parent sprung – 'What fortune, pray?' – Their own,
And better got than Bestia's† from the throne.
Born to no pride, inheriting no strife,
Nor marrying discord in a noble wife,
Stranger to civil and religious rage,
The good man walked innoxious through his age.
No courts he saw, no suits would ever try,
Nor dared an oath,† nor hazarded a lie:
Unlearn'd, he knew no schoolman's* subtle art, theologian
No language but the language of the heart.

*Knight of the post* giver of false evidence
*Knight of the shire* a county MP
*Sappho* again, Lady Mary
*bit* taken in
*Welsted* the poet Leonard Welsted had accused him of callousness to others
*Budgell* Eustace Budgell identified Pope as accusing him in the Grub Street Journal of forging a will
*two Curlls* the original and Lord Hervey
*gentle blood* Hervey's jibe of 'birth obscure' had stung Pope, whose father was a draper
*Bestia* a bribed Roman consul, here probably the Duke of Marlborough, liberally rewarded by Queen Anne
*oath* his father suffered anti-Catholic penalties by refusing to take the oath against the Pope

By nature honest, by experience wise,
Healthy by temperance and by exercise;
His life, though long, to sickness passed unknown,
His death was instant, and without a groan.
Oh grant me thus to live, and thus to die!
Who sprung from kings shall know less joy than I.
  O friend! may each domestic bliss be thine!
Be no unpleasing melancholy mine:
Me, let the tender office long engage
To rock the cradle of reposing age,
With lenient arts extend a mother's breath,
Make languor smile, and smooth the bed of death,†
Explore the thought, explain the asking eye,
And keep awhile one parent from the sky!
On cares like these if length of days attend,
May heaven, to bless those days, preserve my friend,†
Preserve him social, cheerful, and serene,
And just as rich as when he served a queen!
Whether that blessing be denied or given,
Thus far was right, the rest belongs to Heaven.

1731–4 1735

*death* his mother died in 1733, before this poem was published

*friend* Arbuthnot, who had attended Queen Anne

# Lady Mary Wortley Montagu

1689–1762

Lady Mary Pierrepont, a cousin of Henry Fielding, defied her father, the Earl of Kingston, to marry for love the politician and businessman Edward Wortley Montagu. (She later lived over twenty years apart from him on the Continent.) A learned, independent and witty woman, she moved in fashionable social and literary circles, having some reputation from her *Court Poems* (1716). An early friendship with Pope turned to bitter attacks on both sides (see his references to 'Sappho' in *Epistle to Arbuthnot* and *To a Lady*). She is now best remembered for her letters, which reveal a worldly, open-minded intelligence. Her husband was ambassador to Turkey 1716–18, which with her later travels provided a rich vein of material. (The French painter Ingres was influenced by the descriptions in several of her Turkish letters.) Her daughter married the future Prime Minister, Lord Bute.

## *From* LETTERS

### To the Countess of Mar

### *[Turkish Women]*

*Adrianople, 1 April 1717*

I wish to God (dear sister) that you was as regular in letting me have the pleasure of knowing what passes on your side of the globe as I am careful in endeavouring to amuse you by the account of all I see that I think you care to hear of. You content yourself with telling me over and over that the town is very dull. It may possibly be dull to you when everyday does not present you with something new, but for me that am in arrear at least two months' news, all that seems very stale with you would be fresh and sweet here; pray let me into more particulars. I will try to awaken your gratitude by giving you a full and true relation of the novelties of this place, none of which would surprise you more than a sight of my person as I am now in my Turkish habit, though I believe you would be of my opinion that 'tis admirably becoming. I intend to send you my picture; in the meantime accept of it here.

The first piece of my dress is a pair of drawers, very full, that reach to my shoes and conceal the legs more modestly than your petticoats. They are of a thin, rose-colour damask brocaded with silver flowers, my shoes of white kid leather embroidered with gold. Over this hangs my smock of a fine white silk gauze edged with embroidery. This smock has wide sleeves hanging half-way down the arm and is closed at the neck with a diamond button, but the shape and colour of the bosom very well to be distinguished through it. The *antery* is a waistcoat made close to the shape, of white and gold damask, with very long sleeves falling back and fringed with deep gold fringe, and should have diamond or pearl buttons. My caftan of the same stuff with my drawers is a robe exactly fitted to my shape and reaching to my feet, with very long strait falling sleeves. Over this is the girdle of about four fingers broad, which all that can afford have entirely of diamonds or other precious stones. Those that will not be at that expense have it of exquisite embroidery on satin, but it must be fastened before with a clasp of diamonds. The *curdée* is a loose robe they throw off or put on according to the weather, being of a rich brocade (mine is green and gold) either lined with ermine or sables; the sleeves reach very little below the shoulders.

The head-dress is composed of a cap called *talpack*, which is in winter of fine velvet embroidered with pearls or diamonds and in summer of a light, shining silver stuff. This is fixed on one side of the head, hanging a little way down with a gold tassel and bound on either with a circle of diamonds (as I have seen several) or a rich embroidered handkerchief. On the other side of the head the hair is laid flat, and here the ladies are at liberty to show their fancies, some putting flowers, others a plume of heron's feathers, and, in short, what they please, but the most general fashion is a large bouquet of jewels made like natural flowers, that is, the buds of pearl, the roses of different coloured rubies, the jasmines of diamonds, jonquils of topazes, etc., so well set and enamelled 'tis hard to imagine anything of that kind so beautiful. The hair hangs at its full length behind, divided into tresses braided with pearl or riband, which is always in great quantity.

I never saw in my life so many fine heads of hair. I have counted one hundred and ten of these tresses of one lady's, all natural; but it must be owned that every beauty is more common here than with us. 'Tis suprising to see a young woman that is not very handsome. They have naturally the most beautiful complexions in the world and generally large black eyes. I can assure you with great truth that the Court of England (though I believe it the fairest in Christendom) cannot show so many beauties as are under our protection here. They generally shape their eyebrows, and the Greeks and Turks have a custom of putting round their eyes on the inside a black tincture that, at a distance or by candlelight, adds very much to the blackness of them. I fancy many of our ladies would be overjoyed to know this secret, but 'tis too visible by day. They dye their nails rose colour; I own I cannot enough accustom myself to this fashion to find any beauty in it.

As to their morality or good conduct, I can say like Harlequin, ''Tis just as 'tis with you'; and the Turkish ladies don't commit one sin the less for not being Christians. Now I am a little acquainted with their ways, I cannot forbear admiring either the exemplary discretion or extreme stupidity of all the writers that have given accounts of 'em. 'Tis very easy to see they have more liberty than we have, no woman of what rank soever being permitted to go in the streets without two muslins, one that covers her face all but her eyes and another that hides the whole dress of her head and hangs half-way down her back; and their shapes are wholly concealed by a thing they call a *ferigée*, which no woman of any sort appears without. This has strait sleeves that reach to their fingers' ends and it laps all round 'em, not unlike a riding hood. In winter 'tis of cloth, and in summer, plain stuff or silk. You may guess how effectually this disguises them, that there is no distinguishing the great lady from her slave, and 'tis impossible for the most jealous husband to know his wife when he meets her, and no man dare either touch or follow a woman in the street.

This perpetual masquerade gives them entire liberty of following their inclinations without danger of discovery. The most usual method of intrigue is to send an appointment to the lover to meet the lady at a Jew's shop, which are as notoriously convenient as our Indian houses, and yet even those that don't make that use of 'em do not scruple to go to buy penn'orths and tumble over rich goods, which are chiefly to be found amongst that sort of people. The great ladies seldom let their gallants know who they are, and 'tis so difficult to find it out that they can very seldom guess at her name they have corresponded with above half a year together.

You may easily imagine the number of faithful wives very small in a country where they have nothing to fear from their lovers' indiscretion, since we see so many that have the courage to expose themselves to that in this world and all the threatened punishment of the next, which is never preached to the Turkish damsels. Neither have they much to apprehend from the resentment of their husbands, those ladies that are rich having all their money in their own hands, which they take with 'em upon a divorce with an addition which he is obliged to give 'em. Upon the whole, I look upon the Turkish women as the only free people in the empire. The very Divan† pays a respect to 'em, and the Grand

*Divan* council of state

Signior[†] himself, when a pasha[†] is executed, never violates the privileges of the harem (or women's apartment) which remains unsearched entire to the widow. They are queens of their slaves, which the husband has no permission so much as to look upon, except it be an old woman or two that his lady chooses. 'Tis true their law permits them four wives, but there is no instance of a man of quality that makes use of this liberty, or of a woman of rank that would suffer it. When a husband happens to be inconstant (as those things will happen) he keeps his mistress in a house apart and visits her as privately as he can, just as 'tis with you. Amongst all the great men here I only know the *tefterdar* (i.e. treasurer) that keeps a number of she slaves for his own use (that is, on his own side of the house, for a slave once given to serve a lady is entirely at her disposal), and he is spoke of as a libertine, or what we should call a rake, and his wife won't see him, though she continues to live in his house.

Thus you see, dear sister, the manners of mankind do not differ so widely as our voyage writers would make us believe. Perhaps it would be more entertaining to add a few surprising customs of my own invention, but nothing seems to me so agreeable as truth, and I believe nothing so acceptable to you. I conclude with repeating the great truth of my being, dear sister, etc.

## To Sarah Chiswell
## *[Inoculation against Smallpox]*[†]

*Adrianople, 1 April 1717*

. . . Apropos of distempers, I am going to tell you a thing that I am sure will make you wish yourself here. The smallpox, so fatal and so general amongst us, is here entirely harmless by the invention of engrafting (which is the term they give it). There is a set of old women who make it their business to perform the operation. Every autumn, in the month of September, when the great heat is abated, people send to one another to know if any of their family has a mind to have the smallpox. They make parties for this purpose, and when they are met (commonly fifteen or sixteen together) the old woman comes with a nutshell full of the matter of the best sort of smallpox and asks what

*Grand Signior* Sultan (Turkish ruler)
*pasha* high-ranking officer
*Inoculation Against Smallpox* Lady Mary, whose beauty had been attacked by smallpox, was largely responsible for the introduction in Britain of inoculation against the disease. Ironically, Sarah Chiswell died of smallpox in 1726

veins you please to have opened. She immediately rips open that you offer to her with a large needle (which gives you no more pain than a common scratch) and puts into the vein as much venom as can lie upon the head of her needle, and after binds up the little wound with a hollow bit of shell, and in this manner opens four or five veins. The Grecians have commonly the superstition of opening one in the middle of the forehead, in each arm, and on the breast to mark the sign of the cross, but this has a very ill effect, all these wounds leaving little scars, and is not done by those that are not superstitious, who choose to have them in the legs or that part of the arm that is concealed. The children or young patients play together all the rest of the day and are in perfect health till the eighth. Then the fever begins to seize 'em and they keep their beds two days, very seldom three. They have very rarely above twenty or thirty in their faces, which never mark, and in eight days' time they are as well as before their illness. Where they are wounded there remains running sores during the distemper, which I don't doubt is a great relief to it. Every year thousands undergo this operation, and the French ambassador says pleasantly that they take the smallpox here by way of diversion as they take the waters in other countries. There is no example of anyone that has died in it, and you may believe I am very well satisfied of the safety of the experiment since I intend to try it on my dear little son. I am patriot enough to take pains to bring this useful invention into fashion in England, and I should not fail to write to some of our doctors very particularly about it if I knew any one of 'em that I thought had virtue enough to destroy such a considerable branch of their revenue for the good of mankind, but that distemper is too beneficial to them not to expose to all their resentment the hardy wight that should undertake to put an end to it. Perhaps if I live to return I may, however, have courage to war with 'em. Upon this occasion, admire the heroism in the heart of your friend, etc.

## To the Countess of Mar
## *[Female Society in Turkey]*

*Adrianople, 18 April 1717*

I writ to you (dear sister) and to all my other English correspondents by the last ship, and only Heaven can tell when I shall have another opportunity of sending to you; but I cannot forbear writing, though perhaps my letter may lie upon my hands this two months. To confess the truth, my head is so full of my entertainment yesterday that 'tis absolutely necessary for my own repose to give it some vent. Without farther preface I will then begin my story.

I was invited to dine with the Grand Vizier's† lady, and 'twas with a great deal of pleasure I prepared myself for an entertainment which was never given before to any Christian. I thought I should very little satisfy her curiosity (which I did not doubt was a considerable motive to the invitation) by going in a dress she was used to see, and therefore dressed myself in the court habit of Vienna, which is much more magnificent than ours. However, I chose to go *incognito* to avoid any disputes about ceremony, and went in a Turkish coach only attended by my woman that held up my train, and the Greek lady who was my interpretess. I was met at the court door by her black eunuch, who helped me out of the coach with great respect and conducted me through several rooms, where her she-slaves, finely dressed, were ranged on each side. In the innermost, I found the lady sitting on her sofa in a sable vest. She advanced to meet me and presented me half a dozen of her friends with great civility. She seemed a very good woman, near fifty year old. I was surprised to observe so little magnificence in her house, the furniture being all very moderate; and except the habits and number of her slaves nothing about her appeared expensive. She guessed at my thoughts and told me she was no longer of an age to spend either her time or money in superfluities; that her whole expense was in charity, and her employment praying to God. There was no affectation in this speech; both she and her husband are entirely given up to devotion. He never looks upon any other woman; and, what is much more extraordinary, touches no bribes, notwithstanding the example of all his predecessors. He is so scrupulous on this point, he would not accept Mr Wortley's present, till he had been assured over and over 'twas a settled perquisite of his place at the entrance of every ambassador.

She entertained me with all kind of civility till dinner came in, which was served one dish at a time, to a vast number, all finely dressed after their manner, which I do not think so bad as you have perhaps heard it represented. I am a very good judge of their eating, having lived three weeks in the house of an *effendi* at Belgrade who gave us very magnificent dinners dressed by his own cooks, which the first week pleased me extremely; but I own I then begun to grow weary of it, and desired my own cook might add a dish or two after our manner, but I attribute this to custom. I am very much inclined to believe that an Indian that had never tasted of either would prefer their cookery to ours. Their sauces are very high, all the roast very much done. They use a great deal of rich spice. The soup is served for the last dish; and they have at least as great a variety of ragouts† as we have. I was very sorry I could not eat of as many as the good lady would have had me, who was very earnest in serving me of every thing. The treat concluded

*Grand Vizier* chief minister

*ragouts* stewed meats

with coffee and perfumes, which is a high mark of respect; two slaves kneeling censed my hair, clothes and handkerchief. After this ceremony, she commanded her slaves to play and dance, which they did with their guitars in their hands, and she excused to me their want of skill, saying she took no care to accomplish them in the art. I returned her thanks, and soon after took my leave.

I was conducted back in the same manner I entered, and would have gone straight to my own house; but the Greek lady with me earnestly solicited me to visit the *kiyaya's* lady, saying he was the second officer in the empire and ought indeed to be looked upon as the first, the Grand Vizier having only the name while he exercised the authority. I had found so little diversion in this *harem*,† that I had no mind to go into another, but her importunity prevailed with me, and I am extremely glad that I was so complaisant. All things here were with quite another air than at the Grand Vizier's, and the very house confessed the difference between an old devotee and a young beauty. It was nicely clean and magnificent. I was met at the door by two black eunuchs who led me through a long gallery between two ranks of beautiful young girls with their hair finely plaited, almost hanging to their feet, all dressed in fine light damasks brocaded with silver. I was sorry that decency did not permit me to stop to consider them nearer, but that thought was lost upon my entrance into a large room, or rather pavilion, built round with gilded sashes, which were most of 'em thrown up; and the trees planted near them gave an agreeable shade, which hindered the sun from being troublesome, the jessamines and honeysuckles that twisted round their trunks, shedding a soft perfume increased by a white marble fountain playing sweet water in the lower part of the room, which fell into three or four basins with a pleasing sound. The roof was painted with all sorts of flowers falling out of gilded baskets that seemed tumbling down.

On a sofa, raised three steps and covered with fine Persian carpets, sat the *kiyaya's* lady, leaning on cushions of white satin, embroidered; and at her feet sat two young girls about twelve year old, lovely as angels, dressed perfectly rich, and almost covered with jewels. But they were hardly seen near the fair Fatima (for that is her name), so much her beauty effaced every thing. I have seen all that has been called lovely either in England or Germany, and must own that I never saw anything so gloriously beautiful, nor can I recollect a face that would have been taken notice of near hers. She stood up to receive me, saluting me after their fashion, putting her hand to her heart with a sweetness full of majesty that no court breeding could ever give. She ordered cushions to be given me and took care to place me in the corner, which is the

---

*harem* women's quarters

place of honour. I confess, though the Greek lady had before given me a great opinion of her beauty, I was so struck with admiration, that I could not for some time speak to her, being wholly taken up in gazing. That surprising harmony of features! that charming result of the whole! that exact proportion of body! that lovely bloom of complexion unsullied by art! the unutterable enchantment of her smile! But her eyes! large and black, with all the soft languishment of the blue! every turn of her face discovering some new charm! After my first surprise was over, I endeavoured by nicely[†] examining her face, to find out some imperfection, without any fruit of my search but being clearly convinced of the error of that vulgar notion, that a face perfectly regular would not be agreeable, nature having done for her with more success what Apelles[†] is said to have essayed, by a collection of the most exact features to form a perfect face, and to that a behaviour so full of grace and sweetness, such easy motions, with an air so majestic yet free from stiffness or affectation that I am persuaded, could she be suddenly transported upon the most polite throne of Europe, nobody would think her other than born and bred to be a queen, though educated in a country we call barbarous. To say all in a word, our most celebrated English beauties would vanish near her.

She was dressed in a *caftan* of gold brocade flowered with silver, very well fitted to her shape and showing to admiration the beauty of her bosom, only shaded by the thin gauze of her shift. Her drawers were pale pink, green and silver; her slippers white, finely embroidered; her lovely arms adorned with bracelets of diamonds, and her broad girdle set round with diamonds; upon her head a rich Turkish handkerchief of pink and silver, her own fine black hair hanging a great length in various tresses, and on one side of her head some bodkins of jewels. I am afraid you will accuse me of extravagance in this description. I think I have read somewhere that women always speak in rapture when they speak of beauty, but I can't imagine why they should not be allowed to do so. I rather think it virtue to be able to admire without any mixture of desire or envy. The gravest writers have spoken with great warmth of some celebrated pictures and statues. The workmanship of Heaven certainly excels all our weak imitations, and I think has a much better claim to our praise. For me, I am not ashamed to own I took more pleasure in looking on the beauteous Fatima, than the finest piece of sculpture could have given me. She told me the two girls at her feet were her daughters, though she appeared too young to be their mother.

Her fair maids were ranged below the sofa to the number of twenty, and put me in mind of the pictures of the ancient nymphs. I did not think all nature could have furnished such a scene of beauty. She made

*nicely* closely

*Apelles* ancient Greek painter

them a sign to play and dance. Four of them immediately began to play some soft airs on instruments between a lute and a guitar, which they accompanied with their voices, while the others danced by turns. This dance was very different from what I had seen before. Nothing could be more artful, or more proper to raise certain ideas, the tunes so soft, the motions so languishing, accompanied with pauses and dying eyes, half-falling back, and then recovering themselves in so artful a manner that I am very positive the coldest and most rigid prude upon earth could not have looked upon them without thinking of something not to be spoke of. I suppose you may have read that the Turks have no music but what is shocking to the ears, but this account is from those who never heard any but what is played in the streets, and is just as reasonable as if a foreigner should take his ideas of English music from the *bladder and string*, or the *marrow bones and cleavers*. I can assure you that the music is extremely pathetic. 'Tis true I am inclined to prefer the Italian, but perhaps I am partial. I am acquainted with a Greek lady who sings better than Mrs Robinson,† and is very well skilled in both, who gives the preference to the Turkish. 'Tis certain they have very fine natural voices; these were very agreeable.

When the dance was over, four fair slaves came into the room with silver censers in their hands and perfumed the air with amber, aloes-wood, and other scents. After this they served me coffee upon their knees in the finest japan china, with soucoups of silver gilt. The lovely Fatima entertained me all this time in the most polite agreeable manner, calling me often *Uzelle Sultanam*, or the beautiful sultana, and desiring my friendship with the best grace in the world, lamenting that she could not entertain me in my own language. When I took my leave two maids brought in a fine silver basket of embroidered handkerchiefs. She begged I would wear the richest for her sake, and gave the others to my woman and interpretess. I retired through the same ceremonies as before, and could not help fancying I had been some time in Mahomet's paradise, so much was I charmed with what I had seen. I know not how the relation of it appears to you. I wish it may give you part of my pleasure; for I would have my dear sister share in all [my] diversions.

*Mrs Robinson* leading contemporary English singer

## To the Countess of Bute
### *[Female Education]*

170 *Gottolengo,*† *28 January 1753*

Dear Child,

You have given me a great deal of satisfaction by your account of your eldest daughter. I am particularly pleased to hear she is a good arithmetician; it is the best proof of understanding. The knowledge of numbers is one of the chief distinctions between us and brutes. If there is anything in blood you may reasonably expect your children should be endowed with an uncommon share of good sense. Mr Wortley's family and mine have both produced some of the greatest men that have been born in England. I mean Admiral Sandwich, and my great-grandfather who was distinguished by the name of Wise William. I have heard Lord Bute's father mentioned as an extraordinary genius (though he had not many opportunities of showing it), and his uncle the present Duke of Argyle has one of the best heads I ever knew.

I will therefore speak to you as supposing Lady Mary not only capable but desirous of learning. In that case, by all means let her be indulged in it. You will tell me, I did not make it a part of your education. Your prospect was very different from hers, as you had no defect either in mind or person to hinder, and much in your circumstances to attract, the highest offers. It seemed your business to learn how to live in the world, as it is hers to know how to be easy out of it. It is the common error of builders and parents to follow some plan they think beautiful (and perhaps is so) without considering that nothing is beautiful that is misplaced. Hence we see so many edifices raised that the raisers can never inhabit, being too large for their fortunes. Vistas are laid open over barren heaths, and apartments contrived for a coolness very agreeable in Italy but killing in the north of Britain. Thus every woman endeavours to breed her daughter a fine lady, qualifying her for a station in which she will never appear, and at the same time incapacitating her for that retirement to which she is destined. Learning (if she has a real taste for it) will not only make her contented but happy in it. No entertainment is so cheap as reading, nor any pleasure so lasting. She will not want new fashions nor regret the loss of expensive diversions or variety of company if she can be amused with an author in her closet. To render this amusement extensive, she should be permitted to learn the languages. I have heard it lamented that boys lose so many years in mere learning of words. This is no objection to a

---

*Gottolengo* for many years, Lady Mary lived at her house in Northern Italy

girl, whose time is not so precious. She cannot advance herself in any profession, and has therefore more hours to spare; and as you say her memory is good she will be very agreeably employed this way.

There are two cautions to be given on this subject: first, not to think herself learned when she can read Latin or even Greek. Languages are more properly to be called vehicles of learning than learning itself, as may be observed in many schoolmasters, who though perhaps critics in grammar are the most ignorant fellows upon earth. True knowledge consists in knowing things, not words. I would wish her no further a linguist than to enable her to read books in their originals, that are often corrupted and always injured by translations. Two hours application every morning will bring this about much sooner than you can imagine, and she will have leisure enough beside to run over the English poetry, which is a more important part of a woman's education than it is generally supposed. Many a young damsel has been ruined by a fine copy of verses, which she would have laughed at if she had known it had been stolen from Mr Waller.† I remember when I was a girl I saved one of my companions from destruction, who communicated to me an epistle she was quite charmed with. As she had a natural good taste she observed the lines were not so smooth as Prior's† or Pope's, but had more thought and spirit than any of theirs. She was wonderfully delighted with such a demonstration of her lover's sense and passion, and not a little pleased with her own charms, that had force enough to inspire such elegancies. In the midst of this triumph I showed her they were taken from Randolph's† *Poems*, and the unfortunate transcriber was dismissed with the scorn he deserved. To say truth, the poor plagiary was very unlucky to fall into my hands; that author, being no longer in fashion, would have escaped anyone of less universal reading than myself. You should encourage your daughter to talk over with you what she reads, and as you are very capable of distinguishing, take care she does not mistake pert folly for wit and humour, or rhyme for poetry, which are the common errors of young people, and have a train of ill consequences.

The second caution to be given her (and which is most absolutely necessary) is to conceal whatever learning she attains, with as much solicitude as she would hide crookedness or lameness. The parade of it can only serve to draw on her the envy, and consequently the most inveterate hatred of all he and she fools, which will certainly be at least three parts in four of all her acquaintance. The use of knowledge in our sex (beside the amusement of solitude) is to moderate the passions and learn to be contented with a small expense, which are the certain

*Waller* Edmund Waller (1606–87)
*Prior* Matthew Prior (1664–1721)
*Randolph* Thomas Randolph (1605–35), *Poems*, 1638

effects of a studious life and, it may be, preferable even to that fame which men have engrossed to themselves and will not suffer us to share. You will tell me I have not observed this rule myself, but you are mistaken; it is only inevitable accident that has given me any reputation that way. I have always carefully avoided it, and ever thought it a misfortune.

The explanation of this paragraph would occasion a long digression, which I will not trouble you with, it being my present design only to say what I think useful for the instruction of my granddaughter, which I have much at heart. If she has the same inclination (I should say passion) for learning that I was born with, history, geography, and philosophy will furnish her with materials to pass away cheerfully a longer life than is allotted to mortals. I believe there are few heads capable of making Sir Isaac Newton's calculations, but the result of them is not difficult to be understood by a moderate capacity. Do not fear this should make her affect the character of Lady – –, or Lady – –, or Mrs – –. Those women are ridiculous not because they have learning but because they have it not. One thinks herself a complete historian after reading Echard's[†] *Roman History*, another a profound philosopher having got by heart some of Pope's unintelligible essays, and a third an able divine on the strength of Whitefield's[†] sermons. Thus you hear them screaming politics and controversy. It is a saying of Thucydides:[†] Ignorance is bold, and knowledge reserved. Indeed it is impossible to be far advanced in it without being more humbled by a conviction of human ignorance than elated by learning.

At the same time I recommend books I neither exclude work nor drawing. I think it as scandalous for a woman not to know how to use a needle, as for a man not to know how to use a sword. I was once extreme fond of my pencil, and it was a great mortification to me when my father turned off my master, having made a considerable progress for the short time I learned. My over-eagerness in the pursuit of it had brought a weakness on my eyes that made it necessary to leave it off, and all the advantage I got was the improvement of my hand. I see by hers that practice will make her a ready writer. She may attain it by serving you for a secretary when your health or affairs make it troublesome to you to write yourself, and custom will make it an agreeable amusement to her. She cannot have too many for that station of life which will probably be her fate. The ultimate end of your education was to make you a good wife (and I have the comfort to hear that you are one); hers ought to be, to make her happy in a virgin state.

*Echard* Laurence Echard (?1670–1730), British historian

*Whitefield* George Whitefield (1714–70), methodist preacher

*Thucydides* *c* 460–395 BC Greek historian

I will not say it is happier, but it is undoubtedly safer than any marriage. In a lottery where there is (at the lowest computation) ten thousand blanks to a prize it is the most prudent choice not to venture.

I have always been so thoroughly persuaded of this truth that notwithstanding the flattering views I had for you (as I never intended you a sacrifice to my vanity) I thought I owed you the justice to lay before you all the hazards attending matrimony. You may recollect I did so in the strongest manner. Perhaps you may have more success in the instructing your daughter. She has so much company at home she will not need seeking it abroad, and will more readily take the notions you think fit to give her. As you were alone in my family, it would have been thought a great cruelty to suffer you no companions of your own age, especially having so many near relations, and I do not wonder their opinions influenced yours. I was not sorry to see you not determined on a single life, knowing it was not your father's intention, and contented myself with endeavouring to make your home so easy that you might not be in haste to leave it.

I am afraid you will think this a very long and insignificant letter. I hope the kindness of the design will excuse it, being willing to give you every proof in my power that I am your most affectionate mother,

M. Wortley

1763–7, 1965–7

# Samuel Richardson

1689–1761

Humbly born near Derby, Richardson spent most of his life in London, rising from printer's apprentice to become a major figure in the trade, printer of the House of Commons Journals (1742) and Master of the Stationers' Company (1754–5). Out of his writing sample letters suitable for various occasions grew his first novel *Pamela* (1740), a young servant's account in letters and journal of her imprisonment and temptation by her master, who eventually recognises her merits and marries her. The vivid technique of 'writing to the moment' and the socially-challenging subject-matter made the novel one of the sensations of the century, with adaptations and sequels, though its prudential morality and detailing of trivia were attacked by Fielding (p. 295). The centre of a group of female admirers, Richardson was greatly praised by Johnson for his psychological insight. His masterpiece *Clarissa* (1747–8) takes a million words to recount in letters from various correspondents the heroine's moral struggles, rape, and triumphant death: a rare example of successful tragedy in this period. *Sir Charles Grandison* (1753–4), an epistolary novel about a 'good man', was adapted for domestic performance by Jane Austen, a later admirer of Richardson's insight, if not his prolixity. His interest in elaborating emotional conflict at the expense of story has left him the least read of the great novelists.

## *From* PAMELA, OR VIRTUE REWARDED†

### *[An Attack]*

TUESDAY *Night*

For the future, I will always mistrust most, when appearances look fairest. O your poor daughter, what has she not suffered since Sunday night, the time of her worst trial, and fearfullest danger!

*Pamela, or Virtue Rewarded* Pamela keeps for her parents a detailed record of her imprisonment by her master, now in its fortieth day, and of the close watch kept by Mrs Jewkes. Squire B. has seemingly gone off to Stamford

O how I shudder to write you an account of this wicked interval of time! For, my dear parents, will you not be too much frightened and affected with my distress, when I tell you, that his journey to Stamford was all abominable pretence? For he came home privately, and had well-nigh effected all his vile purposes in the ruin of your poor daughter; and that by such a plot as I was not in the least apprehensive of: and you'll hear what a vile unwomanly part that wicked wretch, Mrs Jewkes, acted in it.

Take the dreadful story as well as I can relate it.

The maid Nan is fond of liquor, if she can get at it; and Mrs Jewkes happened, or designed, as is too probable, to leave a bottle of cherry-brandy in her way, and the wench drank more of it than she should; and when she came to lay the cloth, Mrs Jewkes perceived it, and rated at† her most sadly. The wretch has too many faults of her own, to suffer any of the like sort in any body else, if she can help it; and she bade her get out of her sight, when we had supped, and go to bed, to sleep off her liquor, before we came to bed. And so the poor maid went muttering up stairs.

About two hours after, which was near eleven o'clock, Mrs Jewkes and I went up to go to bed; I pleasing myself with what a charming night I should have. We locked both doors, and saw poor Nan, as I thought, sitting fast asleep, in an elbow-chair, in a dark corner of the room, with her apron thrown over her head and neck. But oh! it was my abominable master, as you shall hear by and by. And Mrs Jewkes said, 'There is that beast of a wench fast asleep! I knew she had taken a fine dose.' 'I will wake her,' said I. 'Let her sleep on,' answered she, 'we shall lie better without her.' 'So we shall,' said I; 'but won't she get cold?'

'I hope,' said the vile woman, 'you have no writing tonight.' 'No,' replied I, 'I will go to bed when you go, Mrs Jewkes.' 'That's right,' answered she; 'indeed I wonder what you can find to write about so continually. I am sure you have better conveniences of that kind, and more paper, than I am aware of. Indeed I had intended to rummage† you, if my master had not come down; for I spied a broken tea-cup with ink, which gave me a suspicion: but as he is come, let him look after you, if he will. If you deceive him, it will be his own fault.'

All this time we were undressing; and I fetching a deep sigh, 'What do you sigh for?' said she. 'I am thinking, Mrs Jewkes,' answered I, 'what a sad life I live, and how hard is my lot. I am sure the thief that has robbed is much better off than I, bating† the guilt; and I should, I

*rated at* scolded
*rummage* search
*bating* except for

think, take it for a mercy to be hanged out of the way, rather than live in these cruel apprehensions.'

So, being not sleepy, and in a prattling vein, I began to give a little history of myself, in this manner.

'My poor honest parents,' said I, 'in the first place, took care to instil good principles into my mind, till I was almost twelve years of age; and taught me to prefer goodness and poverty, if they could not be separated, to the highest condition; and they confirmed their lessons by their own practice; for they were of late years remarkably poor, and always as remarkably honest, even to a proverb; for, *As honest as Goodman* ANDREWS, was a bye-word.

'Well, then comes my late dear good lady, and takes a fancy to me, and said she would be the making of me, if I was a good girl: and she put me to sing, to dance, to play on the harpsichord, in order to divert her melancholy hours; and also taught me all manner of fine needle-works; but still this was her lesson, "*My good Pamela, be virtuous, and keep the men at a distance.*" Well, so I did; and yet, though I say it, they all respected me; and would do any thing for me, as if I were a gentlewoman.

'But then, what comes next? Why, it pleased God to take my good lady; and then comes my master: and what says he? Why, in effect, it is "*Be not virtuous*, Pamela."

'So here have I lived above sixteen years in virtue and reputation; and, all at once, when I come to know what is good, and what is evil, I must renounce all the good, all the whole sixteen years innocence, which, next to God's grace, I owed chiefly to my parents and to my lady's good lessons and examples, and choose the evil; and so, in a moment's time, become the vilest of creatures! And all this, for what, I pray? Why, truly, for a pair of diamond earrings, a solitaire, a necklace, and a diamond ring for my finger; which would not become me: for a few paltry fine clothes; which, when I wore them, would make but my former poverty more ridiculous to every body that saw me; especially when they knew the base terms I wore them upon. But, indeed, I was to have a great parcel of guineas beside; I forget how many; for had there been ten times more, they would not have been so much to me, as the honest six guineas you tricked me out of, Mrs Jewkes.

'Well, but then I was to have I know not how many pounds a year for my life; and my poor father (fine encouragement indeed!) was to be the manager for the abandoned prostitute, his daughter: and then (there was the jest of it!) my kind, forgiving, virtuous master would pardon me all my misdeeds.

'And what, pray, are all these violent misdeeds? Why, they are, for daring to adhere to the good lessons that were taught me; for not being contented, when I was run away with, in order to be ruined; but contriving, if my poor wits had been able, to get out of danger, and preserve myself honest.

'Then was he once jealous of poor John,[†] though he knew John was his own creature, and helped to deceive me.

'Then was he outrageous against poor Mr Williams;[†] and him has this good, merciful master thrown into gaol! and for what? Why, truly, for that being a divine, and a good man, he was willing to forego all his expectations of interest, and assist a poor creature, whom he believed innocent!

'But, to be sure, I must be *forward*, *bold*, *saucy*, and what not, to dare to attempt an escape from certain ruin, and an unjust confinement. Poor Mr Williams! how was he drawn in to make marriage proposals to me! O Mrs Jewkes! what a trick was that! The honest gentleman would have had but a poor catch of me, had I consented to be his wife; but he, and *you* too, know I did not want to marry *any body*. I only wanted to go to my poor parents, and not to be laid under an unlawful restraint, and which would not have been attempted, but only that I am a poor destitute young creature, and have no friend that is able to right me.

'So here, Mrs Jewkes,' said I, 'have I given my history in brief. I am very unhappy: and whence my unhappiness? Why, because my master sees something in my person that takes his present fancy; and because I would not be ruined; why, therefore, to choose, I must, and I shall be ruined! And this is all the reason that can be given!'

She heard me run on all this time, while I was undressing, without any interruption; and I said, 'Well, I must go to the two closets, ever since an affair of the closet[†] at the other house, though he is so far off. And I have a good mind to wake this poor maid.' 'No, don't,' said she, 'I charge you. I am very angry with her, and she'll get no harm there; and if she wakes, she will find her way to bed well enough, as there is a candle in the chimney.'

So I looked into the closets; and kneeled down in my own, as I used to do, to say my prayers, and this with my under clothes in my hand; and passed by the supposed sleeping wench, in my return. But little did I think, it was my wicked, wicked master in a gown and petticoat of hers, and her apron over his face and shoulders. To what meannesses will not Lucifer makes his votaries stoop, to gain their abominable ends!

Mrs Jewkes by this time was got to bed, on the further side, as she used to do; and I lay close to her, to make room for the maid, when she should awake. 'Where are the keys?' said I, 'and yet I am not so

*John* another servant
*Mr Williams* a clergyman
*closet* small side-room, where Mr B. once hid

much afraid tonight.' 'Here,' said the wicked woman, 'put your arm under mine, and you shall find them about my wrist, as they used to be.' I did so, and the abominable designer held my hand with her right hand, as my right arm was under her left.

In less than a quarter of an hour, hearing the supposed maid in motion, 'Poor Nan is awake,' said I; 'I hear her stir.' 'Let us go to sleep,' replied she, 'and not mind her: she'll come to bed, when she's quite awake.' 'Poor soul!' said I, 'I'll warrant she will have the headache finely tomorrow for this.' 'Be silent,' answered she, 'and go to sleep; you keep me awake. I never found you in so talkative a humour in my life.' 'Don't chide me,' said I; 'I will say but one thing more: do you think Nan could hear me talk of my master's offers?' 'No, no,' replied she, 'she was dead asleep.' 'I am glad of that,' said I; 'because I would not expose my master to his common servants; and I knew you were no stranger to his *fine* articles.'† 'I think they *were* fine articles,' replied she, 'and you were bewitched you did not close with them: but let us go to sleep.'

So I was silent: and the pretended Nan (O wicked, base, villainous designer! what a plot, what an unexpected plot was this!) seemed to be awakening; and Mrs Jewkes, abhorred creature! said, 'Come, Nan! What, are you awake at last? Prithee come to bed, for Mrs Pamela is in a talking fit, and won't go to sleep one while.'

At that, the pretended she came to the bed-side; and sitting down in a chair concealed by the curtain, began to undress. 'Poor Mrs Ann,' said I, 'I warrant your head aches most sadly! How do you do?' No answer was returned. 'You know I have ordered her not to answer you,' said the abominably wicked woman: this plot, to be sure, was laid when she gave her these orders the night before.

The pretended Nan (how shocking to relate!) then came into bed, trembling like an aspen-leaf; and I (poor fool that I was!) pitied her much. But well might the barbarous deceiver tremble at his vile dissimulation, and base designs.

What words shall I find, my dear mother, (for my father should not see this shocking part) to describe the rest, and my confusion, when the guilty wretch took my left arm, and laid it under his neck as the vile procuress held my right; and then he clasped me round the waist!

'Is the wench mad?' said I. 'Why, how now, confidence?' thinking still it had been Nan. But he kissed me with frightful vehemence; and then his voice broke upon me like a clap of thunder: 'Now, Pamela,' said he, 'is the time of reckoning come, that I have threatened!' I screamed out for help; but there was nobody to help me: and both my

*articles* formal proposal that Pamela be his mistress

hands were secured, as I said. Sure never poor soul was in such agonies as I. 'Wicked man!' said I; 'wicked abominable woman! Good Heaven, this *one* time! this *one* time, good Heaven, deliver me, or strike me dead this moment!' And then I screamed again and again.

'One word with you, Pamela!' said he. 'Hear me but one word! Hitherto you find I offer nothing to you.' 'Is this *nothing*,' said I, 'to be in bed here? To hold my hands between you?'

'Hear me, Pamela.' 'I will hear, if you will this moment leave the bed, and take this vile woman from me!'

Said she (O disgrace of womankind!) 'Don't stand dilly-dallying, sir. She cannot exclaim worse than she has done; and will be quieter when she knows the worst.'

'Silence!' said he to her. 'I must say one word to you, Pamela: it is this; you now see, that you are in my power! You cannot get from me, nor help yourself: yet have I not offered any thing amiss to you. But if you resolve not to comply with my proposals, I will not lose this opportunity. If you do, I will yet leave you. I abhor violence. Your compliance, my dear girl, shall entitle you to all I offered you in my proposals.'

'O sir,' exclaimed I, 'leave me, do but leave me, and I will do any thing I ought to do.' 'Swear then to me,' said he, 'that you will accept my proposals!' And then (for this was all detestable grimace) he put his hand in my bosom.

With struggling, fright, terror, I quite fainted away, and did not come to myself soon; so that they both, from the cold sweats I was in, thought me dying. And I remember no more, than that, when, with great difficulty, they brought me to myself, she was sitting on one side of the bed, with her clothes on; and he on the other, in his gown and slippers.

When I saw them there, I sat up in my bed, nothing about my neck, without any regard to what appearance I must make: and he soothing me with an aspect of pity and concern, I put my hand to his mouth, and said, 'O tell me, yet tell me not, what I have suffered in this distress!' And I talked quite wild, and knew not what; for I was on the point of distraction.

He most solemnly, and with a bitter imprecation, vowed, that he had not offered the least indecency; that he was frightened at the terrible manner I was taken with the fit: that he would desist from his attempt; and begged but to see me easy and quiet, and he would leave me directly, and go to his own bed. 'O then,' said I, 'take with you this most wicked woman, this vile Mrs Jewkes, as an earnest that I may believe you!'

'And will you, sir,' said the wicked wretch, 'for a fit or two, give up such an opportunity as this? I thought you had known the sex better. She is now, you see, quite well again!'

This I heard; more she might say; but I fainted away once more, at these words, and at his clasping his arms about me again. And when I came a little to myself, I saw him sit there, and the maid Nan, holding a smelling-bottle to my nose, and no Mrs Jewkes.

He said, taking my hand, 'Now will I vow to you, my dear Pamela, that I will leave you the moment I see you better, and pacified. Here's Nan knows, and will tell you, my concern for you. I vow to Heaven, that I have not offered any indecency to you. And since I found Mrs Jewkes so offensive to you, I have sent her to the maid's bed. The maid only shall stay with you tonight; and but promise me, that you will compose yourself, and I will leave you.' 'But,' said I, 'will not Nan also hold my hand? And will not she let you come in again?' He swore that he would not return that night. 'Nan,' said he, 'do you go to bed to the dear creature, and say all you can to comfort her: and now, Pamela, give me but your hand, and say you forgive me, and I will leave you to your repose.'

I held out my trembling hand, which he vouchsafed to kiss; and again demanding my forgiveness, 'God forgive you, sir,' said I, 'as you will be just to what you promise!' And he withdrew, with a countenance of remorse, as I hoped; and Nan shut the doors, and, at my request, brought the keys to bed.

This, O my dear parents! was a most dreadful trial. I tremble still to think of it. I hope, as he assures me, he was not guilty of indecency; but have reason to be thankful that I was disabled in my intellects. Since it is but too probable, that all my resistance, and all my strength, otherwise would not have availed me.

I was so weak all day on Monday, that I could not get out of bed. My master showed great tenderness for me; and I hope he is really sorry, and that this will be his last attempt; but he does not say so neither.

He came in the morning, as soon as he heard the door open: and I began to be fearful. He stopped short of the bed, and said, 'Rather than give you apprehensions, I will come no further.' 'Your honour, sir,' said I, 'and your mercy, is all I have to beg.'

He sat down on the side of the bed, and asked kindly, How I did? He bid me be composed; and said, I still looked a little wildly. 'Pray, sir,' said I, 'let me not see this infamous Mrs Jewkes: I cannot bear her in my sight.' 'She shan't come near you all this day, if you will promise to compose yourself.' 'Then, sir, I will try.' He pressed my hand very tenderly, and went out.

What a change does this show! May it be lasting! But, alas! he seems only to have altered his method of proceeding; and retains, I doubt, his wicked purpose!

On Tuesday about ten o'clock, when he heard I was up, he sent for me down into the parlour. As soon as he saw me, he said, 'Come nearer to me, Pamela.' I did, and he took my hand, and said, 'You begin to look well again: I am glad of it. You little rogue,' was his free word, 'how did you frighten me on Sunday night!' 'Sir,' said I, 'pray name not that night'; my eyes overflowing at the remembrance: and I turned my head aside.

'Place some little confidence in me,' said he. 'I know what those charming eyes mean, and you shall not need to explain yourself. I do assure you, that the moment you fainted away, I quitted the bed, and Mrs Jewkes did so too. I put on my gown, and she fetched her smelling-bottle, and we both did all we could to restore you; and my passion for you was all swallowed up in the concern I had for your recovery; for I thought I never saw a fit so strong and violent in my life; and feared we should not bring you to yourself again. My apprehensions for you, might possibly be owing to my folly, and my unacquaintedness with what your sex *can* show when they are in earnest. But this I repeat to you, that your mind may be entirely comforted: all that I offered to you was before you fainted away. You yourself are sensible, that that was rather what might excite your fears, than deserve your censure. You have nothing, therefore, to make yourself uneasy at, or to reproach me with on the occasion you take so much at heart.'

'What you refer to, sir,' said I, 'was very bad: and it was too plain, you had the worst designs.' 'When I tell you the truth in one instance,' replied he, 'you may believe me in the other. I know not, I declare, beyond that lovely bosom, that you are a woman; but that I *did* intend what you call *the worst*, is most certain: and though I would not too much alarm you now, I could curse my weakness and my folly, which makes me own, that I cannot live without you. But, if I am master of myself, and my own resolution, I will not attempt to compel you to any thing.' 'Sir,' said I, 'you may easily keep your resolution, if you will send me out of your way, to my parents; and that is all I beg.'

''Tis a folly to talk of it,' said he. 'You must not, shall not go. And if I could be assured you would not attempt it, your stay here should be made agreeable to you.' 'But to what end, sir, am I to stay?' said I: 'you yourself seem not sure you can keep your own present good resolutions; and what would you think of me, were I to stay to my danger, if I *could* get away in safety? And what will the world –'

'The world, pretty simpleton!' interrupted he: 'what has the world to do between you and me? But I now sent for you for two reasons; the first is, to engage you to promise me for a fortnight to come, that you will not offer to go away without my consent; and this I expect for *your own* sake, that I may give you more liberty. The second, that you will see Mrs Jewkes, and forgive her. She is much concerned, and thinks, that, as all her fault was her obedience to me, it would be very cruel to sacrifice her, as she calls it, to your resentment.'

'As to the first, sir,' said I, 'it is a hard injunction: and as to the second, considering Mrs Jewkes's vile unwomanly wickedness, and her endeavours to instigate you to ruin me, when you, from your returning goodness, seemed to have some compassion for me, it is still harder. But to shew my compliance in all I *can* comply with' (for you know, my dear parents, I might as well make a merit of complying, when my refusal would stand me in no stead) 'I will consent to both.'

'That's my good girl!' said he, and kissed me. 'This is quite prudent, and shows me, that you don't take insolent advantage of my passion for you; and will, perhaps, stand you in more stead than you are aware of.'

He then rung the bell, and said, 'Call down Mrs Jewkes.' She came down, and he took my hand, and put it into hers; and said, 'Mrs Jewkes, I am obliged to you for your diligence and fidelity; but Pamela must be allowed to think *she* is not; because the service I employed you in was not so agreeable to her, as I could have wished she would have thought it; and you were not to favour her, but obey me. But yet I assure you, at the very first word, she has *once* obliged me, by consenting to be reconciled to you; and if she gives me no great cause, I shall not, perhaps, put you on such disagreeable service again. Now, therefore, be you once more bedfellows and board-fellows, as I may say, for some days longer; and see that Pamela sends no letters nor messages out of the house, nor keeps a correspondence unknown to me, especially with that Williams; and, as for the rest, show the dear girl all the respect that is due to one I must love, and who yet, I hope, will deserve my love; and let her be under no unnecessary restraints. But your watchful care is not, however, to cease: and remember, that you are not to disoblige *me*, to oblige *her*; and that I will not, cannot, yet part with her.'

Mrs Jewkes looked very sullen, and as if she would be glad still to do me a good turn, if it lay in her power.

I took courage then to drop a word or two for poor Mr Williams; but he was angry, and said, he could not endure to hear his name, in *my* mouth.

I begged for leave to send a letter to you, my dear father. So I should, he said, if he might read it first. But this did not answer my design; and yet I would have sent you such a letter as he might have seen, if I had been sure my danger was over. But that I cannot; for he now seems to be taking another method: a method which I am still more apprehensive of, than I was of his more open and haughty behaviour; because he may now perhaps resolve to watch an opportunity, and join force with it, when I least think of my danger: for now he seems all kindness. He talks of love without reserve; and makes nothing of allowing himself the liberty of kissing me, which he calls innocent; but which I do not like; since for a master to take such freedoms with a servant, has meaning too much in it, not to alarm.

Just this moment I have a confirmation of what I thought of his designs in his change of behaviour to me; for I overheard him say to the wicked woman, who very likely (for I heard not what she said) had been instigating him again, 'I have begun wrong. Terror does but add to her frost. But she is a charming girl; and may be thawed by kindness. I should have sought to melt her by love.'

What an abominable man is this! Yet his mother so good a woman! He says I must stay a fortnight. What a dangerous fortnight may this be to your girl! But I trust that God will enable me (as is my constant prayer) to be proof against his vileness . . . .

1740

# Philip Dormer Stanhope, Fourth Earl of Chesterfield

1694–1773

Chesterfield, a significant statesman and a friend of Scriblerian writers, is now best remembered as the recipient of Johnson's letter of defiance (p. 346), and for his letters to his natural son (publ. 1774; other letters to a godson publ. 1890). The letters were private advice to an evidently diffident and stupid boy (b. 1732) on how to behave as a gentleman; the degree of calculation and restraint required makes them a fascinating social document. Despite wide respect, Johnson said that they 'teach the morals of a whore and the manners of a dancing-master'. At any rate, they are the elegant product of a worldly mind.

## *From* LETTERS TO HIS NATURAL SON

### *[Polite Behaviour]*

*Bath, March 9, 1748.*

Dear Boy,

I must, from time to time, remind you of what I have often recommended to you, and of what you cannot attend to too much; *sacrifice to the Graces*. The different effects of the same things, said or done, when accompanied or abandoned by them, is almost inconceivable. They prepare the way to the heart; and the heart has such an influence over the understanding, that it is worth while to engage it in our interest. It is the whole of women, who are guided by nothing else: and it has so much to say, even with men, and the ablest men too, that it commonly triumphs in every struggle with the understanding. Monsieur de Rochefoucault, in his *Maxims*,† says, that *l'esprit est souvent la dupe du cœur* [the heart often dupes the mind]. If he had said, instead of *souvent*, *presque toujours* [almost always], I fear he would have been nearer the truth. This being the case, aim at the heart. Intrinsic merit alone will not do; it will gain you the general esteem of

*Maxims* (1665) a work also admired by Swift

all; but not the particular affection, that is, the heart of any. To engage the affection of any particular person, you must, over and above your general merit, have some particular merit to that person, by services done or offered; by expressions of regard and esteem; by complaisance, attentions, etc., for him: and the graceful manner of doing all these things opens the way to the heart, and facilitates, or rather ensures, their effects.

From your own observation, reflect what a disagreeable impression an awkward address, a slovenly figure, an ungraceful manner of speaking whether stuttering, muttering, monotony, or drawling, an unattentive behaviour, etc., make upon you, at first sight, in a stranger, and how they prejudice you against him, though, for aught you know, he may have great intrinsic sense and merit. And reflect, on the other hand, how much the opposites of all these things prepossess you, at first sight, in favour of those who enjoy them. You wish to find all good qualities in them, and are in some degree disappointed if you do not. A thousand little things, not separately to be defined, conspire to form these Graces, this *je ne sais quoi* [something], that always pleases. A pretty person, genteel motions, a proper degree of dress, an harmonious voice, something open and cheerful in the countenance, but without laughing; a distinct and properly varied manner of speaking: all these things, and many others, are necessary ingredients in the composition of the pleasing *je ne sais quoi*, which everybody feels, though nobody can describe. Observe carefully, then, what displeases or pleases you in others, and be persuaded, that, in general, the same thing will please or displease them in you.

Having mentioned laughing, I must particularly warn you against it: and I could heartily wish that you may often be seen to smile, but never heard to laugh while you live. Frequent and loud laughter is the characteristic of folly and ill manners: it is the manner in which the mob express their silly joy at silly things; and they call it being merry. In my mind there is nothing so illiberal, and so ill-bred, as audible laughter. True wit, or sense, never yet made anybody laugh; they are above it: they please the mind, and give a cheerfulness to the countenance. But it is low buffoonery, or silly accidents, that always excite laughter; and that is what people of sense and breeding should show themselves above. A man's going to sit down, in the supposition that he had a chair behind him, and falling down upon his breech for want of one, sets a whole company a laughing, when all the wit in the world would not do it; a plain proof, in my mind, how low and unbecoming a thing laughter is. Not to mention the disagreeable noise that it makes, and the shocking distortion of the face that it occasions. Laughter is easily restrained by a very little reflection; but, as it is generally connected with the idea of gaiety, people do not enough attend to its absurdity. I am neither of a melancholy, nor a cynical disposition; and am as willing, and as apt, to be pleased as anybody; but I am sure that, since I have had the full use of my reason, nobody has ever heard me laugh. Many people, at first from awkwardness and *mauvaise honte* [bashfulness], have got a very disagreeable and silly trick of laughing whenever they speak: and I know a man of very good parts, Mr Waller, who cannot say the commonest thing without laughing; which makes those who do not know him take him at first for a natural fool. . . .

## *[How to Please People]*

*Sept. 5, 1748.*

Berlin will be entirely a new scene to you, and I look upon it in a manner as your first step into the great world: take care that step be not a false one, and that you do not stumble at the threshold. You will there be in more company than you have yet been; manners and attentions will therefore be more necessary. Pleasing in company is the only way of being pleased in it yourself. Sense and knowledge are the first and necessary foundations for pleasing in company, but they will by no means do alone, and they will never be perfectly welcome if they are not accompanied with manners and attentions. You will best acquire these by frequenting the companies of people of fashion; but then you must resolve to acquire them in those companies by proper care and observation; for I have known people who, though they have frequented good company all their lifetime, have done it in so inattentive and unobserving a manner as to be never the better for it, and to remain as disagreeable, as awkward, and as vulgar, as if they had never seen any person of fashion. When you go into good company (by good company is meant the people of the first fashion of the place) observe carefully their turn, their manners, their address, and conform your own to them.

But this is not all, neither; go deeper still; observe their characters, and pry, as far as you can, into both their hearts and their heads. Seek for their particular merit, their predominant passion, or their prevailing weakness; and you will then know what to bait your hook with to catch them. Man is a composition of so many and such various ingredients, that it requires both time and care to analyse him; for, though we have all the same ingredients in our general composition, as reason, will, passion, and appetites; yet the different proportions and combinations of them in each individual, produce that infinite variety of characters which in some particular or other distinguishes every individual from another. Reason ought to direct the whole, but seldom does. And he who addresses himself singly to another man's reason, without endeavouring to engage his heart in his interest also, is no more likely to succeed, than a man who should apply only to a King's nominal minister and neglect his favourite.

La Rochefoucault is I know blamed, but I think without reason, for deriving all our actions from the source of self-love. For my own part, I see a great deal of truth and no harm at all in that opinion. It is certain that we seek our own happiness in everything we do; and it is as certain that we can only find it in doing well, and in conforming all our actions to the rule of right reason, which is the great law of nature. It is only a mistaken self-love that is a blameable motive, when we take the immediate and indiscriminate gratification of a passion or appetite for real happiness. But am I blameable if I do a good action, upon account of the happiness which that honest consciousness will give me? Surely not. On the contrary, that pleasing consciousness is a proof of my virtue. The reflection which is the most censured in Monsieur de la Rochefoucault's book, as a very ill-natured one, is this: *On trouve dans le malheur de son meilleur ami, quelque chose qui ne déplait pas* [there is something not displeasing in our best friend's ill]. And why not? Why may I not feel a very tender and real concern for the misfortune of my friend, and yet at the same time feel a pleasing consciousness of having discharged my duty to him, by comforting and assisting him to the utmost of my power in that misfortune? Give me but virtuous actions, and I will not quibble and chicane about the motives. And I will give anybody their choice of these two truths, which amount to the same thing: He who loves himself best is the honestest man; or, The honestest man loves himself best. . . .

As women are a considerable, or at least a pretty numerous part of company; and as their suffrages go a great way towards establishing a man's character in the fashionable part of the world (which is of great importance to the fortune and figure he proposes to make in it), it is necessary to please them. I will therefore, upon this subject, let you into certain *arcana* [secrets], that will be very useful for you to know, but which you must, with the utmost care, conceal, and never seem to know. Women, then, are only children of a larger growth; they have an entertaining tattle and sometimes wit; but for solid, reasoning good-sense, I never in my life knew one that had it, or who reasoned or acted consequentially for four-and-twenty hours together. Some little passion or humour always breaks in upon their best resolutions. Their beauty neglected or controverted, their age increased, or their supposed understandings depreciated, instantly kindles their little passions, and overturns any system of consequential conduct, that in their most reasonable moments they might have been capable of forming. A man of sense only trifles with them, plays with them, humours and flatters them, as he does with a sprightly, forward child; but he neither consults them about, nor trusts them with, serious matters; though he often makes them believe that he does both; which is the thing in the world that they are proud of; for they love mightily to be dabbling in business (which by the way, they always spoil); and being justly distrustful, that men in general look upon them in a trifling light, they almost adore that man, who talks more seriously to them, and who seems to consult and trust them; I say, who seems, for weak men really do, but wise ones only seem to do it. No flattery is either too high or too low for them. They will greedily swallow the highest, and gratefully accept of the lowest; and you may safely flatter any woman, from her understanding down to the exquisite taste of her fan. Women who are either indisputably beautiful, or indisputably ugly, are best flattered upon the score of their understandings; but those who are in a state of mediocrity are best flattered upon their beauty, or at least their graces; for every woman who is not absolutely ugly, thinks herself handsome; but, not hearing often that she is so, is the more grateful and the more obliged to the few who tell her so; whereas a decided and conscious beauty looks upon every tribute paid to her beauty, only as her due; but wants to shine, and to be considered on the side of her understanding; and a woman who is ugly enough to know that she is so, knows that she has nothing left for it but her understanding, which is consequently (and probably in more senses than one) her weak side.

But these are secrets which you must keep inviolably, if you would not, like Orpheus,† be torn to pieces by the whole sex; on the contrary, a man who thinks of living in the great world, must be gallant, polite, and attentive to please the women. They have, from the weakness of men, more or less influence in all Courts; they absolutely stamp every man's character in the *beau monde* [fashionable world], and make it either current, or cry it down, and stop it in payments. It is, therefore, absolutely necessary to manage, please, and flatter them; and never to discover† the least marks of contempt, which is what they never forgive; but in this they are not singular, for it is the same with men; who will much sooner forgive an injustice than an insult. Every man is not ambitious, or covetous, or passionate; but every man has pride enough in his composition to feel and resent the least slight and contempt. Remember, therefore, most carefully to conceal your contempt, however just, wherever you would not make an implacable enemy. Men are much more unwilling to have their weaknesses and their imperfections known, than their crimes; and, if you hint to a man that you think him silly, ignorant, or even ill-bred or awkward, he will hate you more, and longer, than if you tell him plainly that you think him a rogue. Never yield to that temptation, which to most young men is very strong, of

*Orpheus* legendary Greek hero destroyed by frenzied women

*discover* reveal

exposing other people's weaknesses and infirmities, for the sake either of diverting the company, or of showing your own superiority. You may get the laugh on your side by it, for the present; but you will make enemies by it for ever; and even those who laugh with you then will, upon reflection, fear, and consequently hate you; besides that, it is ill-natured, and a good heart desires rather to conceal than expose other people's weaknesses or misfortunes. If you have wit, use it to please, and not to hurt: you may shine like the sun in the temperate zones, without scorching. Here it is wished for: under the line it is dreaded.

These are some of the hints which my long experience in the great world enables me to give you; and which, if you attend to them, may prove useful to you in your journey through it. I wish it may be a prosperous one; at least, I am sure that it must be your own fault if it is not. . . .

## *[Social Accomplishments]*

*London, January 18, 1750.*

My Dear Friend,

I consider the solid part of your little edifice as so near being finished and completed, that my only remaining care is about the embellishments; and that must now be your principal care too. Adorn yourself with all those graces and accomplishments, which, without solidity, are frivolous; but without which, solidity is, to a great degree, useless. Take one man, with a very moderate degree of knowledge, but with a pleasing figure, a prepossessing address, graceful in all that he says and does, polite, *liant* [winning], and, in short, adorned with all the lesser talents; and take another man, with sound sense and profound knowledge, but without the above-mentioned advantages; the former will not only get the better of the latter, in every pursuit of every kind, but in truth there will be no sort of competition between them. But can every man acquire these advantages? I say Yes, if he please; supposing he is in a situation, and in circumstances, to frequent good company. Attention, observation, and imitation, will most infallibly do it.

When you see a man, whose first *abord* [manner] strikes you, prepossesses you in his favour, and makes you entertain a good opinion of him, you do not know why: analyse that *abord*, and examine, within yourself, the several parts that compose it; and you will generally find it to be the result, the happy assemblage, of modesty unembarrassed, respect without timidity, a genteel, but unaffected attitude of body and limbs, an open, cheerful, but unsmirking countenance, and a dress, by no means negligent, and yet not foppish. Copy him, then, not servilely, but as some of the greatest masters of painting have copied others;

insomuch, that their copies have been equal to the originals, both as to beauty and freedom. When you see a man, who is universally allowed to shine as an agreeable well-bred man, and a fine gentleman (as for example, the Duke de Nivernois), attend to him, watch him carefully; observe in what manner he addresses himself to his superiors, how he lives with his equals, and how he treats his inferiors. Mind his turn of conversation, in the several situations of morning visits, the table, and the evening amusements. Imitate, without mimicking him; and be his duplicate, but not his ape. You will find that he takes care never to say or do anything that can be construed into a slight, or a negligence; or that can, in any degree, mortify people's vanity and self-love; on the contrary, you will perceive that he makes people pleased with him, by making them first pleased with themselves: he shows respect, regard, esteem, and attention, where they are severally proper; he sows them with care, and he reaps them in plenty.

These amiable accomplishments are all to be acquired by use and imitation; for we are, in truth, more than half what we are, by imitation. The great point is, to choose good models, and to study them with care. People insensibly contract, not only the air, the manners, and the vices, of those with whom they commonly converse, but their virtues too, and even their way of thinking. This is so true, that I have known very plain understandings catch a certain degree of wit, by constantly conversing with those who had a great deal. Persist, therefore, in keeping the best company, and you will insensibly become like them; but if you add attention and observation, you will very soon be one of them. This inevitable contagion of company, shows you the necessity of keeping the best, and avoiding all other; for in every one, something will stick. You have hitherto, I confess, had very few opportunities of keeping polite company. Westminster school is, undoubtedly, the seat of illiberal manners and brutal behaviour. Leipzig, I suppose, is not the seat of refined and elegant manners. Venice, I believe, has done something; Rome, I hope, will do a great deal more; and Paris will, I dare say, do all that you want: always supposing, that you frequent the best companies, and in the intention of improving and forming yourself; for, without that intention, nothing will do.

I here subjoin a list of all those necessary, ornamental accomplishments (without which, no man living can either please or rise in the world) which hitherto I fear you want, and which only require your care and attention to possess.

To speak elegantly, whatever language you speak in; without which, nobody will hear you with pleasure, and, consequently, you will speak to very little purpose.

An agreeable and distinct elocution; without which nobody will hear you with patience; this everybody may acquire, who is not born with some imperfection in the organs of speech. You are not; and therefore it is wholly in your power. You need take much less pains for it than Demosthenes did.

A distinguished politeness of manners and address; which common sense, observation, good company, and imitation, will infallibly give you, if you will accept of it.

A genteel carriage, and graceful motions, with the air of a man of fashion. A good dancing-master, with some care on your part, and some imitation of those who excel, will soon bring this about.

To be extremely clean in your person, and perfectly well dressed, according to the fashion, be that what it will. Your negligence of dress, while you were a schoolboy, was pardonable, but would not be so now.

Upon the whole, take it for granted, that, without these accomplishments, all you know, and all you can do, will avail you very little. Adieu!

1774

# James Thomson

1700–48

Brought up in the Scottish borders, Thomson came to London at 25 and eventually became acquainted with the Scriblerus wits: his poetry represents a contemporary alternative to the urban, satiric strain. His four poems on the seasons appeared 1726–30, and the complete work was repeatedly revised to 1746, having great popularity. The blank verse, latinate diction and syntax owe much to Milton. The close study of nature is set in a framework of moral reflection and concern with the great author of the universe. Thomson also wrote dramas and, probably, 'Rule Britannia'. His last work, *The Castle of Indolence* (1748), is an allegory which returns to the stanza used by Spenser in *The Faerie Queene* (1590–6), whose archaic language it echoes.

## THE SEASONS

### From *Summer*

'Tis raging noon; and, vertical, the Sun
Darts on the head direct his forceful rays.
O'er heaven and earth, far as the ranging eye
Can sweep, a dazzling deluge reigns; and all
From pole to pole is undistinguished blaze.
In vain the sight dejected[1] to the ground
Stoops for relief; thence hot ascending steams
And keen reflection pain. Deep to the root
Of vegetation parched, the cleaving fields
And slippery lawn an arid hue disclose,
Blast fancy's blooms, and wither even the soul.
Echo no more returns the cheerful sound
Of sharpening scythe: the mower, sinking, heaps
O'er him the humid hay, with flowers perfumed;
And scarce a chirping grasshopper is heard
Through the dumb mead. Distressful nature pants.
The very streams look languid from afar,

*dejected* (Latin) cast down

Or, through th' unsheltered glade, impatient seem
To hurl into the covert of the grove.
  All-conquering heat, oh, intermit thy wrath!
And on my throbbing temples potent thus
Beam not so fierce! Incessant still you flow,
And still another fervent flood succeeds,
Poured on the head profuse.† In vain I sigh,
And restless turn, and look around for night:
Night is far off; and hotter hours approach.
Thrice happy he, who on the sunless side
Of a romantic mountain, forest-crowned,
Beneath the whole collected shade reclines;
Or in the gelid* caverns, woodbine-wrought — cold
And fresh bedewed with ever-spouting streams,
Sits coolly calm; while all the world without,
Unsatisfied and sick, tosses in noon.
Emblem instructive of the virtuous man,
Who keeps his tempered mind serene and pure,
And every passion aptly harmonized
Amid a jarring world with vice inflamed.
  Welcome, ye shades! ye bowery thickets, hail!
Ye lofty pines! ye venerable oaks!
Ye ashes wild, resounding o'er the steep!
Delicious is your shelter to the soul
As to the hunted hart the sallying spring
Or stream full-flowing, that his swelling sides
Laves as he floats along the herbaged brink.
Cool through the nerves your pleasing comfort glides;
The heart beats glad; the fresh-expanded eye
And ear resume their watch; the sinews knit;
And life shoots swift through all the lightened limbs.
  Around th' adjoining brook, that purls along
The vocal grove, now fretting o'er a rock,
Now scarcely moving through a reedy pool,
Now starting to a sudden stream, and now
Gently diffused into a limpid plain,
A various group the herds and flocks compose,
Rural confusion! On the grassy bank
Some ruminating lie, while others stand
Half in the flood and, often bending, sip
The circling surface. In the middle droops
The strong laborious ox, of honest front,

*profuse* (Latin) poured forth

Which incomposed* he shakes; and from his sides disturbed
The troublous insects lashes with his tail,
Returning still. Amid his subjects safe
Slumbers the monarch-swain, his careless arm
Thrown round his head on downy moss sustained;
Here laid his scrip* with wholesome viands filled, bag
There, listening every noise, his watchful dog.
Light fly his slumbers, if perchance a flight
Of angry gad-flies fasten on the herd,
That startling scatters from the shallow brook
In search of lavish stream. Tossing the foam,
They scorn the keeper's voice, and scour the plain
Through all the bright severity of noon;
While from their labouring breasts a hollow moan
Proceeding runs low-bellowing round the hills.
Oft in this season too, the horse, provoked,
While his big sinews full of spirits swell,
Trembling with vigour, in the heat of blood
Springs the high fence, and o'er the field effused,[†]
Darts on the gloomy flood with steadfast eye
And heart estranged to fear: his nervous* chest, strong
Luxuriant and erect, the seat of strength,
Bears down th' opposing stream; quenchless his thirst,
He takes the river at redoubled draughts,
And with wide nostrils, snorting, skims the wave.
Still let me pierce into the midnight depth
Of yonder grove, of wildest largest growth,
That, forming high in air a woodland choir,
Nods o'er the mount beneath. At every step,
Solemn and slow the shadows blacker fall,
And all is awful listening gloom around.
These are the haunts of meditation, these
The scenes where ancient bards th' inspiring breath
Ecstatic felt, and, from this world retired,
Conversed with angels and immortal forms,
On gracious errands bent – to save the fall
Of virtue struggling on the brink of vice;
In waking whispers and repeated dreams
To hint pure thought, and warn the favoured soul,
For future trials fated, to prepare;
To prompt the poet, who devoted gives
His muse to better themes; to soothe the pangs

*effused* rushing free

Of dying worth, and from the patriot's breast
(Backward to mingle in detested war,
But foremost when engaged) to turn the death;
And numberless such offices of love,
Daily and nightly, zealous to perform. . . .

## From *Winter*†

When from the pallid sky the Sun descends,
With many a spot, that o'er his glaring orb
Uncertain wanders, stained; red fiery streaks
Begin to flush around. The reeling clouds
Stagger with dizzy poise, as doubting yet
Which master to obey; while, rising slow,
Blank in the leaden-coloured east, the moon
Wears a wan circle round her blunted horns.
Seen through the turbid, fluctuating air,
The stars obtuse† emit a shivering ray;
Or frequent seem to shoot athwart the gloom,
And long behind them trail the whitening blaze.
Snatched in short eddies, plays the withered leaf;
And on the flood the dancing feather floats.
With broadened nostrils to the sky upturned,
The conscious heifer snuffs the stormy gale.
Even, as the matron, at her nightly task,
With pensive labour draws the flaxen thread,
The wasted taper and the crackling flame
Foretell the blast. But chief the plumy race,
The tenants of the sky, its changes speak.
Retiring from the downs, where all day long
They picked their scanty fare, a blackening train
Of clamorous rooks thick-urge their weary flight,
And seek the closing shelter of the grove.
Assiduous, in his bower, the wailing owl
Plies his sad song. The cormorant on high
Wheels from the deep, and screams along the land.
Loud shrieks the soaring hern; and with wild wing
The circling sea-fowl cleave the flaky clouds.
Ocean, unequal pressed, with broken tide
And blind commotion heaves; while from the shore,
Eat† into caverns by the restless wave,

Much of the detail is from Virgil, *Georgics* 1
*obtuse* not seen sharply
*Eat* eaten, worn away

And forest-rustling mountain comes a voice
That, solemn-sounding, bids the world prepare.
Then issues forth the storm with sudden burst,
And hurls the whole precipitated air
Down in a torrent. On the passive main
Descends th' ethereal force, and with strong gust
Turns from its bottom the discoloured deep.
Through the black night that sits immense around,
Lashed into foam, the fierce-conflicting brine
Seems o'er a thousand raging waves to burn.
Meantime the mountain-billows, to the clouds
In dreadful tumult swelled, surge above surge,
Burst into chaos with tremendous roar,
And anchored navies from their stations drive
Wild as the winds, across the howling waste
Of mighty waters: now th' inflated wave
Straining they scale, and now impetuous shoot
Into the secret chambers of the deep,
The wintry Baltic thundering o'er their head.
Emerging thence again, before the breath
Of full-exerted heaven they wing their course,
And dart on distant coasts – if some sharp rock
Or shoal insidious break not their career,
And in loose fragments fling them floating round.
    Nor less at land the loosened tempest reigns.
The mountain thunders, and its sturdy sons†
Stoop to the bottom of the rocks they shade.
Lone on the midnight steep, and all aghast,
The dark wayfaring stranger breathless toils,
And often falling, climbs against the blast.
Low waves the rooted forest, vexed, and sheds
What of its tarnished honours† yet remain –
Dashed down and scattered, by the tearing wind's
Assiduous fury, its gigantic limbs.
Thus struggling through the dissipated grove,
The whirling tempest raves along the plain;
And, on the cottage thatched or lordly roof
Keen-fastening, shakes them to the solid base.
Sleep frighted flies; and round the rocking dome,†
For entrance eager, howls the savage blast.
Then too, they say, through all the burdened air

*sturdy sons* strong trees
*tarnished honours* ruined foliage
*dome* (Latin) house

Long groans are heard, shrill sounds, and distant sighs,
That, uttered by the demon of the night,
Warn the devoted* wretch of woe and death. doomed
Huge uproar lords it wide. The clouds, commixed
With stars swift-gliding, sweep along the sky.
All Nature reels: till Nature's King, who oft
Amid tempestuous darkness dwells alone,
And on the wings† of the careering wind
Walks dreadfully serene, commands a calm;
Then straight air, sea, and earth are hushed at once.
As yet 'tis midnight deep. The weary clouds,
Slow-meeting, mingle into solid gloom.
Now, while the drowsy world lies lost in sleep,
Let me associate with the serious Night,
And Contemplation, her sedate compeer;
Let me shake off th' intrusive cares of day,
And lay the meddling senses all aside.
Where now, ye lying vanities of life!
Ye ever-tempting, ever-cheating train!
Where are you now? and what is your amount?
Vexation, disappointment, and remorse.
Sad, sickening thought! and yet deluded man,
A scene of crude disjointed visions past,
And broken slumbers, rises still resolved,
With new-flushed hopes, to run the giddy round.
Father of light and life! thou Good Supreme!
O teach me what is good! teach me Thyself!
Save me from folly, vanity, and vice,
From every low pursuit; and feed my soul
With knowledge, conscious peace, and virtue pure –
Sacred, substantial, never-fading bliss! . . .

1726–46

† *wings . . . walks* Psalm 104.3

# *From* THE CASTLE OF INDOLENCE

## *[The Land of Drowsyhed]*

### CANTO I

*The Castle hight* of* Indolence, called
*And its false luxury;*
*Where for a little time, alas!*
*We lived right jollily*

I

O mortal man, who livest here by toil,
Do not complain of this thy hard estate;
That like an emmet* thou must ever moil* ant toil
Is a sad sentence† of an ancient date:
And, certes* there is for it reason great; certainly
For though sometimes it makes thee weep and wail,
And curse thy stars, and early drudge and late,
Withouten that would come an heavier bale,* trouble
Loose life, unruly passions, and diseases pale.

II

In lowly dale, fast by a river's side,
With woody hill o'er hill encompassed round,
A most enchanting wizard did abide,
Than whom a fiend more fell is nowhere found.
It was, I ween, a lovely spot of ground;
And there a season atween June and May,
Half prankt with spring, with summer half imbrowned,
A listless climate made, where, sooth to say,
No living wight could work, ne carèd even for play.

III

Was nought around but images of rest:
Sleep-soothing groves, and quiet lawns between;
And flowery beds that slumbrous influence kest,* cast
From poppies breathed; and beds of pleasant green,
Where never yet was creeping creature seen.
Meantime unnumbered glittering streamlets played,
And hurlèd everywhere their waters sheen,* bright
That, as they bickered through the sunny glade,
Though restless still themselves, a lulling murmur made.

---

*sentence* on Adam (Genesis 3)

IV

Joined to the prattle of the purling rills,
Were heard the lowing herds along the vale,
And flocks loud-bleating from the distant hills,
And vacant shepherds piping in the dale:
And now and then sweet Philomel* would wail, — the nightingale
Or stock-doves plain amid the forest deep,
That drowsy rustled to the sighing gale;
And still a coil the grasshopper did keep:
Yet all these sounds yblent* inclinèd all to sleep. — blended

V

Full in the passage of the vale, above,
A sable, silent, solemn forest stood:
Where nought but shadowy forms were seen to move,
As Idless* fancied in her dreaming mood. — Idleness
And up the hills, on either side, a wood
Of blackening pines, ay waving to and fro,
Sent forth a sleepy horror through the blood;
And where this valley winded out, below,
The murmuring main was heard, and scarcely heard, to flow.

VI

A pleasing land of drowsyhed it was:
Of dreams that wave before the half-shut eye;
And of gay castles in the clouds that pass,
For ever flushing round a summer sky:
There eke the soft delights, that witchingly
Instil a wanton sweetness through the breast,
And the calm pleasures always hovered nigh;
But whate'er smacked of noyance, or unrest,
Was far far off expelled from this delicious nest.

VII

The landskip such, inspiring perfect ease;
Where Indolence (for so the wizard hight)
Close-hid his castle mid embowering trees,
That half shut out the beams of Phoebus bright,
And made a kind of checkered day and night.
Meanwhile, unceasing at the massy gate,
Beneath a spacious palm, the wicked wight
Was placed; and, to his lute, of cruel fate
And labour harsh complained, lamenting man's estate. . . .

1748

# Henry Fielding

1707–54

Fielding, the son of a general, was educated at Eton beside such future statesmen as the elder Pitt. He studied abroad at Leyden (1728–9) and returned to London to write many farces and dramatic satires (*The Life and Death of Tom Thumb the Great*, 1731; *The Historical Register for 1736*). The political censorship of the 1737 Licensing Act ended his theatre career, although he carried some of its techniques into his fiction. In *Shamela* (1741) he ridiculed the dubious morality and dramatic style of Richardson's novel; *Joseph Andrews* (1742), a more positive account of Pamela's 'brother', and *Tom Jones* (1749), offered his view of the novel as 'a comic epic poem in prose'; *Amelia* (1751) is more domestic and pathetic in treatment. Fielding had meanwhile taken to journalism, including the anti-Stuart *The Jacobite's Journal*, and continued to attack hypocrisy in his ironic celebration of the thief-taker, *Jonathan Wild the Great* (1743). Having read for the bar, he became Justice of the Peace for Westminster and then Middlesex (1749), and as Bow Street magistrate worked with his half-brother, Sir John, to stamp out street disorder and legal corruption, and promote the welfare of the poor. *The Journal of a Voyage to Lisbon* (1755) is a surprisingly lively account of an unsuccessful attempt to throw off his fatal illness.

## *From* SHAMELA†

## LETTER VI *[True Confessions]*

SHAMELA ANDREWS *to* HENRIETTA MARIA HONORA ANDREWS.

O Madam, I have strange things to tell you! As I was reading in that charming book about the Dealings,† in comes my master – to be sure he is a precious one. 'Pamela,' says he, 'what book is that? I warrant you Rochester's poems.'† 'No, forsooth,' says I, as pertly as I could;

*Shamela* Fielding ridicules the style and morality of the original by offering the 'true' account of Pamela

*Dealings* of God with the Methodist, George Whitefield

*Rochester's poems* that is, pornography

'why how now, Saucy Chops, Boldface,' says he – 'Mighty pretty words,' says I, pert again. – 'Yes (says he), you are a d – d, impudent, stinking, cursed, confounded jade, and I have a great mind to kick your a – .' 'You, kiss' – says I. 'Agad,' says he, 'and so I will;' with that he caught me in his arms, and kissed me till he made my face all over fire. Now this served purely, you know, to put upon the fool for anger. O! What precious fools men are! And so I flung from him in a mighty rage, and pretended as how I would go out at the door; but when I came to the end of the room, I stood still, and my master cried out, 'Hussy, Slut, Saucebox, Boldface, come hither' – 'Yes, to be sure,' says I; 'why don't you come,' says he; 'what should I come for?' says I; 'if you don't come to me, I'll come to you,' says he; 'I shan't come to you, I assure you,' says I. Upon which he run up, caught me in his arms, and flung me upon a chair, and began to offer to touch my under-petticoat. 'Sir,' says I, 'you had better not offer to be rude;' 'well,' says he, 'no more I won't then;' and away he went out of the room. I was so mad to be sure I could have cried.

*Oh what a prodigious vexation it is to a woman to be made a fool of!*

Mrs Jervis, who had been without, harkening, now came to me. She burst into a violent laugh the moment she came in. 'Well,' says she, as soon as she could speak, 'I have reason to bless myself that I am an old woman. Ah child! if you had known the jolly blades of my age, you would not have been left in the lurch in this manner.' 'Dear Mrs Jervis,' says I, 'don't laugh at one;' and to be sure I was a little angry with her. – 'Come,' says she, 'my dear honeysuckle, I have one game to play for you; he shall see you in bed; he shall, my little rosebud, he shall see those pretty, little, white, round, panting' – and offered to pull off my handkerchief.† – 'Fie, Mrs Jervis,' says I, 'you make me blush,' and upon my fackins,† I believe she did. She went on thus: 'I know the squire likes you, and notwithstanding the awkwardness of his proceeding, I am convinced hath some hot blood in his veins, which will not let him rest, till he hath communicated some of his warmth to thee, my little angel; I heard him last night at our door, trying if it was open; now tonight I will take care it shall be so; I warrant that he makes the second trial; which if he doth, he shall find us ready to receive him. I will at first counterfeit sleep, and after a swoon; so that he will have you naked in his possession: and then if you are disappointed, a plague of all young squires, say I.' – 'And so, Mrs Jervis,' says I, 'you would have me yield myself to him, would you; you would have me be a second time a fool for nothing. Thank you for that, Mrs Jervis.' 'For nothing! marry forbid,' says she, 'you know he

*handkerchief* covering her breast    *my fackins* my faith

hath large sums of money, besides abundance of fine things; and do you think, when you have inflamed him, by giving his hand a liberty with that charming person; and that you know he may easily think he obtains against your will, he will not give anything to come at all?' – 'This will not do, Mrs Jervis,' answered I. 'I have heard my mamma say (and so you know, Madam, I have), that in her youth, fellows have often taken away in the morning what they gave over night. No, Mrs Jervis, nothing under a regular taking into keeping, a settled settlement,[†] for me, and all my heirs, all my whole lifetime, shall do the business – or else crosslegged is the word, faith, with Sham'; and then I snapt my fingers.

*Thursday Night, Twelve o'Clock.*

Mrs Jervis and I are just in bed, and the door unlocked; if my master should come – Odsbobs! I hear him just coming in at the door. You see I write in the present tense, as Parson Williams says. Well, he is in bed between us, we both shamming a sleep; he steals his hand into my bosom, which I, as if in my sleep, press close to me with mine, and then pretend to awake. – I no sooner see him, but I scream out to Mrs Jervis, she feigns likewise but just to come to herself; we both begin, she to becall, and I to bescratch very liberally. After having made a pretty free use of my fingers, without any great regard to the parts I attacked, I counterfeit a swoon. Mrs Jervis then cries out, 'O sir, what have you done? you have murthered poor Pamela: she is gone, she is gone.' –

*O what a difficulty it is to keep one's countenance, when a violent laugh desires to burst forth!*

The poor Booby, frightened out of his wits, jumped out of bed, and, in his shirt, sat down by my bed-side, pale and trembling, for the moon shone, and I kept my eyes wide open, and pretended to fix them in my head. Mrs Jervis applied lavender water, and hartshorn,[†] and this for a full half hour; when thinking I had carried it on long enough, and being likewise unable to continue the sport any longer, I began by degrees to come to myself.

The squire, who had sat all this while speechless, and was almost really in that condition which I feigned, the moment he saw me give symptoms of recovering my senses, fell down on his knees; and 'O Pamela,' cried he, 'can you forgive me, my injured maid? By heaven, I know not whether you are a man or a woman, unless by your swelling breasts. Will you promise to forgive me?' 'I forgive you! D – n you,' says I; 'and d – n you,' says he, 'if you come to that. I wish I had never seen your bold face, saucy sow' – and so went out of the room.

*settlement* formal transfer of property *hartshorn* an ammonia restorative

*O what a silly fellow is a bashful young lover!*

He was no sooner out of hearing, as we thought, than we both burst into a violent laugh. 'Well,' says Mrs Jervis, 'I never saw anything better acted than your part: but I wish you may not have discouraged him from any future attempt; especially since his passions are so cool, that you could prevent his hands going further than your bosom.' 'Hang him,' answered I, 'he is not quite so cold as that, I assure you; our hands, on neither side, were idle in the scuffle, nor have left us any doubt of each other as to that matter.' . . .

1741

# *From* JOSEPH ANDREWS†

## CHAPTER 12 *[Good Neighbours]*

*Containing many surprising Adventures, which Joseph Andrews met with on the Road, scarce credible to those who have never travelled in a Stage-Coach.*

Nothing remarkable happened on the road, 'till their arrival at the inn, to which the horses were ordered; whither they came about two in the morning. The moon then shone very bright, and Joseph making his friend a present of a pint of wine, and thanking him for the favour of his horse, notwithstanding all entreaties to the contrary, proceeded on his journey on foot.

He had not gone above two miles, charmed with the hopes of shortly seeing his beloved Fanny, when he was met by two fellows in a narrow lane, and ordered to stand and deliver. He readily gave them all the money he had, which was somewhat less than two pounds; and told them he hoped they would be so generous as to return him a few shillings, to defray his charges on his way home.

One of the ruffians answered with an oath, 'Yes, we'll give you something presently: but first strip and be d – n'd to you.' – 'Strip', cried the other, 'or I'll blow your brains to the Devil.' Joseph, remembering that he had borrowed his coat and breeches of a friend;

*Joseph Andrews* The novel begins as the story of 'Pamela's brother', who is cast out of the domestic service of Lady Booby for rejecting her lustful advances (the situation parodies that in Richardson's novel). Joseph sets out from London for Somerset, to find his true love, Fanny. The extract shows the antithesis of *Pamela* in its external narrator's clear control of its styles; the economy and irony owe much to Swift

and that he should be ashamed of making any excuse for not returning them, replied, he hoped they would not insist on his clothes, which were not worth much; but consider the coldness of the night. 'You are cold, are you, you rascal!' says one of the robbers, 'I'll warm you with a vengeance;' and damning his eyes, snapped a pistol at his head: which he had no sooner done, than the other levelled a blow at him with his stick, which Joseph, who was expert at cudgel-playing, caught with his, and returned the favour so successfully on his adversary, that he laid him sprawling at his feet, and at the same instant received a blow from behind, with the butt-end of a pistol from the other villain, which felled him to the ground, and totally deprived him of his senses.

The thief who had been knocked down had now recovered himself; and both together fell to be-labouring poor Joseph with their sticks, till they were convinced they had put an end to his miserable being: they then stripped him entirely naked, threw him into a ditch, and departed with their booty.

The poor wretch, who lay motionless a long time, just began to recover his senses as a stage-coach came by. The postilion[†] hearing a man's groans, stopped his horses, and told the coachman, 'he was certain there was a *dead* man lying in the ditch, for he heard him groan.' 'Go on, sirrah,' says the coachman, 'we are confounded late, and have no time to look after dead men.' A lady, who heard what the postilion said, and likewise heard the groan, called eagerly to the coachman, 'to stop and see what was the matter.' Upon which he bid the postilion 'alight, and look into the ditch.' He did so, and returned, 'that there was a man sitting upright as naked as ever he was born,' – 'O J-sus,' cried the lady, 'A naked man! Dear coachman, drive on and leave him.' Upon this the gentlemen got out of the coach; and Joseph begged them, 'to have mercy upon him: for that he had been robbed, and almost beaten to death.' 'Robbed,' cries an old gentleman; 'let us make all the haste imaginable, or we shall be robbed too.' A young man, who belonged to the law, answered, 'he wished they had passed by without taking any notice: but that now they might be proved to have been *last in his company*; if he should die, they might be called to some account for his murder. He therefore thought it advisable to save the poor creature's life, for their own sakes, if possible; at least, if he died, to prevent the jury's finding *that they fled*[†] *for it.* He was therefore *of opinion*, to take the man into the coach, and carry him to the next inn.' The lady insisted, 'that he should not come into the coach. That if they lifted him in, she would herself alight: for she had rather stay in that

*postilion* riding on one of the horses
*fled* flight from the scene could result in punishment

place to all eternity, than ride with a naked man.' The coachman objected, 'that he could not suffer him to be taken in, unless some body would pay a shilling for his carriage the four miles.' Which the two gentlemen refused to do; but the lawyer, who was afraid of some mischief happening to himself if the wretch was left behind in that condition, saying, 'no man could be too cautious in these matters, and that he remembered very extraordinary cases in the books,' threatened the coachman, and bid him deny taking him up at his peril; 'for that if he died, he should be indicted for his murder, and if he lived, and brought an action against him, he would willingly take a brief in it.' These words had a sensible effect on the coachman, who was well acquainted with the person who spoke them; and the old gentleman abovementioned, thinking the naked man would afford him frequent opportunities of showing his wit to the lady, offered to join with the company in giving a mug of beer for his fare; till partly alarmed by the threats of the one, and partly by the promises of the other, and being perhaps a *little* moved with compassion at the poor creature's condition, who stood bleeding and shivering with the cold, he at length agreed; and Joseph was now advancing to the coach, where seeing the lady, who held the sticks of her fan before her eyes, he absolutely refused, miserable as he was, to enter, unless he was furnished with sufficient covering, to prevent giving the least offence to decency. So perfectly modest was this young man; such mighty effects had the spotless example of the amiable Pamela, and the excellent sermons of Mr Adams wrought upon him.

Though there were several great coats about the coach, it was not easy to get over this difficulty which Joseph had started. The two gentlemen complained they were cold, and could not spare a rag; the man of wit saying, with a laugh, *that charity began at home*; and the coachman, who had two great coats spread under him, refused to lend either, lest they should be made bloody; the lady's footman desired to be excused for the same reason, which the lady herself, notwithstanding her abhorrence of a naked man, approved: and it is more than probable, poor Joseph who obstinately adhered to his modest resolution, must have perished, unless the postilion (a lad who hath been since transported† for robbing a hen-roost) had voluntarily stripped off a great coat, his only garment, at the same time swearing a great oath (for which he was rebuked by the passengers) 'that he would rather ride in his shirt all his life, than suffer a fellow-creature to lie in so miserable a condition.'

Joseph, having put on the great coat, was lifted into the coach, which now proceeded on its journey. He declared himself almost dead with the cold, which gave the man of wit an occasion to ask the lady, if she

*transported* to a penal colony

could not accommodate him with a dram. She answered with some resentment, 'she wondered at his asking her such a question;' but assured him, 'she never tasted any such thing.'

The lawyer was enquiring into the circumstances of the robbery, when the coach stopped, and one of the ruffians, putting a pistol in, demanded their money of the passengers; who readily gave it them; and the lady, in her fright, delivered up a little silver bottle, of about a half-pint size, which the rogue clapping it to his mouth, and drinking her health, declared held some of the best nantes[†] he had ever tasted: this the lady afterwards assured the company was the mistake of her maid, for that she had ordered her to fill the bottle with Hungary water.[†]

As soon as the fellows were departed, the lawyer, who had, it seems, a case of pistols in the seat of the coach, informed the company, that if it had been day-light, and he could have come at his pistols, he would not have submitted to the robbery; he likewise set forth, that he had often met highwaymen when he travelled on horseback, but none ever durst attack him; concluding, that if he had not been more afraid for the lady than for himself, he should not have now parted with his money so easily.

As wit is generally observed to love to reside in empty pockets, so the gentleman, whose ingenuity we have above remarked, as soon as he had parted with his money, began to grow wonderfully facetious. He made frequent allusions to Adam and Eve, and said many excellent things on figs and figleaves; which perhaps gave more offence to Joseph than to any other in the company.

The lawyer likewise made several very pretty jests, without departing from his profession. He said, 'if Joseph and the lady were alone, he would be the more capable of making a *conveyance*[†] to her, as his *affairs* were not *fettered* with any *incumbrance*; he'd warrant, he soon suffered a *recovery* by a writ of *entry*, which was the proper way to create *heirs in tail*; that for his own part, he would engage to make so *firm a settlement* in a coach, that there should be no danger of an *ejectment*;'[†] with an inundation of the like gibberish, which he continued to vent till the coach arrived at an inn, where one servant-maid only was up in readiness to attend the coachman, and furnish him with cold meat and a dram. Joseph desired to alight, and that he might have a bed prepared for him, which the maid readily promised to perform; and being a good-natured wench, and not so squeamish as the lady had been, she clapped a large faggot on the fire, and furnishing Joseph with a great coat belonging to one of the hostlers, desired him to sit down

*nantes* brandy
*Hungary water* medicinal flower-water
*conveyance . . . ejectment* legal terms, here with sexual innuendo

and warm himself, whilst she made his bed. The coachman, in the mean time, took an opportunity to call up a surgeon, who lived within a few doors: after which, he reminded his passengers how late they were, and after they had taken leave of Joseph, hurried them off as fast as he could.

The wench soon got Joseph to bed, and promised to use her interest to borrow him a shirt; but imagined, as she afterwards said, by his being so bloody, that he must be a dead man: she ran with all speed to hasten the surgeon, who was more than half dressed, apprehending that the coach had been overturned and some gentleman or lady hurt. As soon as the wench had informed him at his window, that it was a poor foot passenger who had been stripped of all he had, and almost murdered, he chid her for disturbing him so early, slipped off his clothes again, and very quietly returned to bed and to sleep.

Aurora† now began to show her blooming cheeks over the hills, whilst ten millions of feathered songsters, in jocund chorus, repeated odes† a thousand times sweeter than those of our Laureate, and sung both *the day and the song*; when the master of the inn, Mr Tow-wouse, arose, and learning from his maid an account of the robbery, and the situation of his poor naked guest, he shook his head, and cried, 'Good-lack-a-day!' and then ordered the girl to carry him one of his own shirts.

Mrs Tow-wouse was just awake, and had stretched out her arms in vain to fold her departed husband, when the maid entered the room. 'Who's there? Betty?' 'Yes madam.' 'Where's your master?' 'He's without, madam; he hath sent me for a shirt to lend to a poor naked man, who hath been robbed and murdered.' 'Touch one, if you dare, you slut,' said Mrs Tow-wouse, 'your master is a pretty sort of a man to take in naked vagabonds, and clothe them with his own clothes. I shall have no such doings. – If you offer to touch any thing, I will throw the chamber-pot at your head. Go, send your master to me.' 'Yes madam,' answered Betty. As soon as he came in, she thus began: 'What the Devil do you mean by this, Mr Tow-wouse? Am I to buy shirts to lend to a set of scabby rascals?' 'My dear,' said Mr Tow-wouse, 'this is a poor wretch.' 'Yes,' says she, 'I know it is a poor wretch, but what the Devil have we to do with poor wretches? The law makes us provide for too many already. We shall have thirty or forty poor wretches in red coats† shortly.' 'My dear,' cries Tow-wouse, 'this man hath been robbed of all he hath.' 'Well then,' says she, 'where's his money to pay

*Aurora* goddess of dawn
*odes* official productions by the Poet Laureate, Colley Cibber. F. echoes his own recent parody
*red coats* soldiers billeted on them

his reckoning? Why doth not such a fellow go to an ale-house? I shall send him packing as soon as I am up, I assure you.' 'My dear,' said he, 'common charity won't suffer you to do that.' 'Common charity, a f – t!' says she, 'common charity teaches us to provide for ourselves, and our families; and I and mine won't be ruined by your charity, I assure you.' 'Well,' says he, 'my dear, do as you will when you are up, you know I never contradict you.' 'No,' says she, 'if the Devil was to contradict me, I would make the house too hot to hold him.'

With such like discourses they consumed near half an hour, whilst Betty provided a shirt from the hostler, who was one of her sweethearts, and put it on poor Joseph. The surgeon had likewise at last visited him, had washed and dressed his wounds, and was now come to acquaint Mr Tow-wouse, that his guest was in such extreme danger of his life, that he scarce saw any hopes of his recovery. – 'Here's a pretty kettle of fish,' cries Mrs Tow-wouse, 'you have brought upon us! We are like to have a funeral at our own expense.' Tow-wouse (who notwithstanding his charity, would have given his vote as freely as he ever did at an election, that any other house in the kingdom, should have had quiet possession of his guest) answered, 'My dear, I am not to blame: he was brought hither by the stage-coach; and Betty had put him to bed before I was stirring.' 'I'll Betty her,' says she – At which, with half her garments on, the other half under her arm, she sallied out in quest of the unfortunate Betty, whilst Tow-wouse and the surgeon went to pay a visit to poor Joseph, and enquire into the circumstance of this melancholy affair.

1742

# *From* TOM JONES†

## BOOK V, CHAPTER X *[Caught in the Act]*

*Shewing the Truth of many Observations of* Ovid, *and of other more grave Writers, who have proved, beyond Contradiction, that Wine is often the Fore-runner of Incontinency.*

Jones retired from the company, in which we have seen him engaged, into the fields, where he intended to cool himself by a walk in the open air, before he attended Mr Allworthy. There, whilst he renewed those meditations on his dear Sophia, which the dangerous illness of his friend and benefactor had for some time interrupted, an accident happened, which with sorrow we relate, and with sorrow, doubtless, will it be read; however, that historic truth to which we profess so inviolable an attachment, obliges us to communicate it to posterity.

It was now a pleasant evening in the latter end of June, when our hero was walking in a most delicious grove, where the gentle breezes fanning the leaves, together with the sweet trilling of a murmuring stream, and the melodious notes of nightingales formed all together the most enchanting harmony. In this scene, so sweetly accommodated to love, he meditated on his dear Sophia. While his wanton fancy roved unbounded over all her beauties, and his lively imagination painted the charming maid in various ravishing forms, his warm heart melted with tenderness, and at length throwing himself on the ground by the side of a gently murmuring brook, he broke forth into the following ejaculation.

'O Sophia, would heaven give thee to my arms, how blest would be my condition! Curst be that fortune which sets a distance between us. Was I but possessed of thee, one only suit of rags thy whole estate, is there a man on earth whom I would envy! How contemptible would the brightest Circassian† beauty, dressed in all the jewels of the Indies, appear to my eyes! But why do I mention another woman? could I think my eyes capable of looking at any other with tenderness, these hands should tear them from my head. No, my Sophia, if cruel fortune separates us for ever, my soul shall dote on thee alone. The chastest constancy will I ever preserve to thy image. Though I should never have possession of thy charming person, still shalt thou alone have possession of my thoughts, my love, my soul. Oh! my fond heart is so wrapped in

*Tom Jones* Tom Jones, a foundling brought up by Squire Allworthy, is a warm-blooded lad; Blifil, his calculating half-brother; Thwackum, a clergyman. Tom is attracted by Molly, but loves Sophia, daughter of Squire Western

that tender bosom, that the brightest beauties would for me have no charms, nor would a hermit be colder in their embraces. Sophia, Sophia alone shall be mine. What raptures are in that name! I will engrave it on every tree.'

At these words he started up, and beheld – not his Sophia – no, nor a Circassian[†] maid richly and elegantly attired for the Grand Signior's seraglio.[†] No; without a gown, in a shift that was somewhat of the coarsest, and none of the cleanest, bedewed likewise with some odoriferous effluvia, the produce of the day's labour, with a pitch-fork in her hand, Molly Seagrim approached. Our hero had his pen-knife in his hand, which he had drawn for the before-mentioned purpose, of carving on the bark; when the girl coming near him cried out with a smile, 'You don't intend to kill me, Squire, I hope!' 'Why should you think I would kill you?' answered Jones. 'Nay,' replied she, 'after your cruel usage of me when I saw you last, killing me would, perhaps, be too great kindness for me to expect.'

Here ensued a parley, which, as I do not think myself obliged to relate it, I shall omit. It is sufficient that it lasted a full quarter of an hour, at the conclusion of which they retired into the thickest part of the grove.

Some of my readers may be inclined to think this event unnatural. However, the fact is true; and, perhaps, may be sufficiently accounted for, by suggesting that Jones probably thought one woman better than none, and Molly as probably imagined two men to be better than one. Besides the before-mentioned motive assigned to the present behaviour of Jones, the reader will be likewise pleased to recollect in his favour, that he was not at this time perfect master of that wonderful power of reason, which so well enables grave and wise men to subdue their unruly passions, and to decline any of these prohibited amusements. Wine now had totally subdued this power in Jones. He was, indeed, in a condition, in which if reason had interposed, though only to advise, she might have received the answer which one Cleostratus gave many years ago to a silly fellow who asked him if he was not ashamed to be drunk? 'Are not you,' said Cleostratus, 'ashamed to admonish a drunken man?' – To say the truth, in a court of justice, drunkenness must not be an excuse, yet in a court of conscience it is greatly so; and therefore Aristotle, who commends the laws of Pittacus, by which drunken men received double punishment for their crimes, allows there is more of policy than justice in that law. Now, if there are any transgressions pardonable from drunkenness, they are certainly such as Mr Jones was at present guilty of; on which head I could pour forth a vast profusion of learning, if I imagined it would either entertain my reader, or teach him any thing more than he knows already. For his sake, therefore, I

*Circassian* handsome inhabitant of Caucasus *seraglio* harem shall keep my learning to myself, and return to my history.

It hath been observed, that fortune seldom doth things by halves. To say truth, there is no end to her freaks whenever she is disposed to gratify or displease. No sooner had our hero retired with his Dido, but

*Speluncam* Blifil, *Dux et Divinus eandem*
*Deveniunt.*† [Blifil and the parson come to the same cave]

the parson and the young squire, who were taking a serious walk, arrived at the stile which leads into the grove, and the latter caught a view of the lovers, just as they were sinking out of sight.

Blifil knew Jones very well, though he was at above a hundred yards distance, and he was as positive to the sex of his companion, though not to the individual person. He started; blessed himself, and uttered a very solemn ejaculation.

Thwackum expressed some surprise at these sudden emotions, and asked the reason of them. To which Blifil answered, 'he was certain he had seen a fellow and wench retire together among the bushes, which he doubted not was with some wicked purpose.' As to the name of Jones he thought proper to conceal it, and why he did so must be left to the judgment of the sagacious reader: for we never choose to assign motives to the actions of men, when there is any possibility of our being mistaken.

The parson, who was not only strictly chaste in his own person, but a great enemy to the opposite vice in all others, fired at this information. He desired Mr Blifil to conduct him immediately to the place, which as he approached, he breathed forth vengeance mixed with lamentations; nor did he refrain from casting some oblique reflections on Mr Allworthy, insinuating that the wickedness of the country was principally owing to the encouragement he had given to vice, by having exerted such kindness to a bastard, and by having mitigated that just and wholesome rigour of the law, which allots a very severe punishment to loose wenches.

The way, through which our hunters were to pass in pursuit of their game, was so beset with briars, that it greatly obstructed their walk, and caused, besides, such a rustling that Jones had sufficient warning of their arrival, before they could surprise him; nay, indeed, so incapable was Thwackum of concealing his indignation, and such vengeance did he mutter forth every step he took, that this alone must have abundantly satisfied Jones, that he was (to use the language of sportsmen) *found sitting*.

---

*Speluncam . . . Deveniunt* parodies Virgil on the love of Dido and Aeneas (*Aeneid*, IV)

# CHAPTER XI

*In which a Simile in Mr* Pope's *Period of a Mile, introduces as bloody a Battle as can possibly be fought, without the Assistance of Steel or* cold *Iron.*

As in the season of RUTTING (an uncouth phrase, by which the vulgar denote that gentle dalliance, which in the well-wooded forest of Hampshire, passes between lovers of the ferine[†] kind) if while the lofty crested stag meditates the amorous sport, a couple of puppies, or any other beasts of hostile note, should wander so near the temple of Venus Ferina, that the fair hind should shrink from the place, touched with that somewhat, either of fear or frolic, of nicety or skittishness with which Nature hath bedecked all females, or hath, at least, instructed them how to put it on; lest, through the indelicacy of males, the Samean[†] mysteries should be pried into by unhallowed eyes: for at the celebration of these rites, the female priestess cries out with her in Virgil[†] (who was then probably hard at work on such celebration)

> – *Procul, O procul este, profani;*
> *Proclamat Vates, totoque absistite Luco.*
> – Far hence be souls profane,
> The Sibyl cried, and from the grove abstain.
>
> DRYDEN.

If, I say, while these sacred rites, which are in common to *Genus omne Animantium* [all living creatures], are in agitation between the stag and his mistress, any hostile beasts should venture too near, on the first hint given by the frightened hind, fierce and tremendous rushes forth the stag to the entrance of the thicket; there stands he sentinel over his love, stamps the ground with his foot, and with his horns brandished aloft in air, proudly provokes the apprehended foe to combat.

Thus, and more terrible, when he perceived the enemy's approach, leaped forth our hero. Many a step advanced he forwards, in order to conceal the trembling hind, and, if possible, to secure her retreat. And now Thwackum having first darted some livid lightning from his fiery eyes, began to thunder forth, 'Fie upon it! Fie upon it! Mr Jones. Is it possible you should be the person!' 'You see,' answered Jones, 'it is possible I should be here.' 'And who,' said Thwackum, 'is that wicked slut with you?' 'If I have any wicked slut with me,' cries Jones, 'it is possible I shall not let you know who she is.' 'I command you to tell

*ferine* wild-animal
*Samean* of Samos, sacred to Juno, Roman goddess of marriage
*Virgil* in *Aeneid*, VI, at entrance of the underworld

me immediately,' says Thwackum, 'and I would not have you imagine, young man, that your age, though it hath somewhat abridged the purpose of tuition, hath totally taken away the authority of the master. The relation of the master and scholar is indelible, as, indeed, all other relations are: for they all derive their original from Heaven. I would have you think yourself, therefore, as much obliged to obey me now, as when I taught you your first rudiments.' 'I believe you would,' cries Jones, 'but that will not happen, unless you had the same birchen argument to convince me.' 'Then I must tell you plainly,' said Thwackum, 'I am resolved to discover the wicked wretch.' 'And I must tell you plainly,' returned Jones, 'I am resolved you shall not.' Thwackum then offered† to advance, and Jones laid hold of his arms; which Mr Blifil endeavoured to rescue, declaring 'he would not see his old master insulted.'

Jones now finding himself engaged with two, thought it necessary to rid himself of one of his antagonists as soon as possible. He therefore, applied to the weakest first; and letting the parson go, he directed a blow at the young squire's breast, which luckily taking place, reduced him to measure his length on the ground.

Thwackum was so intent on the discovery, that the moment he found himself at liberty he stepped forward directly into the fern, without any great consideration of what might, in the mean time, befall his friend; but he had advanced a very few paces into the thicket, before Jones having defeated Blifil, overtook the parson, and dragged him backward by the skirt of his coat.

This parson had been a champion in his youth, and had won much honour by his fist, both at school and at the university. He had now, indeed, for a great number of years, declined the practice of that noble art; yet was his courage full as strong as his faith, and his body no less strong than either. He was moreover, as the reader may, perhaps, have conceived, somewhat irascible in his nature. When he looked back, therefore, and saw his friend stretched out on the ground, and found himself at the same time so roughly handled by one who had formerly been only passive in all conflicts between them (a circumstance which highly aggravated the whole), his patience at length gave way; he threw himself into a posture of offence, and collecting all his force, attacked Jones in the front, with as much impetuosity as he had formerly attacked him in the rear.

Our hero received the enemy's attack with the most undaunted intrepidity, and his bosom resounded with the blow. This he presently returned with no less violence, aiming likewise at the parson's breast; but he dexterously drove down the fist of Jones, so that it reached only

*offered* attempted

his belly, where two pounds of beef and as many of pudding were then deposited, and whence consequently no hollow sound could proceed. Many lusty blows, much more pleasant as well as easy to have seen, than to read or describe, were given on both sides; at last a violent fall in which Jones had thrown his knees into Thwackum's breast, so weakened the latter, that victory had been no longer dubious, had not Blifil, who had now recovered his strength, again renewed the fight, and, by engaging with Jones, given the parson a moment's time to shake his ears, and to regain his breath.

And now both together attacked our hero, whose blows did not retain that force with which they had fallen at first; so weakened was he by his combat with Thwackum: for though the pedagogue chose rather to play solos on the human instrument, and had been lately used to those only, yet he still retained enough of his ancient knowledge to perform his part very well in a duet.

The victory, according to modern custom, was like to be decided by numbers, when, on a sudden, a fourth pair of fists appeared in the battle, and immediately paid their compliments to the parson; the owner of them, at the same time, crying out, 'Are you not ashamed and be d – nd to you, to fall two of you upon one?'

The battle,† which was of the kind, that for distinction's sake is called royal,† now raged with the utmost violence during a few minutes; till Blifil being a second time laid sprawling by Jones, Thwackum condescended to apply for quarter to his new antagonist, who was now found to be Mr Western himself: for in the heat of the action none of the combatants had recognised him.

In fact, that honest squire, happening in his afternoon's walk with some company, to pass through the field where the bloody battle was fought, and having concluded from seeing three men engaged, that two of them must be on a side, he hastened from his companions, and with more gallantry than policy, espoused the cause of the weaker party. By which generous proceeding, he very probably prevented Mr Jones from becoming a victim to the wrath of Thwackum, and to the pious friendship which Blifil bore his old master: for besides the disadvantage of such odds, Jones had not yet sufficiently recovered the former strength of his broken arm. This reinforcement, however, soon put an end to the action, and Jones with his ally obtained the victory.

1749

*battle . . . royal* general struggle

# Samuel Johnson

## 1709–84

Johnson suffered early from defective eyesight and from scrofula, for which he was 'touched' for a cure by Queen Anne. His unusual knowledge as the son of a Lichfield bookseller took him to Pembroke College, Oxford, which poverty forced him to leave. After unsuccessful schoolteaching in the Midlands and marriage in 1734 to a much older widow, he went with his pupil David Garrick (the future actor) to London, where he contributed a wide range of work, including his own versions of the parliamentary debates, to *The Gentleman's Magazine*. In the Grub-Street world of hack-writers, he slowly became known as versatile, learned and independent: his poem *London* (1738) attracted Pope's attention; another imitation of Juvenal *The Vanity of Human Wishes*, his first signed work, and his tragedy *Irene* appeared in 1749. Johnson's periodical essay series *The Rambler* (1750–2) and *The Idler* (1758–60) established his reputation as literary critic and moralist, consolidated by his eastern tale *Rasselas, Prince of Abyssinia* (1759). For some years he worked on his great English *Dictionary*, drawing on his wide reading: its publication in 1755 won public recognition and allowed him to repudiate the tardy patronage of Lord Chesterfield in a gesture symbolic of the professional writer's independence. This learning also benefited his edition of Shakespeare (1765), with its famous Preface.

Despite his tendency to melancholy, Johnson was a sociable man, the centre of various groups, notably the famous Club (1764), which comprised leading men of arts and public life (Reynolds, Garrick, Burke, Gibbon, Boswell, Goldsmith, Sheridan, C. J. Fox). His last twenty years, including his journey to the Hebrides in 1773, were documented in vivid detail by James Boswell in the *Life* (1791) and the *Tour* (1785). In the 1770s Johnson wrote political pamphlets on the Falkland Islands and against the American colonists' demands; his last major work was the series of prefaces known as the *Lives* of the English poets from the mid-seventeenth century to his own time, which embody his interest in literature and biography.

Johnson's large miscellaneous output, often hastily produced for money or as a favour to a friend, almost always displays unexpected knowledge and a vigorous mind. A sincere Christian tortured by dark fears (he was haunted by Christ's parable of the talents), he became more regarded in the nineteenth century as the moralist-conversationalist recorded by Boswell than the exponent of an allegedly cumbrous prose style. His restored reputation as a critic stands beside his great humanity: a friend of the derelict, he understood human frailty.

# THE VANITY OF HUMAN WISHES†

## *The Tenth Satire of Juvenal Imitated*

Let observation with extensive view,
Survey mankind, from China to Peru,†
Remark each anxious toil, each eager strife,
And watch the busy scenes of crowded life;
Then say how hope and fear, desire and hate,
O'erspread with snares the clouded maze of fate,
Where wavering man, betrayed by venturous pride,
To tread the dreary paths without a guide,
As treacherous phantoms in the mist delude,
Shuns fancied ills, or chases airy good:
How rarely reason guides the stubborn choice,
Rules the bold hand, or prompts the suppliant voice;
How nations sink, by darling schemes oppressed,
When vengeance listens to the fool's request.
Fate wings† with every wish th' afflictive dart,
Each gift of nature, and each grace of art,
With fatal heat impetuous courage glows,
With fatal sweetness elocution flows,
Impeachment stops the speaker's powerful breath,
And restless fire precipitates† on death.
    But scarce observed, the knowing and the bold
Fall in the general massacre of gold;

*The Vanity of Human Wishes* Johnson 'imitates' the first-century Roman satirist by converting his stoicism into Christianity, his historical portraits into modern examples (Hannibal into Charles XII of Sweden: images of struggle and warfare recur). In style he aims at the original's 'declamatory grandeur'

*from China . . . Peru* from east to west, everywhere

*wings* gives feathers to ensure accuracy on target

*precipitates* rushes down

Wide-wasting pest! that rages unconfined,
And crowds with crimes the records of mankind;
For gold his sword the hireling ruffian draws,
For gold the hireling judge distorts the laws;
Wealth heaped on wealth, nor truth nor safety buys,
The dangers gather as the treasures rise.
  Let history tell where rival kings command,
And dubious title shakes the madded land,
When statutes glean† the refuse of the sword,
How much more safe the vassal than the lord;
Low skulks the hind beneath the rage of power,
And leaves the wealthy traitor in the Tower,†
Untouched his cottage, and his slumbers sound,
Though confiscation's vultures hover round.
  The needy traveller, serene and gay,
Walks the wild heath, and sings his toil away.
Does envy seize thee? crush th' upbraiding joy,
Increase his riches and his peace destroy;
Now fears in dire vicissitude invade,
The rustling brake alarms, and quivering shade,
Nor light nor darkness bring his pain relief,
One shows the plunder, and one hides the thief.
  Yet still one general cry the skies assails,
And gain and grandeur load the tainted gales;
Few know the toiling statesman's fear or care,
Th' insidious rival and the gaping heir.
  Once more, Democritus,† arise on earth,
With cheerful wisdom and instructive mirth,
See motley† life in modern trappings dressed,
And feed with varied fools th' eternal jest:
Thou who couldst laugh where want enchained caprice,
Toil crushed conceit, and man was of a piece;
Where wealth unloved without a mourner died,
And scarce a sycophant was fed by pride;
Where ne'er was known the form of mock debate,
Or seen a new-made mayor's unwieldy state;
Where change of favourites made no change of laws,
And senates heard before they judged a cause;
How wouldst thou shake at Britain's modish tribe,
Dart the quick taunt, and edge the piercing gibe!

*statutes glean* laws ruin those spared by war
*Tower* Tower of London: a prison
*Democritus* Greek 'laughing philosopher' of mankind's follies (*c.* 460–370 BC)
*motley* varied, but also the dress of a fool

Attentive truth and nature to descry,
And pierce each scene with philosophic eye.
To thee were solemn toys or empty show,
The robes of pleasure and the veils of woe:
All aid the farce, and all thy mirth maintain,
Whose joys are causeless, or whose griefs are vain.
  Such was the scorn that filled the sage's mind,
Renewed at every glance on humankind;
How just that scorn ere yet thy voice declare,
Search every state, and canvass every prayer.
  Unnumbered suppliants crowd Preferment's[†] gate,
Athirst for wealth, and burning to be great;
Delusive fortune hears th' incessant call,
They mount, they shine, evaporate, and fall.[†]
On every stage the foes of peace attend,
Hate dogs their flight, and insult mocks their end.
Love ends with hope, the sinking statesman's door
Pours in the morning worshipper no more:
For growing names the weekly scribbler lies,
To growing wealth the dedicator flies,
From every room descends the painted face,
That hung the bright Palladium[†] of the place,
And smoked in kitchens, or in auctions sold,
To better features yields the frame of gold:
For now no more we trace in every line
Heroic worth, benevolence divine:
The form distorted justifies the fall,
And detestation rids th' indignant wall.
  But will not Britain hear the last appeal,
Sign her foes' doom, or guard her favourites' zeal?
Through freedom's sons no more remonstrance rings,
Degrading nobles and controlling kings;
Our supple tribes repress their patriot throats,
And ask no questions but the price of votes:
With weekly libels[†] and septennial ale,[†]
Their wish is full to riot and to rail.
  In full-blown dignity, see Wolsey[†] stand,
Law in his voice, and fortune in his hand:

*Preferment* advancement to office (here, also its bestower)

*evaporate . . . fall* the image may be of a shooting star, or firework

*Palladium* the image of the goddess Pallas Athena, which protected Troy

*libels* scurrilous campaign literature

*septennial ale* bribes to the parliamentary electors at seven-year intervals

*Wolsey* the first of a series of representatives of different modes of life. Cardinal Wolsey (*c.* 1475–1530), Lord Chancellor to Henry VIII, fell from his great religious and secular power

To him the church, the realm, their powers consign,
Through him the rays of regal bounty shine,
Turned by his nod the stream of honour flows,
His smile alone security bestows:
Still to new heights his restless wishes tower,
Claim leads to claim, and power advances power;
Till conquest unresisted ceased to please,
And rights submitted, left him none to seize.
At length his sovereign frowns – the train of state
Mark the keen glance, and watch the sign to hate.
Where'er he turns he meets a stranger's eye,
His suppliants scorn him, and his followers fly;
At once is lost the pride of aweful state,
The golden canopy, the glittering plate,
The regal palace, the luxurious board,
The liveried[†] army, and the menial lord.
With age, with cares, with maladies oppressed,
He seeks the refuge of monastic rest.
Grief aids disease, remembered folly stings,
And his last sighs reproach the faith of kings.
  Speak thou, whose thoughts at humble peace repine,
Shall Wolsey's wealth, with Wolsey's end be thine?
Or liv'st thou now, with safer pride content,
The wisest justice on the banks of Trent?[†]
For why did Wolsey near the steeps of fate,
On weak foundations raise th' enormous weight?
Why but to sink beneath misfortune's blow,
With louder ruin to the gulfs below?
  What gave great Villiers[†] to th' assassin's knife,
And fixed disease on Harley's[†] closing life?
What murdered Wentworth,[†] and what exiled Hyde,[†]
By kings protected, and to kings allied?
What but their wish indulged in courts to shine,
And power too great to keep, or to resign?
  When first the college rolls receive his name,
The young enthusiast[†] quits his ease for fame;
Through all his veins the fever of renown
Burns from the strong contagion of the gown;

*liveried* uniformed servants
*Trent* Midland river
*Villiers* George, Duke of Buckingham, favourite of James I, murdered 1628
*Harley* Robert Harley, Earl of Oxford, Lord Treasurer until Queen Anne's death (1714), then imprisoned
*Wentworth* Thomas Wentworth, Earl of Strafford, adviser to Charles I, executed 1641
*Hyde* Edward Hyde, Earl of Clarendon, Lord Chancellor under Charles II, father-in-law of James II, exiled 1667
*enthusiast* as usual in this period, pejorative: a zealot, fanatic

O'er Bodley's dome[†] his future labours spread,
And Bacon's[†] mansion trembles o'er his head.
Are these thy views? proceed, illustrious youth,
And virtue guard thee to the throne of truth!
Yet should thy soul indulge the generous heat,
Till captive science yields her last retreat;
Should reason guide thee with her brightest ray,
And pour on misty doubt resistless day;
Should no false kindness lure to loose delight,
Nor praise relax, nor difficulty fright;
Should tempting novelty thy cell refrain,
And sloth effuse her opiate fumes in vain;
Should beauty blunt on fops her fatal dart,
Nor claim the triumph of a lettered heart;
Should no disease thy torpid veins invade,
Nor melancholy's phantoms haunt thy shade;
Yet hope not life from grief or danger free,
Nor think the doom of man reversed for thee:
Deign on the passing world to turn thine eyes,
And pause awhile from letters, to be wise;
There mark what ills the scholar's life assail,
Toil, envy, want, the patron,[†] and the jail.
See nations slowly wise, and meanly just,
To buried merit raise the tardy bust.
If dreams yet flatter, once again attend,
Hear Lydiat's[†] life, and Galileo's[†] end.
   Nor deem, when learning her last prize bestows,
The glittering eminence exempt from foes;
See when the vulgar 'scape, despised or awed,
Rebellion's vengeful talons seize on Laud.[†]
From meaner minds, though smaller fines content,
The plundered palace or sequestered rent;
Marked out by dangerous parts he meets the shock,
And fatal learning leads him to the block:
Around his tomb let art and genius weep,
But hear his death, ye blockheads, hear and sleep.
   The festal blazes, the triumphal show,

*Bodley's dome* Bodleian Library, Oxford (*dome*: buildings)
*Bacon* there was a legend that the study of Roger Bacon, Oxford philosopher and scientist (d.1292), would collapse on its bridge when a greater man passed under
*patron* changed from the earlier 'garret': see headnote on Chesterfield
*Lydiat* Thomas Lydiat, mathematician, died poor in 1646
*Galileo* the astronomer Galileo was imprisoned by the Inquisition, and died blind (1642)
*Laud* William Laud, Chancellor of Oxford University, Archbishop of Canterbury, executed 1645

The ravished standard, and the captive foe,
The senate's thanks, the gazette's pompous tale,
With force resistless o'er the brave prevail.
Such bribes the rapid Greek† o'er Asia whirled,
For such the steady Romans shook the world;
For such in distant lands the Britons shine,
And stain with blood the Danube or the Rhine;
This power has praise, that virtue scarce can warm,
Till fame supplies the universal charm.
Yet reason frowns on war's unequal game,
Where wasted nations raise a single name,
And mortgaged states their grandsires' wreaths regret,
From age to age in everlasting debt;
Wreaths which at last the dear-bought right convey
To rust on medals, or on stones decay.
   On what foundation stands the warrior's pride,
How just his hopes let Swedish Charles† decide;
A frame of adamant, a soul of fire,
No dangers fright him, and no labours tire;
O'er love, o'er fear, extends his wide domain,
Unconquered lord of pleasure and of pain;
No joys to him pacific sceptres yield,
War sounds the trump, he rushes to the field;
Behold surrounding kings their power combine,
And one capitulate, and one resign;
Peace courts his hand, but spreads her charms in vain;
'Think nothing gained,' he cries, ''till nought remain,
'On Moscow's walls till Gothic standards fly,
'And all be mine beneath the polar sky.'
The march begins in military state,
And nations on his eye suspended wait;
Stern famine guards the solitary coast,
And winter barricades the realms of frost;
He comes, not want and cold his course delay; –
Hide, blushing glory, hide Pultowa's day:
The vanquished hero leaves his broken bands,
And shows his miseries in distant lands;
Condemned a needy supplicant to wait,
While ladies interpose, and slaves debate.

*rapid Greek* Alexander the Great (356–323 BC)
*Charles . . . Pultowa* Charles XII of Sweden (1682–1718); Frederick IV of Denmark capitulated in 1700, Augustus II of Poland abdicated in 1706 (l.200); defeated by Russia at Poltava (1709), C. went to Turkey; killed at Frederikshald, Norway, possibly by his own side

But did not chance at length her error mend?
Did no subverted empire mark his end?
Did rival monarchs give the fatal wound?
Or hostile millions press him to the ground?
His fall was destined to a barren strand,
A petty fortress, and a dubious hand;
He left the name, at which the world grew pale,
To point a moral, or adorn a tale.
  All times their scenes of pompous woes afford,
From Persia's tyrant[†] to Bavaria's lord.
In gay hostility, and barbarous pride,
With half mankind embattled at his side,
Great Xerxes comes to seize the certain prey,
And starves exhausted regions in his way;
Attendant Flattery counts his myriads o'er,
Till counted myriads soothe his pride no more;
Fresh praise is tried till madness fires his mind,
The waves he lashes, and enchains the wind;
New powers are claimed, new powers are still bestowed,
Till rude resistance lops the spreading god;
The daring Greeks deride the martial show,
And heap their valleys with the gaudy foe;
Th' insulted sea with humbler thoughts he gains,
A single skiff to speed his flight remains;
Th' incumbered oar scarce leaves the dreaded coast
Through purple billows and a floating host.
  The bold Bavarian[†] in a luckless hour,
Tries the dread summits of Caesarean power,
With unexpected legions bursts away,
And sees defenceless realms receive his sway;
Short sway! fair Austria[†] spreads her mournful charms,
The queen, the beauty, sets the world in arms;
From hill to hill the beacon's rousing blaze
Spreads wide the hope of plunder and of praise;
The fierce Croatian,[†] and the wild Hussar,[†]
And all the sons of ravage crowd the war;
The baffled prince in honour's flattering bloom
Of hasty greatness finds the fatal doom,

*Persia's tyrant* Xerxes the Great punished the sea for destroying his boat-bridge; defeated by the Greeks in the sea battle of Salamis, 480 BC

*bold Bavarian . . . Hussar* Charles Albert (1697–1745), Elector of Bavaria, became Holy Roman Emperor (l.242) despite the claims of Maria Theresa, *fair Austria*; his reign was short and unhappy. *Croatian*: with *Hussar*, troops of Austrian Empire

His foes' derision, and his subjects' blame,
And steals to death from anguish and from shame.
Enlarge my life with multitude of days,
In health, in sickness, thus the suppliant prays;
Hides from himself his state, and shuns to know
That life protracted is protracted woe.
Time hovers o'er, impatient to destroy,
And shuts up all the passages of joy:
In vain their gifts the bounteous seasons pour,
The fruit autumnal, and the vernal flower,
With listless eyes the dotard views the store,
He views, and wonders that they please no more;
Now pall the tasteless meats and joyless wines,
And luxury with sighs her slave resigns.
Approach, ye minstrels, try the soothing strain,
Diffuse the tuneful lenitives† of pain:
No sounds, alas, would touch th' impervious ear,
Though dancing mountains witnessed Orpheus† near;
Nor lute nor lyre his feeble powers attend,
Nor sweeter music of a virtuous friend,
But everlasting dictates crowd his tongue,
Perversely grave, or positively wrong.
The still returning tale, and lingering jest,
Perplex the fawning niece and pampered guest,
While growing hopes scarce awe the gathering sneer,
And scarce a legacy can bribe to hear;
The watchful guests still hint the last offence,
The daughter's petulance, the son's expense,
Improve his heady rage with treacherous skill,
And mould his passions till they make his will.
Unnumbered maladies his joints invade,
Lay siege to life and press the dire blockade;
But unextinguished avarice still remains,
And dreaded losses aggravate his pains;
He turns, with anxious heart and crippled hands,
His bonds of debt, and mortgages of lands;
Or views his coffers with suspicious eyes,
Unlocks his gold, and counts it till he dies.
But grant the virtues of a temperate prime,
Bless with an age exempt from scorn or crime;

*lenitives* soothing medicines
*Orpheus* Greek bard, whose music moved mountains

An age that melts with unperceived decay,
And glides in modest innocence away;
Whose peaceful day benevolence endears,
Whose night congratulating conscience cheers;
The general favourite as the general friend:
Such age there is, and who shall wish its end?
  Yet even on this her load misfortune flings,
To press the weary minutes' flagging wings:
New sorrow rises as the day returns,
A sister sickens, or a daughter mourns.
Now kindred merit fills the sable bier,
Now lacerated friendship claims a tear.
Year chases year, decay pursues decay,
Still drops some joy from withering life away;
New forms arise, and different views engage,
Superfluous lags the veteran on the stage,
Till pitying nature signs the last release,
And bids afflicted worth retire to peace.
  But few there are whom hours like these await,
Who set unclouded in the gulfs of Fate.
From Lydia's monarch† should the search descend,
By Solon† cautioned to regard his end,
In life's last scene what prodigies surprise,
Fears of the brave, and follies of the wise?
From Marlborough's† eyes the streams of dotage flow,
And Swift† expires a driveller and a show.
  The teeming mother, anxious for her race,
Begs for each birth the fortune of a face:
Yet Vane† could tell what ills from beauty spring;
And Sedley† cursed the form that pleased a king.
Ye nymphs of rosy lips and radiant eyes,
Whom pleasure keeps too busy to be wise,
Whom joys with soft varieties invite,
By day the frolic, and the dance by night,
Who frown with vanity, who smile with art,
And ask the latest fashion of the heart,

*Lydia's monarch . . . Solon* the rich King Croesus, whom the Greek philosopher Solon advised that no man is happy until dead

*Marlborough* John Churchill, Duke of Marlborough (1650–1722), the great Whig victor of Blenheim, suffered from strokes after 1716

*Swift* M's political enemy, was declared of unsound mind in 1742 and had died as recently as 1745

*Vane* Anne Vane (1705–36), mistress of Frederick, Prince of Wales

*Sedley* Catherine Sedley (1657–1717), mistress of James II. (Both Vane and Sedley seem actually to have been ugly.)

What care, what rules your heedless charms shall save,
Each nymph your rival, and each youth your slave?
Against your fame with fondness hate combines,
The rival batters, and the lover mines.
With distant voice neglected virtue calls,
Less heard and less, the faint remonstrance falls;
Tired with contempt, she quits the slippery reign,
And pride and prudence take her seat in vain.
In crowd at once, where none the pass defend,
The harmless freedom, and the private friend.
The guardians yield, by force superior plied;
By interest, prudence; and by flattery, pride,
Now beauty falls betrayed, despised, distressed,
And hissing infamy proclaims the rest.

Where then shall hope and fear their objects find?
Must dull suspense† corrupt the stagnant mind?
Must helpless man, in ignorance sedate,
Roll darkling down the torrent of his fate?
Must no dislike alarm, no wishes rise,
No cries attempt the mercies of the skies?
Enquirer, cease, petitions yet remain,
Which heaven may hear, nor deem religion vain.
Still raise for good the supplicating voice,
But leave to heaven the measure and the choice,
Safe in his power, whose eyes discern afar
The secret ambush of a specious prayer.
Implore his aid, in his decisions rest,
Secure whate'er he gives, he gives the best.
Yet when the sense of sacred presence fires,
And strong devotion to the skies aspires,
Pour forth thy fervours for a healthful mind,†
Obedient passions, and a will resigned;
For love, which scarce collective man can fill;
For patience sovereign o'er transmuted ill;
For faith, that panting for a happier seat,
Counts death kind nature's signal of retreat:
These goods for man the laws of heaven ordain,
These goods he grants, who grants the power to gain;
With these celestial wisdom calms the mind,
And makes the happiness she does not find.

1749

*suspense* suspension of judgment
*healthful mind* Johnson's version of Juvenal's 'mens sana in corpore sano'; the religious hope is his addition to the pagan model

# THE RAMBLER,† No. 4 Saturday, March 31, 1750

## *[Morality in Fiction]*

The works of fiction with which the present generation seems more particularly delighted are such as exhibit life in its true state, diversified only by accidents that daily happen in the world, and influenced by passions and qualities which are really to be found in conversing with mankind.

This kind of writing may be termed not improperly the comedy of romance, and is to be conducted nearly by the rules of comic poetry. Its province is to bring about natural events by easy means, and to keep up curiosity without the help of wonder: it is therefore precluded from the machines and expedients of the heroic romance, and can neither employ giants to snatch away a lady from the nuptial rites, nor knights to bring her back from captivity: it can neither bewilder its personages in deserts nor lodge them in imaginary castles.

I remember a remark made by Scaliger† upon Pontanus,† that all his writings are filled with the same images; and that if you take from him his lilies and his roses, his satyrs and his dryads, he will have nothing left that can be called poetry. In like manner, almost all the fictions of the last age will vanish if you deprive them of a hermit and a wood, a battle and a shipwreck.

Why this wild strain of imagination found reception so long in polite and learned ages, it is not easy to conceive; but we cannot wonder that, while readers could be procured, the authors were willing to continue it: for when a man had by practice gained some fluency of language, he had no further care than to retire to his closet, let loose his invention, and heat his mind with incredibilities; a book was thus produced without fear of criticism, without the toil of study, without knowledge of nature, or acquaintance with life.

The task of our present writers is very different; it requires, together with that learning which is to be gained from books, that experience which can never be attained by solitary diligence, but must arise from general converse, and accurate observation of the living world. Their performances have, as Horace expresses it, *plus oneris quantum veniae minus*, little indulgence, and therefore more difficulty. They are engaged in portraits of which every one knows the original, and can detect any

*The Rambler, No. 4* J. here contrasts the older form of romance with the realism of the novel, whose recent heroes included Fielding's Tom Jones

*Scaliger* 1484–1558, critic

*Pontanus* 1426–1503, wrote in Latin about woodland spirits and nymphs

deviation from exactness of resemblance. Other writings are safe, except from the malice of learning, but these are in danger from every common reader; as the slipper ill executed was censured by a shoemaker who happened to stop in his way at the Venus of Apelles.†

But the fear of not being approved as just copiers of human manners is not the most important concern that an author of this sort ought to have before him. These books are written chiefly to the young, the ignorant, and the idle, to whom they serve as lectures of conduct, and introductions into life. They are the entertainment of minds unfurnished with ideas, and therefore easily susceptible of impressions; not fixed by principles, and therefore easily following the current of fancy; not informed by experience, and consequently open to every false suggestion and partial account.

That the highest degree of reverence should be paid to youth, and that nothing indecent should be suffered to approach their eyes or ears, are precepts extorted by sense and virtue from an ancient writer, by no means eminent for chastity of thought. The same kind, though not the same degree, of caution, is required in every thing which is laid before them, to secure them from unjust prejudices, perverse opinions, and incongruous combinations of images.

In the romances formerly written, every transaction and sentiment was so remote from all that passes among men that the reader was in very little danger of making any applications to himself; the virtues and crimes were equally beyond his sphere of activity; and he amused himself with heroes and with traitors, deliverers and persecutors, as with beings of another species, whose actions were regulated upon motives of their own, and who had neither faults nor excellencies in common with himself.

But when an adventurer is levelled with the rest of the world, and acts in such scenes of the universal drama as may be the lot of any other man, young spectators fix their eyes upon him with closer attention, and hope by observing his behaviour and success to regulate their own practices, when they shall be engaged in the like part.

For this reason these familiar histories may perhaps be made of greater use than the solemnities of professed morality, and convey the knowledge of vice and virtue with more efficacy than axioms and definitions. But if the power of example is so great as to take possession of the memory by a kind of violence, and produce effects almost without the intervention of the will, care ought to be taken that, when the choice is unrestrained, the best examples only should be exhibited; and that

*Apelles* Greek painter (fourth century BC): he altered the slipper, then told the cobbler to 'stick to his last'

which is likely to operate so strongly should not be mischievous or uncertain in its effects.

The chief advantage which these fictions have over real life is that their authors are at liberty, though not to invent, yet to select objects, and to cull from the mass of mankind those individuals upon which the attention ought most to be employed, as a diamond, though it cannot be made, may be polished by art, and placed in such a situation as to display that lustre which before was buried among common stones.

It is justly considered as the greatest excellency of art to imitate nature; but it is necessary to distinguish those parts of nature which are most proper for imitation: greater care is still required in representing life, which is so often discoloured by passion, or deformed by wickedness. If the world be promiscuously described, I cannot see of what use it can be to read the account; or why it may not be as safe to turn the eye immediately upon mankind, as upon a mirror which shows all that presents itself without discrimination.

It is therefore not a sufficient vindication of a character that it is drawn as it appears, for many characters ought never to be drawn; nor of a narrative that the train of events is agreeable to observation and experience, for that observation which is called knowledge of the world will be found much more frequently to make men cunning than good. The purpose of these writings is surely not only to show mankind, but to provide that they may be seen hereafter with less hazard; to teach the means of avoiding the snares which are laid by treachery for innocence without infusing any wish for that superiority with which the betrayer flatters his vanity; to give the power of counteracting fraud without the temptation to practise it; to initiate youth by mock encounters in the art of necessary defence, and to increase prudence without impairing virtue.

Many writers, for the sake of following nature, so mingle good and bad qualities in their principal personages that they are both equally conspicuous; and as we accompany them through their adventures with delight, and are led by degrees to interest ourselves in their favour, we lose the abhorrence of their faults, because they do not hinder our pleasure, or perhaps, regard them with some kindness for being united with so much merit.

There have been men indeed splendidly wicked, whose endowments threw a brightness on their crimes, and whom scarce any villainy made perfectly detestable, because they never could be wholly divested of their excellencies; but such have been in all ages the great corrupters of the world, and their resemblance ought no more to be preserved than the art of murdering without pain.

Some have advanced, without due attention to the consequences of this notion, that certain virtues have their correspondent faults, and therefore that to exhibit either apart is to deviate from probability. Thus men are observed by Swift to be 'grateful in the same degree as they are resentful'. This principle, with others of the same kind, supposes man to act from a brute impulse, and pursue a certain degree of inclination without any choice of the object; for, otherwise, though it should be allowed that gratitude and resentment arise from the same constitution of the passions, it follows not that they will be equally indulged when reason is consulted; yet unless that consequence be admitted, this sagacious maxim becomes an empty sound, without any relation to practice or to life.

Nor is it evident that even the first motions to these effects are always in the same proportion. For pride, which produces quickness of resentment, will obstruct gratitude, by unwillingness to admit that inferiority which obligation implies; and it is very unlikely that he who cannot think he receives a favour will acknowledge or repay it.

It is of the utmost importance to mankind that positions of this tendency should be laid open and confuted; for while men consider good and evil as springing from the same root, they will spare the one for the sake of the other, and in judging, if not of others at least of themselves, will be apt to estimate their virtues by their vices. To this fatal error all those will contribute who confound the colours of right and wrong, and instead of helping to settle their boundaries, mix them with so much art that no common mind is able to disunite them.

In narratives where historical veracity has no place, I cannot discover why there should not be exhibited the most perfect idea of virtue; of virtue not angelical, nor above probability, for what we cannot credit we shall never imitate, but the highest and purest that humanity can reach, which, exercised in such trials as the various revolutions of things shall bring upon it, may, by conquering some calamities, and enduring others, teach us what we may hope, and what we can perform. Vice, for vice is necessary to be shown, should always disgust; nor should the graces of gaiety, or the dignity of courage, be so united with it as to reconcile it to the mind. Wherever it appears, it should raise hatred by the malignity of its practices, and contempt by the meanness of its stratagems; for while it is supported by either parts or spirit, it will be seldom heartily abhorred. The Roman tyrant† was content to be hated, if he was but feared; and there are thousands of the readers of romances willing to be thought wicked if they may be allowed to be wits. It is therefore to be steadily inculcated that virtue is the highest proof of

*Roman tyrant* the Emperor Caligula (AD 12–41) said: 'oderint dum metuant'

understanding, and the only solid basis of greatness; and that vice is the natural consequence of narrow thoughts, that it begins in mistake, and ends in ignominy.

1750

# A DICTIONARY OF THE ENGLISH LANGUAGE

## *From the* Preface

It is the fate of those who toil at the lower employments of life to be rather driven by the fear of evil than attracted by the prospect of good; to be exposed to censure, without hope of praise; to be disgraced by miscarriage, or punished for neglect, where success would have been without applause, and diligence without reward.

Among these unhappy mortals is the writer of dictionaries; whom mankind have considered, not as the pupil, but the slave of science, the pioneer† of literature, doomed only to remove rubbish and clear obstructions from the paths through which learning and genius press forward to conquest and glory, without bestowing a smile on the humble drudge that facilitates their progress. Every other author may aspire to praise; the lexicographer can only hope to escape reproach, and even this negative recompense has been yet granted to very few.

I have, notwithstanding this discouragement, attempted a dictionary of the English language, which, while it was employed in the cultivation of every species of literature, has itself been hitherto neglected; suffered to spread, under the direction of chance, into wild exuberance, resigned to the tyranny of time and fashion, and exposed to the corruptions of ignorance, and caprices of innovation.

When I took the first survey of my undertaking, I found our speech copious without order, and energetic without rules: wherever I turned my view, there was perplexity to be disentangled, and confusion to be regulated; choice was to be made out of boundless variety, without any established principle of selection; adulterations were to be detected, without a settled test of purity, and modes of expression to be rejected or received, without the suffrages of any writers of classical reputation or acknowledged authority.

*pioneer* military engineer

Having therefore no assistance but from general grammar, I applied myself to the perusal of our writers; and noting whatever might be of use to ascertain or illustrate any word or phrase, accumulated in time the materials of a dictionary, which, by degrees, I reduced to method, establishing to myself, in the progress of the work, such rules as experience and analogy suggested to me; experience, which practice and observation were continually increasing; and analogy, which, though in some words obscure, was evident in others.

In adjusting the orthography,† which has been to this time unsettled and fortuitous, I found it necessary to distinguish those irregularities that are inherent in our tongue, and perhaps coeval with it, from others which the ignorance or negligence of later writers has produced. Every language has its anomalies, which, though inconvenient, and in themselves once unnecessary, must be tolerated among the imperfections of human things, and which require only to be registered, that they may not be increased, and ascertained, that they may not be confounded: but every language has likewise its improprieties and absurdities, which it is the duty of the lexicographer to correct or proscribe. . . .

The solution of all difficulties, and the supply of all defects, must be sought in the examples subjoined to the various senses of each word, and ranged according to the time of their authors.

When first I collected these authorities, I was desirous that every quotation should be useful to some other end than the illustration of a word; I therefore extracted from philosophers principles of science; from historians remarkable facts; from chemists complete processes; from divines striking exhortations; and from poets beautiful descriptions. Such is design, while it is yet at a distance from execution. When the time called upon me to range this accumulation of elegance and wisdom into an alphabetical series, I soon discovered that the bulk of my volumes would fright away the student, and was forced to depart from my scheme of including all that was pleasing or useful in English literature, and reduce my transcripts very often to clusters of words in which scarcely any meaning is retained: thus to the weariness of copying, I was condemned to add the vexation of expunging. Some passages I have yet spared which may relieve the labour of verbal searches, and intersperse with verdure and flowers the dusty deserts of barren philology.

The examples, thus mutilated, are no longer to be considered as conveying the sentiments or doctrine of their authors; the word for the sake of which they are inserted, with all its appendant clauses, has been carefully preserved, but it may sometimes happen, by hasty detruncation,

*orthography* spelling

that the general tendency of the sentence may be changed: the divine may desert his tenets, or the philosopher his system.

Some of the examples have been taken from writers who were never mentioned as masters of elegance, or models of style; but words must be sought where they are used; and in what pages eminent for purity can terms of manufacture or agriculture be found? Many quotations serve no other purpose than that of proving the bare existence of words, and are therefore selected with less scrupulousness than those which are to teach their structures and relations.

My purpose was to admit no testimony of living authors, that I might not be misled by partiality, and that none of my contemporaries might have reason to complain; nor have I departed from this resolution but when some performance of uncommon excellence excited my veneration, when my memory supplied me from late books with an example that was wanting, or when my heart, in the tenderness of friendship, solicited admission for a favourite name.

So far have I been from any care to grace my pages with modern decorations that I have studiously endeavoured to collect examples and authorities from the writers before the Restoration, whose works I regard as *the wells of English undefiled*, as the pure sources of genuine diction. Our language, for almost a century, has, by the concurrence of many causes, been gradually departing from its original Teutonic† character, and deviating towards a Gallic† structure and phraseology, from which it ought to be our endeavour to recall it, by making our ancient volumes the ground-work of style, admitting among the additions of later times only such as may supply real deficiencies, such as are readily adopted by the genius of our tongue, and incorporate easily with our native idioms.

But as every language has a time of rudeness antecedent to perfection, as well as of false refinement and declension, I have been cautious lest my zeal for antiquity might drive me into times too remote, and crowd my book with words now no longer understood. I have fixed Sidney's† work for the boundary beyond which I make few excursions. From the authors which rose in the time of Elizabeth, a speech might be formed adequate to all the purposes of use and elegance. If the language of theology were extracted from Hooker and the translation of the Bible; the terms of natural knowledge from Bacon; the phrases of policy, war, and navigation from Raleigh; the dialect of poetry and fiction from Spenser and Sidney; and the diction of common life from Shakespeare, few ideas would be lost to mankind for want of English words in which they might be expressed. . . .

---

*Teutonic* Anglo-Saxon
*Gallic* French
*Sidney* Sir Philip Sidney (1554–86), statesman and author

Of the event of this work, for which, having laboured it with so much application, I cannot but have some degree of parental fondness, it is natural to form conjectures. Those who have been persuaded to think well of my design will require that it should fix our language, and put a stop to those alterations which time and chance have hitherto been suffered to make in it without opposition. With this consequence I will confess that I flattered myself for a while; but now begin to fear that I have indulged expectation which neither reason nor experience can justify. When we see men grow old and die at a certain time one after another, from century to century, we laugh at the elixir that promises to prolong life to a thousand years; and with equal justice may the lexicographer be derided who being able to produce no example of a nation that has preserved their words and phrases from mutability shall imagine that his dictionary can embalm his language, and secure it from corruption and decay, that it is in his power to change sublunary nature, or clear the world at once from folly, vanity, and affectation. . . .

In hope of giving longevity to that which its own nature forbids to be immortal, I have devoted this book, the labour of years, to the honour of my country, that we may no longer yield the palm of philology without a contest to the nations of the continent. The chief glory of every people arises from its authors: whether I shall add any thing by my own writings to the reputation of English literature must be left to time: much of my life has been lost under the pressure of disease; much has been trifled away; and much has always been spent in provision for the day that was passing over me; but I shall not think my employment useless or ignoble, if by my assistance foreign nations, and distant ages, gain access to the propagators of knowledge, and understand the teachers of truth; if my labours afford light to the repositories of science, and add celebrity to Bacon, to Hooker, to Milton, and to Boyle. . . .

In this work, when it shall be found that much is omitted, let it not be forgotten that much likewise is performed; and though no book was ever spared out of tenderness to the author, and the world is little solicitous to know whence proceeded the faults of that which it condemns; yet it may gratify curiosity to inform it that the *English Dictionary* was written with little assistance of the learned, and without any patronage of the great; not in the soft obscurities of retirement, or under the shelter of academic bowers, but amidst inconvenience and distraction, in sickness and in sorrow: and it may repress the triumph of malignant criticism to observe that if our language is not here fully displayed, I have only failed in an attempt which no human powers have hitherto completed. If the lexicons of ancient tongues, now immutably fixed, and comprised in a few volumes, be yet, after the toil of successive ages, inadequate and delusive; if the aggregated knowledge and co-operating diligence of the Italian academicians did not secure them from the censure of Beni; if the embodied critics of France, when fifty years had been spent upon their work, were obliged to change its economy, and give their second edition another form, I may surely be contented without the praise of perfection, which, if I could obtain, in this gloom of solitude, what would it avail me? I have protracted my work till most of those whom I wished to please have sunk into the grave,† and success and miscarriage are empty sounds: I therefore dismiss it with frigid tranquillity, having little to fear or hope from censure or from praise.

1755

## *From* RASSELAS†

## Chap. VI *A Dissertation on the Art of Flying*

Among the artists that had been allured into the happy valley, to labour for the accommodation and pleasure of its inhabitants, was a man eminent for his knowledge of the mechanic powers, who had contrived many engines both of use and recreation. By a wheel, which the stream turned, he forced the water into a tower, whence it was distributed to all the apartments of the palace. He erected a pavilion in the garden, around which he kept the air always cool by artificial showers. One of the groves, appropriated to the ladies, was ventilated by fans, to which the rivulet that run through it gave a constant motion; and instruments of soft music were placed at proper distances, of which some played by the impulse of the wind, and some by the power of the stream.

This artist was sometimes visited by Rasselas, who was pleased with every kind of knowledge, imagining that the time would come when all his acquisitions should be of use to him in the open world. He came one day to amuse himself in his usual manner, and found the master busy in building a sailing chariot: he saw that the design was practicable upon a level surface, and with expressions of great esteem solicited its completion. The workman was pleased to find himself so much regarded by the prince, and resolved to gain yet higher honours. 'Sir,' said he, 'you have seen but a small part of what the mechanic sciences can perform. I have been long of opinion that, instead of the tardy

*grave* J's wife had died in 1752

*Rasselas* Rasselas, son of the Abyssinian emperor, is confined in the 'happy valley', but hopes some day to see the outside world

conveyance of ships and chariots, man might use the swifter migration of wings; that the fields of air are open to knowledge, and that only ignorance and idleness need crawl upon the ground.'

This hint rekindled the prince's desire of passing the mountains; having seen what the mechanist had already performed, he was willing to fancy that he could do more; yet resolved to inquire further before he suffered hope to afflict him by disappointment. 'I am afraid,' said he to the artist, 'that your imagination prevails over your skill, and that you now tell me rather what you wish than what you know. Every animal has his element assigned him; the birds have the air, and man and beasts the earth.' 'So,' replied the mechanist, 'fishes have the water, in which yet beasts can swim by nature, and men by art. He that can swim needs not despair to fly: to swim is to fly in a grosser fluid, and to fly is to swim in a subtler. We are only to proportion our power of resistance to the different density of the matter through which we are to pass. You will be necessarily upborne by the air, if you can renew any impulse upon it faster than the air can recede from the pressure.'

'But the exercise of swimming,' said the prince, 'is very laborious; the strongest limbs are soon wearied; I am afraid the act of flying will be yet more violent, and wings will be of no great use, unless we can fly further than we can swim.'

'The labour of rising from the ground,' said the artist, 'will be great, as we see it in the heavier domestic fowls; but, as we mount higher, the earth's attraction, and the body's gravity, will be gradually diminished, till we shall arrive at a region where the man will float in the air without any tendency to fall: no care will then be necessary but to move forwards, which the gentlest impulse will effect. You, sir, whose curiosity is so extensive, will easily conceive with what pleasure a philosopher, furnished with wings, and hovering in the sky, would see the earth, and all its inhabitants, rolling beneath him, and presenting to him successively, by its diurnal† motion, all the countries within the same parallel. How must it amuse the pendent spectator to see the moving scene of land and ocean, cities and deserts! To survey with equal security the marts of trade, and the fields of battle; mountains infested by barbarians, and fruitful regions gladdened by plenty, and lulled by peace! How easily shall we then trace the Nile through all his passage; pass over to distant regions, and examine the face of nature from one extremity of the earth to the other!'

'All this,' said the prince, 'is much to be desired, but I am afraid that no man will be able to breathe in these regions of speculation and tranquillity. I have been told that respiration is difficult upon lofty mountains, yet from these precipices, though so high as to produce

*diurnal* daily

great tenuity of the air, it is very easy to fall: therefore I suspect that from any height where life can be supported there may be danger of too quick descent.'

'Nothing,' replied the artist, 'will ever be attempted, if all possible objections must be first overcome. If you will favour my project I will try the first flight at my own hazard. I have considered the structure of all volant† animals, and find the folding continuity of the bat's wings most easily accommodated to the human form. Upon this model I shall begin my task tomorrow, and in a year expect to tower into the air beyond the malice or pursuit of man. But I will work only on this condition, that the art shall not be divulged, and that you shall not require me to make wings for any but ourselves.'

'Why,' said Rasselas, 'should you envy others so great an advantage? All skill ought to be exerted for universal good; every man has owed much to others, and ought to repay the kindness that he has received.'

'If men were all virtuous,' returned the artist, 'I should with great alacrity teach them all to fly. But what would be the security of the good, if the bad could at pleasure invade them from the sky? Against an army sailing through the clouds neither walls, nor mountains, nor seas, could afford any security. A flight of northern savages might hover in the wind, and light at once with irresistible violence upon the capital of a fruitful region that was rolling under them. Even this valley, the retreat of princes, the abode of happiness, might be violated by the sudden descent of some of the naked nations that swarm on the coast of the southern sea.'

The prince promised secrecy, and waited for the performance, not wholly hopeless of success. He visited the work from time to time, observed its progress, and remarked many ingenious contrivances to facilitate motion, and unite levity with strength. The artist was every day more certain that he should leave vultures and eagles behind him, and the contagion of his confidence seized upon the prince.

In a year the wings were finished, and, on a morning appointed, the maker appeared furnished for flight on a little promontory: he waved his pinions a while to gather air, then leaped from his stand, and in an instant dropped into the lake. His wings, which were of no use in the air, sustained him in the water, and the prince drew him to land, half dead with terror and vexation.

*volant* flying

## Chap. X *A Dissertation upon Poetry*

[The poet Imlac tells of his experience in the outside world.]

'Wherever I went, I found that poetry was considered as the highest learning, and regarded with a veneration somewhat approaching to that which man would pay to the angelic nature. And it yet fills me with wonder that, in almost all countries, the most ancient poets are considered as the best: whether it be that every other kind of knowledge is an acquisition gradually attained, and poetry is a gift conferred at once; or that the first poetry of every nation surprised them as a novelty, and retained the credit by consent which it received by accident at first: or whether, as the province of poetry is to describe nature and passion, which are always the same, the first writers took possession of the most striking objects for description, and the most probable occurrences for fiction, and left nothing to those that followed them but transcription of the same events, and new combinations of the same images. Whatever be the reason, it is commonly observed that the early writers are in possession of nature, and their followers of art: that the first excel in strength and invention, and the latter in elegance and refinement.

'I was desirous to add my name to this illustrious fraternity. I read all the poets of Persia and Arabia, and was able to repeat by memory the volumes that are suspended in the mosque of Mecca.† But I soon found that no man was ever great by imitation. My desire of excellence impelled me to transfer my attention to nature and to life. Nature was to be my subject, and men to be my auditors. I could never describe what I had not seen: I could not hope to move those with delight or terror whose interests and opinions I did not understand.

'Being now resolved to be a poet, I saw every thing with a new purpose; my sphere of attention was suddenly magnified: no kind of knowledge was to be overlooked. I ranged mountains and deserts for images and resemblances, and pictured upon my mind every tree of the forest and flower of the valley. I observed with equal care the crags of the rock and the pinnacles of the palace. Sometimes I wandered along the mazes of the rivulet, and sometimes watched the changes of the summer clouds. To a poet nothing can be useless. Whatever is beautiful, and whatever is dreadful, must be familiar to his imagination: he must be conversant with all that is awfully vast or elegantly little. The plants of the garden, the animals of the wood, the minerals of the earth, and meteors of the sky, must all concur to store his mind with inexhaustible variety: for every idea is useful for the enforcement or decoration of moral or religious truth; and he who knows most will have most power

*Mecca* Muslim sacred place

of diversifying his scenes, and of gratifying his reader with remote allusions and unexpected instruction.

'All the appearances of nature I was therefore careful to study, and every country which I have surveyed has contributed something to my poetical powers.'

'In so wide a survey,' said the prince, 'you must surely have left much unobserved. I have lived, till now, within the circuit of these mountains, and yet cannot walk abroad without the sight of something which I had never beheld before, or never heeded.'

'The business of a poet,' said Imlac, 'is to examine, not the individual, but the species; to remark general properties and large appearances; he does not number the streaks of the tulip, or describe the different shades in the verdure of the forest. He is to exhibit in his portraits of nature such prominent and striking features as recall the original to every mind; and must neglect the minuter discriminations, which one may have remarked, and another have neglected, for those characteristics which are alike obvious to vigilance and carelessness.

'But the knowledge of nature is only half the task of a poet; he must be acquainted likewise with all the modes of life. His character requires that he estimate the happiness and misery of every condition; observe the power of all the passions in all their combinations, and trace the changes of the human mind as they are modified by various institutions and accidental influences of climate or custom, from the spriteliness of infancy to the despondence of decrepitude. He must divest himself of the prejudices of his age or country; he must consider right and wrong in their abstracted and invariable state; he must disregard present laws and opinions, and rise to general and transcendental truths, which will always be the same: he must therefore content himself with the slow progress of his name; contemn the applause of his own time, and commit his claims to the justice of posterity. He must write as the interpreter of nature, and the legislator of mankind, and consider himself as presiding over the thoughts and manners of future generations; as a being superior to time and place.

'His labour is not yet at an end: he must know many languages and many sciences; and, that his style may be worthy of his thoughts, must, by incessant practice, familiarise to himself every delicacy of speech and grace of harmony.'

1759

# *From* PREFACE TO SHAKESPEARE[†]

Nothing can please many, and please long, but just representations of general nature. Particular manners can be known to few, and therefore few only can judge how nearly they are copied. The irregular combinations of fanciful invention may delight a while, by that novelty of which the common satiety of life sends us all in quest; but the pleasures of sudden wonder are soon exhausted, and the mind can only repose on the stability of truth.

Shakespeare is above all writers, at least above all modern writers, the poet of nature; the poet that holds up to his readers a faithful mirror of manners and of life. His characters are not modified by the customs of particular places, unpractised by the rest of the world; by the peculiarities of studies or professions, which can operate but upon small numbers; or by the accidents of transient fashions or temporary opinions: they are the genuine progeny of common humanity, such as the world will always supply, and observation will always find. His persons act and speak by the influence of those general passions and principles by which all minds are agitated, and the whole system of life is continued in motion. In the writings of other poets a character is too often an individual; in those of Shakespeare it is commonly a species.

It is from this wide extension of design that so much instruction is derived. It is this which fills the plays of Shakespeare with practical axioms and domestic wisdom. It was said of Euripides[†] that every verse was a precept; and it may be said of Shakespeare that from his works may be collected a system of civil and economical prudence. Yet his real power is not shown in the splendour of particular passages, but by the progress of his fable, and the tenor of his dialogue; and he that tries to recommend him by select quotations will succeed like the pedant in Hierocles,[†] who, when he offered his house to sale, carried a brick in his pocket as a specimen.

It will not easily be imagined how much Shakespeare excels in accommodating his sentiments to real life but by comparing him with other authors. It was observed of the ancient schools of declamation that the more diligently they were frequented, the more was the student disqualified for the world, because he found nothing there which he should ever meet in any other place. The same remark may be applied

*Preface to Shakespeare* Johnson's edition of Shakespeare (1765) had detailed notes and a brief general comment on each play. The great Preface takes up many current topics: the relation of art to life; the mixing of tragedy and comedy; the dramatic 'unities' of time and place. In his usual manner, Johnson assesses his author's virtues and faults; his views, often shocking to the modern reader, are carefully considered and profoundly aware of the functions of literature; the plays had survived by their wide appeal to human experience rather than dramatic theory

*Euripides* Greek tragedian (fifth century BC)

*Hierocles* Greek philosopher (fifth century AD)

to every stage but that of Shakespeare. The theatre, when it is under any other direction, is peopled by such characters as were never seen, conversing in a language which was never heard, upon topics which will never arise in the commerce of mankind. But the dialogue of this author is often so evidently determined by the incident which produces it, and is pursued with so much ease and simplicity, that it seems scarcely to claim the merit of fiction, but to have been gleaned by diligent selection out of common conversation, and common occurrences.

Upon every other stage the universal agent is love, by whose power all good and evil is distributed, and every action quickened or retarded. To bring a lover, a lady, and a rival into the fable; to entangle them in contradictory obligations, perplex them with oppositions of interest, and harass them with violence of desires inconsistent with each other; to make them meet in rapture and part in agony; to fill their mouths with hyperbolical joy and outrageous sorrow; to distress them as nothing human ever was distressed; to deliver them as nothing human ever was delivered is the business of a modern dramatist. For this, probability is violated, life is misrepresented, and language is depraved. But love is only one of many passions, and as it has no great influence upon the sum of life, it has little operation in the dramas of a poet who caught his ideas from the living world, and exhibited only what he saw before him. He knew that any other passion, as it was regular or exorbitant, was a cause of happiness or calamity.

Characters thus ample and general were not easily discriminated and preserved, yet perhaps no poet ever kept his personages more distinct from each other. I will not say with Pope that every speech may be assigned to the proper speaker, because many speeches there are which have nothing characteristical; but perhaps, though some may be equally adapted to every person, it will be difficult to find any that can be properly transferred from the present possessor to another claimant. The choice is right, when there is reason for choice.

Other dramatists can only gain attention by hyperbolical or aggravated characters, by fabulous and unexampled excellence or depravity, as the writers of barbarous romances invigorated the reader by a giant and a dwarf; and he that should form his expectations of human affairs from the play, or from the tale, would be equally deceived. Shakespeare has no heroes; his scenes are occupied only by men, who act and speak as the reader thinks that he should himself have spoken or acted on the same occasion. Even where the agency is supernatural the dialogue is level with life. Other writers disguise the most natural passions and most frequent incidents; so that he who contemplates them in the book will not know them in the world: Shakespeare approximates† the

*approximates* brings near

remote, and familiarises the wonderful; the event which he represents will not happen, but if it were possible, its effects would probably be such as he has assigned; and it may be said that he has not only shown human nature as it acts in real exigences, but as it would be found in trials to which it cannot be exposed.

This therefore is the praise of Shakespeare, that his drama is the mirror of life; that he who has mazed[†] his imagination, in following the phantoms which other writers raise up before him, may here be cured of his delirious ecstasies, by reading human sentiments in human language; by scenes from which a hermit may estimate the transactions of the world, and a confessor predict the progress of the passions.

His adherence to general nature has exposed him to the censure of critics, who form their judgments upon narrower principles. Dennis[†] and Rymer[†] think his Romans not sufficiently Roman; and Voltaire[†] censures his kings as not completely royal. Dennis is offended that Menenius, a senator of Rome, should play the buffoon; and Voltaire perhaps thinks decency violated when the Danish usurper is represented as a drunkard. But Shakespeare always makes nature predominate over accident; and if he preserves the essential character, is not very careful of distinctions superinduced and adventitious. His story requires Romans or kings, but he thinks only on men. He knew that Rome, like every other city, had men of all dispositions; and wanting a buffoon, he went into the senate-house for that which the senate-house would certainly have afforded him. He was inclined to show an usurper and a murderer not only odious but despicable; he therefore added drunkenness to his other qualities, knowing that kings love wine like other men, and that wine exerts its natural power upon kings. These are the petty cavils of petty minds; a poet overlooks the casual distinction of country and condition, as a painter, satisfied with the figure, neglects the drapery.

The censure which he has incurred by mixing comic and tragic scenes, as it extends to all his works, deserves more consideration. Let the fact be first stated, and then examined.

Shakespeare's plays are not in the rigorous and critical sense either tragedies or comedies, but compositions of a distinct kind; exhibiting the real state of sublunary[†] nature, which partakes of good and evil, joy and sorrow, mingled with endless variety of proportion and innumerable modes of combination; and expressing the course of the world, in which the loss of one is the gain of another; in which, at the

*mazed* confused

*Dennis* John Dennis, *Essay on Shakespeare* (1712)

*Rymer* Thomas Rymer, *A Short View of Tragedy* (1692; it included a notorious attack on *Othello*)

*Voltaire* 1694–1778, French neo-classical critic

*sublunary* beneath the moon, on earth

same time, the reveller is hasting to his wine, and the mourner burying his friend; in which the malignity of one is sometimes defeated by the frolic of another; and many mischiefs and many benefits are done and hindered without design.

Out of this chaos of mingled purposes and casualties the ancient poets, according to the laws which custom had prescribed, selected some the crimes of men, and some their absurdities; some the momentous vicissitudes of life, and some the lighter occurrences; some the terror of distress, and some the gaieties of prosperity. Thus rose the two modes of imitation known by the names of tragedy and comedy, compositions intended to promote different ends by contrary means, and considered as so little allied that I do not recollect among the Greeks or Romans a single writer who attempted both.

Shakespeare has united the powers of exciting laughter and sorrow not only in one mind but in one composition. Almost all his plays are divided between serious and ludicrous characters, and, in the successive evolutions of the design, sometimes produce seriousness and sorrow, and sometimes levity and laughter.

That this is a practice contrary to the rules of criticism† will be readily allowed; but there is always an appeal open from criticism to nature. The end of writing is to instruct; the end of poetry is to instruct by pleasing. That the mingled drama may convey all the instruction of tragedy or comedy cannot be denied, because it includes both in its alternations of exhibition, and approaches nearer than either to the appearance of life, by showing how great machinations and slender designs may promote or obviate one another, and the high and the low co-operate in the general system by unavoidable concatenation. . . .

Shakespeare engaged in dramatic poetry with the world open before him; the rules of the ancients were yet known to few; the public judgment was unformed; he had no example of such fame as might force him upon imitation, nor critics of such authority as might restrain his extravagance. He therefore indulged his natural disposition, and his disposition, as Rymer has remarked, led him to comedy. In tragedy he often writes with great appearance of toil and study what is written at last with little felicity; but in his comic scenes, he seems to produce without labour what no labour can improve. In tragedy he is always struggling after some occasion to be comic, but in comedy he seems to repose, or to luxuriate, as in a mode of thinking congenial to his nature. In his tragic scenes there is always something wanting, but his comedy often surpasses expectation or desire. His comedy pleases by the thoughts and the language, and his tragedy for the greater part by

*rules of criticism* formulations based on ancient writers' practice

incident and action. His tragedy seems to be skill, his comedy to be instinct.

The force of his comic scenes has suffered little diminution from the changes made by a century and a half in manners or in words. As his personages act upon principles arising from genuine passion, very little modified by particular forms, their pleasures and vexations are communicable to all times and to all places; they are natural, and therefore durable; the adventitious peculiarities of personal habits are only superficial dyes, bright and pleasing for a little while, yet soon fading to a dim tint, without any remains of former lustre; but the discriminations of true passion are the colours of nature; they pervade the whole mass, and can only perish with the body that exhibits them. The accidental compositions of heterogeneous modes are dissolved by the chance which combined them; but the uniform simplicity of primitive† qualities neither admits increase, nor suffers decay. The sand heaped by one flood is scattered by another, but the rock always continues in its place. The stream of time, which is continually washing the dissoluble fabrics of other poets, passes without injury by the adamant† of Shakespeare. . . .

Shakespeare with his excellencies has likewise faults, and faults sufficient to obscure and overwhelm any other merit. I shall show them in the proportion in which they appear to me, without envious malignity or superstitious veneration. No question can be more innocently discussed than a dead poet's pretensions to renown; and little regard is due to that bigotry which sets candour higher than truth.

His first defect is that to which may be imputed most of the evil in books or in men. He sacrifices virtue to convenience, and is so much more careful to please than to instruct that he seems to write without any moral purpose. From his writings indeed a system of social duty may be selected, for he that thinks reasonably must think morally; but his precepts and axioms drop casually from him; he makes no just distribution of good or evil, nor is always careful to show in the virtuous a disapprobation of the wicked; he carries his persons indifferently through right and wrong, and at the close dismisses them without further care, and leaves their examples to operate by chance. This fault the barbarity of his age cannot extenuate; for it is always a writer's duty to make the world better, and justice is a virtue independent on time or place.

The plots are often so loosely formed that a very slight consideration may improve them, and so carelessly pursued that he seems not always fully to comprehend his own design. He omits opportunities of instructing or delighting which the train of his story seems to force

*primitive* basic, essential    *adamant* hard stone

upon him, and apparently rejects those exhibitions which would be more affecting, for the sake of those which are more easy.

It may be observed that in many of his plays the latter part is evidently neglected. When he found himself near the end of his work, and in view of his reward, he shortened the labour, to snatch the profit. He therefore remits his efforts where he should most vigorously exert them, and his catastrophe is improbably produced or imperfectly represented. . . .

In his comic scenes he is seldom very successful when he engages his characters in reciprocations of smartness and contests of sarcasm; their jests are commonly gross, and their pleasantry licentious; neither his gentlemen nor his ladies have much delicacy, nor are sufficiently distinguished from his clowns by any appearance of refined manners. Whether he represented the real conversation of his time is not easy to determine; the reign of Elizabeth is commonly supposed to have been a time of stateliness, formality, and reserve, yet perhaps the relaxations of that severity were not very elegant. There must, however, have been always some modes of gaiety preferable to others, and a writer ought to choose the best.

In tragedy his performance seems constantly to be worse as his labour is more. The effusions of passion which exigence forces out are for the most part striking and energetic; but whenever he solicits his invention, or strains his faculties, the offspring of his throes is tumour, meanness, tediousness, and obscurity.

In narration he affects a disproportionate pomp of diction and a wearisome train of circumlocution, and tells the incident imperfectly in many words which might have been more plainly delivered in few. Narration in dramatic poetry is naturally tedious as it is unanimated and inactive, and obstructs the progress of the action; it should therefore always be rapid, and enlivened by frequent interruption. Shakespeare found it an encumbrance, and instead of lightening it by brevity, endeavoured to recommend it by dignity and splendour.

His declamations or set speeches are commonly cold and weak, for his power was the power of nature; when he endeavoured, like other tragic writers, to catch opportunities of amplification, and instead of inquiring what the occasion demanded, to show how much his stores of knowledge could supply, he seldom escapes without the pity or resentment of his reader.

It is incident to him to be now and then entangled with an unwieldy sentiment which he cannot well express, and will not reject; he struggles with it a while, and if it continues stubborn, comprises it in words such as occur, and leaves it to be disentangled and evolved by those who have more leisure to bestow upon it.

Not that always where the language is intricate the thought is subtle, or the image always great where the line is bulky; the equality of words to things is very often neglected, and trivial sentiments and vulgar ideas disappoint the attention to which they are recommended by sonorous epithets and swelling figures.

But the admirers of this great poet have most reason to complain when he approaches nearest to his highest excellence, and seems fully resolved to sink them in dejection, and mollify them with tender emotions by the fall of greatness, the danger of innocence, or the crosses of love. What he does best, he soon ceases to do. He is not long soft and pathetic without some idle conceit,† or contemptible equivocation.† He no sooner begins to move than he counteracts himself; and terror and pity, as they are rising in the mind, are checked and blasted by sudden frigidity.

A quibble† is to Shakespeare what luminous vapours are to the traveller; he follows it at all adventures, it is sure to lead him out of his way, and sure to engulf him in the mire. It has some malignant power over his mind, and its fascinations are irresistible. Whatever be the dignity or profundity of his disquisition, whether he be enlarging knowledge or exalting affection, whether he be amusing attention with incidents, or enchaining it in suspense, let but a quibble spring up before him, and he leaves his work unfinished. A quibble is the golden apple† for which he will always turn aside from his career, or stoop from his elevation. A quibble, poor and barren as it is, gave him such delight that he was content to purchase it by the sacrifice of reason, propriety and truth. A quibble was to him the fatal Cleopatra for which he lost the world, and was content to lose it.

It will be thought strange that, in enumerating the defects of this writer, I have not yet mentioned his neglect of the unities;† his violation of those laws which have been instituted and established by the joint authority of poets and of critics.

For his other deviations from the art of writing, I resign him to critical justice, without making any other demand in his favour than that which must be indulged to all human excellence; that his virtues be rated with his failings. But from the censure which this irregularity may bring upon him, I shall, with due reverence to that learning which I must oppose, adventure to try how I can defend him.

His histories, being neither tragedies nor comedies, are not subject to any of their laws; nothing more is necessary to all the praise which they expect than that the changes of action be so prepared as to be

*conceit* witty comparison
*equivocation* double meaning
*quibble* pun. J. was unsympathetic to such wit and ambiguity: see Life of Cowley (p. 350)
*golden apple* for this Atalanta lost her race
*unities* principles that a single united action should happen in one day in one place

understood, that the incidents be various and affecting, and the characters consistent, natural, and distinct. No other unity is intended, and therefore none is to be sought.

In his other works he has well enough preserved the unity of action. He has not, indeed, an intrigue regularly perplexed and regularly unravelled; he does not endeavour to hide his design only to discover it, for this is seldom the order of real events, and Shakespeare is the poet of nature. But his plan has commonly what Aristotle† requires, a beginning, a middle, and an end; one event is concatenated with another, and the conclusion follows by easy consequence. There are perhaps some incidents that might be spared, as in other poets there is much talk that only fills up time upon the stage; but the general system makes gradual advances, and the end of the play is the end of expectation.

To the unities of time and place he has shown no regard, and perhaps a nearer view of the principles on which they stand will diminish their value, and withdraw from them the veneration which, from the time of Corneille,† they have very generally received, by discovering that they have given more trouble to the poet than pleasure to the auditor.

The necessity of observing the unities of time and place arises from the supposed necessity of making the drama credible. The critics hold it impossible that an action of months or years can be possibly believed to pass in three hours; or that the spectator can suppose himself to sit in the theatre, while ambassadors go and return between distant kings, while armies are levied and towns besieged, while an exile wanders and returns, or till he whom they saw courting his mistress shall lament the untimely fall of his son. The mind revolts from evident falsehood, and fiction loses its force when it departs from the resemblance of reality.

From the narrow limitation of time necessarily arises the contraction of place. The spectator who knows that he saw the first act at Alexandria cannot suppose that he sees the next at Rome, at a distance to which not the dragons of Medea† could, in so short a time, have transported him; he knows with certainty that he has not changed his place; and he knows that place cannot change itself; that what was a house cannot become a plain; that what was Thebes can never be Persepolis.

Such is the triumphant language with which a critic exults over the misery of an irregular poet, and exults commonly without resistance or reply. It is time therefore to tell him, by the authority of Shakespeare, that he assumes as an unquestionable principle a position which, while

*Aristotle* fourth century BC Greek, greatest critic of antiquity (*Poetics*)

*Corneille* French neo-classical dramatist (1606–84)

*Medea* character in Greek mythology and tragedy

his breath is forming it into words, his understanding pronounces to be false. It is false that any representation is mistaken for reality; that any dramatic fable in its materiality was ever credible, or, for a single moment, was ever credited. . . .

The truth is that the spectators are always in their senses, and know, from the first act to the last, that the stage is only a stage, and that the players are only players. They come to hear a certain number of lines recited with just gesture and elegant modulation. The lines relate to some action, and an action must be in some place; but the different actions that complete a story may be in places very remote from each other; and where is the absurdity of allowing that space to represent first Athens, and then Sicily, which was always known to be neither Sicily nor Athens, but a modern theatre?

By supposition, as place is introduced, time may be extended; the time required by the fable elapses for the most part between the acts; for, of so much of the action as is represented, the real and poetical duration is the same. If, in the first act, preparations for war against Mithridates are represented to be made in Rome, the event of the war may, without absurdity, be represented, in the catastrophe, as happening in Pontus; we know that there is neither war, nor preparation for war; we know that we are neither in Rome nor Pontus; that neither Mithridates nor Lucullus are before us. The drama exhibits successive imitations of successive actions, and why may not the second imitation represent an action that happened years after the first, if it be so connected with it that nothing but time can be supposed to intervene? Time is, of all modes of existence, most obsequious[†] to the imagination; a lapse of years is as easily conceived as a passage of hours. In contemplation we easily contract the time of real actions, and therefore willingly permit it to be contracted when we only see their imitation.

It will be asked how the drama moves, if it is not credited. It is credited with all the credit due to a drama. It is credited, whenever it moves, as a just picture of a real original; as representing to the auditor what he would himself feel if he were to do or suffer what is there feigned to be suffered or to be done. The reflection that strikes the heart is not that the evils before us are real evils, but that they are evils to which we ourselves may be exposed. If there be any fallacy, it is not that we fancy the players but that we fancy ourselves unhappy for a moment; but we rather lament the possibility than suppose the presence of misery, as a mother weeps over her babe when she remembers that death may take it from her. The delight of tragedy proceeds from our consciousness of fiction; if we thought murders and treasons real, they would please no more.

*obsequious* compliant

Imitations produce pain or pleasure, not because they are mistaken for realities, but because they bring realities to mind. When the imagination is recreated by a painted landscape, the trees are not supposed capable to give us shade, or the fountains coolness; but we consider how we should be pleased with such fountains playing beside us, and such woods waving over us. We are agitated in reading the history of Henry the Fifth, yet no man takes his book for the field of Agincourt. A dramatic exhibition is a book recited with concomitants that increase or diminish its effect. Familiar comedy is often more powerful on the theatre than in the page; imperial tragedy is always less. The humour of Petruchio[†] may be heightened by grimace; but what voice or what gesture can hope to add dignity or force to the soliloquy of Cato?[†]

A play read affects the mind like a play acted. It is therefore evident that the action is not supposed to be real, and it follows that between the acts a longer or shorter time may be allowed to pass, and that no more account of space or duration is to be taken by the auditor of a drama than by the reader of a narrative, before whom may pass in an hour the life of a hero, or the revolutions of an empire.

Whether Shakespeare knew the unities, and rejected them by design, or deviated from them by happy ignorance, it is, I think, impossible to decide, and useless to inquire. We may reasonably suppose that, when he rose to notice, he did not want the counsels and admonitions of scholars and critics, and that he at last deliberately persisted in a practice which he might have begun by chance. . . .

## *From* General Note on *King Lear*[†]

But though this moral be incidentally enforced, Shakespeare has suffered the virtue of Cordelia to perish in a just cause, contrary to the natural ideas of justice, to the hope of the reader, and, what is yet more strange, to the faith of chronicles.[†] Yet this conduct is justified by the Spectator, who blames Tate for giving Cordelia success and happiness in his alteration, and declares that in his opinion *the tragedy has lost half its beauty*. Dennis has remarked, whether justly or not, that, to secure the favourable reception of *Cato, the town was poisoned with much false and abominable criticism*, and that endeavours had been used to discredit and decry poetical justice. A play in which the wicked

*Petruchio* in *The Taming of the Shrew*
*Cato* in Addison's tragedy
*General Note on King Lear* In his comment on *King Lear*, usually performed with a happy ending in Nahum Tate's 1681 adaptation, Johnson is concerned that the consequence of evil be clearly demonstrated
*chronicles* Shakespeare's sources

prosper, and the virtuous miscarry, may doubtless be good, because it is a just representation of the common events of human life: but since all reasonable beings naturally love justice, I cannot easily be persuaded that the observation of justice makes a play worse; or, that if other excellencies are equal, the audience will not always rise better pleased from the final triumph of persecuted virtue.

In the present case the public has decided. Cordelia, from the time of Tate, has always retired with victory and felicity. And, if my sensations could add any thing to the general suffrage, I might relate that I was many years ago so shocked by Cordelia's death that I know not whether I ever endured to read again the last scenes of the play till I undertook to revise them as an editor. . .

1765

## *From* A JOURNEY TO THE WESTERN ISLANDS OF SCOTLAND

### *[Highland Scenery]*

We were now in the bosom of the Highlands, with full leisure to contemplate the appearance and properties of mountainous regions, such as have been, in many countries, the last shelters of national distress, and are everywhere the scenes of adventures, stratagems, surprises and escapes. . . .

Of the hills many may be called with Homer's Ida *abundant in springs*, but few can deserve the epithet which he bestows upon Pelion by *waving their leaves*. They exhibit very little variety, being almost wholly covered with dark heath, and even that seems to be checked in its growth. What is not heath is nakedness, a little diversified by now and then a stream rushing down the steep. An eye accustomed to flowery pastures and waving harvests is astonished and repelled by this wide extent of hopeless sterility. The appearance is that of matter incapable of form or usefulness, dismissed by nature from her care and disinherited of her favours, left in its original elemental state, or quickened only with one sullen power of useless vegetation.

It will very readily occur that this uniformity of barrenness can afford very little amusement to the traveller; that it is easy to sit at home and conceive rocks and heath, and waterfalls; and that these journeys are useless labours, which neither impregnate the imagination, nor enlarge the understanding. It is true that of far the greater part of things, we must content ourselves with such knowledge as decription may exhibit, or analogy supply; but it is true likewise that these ideas are always incomplete, and that at least, till we have compared them with realities, we do not know them to be just. As we see more, we become possessed of more certainties, and consequently gain more principles of reasoning, and found a wider basis of analogy.

Regions mountainous and wild, thinly inhabited, and little cultivated, make a great part of the earth, and he that has never seen them must live unacquainted with much of the face of nature, and with one of the great scenes of human existence.

As the day advanced towards noon, we entered a narrow valley not very flowery, but sufficiently verdant. Our guides told us that the horses could not travel all day without rest or meat,[†] and entreated us to stop here, because no grass would be found in any other place. The request was reasonable and the argument cogent. We therefore willingly dismounted and diverted ourselves as the place gave us opportunity.

I sat down on a bank such as a writer of romance might have delighted to feign. I had indeed no trees to whisper over my head, but a clear rivulet streamed at my feet. The day was calm, the air soft, and all was rudeness, silence, and solitude. Before me, and on either side, were high hills, which by hindering the eye from ranging, forced the mind to find entertainment for itself. Whether I spent the hour well I know not; for here I first conceived the thought of this narration.

We were in this place at ease and by choice, and had no evils to suffer or to fear; yet the imaginations excited by the view of an unknown and untravelled wilderness are not such as arise in the artificial solitude of parks and gardens, a flattering notion of self-sufficiency, a placid indulgence of voluntary delusions, a secure expansion of the fancy, or a cool concentration of the mental powers. The phantoms which haunt a desert are want, and misery, and danger; the evils of dereliction rush upon the thoughts; man is made unwillingly acquainted with his own weakness, and meditation shows him only how little he can sustain, and how little he can perform. There were no traces of inhabitants, except a rude pile of clods called a summer hut, in which a herdsman had rested in the favourable seasons. Whoever had been in the place where I then sat, unprovided with provisions and ignorant of the country, might, at least before the roads were made, have wandered among the rocks till he had perished with hardship, before he could have found either food or shelter. Yet what are these hillocks to the ridges of Taurus,[†] or these spots of wildness to the deserts of America?

1775

*meat* food

*Taurus* mountain-range in Turkey

# *From* LETTERS

## To the Earl of Chesterfield[†]

February 1755

My Lord

I have been lately informed by the proprietor of *The World* that two papers in which my Dictionary is recommended to the public were written by your Lordship. To be so distinguished is an honour which, being very little accustomed to favours from the great, I know not well how to receive, or in what terms to acknowledge.

When upon some slight encouragement I first visited your Lordship, I was overpowered like the rest of mankind by the enchantment of your address, and could not forbear to wish that I might boast myself *le vainqueur du vainqueur de la terre* [the conqueror of the world's conqueror], that I might obtain that regard for which I saw the world contending, but I found my attendance so little encouraged that neither pride nor modesty would suffer me to continue it. When I had once addressed your Lordship in public, I had exhausted all the art of pleasing which a retired and uncourtly scholar can possess. I had done all that I could, and no man is well pleased to have his all neglected, be it ever so little.

Seven years, My Lord, have now passed since I waited in your outward rooms or was repulsed from your door, during which time I have been pushing on my work through difficulties of which it is useless to complain, and have brought it at last to the verge of publication without one act of assistance, one word of encouragement, or one smile of favour. Such treatment I did not expect, for I never had a patron before.

The shepherd in Virgil grew at last acquainted with Love, and found him a native of the rocks.[†] Is not a patron, My Lord, one who looks with unconcern on a man struggling for life in the water and when he has reached ground encumbers him with help? The notice which you have been pleased to take of my labours, had it been early, had been kind; but it has been delayed till I am indifferent and cannot enjoy it, till I am solitary and cannot impart it, till I am known and do not want it.

I hope it is no very cynical asperity not to confess obligation where no benefit has been received, or to be unwilling that the public should

---

*Letter to Earl of Chesterfield* Johnson felt that Chesterfield [q.v.] had neglected his early struggles on the *Dictionary*, only to associate himself with the completed work

*rocks* harsh and barren

consider me as owing that to a patron which Providence has enabled me to do for myself.

Having carried on my work thus far with so little obligation to any favourer of learning, I shall not be disappointed though I should conclude it, if less be possible, with less, for I have been long wakened from that dream of hope in which I once boasted myself with so much exultation, My Lord,

Your Lordship's most humble, most obedient servant,

Sam: Johnson

## To James Macpherson[†]

Mr James Macpherson – I received your foolish and impudent note. Whatever insult is offered me I will do my best to repel, and what I cannot do for myself the law will do for me. I will not desist from detecting what I think a cheat from any fear of the menaces of a ruffian.

You want me to retract. What shall I retract? I thought your book an imposture from the beginning, I think it upon yet surer reasons an imposture still. For this opinion I give the public my reasons, which I here dare you to refute.

But however I may despise you, I reverence truth and if you can prove the genuineness of the work I will confess it. Your rage I defy, your abilities since your Homer[†] are not so formidable, and what I have heard of your morals disposes me to pay regard not to what you shall say, but to what you can prove.

You may print this if you will.

Sam: Johnson

January 20, 1775

## To the Revd William Dodd[†]

Dear Sir

That which is appointed for all men is now coming upon you. Outward circumstances, the eyes and the thoughts of men, are below the notice of an immortal being about to stand the trial for eternity before the Supreme Judge of heaven and earth. Be comforted: your crime, morally or religiously considered, has no very deep dye of

*Letter to James Macpherson* Johnson did not conceal his view that Macpherson (see p. 470) had invented, not translated from Gaelic, the poems of Ossian

*Homer* *Iliad* translation (1773)

*Letter to Revd. William Dodd* A leading clergyman, Dodd had forged a bond in the name of the 5th Earl of Chesterfield. He was duly hanged despite Johnson's intense campaign to save him

turpitude. It corrupted no man's principles; it attacked no man's life. It involved only a temporary and reparable injury. Of this, and of all other sins, you are earnestly to repent; and may God, who knoweth our frailty and desireth not our death, accept your repentance, for the sake of his Son JESUS CHRIST our Lord.

In requital of those well-intended offices† which you are pleased so emphatically to acknowledge, let me beg that you make in your devotions one petition for my eternal welfare.

I am, dear Sir, your affectionate servant,

Sam: Johnson

June 26, 1777

## *From* PRAYERS AND MEDITATIONS†

SEPT. 18. 1764 ABOUT 6. EVENING. This is my fifty-sixth birthday, the day on which I have concluded fifty-five years.

I have outlived many friends. I have felt many sorrows. I have made few improvements. Since my resolution formed last Easter, I have made no advancement in knowledge or in goodness; nor do I recollect that I have endeavoured it. I am dejected but not hopeless.

O God, for Jesus Christ's sake, have mercy upon me.

7 IN THE EVENING. I went to church, prayed *to be loosed from the chain of my sins*. . . . I am beset with scruples and troublesome thoughts.

I have now spent fifty-five years in resolving, having from the earliest time almost that I can remember been forming schemes of a better life. I have done nothing; the need of doing therefore is pressing, since the time of doing is short. O God, grant me to resolve aright, and to keep my resolution for Jesus Christ's sake. Amen.

MARCH 30. EASTER DAY 1777 1^ma^ MANE.† The day is now come again in which, by a custom which since the death of my wife I have by the Divine assistance always observed, I am to renew the great covenant with my Maker and my Judge. I humbly hope to perform it better. I hope for more efficacy of resolution, and more diligence of endeavour. When I survey my past life, I discover nothing but a barren waste of time with some disorders of body, and disturbances of the mind very

*offices* Johnson's attentions

*Prayers and Meditations* These remains of private papers, published after his death, touchingly show Johnson's spiritual struggles

*1^ma^ mane* (Latin) one in the morning

near to madness; which I hope he that made me, will suffer to extenuate many faults, and excuse many deficiencies. Yet much remains to be repented and reformed. I hope that I refer more to God than in former times, and consider more what submission is due to his dispensations. But I have very little reformed my practical life, and the time in which I can struggle with habits cannot be now expected to be long. Grant, O God, that I may no longer resolve in vain, or dream away the life which thy indulgence gives me, in vacancy and uselessness.

1785

# *From* THE LIVES OF THE POETS

## *From* 'Life of Cowley': The Metaphysical Poets

Cowley, like other poets who have written with narrow views and, instead of tracing intellectual pleasure to its natural sources in the mind of man, paid their court to temporary prejudices, has been at one time too much praised and too much neglected at another.

Wit, like all other things subject by their nature to the choice of man, has its changes and fashions, and at different times takes different forms. About the beginning of the seventeenth century appeared a race of writers that may be termed the metaphysical[†] poets, of whom in a criticism on the works of Cowley it is not improper to give some account.

The metaphysical poets were men of learning, and to show their learning was their whole endeavour; but, unluckily resolving to show it in rhyme, instead of writing poetry they only wrote verses, and very often such verses as stood the trial of the finger better than of the ear; for the modulation was so imperfect that they were only found to be verses by counting the syllables.

If the father of criticism[†] has rightly denominated poetry *τέχνη μιμητική*, *an imitative art*, these writers will without great wrong lose their right to the name of poets, for they cannot be said to have imitated any thing: they neither copied nature nor life; neither painted the forms of matter nor represented the operations of intellect.

Those however who deny them to be poets allow them to be wits. Dryden confesses of himself and his contemporaries that they fall below Donne in wit, but maintains that they surpass him in poetry.

---

*metaphysical* abstractly philosophical     *father of criticism* Aristotle in *Poetics*

If wit be well described by Pope† as being 'that which has been often thought, but was never before so well expressed', they certainly never attained nor ever sought it, for they endeavoured to be singular in their thoughts, and were careless of their diction. But Pope's account of wit is undoubtedly erroneous; he depresses it below its natural dignity, and reduces it from strength of thought to happiness of language.

If by a more noble and more adequate conception that be considered as wit which is at once natural and new, that which though not obvious is, upon its first production, acknowledged to be just; if it be that which he that never found it wonders how he missed; to wit of this kind the metaphysical poets have seldom risen. Their thoughts are often new, but seldom natural; they are not obvious, but neither are they just; and the reader, far from wondering that he missed them, wonders more frequently by what perverseness of industry they were ever found.

But wit, abstracted from its effects upon the hearer, may be more rigorously and philosophically considered as a kind of *discordia concors* [harmonious discord]; a combination of dissimilar images, or discovery of occult resemblances in things apparently unlike. Of wit, thus defined, they have more than enough. The most heterogeneous ideas are yoked by violence together; nature and art are ransacked for illustrations, comparisons, and allusions; their learning instructs, and their subtlety surprises; but the reader commonly thinks his improvement dearly bought, and, though he sometimes admires, is seldom pleased.

From this account of their compositions it will be readily inferred that they were not successful in representing or moving the affections. As they were wholly employed on something unexpected and surprising they had no regard to that uniformity of sentiment which enables us to conceive and to excite the pains and the pleasure of other minds: they never enquired what on any occasion they should have said or done, but wrote rather as beholders than partakers of human nature; as beings looking upon good and evil, impassive and at leisure; as Epicurean† deities making remarks on the actions of men and the vicissitudes of life, without interest and without emotion. Their courtship was void of fondness and their lamentation of sorrow. Their wish was only to say what they hoped had been never said before.

Nor was the sublime more within their reach than the pathetic; for they never attempted that comprehension and expanse of thought which at once fills the whole mind, and of which the first effect is sudden astonishment, and the second rational admiration. Sublimity is produced by aggregation, and littleness by dispersion. Great thoughts are always

*Pope* *Essay on Criticism* l.298, loosely quoted
*Epicurean* Epicurus (341–279 BC): Greek philosopher of pleasure in repose

general, and consist in positions not limited by exceptions, and in descriptions not descending to minuteness. It is with great propriety that subtlety, which in its original import means exility† of particles, is taken in its metaphorical meaning for nicety of distinction. Those writers who lay on the watch for novelty could have little hope of greatness; for great things cannot have escaped former observation. Their attempts were always analytic: they broke every image into fragments, and could no more represent by their slender conceits and laboured particularities the prospects of nature or the scenes of life than he who dissects a sunbeam with a prism can exhibit the wide effulgence of a summer noon.

What they wanted however of the sublime they endeavoured to supply by hyperbole;† their amplification had no limits: they left not only reason but fancy behind them, and produced combinations of confused magnificence that not only could not be credited, but could not be imagined.

Yet great labour directed by great abilities is never wholly lost: if they frequently threw away their wit upon false conceits, they likewise sometimes struck out unexpected truth: if their conceits were far-fetched, they were often worth the carriage. To write on their plan it was at least necessary to read and think. No man could be born a metaphysical poet, nor assume the dignity of a writer by descriptions copied from descriptions, by imitations borrowed from imitations, by traditional imagery and hereditary similes, by readiness of rhyme and volubility of syllables.

In perusing the works of this race of authors the mind is exercised either by recollection or enquiry; either something already learned is to be retrieved, or something new is to be examined. If their greatness seldom elevates, their acuteness often surprises; if the imagination is not always gratified, at least the powers of reflection and comparison are employed; and in the mass of materials, which ingenious absurdity has thrown together, genuine wit and useful knowledge may be sometimes found, buried perhaps in grossness of expression, but useful to those who know their value, and such as, when they are expanded to perspicuity and polished to elegance, may give lustre to works which have more propriety though less copiousness of sentiment.†

This kind of writing, which was, I believe, borrowed from Marino† and his followers, had been recommended by the example of Donne, a man of very extensive and various knowledge, and by Jonson, whose manner resembled that of Donne more in the ruggedness of his lines than in the cast of his sentiments. . . .

*exility* slenderness
*hyperbole* vast exaggeration
*sentiment* thought
*Marino* 1569–1625, Italian poet

## *From* 'Life of Milton': Milton's Politics

His political notions were those of an acrimonious and surly republican, for which it is not known that he gave any better reason than that *a popular government was the most frugal; for the trappings of a monarchy would set up an ordinary commonwealth*. It is surely very shallow policy, that supposes money to be the chief good; and even this, without considering that the support and expense of a court is, for the most part, only a particular kind of traffic, by which money is circulated, without any national impoverishment.

Milton's republicanism was, I am afraid, founded in an envious hatred of greatness, and a sullen desire of independence; in petulance impatient of control, and pride disdainful of superiority. He hated monarchs in the state, and prelates in the church; for he hated all whom he was required to obey. It is to be suspected, that his predominant desire was to destroy rather than establish, and that he felt not so much the love of liberty as repugnance to authority.

It has been observed, that they who most loudly clamour for liberty do not most liberally grant it. What we know of Milton's character in domestic relations is, that he was severe and arbitrary. His family consisted of women; and there appears in his books something like a Turkish contempt of females, as subordinate and inferior beings. That his own daughters might not break the ranks, he suffered them to be depressed by a mean and penurious education. He thought woman made only for obedience, and man only for rebellion. . . .

## *[Lycidas]*

One of the poems on which much praise has been bestowed is *Lycidas*; of which the diction is harsh,† the rhymes uncertain, and the numbers unpleasing. What beauty there is we must therefore seek in the sentiments and images. It is not to be considered as the effusion of real passion; for passion runs not after remote allusions and obscure opinions. Passion plucks no berries from the myrtle and ivy, nor calls upon Arethuse and Mincius, nor tells of 'rough satyrs and fauns with cloven heel'. Where there is leisure for fiction there is little grief.

In this poem there is no nature, for there is no truth; there is no art, for there is nothing new. Its form is that of a pastoral, easy, vulgar,† and therefore disgusting:† whatever images it can supply are long ago exhausted; and its inherent improbability always forces dissatisfaction

*harsh* strained
*vulgar* commonplace
*disgusting* distasteful

on the mind. When Cowley tells of Hervey that they studied together, it is easy to suppose how much he must miss the companion of his labours and the partner of his discoveries; but what image of tenderness can be excited by these lines!

> We drove afield, and both together heard
> What time the grey fly winds her sultry horn,
> Battening our flocks with the fresh dews of night.

We know that they never drove afield, and that they had no flocks to batten; and though it be allowed that the representation may be allegorical, the true meaning is so uncertain and remote that it is never sought because it cannot be known when it is found.

Among the flocks and copses and flowers appear the heathen deities, Jove and Phoebus, Neptune and Æolus, with a long train of mythological imagery, such as a college easily supplies. Nothing can less display knowledge or less exercise invention than to tell how a shepherd has lost his companion and must now feed his flocks alone, without any judge of his skill in piping; and how one god asks another god what is become of Lycidas, and how neither god can tell. He who thus grieves will excite no sympathy; he who thus praises will confer no honour.

This poem has yet a grosser fault. With these trifling fictions are mingled the most awful and sacred truths, such as ought never to be polluted with such irreverent combinations. The shepherd likewise is now a feeder of sheep, and afterwards an ecclesiastical pastor, a superintendent of a Christian flock. Such equivocations are always unskilful; but here they are indecent, and at least approach to impiety, of which, however, I believe the writer not to have been conscious.

Such is the power of reputation justly acquired that its blaze drives away the eye from nice examination. Surely no man could have fancied that he read *Lycidas* with pleasure had he not known its author. . . .

## *[Paradise Lost]*

Those little pieces may be dispatched without much anxiety; a greater work calls for greater care. I am now to examine *Paradise Lost*, a poem which, considered with respect to design, may claim the first place, and with respect to performance the second, among the productions of the human mind.

By the general consent of critics, the first praise of genius is due to the writer of an epic poem, as it requires an assemblage of all the powers which are singly sufficient for other compositions. Poetry is the art of uniting pleasure with truth, by calling imagination to the help of reason. Epic poetry undertakes to teach the most important truths by the most pleasing precepts, and therefore relates some great event in the most affecting manner. History must supply the writer with the rudiments of narration, which he must improve and exalt by a nobler art, must animate by dramatic energy, and diversify by retrospection and anticipation; morality must teach him the exact bounds and different shades of vice and virtue; from policy and the practice of life he has to learn the discriminations of character and the tendency of the passions, either single or combined; and physiology must supply him with illustrations and images. To put these materials to poetical use is required an imagination capable of painting nature and realising fiction. Nor is he yet a poet till he has attained the whole extension of his language, distinguished all the delicacies of phrase, and all the colours of words, and learned to adjust their different sounds to all the varieties of metrical modulation.

Bossu† is of opinion that the poet's first work is to find a *moral*, which his fable is afterwards to illustrate and establish. This seems to have been the process only of Milton: the moral of other poems is incidental and consequent; in Milton's only it is essential and intrinsic. His purpose was the most useful and the most arduous: 'to vindicate† the ways of God to man'; to show the reasonableness of religion, and the necessity of obedience to the Divine Law.

To convey this moral there must be a *fable*, a narration artfully constructed so as to excite curiosity and surprise expectation. In this part of his work Milton must be confessed to have equalled every other poet. He has involved in his account of the Fall of Man the events which preceded, and those that were to follow it: he has interwoven the whole system of theology with such propriety that every part appears to be necessary, and scarcely any recital is wished shorter for the sake of quickening the progress of the main action.

The subject of an epic poem is naturally an event of great importance. That of Milton is not the destruction of a city, the conduct of a colony, or the foundation of an empire. His subject is the fate of worlds, the revolutions of heaven and of earth; rebellion against the Supreme King raised by the highest order of created beings; the overthrow of their host and the punishment of their crime; the creation of a new race of reasonable creatures; their original happiness and innocence, their forfeiture of immortality, and their restoration to hope and peace.

Great events can be hastened or retarded only by persons of elevated dignity. Before the greatness displayed in Milton's poem all other greatness shrinks away. The weakest of his agents are the highest and

*Bossu* French critic on epic (1675)
*vindicate* *Paradise Lost*, I.26 has 'justify . . . men'

noblest of human beings, the original parents of mankind; with whose actions the elements consented; on whose rectitude or deviation of will depended the state of terrestrial nature and the condition of all the future inhabitants of the globe.

Of the other agents in the poem the chief are such as it is irreverence to name on slight occasions. The rest were lower powers;

of which the least could wield
Those elements, and arm him with the force
Of all their regions;

powers which only the control of Omnipotence restrains from laying creation waste, and filling the vast expanse of space with ruin and confusion. To display the motives and actions of beings thus superior, so far as human reason can examine them or human imagination represent them, is the task which this mighty poet has undertaken and performed.

In the examination of epic poems much speculation is commonly employed upon the *characters*. The characters in the *Paradise Lost* which admit of examination are those of angels and of man; of angels good and evil, of man in his innocent and sinful state.

Among the angels the virtue of Raphael is mild and placid, of easy condescension and free communication; that of Michael is regal and lofty, and, as may seem, attentive to the dignity of his own nature. Abdiel and Gabriel appear occasionally, and act as every incident requires; the solitary fidelity of Abdiel is very amiably painted.

Of the evil angels the characters are more diversified. To Satan, as Addison observes, such sentiments are given as suit 'the most exalted and most depraved being'. Milton has been censured by Clarke for the impiety which sometimes breaks from Satan's mouth. For there are thoughts, as he justly remarks, which no observation of character can justify, because no good man would willingly permit them to pass, however transiently, through his own mind. To make Satan speak as a rebel, without any such expressions as might taint the reader's imagination, was indeed one of the great difficulties in Milton's undertaking, and I cannot but think that he has extricated himself with great happiness. There is in Satan's speeches little that can give pain to a pious ear. The language of rebellion cannot be the same with that of obedience. The malignity of Satan foams in haughtiness and obstinacy; but his expressions are commonly general, and no otherwise offensive than as they are wicked.

The other chiefs of the celestial rebellion are very judiciously discriminated in the first and second books; and the ferocious character of Moloch appears, both in the battle and the council, with exact consistency.

To Adam and to Eve are given during their innocence such sentiments as innocence can generate and utter. Their love is pure benevolence and mutual veneration; their repasts are without luxury and their diligence without toil. Their addresses to their Maker have little more than the voice of admiration and gratitude. Fruition left them nothing to ask, and innocence left them nothing to fear.

But with guilt enter distrust and discord, mutual accusation, and stubborn self-defence; they regard each other with alienated minds, and dread their Creator as the avenger of their transgression. At last they seek shelter in his mercy, soften to repentance, and melt in supplication. Both before and after the Fall the superiority of Adam is diligently sustained.

Of the *probable* and the *marvellous*,[†] two parts of a vulgar epic poem which immerge the critic in deep consideration, the *Paradise Lost* requires little to be said. It contains the history of a miracle, of Creation and Redemption; it displays the power and the mercy of the Supreme Being: the probable therefore is marvellous, and the marvellous is probable. The substance of the narrative is truth; and as truth allows no choice, it is, like necessity, superior to rule. To the accidental or adventitious parts, as to every thing human, some slight exceptions may be made. But the main fabric is immovably supported.

It is justly remarked by Addison that this poem has, by the nature of its subject, the advantage above all others, that it is universally and perpetually interesting. All mankind will, through all ages, bear the same relation to Adam and to Eve, and must partake of that good and evil which extend to themselves.

Of the *machinery*,[†] so called from Θεὸς ἀπὸ μηχανῆς [god from the machine], by which is meant the occasional interposition of supernatural power, another fertile topic of critical remarks, here is no room to speak, because every thing is done under the immediate and visible direction of Heaven; but the rule is so far observed that no part of the action could have been accomplished by any other means. . . .

The thoughts which are occasionally called forth in the progress are such as could only be produced by an imagination in the highest degree fervid and active, to which materials were supplied by incessant study and unlimited curiosity. The heat of Milton's mind might be said to sublimate[†] his learning, to throw off into his work the spirit of science, unmingled with its grosser parts.

He had considered creation in its whole extent, and his descriptions are therefore learned. He had accustomed his imagination to unrestrained indulgence, and his conceptions therefore were extensive. The character-

---

*marvellous* 'exceeding natural power' (Johnson)

*machinery* a feature of Greek drama

*sublimate* purify by heat

istic quality of his poem is sublimity. He sometimes descends to the elegant, but his element is the great. He can occasionally invest himself with grace; but his natural port is gigantic loftiness. He can please when pleasure is required; but it is his peculiar power to astonish.

He seems to have been well acquainted with his own genius, and to know what it was that Nature had bestowed upon him more bountifully than upon others; the power of displaying the vast, illuminating the splendid, enforcing the awful, darkening the gloomy, and aggravating the dreadful: he therefore chose a subject on which too much could not be said, on which he might tire his fancy without the censure of extravagance.

The appearances of nature and the occurrences of life did not satiate his appetite of greatness. To paint things as they are requires a minute attention, and employs the memory rather than the fancy. Milton's delight was to sport in the wide regions of possibility; reality was a scene too narrow for his mind. He sent his faculties out upon discovery, into worlds where only imagination can travel, and delighted to form new modes of existence, and furnish sentiment and action to superior beings, to trace the counsels of hell, or accompany the choirs of heaven.

But he could not be always in other worlds: he must sometimes revisit earth, and tell of things visible and known. When he cannot raise wonder by the sublimity of his mind he gives delight by its fertility.

Whatever be his subject he never fails to fill the imagination. But his images and descriptions of the scenes or operations of nature do not seem to be always copied from original form, nor to have the freshness, raciness, and energy of immediate observation. He saw nature, as Dryden expresses it, 'through the spectacles of books'; and on most occasions calls learning to his assistance. . . .

The defects and faults of *Paradise Lost*, for faults and defects every work of man must have, it is the business of impartial criticism to discover. As in displaying the excellence of Milton I have not made long quotations, because of selecting beauties there had been no end, I shall in the same general manner mention that which seems to deserve censure; for what Englishman can take delight in transcribing passages which, if they lessen the reputation of Milton, diminish in some degree the honour of our country? . . .

The plan of *Paradise Lost* has this inconvenience, that it comprises neither human actions nor human manners. The man and woman who act and suffer are in a state which no other man or woman can ever know. The reader finds no transaction in which he can be engaged, beholds no condition in which he can by any effort of imagination place himself; he has, therefore, little natural curiosity or sympathy.

We all, indeed, feel the effects of Adam's disobedience; we all sin like Adam, and like him must all bewail our offences; we have restless and insidious enemies in the fallen angels, and in the blessed spirits we have guardians and friends; in the Redemption of mankind we hope to be included: in the description of heaven and hell we are surely interested, as we are all to reside hereafter either in the regions of horror or of bliss.

But these truths are too important to be new: they have been taught to our infancy; they have mingled with our solitary thoughts and familiar conversation, and are habitually interwoven with the whole texture of life. Being therefore not new they raise no unaccustomed emotion in the mind: what we knew before we cannot learn; what is not unexpected cannot surprise.

Of the ideas suggested by these awful scenes, from some we recede with reverence, except when stated hours require their association; and from others we shrink with horror or admit them only as salutary inflictions, as counterpoises to our interests and passions. Such images rather obstruct the career of fancy than incite it.

Pleasure and terror are indeed the genuine sources of poetry; but poetical pleasure must be such as human strength and fortitude may combat. The good and evil of Eternity are too ponderous for the wings of wit; the mind sinks under them in passive helplessness, content with calm belief and humble adoration.

Known truths however may take a different appearance, and be conveyed to the mind by a new train of intermediate images. This Milton has undertaken, and performed with pregnancy and vigour of mind peculiar to himself. Whoever considers the few radical[†] positions which the Scriptures afforded him will wonder by what energetic operations he expanded them to such extent and ramified them to so much variety, restrained as he was by religious reverence from licentiousness of fiction.

Here is a full display of the united force of study and genius; of a great accumulation of materials, with judgement to digest and fancy to combine them: Milton was able to select from nature or from story, from ancient fable or from modern science, whatever could illustrate or adorn his thoughts. An accumulation of knowledge impregnated his mind, fermented by study and exalted by imagination.

It has been therefore said without an indecent hyperbole by one of his encomiasts, that in reading *Paradise Lost* we read a book of universal knowledge.

But original deficience cannot be supplied. The want of human interest is always felt. *Paradise Lost* is one of the books which the reader admires and lays down, and forgets to take up again. None ever

*radical* basic (the Genesis account is brief)

wished it longer than it is. Its perusal is a duty rather than a pleasure. We read Milton for instruction, retire harassed and overburdened, and look elsewhere for recreation; we desert our master, and seek for companions. . . .

Through all his greater works there prevails an uniform peculiarity of *diction*, a mode and cast of expression which bears little resemblance to that of any former writer, and which is so far removed from common use that an unlearned reader when he first opens his book finds himself surprised by a new language.

This novelty has been, by those who can find nothing wrong in Milton, imputed to his laborious endeavours after words suitable to the grandeur of his ideas. 'Our language,' says Addison, 'sunk under him.' But the truth is, that both in prose and verse, he had formed his style by a perverse and pedantic principle. He was desirous to use English words with a foreign idiom. This in all his prose is discovered and condemned, for there judgement operates freely, neither softened by the beauty nor awed by the dignity of his thoughts; but such is the power of his poetry that his call is obeyed without resistance, the reader feels himself in captivity to a higher and a nobler mind, and criticism sinks in admiration. . . .

Poetry may subsist without rhyme, but English poetry will not often please; nor can rhyme ever be safely spared but where the subject is able to support itself. Blank verse makes some approach to that which is called the 'lapidary† style'; has neither the easiness of prose nor the melody of numbers, and therefore tires by long continuance. Of the Italian writers without rhyme whom Milton alleges as precedents not one is popular; what reason could urge in its defence has been confuted by the ear.

But whatever the advantage of rhyme I cannot prevail on myself to wish that Milton had been a rhymer, for I cannot wish his work to be other than it is; yet like other heroes he is to be admired rather than imitated. He that thinks himself capable of astonishing may write blank verse, but those that hope only to please must condescend to rhyme.

The highest praise of genius is original invention. Milton cannot be said to have contrived the structure of an epic poem, and therefore owes reverence to that vigour and amplitude of mind to which all generations must be indebted for the art of poetical narration, for the texture of the fable, the variation of incidents, the interposition of dialogue, and all the stratagems that surprise and enchain attention. But of all the borrowers from Homer, Milton is perhaps the least indebted. He was naturally a thinker for himself, confident of his own abilities and disdainful of help or hindrance; he did not refuse admission

*lapidary* monumental

to the thoughts or images of his predecessors, but he did not seek them. From his contemporaries he neither courted nor received support; there is in his writings nothing by which the pride of other authors might be gratified or favour gained, no exchange of praise nor solicitation of support. His great works were performed under discountenance and in blindness, but difficulties vanished at his touch; he was born for whatever is arduous; and his work is not the greatest of heroic poems, only because it is not the first.

## *From* 'Life of Pope': Comparison with Dryden

Of his intellectual character the constituent and fundamental principle was good sense, a prompt and intuitive perception of consonance† and propriety. He saw immediately, of his own conceptions, what was to be chosen, and what to be rejected; and, in the works of others, what was to be shunned, and what was to be copied.

But good sense alone is a sedate and quiescent quality, which manages its possessions well, but does not increase them; it collects few materials for its own operations, and preserves safety, but never gains supremacy. Pope had likewise genius; a mind active, ambitious, and adventurous, always investigating, always aspiring; in its widest searches still longing to go forward, in its highest flights still wishing to be higher; always imagining something greater than it knows, always endeavouring more than it can do.

To assist these powers he is said to have had great strength and exactness of memory. That which he had heard or read was not easily lost; and he had before him not only what his own meditation suggested, but what he had found in other writers that might be accommodated to his present purpose.

These benefits of nature he improved by incessant and unwearied diligence; he had recourse to every source of intelligence, and lost no opportunity of information; he consulted the living as well as the dead; he read his compositions to his friends, and was never content with mediocrity when excellence could be attained. He considered poetry as the business of his life, and, however he might seem to lament his occupation, he followed it with constancy: to make verses was his first labour, and to mend them was his last.

From his attention to poetry he was never diverted. If conversation offered anything that could be improved he committed it to paper; if a thought, or perhaps an expression more happy than was common, rose

*consonance* harmony

to his mind, he was careful to write it; an independent distich† was preserved for an opportunity of insertion, and some little fragments have been found containing lines, or parts of lines, to be wrought upon at some other time.

He was one of those few whose labour is their pleasure, he was never elevated to negligence, nor wearied to impatience; he never passed a fault unamended by indifference, nor quitted it by despair. He laboured his works first to gain reputation, and afterwards to keep it.

Of composition there are different methods. Some employ at once memory and invention, and, with little intermediate use of the pen, form and polish large masses by continued meditation, and write their productions only when, in their own opinion, they have completed them. It is related of Virgil that his custom was to pour out a great number of verses in the morning, and pass the day in retrenching exuberances and correcting inaccuracies. The method of Pope, as may be collected from his translation, was to write his first thoughts in his first words, and gradually to amplify, decorate, rectify, and refine them.

With such faculties and such dispositions he excelled every other writer in *poetical prudence*; he wrote in such a manner as might expose him to few hazards. He used almost always the same fabric† of verse; and, indeed, by those few essays which he made of any other, he did not enlarge his reputation. Of this uniformity the certain consequence was readiness and dexterity. By perpetual practice language had in his mind a systematical arrangement; having always the same use for words, he had words so selected and combined as to be ready at his call. This increase of facility he confessed himself to have perceived in the progress of his translation.

But what was yet of more importance, his effusions were always voluntary, and his subjects chosen by himself. His independence secured him from drudging at a task, and labouring upon a barren topic: he never exchanged praise for money, nor opened a shop of condolence or congratulation. His poems, therefore, were scarce ever temporary. He suffered coronations and royal marriages to pass without a song, and derived no opportunities from recent events, nor any popularity from the accidental disposition of his readers. He was never reduced to the necessity of soliciting the sun to shine upon a birthday, of calling the Graces and Virtues to a wedding, or of saying what multitudes have said before him. When he could produce nothing new, he was at liberty to be silent.

His publications were for the same reason never hasty. He is said to have sent nothing to the press till it had lain two years under his inspection: it is at least certain that he ventured nothing without nice

*distich* verse couplet

*same fabric* heroic couplets

examination. He suffered the tumult of imagination to subside, and the novelties of invention to grow familiar. He knew that the mind is always enamoured of its own productions, and did not trust his first fondness. He consulted his friends, and listened with great willingness to criticism; and, what was of more importance, he consulted himself, and let nothing pass against his own judgement.

He professed to have learned his poetry from Dryden, whom, whenever an opportunity was presented, he praised through his whole life with unvaried liberality; and perhaps his character may receive some illustration if he be compared with his master.

Integrity of understanding and nicety of discernment were not allotted in a less proportion to Dryden than to Pope. The rectitude of Dryden's mind was sufficiently shown by the dismission of his poetical prejudices, and the rejection of unnatural thoughts and rugged numbers. But Dryden never desired to apply all the judgement that he had. He wrote, and professed to write, merely for the people; and when he pleased others, he contented himself. He spent no time in struggles to rouse latent powers; he never attempted to make that better which was already good, nor often to mend what he must have known to be faulty. He wrote, as he tells us, with very little consideration; when occasion or necessity called upon him, he poured out what the present moment happened to supply, and, when once it had passed the press, ejected it from his mind; for when he had no pecuniary interest, he had no further solicitude.

Pope was not content to satisfy; he desired to excel, and therefore always endeavoured to do his best: he did not court the candour, but dared the judgement of his reader, and, expecting no indulgence from others, he showed none to himself. He examined lines and words with minute and punctilious observation, and retouched every part with indefatigable diligence, till he had left nothing to be forgiven.

For this reason he kept his pieces very long in his hands, while he considered and reconsidered them. The only poems which can be supposed to have been written with such regard to the times as might hasten their publication were the two satires of *Thirty-eight*,† of which Dodsley† told me that they were brought to him by the author that they might be fairly copied. 'Almost every line,' he said, 'was then written twice over; I gave him a clean transcript, which he sent some time afterwards to me for the press, with almost every line written twice over a second time.'

His declaration that his care for his works ceased at their publication was not strictly true. His parental attention never abandoned them;

*Thirty-eight* known as *The Epilogue to the Satires*

*Dodsley* Robert Dodsley (1703–64), publisher

what he found amiss in the first edition, he silently corrected in those that followed. He appears to have revised the *Iliad*, and freed it from some of its imperfections; and the *Essay on Criticism* received many improvements after its first appearance. It will seldom be found that he altered without adding clearness, elegance, or vigour. Pope had perhaps the judgement of Dryden; but Dryden certainly wanted the diligence of Pope.

In acquired knowledge the superiority must be allowed to Dryden, whose education was more scholastic, and who before he became an author had been allowed more time for study, with better means of information. His mind has a larger range, and he collects his images and illustrations from a more extensive circumference of science. Dryden knew more of man in his general nature, and Pope in his local manners. The notions of Dryden were formed by comprehensive speculation, and those of Pope by minute attention. There is more dignity in the knowledge of Dryden, and more certainty in that of Pope.

Poetry was not the sole praise of either, for both excelled likewise in prose; but Pope did not borrow his prose from his predecessor. The style of Dryden is capricious and varied, that of Pope is cautious and uniform; Dryden obeys the motions of his own mind, Pope constrains his mind to his own rules of composition. Dryden is sometimes vehement and rapid; Pope is always smooth, uniform, and gentle. Dryden's page is a natural field, rising into inequalities, and diversified by the varied exuberance of abundant vegetation; Pope's is a velvet lawn, shaven by the scythe, and levelled by the roller.

Of genius, that power which constitutes a poet; that quality without which judgement is cold and knowledge is inert; that energy which collects, combines, amplifies, and animates – the superiority must, with some hesitation, be allowed to Dryden. It is not to be inferred that of this poetical vigour Pope had only a little, because Dryden had more, for every other writer since Milton must give place to Pope; and even of Dryden it must be said that if he has brighter paragraphs, he has not better poems. Dryden's performances were always hasty, either excited by some external occasion, or extorted by domestic necessity; he composed without consideration, and published without correction. What his mind could supply at call, or gather in one excursion, was all that he sought, and all that he gave. The dilatory caution of Pope enabled him to condense his sentiments, to multiply his images, and to accumulate all that study might produce, or chance might supply. If the flights of Dryden therefore are higher, Pope continues longer on the wing. If of Dryden's fire the blaze is brighter, of Pope's the heat is more regular and constant. Dryden often surpasses expectation, and Pope never falls below it. Dryden is read with frequent astonishment, and Pope with perpetual delight.

This parallel will, I hope, when it is well considered, be found just; and if the reader should suspect me, as I suspect myself, of some partial fondness for the memory of Dryden, let him not too hastily condemn me; for meditation and enquiry may, perhaps, show him the reasonableness of my determination. . . .

New sentiments and new images others may produce, but to attempt any further improvement of versification will be dangerous. Art and diligence have now done their best, and what shall be added will be the effort of tedious toil and needless curiosity.

After all this it is surely superfluous to answer the question† that has once been asked, 'Whether Pope was a poet?' otherwise than by asking in return, 'If Pope be not a poet, where is poetry to be found?' To circumscribe poetry by a definition will only show the narrowness of the definer, though a definition which shall exclude Pope will not easily be made. Let us look round upon the present time, and back upon the past; let us enquire to whom the voice of mankind has decreed the wreath of poetry; let their productions be examined and their claims stated, and the pretensions of Pope will be no more disputed. Had he given the world only his version the name of poet must have been allowed him; if the writer of the *Iliad* were to class his successors he would assign a very high place to his translator, without requiring any other evidence of genius.

## *From* 'Life of Gray': Gray's Poetry

Gray's poetry is now to be considered, and I hope not to be looked on as an enemy to his name if I confess that I contemplate it with less pleasure than his life. . . .

The poem on the Cat was doubtless by its author considered as a trifle, but it is not a happy trifle. In the first stanza 'the azure flowers that blow' show resolutely a rhyme is sometimes made when it cannot easily be found. Selima, the Cat, is called a nymph, with some violence both to language and sense; but there is good use made of it when it is done; for of the two lines,

> What female heart can gold despise?
> What cat's averse to fish?

the first relates merely to the nymph, and the second only to the cat. The sixth stanza contains a melancholy truth, that 'a favourite has no friend', but the last ends in a pointed sentence of no relation to the

*the question* raised in Joseph Warton's *Essay on Pope* (Vol. 1, 1756)

purpose; if what glistered had been 'gold', the cat would not have gone into the water; and, if she had, would not less have been drowned.

The *Prospect of Eton College* suggests nothing to Gray which every beholder does not equally think and feel. His supplication to Father Thames to tell him who drives the hoop or tosses the ball is useless and puerile. Father Thames has no better means of knowing than himself. His epithet 'buxom health' is not elegant; he seems not to understand the word. Gray thought his language more poetical as it was more remote from common use: finding in Dryden 'honey redolent of Spring', an expression that reaches the utmost limits of our language, Gray drove it a little more beyond common apprehension, by making 'gales' to be 'redolent of joy and youth'. . . .

My process has now brought me to the 'Wonderful Wonder of Wonders', the two Sister Odes; by which, though either vulgar ignorance or common sense at first universally rejected them, many have been since persuaded to think themselves delighted. I am one of those that are willing to be pleased, and therefore would gladly find the meaning of the first stanza of *The Progress of Poetry*. . . .

To select a singular event, and swell it to a giant's bulk by fabulous appendages of spectres and predictions, has little difficulty, for he that forsakes the probable may always find the marvellous. And it has little use: we are affected only as we believe; we are improved only as we find something to be imitated or declined. I do not see that *The Bard* promotes any truth, moral or political.

His stanzas are too long, especially his epodes; the ode is finished before the ear has learned its measures, and consequently before it can receive pleasure from their consonance and recurrence.

Of the first stanza the abrupt beginning has been celebrated; but technical beauties can give praise only to the inventor. It is in the power of any man to rush abruptly upon his subject that has read the ballad of *Johnny Armstrong*,

Is there ever a man in all Scotland –.

The initial resemblances, or alliterations, 'ruin', 'ruthless', 'helm nor hauberk', are below the grandeur of a poem that endeavours at sublimity.

In the second stanza the Bard is well described; but in the third we have the puerilities of obsolete mythology. When we are told that Cadwallo 'hushed the stormy main', and that Modred 'made huge Plinlimmon bow his cloud-topped head', attention recoils from the repetition of a tale that, even when it was first heard, was heard with scorn.

The 'weaving' of the 'winding sheet' he borrowed, as he owns, from the northern Bards; but their texture, however, was very properly the work of female powers, as the art of spinning the thread of life in another mythology. Theft is always dangerous; Gray has made weavers of his slaughtered bards by a fiction outrageous and incongruous. They are then called upon to 'Weave the warp, and weave the woof' perhaps with no great propriety; for it is by crossing the woof with the warp that men weave the web or piece; and the first line was dearly bought by the admission of its wretched correspondent, 'Give ample room and verge enough'. He has, however, no other line as bad.

The third stanza of the second ternary† is commended, I think, beyond its merit. The personification is indistinct. Thirst and Hunger are not alike, and their features, to make the imagery perfect, should have been discriminated. We are told, in the same stanza, how 'towers' are 'fed'. But I will no longer look for particular faults; yet let it be observed that the ode might have been concluded with an action of better example: but suicide is always to be had without expense of thought.

These odes are marked by glittering accumulations of ungraceful ornaments: they strike, rather than please; the images are magnified by affectation; the language is laboured into harshness. The mind of the writer seems to work with unnatural violence. 'Double, double, toil and trouble.'† He has a kind of strutting dignity, and is tall by walking on tiptoe. His art and his struggle are too visible, and there is too little appearance of ease and nature.

To say that he has no beauties would be unjust: a man like him, of great learning and great industry, could not but produce something valuable. When he pleases least, it can be said that a good design was ill directed.

His translations of Northern and Welsh Poetry deserve praise: the imagery is preserved, perhaps often improved; but the language is unlike the language of other poets.

In the character of his *Elegy* I rejoice to concur with the common reader; for by the common sense of readers uncorrupted with literary prejudices, after all the refinements of subtlety and the dogmatism of learning, must be finally decided all claim to poetical honours. The *Churchyard* abounds with images which find a mirror in every mind, and with sentiments to which every bosom returns an echo. The four stanzas beginning 'Yet even these bones' are to me original: I have never seen the notions in any other place; yet he that reads them here persuades himself that he has always felt them. Had Gray written often thus it had been vain to blame, and useless to praise him.

1779–81

*ternary* group of three

*'Double . . . trouble'* *Macbeth*, IV.i.10

# TO SIR JOHN LADE, ON HIS COMING OF AGE†

## (A SHORT SONG OF CONGRATULATION)

Long-expected one and twenty
Lingering year at last is flown,
Pomp and pleasure, pride and plenty,
Great Sir John, are all your own.

Loosened from the minor's tether,
Free to mortgage or to sell,
Wild as wind, and light as feather,
Bid the slaves of thrift farewell.

Call the Bettys, Kates, and Jennys,
Every name that laughs at care,
Lavish of your grandsire's guineas,
Show the spirit of an heir.

All that prey on vice and folly
Joy to see their quarry fly,
Here the gamester light and jolly,
There the lender grave and sly.

Wealth, Sir John, was made to wander,
Let it wander as it will;
See the jockey, see the pander,
Bid them come, and take their fill.

When the bonny blade carouses,
Pockets full, and spirits high,
What are acres? What are houses?
Only dirt, or wet or dry.

If the guardian or the mother
Tell the woes of wilful waste,
Scorn their counsel and their pother,
You can hang or drown at last.

1780

*To Sir John Lade* Lade did indeed squander the inheritance he had just come into, and married the former mistress of a notorious highwayman; but he lived into old age

# ON THE DEATH OF DR ROBERT LEVET†

Condemned to hope's delusive mine,
As on we toil from day to day,
By sudden blasts, or slow decline,
Our social comforts drop away.

Well tried through many a varying year,
See Levet to the grave descend;
Officious, innocent, sincere,†
Of every friendless name the friend.

Yet still he fills affection's eye,
Obscurely wise, and coarsely kind;
Nor, lettered arrogance, deny
Thy praise to merit unrefined.

When fainting nature called for aid,
And hovering death prepared the blow,
His vigorous remedy displayed
The power of art without the show.

In misery's darkest caverns known,
His useful care was ever nigh,
Where hopeless anguish poured his groan,
And lonely want retired to die.

No summons mocked by chill delay,
No petty gain disdained by pride,
The modest wants of every day
The toil of every day supplied.

His virtues walked their narrow round,
Nor made a pause, nor left a void;
And sure th' Eternal Master found
The single talent† well employed.

*On the Death of Dr Robert Levet* Levet (1705–82), a member of Johnson's strange household, worked among the poor as an unqualified physician

*officious* doing good offices; *sincere*: honest; *lettered*: learned

*single talent* Jesus' parable (Matthew 25.14–30)

The busy day, the peaceful night,
Unfelt, uncounted, glided by;
His frame was firm, his powers were bright,
Though now his eightieth year was nigh.

Then with no throbbing fiery pain,
No cold gradations of decay,
Death broke at once the vital chain,
And freed his soul the nearest way.

1783

# Laurence Sterne

## 1713–68

Sterne was born in Ireland, the son of an army ensign, but lived in England after 1723. After Jesus College, Cambridge, he was ordained in the Church of England, holding a Yorkshire living from 1738, and marrying. Nearly twenty years later, he wrote *A Political Romance* (1759), a satire on local church politics, and began his novel *The Life and Opinions of Tristram Shandy, Gentleman*, the first two volumes of which were published at York in 1759. From 1760, Sterne was lionised in London society as his eccentric fiction created a sensation: nine volumes were published at intervals until 1767. He published his sermons, and travelled in France (1762–4; and, with Italy, 1765). Always an admirer of women, and now physically apart from his wife, he marked his 'separation' from a new love, Mrs Draper, in the unpublished *Journal to Eliza*. His continental experience was used in *A Sentimental Journey through France and Italy* (1768), from which the cultivation of emotional experience was widely imitated. *Tristram Shandy*, an extraordinary blend of traditional learning and technical innovation, wittily parodies as a precursor of modernism the conventions of the new novel form: although it does have action and characters, it disrupts narrative chronology, jumping to disgressions through associations of ideas; the ineffectual narrator-hero is not born until Volume III; the reader is constantly made aware of the physical book. Sterne's pathos and wit, combined with a vein of sexual innuendo often thought unsuitable for a clergyman, make the novel unique. The extracts preserve the original's typographical eccentricity.

## *From* TRISTRAM SHANDY

### Volume 1

#### CHAPTER I *[Begetting]*

I wish either my father or my mother, or indeed both of them, as they were in duty both equally bound to it, had minded what they were about when they begot me; had they duly consider'd how much depended upon what they were then doing; – that not only the production of a rational Being was concern'd in it, but that possibly the happy formation and temperature of his body, perhaps his genius and the very cast of his mind; – and, for aught they knew to the contrary, even the fortunes of his whole house might take their turn from the humours† and dispositions which were then uppermost: – Had they duly weighed and considered all this, and proceeded accordingly, – I am verily persuaded I should have made a quite different figure in the world, from that, in which the reader is likely to see me. – Believe me, good folks, this is not so inconsiderable a thing as many of you may think it; – you have all, I dare say, heard of the animal spirits,† as how they are transfused from father to son, &c. &c – and a great deal to that purpose: – Well, you may take my word, that nine parts in ten of a man's sense or his nonsense, his success and miscarriages in this world depend upon their motions and activity, and the different tracks and trains you put them into; so that when they are once set a-going, whether right or wrong, 'tis not a halfpenny matter, – away they go cluttering like hey-go-mad; and by treading the same steps over and over again, they presently make a road of it, as plain and as smooth as a garden walk which, when they are once used to, the Devil himself sometimes shall not be able to drive them off it.

*Pray, my dear*, quoth my mother, *have you not forgot to wind up the clock? – Good G – !* cried my father, making an exclamation, but taking care to moderate his voice at the same time, – *Did ever woman, since the creation of the world, interrupt a man with such a silly question?* Pray, what was your father saying? – Nothing.

[Chapter Two explains that the question dispersed the animal spirits which should have safely conducted the spermatozoon]

## CHAPTER III

To my uncle Mr *Toby Shandy* do I stand indebted for the preceding anecdote, to whom my father, who was an excellent natural philosopher,† and much given to close reasoning upon the smallest matters, had oft, and heavily, complain'd of the injury; but once more particularly, as my uncle *Toby* well remember'd, upon his observing a most unaccoun-

*humours* traditionally, human temperament depended on the relationship in the body between the elements of phlegm, blood, choler, melancholy

*animal spirits* traditional bodily source of sensation and motion

*natural philosopher* student of natural phenomena, scientist

table obliquity, (as he call'd it) in my manner of setting up my top, and justifying the principles upon which I had done it, – the old gentleman shook his head, and in a tone more expressive by half of sorrow than reproach, – he said his heart all along foreboded, and he saw it verified in this, and from a thousand other observations he had made upon me, That I should neither think nor act like any other man's child: – *But alas!* continued he, shaking his head a second time, and wiping away a tear which was trickling down his cheeks, *My Tristram's misfortunes began nine months before ever he came into the world.*

– My mother, who was sitting by, look'd up, – but she knew no more than her backside what my father meant, – but my uncle, Mr *Toby Shandy*, who had been often informed of the affair, – understood him very well.

## CHAPTER IV

I know there are readers in the world, as well as many other good people in it, who are no readers at all, – who find themselves ill at ease, unless they are let into the whole secret from first to last, of every thing which concerns you.

It is in pure compliance with this humour of theirs, and from a backwardness in my nature to disappoint any one soul living, that I have been so very particular already. As my life and opinions are likely to make some noise in the world, and, if I conjecture right, will take in all ranks, professions, and denominations of men whatever, – be no less read than the *Pilgrim's Progress* itself – and, in the end, prove the very thing which *Montaigne* dreaded his essays should turn out, that is, a book for a parlour-window; – I find it necessary to consult every one a little in his turn; and therefore must beg pardon for going on a little further in the same way: For which cause, right glad I am, that I have begun the history of myself in the way I have done; and that I am able to go on tracing every thing in it, as *Horace*† says, *ab Ovo.*

*Horace*, I know, does not recommend this fashion altogether: But that gentleman is speaking only of an epic poem or a tragedy; – (I forget which) – besides, if it was not so, I should beg Mr *Horace*'s pardon; – for in writing what I have set about, I shall confine myself neither to his rules, not to any man's rules that ever lived.

To such, however, as do not choose to go so far back into these things, I can give no better advice, than that they skip over the remaining

*Horace* his *Art of Poetry* praised Homer for not starting to relate the Trojan War from the egg which produced Helen, cause of the war

part of this Chapter; for I declare before hand, 'tis wrote only for the curious and inquisitive.

——— Shut the door. ———

I was begot in the night, betwixt the first *Sunday* and the first *Monday* in the month of *March*, in the year of our Lord one thousand seven hundred and eighteen. I am positive I was. – But how I came to be so very particular in my account of a thing which happened before I was born, is owing to another small anecdote known only in our own family, but now made public for the better clearing up this point.

My father, you must know, who was originally a *Turky* merchant, but had left off business for some years, in order to retire to, and die upon, his paternal estate in the county of –, was, I believe, one of the most regular men in every thing he did, whether 'twas matter of business, or matter of amusement, that ever lived. As a small specimen of this extreme exactness of his, to which he was in truth a slave, – he had made it a rule for many years of his life, – on the first *Sunday night* of every month throughout the whole year, – as certain as ever the *Sunday night* came, – to wind up a large house-clock which we had standing upon the back-stairs head, with his own hands: – And being somewhere between fifty and sixty years of age, at the time I have been speaking of, – he had likewise gradually brought some other little family concernments to the same period, in order, as he would often say to my uncle *Toby*, to get them all out of the way at one time, and be no more plagued and pester'd with them the rest of the month.

It was attended but with one misfortune, which, in a great measure, fell upon myself, and the effects of which I fear I shall carry with me to my grave; namely, that, from an unhappy association of ideas which have no connection in nature, it so fell out at length, that my poor mother could never hear the said clock wound up, – the thoughts of some other things unavoidably popp'd into her head, – *& vice versâ:* – which strange combination of ideas, the sagacious *Locke*,† who certainly understood the nature of these things better than most men, affirms to have produced more wry actions than all other sources of prejudice whatsoever.

But this by the bye.

Now it appears, by a memorandum in my father's pocket-book, which now lies upon the table, 'That on *Lady-Day*,† which was on the 25th of the same month in which I date my geniture, – my father set out upon his journey to *London* with my eldest brother *Bobby*, to fix him at *Westminster* school;' and, as it appears from the same authority,

*Locke* his theory of the association of ideas in his *Essay concerning Human Understanding* (1690) influenced the bold narrative jumps in Sterne's novel (see Vol. 2, Chap. 8 below)

*Lady-Day* 25 March, feast of the Annunciation of the Virgin Mary

'That he did not get down to his wife and family till the *second week* in *May* following,' – it brings the thing almost to a certainty. However, what follows in the beginning of the next chapter puts it beyond all possibility of doubt.

– But pray, Sir, What was your father doing all *December*, – *January*, and *February*? – Why, Madam, – he was all that time afflicted with a Sciatica.[†]

[Tristram returns from a series of digressions into his uncle's military career]

# Volume 2

## CHAPTER VIII *[Time and Distance]*

It is about an hour and a half's tolerable good reading since my uncle *Toby* rung the bell, when *Obadiah* was order'd to saddle a horse, and go for Dr *Slop*, the man-midwife; – so that no one can say, with reason, that I have not allowed *Obadiah* time enough, poetically speaking, and considering the emergency too, both to go and come; – tho', morally and truly speaking, the man, perhaps, has scarce had time to get on his boots.

If the hypercritick[†] will go upon this; and is resolved after all to take a pendulum, and measure the true distance betwixt the ringing of the bell and the rap at the door; – and, after finding it to be no more than two minutes, thirteen seconds, and three fifths, – should take upon him to insult over me for such a breach in the unity, or rather probability, of time; – I would remind him, that the idea of duration[†] and of its simple modes, is got merely from the train and succession of our ideas, – and is the true scholastick pendulum, – and by which, as a scholar, I will be tried in this matter, – abjuring and detesting the jurisdiction of all other pendulums whatever.

I would, therefore, desire him to consider that it is but poor eight miles from *Shandy-Hall* to Dr *Slop*, the man-midwife's house; – and that whilst *Obadiah* has been going those said miles and back, I have brought my uncle *Toby* from *Namur*,[†] quite across all *Flanders*, into *England*: – That I have had him ill upon my hands near four years; – and have since travelled him and Corporal *Trim*, in a chariot and four, a journey of near two hundred miles down into *Yorkshire*; – all which put together, must have prepared the reader's imagination for the

*Sciatica* inflamed thigh-nerve
*hypercritick* excessively critical person
*idea of duration* Tristram contrasts mechanical time with our subjective experience of it, which is flexible
*Namur* where Toby was wounded in the groin (1695) during the French wars

entrance of Dr *Slop* upon the stage, – as much, at least, (I hope) as a dance, a song, or a concerto between the acts.

If my hypercritick is intractable, – alledging, that two minutes and thirteen seconds are no more than two minutes and thirteen seconds, – when I have said all I can about them; – and that this plea, tho' it might save me dramatically, will damn me biographically, rendering my book, from this very moment, a profess'd ROMANCE,[†] which, before, was a book apocryphal:[†] – If I am thus pressed – I then put an end to the whole objection and controversy about it all at once, – by acquainting him, that *Obadiah* had not got above threescore yards from the stable-yard before he met with Dr *Slop*; – and indeed he gave a dirty proof that he had met with him, – and was within an ace of giving a tragical one too.

Imagine to yourself; – but this had better begin a new chapter.

# Volume 2

## CHAPTER XII *[Hobby-Horse]*

Your sudden and unexpected arrival, quoth my uncle *Toby*, addressing himself to Dr *Slop*, (all three of them sitting down to the fire together, as my uncle *Toby* began to speak) – instantly brought the great *Stevinus* into my head, who, you must know, is a favourite author with me. – Then added my father, making use of the argument *Ad Crumenam*,[†] – I will lay twenty guineas to a single crown piece, (which will serve to give away to *Obadiah* when he gets back) that this name *Stevinus* was some engineer or other, – or has wrote something or other, either directly or indirectly, upon the science of fortification.[†]

He has so, – replied my uncle *Toby*. – I knew it, said my father; – tho', for the soul of me, I cannot see what kind of connection there can be betwixt Dr *Slop*'s sudden coming, and a discourse upon fortification; – yet I fear'd it. – Talk of what we will, brother, – or let the occasion be never so foreign or unfit for the subject, – you are sure to bring it in: I would not, brother *Toby*, continued my father, – I declare I would not have my head so full of curtins and horn-works. – That, I dare say, you would not, quoth Dr *Slop*, interrupting him, and laughing most immoderately at his pun.[†]

*Dennis* the critick could not detest and abhor a pun, or the insinuation

---

*Romance* absurd fiction
*apocryphal* of doubtful authority
*Ad Crumenam* to the purse
*fortification* Toby is obsessed with recreating in the bowling-green the military building from France
*pun* the military terms also suggest sex

of a pun, more cordially than my father; – he would grow testy upon it at any time; – but to be broke in upon by one, in a serious discourse, was as bad, he would say, as a fillip upon the nose; – he saw no difference.

Sir, quoth my uncle *Toby*, addressing him to Dr *Slop*, – the curtins my brother *Shandy* mentions here, have nothing to do with bed-steads; – tho', I know, *Du Cange* says, 'That bed-curtains, in all probability, have taken their name from them;' – nor have the horn-works, he speaks of, any thing in the world to do with the horn-works of cuckoldom: – But the *curtin*, Sir, is the word we use in fortification, for that part of the wall or rampart which lies between the two bastions and joins them. – Beseigers seldom offer to carry on their attacks directly against the curtin, for this reason, because they are so well *flanked*; ('tis the case of other curtins, quoth Dr *Slop*, laughing) however, continued my uncle *Toby*, to make them sure, we generally choose to place ravelins before them, taking care only to extend them beyond the fossé or ditch: – The common men, who know very little of fortification, confound the ravelin and the half-moon together, – tho' they are very different things; – not in their figure or construction, for we make them exactly alike in all points; – for they always consist of two faces, making a salient angle, with the gorges, not straight, but in form of a crescent. – Where then lies the difference? (quoth my father, a little testily) – In their situations, answered my uncle *Toby*: – For when a ravelin, brother, stands before the curtin, it is a ravelin; and when a ravelin stands before a bastion, then the ravelin is not a ravelin; – it is a half-moon; a half-moon likewise is a half-moon, and no more, so long as it stands before its bastion; – but was it to change place, and get before the curtin, – 'twould be no longer a half-moon; a half-moon, in that case, is not a half-moon; – 'tis no more than a ravelin. – I think, quoth my father, that the noble science of defence has its weak sides, – as well as others.

– As for the horn-works (high! ho! sigh'd my father) which, continued my uncle *Toby*, my brother was speaking of, they are a very considerable part of an outwork; – they are called by the *French* engineers, *Ouvrage á corne*, and we generally make them to cover such places as we suspect to be weaker than the rest; – 'tis form'd by two epaulments or demi-bastions, – they are very pretty, and if you will take a walk, I'll engage to shew you one well worth your trouble. – I own, continued my uncle *Toby*, when we crown them, – they are much stronger, but then they are very expensive, and take up a great deal of ground; so that, in my opinion, they are most of use to cover or defend the head of a camp; otherwise the double tenaille – By the mother who bore us! – brother *Toby*, quoth my father, not able to hold out any longer, – you would provoke a saint; – here have you got us, I know not how, not only souse into the middle of the old subject again: – But so full is your head of these confounded works, that tho' my wife is this moment in the pains of labour, – and you hear her cry out, – yet nothing will serve you but to carry off the man-midwife. – *Accoucheur*, – if you please, quoth Dr *Slop*. – With all my heart, replied my father, I don't care what they call you, – but I wish the whole science of fortification, with all its inventors, at the Devil; – it has been the death of thousands, – and it will be mine, in the end. – I would not, I would not, brother *Toby*, have my brains so full of saps, mines, blinds, gabions, palisadoes, ravelins, half-moons, and such trumpery, to be proprietor of *Namur*, and of all the towns in *Flanders* with it.

My uncle *Toby* was a man patient of injuries; – not from want of courage, – I have told you in the fifth chapter of this second book, 'That he was a man of courage:' – And will add here, that where just occasions presented, or called it forth, – I know no man under whose arm I would sooner have taken shelter; nor did this arise from any insensibility or obtuseness of his intellectual parts; – for he felt this insult of my father's as feelingly as a man could do; – but he was of a peaceful, placid nature, – no jarring element in it, – all was mix'd up so kindly within him; my uncle *Toby* had scarce a heart to retalliate upon a fly.

– Go, – says he, one day at dinner, to an over-grown one which had buzz'd about his nose, and tormented him cruelly all dinner-time, – and which, after infinite attempts, he had caught at last, as it flew by him; – I'll not hurt thee, says my uncle *Toby*, rising from his chair, and going a-cross the room, with the fly in his hand, – I'll not hurt a hair of thy head: – Go, says he, lifting up the sash, and opening his hand as he spoke to let it escape; – go poor Devil, get thee gone, why should I hurt thee? – This world surely is wide enough to hold both thee and me.

I was but ten years old when this happened; – but whether it was, that the action itself was more in unison to my nerves at that age of pity, which instantly set my whole frame into one vibration of most pleasurable sensation; – or how far the manner and expression of it might go towards it; – or in what degree, or by what secret magick, – a tone of voice and harmony of movement, attuned by mercy, might find a passage to my heart, I know not; – this I know, that the lesson of universal good-will then taught and imprinted by my uncle *Toby*, has never since been worn out of my mind: And tho' I would not depreciate what the study of the *Literæ humaniores*,† at the university, have done for me in that respect, or discredit the other helps of an expensive education bestowed upon me, both at home and abroad

*Literae humaniores* classical literature and philosophy

since; – yet I often think that I owe one half of my philanthropy to that one accidental impression.

☞This is to serve for parents and governors instead of a whole volume upon the subject.

I could not give the reader this stroke in my uncle *Toby*'s picture, by the instrument with which I drew the other parts of it, – that taking in no more than the mere HOBBY-HORSICAL likeness; – this is a part of his moral character. My father, in this patient endurance of wrongs, which I mention, was very different, as the reader must long ago have noted; he had a much more acute and quick sensibility of nature, attended with a little soreness of temper; tho' this never transported him to any thing which looked like malignancy; – yet, in the little rubs and vexations of life, 'twas apt to shew itself in a drollish and witty kind of peevishness: – He was, however, frank and generous in his nature, – at all times open to conviction; and in the little ebullitions of this subacid† humour towards others, but particularly towards my uncle *Toby*, whom he truly loved; – he would feel more pain, ten times told, (except in the affair of my aunt *Dinah*, or where an hypothesis was concerned) than what he ever gave.

The characters of the two brothers, in this view of them, reflected light upon each other, and appear'd with great advantage in this affair which arose about *Stevinus*.

I need not tell the reader, if he keeps a HOBBY-HORSE,† – that a man's HOBBY-HORSE is as tender a part as he has about him; and that these unprovoked strokes, at my uncle *Toby's* could not be unfelt by him. – No; – as I said above, my uncle *Toby* did feel them, and very sensibly too.

Pray, Sir, what said he? – How did he behave? – Oh, Sir! – it was great: For as soon as my father had done insulting his HOBBY-HORSE, – he turned his head, without the least emotion, from Dr *Slop*, to whom he was addressing his discourse, and look'd up into my father's face, with a countenance spread over with so much good nature; – so placid; – so fraternal; so inexpressibly tender towards him; – it penetrated my father to his heart: He rose up hastily from his chair, and seizing hold of both my uncle *Toby's* hands as he spoke: – Brother *Toby*, said he, – I beg thy pardon; – forgive, I pray thee, this rash humour which my mother gave me. – My dear, dear brother, answer'd my uncle *Toby*, rising up by my father's help, say no more about it; – you are heartily welcome, had it been ten times as much, brother. But 'tis ungenerous, replied my father, to hurt any man; – a brother worse; – but to hurt a brother of such gentle manners, – so unprovoking, – and so unresenting; – 'tis base: – By heaven, 'tis cowardly. – You are heartily

*subacid* rather sharp

*hobby-horse* cherished obsession

welcome, brother, quoth my uncle *Toby*, – had it been fifty times as much. – Besides, what have I to do, my dear *Toby*, cried my father, either with your amusements or your pleasures, unless it was in my power (which it is not) to increase their measure?

– Brother *Shandy*, answer'd my uncle *Toby*, looking wistfully in his face, – you are much mistaken in this point; for you do increase my pleasure very much, in begetting children for the *Shandy* Family at your time of life. – But, by that, Sir, quoth Dr *Slop*, Mr *Shandy* increases his own. – Not a jot, quoth my father.

### CHAPTER XIII

My brother does it, quoth my uncle *Toby*, out of *principle*. – In a family-way, I suppose, quoth Dr *Slop*. – Pshaw! – said my father, – 'tis not worth talking of.

1760–7

# *From* A SENTIMENTAL JOURNEY THROUGH FRANCE AND ITALY[†]

## THE PULSE

### PARIS

Hail ye small sweet courtesies of life, for smooth do ye make the road of it! like grace and beauty which beget inclinations to love at first sight; 'tis ye who open this door and let the stranger in.

' – Pray, Madame,' said I, 'have the goodness to tell me which way I must turn to go to the Opera comique:' – 'Most willingly, Monsieur,' said she, laying aside her work –

I had given a cast with my eye into half a dozen shops as I came along in search of a face not likely to be disordered by such an interruption; till at last, this hitting my fancy, I had walked in.

She was working a pair of ruffles as she sat in a low chair on the far side of the shop facing the door –

*A Sentimental Journey through France and Italy* The narrator, Parson Yorick (taken from *Tristram Shandy*), values moments of spiritual contact on his travels

' – *Tres volentieres*; most willingly,' said she, laying her work down upon a chair next her, and rising up from the low chair she was sitting in, with so cheerful a movement and so cheerful a look, that had I been laying out fifty louis d'ors with her, I should have said – 'This woman is grateful.'

'You must turn, Monsieur,' said she, going with me to the door of the shop, and pointing the way down the street I was to take – 'you must turn first to your left hand – *mais prenez guarde* [take care] – there are two turns; and be so good as to take the second – then go down a little way and you'll see a church, and when you are past it, give yourself the trouble to turn directly to the right, and that will lead you to the foot of the *pont neuf* [new bridge] which you must cross – and there, any one will do himself the pleasure to show you – '

She repeated her instructions three times over to me with the same good natured patience the third time as the first; – and if *tones and manners* have a meaning, which certainly they have, unless to hearts which shut them out – she seemed really interested, that I should not lose myself.

I will not suppose it was the woman's beauty, notwithstanding she was the handsomest grisset,† I think, I ever saw, which had much to do with the sense I had of her courtesy; only I remember, when I told her how much I was obliged to her, that I looked very full in her eyes – and that I repeated my thanks as often as she had done her instructions.

I had not got ten paces from the door, before I found I had forgot every tittle of what she had said – so looking back, and seeing her still standing in the door of the shop as if to look whether I went right or not – I returned back, to ask her whether the first turn was to my right or left – for that I had absolutely forgot. – 'Is it possible!' said she, half laughing. – ' 'Tis very possible,' replied I, 'when a man is thinking more of a woman, than of her good advice.'

As this was the real truth – she took it, as every woman takes a matter of right, with a slight courtesy.

' – *Attendez!*' said she, laying her hand upon my arm to detain me, whilst she called a lad out of the back-shop to get ready a parcel of gloves. 'I am just going to send him,' said she, 'with a packet into that quarter, and if you will have the complaisance to step in, it will be ready in a moment, and he shall attend you to the place.' – So I walked in with her to the far side of the shop, and taking up the ruffle in my hand which she laid upon the chair, as if I had a mind to sit, she sat down herself in her low chair, and I instantly sat myself down besides her.

' – He will be ready, Monsieur,' said she, 'in a moment – ' 'And in

*grisset* grey-clad milliner

that moment,' replied I, 'most willingly would I say something very civil to you for all these courtesies. Anyone may do a casual act of good nature, but a continuation of them shows it is a part of the temperature; and certainly,' added I, 'if it is the same blood which comes from the heart, which descends to the extremes (touching her wrist) I am sure you must have one of the best pulses of any woman in the world – ' 'Feel it,' said she, holding out her arm. So laying down my hat, I took hold of her fingers in one hand, and applied the two fore-fingers of my other to the artery –

– Would to heaven! my dear Eugenius,† thou hadst passed by, and beheld me sitting in my black coat, and in my lackadaisical manner, counting the throbs of it, one by one, with as much true devotion as if I had been watching the critical ebb or flow of her fever – How wouldst thou have laughed and moralised upon my new profession? – and thou shouldst have laughed and moralised on – Trust me, my dear Eugenius, I should have said, 'there are worse occupations in this world *than feeling a woman's pulse.*' – 'But a grisset's!' thou wouldst have said – 'and in an open shop! Yorick – '

– So much the better: for when my views are direct, Eugenius, I care not if all the world saw me feel it.

## THE HUSBAND

### PARIS

I had counted twenty pulsations, and was going on fast towards the fortieth, when her husband coming unexpected from a back parlour into the shop put me a little out in my reckoning – 'Twas no body but her husband, she said – so I began a fresh score – 'Monsieur is so good,' quoth she, 'as he passed by us, as to give himself the trouble of feeling my pulse –' The husband took off his hat, and making me a bow, said, I did him too much honour – and having said that, he put on his hat and walked out.

'Good God!' said I to myself, as he went out – 'and can this man be the husband of this woman?'

Let it not torment the few who know what must have been the grounds of this exclamation, if I explain it to those who do not.

In London a shopkeeper and a shopkeeper's wife seem to be one bone and one flesh: in the several endowments of mind and body, sometimes the one, sometimes the other has it, so as in general to be upon a par, and to tally with each other as nearly as man and wife need to do.

---

*Eugenius* 'Yorick's' friend, also mentioned in *Tristram Shandy*

In Paris, there are scarce two orders of beings more different: for the legislative and executive powers of the shop not resting in the husband, he seldom comes there – in some dark and dismal room behind, he sits commerceless in his thrum† night-cap, the same rough son of nature that nature left him.

The genius of a people where nothing but the monarchy is *salique*,† having ceded this department, with sundry others, totally to the women – by a continual higgling with customers of all ranks and sizes from morning to night, like so many rough pebbles shook long together in a bag, by amicable collisions, they have worn down their asperities and sharp angles, and not only become round and smooth, but will receive, some of them, a polish like a brilliant – Monsieur *le Mari* [husband] is little better than the stone under your foot –

– Surely – surely man! it is not good for thee to sit alone – thou wast made for social intercourse and gentle greetings, and this improvement of our natures from it, I appeal to, as my evidence.

'– And how does it beat, Monsieur?' said she. – 'With all the benignity,' said I, looking quietly in her eyes, 'that I expected – ' She was going to say something civil in return – but the lad came into the shop with the gloves – '*A propos* [opportune],' said I; 'I want a couple of pair myself.'

## THE GLOVES
### PARIS

The beautiful grisset rose up when I said this, and going behind the counter, reached down a parcel and untied it: I advanced to the side over-against her: they were all too large. The beautiful grisset measured them one by one across my hand – It would not alter the dimensions – She begged I would try a single pair, which seemed to be the least – She held it open – my hand slipped into it at once – 'It will not do,' said I, shaking my head a little – 'No,' said she, doing the same thing.

There are certain combined looks of simple subtlety – where whim, and sense, and seriousness, and nonsense, are so blended, that all the languages of Babel† set loose together could not express them – they are communicated and caught so instantaneously, that you can scarce say which party is the infecter. I leave it to your men of words to swell pages about it – it is enough in the present to say again, the gloves would not do; so folding our hands within our arms, we both lolled upon the counter – it was narrow, and there was just room for the parcel to lay between us.

*thrum* thread or canvas
*salique* law forbidding woman monarch
*Babel* place of confused languages (Genesis 11)

The beautiful grisset looked sometimes at the gloves, then sideways to the window, then at the gloves – and then at me. I was not disposed to break silence – I followed her example: so I looked at the gloves, then to the window, then at the gloves, and then at her – and so on alternately.

I found I lost considerably in every attack – she had a quick black eye, and shot through two such long and silken eye-lashes with such penetration, that she looked into my very heart and reins† – It may seem strange, but I could actually feel she did –

' – It is no matter,' said I, taking up a couple of the pairs next me, and putting them into my pocket.

I was sensible the beautiful grisset had not asked above a single livre† above the price – I wished she had asked a livre more, and was puzzling my brains how to bring the matter about – 'Do you think, my dear Sir,' said she, mistaking my embarrassment, 'that I could ask a *sous* too much of a stranger – and of a stranger whose politeness, more than his want of gloves, has done me the honour to lay himself at my mercy? – *M'en croyez capable?*' – 'Faith! not I,' said I; 'and if you were, you are welcome' – So counting the money into her hand, and with a lower bow than one generally makes to a shopkeeper's wife, I went out, and her lad with his parcel followed me.

1768

*reins* kidneys (seat of emotion)

*livre* about a franc (a sou is much less)

# Thomas Gray

## 1716–71

Gray was the son of a London scrivener. At Eton, he first met Horace Walpole (see below) with whom he travelled on the continent in 1739–41. Most of his adult life, apart from travels, was spent at Cambridge, where he moved in 1756 from Peterhouse to Pembroke. A bachelor and a quiet scholar, he declined the Poet Laureateship, but became Professor of Modern History (never lecturing). In contrast to professional writers, he published little of his slender output. His learning is seen in his attempts to recapture the sublime energy and drama of the Greek lyric poet, Pindar (fifth century BC), in the abruptness of the odes; elsewhere he shows the influence of the 'new' poetic material he found in Old Norse and Welsh, in contrast to the 'Augustan' tradition; but the common humanity of the *Elegy* has always had the widest appeal. Gray believed that 'the language of the age is never the language of poetry'; his styles are sophisticated and allusive. His interest in the picturesque led him on the new tourist route to Scotland and the Lake District. His letters are among the less formal and most attractive of the century. Johnson's criticism (see above) was highly controversial.

## ODE ON A DISTANT PROSPECT OF ETON COLLEGE†

Ye distant spires, ye antique towers,
That crown the watery glade,
Where grateful science† still adores
Her Henry's holy shade;
And ye that from the stately brow
Of Windsor's heights th' expanse below

*Ode on a Distant Prospect of Eton College* Within the previous fifteen months, Gray had quarrelled with Walpole, and had suffered the death of another Eton friend, Richard West. The physical situation of the school across the river from Windsor Castle, and its foundation by King Henry VI in 1440, provide Gray's starting-point. A Greek epigraph said: 'I am a man, reason enough for being unhappy'

*science* learning in general

Of grove, of lawn, of mead survey,
Whose turf, whose shade, whose flowers among
Wanders the hoary Thames along
His silver-winding way.

Ah, happy hills, ah, pleasing shade,
Ah, fields beloved in vain,
Where once my careless childhood strayed,
A stranger yet to pain!
I feel the gales, that from ye blow,
A momentary bliss bestow,
As waving fresh their gladsome wing,
My weary soul they seem to soothe,
And, redolent of joy and youth,
To breathe a second spring.

Say, Father Thames, for thou hast seen
Full many a sprightly race
Disporting on thy margent* green — brink
The paths of pleasure trace,
Who foremost now delight to cleave
With pliant arm thy glassy wave?
The captive linnet which enthral?†
What idle progeny succeed
To chase the rolling circle's speed,
Or urge the flying ball?

While some on earnest business bent
Their murmuring labours ply
'Gainst graver hours, that bring constraint
To sweeten liberty:
Some bold adventurers disdain
The limits of their little reign,
And unknown regions dare descry:
Still as they run they look behind,
They hear a voice in every wind,
And snatch a fearful joy.

Gay hope is theirs by fancy fed,
Less pleasing when possessed;
The tear forgot as soon as shed,
The sunshine of the breast:

*enthral* hold in bondage

Theirs buxom health of rosy hue,
Wild wit, invention ever-new,
And lively cheer of vigour born;
The thoughtless day, the easy night,
The spirits pure, the slumbers light,
That fly th' approach of morn.

Alas, regardless of their doom
The little victims play!
No sense have they of ills to come,
Nor care beyond today:
Yet see how all around 'em wait
The ministers† of human fate,
And black misfortune's baleful train!
Ah, show them, where in ambush stand
To seize their prey the murderous band!
Ah, tell them, they are men!

These shall the fury passions tear,
The vultures of the mind,
Disdainful anger, pallid fear,
And shame that skulks behind;
Or pining love shall waste their youth,
Or jealousy with rankling tooth,
That inly gnaws the secret heart,
And envy wan, and faded care,
Grim-visaged comfortless despair,
And sorrow's piercing dart.

Ambition this shall tempt to rise,
Then whirl the wretch from high,
To bitter scorn a sacrifice,
And grinning infamy.
The stings of falsehood those shall try,
And hard unkindness' altered eye,
That mocks the tear it forced to flow;
And keen remorse with blood defiled,
And moody madness laughing wild
Amid severest woe.

*ministers* agents, instruments (the personified abstracts)

Lo, in the vale of years beneath
A grisly troop are seen,
The painful family of death,
More hideous than their queen:
This racks the joints, this fires the veins,
That every labouring sinew strains,
Those in the deeper vitals rage:
Lo, poverty, to fill the band,
That numbs the soul with icy hand,
And slow-consuming age.

To each his sufferings: all are men,
Condemned alike to groan;
The tender for another's pain,
Th' unfeeling for his own.
Yet ah! why should they know their fate?
Since sorrow never comes too late,
And happiness too swiftly flies.
Thought would destroy their paradise.
No more; where ignorance is bliss,
'Tis folly to be wise.

1742 1747

# SONNET ON THE DEATH OF MR RICHARD WEST†

In vain to me the smiling mornings shine,
And reddening Phoebus† lifts his golden fire:
The birds in vain their amorous descant join,
Or cheerful fields resume their green attire:
These ears, alas! for other notes repine,
A different object do these eyes require.
My lonely anguish melts no heart but mine;
And in my breast the imperfect joys expire.
Yet morning smiles the busy race to cheer,

*Sonnet of the Death of Mr Richard West* Gray's close friend had died two months before. In the 1800 Preface to *Lyrical Ballads*, Wordsworth criticises the poem's artificial diction

*Phoebus* Apollo, the sun god

And new-born pleasure brings to happier men:
The fields to all their wonted tribute bear;
To warm their little loves the birds complain.
I fruitless mourn to him that cannot hear,
And weep the more because I weep in vain.

1742 1775

# ODE ON THE DEATH OF A FAVOURITE CAT, DROWNED IN A TUB OF GOLD FISHES†

'Twas on a lofty vase's side,
Where China's gayest art had dyed
The azure flowers, that blow;
Demurest of the tabby kind,
The pensive Selima reclined,
Gazed on the lake below.

Her conscious tail her joy declared;
The fair round face, the snowy beard,
The velvet of her paws,
Her coat that with the tortoise vies,
Her ears of jet and emerald eyes,
She saw; and purred applause.†

Still had she gazed; but 'midst the tide
Two angel forms were seen to glide,
The genii† of the stream:
Their scaly armour's Tyrian† hue
Through richest purple to the view
Betrayed a golden gleam.

*Ode on the Death of a Favourite Cat* One of Horace Walpole's cats had recently drowned. Gray plays with various stylistic levels, using mock-heroic and animal fable

*purred applause* suggests Eve's of her reflection (*Paradise Lost*, IV.456–66)

*genii* presiding spirits

*Tyrian* purple (from ancient Tyre)

The hapless nymph with wonder saw:
A whisker first and then a claw,
With many an ardent wish,
She stretched in vain to reach the prize.
What female heart can gold despise?
What cat's averse to fish?

Presumptuous maid! with looks intent
Again she stretched, again she bent,
Nor knew the gulf between.
(Malignant Fate sat by and smiled)
The slippery verge her feet beguiled,
She tumbled headlong in.

Eight times emerging from the flood
She mewed to every watery god,
Some speedy aid to send.
No dolphin† came, no nereid* stirred: sea-nymph
Nor cruel Tom nor Susan heard.
A favourite has no friend!

From hence, ye beauties, undeceived,
Know, one false step is ne'er retrieved,
And be with caution bold.
Not all that tempts your wandering eyes
And heedless hearts is lawful prize;
Nor all that glisters gold.

1747 1748

# ELEGY WRITTEN IN A COUNTRY CHURCHYARD†

The curfew† tolls the knell of parting day,
The lowing herd wind slowly o'er the lea,
The ploughman homeward plods his weary way,
And leaves the world to darkness and to me.

*dolphin* in Greek legend, one rescued Arion from the sea

*Elegy written in a Country Churchyard* No specific churchyard may be intended: Gray was familiar with the visual properties of the 'graveyard' poetry of the 1740s, such as Robert Blair's *The Grave* (1743), and Edward Young's *Night Thoughts* (1742–5). Revised from the original drafts to give a complex view of the poet-figure, the *Elegy* was an instant popular success in its exploration of basic human themes, and its relation of imagery to emotion

*curfew* signal bell

Now fades the glimmering landscape on the sight,
And all the air a solemn stillness holds,
Save where the beetle wheels his droning flight,
And drowsy tinklings lull the distant folds;

Save that from yonder ivy-mantled tower
The moping owl does to the moon complain
Of such as, wandering near her secret bower,
Molest her ancient solitary reign.

Beneath those rugged elms, that yew-tree's shade,
Where heaves the turf in many a mouldering heap,
Each in his narrow cell for ever laid,
The rude† forefathers of the hamlet sleep.

The breezy call of incense-breathing morn,
The swallow twittering from the straw-built shed,
The cock's shrill clarion or the echoing horn,
No more shall rouse them from their lowly bed.

For them no more the blazing hearth shall burn,
Or busy housewife ply her evening care:
No children run to lisp their sire's return,
Or climb his knees the envied kiss to share.

Oft did the harvest to their sickle yield,
Their furrow oft the stubborn glebe* has broke;     field
How jocund did they drive their team afield!
How bowed the woods beneath their sturdy stroke!

Let not ambition mock their useful toil,
Their homely joys and destiny obscure;
Nor grandeur hear, with a disdainful smile,
The short and simple annals of the poor.

The boast of heraldry, the pomp of power,
And all that beauty, all that wealth e'er gave,
Awaits alike the inevitable hour.†
The paths of glory lead but to the grave.

---

*rude* simple, uneducated

*awaits . . . hour* 'hour' is the verb's subject, as word order imitates action

Nor you, ye proud, impute to these the fault,
If memory o'er their tomb no trophies† raise,
Where through the long-drawn aisle and fretted† vault
The pealing anthem swells the note of praise.

Can storied† urn or animated* bust — lifelike
Back to its mansion call the fleeting breath?
Can honour's voice provoke the silent dust,
Or flattery soothe the dull cold ear of death?

Perhaps in this neglected spot is laid
Some heart once pregnant with celestial fire;
Hands that the rod of empire might have swayed,
Or waked to ecstasy the living lyre.

But knowledge to their eyes her ample page
Rich with the spoils of time did ne'er unroll;
Chill penury repressed their noble rage,* — passion
And froze the genial* current of the soul. — spirited

Full many a gem of purest ray serene
The dark unfathomed caves of ocean bear:
Full many a flower is born to blush unseen
And waste its sweetness on the desert air.

Some village-Hampden† that with dauntless breast
The little tyrant of his fields withstood;
Some mute inglorious Milton† here may rest,
Some Cromwell† guiltless of his country's blood.

Th' applause of listening senates† to command,
The threats of pain and ruin to despise,
To scatter plenty o'er a smiling land,
And read their history in a nation's eyes,

Their lot forbade: nor circumscribed alone
Their growing virtues, but their crimes confined;
Forbade to wade through slaughter to a throne,
And shut the gates of mercy on mankind,

---

*trophies* elaborate monuments
*fretted* with carved patterns
*storied* showing a narrative
*Hampden . . . Cromwell* John Hampden (1594–1643), an MP, defied Charles I; Milton and Cromwell are other seventeenth-century types of fame
*senates* political assemblies

The struggling pangs of conscious truth to hide,
To quench the blushes of ingenuous shame,†
Or heap the shrine of luxury and pride
With incense kindled at the muse's flame.

Far from the madding† crowd's ignoble strife
Their sober wishes never learned to stray;
Along the cool sequestered vale of life
They kept the noiseless tenor of their way.

Yet ev'n these bones from insult to protect
Some frail memorial† still erected nigh,
With uncouth rhymes and shapeless sculpture decked,
Implores the passing tribute of a sigh.

Their name, their years, spelt by th' unlettered muse,
The place of fame and elegy supply:
And many a holy text around she strews,
That teach the rustic moralist to die.

For who to dumb forgetfulness a prey,
This pleasing anxious being e'er resigned,
Left the warm precincts of the cheerful day,
Nor cast one longing lingering look behind?

On some fond breast the parting soul relies,
Some pious drops the closing eye requires;
Ev'n from the tomb the voice of Nature cries,
Ev'n in our ashes live their wonted fires.

For thee† who, mindful of th' unhonoured dead,
Dost in these lines their artless tale relate;
If chance, by lonely contemplation led,
Some kindred spirit shall inquire thy fate,

Haply some hoary-headed swain may say,
'Oft have we seen him at the peep of dawn
Brushing with hasty steps the dews away
To meet the sun upon the upland lawn.

*ingenuous shame* natural sense of honour
*madding* acting madly
*frail memorial* unsophisticated tombstone, with simple inscription
*for thee . . .* these stanzas imagine a rustic describing to a third party the life and death of the isolated poet-figure whose own epitaph is then offered

'There at the foot of yonder nodding beech
That wreathes its old fantastic roots so high,
His listless length at noontide would he stretch,
And pore upon the brook that babbles by.

'Hard by yon wood, now smiling as in scorn,
Muttering his wayward fancies he would rove,
Now drooping, woeful wan, like one forlorn,
Or crazed with care, or crossed in hopeless love.

'One morn I missed him on the customed hill,
Along the heath and near his favourite tree;
Another came; nor yet beside the rill,
Nor up the lawn, nor at the wood was he;

'The next with dirges due in sad array
Slow through the church-way path we saw him borne.
Approach and read (for thou canst read) the lay,
Graved on the stone beneath yon aged thorn.'

THE EPITAPH

*Here rests his head upon the lap of earth*
*A youth to fortune and to fame unknown.*
*Fair science* frowned not on his humble birth,* learning
*And melancholy marked him for her own.*

*Large was his bounty and his soul sincere,*
*Heaven did a recompense as largely send:*
*He gave to misery all he had, a tear,*
*He gained from heaven ('twas all he wished) a friend.*

*No farther seek his merits to disclose,*
*Or draw his frailties from their dread abode*
*(There they alike in trembling hope repose),*
*The bosom of his Father and his God.*

*c.* 1746–50 1751

# THE BARD. A PINDARIC ODE†

I. 1

'Ruin seize thee, ruthless king!
Confusion on thy banners wait,
Though fanned by conquest's crimson wing
They mock the air with idle state.
Helm nor hauberk's† twisted mail,
Nor even thy virtues, tyrant, shall avail
To save thy secret soul from nightly fears,
From Cambria's† curse, from Cambria's tears!'
Such were the sounds, that o'er the crested pride
Of the first Edward scattered wild dismay,
As down the steep of Snowdon's† shaggy side
He wound with toilsome march his long array.
Stout Glo'ster stood aghast in speechless trance:
'To arms!', cried Mortimer and couched his quivering lance.

I. 2

On a rock, whose haughty brow
Frowns o'er old Conway's† foaming flood,
Robed in the sable garb of woe,
With haggard† eyes the poet stood
(Loose his beard and hoary hair
Streamed, like a meteor, to the troubled air);
And, with a master's hand and prophet's fire,
Struck the deep sorrows of his lyre.
'Hark, how each giant-oak and desert cave
Sighs to the torrent's awful voice beneath!
O'er thee, oh King! their hundred arms they wave,
Revenge on thee in hoarser murmurs breathe;
Vocal no more, since Cambria's fatal day,
To high-born Hoel's† harp, or soft Llewellyn's† lay.

---

*The Bard. A Pindaric Ode* Like 'The Progress of Poesy' (1757), this is a consciously difficult poem, later annotated by Gray. He imitates the form of Pindar's odes, grouping his stanzas in threes: the first two, strophe and antistrophe, are different from the epode; there is a complex metrical and rhyming pattern. The sublime emotions, obscure allusions and rapid transitions imitate the original. The subject combines Gray's interests in Welsh poetry and in the function of literature. He imagines King Edward I in 1283, after the conquest of Wales, confronted by the last bard, who laments his fellow-poets, and is joined by their spirits in prophesying ruin to Edward's line, until the accession of the Welsh Tudor, Henry VII, followed by a flowering of literature. The bard then commits suicide

*hauberk* chain-mail coat

*Cambria* Wales; Mount *Snowdon* and the river *Conway* are in the north

*haggard* 'from an unreclaimed hawk . . . looks wild' (Gray)

*Hoel . . . Modred* real Welsh names, but not historical bards

I. 3

'Cold is Cadwallo's† tongue,
That hushed the stormy main:
Brave Urien† sleeps upon his craggy bed:
Mountains, ye mourn in vain
Modred,† whose magic song
Made huge Plinlimmon† bow his cloud-topped head.
On dreary Arvon's† shore they lie,
Smeared with gore and ghastly pale:
Far, far aloof th' affrighted ravens sail;
The famished eagle screams and passes by.
Dear lost companions of my tuneful art,
Dear as the light that visits these sad eyes,
Dear as the ruddy drops that warm my heart,
Ye died amidst your dying country's cries –
No more I weep. They do not sleep.
On yonder cliffs, a grisly band,
I see them sit, they linger yet,
Avengers of their native land;
With me in dreadful harmony they join,
And weave with bloody hands the tissue of thy line.'

II. 1

'Weave the warp† and weave the woof,
The winding-sheet† of Edward's race.
Give ample room and verge enough
The characters† of hell to trace.
Mark the year and mark the night,
When Severn† shall re-echo with affright
The shrieks of death, through Berkeley's† roofs that ring,
Shrieks of an agonizing King!
She-wolf of France, with unrelenting fangs,
That tearest the bowels of thy mangled mate,
From thee be born who o'er thy country hangs
The scourge† of heaven. What terrors round him wait!
Amazement in his van,† with flight combined,
And sorrow's faded form, and solitude behind.

*Plinlimmon* mountain in south
*Arvon* Caernarvon, North Wales
*Weave the warp* the collective prophecy of the bards runs to l.100
*winding-sheet . . . characters* corpse wrapper, marked with 'characters', signs
*Severn . . . heaven* Edward II was murdered in 1327 at *Berkeley* Castle, by the river Severn, through his French Queen, whose son, Edward III, *scourged* France
*van* vanguard, front of the army

II. 2

'Mighty victor,† mighty lord,
Low on his funeral couch he lies!
No pitying heart, no eye, afford
A tear to grace his obsequies.
Is the sable warrior fled?
Thy son is gone. He rests among the dead.
The swarm that in thy noon-tide beam were born?
Gone to salute the rising morn.
Fair laughs the morn and soft the zephyr blows,
While proudly riding o'er the azure realm
In gallant trim the gilded vessel† goes;
Youth on the prow and pleasure at the helm,
Regardless of the sweeping whirlwind's sway,
That, hushed in grim repose, expects his evening-prey.

II. 3

'Fill high the sparkling bowl,
The rich repast prepare,
Reft of a crown, he yet may share the feast:
Close by the regal chair
Fell thirst and famine scowl
A baleful smile upon their baffled guest.
Heard ye the din of battle bray,
Lance to lance and horse to horse?
Long years of havoc† urge their destined course,
And through the kindred squadrons mow their way.
Ye towers of Julius,† London's lasting shame,
With many a foul and midnight murder fed,
Revere his consort's† faith, his father's† fame,
And spare the meek usurper's holy head.
Above, below, the rose of snow,
Twined with her blushing foe, we spread:
The bristled Boar† in infant-gore
Wallows beneath the thorny shade.

*mighty victor* Edward III died wretched in 1377, after his son, the Black Prince (d. 1376)

*gilded vessel* in the reign of Richard II, who was eventually starved to death in 1400 (1.81)

*years of havoc* the wars of York and Lancaster, the white and red roses

*Julius . . . father's* Caesar, reputed founder of Tower of London, where the holy but Lancastrian Henry VI was murdered in 1471; his father was the warrior Henry V, his *consort* a heroic woman

*bristled Boar* Richard III, alleged murderer of his nephews, was defeated in 1485 by the Tudor Henry VII, to end the wars

Now, brothers, bending o'er th' accursed loom,
Stamp we our vengeance deep, and ratify his doom.

III. 1

'Edward, lo! to sudden fate
(Weave we the woof. The thread is spun)
Half of thy heart we consecrate.†
(The web is wove. The work is done.)'
'Stay, oh stay! nor thus forlorn
Leave me unblessed, unpitied, here to mourn;
In yon bright track, that fires the western skies,
They melt, they vanish from my eyes.
But oh! what solemn scenes on Snowdon's height
Descending slow their glittering skirts unroll?
Visions of glory, spare my aching sight,
Ye unborn ages, crowd not on my soul!
No more our long-lost Arthur† we bewail.
All-hail, ye genuine kings, Britannia's issue, hail!

III. 2

'Girt with many a baron bold
Sublime their starry fronts they rear;
And gorgeous dames, and statesmen old
In bearded majesty, appear.
In the midst a form divine!†
Her eye proclaims her of the Briton-line;
Her lion-port, her awe-commanding face,
Attempered sweet to virgin-grace.
What strings symphonious tremble in the air,
What strains of vocal transport round her play!
Hear from the grave, great Taliessin, hear;
They breathe a soul to animate thy clay.
Bright rapture calls and, soaring as she sings,
Waves in the eye of heaven her many-coloured wings.

*consecrate* doom (Edward's wife died several years later)
*Arthur* the expected return of the Briton, King Arthur, was associated with the Welsh ancestry of the new Tudors
*form divine* Queen Elizabeth I, in whose reign (1558–1603) literature revives

III. 3

'The verse adorn again
Fierce war and faithful love,
And truth severe, by fairy fiction[†] dressed.
In buskined[†] measures move
Pale-grief and pleasing pain,
With horror, tyrant of the throbbing breast.
A voice[†] as of the cherub-choir
Gales from blooming Eden bear;
And distant warblings lessen on my ear,
That lost in long futurity expire.
Fond[†] impious man, thinkest thou yon sanguine cloud,
Raised by thy breath, has quenched the orb of day?
Tomorrow he repairs the golden flood,
And warms the nations with redoubled ray.
Enough for me: with joy I see
The different doom our fates assign.
Be thine despair and sceptred care;
To triumph,[†] and to die are mine.'
He spoke, and headlong from the mountain's height
Deep in the roaring tide he plunged to endless night.

1755–7 1757

## *From* JOURNAL IN THE LAKE DISTRICT, 1769[†]

Oct: 3. Wind at SE; a heavenly day. Rose at seven, and walked out under the conduct of my landlord to Borrowdale. The grass was covered with a hoar-frost, which soon melted, & exhaled in a thin bluish smoke. Crossed the meadows obliquely, catching a diversity of views among the hills over the lake & islands, and changing prospect at every ten paces, left Cockshot and Castlehill (which we formerly mounted) behind

---

*fairy fiction* Edmund Spenser's *The Faerie Queen* (1590–6)
*buskined* dressed for tragedy (suggesting Shakespeare)
*A voice* Milton, in *Paradise Lost* (1667)
*Fond* foolish (as the king's cloud of blood only briefly hides the sun)
*triumph* in his liberty, and in his link with future poets; Johnson is severe on the morality, as on much else in the poem
*Journal in the Lake District, 1769* Gray was in Cumberland, near Derwent Water

me, & drew near the foot of Walla Crag, whose bare & rocky brow, cut perpendicularly down above 400 feet, as I guess, awfully overlooks the way: our path here tends to the left, & the ground gently rising, & covered with a glade of scattering trees & bushes on the very margin of the water, opens both ways the most delicious view, that my eyes ever beheld. Behind you are the magnificent heights of Walla Crag; opposite lie the thick hanging woods of Lord Egremont, & Newland Valley, with green & smiling fields embosomed in the dark cliffs; to the left the jaws of Borrowdale, with that turbulent chaos of mountain behind mountain rolled in confusion; beneath you, & stretching far away to the right the shining purity of the Lake, just ruffled by the breeze enough to show it is alive, reflecting rocks, woods, fields, & inverted tops of mountains, with the white buildings of Keswick, Crosthwaite church, & Skiddaw for a background at distance. Oh Doctor![†] I never wished more for you; & pray think, how the glass played its part in such a spot, which is called Carf-close-reeds: I choose to set down these barbarous names, that anybody may enquire on the place, & easily find the particular station that I mean. This scene continues to Barrowgate, & a little farther, passing a brook called Barrowbeck, we entered Borrowdale. The crags, named Lodore Banks now begin to impend terribly over your way; & more terribly, when you hear, that three years since an immense mass of rock tumbled at once from the brow, & barred all access to the dale (for this is the only road) till they could work their way through it. Luckily no one was passing at the time of this fall; but down the side of the mountain, & far into the lake lie dispersed the huge fragments of this ruin in all shapes & in all directions. Something farther we turned aside into a coppice, ascending a little in front of Lodore waterfall. The height appears to be about 200 feet, the quantity of water not great, though (these three days excepted) it had rained daily in the hills for near two months before: but then the stream was nobly broken, leaping from rock to rock, & foaming with fury. On one side a towering crag, that spired up to equal, if not overtop, the neighbouring cliffs (this lay all in shade & darkness) on the other hand a rounder broader projecting hill shagged with wood & illumined by the sun, which glanced sideways on the upper part of the cataract. The force of the water wearing a deep channel in the ground hurries away to join the lake. We descended again, and passed the stream over a rude bridge. Soon after we came under Gowder Crag, a hill more formidable to the eye & to the apprehension than that of Lodore; the rocks atop, deep-cloven perpendicularly by the rains, hanging loose & nodding forwards, seem just starting from their base in shivers: the whole way down & the road on

*Doctor* Thomas Wharton (d. 1794)

both sides is strewed with piles of the fragments strangely thrown across each other & of a dreadful bulk. The place reminds one of those passes in the Alps, where the guides tell you to move on with speed, & say nothing, lest the agitation of the air should loosen the snows above, and bring down a mass, that would overwhelm a caravan. I took their counsel here and hastened on in silence.

Non ragioniam di lor; ma guarda, e passa![†]
[Let us not speak of them; but look and pass on!]

*Non ragioniam . . . passa!* Dante, Italian poet (1265–1321): *Inferno*, III.51

# Horace Walpole, Fourth Earl of Orford

1717–97

Son of the Prime Minister, Sir Robert, Walpole was educated at Eton with Thomas Gray, with whom he made a troubled continental journey, 1739–41; after reconciliation, he published Gray's Pindaric Odes at his printing press at Strawberry Hill, outside London. This famous house (now part of a teachers' college) was elaborately decorated by him as a mock 'Gothic' castle, and became a tourist site. Inspired by a dream, Walpole wrote the first 'Gothic' novel *The Castle of Otranto* (1764) and set the vogue for medieval dungeons, ghosts and persecuted heroines; his other writings include pioneer work on the visual arts, and a defence of Richard III. Walpole's political career was insignificant, but his access to high places proved valuable for his manuscript Memoirs of the reigns of George II and III. His masterpiece is his huge correspondence with a series of friends to whom he directed as appropriate his society gossip, literary anecdote (he looked down on Johnson and Boswell), political commentary, and autobiography. Now available in the great Yale edition, the letters are self-conscious works of art which keep one eye on future readers.

## *From* LETTERS

### To Richard West, c. Friday 15 May 1739, from Paris

*[Pomp and Piety]*

Dear West,

I should think myself to blame not to try to divert you, when you tell me I can. . . . Stand by, clear the way, make room for the pompous appearance of Versailles le grand! But no: it fell so short of my idea of it, mine, that I have resigned to Gray the office of writing its panegyric. He likes it. They say I am to like it better next Sunday; when the sun is to shine, the King is to be fine, the waterworks are to play, and the new Knights of the Holy Ghost are to be installed! Ever since Wednesday, the day we were there, we have done nothing but dispute about it. They say, we did not see it to advantage, that we ran through the apartments, saw the garden *en passant*, and slubbered over Trianon. I say, we saw nothing. However, we had time to see that the great front is a lumber of littleness, composed of black brick, stuck full of bad old busts, and fringed with gold rails. The rooms are all small, except the great gallery, which is noble, but totally wainscoted with looking-glass. The garden is littered with statues and fountains, each of which has its tutelary deity. In particular, the elementary God of Fire solaces himself in one. In another, Enceladus, in lieu of a mountain, is overwhelmed with many waters. There are avenues of water-pots, who disport themselves much in squirting up cascadelins. In short, 'tis a garden for a great child. Such was Louis Quatorze, who is here seen in his proper colours, where he commanded in person, unassisted by his armies and generals, and left to the pursuit of his own puerile ideas of glory.

We saw last week a place of another kind, and which has more the air of what it would be, than anything I have yet met with: it was the convent of the Chartreux. All the conveniencies, or rather (if there was such a word) all the *adaptments* are assembled here, that melancholy, meditation, selfish devotion, and despair would require. But yet 'tis pleasing. Soften the terms, and mellow the uncouth horror that reigns here, but a little, and 'tis a charming solitude. It stands on a large space of ground, is old and irregular. The chapel is gloomy: behind it, through some dark passages, you pass into a large obscure hall, which looks like a combination-chamber for some hellish council. The large cloister surrounds their burying-ground. The cloisters are very narrow, and very long, and let into the cells, which are built like little huts detached from each other. We were carried into one, where lived a middle-aged man not long initiated into the order. He was extremely civil, and called himself Dom Victor. We have promised to visit him often. Their habit is all white: but besides this, he was infinitely clean in his person; and his apartment and garden, which he keeps and cultivates without any assistance, was neat to a degree. He has four little rooms, furnished in the prettiest manner, and hung with good prints. One of them is a library, and another a gallery. He has several canary-birds disposed in a pretty manner in breeding-cages. In his garden was a bed of good tulips in bloom, flowers and fruit-trees, and all neatly kept. They are permitted at certain hours to talk to strangers, but never to one another, or to go out of their convent. But what we chiefly went to see was the small cloister, with the history of St Bruno, their founder, painted by Le Soeur. It consists of twenty-two pictures, the figures a good deal less than life. But sure they are amazing! I don't know what Raphael may be in Rome, but these pictures excel all I have seen in Paris and England. The figure of the dead man who spoke at his burial, contains all the strongest and horridest ideas, of ghastliness, hypocrisy discovered, and the height of damnation; pain and cursing. A Benedictine monk, who was there at the same time, said to me of this picture: *C'est une fable, mais on la croyait autrefois* [It's only a story, but they used to believe it]. Another, who showed me relics in one of their churches, expressed as much ridicule for them. The pictures I have been speaking of are ill preserved, and some of the finest heads defaced, which was done at first by a rival of Le Soeur's. – Adieu! dear West, take care of your health; and some time or other we will talk over all these things with more pleasure than I have had in seeing them.

Yours ever.

## To Richard West From a hamlet among the mountains of Savoy, Sept. 28, 1739

## *[Wild Nature]*

Precipices, mountains, torrents, wolves, rumblings, Salvator Rosa† – the pomp of our park and the meekness of our palace! Here we are, the lonely lords of glorious desolate prospects. I have kept a sort of resolution which I made, of not writing to you as long as I stayed in France: I am now a quarter of an hour out of it, and write to you. Mind, 'tis three months since we heard from you. I begin this letter among the clouds; where I shall finish, my neighbour heaven probably knows: 'tis an odd wish in a mortal letter, to hope not to finish it on this side the atmosphere. You will have a billet tumble to you from the stars when you least think of it; and that I should write it too! Lord, how potent that sounds! But I am to undergo many transmigrations before I come to 'yours ever.' Yesterday I was a shepherd of Dauphiné; today an Alpine savage; tomorrow a Carthusian monk; and Friday a Swiss Calvinist. I have one quality which I find remains with me in all worlds and in all ethers; I brought it with me from your world, and am admired for it in this, 'tis my esteem for you: this is a common thought among you, and you will laugh at it, but it is new here; as new to remember one's friends in the world one has left, as for you to remember those you have lost.

Aix in Savoy, Sept. 30th.

We are this minute come in here, and here's an awkward abbé this minute come in to us. I asked him if he would sit down. *Oui, oui, oui.* He has ordered us a radish soup for supper, and has brought a

*Salvator Rosa* 1615–73; dramatic landscape painter

chessboard to play with Mr Conway. I have left 'em in the act, and am set down to write to you. Did you ever see anything like the prospect we saw yesterday? I never did. We rode three leagues to see the Grande Chartreuse; expected bad roads, and the finest convent in the kingdom. We were disappointed pro and con. The building is large and plain, and has nothing remarkable but its primitive simplicity: they entertained us in the neatest manner, with eggs, pickled salmon, dried fish, conserves, cheese, butter, grapes and figs, and pressed us mightily to lie there. We tumbled into the hands of a lay-brother, who, unluckily having the charge of the meal and bran, showed us little besides. They desired us to set down our names in the list of strangers, where, among others, we found two mottoes of our countrymen for whose stupidity and brutality we blushed. . . . But the road, West, the road! winding round a prodigious mountain, and surrounded with others, all shagged with hanging woods, obscured with pines or lost in clouds! Below, a torrent breaking through cliffs, and tumbling through fragments of rocks! Sheets of cascades forcing their silver speed down channelled precipices, and hasting into the roughened river at the bottom! Now and then an old foot-bridge, with a broken rail, a leaning cross, a cottage, or the ruin of an hermitage! This sounds too bombast and too romantic to one that has not seen it, too cold for one that has. If I could send you my letter post between two lovely tempests that echoed each other's wrath, you might have some idea of this noble roaring scene, as you were reading it. Almost on the summit, upon a fine verdure, but without any prospect, stands the Chartreuse. We stayed there two hours, rode back through this charming picture, wished for a painter, wished to be poets! Need I tell you we wished for you?

Good night!

## To George Montagu, Thursday 13 November 1760

### *[The Burial of King George II]*

Even the honeymoon of a new reign don't produce events every day. There is nothing but the common toying of addresses and kissing hands. . . . For the King himself he seems all good-nature, and wishing to satisfy everybody. All his speeches are obliging. I saw him again yesterday, and was surprised to find the levee room had lost so entirely the air of the lion's den. This young man don't stand in one spot, with his eyes fixed royally on the ground, and dropping bits of German news. He walks about and speaks to everybody. I saw him afterwards on the throne, where he is graceful and genteel, sits with dignity, and reads his answers to addresses well. . . .

Do you know I had the curiosity to go to the burying t'other night; I had never seen a royal funeral. Nay, I walked as a rag of quality, which I found would be, and so it was, the easiest way of seeing it. It is absolutely a noble sight. The Prince's Chamber hung with purple and a quantity of silver lamps, the coffin under a canopy of purple velvet, and six vast chandeliers of silver on high stands had a very good effect: the ambassador from Tripoli and his son were carried to see that chamber. The procession through a line of foot-guards, every seventh man bearing a torch, the horse-guards lining the outside, their officers with drawn sabres and crape sashes, on horseback, the drums muffled, the fifes, bells tolling and minute guns, all this was very solemn. But the charm was the entrance of the Abbey,† where we were received by the Dean and chapter in rich copes, the choir and almsmen all bearing torches; the whole Abbey so illuminated, that one saw it to greater advantage than by day; the tombs, long aisles, and fretted roof all appearing distinctly, and with the happiest chiaroscuro. There wanted nothing but incense, and little chapels here and there with priests saying mass for the repose of the defunct – yet one could not complain of its not being Catholic enough. I had been in dread of being coupled with some boy of ten years old – but the heralds were not very accurate, and I walked with George Grenville, taller and older enough to keep me in countenance. When we came to the chapel of Henry VII all solemnity and decorum ceased – no order was observed, people sat or stood where they could or would, the yeomen of the guard were crying out for help, oppressed by the immense weight of the coffin, the Bishop read sadly, and blundered in the prayers, the fine chapter, *Man that is born of a woman*, was chanted not read, and the anthem, besides being unmeasurably tedious, would have served as well for a nuptial. The real serious part was the figure of the Duke of Cumberland, heightened by a thousand melancholy circumstances. He had a dark brown adonis,† and a cloak of black cloth with a train of five yards. Attending the funeral of a father, how little reason soever he had to love him, could not be pleasant. His leg extremely bad, yet forced to stand upon it near two hours, his face bloated and distorted with his late paralytic stroke, which has affected too one of his eyes, and placed over the mouth of the vault, into which in all probability he must himself so soon descend – think how unpleasant a situation! He bore it all with a firm and unaffected countenance. This grave scene was fully contrasted by the burlesque Duke of Newcastle – he fell into a fit of crying the moment he came into the chapel and flung himself back in a stall, the Archbishop hovering over him with a smelling bottle – but in two minutes his curiosity got the better of his hypocrisy and he ran about the chapel

*Abbey* Westminster Abbey

*adonis* kind of wig

with his glass to spy who was or was not there, spying with one hand and mopping his eyes with t'other. Then returned the fear of catching cold, and the Duke of Cumberland, who was sinking with heat, felt himself weighed down, and turning round, found it was the Duke of Newcastle standing upon his train to avoid the chill of the marble. It was very theatric to look down into the vault, where the coffin lay, attended by mourners with lights. Clavering, the Groom of the Bedchamber, refused to sit up with the body, and was dismissed by the King's order.

I have nothing more to tell you but a trifle, a very trifle – the King of Prussia has totally defeated Marshal Daun. This which would have been prodigious news a month ago, is nothing today; it only takes its turn among the questions, 'Who is to be Groom of the Bedchamber?' 'What is Sir T. Robinson to have?' I have been at Leicester Fields today; the crowd was immoderate; I don't believe it will continue so. Good night.

Yours ever

H. W.

# Tobias George Smollett

1721–71

Born near Loch Lomond in Scotland, Smollett failed in his early medical career, and joined a naval expedition against the Spaniards in the West Indies, whose horrors he graphically described in his first novel, *Roderick Random* (1748). *Peregrine Pickle* (1751) and *Ferdinand Fathom* (1753) continued his accounts of violence and black humour in an often cruel world; he also translated his gentler master, Cervantes (1755). Major non-fiction included editing the *Critical Review* (1756–63), and a best-selling *Complete History of England* (1757–8); he was a vigorous literary and political controversialist, receiving a three-month prison sentence for libel. His *Travels through France and Italy* (1766) delight by abrasive attitudes, which made Sterne call him 'Smelfungus' in his *Sentimental Journey*. Smollett died in Italy, having published his most genial novel, the epistolary *Expedition of Humphry Clinker* (1771), in which a family and their servants relate in a variety of styles their travels through England and Scotland, back to Wales. Dickens was a great reader of Smollett, and learned from his techniques of character portrayal.

## *From* THE EXPEDITION OF HUMPHRY CLINKER†

### *[The Pleasures of Bath and London]*

To Dr. LEWIS from Matthew Bramble

You ask me, why I don't take the air a-horseback, during this fine weather? – In which of the avenues of this paradise would you have

*The Expedition of Humphry Clinker* The central figure, Matthew Bramble, a crusty but warm-hearted squire, writes about his experiences in the fashionable resort of Bath, and in London. Lydia is his niece, Tabitha his sister

me take that exercise? Shall I commit myself to the high-roads of London or Bristol, to be stifled with dust, or pressed to death in the midst of post-chaises, flying-machines,† waggons, and coal-horses; besides the troops of fine gentlemen that take to the high-way, to show their horsemanship; and the coaches of fine ladies, who go thither to show their equipages? Shall I attempt the Downs, and fatigue myself to death in climbing up an eternal ascent, without any hopes of reaching the summit? Know then, I have made divers desperate leaps at those upper regions; but always fell backward into this vapour-pit,† exhausted and dispirited by those ineffectual efforts; and here we poor valetudinarians pant and struggle, like so many Chinese gudgeons,† gasping in the bottom of a punch-bowl. By Heaven, it is a kind of enchantment! If I do not speedily break the spell, and escape, I may chance to give up the ghost in this nauseous stew of corruption – It was but two nights ago, that I had like to have made my public exit, at a minute's warning. One of my greatest weaknesses is that of suffering myself to be overruled by the opinion of people, whose judgment I despise – I own, with shame and confusion of face, that importunity of any kind I cannot resist. This want of courage and constancy is an original flaw in my nature, which you must have often observed with compassion, if not with contempt. I am afraid some of our boasted virtues may be traced up to this defect. –

Without further preamble, I was persuaded to go to a ball, on purpose to see Liddy dance a minuet with a young petulant jackanapes, the only son of a wealthy undertaker† from London, whose mother lodges in our neighbourhood, and has contracted an acquaintance with Tabby. I sat a couple of long hours, half stifled, in the midst of a noisome crowd; and could not help wondering, that so many hundreds of those that rank as rational creatures, could find entertainment in seeing a succession of insipid animals, describing the same dull figure for a whole evening, on an area, not much bigger than a tailor's shop-board. If there had been any beauty, grace, activity, magnificent dress, or variety of any kind, howsoever absurd, to engage the attention, and amuse the fancy, I should not have been surprised; but there was no such object: it was a tiresome repetition of the same languid, frivolous scene, performed by actors that seemed to sleep in all their motions – The continual swimming of those phantoms before my eyes, gave me a swimming of the head; which was also affected by the fouled air, circulating through such a number of rotten human bellows – I therefore retreated towards the door, and stood in the passage to the next room, talking to my

*flying-machines* rapid coaches
*vapour-pit* Bath lies in the valley of the River Avon
*gudgeons* small fish
*undertaker* contractor

friend Quin; when an end being put to the minuets, the benches were removed to make way for the country-dances; and the multitude rising at once, the whole atmosphere was put in commotion. Then, all of a sudden, came rushing upon me an Egyptian gale, so impregnated with pestilential vapours, that my nerves were overpowered, and I dropped senseless upon the floor.

You may easily conceive what a clamour and confusion this accident must have produced, in such an assembly – I soon recovered, however, and found myself in an easy chair, supported by my own people – Sister Tabby, in her great tenderness, had put me to the torture, squeezing my head under her arm, and stuffing my nose with spirit of hartshorn, till the whole inside was excoriated. I no sooner got home, than I sent for doctor Ch –, who assured me, I needed not be alarmed, for my swooning was entirely occasioned by an accidental impression of fetid effluvia upon nerves of uncommon sensibility. I know not how other people's nerves are constructed; but one would imagine they must be made of very coarse materials, to stand the shock of such a horrid assault. It was, indeed, *a compound of villainous smells*, in which the most violent stinks, and the most powerful perfumes, contended for the mastery. Imagine to yourself a high exalted essence of mingled odours, arising from putrid gums, imposthumated lungs, sour flatulencies, rank arm-pits, sweating feet, running sores and issues, plasters, ointments, and embrocations, hungary-water, spirit of lavender, assafœtida drops, musk, hartshorn, and sal volatile; besides a thousand frowzy steams, which I could not analyse. Such, O Dick! is the fragrant æther we breathe in the polite assemblies of Bath – Such is the atmosphere I have exchanged for the pure, elastic, animating air of the Welsh mountains – *O Rus, quando te aspiciam*† [oh countryside, when shall I see you]. – I wonder what the devil possessed me –

But few words are best: I have taken my resolution – You may well suppose I don't intend to entertain the company with a second exhibition – I have promised, in an evil hour, to proceed to London, and that promise shall be performed; but my stay in the metropolis shall be brief. . . .

To Dr. LEWIS from Matthew Bramble

Dear Doctor,

London is literally new to me; new in its streets, houses, and even in its situation; as the Irishman said, 'London is now gone out of town.' What I left open fields, producing hay and corn, I now find covered with streets, and squares, and palaces, and churches. I am credibly

*O Rus . . . aspiciam* Horace, *Satires*, II.6.60

informed, that in the space of seven years, eleven thousand new houses have been built in one quarter of Westminster, exclusive of what is daily added to other parts of this unwieldy metropolis. Pimlico and Knightsbridge are now almost joined to Chelsea and Kensington; and if this infatuation continues for half a century, I suppose the whole county of Middlesex will be covered with brick.

It must be allowed, indeed, for the credit of the present age, that London and Westminster are much better paved and lighted than they were formerly. The new streets are spacious, regular, and airy; and the houses generally convenient. The Bridge at Blackfriars is a noble monument of taste and public-spirit – I wonder how they stumbled upon a work of such magnificence and utility. But, notwithstanding these improvements, the capital is become an overgrown monster; which, like a dropsical head, will in time leave the body and extremities without nourishment and support. The absurdity will appear in its full force, when we consider, that one sixth part of the natives of this whole extensive kingdom is crowded within the bills† of mortality. What wonder that our villages are depopulated, and our farms in want of day-labourers? The abolition of small farms, is but one cause of the decrease of population. Indeed, the incredible increase of horses and black cattle, to answer the purposes of luxury, requires a prodigious quantity of hay and grass, which are raised and managed without much labour; but a number of hands will always be wanted for the different branches of agriculture, whether the farms be large or small. The tide of luxury has swept all the inhabitants from the open country – The poorest squire, as well as the richest peer, must have his house in town, and make a figure with an extraordinary number of domestics. The plough-boys, cow-herds, and lower hinds, are debauched and seduced by the appearance and discourse of those coxcombs in livery, when they make their summer excursions. They desert their dirt and drudgery, and swarm up to London, in hopes of getting into service, where they can live luxuriously and wear fine clothes, without being obliged to work; for idleness is natural to man – Great numbers of these, being disappointed in their expectation, become thieves and sharpers; and London being an immense wilderness, in which there is neither watch nor ward of any signification, nor any order or police, affords them lurking-places as well as prey.

There are many causes that contribute to the daily increase of this enormous mass; but they may be all resolved into the grand source of luxury and corruption – About five and twenty years ago, very few, even of the most opulent citizens of London, kept any equipage, or

*within the bills* in the area of London death statistics

even any servants in livery. Their tables produced nothing but plain boiled and roasted, with a bottle of port and a tankard of beer. At present, every trader in any degree of credit, every broker and attorney, maintains a couple of footmen, a coachman, and postilion. He has his town-house, and his country-house, his coach, and his postchaise. His wife and daughters appear in the richest stuffs, bespangled with diamonds. They frequent the court, the opera, the theatre, and the masquerade. They hold assemblies at their own houses: they make sumptuous entertainments, and treat with the richest wines of Bordeaux, Burgundy, and Champagne. The substantial tradesman, who wont to pass his evenings at the ale-house for fourpence half-penny, now spends three shillings at the tavern, while his wife keeps card-tables at home; she must likewise have fine clothes, her chaise, or pad,[†] with country lodgings, and go three times a week to public diversions. Every clerk, apprentice, and even waiter of tavern or coffee-house, maintains a gelding by himself, or in partnership, and assumes the air and apparel of a petit maitre – The gayest places of public entertainment are filled with fashionable figures; which, upon inquiry, will be found to be journeymen tailors, serving-men, and abigails,[†] disguised like their betters.

In short, there is no distinction or subordination left – The different departments of life are jumbled together – The hod-carrier, the low mechanic, the tapster, the publican, the shop-keeper, the pettifogger,[†] the citizen, and courtier, *all tread upon the kibes of one another*: actuated by the demons of profligacy and licentiousness, they are seen every where, rambling, riding, rolling, rushing, justling, mixing, bouncing, cracking, and crashing in one vile ferment of stupidity and corruption – All is tumult and hurry; one would imagine they were impelled by some disorder of the brain, that will not suffer them to be at rest. The foot-passengers run along as if they were pursued by bailiffs. The porters and chairmen trot with their burdens. People, who keep their own equipages, drive through the streets at full speed. Even citizens, physicians, and apothecaries, glide in their chariots like lightning. The hackney-coachmen make their horses smoke, and the pavement shakes under them; and I have actually seen a waggon pass through Piccadilly at the hand-gallop. In a word, the whole nation seems to be running out of their wits.

The diversions of the times are not ill suited to the genius of this incongruous monster, called the *public*. Give it noise, confusion, glare, and glitter; it has no idea of elegance and propriety – What are the amusements at Ranelagh?[†] One half of the company are following one

*pad* horse
*abigails* lady's-maids
*pettifogger* low practitioner
*Ranelagh* pleasure garden in Chelsea

another's tails, in an eternal circle; like so many blind asses in an olive-mill, where they can neither discourse, distinguish, nor be distinguished; while the other half are drinking hot water, under the denomination of tea, till nine or ten o'clock at night, to keep them awake for the rest of the evening. As for the orchestra, the vocal music especially, it is well for the performers that they cannot be heard distinctly. Vauxhall† is a composition of baubles, overcharged with paltry ornaments, ill conceived, and poorly executed; without any unity of design, or propriety of disposition. It is an unnatural assembly of objects, fantastically illuminated in broken masses; seemingly contrived to dazzle the eyes and divert the imagination of the vulgar – Here a wooden lion, there a stone statue; in one place, a range of things like coffee-house boxes, covered a-top; in another, a parcel of ale-house benches; in a third, a puppet-show representation of a tin cascade; in a fourth, a gloomy cave of a circular form, like a sepulchral vault half lighted; in a fifth, a scanty slip of grass-plat, that would not afford pasture sufficient for an ass's colt. The walks, which nature seems to have intended for solitude, shade, and silence, are filled with crowds of noisy people, sucking up the nocturnal rheums of an aguish climate; and through these gay scenes, a few lamps glimmer like so many farthing candles.

When I see a number of well-dressed people, of both sexes, sitting on the covered benches, exposed to the eyes of the mob; and, which is worse, to the cold, raw, night-air, devouring sliced beef, and swilling port, and punch, and cider, I can't help compassionating their temerity, while I despise their want of taste and decorum; but, when they course along those damp and gloomy walks, or crowd together upon the wet gravel, without any other cover than the cope of Heaven, listening to a song, which one half of them cannot possibly hear, how can I help supposing they are actually possessed by a spirit, more absurd and pernicious than any thing we meet with in the precincts of Bedlam? In all probability, the proprietors of this, and other public gardens of inferior note, in the skirts of the metropolis, are, in some shape, connected with the faculty of physic, and the company of undertakers; for, considering that eagerness in the pursuit of what is called pleasure, which now predominates through every rank and denomination of life, I am persuaded, that more gouts, rheumatisms, catarrhs, and consumptions are caught in these nocturnal pastimes, *sub dio* [in the open], than from all the risks and accidents to which a life of toil and danger is exposed.

These, and other observations, which I have made in this excursion, will shorten my stay at London, and send me back with a double relish to my solitude and mountains. . . .

---

*Vauxhall* ornamental musical gardens

[Win Jenkins, Tabitha's servant, sends letters whose comic illiteracy is reinforced by creative ambiguities of domestic language which undermine her religious and sexual attitudes: *pyebill*/Bible; *light of grease*/grace; *bride's fever*/favour]

## *[A Domestic Epistle]*

To Mrs MARY JONES, at Brambleton-hall

Dear Mary Jones,

Miss Liddy is so good as to unclose me in a kiver as fur as Gloster, and the carrier will bring it to hand – God send us all safe to Monmouthshire, for I'm quite jaded with rambling – 'Tis a true saying, *live and learn* – O woman, what chuckling and changing have I seen! – Well, there's nothing sartain in this world – Who would have thought that mistriss, after all the pains taken for the good of her prusias sole, would go for to throw away her poor body? that she would cast the heys of infection upon such a carrying-crow as Lashmihago! as old as Matthewsullin, as dry as a red herring, and as pore as a starved veezel – O, Molly! hadst thou seen him come down the ladder, in a shurt so scanty, that it could not kiver his nakedness! – The young 'squire called him Dunquickset; but he looked for all the world like Cradoc-ap Morgan, the ould tinker, that suffered at Abergany for steeling of kettle – Then he's a profane scuffle, and, as Mr Clinker says, no better than an impfiddle, continually playing upon the pyebill[†] and the new-burth – I doubt he has as little manners as money; for he can't say a civil word, much more make me a present of a pair of gloves for good-will; but he looks as if he wanted to be very forewood and familiar – O! that ever a gentlewoman of years and discretion should tare her air, and cry and disporridge herself for such a nubjack! as the song goes –

I vow she wou'd fain have a burd
That bids such a price for an owl.

but, for sartain, he must have dealt with some Scotch musician to bring her to this pass – As for me, I put my trust in the Lord; and I have got a slice of witch elm sowed in the gathers of my under petticoat; and Mr Clinker assures me, that by the new light of grease,[†] I may deify the devil and all his works – But I nose what I nose – If mistress should take up with Lashmyhago, this is no sarvice for me – Thank God, there's no want of places; and if it wan't for wan thing, I would – but, no matter – Madam Baynar's woman has twenty good pounds a-year and parquisites; and dresses like a parson of distinkson – I dined with her and the valley de shambles, with bags and golden jackets; but there was nothing kimfittable to eat, being as how they live upon board, and having nothing but a piss of could cuddling tart and some blamangey, I was tuck with the cullick and a murcy it was that mistress had her viol of assings in the cox.

But, as I was saying, I think for sartain this match will go forewood; for things are come to a creesus; and I have seen with my own hays, such smuggling – But I scorn for to exclose the secrets of the family; and if it wance comes to marrying, who nose but the frolick may go round – I believes as how, Miss Liddy would have no reversion if her swan would appear; and you would be surprised, Molly, to receive a bride's fever† from your humble sarvant – but this is all suppository, dear girl; and I have sullenly promised to Mr Clinker, that neither man, woman, nor child, shall no that arrow said a civil thing to me in the way of infection – I hopes to drink your health at Brambleton-hall, in a horn of October, before the month be out – Pray let my bed be turned once a-day, and the windore opened, while the weather is dry; and burn a few billets with some brush in the footman's garret, and see their mattrash be dry as a bone; for both our gentlemen have got a sad could by lying in damp shits at sir Tummas Ballfart's. No more at present, but my sarvice to Saul and the rest of our fellow-sarvents, being,

Dear Mary Jones,
always yours,
WIN. JENKINS

Oct. 4.

1771

# Christopher Smart

1722–71

One of the most remarkable poetic talents of the century, Smart showed his classical scholarship as a Cambridge undergraduate. A friend of Johnson, he published georgic and satiric poetry in the 1750s, but for most of the period 1757–63 was confined in places for the insane. *A Song to David* (1763) praises God in mystically patterned groups of stanzas; David, king and psalmist, had praised God to the harp. *Jubilate Agno* (Rejoice in the Lamb), evidently written during his madness, was not published until 1939. In lines of varying length and rhythm, it praises God's creation in structures based on the antiphonal responses of Hebrew poetry. The diction and imagery of these poems are extraordinarily rich combinations of scientific and biblical materials; in many respects they are far from the high Augustan verse style of the period, although his minor poems show the influence of Pope (Smart also translated Horace). He died in a debtors' prison. His reputation has risen greatly in this century, partly helped by the fresh publication.

## *From* JUBILATE AGNO Fragment B

### *[My Cat Jeoffry]*

For I will consider my Cat Jeoffry.
For he is the servant of the Living God duly and daily serving him.
For at the first glance of the glory of God in the East he worships in his way.
For is this done by wreathing his body seven times round with elegant quickness.
For then he leaps up to catch the musk, which is the blessing of God upon his prayer.
For he rolls upon prank to work it in.
For having done duty and received blessing he begins to consider himself.
For this he performs in ten degrees.

For first he looks upon his fore-paws to see if they are clean.
For secondly he kicks up behind to clear away there.
For thirdly he works it upon stretch with the fore paws extended.
For fourthly he sharpens his paws by wood.
For fithly he washes himself.
For Sixthly he rolls upon wash.
For Seventhly he fleas himself, that he may not be interrupted upon the beat.
For Eighthly he rubs himself against a post.
For Ninthly he looks up for his instructions.
For Tenthly he goes in quest of food.
For having considered God and himself he will consider his neighbour.
For if he meets another cat he will kiss her in kindness.
For when he takes his prey he plays with it to give it chance.
For one mouse in seven escapes by his dallying.
For when his day's work is done his business more properly begins.
For he keeps the Lord's watch in the night against the adversary.
For he counteracts the powers of darkness by his electrical skin and glaring eyes.
For he counteracts the Devil, who is death, by brisking about the life.
For in his morning orisons he loves the sun and the sun loves him.
For he is of the tribe of Tiger.
For the Cherub Cat is a term of the Angel Tiger.
For he has the subtlety and hissing of a serpent, which in goodness he suppresses.
For he will not do destruction, if he is well-fed, neither will he spit without provocation.
For he purrs in thankfulness, when God tells him he's a good Cat.
For he is an instrument for the children to learn benevolence upon.
For every house is incomplete without him and a blessing is lacking in the spirit.
For the Lord† commanded Moses concerning the cats at the departure of the Children of Israel from Egypt.
For every family had one cat at least in the bag.
For the English Cats are the best in Europe.
For he is the cleanest in the use of his fore-paws of any quadrupede.
For the dexterity of his defence is an instance of the love of God to him exceedingly.
For he is the quickest to his mark of any creature.
For he is tenacious of his point.
For he is a mixture of gravity and waggery.
For he knows that God is his Saviour.

*the Lord* Exodus 12.32 does not mention cats

For there is nothing sweeter than his peace when at rest.
For there is nothing brisker than his life when in motion.
For he is of the Lord's poor and so indeed is he called by benevolence perpetually – Poor Jeoffry! poor Jeoffry! the rat has bit thy throat.
For I bless the name of the Lord Jesus that Jeoffry is better.
For the divine spirit comes about his body to sustain it in complete cat.
For his tongue is exceeding pure so that it has in purity what it wants in music.
For he is docile and can learn certain things.
For he can set up with gravity which is patience upon approbation.
For he can fetch and carry, which is patience in employment.
For he can jump over a stick which is patience upon proof positive.
For he can spraggle[†] upon waggle at the word of command.
For he can jump from an eminence into his master's bosom.
For he can catch the cork and toss it again.
For he is hated by the hypocrite and miser.
For the former is afraid of detection.
For the latter refuses the charge.
For he camels his back to bear the first notion of business.
For he is good to think on, if a man would express himself neatly.
For he made a great figure in Egypt for his signal services.
For he killed the Ichneumon[†]-rat very pernicious by land.
For his ears are so acute that they sting again.
For from this proceeds the passing quickness of his attention.
For by stroking of him I have found out electricity.
For I perceived God's light about him both wax and fire.
For the Electrical fire is the spiritual substance, which God sends from heaven to sustain the bodies both of man and beast.
For God has blessed him in the variety of his movements.
For, though he cannot fly, he is an excellent clamberer.
For his motions upon the face of the earth are more than any other quadrupede.
For he can tread to all the measures upon the music.
For he can swim for life.
For he can creep.

1758–63 1939

*spraggle* sprawl, stretch *Ichneumon* animal like a weasel

# *From* A SONG TO DAVID

## [God's Creation]

XVIII

He† sung of God – the mighty source
Of all things – the stupendous force
On which all strength depends;
From whose right arm, beneath whose eyes,
All period, power, and enterprise
Commences, reigns, and ends.

XIX

Angels – their ministry and meed,
Which to and fro with blessings speed,
Or with their citterns† wait;
Where Michael† with his millions bows,
Where dwells the seraph† and his spouse,
The cherub† and her mate.

XX

Of man – the semblance and effect
Of God and Love – the Saint elect
For infinite applause –
To rule the land, and briny broad,
To be laborious in his laud,
And heroes in his cause.

XXI

The world – the clustering spheres† he made,
The glorious light, the soothing shade,
Dale, champaign,† grove, and hill;
The multitudinous abyss,
Where secrecy remains in bliss,
And wisdom hides her skill.

XXII

Trees, plants, and flowers – of virtuous root;
Gem* yielding blossom, yielding fruit, bud
Choice gums and precious balm;
Bless ye the nosegay in the vale,

---

*He* King David, the psalmist
*citterns* here, harps
*Michael* leader of angels (*seraph* and *cherub*)
*spheres* carrying the planets
*champaign* open country

And with the sweetners of the gale
 Enrich the thankful psalm.

XXIII

Of fowl – e'en every beak and wing
Which cheer the winter, hail the spring,
 That live in peace or prey;
They that make music, or that mock,
The quail, the brave domestic cock,
 The raven, swan, and jay.

XXIV

Of fishes – every size and shape,
Which nature frames of light escape,
 Devouring man to shun:
The shells are in the wealthy deep,
The shoals upon the surface leap,
 And love the glancing sun.

XXV

Of beasts – the beaver plods his task;
While the sleek tigers roll and bask,
 Nor yet the shades arouse:
Her cave the mining coney scoops;
Where o'er the mead the mountain stoops,
 The kids exult and browse.

XXVI

Of gems – their virtue and their price,
Which hid in earth from man's device,
 Their darts of lustre sheathe;
The jasper of the master's stamp,
The topaz blazing like a lamp
 Among the mines beneath.

XXVII

Blest was the tenderness he felt
When to his graceful harp he knelt,
 And did for audience call;
When Satan with his hand he quelled,
And in serene suspense he held
 The frantic throes of Saul.†

*Saul* David's music expelled an evil spirit from the King of Israel (I Samuel 16.23)

XXVIII

His furious foes no more maligned
As he such melody divined,
  And sense and soul detained;
Now striking strong, now soothing soft,
He sent the godly sounds aloft,
  Or in delight refrained. . . .

## *[Adoration]*

XLIX

O DAVID, highest in the list
Of worthies, on God's ways insist,
  The genuine word repeat:
Vain are the documents of men,
And vain the flourish of the pen
  That keeps the fool's conceit.

L

PRAISE above all – for praise prevails;
Head up the measure, load the scales,
  And good to goodness add:
The generous soul her Saviour aids,
But peevish obloquy degrades;
  The Lord is great and glad.

LI

For ADORATION all the ranks
Of angels yield eternal thanks,
  And DAVID in the midst;
With God's good poor, which, last and least
In man's esteem, thou to thy feast,†
  O blessed bride-groom, bidst.

LII

For ADORATION seasons change,
And order, truth, and beauty range,
  Adjust, attract, and fill:
The grass the polyanthus checks;
And polished porphyry† reflects,
  By the descending rill.

*feast* see Luke 14.7–21 *porphyry* variegated stone

LIII

Rich almonds colour to the prime
For ADORATION; tendrils climb,
And fruit-trees pledge their gems;
And Ivis* with her gorgeous vest hummingbird
Builds for her eggs her cunning nest,
And bell-flowers bow their stems.

LIV

With vinous syrup cedars spout;
From rocks pure honey gushing out,
For ADORATION springs:
All scenes of painting crowd the map
Of nature; to the mermaid's pap
The scaled infant clings.

LV

The spotted ounce* and playsome cubs lynx
Run rustling 'mongst the flowering shrubs,
And lizards feed the moss;
For ADORATION beasts embark,
While waves upholding halcyon's* ark kingfisher
No longer roar and toss.

LVI

While Israel sits beneath his fig,
With coral root and amber sprig
The weaned adventurer sports;
Where to the palm the jasmin cleaves,
For ADORATION 'mongst the leaves
The gale his peace reports.

LVII

Increasing days their reign exalt,
Nor in the pink and mottled vault
Th' opposing spirits tilt;
And, by the coasting reader spied,
The silverlings and crusions* glide fish
For ADORATION gilt.

LVIII

For ADORATION ripening canes
And cocoa's purest milk detains
The western pilgrim's staff;

Where rain in clasping boughs inclosed,
And vines with oranges disposed,
Embower the social laugh.

LIX

Now labour his reward receives,
For ADORATION counts his sheaves
To peace, her bounteous prince;
The nectarine his strong tint imbibes,
And apples of ten thousand tribes,
And quick peculiar quince.

LX

The wealthy crops of whitening rice,
'Mongst thyine* woods and groves of spice, gum-tree
For ADORATION grow;
And, marshalled in the fencèd land,
The peaches and pomegranates stand,
Where wild carnations blow.

LXI

The laurels with the winter strive;
The crocus burnishes alive
Upon the snow-clad earth:
For ADORATION myrtles stay
To keep the garden from dismay,
And bless the sight from dearth.

LXII

The pheasant shows his pompous neck;
And ermine, jealous of a speck,
With fear eludes offence:
The sable, with his glossy pride,
For ADORATION is descried,
Where frosts the wave condense.

LXIII

The cheerful holly, pensive yew,
And holy thorn, their trim renew;
The squirrel hoards his nuts:
All creatures batten o'er their stores,
And careful nature all her doors
For ADORATION shuts.

LXIV

For ADORATION, DAVID's psalms
Lift up the heart to deeds of alms;
And he, who kneels and chants,
Prevails his passions to control,
Finds meat and medicine to the soul,
Which for translation† pants.

LXV

For ADORATION, beyond match,
The scholar† bulfinch aims to catch
The soft flute's ivory touch;
And, careless on the hazel spray,
The daring redbreast keeps at bay
The damsel's greedy clutch.

LXVI

For ADORATION, in the skies,
The Lord's philosopher† espies
The Dog, the Ram, and Rose;
The planets ring, Orion's sword;
Nor is his greatness less adored
In the vile worm that glows.

LXVII

For ADORATION on the strings†
The western breezes work their wings,
The captive ear to soothe –
Hark! 'tis a voice – how still, and small –
That makes the cataracts to fall,
Or bids the sea be smooth.

LXVIII

For ADORATION, incense comes
From bezoar,† and Arabian gums;
And on the civet's fur.
But as for prayer, or ere it faints,
Far better is the breath of saints
Than galbanum† and myrrh.

*translation* removal (to heaven)
*scholar* taught to mimic
*philosopher* the astronomer sees God's works in the constellations following
*strings* the Aeolian harp is stirred by the wind
*bezoar* scented medicinal stone
*galbanum* like myrrh, a scented gum

### LXIX

For ADORATION from the down,
Of damsons to th' anana's* crown, — *pineapple*
 God sends to tempt the taste;
And while the luscious zest invites,
The sense, that in the scene delights,
 Commands desire be chaste.

### LXX

For ADORATION, all the paths
Of grace are open, all the baths
 Of purity refresh;
And all the rays of glory beam
To deck the man of God's esteem,
 Who triumphs o'er the flesh.

### LXXI

For ADORATION, in the dome
Of Christ the sparrows find an home;
 And on his olives perch:
The swallow also dwells with thee,
O man of God's humility,
 Within his Saviour CHURCH.

### LXXII

Sweet is the dew that falls betimes,
And drops upon the leafy limes;
 Sweet Hermon's† fragrant air:
Sweet is the lily's silver bell,
And sweet the wakeful tapers smell
 That watch for early prayer.

### LXXIII

Sweet the young nurse with love intense,
Which smiles o'er sleeping innocence;
 Sweet when the lost arrive:
Sweet the musician's ardour beats,
While his vague mind's in quest of sweets,
 The choicest flowers to hive.

---

† *Hermon* biblical mountain (Psalm 133)

LXXIV

Sweeter in all the strains of love,
The language of thy turtle dove,
  Paired to thy swelling chord;
Sweeter with every grace endued,
The glory of thy gratitude,
  Respired unto the Lord.

LXXV

Strong is the horse upon his speed;
Strong in pursuit the rapid glede,†
  Which makes at once his game:
Strong the tall ostrich on the ground;
Strong through the turbulent profound
  Shoots xiphias* to his aim. sword-fish

LXXVI

Strong is the lion – like a coal
His eye-ball – like a bastion's mole†
  His chest against the foes:
Strong, the gier-eagle* on his sail, vulture
Strong against tide, th' enormous whale
  Emerges as he goes.

LXXVII

But stronger still, in earth and air,
And in the sea, the man of prayer;
  And far beneath the tide;
And in the seat to faith assigned,
Where ask is have, where seek is find,
  Where knock is open wide.

LXXVIII

Beauteous the fleet before the gale;
Beauteous the multitudes in mail,†
  Ranked arms and crested heads:
Beauteous the garden's umbrage mild,
Walk, water, meditated wild,
  And all the bloomy beds.

---

*glede* a bird of prey
*bastion's mole* tower's strong wall
*mail* soldiers' chain armour

### LXXIX

Beauteous the moon full on the lawn;
And beauteous, when the veil's withdrawn,
 The virgin to her spouse:
Beauteous the temple decked and filled,
When to the heaven of heavens they build
 Their heart-directed vows.

### LXXX

Beauteous, yea beauteous more than these,
The shepherd king† upon his knees,
 For his momentous trust;
With wish of infinite conceit,
For man, beast, mute,* the small and great, fish
 And prostrate dust to dust.

### LXXXI

Precious the bounteous widow's mite;
And precious, for extreme delight,
 The largess from the churl:
Precious the ruby's blushing blaze,
And alba's† blest imperial rays,
 And pure cerulean pearl.

### LXXXII

Precious the penitential tear;
And precious is the sigh sincere,
 Acceptable to God:
And precious are the winning flowers,
In gladsome Israel's feast of bowers,
 Bound on the hallowed sod.

### LXXXIII

More precious that diviner part
Of David, even the Lord's own heart,
 Great, beautiful, and new:
In all things where it was intent,
In all extremes, in each event,
 Proof – answering true to true.

*shepherd king* David himself (I Samuel 16.11) *alba* white stone from God (Revelation 2.17)

LXXXIV

Glorious the sun in mid career;
Glorious th' assembled fires appear;
  Glorious the comet's train:
Glorious the trumpet and alarm;
Glorious th' almighty stretched-out arm;
  Glorious th' enraptured main:

LXXXV

Glorious the northern lights astream;
Glorious the song, when God's the theme;
  Glorious the thunder's roar:
Glorious hosanna from the den;
Glorious the catholic* amen; universal
  Glorious the martyr's gore:

LXXXVI

Glorious – more glorious is the crown
Of Him that brought salvation down
  By meekness, called thy Son;
Thou at stupendous truth believed,
And now the matchless deed's achieved,
  DETERMINED, DARED, and DONE.

1763

# Adam Smith

1723–90

Smith was educated at Glasgow University and at Balliol College, Oxford. His academic and literary career, at the start of the Scottish Enlightenment's leadership of Europe, shows the range and versatility of learned men of the period. Having lectured on rhetoric and belles-lettres, he became Professor of Logic and then Moral Philosophy (1752) at Glasgow, and published his *Theory of Moral Sentiments* in 1759. Leaving his chair, he travelled as tutor to the Duke of Buccleuch on the Continent, where he developed his interest in political economy, later given its fullest expression in his major work *An Inquiry into the Nature and Causes of the Wealth of Nations* (1776). He wrote also on aesthetic topics, and was a member of Johnson's Club. In Smith's view, individual self-interests accumulate to the public benefit: here he demonstrates the value of the division of labour in an apparently simple manufacturing process.

## *From* THE WEALTH OF NATIONS

### *[The Division of Labour]*

The effects of the division of labour, in the general business of society, will be more easily understood by considering in what manner it operates in some particular manufactures. It is commonly supposed to be carried furthest in some very trifling ones; not perhaps that it really is carried further in them than in others of more importance: but in those trifling manufactures which are destined to supply the small wants of but a small number of people, the whole number of workmen must necessarily be small; and those employed in every different branch of the work can often be collected into the same workhouse, and placed at once under the view of the spectator. In those great manufactures, on the contrary, which are destined to supply the great wants of the great body of the people, every different branch of the work employs so great a number of workmen, that it is impossible to collect them all into the same workhouse. We can seldom see more, at one time, than those employed in one single branch. Though in such manufactures, therefore, the work may really be divided into a much greater number of parts, than in those of a more trifling nature, the division is not near so obvious, and has accordingly been much less observed.

To take an example, therefore, from a very trifling manufacture, but one in which the division of labour has been very often taken notice of, the trade of a pin-maker: a workman not educated to this business (which the division of labour has rendered a distinct trade), nor acquainted with the use of the machinery employed in it (to the invention of which the same division of labour has probably given occasion), could scarce, perhaps, with his utmost industry, make one pin a day, and certainly could not make twenty. But in the way in which this business is now carried on, not only the whole work is a peculiar trade, but it is divided into a number of branches, of which the greater part are likewise peculiar trades. One man draws out the wire; another straights it; a third cuts it; a fourth points it; a fifth grinds it at the top for receiving the head; to make the head requires two or three distinct operations; to put it on is a peculiar business; to whiten the pins is another; it is even a trade by itself to put them into the paper; and the important business of making a pin, is in this manner, divided into about eighteen distinct operations, which in some manufactories, are all performed by distinct hands though in others the same man will sometimes perform two or three of them. I have seen a small manufactory of this kind, where ten men only were employed, and where some of them consequently performed two or three distinct operations. But though they were very poor, and therefore but indifferently accommodated with the necessary machinery they could, when they exerted themselves, make among them about twelve pounds of pins a day. There are in a pound upwards of four thousand pins of a middling size. Those ten persons, therefore, could make among them upwards of forty-eight thousand pins in a day. Each person, therefore, making a tenth part of forty-eight thousand pins, might be considered as making four thousand eight hundred pins in a day. But if they had all wrought separately and independently, and without any of them having been educated to this pecular business, they certainly could not each of them have made twenty, perhaps not one pin a day; that is, certainly, not the two hundred and fortieth, perhaps not the four thousand eight hundredth, part of what they are at present capable of performing, in consequence of a proper division and combination of their different operations.

1776

# Sir Joshua Reynolds

## 1729–92

After study in Italy (1750–2), Reynolds quickly rose to profitable domination of English painting, especially of portraiture, to which he brought wide historical knowledge and the grand style. A leading member of the Johnson circle, he painted many of its celebrities. As first President of the Royal Academy he gave a series of *Discourses* (1769–90) on art and aesthetic theory, which had much in common with current literary criticism. William Blake offered a detailed refutation of his values in extensive annotations of the texts.

## *From* DISCOURSES ON ART, No. 3

### *[Nature and the Grand Style]*

The wish of the genuine painter must be more extensive: instead of endeavouring to amuse mankind with the minute neatness of his imitations, he must endeavour to improve them by the grandeur of his ideas; instead of seeking praise, by deceiving the superficial sense of the spectator, he must strive for fame, by captivating the imagination.

The principle now laid down, that the perfection of this art does not consist in mere imitation, is far from being new or singular. It is, indeed, supported by the general opinion of the enlightened part of mankind. The poets, orators, and rhetoricians of antiquity, are continually enforcing this position; that all the arts receive their perfection from an ideal beauty, superior to what is to be found in individual nature. They are ever referring to the practice of the painters and sculptors of their times, particularly Phidias† (the favourite artist of antiquity), to illustrate their assertions. As if they could not sufficiently express their admiration of his genius by what they knew, they have recourse to poetical enthusiasm. They call it inspiration; a gift from heaven. The artist is supposed to have ascended the celestial regions, to furnish his mind with this perfect idea of beauty. . . .

*Phidias* *c.* 490–448 BC; Greek sculptor

The Moderns are not less convinced than the Ancients of this superior power existing in the art; nor less sensible of its effects. Every language has adopted terms expressive of this excellence. The *gusto grande* of the Italians, the *beau ideal* of the French, and the *great style*, *genius* and *taste* among the English, are but different appellations of the same thing. It is this intellectual dignity, they say, that ennobles the painter's art; that lays the line between him and the mere mechanic; and produces those great effects in an instant, which eloquence and poetry, by slow and repeated efforts, are scarcely able to attain.

Such is the warmth with which both the Ancients and Moderns speak of this divine principle of the art; but, as I have formerly observed, enthusiastic admiration seldom promotes knowledge. Though a student by such praise may have his attention roused, and a desire excited, of running in this great career; yet it is possible that what has been said to excite, may only serve to deter him. He examines his own mind, and perceives there nothing of that divine inspiration, with which, he is told, so many others have been favoured. He never travelled to heaven to gather new ideas; and he finds himself possessed of no other qualifications than what mere common observation and a plain understanding can confer. Thus he becomes gloomy amidst the splendour of figurative declamation, and thinks it hopeless, to pursue an object which he supposes out of the reach of human industry.

But on this, as upon many other occasions, we ought to distinguish how much is to be given to enthusiasm, and how much to reason. We ought to allow for, and we ought to commend, that strength of vivid expression, which is necessary to convey, in its full force, the highest sense of the most complete effect of art; taking care at the same time, not to lose in terms of vague admiration, that solidity and truth of principle, upon which alone we can reason, and may be enabled to practise.

It is not easy to define in what this great style consists; nor to describe, by words, the proper means of acquiring it, if the mind of the student should be at all capable of such an acquisition. Could we teach taste or genius by rules, they would be no longer taste and genius. But though there neither are, nor can be, any precise invariable rules for the exercise, or the acquisition, of these great qualities, yet we may truly say that they always operate in proportion to our attention in observing the works of nature, to our skill in selecting, and to our care in digesting, methodising, and comparing our observations. There are many beauties in our art, that seem, at first, to lie without the reach of precept, and yet may easily be reduced to practical principles. Experience is all in all; but it is not every one who profits by experience; and most people err, not so much from want of capacity to find their object, as from not knowing what object to pursue. This great ideal perfection and beauty are not to be sought in the heavens, but upon the earth. They are about us, and upon every side of us. But the power of discovering what is deformed in nature, or in other words, what is particular and uncommon, can be acquired only by experience; and the whole beauty and grandeur of the art consists, in my opinion, in being able to get above all singular forms, local customs, particularities, and details of every kind.

All the objects which are exhibited to our view by nature, upon close examination will be found to have their blemishes and defects. The most beautiful forms have something about them like weakness, minuteness, or imperfection. But it is not every eye that perceives these blemishes. It must be an eye long used to the contemplation and comparison of these forms; and which, by a long habit of observing what any set of objects of the same kind have in common, has acquired the power of discerning what each wants in particular. This long laborious comparison should be the first study of the painter, who aims at the greatest style. By this means, he acquires a just idea of beautiful forms; he corrects nature by herself, her imperfect state by her more perfect. His eye being enabled to distinguish the accidental deficiencies, excrescences, and deformities of things, from their general figures, he makes out an abstract idea of their forms more perfect than any one original; and what may seem a paradox, he learns to design naturally by drawing his figures unlike to any one object. This idea of the perfect state of nature, which the artist calls the Ideal Beauty, is the great leading principle, by which works of genius are conducted. By this Phidias acquired his fame. He wrought upon a sober principle, what has so much excited the enthusiasm of the world; and by this method you, who have courage to tread the same path, may acquire equal reputation.

This is the idea which has acquired, and which seems to have a right to the epithet of *divine*; as it may be said to preside, like a supreme judge, over all the productions of nature; appearing to be possessed of the will and intention of the Creator, as far as they regard the external form of living beings. When a man once possesses this idea in its perfection, there is no danger, but that he will be sufficiently warmed by it himself, and be able to warm and ravish every one else.

Thus it is from a reiterated experience, and a close comparison of the objects in nature, that an artist becomes possessed of the idea of that central form, if I may so express it, from which every deviation is deformity. But the investigation of this form, I grant, is painful. . . .

1770

# *From* DISCOURSES ON ART, No. 7
## *[Nature and Taste]*

We will take it for granted, that reason is something invariable and fixed in the nature of things; and without endeavouring to go back to an account of first principles, which for ever will elude our search, we will conclude, that whatever goes under the name of taste, which we can fairly bring under the dominion of reason, must be considered as equally exempt from change. If therefore, in the course of this enquiry, we can show that there are rules for the conduct of the artist which are fixed and invariable, it follows of course, that the art of the connoisseur, or, in other words, taste, has likewise invariable principles.

Of the judgment which we make on the works of art, and the preference that we give to one class of art over another, if a reason be demanded, the question is perhaps evaded by answering, I judge from my taste; but it does not follow that a better answer cannot be given, though, for common gazers, this may be sufficient. Every man is not obliged to investigate the causes of his approbation or dislike.

The arts would lie open for ever to caprice and casualty, if those who are to judge of their excellencies had no settled principles by which they are to regulate their decisions, and the merit or defect of performances were to be determined by unguided fancy. And indeed we may venture to assert, that whatever speculative knowledge is necessary to the artist, is equally and indispensably necessary to the connoisseur.

The first idea that occurs in the consideration of what is fixed in art, or in taste, is that presiding principle of which I have so frequently spoken in former discourses – the general idea of nature. The beginning, the middle, and the end of every thing that is valuable in taste, is comprised in the knowledge of what is truly nature; for whatever notions are not conformable to those of nature, or universal opinion, must be considered as more or less capricious.

My notion of nature comprehends not only the forms which nature produces, but also the nature and internal fabric and organisation, as I may call it, of the human mind and imagination. The terms beauty, or nature, which are general ideas, are but different modes of expressing the same thing, whether we apply these terms to statues, poetry, or picture. Deformity is not nature, but an accidental deviation from her accustomed practice. This general idea therefore ought to be called Nature, and nothing else, correctly speaking, has a right to that name. But we are so far from speaking, in common conversation, with any such accuracy, that, on the contrary, when we criticise Rembrandt† and

*Rembrandt* 1609–69; Dutch painter

other Dutch painters, who introduced into their historical pictures exact representations of individual objects with all their imperfections, we say – though it is not in a good taste, yet it is nature.

This misapplication of terms must be very often perplexing to the young student. Is not art, he may say, an imitation of nature? Must he not therefore who imitates her with the greatest fidelity, be the best artist? By this mode of reasoning Rembrandt has a higher place than Raphael.† But a very little reflection will serve to show us that these particularities cannot be nature: for how can that be the nature of man, in which no two individuals are the same?

It plainly appears, that as a work is conducted under the influence of general ideas, or partial, it is principally to be considered as the effect of a good or bad taste.

As beauty therefore does not consist in taking what lies immediately before you, so neither, in our pursuit of taste, are those opinions which we first received and adopted, the best choice, or the most natural to the mind and imagination. In the infancy of our knowledge we seize with greediness the good that is within our reach; it is by after consideration, and in consequence of discipline, that we refuse the present for a greater good at a distance. The nobility or elevation of all arts, like the excellency of virtue itself, consists in adopting this enlarged and comprehensive idea; and all criticism built upon the more confined view of what is natural, may properly be called *shallow* criticism, rather than false: its defect is, that the truth is not sufficiently extensive. . . .

1776

## *From* DISCOURSES ON ART, No. 11

### *[Genius in Art]*

The highest ambition of every artist is to be thought a man of genius. As long as this flattering quality is joined to his name he can bear with patience the imputation of carelessness, incorrectness, or defects of whatever kind.

So far indeed is the presence of genius from implying an absence of faults, that they are considered by many as its inseparable companions. Some go such lengths as to take indications from them, and not only

*Raphael* 1483–1520; Italian Renaissance painter

excuse faults on account of genius, but presume genius from the existence of certain faults.

It is certainly true, that a work may justly claim the character of genius, though full of errors; and it is equally true, that it may be faultless, and yet not exhibit the least spark of genius. This naturally suggests an enquiry, a desire at least of enquiring, what qualities of a work and of a workman may justly entitle a painter to that character.

I have in a former discourse [3] endeavoured to impress you with a fixed opinion, that a comprehensive and critical knowledge of the works of nature is the only source of beauty and grandeur. But when we speak to painters we must always consider this rule, and all rules, with a reference to the mechanical practice of their own particular art. It is not properly in the learning, the taste, and the dignity of the ideas, that genius appears as belonging to a painter. There is a genius particular and appropriated to his own trade (as I may call it), distinguished from all others. For that power, which enables the artist to conceive his subject with dignity, may be said to belong to general education; and is as much the genius of a poet, or the professor of any other liberal art, or even a good critic in any of those arts, as of a painter. Whatever sublime ideas may fill his mind, he is a painter only as he can put in practice what he knows, and communicate those ideas by visible representation.

If my expression can convey my idea, I wish to distinguish excellence of this kind by calling it the genius of mechanical performance. This genius consists, I conceive, in the power of expressing that which employs your pencil, whatever it may be, *as a whole*; so that the general effect and power of the whole may take possession of the mind, and for a while suspend the consideration of the subordinate and particular beauties or defects.

The advantage of this method of considering objects is what I wish now more particularly to enforce. At the same time I do not forget that a painter must have the power of contracting as well as dilating his sight; because he that does not at all express particulars, expresses nothing; yet it is certain, that a nice discrimination of minute circumstances, and a punctilious delineation of them, whatever excellence it may have (and I do not mean to detract from it), never did confer on the artist the character of genius.

Beside those minute differences in things which are frequently not observed at all, and, when they are, make little impression, there are in all considerable objects great characteristic distinctions, which press strongly on the senses, and therefore fix the imagination. These are by no means, as some persons think, an aggregate of all the small discriminating particulars; nor will such an accumulation of particulars ever express them. These answer to what I have heard great lawyers call the leading points in a case, or the leading cases relative to those points.

The detail of particulars, which does not assist the expression of the main characteristic, is worse than useless, it is mischievous, as it dissipates the attention, and draws it from the principal point. It may be remarked, that the impression which is left on our mind, even of things which are familiar to us, is seldom more than their general effect; beyond which we do not look in recognising such objects. To express this in painting, is to express what is congenial and natural to the mind of man, and what gives him by reflection his own mode of conceiving. The other presupposes *nicety* and *research*, which are only the business of the curious and attentive, and therefore does not speak to the general sense of the whole species; in which common, and, as I may so call it, mother tongue, every thing grand and comprehensive must be uttered.

I do not mean to prescribe what degree of attention ought to be paid to the minute parts; this it is hard to settle. We are sure that it is expressing the general effect of the whole which alone can give to objects their true and touching character; and wherever this is observed, whatever else may be neglected, we acknowledge the hand of a master. We may even go further, and observe, that when the general effect only is presented to us by a skilful hand, it appears to express the object represented in a more lively manner than the minutest resemblance would do. . . .

1782

# Edmund Burke

1729–97

Educated at Trinity College, Dublin, Burke came to London for a law career. He became an MP in 1765, and had a great reputation as an orator (speeches before and on the American war; on India; like Sheridan, he spoke in the impeachment of Warren Hastings). He supported liberal causes (Catholic emancipation; abolition of the slave trade) but criticised violent social change in *Reflections on the Revolution in France* (1790), his best-known political work. His literary interests appear in his friendships, as founder-member of Johnson's Club, in his help of Crabbe, in his work for the *Annual Register* (which published poetry as well as records of events), and in his *Philosophical Enquiry into the Origin of our Ideas of the Sublime and Beautiful* (1757). This major work of aesthetic theory explores the literary value of vastness, obscurity, terror; it extended the debate about *Paradise Lost*, and provided a critical background for the novelties of such works as Gray's Odes and the Gothic novel. As opposed to the lofty, emotional sublime, the beautiful is seen as small and highly-finished.

## *From* PHILOSOPHICAL ENQUIRY INTO THE ORIGIN OF OUR IDEAS OF THE SUBLIME AND BEAUTIFUL

### Part I SECTION VII Of the SUBLIME

Whatever is fitted in any sort to excite the ideas of pain, and danger, that is to say, whatever is in any sort terrible, or is conversant about terrible objects, or operates in a manner analogous to terror, is a source of the *sublime*; that is, it is productive of the strongest emotion which the mind is capable of feeling. I say the strongest emotion, because I am satisfied the ideas of pain are much more powerful than those which enter on the part of pleasure. . . .

When danger or pain press too nearly, they are incapable of giving any delight, and are simply terrible; but at certain distances, and with certain modifications, they may be, and they are delightful, as we every day experience. The cause of this I shall endeavour to investigate hereafter.

## *[Terror, Obscurity, Power]*

### Part II SECTION I Of the passion caused by the SUBLIME

The passion caused by the great and sublime in *nature*, when those causes operate most powerfully, is Astonishment; and astonishment is that state of the soul, in which all its motions are suspended, with some degree of horror. In this case the mind is so entirely filled with its object, that it cannot entertain any other, nor by consequence reason on that object which employs it. Hence arises the great power of the sublime, that far from being produced by them, it anticipates our reasonings, and hurries us on by an irresistible force. Astonishment, as I have said, is the effect of the sublime in its highest degree; the inferior effects are admiration, reverence and respect.

### SECTION II TERROR

No passion so effectually robs the mind of all its powers of acting and reasoning as fear. For fear being an apprehension of pain or death, it operates in a manner that resembles actual pain. Whatever therefore is terrible, with regard to sight, is sublime too, whether this cause of terror, be endued with greatness of dimensions or not; for it is impossible to look on any thing as trifling, or contemptible, that may be dangerous. There are many animals, who though far from being large, are yet capable of raising ideas of the sublime, because they are considered as objects of terror. As serpents and poisonous animals of almost all kinds. And to things of great dimensions, if we annex an adventitious idea of terror, they become without comparison greater. A level plain of a vast extent on land, is certainly no mean idea; the prospect of such a plain may be as extensive as a prospect of the ocean; but can it ever fill the mind with any thing so great as the ocean itself? This is owing to several causes, but it is owing to none more than this, that the ocean is an object of no small terror. Indeed terror is in all cases whatsoever, either more openly or latently the ruling principle of the sublime. . .

### SECTION III OBSCURITY

To make any thing very terrible, obscurity seems in general to be necessary. When we know the full extent of any danger, when we can accustom our eyes to it, a great deal of the apprehension vanishes. Every one will be sensible of this, who considers how greatly night adds to our dread, in all cases of danger, and how much the notions of ghosts and goblins, of which none can form clear ideas, affect minds, which give credit to the popular tales concerning such sorts of beings. Those despotic governments, which are founded on the passions of men, and principally upon the passion of fear, keep their chief as much as may be from the public eye. The policy has been the same in many cases of religion. Almost all the heathen temples were dark. Even in the barbarous temples of the Americans at this day, they keep their idol in a dark part of the hut, which is consecrated to his worship. For this purpose too the druids performed all their ceremonies in the bosom of the darkest woods, and in the shade of the oldest and most spreading oaks. No person seems better to have understood the secret of heightening, or of setting terrible things, if I may use the expression, in their strongest light by the force of a judicious obscurity, than Milton. His description† of Death in the second book is admirably studied; it is astonishing with what a gloomy pomp, with what a significant and expressive uncertainty of strokes and colouring he has finished the portrait of the king of terrors.

The other shape,
If shape it might be called that shape had none
Distinguishable, in member, joint, or limb;
Or substance might be called that shadow seemed,
For each seemed either; black he stood as night;
Fierce as ten furies; terrible as hell;
And shook a deadly dart. What seemed his head
The likeness of a kingly crown had on.

In this description† all is dark, uncertain, confused, terrible, and sublime to the last degree.

## SECTION IV Of the difference between CLEARNESS and OBSCURITY with regard to the passions

It is one thing to make an idea clear, and another to make it *affecting* to the imagination. If I make a drawing of a palace, or a temple, or a landscape, I present a very clear idea of those objects; but then (allowing for the effect of imitation which is something) my picture can at most affect only as the palace, temple, or landscape would have affected in the reality. On the other hand, the most lively and spirited verbal

*description* *Paradise Lost*, II.666–73

description I can give, raises a very obscure and imperfect *idea* of such objects; but then it is in my power to raise a stronger *emotion* by the description than I could do by the best painting. This experience constantly evinces. The proper manner of conveying the *affections* of the mind from one to another, is by words; there is a great insufficiency in all other methods of communication; and so far is a clearness of imagery from being absolutely necessary to an influence upon the passions, that they may be considerably operated upon without presenting any image at all, by certain sounds adapted to that purpose; of which we have a sufficient proof in the acknowledged and powerful effects of instrumental music. In reality a great clearness helps but little towards affecting the passions, as it is in some sort an enemy to all enthusiasms whatsoever. . . .

Among the common sort of people, I never could perceive that painting had much influence on their passions. It is true that the best sorts of painting, as well as the best sorts of poetry, are not much understood in that sphere. But it is most certain, that their passions are very strongly roused by a fanatic preacher, or by the ballads† of Chevy Chase, or the children in the wood, and by other little popular poems and tales that are current in that rank of life. I do not know of any paintings, bad or good, that produce the same effect. So that poetry with all its obscurity, has a more general as well as a more powerful dominion over the passions than the other art. And I think there are reasons in nature why the obscure idea, when properly conveyed, should be more affecting than the clear. It is our ignorance of things that causes all our admiration, and chiefly excites our passions. Knowledge and acquaintance make the most striking causes affect but little. It is thus with the vulgar, and all men are as the vulgar in what they do not understand. The ideas of eternity, and infinity, are among the most affecting we have, and yet perhaps there is nothing of which we really understand so little, as of infinity and eternity. We do not any where meet a more sublime description than this justly celebrated one of Milton, wherein he gives the portrait† of Satan with a dignity so suitable to the subject.

He above the rest
In shape and gesture proudly eminent
Stood like a tower; his form had yet not lost
All her original brightness, nor appeared
Less than archangel ruin'd, and th' excess
Of glory obscured: as when the sun new ris'n
Looks through the horizontal misty air
Shorn of his beams; or from behind the moon

*ballads* see Addison's *Spectator* 70 *portrait* *PL*, I.589–99

In dim eclipse disastrous twilight sheds
On half the nations; and with fear of change
Perplexes monarchs.

Here is a very noble picture; and in what does this poetical picture consist? in images of a tower, an archangel, the sun rising through mists, or in an eclipse, the ruin of monarchs, and the revolutions of kingdoms. The mind is hurried out of itself, by a crowd of great and confused images; which affect because they are crowded and confused. For separate them, and you lose much of the greatness, and join them, and you infallibly lose the clearness. The images raised by poetry are always of this obscure kind; though in general the effects of poetry are by no means to be attributed to the images it raises; which point we shall examine more at large hereafter. But painting, when we have allowed for the pleasure of imitation, can only affect simply by the images it presents; and even in painting a judicious obscurity in some things contributes to the effect of the picture; because the images in painting are exactly similar to those in nature; and in nature dark, confused, uncertain images have a greater power on the fancy to form the grander passions than those have which are more clear and determinate. . . .

I am sensible that this idea has met with opposition,† and is likely still to be rejected by several. But let it be considered that hardly any thing can strike the mind with its greatness, which does not make some sort of approach towards infinity; which nothing can do whilst we are able to perceive its bounds; but to see an object distinctly, and to perceive its bounds, is one and the same thing. A clear idea is therefore another name for a little idea. There is a passage in the book of Job† amazingly sublime, and this sublimity is principally due to the terrible uncertainty of the thing described. *In thoughts from the visions of the night, when deep sleep falleth upon men, fear came upon me and trembling, which made all my bones to shake. Then a spirit passed before my face. The hair of my flesh stood up. It stood still*, but I could not discern the form thereof; *an image was before mine eyes; there was silence; and I heard a voice, – Shall mortal man be more just than God?* We are first prepared with the utmost solemnity for the vision; we are first terrified, before we are let even into the obscure cause of our emotion; but when this grand cause of terror makes its appearance, what is it? is it not, wrapt up in the shades of its own incomprehensible darkness, more awful, more striking, more terrible, than the liveliest description, than the clearest painting could possible represent it? . . .

---

*opposition* to the first edition *Job* 4.13–17

## SECTION V POWER

Besides these things which *directly* suggest the idea of danger, and those which produce a similar effect from a mechanical cause, I know of nothing sublime which is not some modification of power. And this branch rises as naturally as the other two branches, from terror, the common stock of every thing that is sublime. The idea of power at first view seems of the class of these indifferent ones, which may equally belong to pain or to pleasure. But in reality, the affection arising from the idea of vast power, is extremely remote from that neutral character. For first, we must remember, that the idea of pain, in its highest degree, is much stronger than the highest degree of pleasure; and that it preserves the same superiority through all the subordinate gradations. From hence it is, that where the chances for equal degrees of suffering or enjoyment are in any sort equal, the idea of the suffering must always be prevalent. And indeed the ideas of pain, and above all of death, are so very affecting, that whilst we remain in the presence of whatever is supposed to have the power of inflicting either, it is impossible to be perfectly free from terror. Again, we know by experience, that for the enjoyment of pleasure, no great efforts of power are at all necessary; nay we know, that such efforts would go a great way towards destroying our satisfaction: for pleasure must be stolen, and not forced upon us; pleasure follows the will; and therefore we are generally affected with it by many things of a force greatly inferior to our own. But pain is always inflicted by a power in some way superior, because we never submit to pain willingly. So that strength, violence, pain and terror, are ideas that rush in upon the mind together. . . .

Let us look at another strong animal in the two distinct lights in which we may consider him. The horse in the light of an useful beast, fit for the plough, the road, the draught, in every social useful light the horse has nothing of the sublime; but is it thus that we are affected with him, *whose neck*[†] *is clothed with thunder, the glory of whose nostrils is terrible, who swalloweth the ground with fierceness and rage, neither believeth that it is the sound of the trumpet?* In this description the useful character of the horse entirely disappears, and the terrible and sublime blaze out together. We have continually about us animals of a strength that is considerable, but not pernicious. Amongst these we never look for the sublime: it comes upon us in the gloomy forest, and in the howling wilderness, in the form of the lion, the tiger, the panther, or rhinoceros. Whenever strength is only useful, and employed for our benefit or our pleasure, then it is never sublime; for nothing can act agreeably to us, that does not act in conformity to our will; but

*whose neck* Job 39

to act agreeably to our will, it must be subject to us; and therefore can never be the cause of a grand and commanding conception. The description of the wild ass, in Job, is worked up into no small sublimity, merely by insisting on his freedom, and his setting mankind at defiance; otherwise the description of such an animal could have had nothing noble in it. . . .

## SECTION VII VASTNESS

Greatness of dimension, is a powerful cause of the sublime. This is too evident, and the observation too common, to need any illustration; it is not so common, to consider in what ways greatness of dimension, vastness of extent, or quantity, has the most striking effect. For certainly, there are ways, and modes, wherein the same quantity of extension shall produce greater effects than it is found to do in others. Extension is either in length, height, or depth. Of these the length strikes least; an hundred yards of even ground will never work such an effect as a tower an hundred yards high, or a rock or mountain of that altitude. I am apt to imagine likewise, that height is less grand than depth; and that we are more struck at looking down from a precipice, than at looking up at an object of equal height, but of that I am not very positive. A perpendicular has more force in forming the sublime, than an inclined plane; and the effects of a rugged and broken surface seem stronger than where it is smooth and polished. . . . However, it may not be amiss to add to these remarks upon magnitude; that, as the great extreme of dimension is sublime, so the last extreme of littleness is in some measure sublime likewise; when we attend to the infinite divisibility of matter, when we pursue animal life into these excessively small, and yet organised beings, that escape the nicest inquisition of the sense, when we push our discoveries yet downward, and consider those creatures so many degrees yet smaller, and the still diminishing scale of existence, in tracing which the imagination is lost as well as the sense, we become amazed and confounded at the wonders of minuteness; nor can we distinguish in its effect this extreme of littleness from the vast itself. For division must be infinite as well as addition; because the idea of a perfect unity can no more be arrived at, than that of a complete whole to which nothing may be added.

## SECTION VIII INFINITY

Another source of the sublime, is *infinity*; if it does not rather belong to the last. Infinity has a tendency to fill the mind with that sort of delightful horror, which is the most genuine effect, and truest test of the sublime. There are scarce any things which can become the objects of our senses that are really, and in their own nature infinite. But the eye not being able to perceive the bounds of many things, they seem to be infinite, and they produce the same effects as if they were really so. We are deceived in the like manner, if the parts of some large object are so continued to any indefinite number, that the imagination meets no check which may hinder its extending them at pleasure.

Whenever we repeat any idea frequently, the mind by a sort of mechanism repeats it long after the first cause has ceased to operate. After whirling about; when we sit down, the objects about us still seem to whirl. After a long succession of noises, as the fall of waters, or the beating of forge hammers, the hammers beat and the water roars in the imagination long after the first sounds have ceased to affect it; and they die away at last by gradations which are scarcely perceptible. . . .

## SECTION XII DIFFICULTY

Another source of greatness is *Difficulty*. When any work seems to have required immense force and labour to effect it, the idea is grand. Stonehenge, neither for disposition nor ornament, has any thing admirable; but those huge rude masses of stone, set on end, and piled each on other, turn the mind on the immense force necessary for such a work. Nay the rudeness of the work increases this cause of grandeur, as it excludes the idea of art, and contrivance; for dexterity produces another sort of effect which is different enough from this. . . .

## SECTION XIV LIGHT

. . . Darkness is more productive of sublime ideas than light. Our great poet† was convinced of this; and indeed so full was he of this idea, so entirely possessed with the power of a well managed darkness, that, in describing the appearance of the Deity, amidst that profusion of magnificent images, which the grandeur of his subject provokes him to pour out upon every side, he is far from forgetting the obscurity which surrounds the most incomprehensible of all beings, but

– – With the majesty of *darkness* round
Circles his throne.

And what is no less remarkable, our author had the secret of preserving this idea, even when he seemed to depart the farthest from it, when he describes the light and glory which flows from the divine presence; a light which by its very excess is converted into a species of darkness,

---

*great poet* in *Paradise Lost*, II.266–7; III.380

*Dark* with excessive *light* thy skirts appear.

Here is an idea not only poetical in an high degree, but strictly and philosophically just. . . .

## Part III SECTION XXVII The SUBLIME and BEAUTIFUL compared

On closing this general view of beauty, it naturally occurs, that we should compare it with the sublime; and in this comparison there appears a remarkable contrast. For sublime objects are vast in their dimensions, beautiful ones comparatively small; beauty should be smooth, and polished; the great, rugged and negligent; beauty should shun the right line, yet deviate from it insensibly; the great in many cases loves the right line, and when it deviates, it often makes a strong deviation; beauty should not be obscure; the great ought to be dark and gloomy; beauty should be light and delicate; the great ought to be solid, and even massive. They are indeed ideas of a very different nature, one being founded on pain, the other on pleasure; and however they may vary afterwards from the direct nature of their causes, yet these causes keep up an eternal distinction between them, a distinction never to be forgotten by any whose business it is to affect the passions. In the infinite variety of natural combinations we must expect to find the qualities of things the most remote imaginable from each other united in the same object. We must expect also to find combinations of the same kind in the works of art. But when we consider the power of an object upon our passions, we must know that when any thing is intended to affect the mind by the force of some predominant property, the affection produced is like to be the more uniform and perfect, if all the other properties or qualities of the object be of the same nature, and tending to the same design as the principal;

If black, and white blend, soften, and unite,
A thousand ways, are there no black and white?†

If the qualities of the sublime and beautiful are sometimes found united, does this prove, that they are the same, does it prove, that they are any way allied, does it prove even that they are not opposite and contradictory? Black and white may soften, may blend, but they are not therefore the same. Nor when they are so softened and blended with each other, or with different colours, is the power of black as black, or of white as white, so strong as when each stands uniform and distinguished.

*If black . . . white* Pope, *Essay on Man,* II.213–14

## *[Reality, Words, Passions]*

### Part V SECTION V

. . . In reality poetry and rhetoric do not succeed in exact description so well as painting does; their business is to affect rather by sympathy than imitation; to display rather the effect of things on the mind of the speaker, or of others, than to present a clear idea of the things themselves. This is their most extensive province, and that in which they succeed the best.

### SECTION VI POETRY not strictly an imitative art

Hence we may observe that poetry, taken in its most general sense, cannot with strict propriety be called an art of imitation. It is indeed an imitation so far as it describes the manners and passions of men which their words can express . . . There it is strictly imitation; and all merely *dramatic* poetry is of this sort. But *descriptive* poetry operates chiefly by *substitution*; by the means of sounds, which by custom have the effect of realities. Nothing is an imitation further than as it resembles some other thing; and words undoubtedly have no sort of resemblance to the ideas for which they stand.

### SECTION VII How WORDS influence the passions

Now, as words affect, not by any original power, but by representation, it might be supposed, that their influence over the passions should be but light; yet it is quite otherwise; for we find by experience that eloquence and poetry are as capable, nay indeed much more capable of making deep and lively impressions than any other arts, and even than nature itself in very many cases. And this arises chiefly from these three causes. First, that we take an extraordinary part in the passions of others, and that we are easily affected and brought into sympathy by any tokens which are shewn of them; and there are no tokens which can express all the circumstances of most passions so fully as words; so that if a person speaks upon any subject, he can not only convey the subject to you, but likewise the manner in which he is himself affected by it. Certain it is, that the influence of most things on our passions is not so much from the things themselves, as from our opinions concerning them; and these again depend very much on the opinions of other men, conveyable for the most part by words only. Secondly; there are many things of a very affecting nature, which can seldom occur in the reality, but the words which represent them often do; and thus they have an opportunity of making a deep impression and taking root in the mind, whilst the idea of the reality was transient; and to some perhaps never really occurred in any shape, to whom it is notwithstanding very affecting, as war, death, famine, &c. Besides, many ideas have never been at all presented to the senses of any men but by words, as God, angels, devils, heaven and hell, all of which have however a great influence over the passions. Thirdly; by words we have it in our power to make such *combinations* as we cannot possibly do otherwise. By this power of combining we are able, by the addition of well-chosen circumstances, to give a new life and force to the simple object. In painting we may represent any fine figure we please; but we never can give it those enlivening touches which it may receive from words. To represent an angel in a picture, you can only draw a beautiful young man winged; but what painting can furnish out any thing so grand as the addition of one word, "the angel of the *Lord?*" It is true, I have here no clear idea, but these words affect the mind more than the sensible image did, which is all I contend for. . . .

As a further instance, let us consider those lines of Milton,[†] where he describes the travels of the fallen angels through their dismal habitation,

> ---- O'er many a dark and dreary vale
> They pass'd, and many a region dolorous;
> O'er many a frozen, many a fiery Alp;
> Rock, caves, lakes, fens, bogs, dens and shades of death,
> A universe of death.

Here is displayed the force of union in

> Rocks, caves, lakes, dens, bogs, fens and shades;

which yet would lose the greatest part of their effect, if they were not the

> Rocks, caves, lakes, dens, bogs, fens and shades ----
> ---- of *Death*.

This idea or this affection caused by a word, which nothing but a word could annex to the others, raises a very great degree of the sublime; and this sublime is raised yet higher by what follows, a '*universe of Death*.' Here are again two ideas not presentable but by language; and an union of them great and amazing beyond conception; if they may properly be called ideas which present no distinct image to the mind; – but still it will be difficult to conceive how words can move the passions which belong to real objects, without representing these objects clearly. This is difficult to us, because we do not sufficiently distinguish, in our observations upon language, between a clear expression, and a strong

*Milton* *Paradise Lost*, II.618–22

expression. These are frequently confounded with each other, though they are in reality extremely different. The former regards the understanding; the latter belongs to the passions. The one describes a thing as it is; the other describes it as it is felt. Now, as there is a moving tone of voice, an impassioned countenance, an agitated gesture, which affect independently of the things about which they are exerted, so there are words, and certain dispositions of words, which being peculiarly devoted to passionate subjects, and always used by those who are under the influence of any passion; they touch and move us more than those which far more clearly and distinctly express the subject matter. We yield to sympathy, what we refuse to description. . . .

1756–7

# Oliver Goldsmith

## *c.* 1730–74

Goldsmith was born in Ireland, and educated at Trinity College, Dublin, and in Edinburgh, before wandering on the continent in the mid-1750s. Despite his medical studies, he had to support himself in London by voluminous literary hack-work: reviews, histories, biographies (*Life of Nash*, 1762). The famous *Chinese Letters* republished as *The Citizen of the World* (1762) are satirical essays describing English life and characters. His short novel *The Vicar of Wakefield* (1766) tests a simple clergyman and father in a corrupt world. Two 'laughing comedies', *The Good-Natured Man* (1768) and *She Stoops to Conquer* (1773), reacted against the sentimental vogue, and are still performed. A man of wide knowledge, Goldsmith was a member of Johnson's prestigious Club, and encouraged by leading members. His major poems, *The Traveller* (1764) and *The Deserted Village* (1770), develop the form of the heroic couplet. His 'Auburn' may combine childhood memories of Ireland with observations of English rural depopulation arising from recent economic and moral change: the money-making and private pleasure associated with great estates seemed to force out the traditional peasantry.

## AN ELEGY ON THE DEATH OF A MAD DOG

Good people all, of every sort,
    Give ear unto my song;
And if you find it wonderous short,
    It cannot hold you long.

In Islington there was a man,
    Of whom the world might say
That still a godly race he ran,
    Whene'er he went to pray.

A kind and gentle heart he had,
To comfort friends and foes;
The naked every day he clad,
When he put on his clothes.

And in that town a dog was found,
As many dogs there be,
Both mongrel, puppy, whelp and hound,
And curs of low degree.

This dog and man at first were friends;
But when a pique began,
The dog, to gain some private ends,
Went mad and bit the man.

Around from all the neighbouring streets
The wondering neighbours ran,
And swore the dog had lost his wits,
To bite so good a man.

The wound it seemed both sore and sad
To every Christian eye;
And while they swore the dog was mad,
They swore the man would die.

But soon a wonder came to light,
That showed the rogues they lied:
The man recovered of the bite,
The dog it was that died.

1766

## [SONG]

When lovely woman stoops to folly,
And finds too late that men betray,
What charm can soothe her melancholy,
What art can wash her guilt away?

The only art her guilt to cover,
To hide her shame from every eye,
To give repentance to her lover,
And wring his bosom – is to die.

1766

# THE DESERTED VILLAGE

Sweet Auburn, loveliest village of the plain,
Where health and plenty cheered the labouring swain,
Where smiling spring its earliest visit paid,
And parting summer's lingering blooms delayed;
Dear lovely bowers of innocence and ease,
Seats of my youth, when every sport could please,
How often have I loitered o'er thy green,
Where humble happiness endeared each scene;
How often have I paused on every charm,
The sheltered cot,* the cultivated farm, cottage
The never-failing brook, the busy mill,
The decent† church that topped the neighbouring hill,
The hawthorn bush, with seats beneath the shade,
For talking age and whispering lovers made.
How often have I blessed the coming day,
When toil remitting lent its turn to play,
And all the village train, from labour free,
Led up their sports beneath the spreading tree,
While many a pastime circled in the shade,
The young contending as the old surveyed;
And many a gambol frolicked o'er the ground,
And sleights of art and feats of strength went round.
And still as each repeated pleasure tired,
Succeeding sports the mirthful band inspired;
The dancing pair that simply sought renown
By holding out to tire each other down;
The swain mistrustless of his smutted face,
While secret laughter tittered round the place;
The bashful virgin's sidelong looks of love,
The matron's glance that would those looks reprove.
These were thy charms, sweet village; sports like these,
With sweet succession, taught even toil to please;
These round thy bowers their cheerful influence shed,
These were thy charms – but all these charms are fled.
Sweet smiling village, loveliest of the lawn,†
Thy sports are fled and all thy charms withdrawn;
Amidst thy bowers the tyrant's hand is seen,
And desolation saddens all thy green:

*decent* suitable, in harmony
*lawn* plain, as in 1.1. It is now only part-cultivated (l.40)

One only master grasps the whole domain,
And half a tillage stints thy smiling plain;
No more thy glassy brook reflects the day,
But, choked with sedges, works its weedy way.
Along thy glades, a solitary guest,
The hollow-sounding bittern guards its nest;
Amidst thy desert walks the lapwing flies,
And tires their echoes with unvaried cries.
Sunk are thy bowers in shapeless ruin all,
And the long grass o'ertops the mouldering wall;
And trembling, shrinking from the spoiler's hand,
Far, far away, thy children leave the land.
Ill fares the land, to hastening ills a prey,
Where wealth accumulates and men decay;
Princes and lords may flourish or may fade;
A breath can make them, as a breath has made;
But a bold peasantry, their country's pride,
When once destroyed, can never be supplied.
A time there was, ere England's griefs began,
When every rood† of ground maintained its man;
For him light labour spread her wholesome store,
Just gave what life required, but gave no more.
His best companions, innocence and health;
And his best riches, ignorance of wealth.
But times are altered; trade's unfeeling train
Usurp the land and dispossess the swain;
Along the lawn, where scattered hamlets rose,
Unwieldy wealth and cumbrous pomp repose;
And every want to opulence allied,
And every pang that folly pays to pride.
These gentle hours that plenty bade to bloom,
Those calm desires that asked but little room,
Those healthful sports that graced the peaceful scene,
Lived in each look and brightened all the green;
These, far departing, seek a kinder shore,
And rural mirth and manners are no more.
Sweet Auburn! parent of the blissful hour,
Thy glades forlorn confess the tyrant's power.
Here as I take my solitary rounds,
Amidst thy tangling walks and ruined grounds,
And, many a year elapsed, return to view
Where once the cottage stood, the hawthorn grew,

*rood* traditional land-measurement

Remembrance wakes with all her busy train,
Swells at my breast, and turns the past to pain.
In all my wanderings round this world of care,
In all my griefs – and God has given my share –
I still had hopes my latest hours to crown,
Amidst these humble bowers to lay me down;
To husband out life's taper at the close,
And keep the flame from wasting by repose.
I still had hopes, for pride attends us still,
Amidst the swains to show my book-learned skill,
Around my fire an evening group to draw,
And tell of all I felt, and all I saw;
And, as an hare, whom hounds and horns pursue,
Pants to the place from whence at first she flew,
I still had hopes, my long vexations past,
Here to return – and die at home at last.
O blest retirement, friend to life's decline,
Retreats from care that never must be mine,
How happy he who crowns in shades like these
A youth of labour with an age of ease;
Who quits a world where strong temptations try,
And, since 'tis hard to combat, learns to fly.
For him no wretches, born to work and weep,
Explore the mine or tempt the dangerous deep;
No surly porter stands in guilty state
To spurn imploring famine from the gate;
But on he moves to meet his latter end,
Angels around befriending virtue's friend;
Bends to the grave with unperceived decay,
While resignation gently slopes the way;
And, all his prospects brightening to the last,
His heaven commences ere the world be past!
Sweet was the sound when oft at evening's close
Up yonder hill the village murmur rose;
There as I passed with careless steps and slow,
The mingling notes came softened from below;
The swain responsive as the milkmaid sung,
The sober herd that lowed to meet their young;
The noisy geese that gabbled o'er the pool,
The playful children just let loose from school;
The watchdog's voice that bayed the whispering wind,
And the loud laugh that spoke the vacant mind;
These all in sweet confusion sought the shade,
And filled each pause the nightingale had made.

But now the sounds of population fail,
No cheerful murmurs fluctuate in the gale,
No busy steps the grass-grown foot-way tread,
For all the bloomy flush of life is fled.
All but yon widowed, solitary thing
That feebly bends beside the plashy spring;
She, wretched matron, forced, in age, for bread,
To strip the brook with mantling† cresses spread,
To pick her wintry faggot from the thorn,
To seek her nightly shed and weep till morn;
She only left of all the harmless train,
The sad historian of the pensive plain.
  Near yonder copse, where once the garden smiled,
And still where many a garden flower grows wild;
There, where a few torn shrubs the place disclose,
The village preacher's modest mansion rose.
A man he was to all the country dear,
And passing rich with forty pounds a year;
Remote from towns he ran his godly race,
Nor e'er had changed, nor wished to change, his place;†
Unpractised he to fawn, or seek for power,
By doctrines fashioned to the varying hour;
Far other aims his heart had learned to prize,
More skilled to raise the wretched than to rise.
His house was known to all the vagrant train,
He chid their wanderings, but relieved their pain;
The long-remembered beggar was his guest,
Whose beard descending swept his aged breast;
The ruined spendthrift, now no longer proud,
Claimed kindred there and had his claims allowed;
The broken soldier, kindly bade to stay,
Sat by his fire and talked the night away;
Wept o'er his wounds, or tales of sorrow done,
Shouldered his crutch and showed how fields were won.
Pleased with his guests, the good man learned to glow,
And quite forgot their vices in their woe;
Careless their merits or their faults to scan,
His pity gave ere charity began.
  Thus to relieve the wretched was his pride,
And even his failings leaned to virtue's side;

*mantling* covering; in l.248, it means 'frothing'

*place* appointment; ll.145–6 refer to the influence of lay patrons of church livings

But in his duty prompt at every call,
He watched and wept, he prayed and felt, for all.
And, as a bird each fond endearment tries
To tempt its new-fledged offspring to the skies,
He tried each art, reproved each dull delay,
Allured to brighter worlds, and led the way.
    Beside the bed where parting life was laid,
And sorrow, guilt, and pain by turns dismayed,
The reverend champion stood. At his control,
Despair and anguish fled the struggling soul;
Comfort came down the trembling wretch to raise,
And his last faltering accents whispered praise.
    At church, with meek and unaffected grace,
His looks adorned the venerable place;
Truth from his lips prevailed with double sway,
And fools, who came to scoff, remained to pray.
The service past, around the pious man,
With steady zeal each honest rustic ran;
Even children followed with endearing wile,
And plucked his gown, to share the good man's smile.
His ready smile a parent's warmth expressed,
Their welfare pleased him and their cares distressed;
To them his heart, his love, his griefs were given,
But all his serious thoughts had rest in heaven.
As some tall cliff, that lifts its awful form,
Swells from the vale, and midway leaves the storm,
Though round its breast the rolling clouds are spread,
Eternal sunshine settles on its head.
    Beside yon straggling fence that skirts the way,
With blossomed furze† unprofitably gay,
There, in his noisy mansion, skilled to rule,
The village master taught his little school;
A man severe he was and stern to view;
I knew him well, and every truant knew;
Well had the boding tremblers learned to trace
The day's disasters in his morning face;
Full well they laughed with counterfeited glee
At all his jokes, for many a joke had he;
Full well the busy whisper, circling round,
Conveyed the dismal tidings when he frowned;
Yet he was kind or, if severe in aught,
The love he bore to learning was in fault;

*furze* gorse, grown here for pleasure, not profit

The village all declared how much he knew;
'Twas certain he could write and cipher* too; calculate
Lands he could measure, terms and tides† presage,
And even the story ran that he could gauge.†
In arguing too, the parson owned his skill,
For even though vanquished, he could argue still;
While words of learned length and thundering sound
Amazed the gazing rustics ranged around,
And still they gazed, and still the wonder grew,
That one small head could carry all he knew.
  But past is all his fame. The very spot
Where many a time he triumphed is forgot.
Near yonder thorn, that lifts its head on high,
Where once the signpost caught the passing eye,
Low lies that house† where nutbrown draughts† inspired,
Where greybeard mirth and smiling toil retired,
Where village statesmen talked with looks profound,
And news much older than their ale went round.
Imagination fondly stoops to trace
The parlour splendours of that festive place;
The white-washed wall, the nicely-sanded floor,
The varnished clock that clicked behind the door;
The chest contrived a double debt to pay,
A bed by night, a chest of drawers by day;
The pictures placed for ornament and use,
The twelve good rules,† the royal game of goose,†
The hearth, except when winter chilled the day,
With aspen boughs and flowers and fennel gay;
While broken teacups, wisely kept for show,
Ranged o'er the chimney, glistened in a row.
  Vain, transitory splendours! Could not all
Reprieve the tottering mansion from its fall!
Obscure it sinks, nor shall it more impart
An hour's importance to the poor man's heart;
Thither no more the peasant shall repair
To sweet oblivion of his daily care;
No more the farmer's news, the barber's tale,
No more the woodman's ballad shall prevail;
No more the smith his dusky brow shall clear,
Relax his ponderous strength and lean to hear;

*terms and tides* legal and religious seasons and festivals
*gauge* measure liquids
*house* the village inn
*draughts* of ale
*rules* of Charles I, on behaviour, often reprinted
*goose* a board game using dice and counters

The host himself no longer shall be found
Careful to see the mantling bliss go round;
Nor the coy maid, half willing to be pressed,
Shall kiss the cup to pass it to the rest.
  Yes! let the rich deride, the proud disdain,
These simple blessings of the lowly train;
To me more dear, congenial to my heart,
One native charm than all the gloss of art;
Spontaneous joys, where nature has its play,
The soul adopts and owns their firstborn sway;
Lightly they frolic o'er the vacant mind,
Unenvied, unmolested, unconfined
But the long pomp, the midnight masquerade,
With all the freaks of wanton wealth arrayed,
In these, ere triflers half their wish obtain,
The toiling pleasure sickens into pain;
And, even while fashion's brightest arts decoy,
The heart distrusting asks, if this be joy.
  Ye friends to truth, ye statesmen who survey
The rich man's joys increase, the poor's decay,
'Tis yours to judge how wide the limits stand
Between a splendid and an happy land.
Proud swells the tide with loads of freighted ore,
And shouting Folly hails them from her shore;
Hoards, even beyond the miser's wish, abound,
And rich men flock from all the world around.
Yet count our gains. This wealth is but a name
That leaves our useful products still the same.
Not so the loss. The man of wealth and pride
Takes up a space that many poor supplied;
Space for his lake, his park's extended bounds,
Space for his horses, equipage and hounds;
The robe that wraps his limbs in silken sloth
Has robbed the neighbouring fields of half their growth;
His seat, where solitary sports are seen,
Indignant spurns the cottage from the green;
Around the world each needful product flies,
For all the luxuries the world supplies;
While thus the land, adorned for pleasure all,
In barren splendour feebly waits the fall.
  As some fair female unadorned and plain,
Secure to please while youth confirms her reign,
Slights every borrowed charm that dress supplies,
Nor shares with art the triumph of her eyes;

But when those charms are passed, for charms are frail,
When time advances and when lovers fail,
She then shines forth, solicitous to bless,
In all the glaring impotence of dress;
Thus fares the land, by luxury betrayed,
In nature's simplest charms at first arrayed;
But verging to decline, its splendours rise,
Its vistas† strike, its palaces surprise;
While scourged by famine from the smiling land,
The mournful peasant leads his humble band;
And while he sinks without one arm to save,
The country blooms – a garden and a grave.
  Where then, ah, where shall poverty reside,
To 'scape the pressure of contiguous pride?
If to some common's fenceless limits strayed,
He drives his flock to pick the scanty blade,
Those fenceless fields the sons of wealth divide,
And even the bare-worn common is denied.
  If to the city sped – what waits him there?
To see profusion that he must not share;
To see ten thousand baneful arts combined
To pamper luxury and thin mankind;
To see those joys the sons of pleasure know
Extorted from his fellow-creature's woe.
Here, while the courtier glitters in brocade,
There the pale artist* plies the sickly trade; workman
Here, while the proud their long-drawn pomps display,
There the black gibbet† glooms beside the way.
The dome where pleasure holds her midnight reign
Here, richly decked, admits the gorgeous train;
Tumultuous grandeur crowds the blazing square,
The rattling chariots clash, the torches glare;
Sure scenes like these no troubles e'er annoy!
Sure these denote one universal joy!
Are these thy serious thoughts? – Ah, turn thine eyes
Where the poor, houseless, shivering female lies.
She once, perhaps, in village plenty blessed,
Has wept at tales of innocence distressed;
Her modest looks the cottage might adorn,
Sweet as the primrose peeps beneath the thorn;

*vistas* man-made prospects in landscape gardens

*gibbet* after public execution, bodies were often publicly displayed

Now lost to all; her friends, her virtue fled,
Near her betrayer's door she lays her head,
And, pinched with cold and shrinking from the shower,
With heavy heart deplores that luckless hour,
When idly first, ambitious of the town,
She left her wheel† and robes of country brown.
   Do thine, sweet Auburn, thine, the loveliest train,
Do thy fair tribes participate her pain?
Even now, perhaps, by cold and hunger led,
At proud men's doors they ask a little bread!
   Ah, no. To distant climes, a dreary scene,
Where half the convex world intrudes between,
Through torrid tracts with fainting steps they go,
Where wild Altama† murmurs to their woe.
Far different there from all that charmed before
The various terrors of that horrid shore:
Those blazing suns that dart a downward ray,
And fiercely shed intolerable day;
Those matted woods where birds forget to sing,
But silent bats in drowsy clusters cling;
Those poisonous fields with rank luxuriance crowned,
Where the dark scorpion gathers death around;
Where at each step the stranger fears to wake
The rattling terrors of the vengeful snake;
Where crouching tigers† wait their hapless prey,
And savage men more murderous still than they;
While oft in whirls the mad tornado flies,
Mingling the ravaged landscape with the skies.
Far different these from every former scene,
The cooling brook, the grassy-vested green,
The breezy covert of the warbling grove,
That only sheltered thefts of harmless love.
   Good heaven! what sorrows gloomed that parting day
That called them from their native walks away;
When the poor exiles, every pleasure past,
Hung round their bowers and fondly looked their last,
And took a long farewell, and wished in vain
For seats like these beyond the western main;
And shuddering still to face the distant deep,
Returned and wept, and still returned to weep.

*wheel* spinning-wheel, symbol of rural economy

*Altama* Altamaha river in Georgia, now USA

*tigers* G. calls the cougar the 'American tiger'

The good old sire the first prepared to go
To new-found worlds, and wept for others' woe;
But for himself, in conscious virtue brave,
He only wished for worlds beyond the grave.
His lovely daughter, lovelier in her tears,
The fond companion of his helpless years,
Silent went next, neglectful of her charms,
And left a lover's for a father's arms.
With louder plaints the mother spoke her woes,
And blessed the cot where every pleasure rose;
And kissed her thoughtless babes with many a tear,
And clasped them close, in sorrow doubly dear;
Whilst her fond husband strove to lend relief
In all the silent manliness of grief.
O luxury! thou cursed by heaven's decree,
How ill exchanged are things like these for thee!
How do thy potions with insidious joy
Diffuse their pleasures only to destroy!
Kingdoms, by thee to sickly greatness grown,
Boast of a florid vigour not their own.
At every draught more large and large they grow,
A bloated mass of rank unwieldy woe;
Till sapped their strength, and every part unsound,
Down, down they sink, and spread a ruin round.
Even now the devastation is begun,
And half the business of destruction done;
Even now, methinks, as pondering here I stand,
I see the rural virtues leave the land.
Down where yon anchoring vessel spreads the sail
That idly waiting flaps with every gale,
Downward they move, a melancholy band,
Pass from the shore and darken all the strand.
Contented toil and hospitable care,
And kind connubial tenderness are there;
And piety, with wishes placed above,
And steady loyalty and faithful love.
And thou, sweet Poetry, thou loveliest maid,
Still first to fly where sensual joys invade;
Unfit in these degenerate times of shame
To catch the heart or strike for honest fame;
Dear charming nymph, neglected and decried,
My shame in crowds, my solitary pride;
Thou source of all my bliss and all my woe,
That found'st me poor at first and keep'st me so;

Thou guide by which the nobler arts excel,
Thou nurse of every virtue, fare thee well.
Farewell, and oh, where'er thy voice be tried,
On Torno's† cliffs or Pambamarca's† side,
Whether where equinoctial fervours glow,
Or winter wraps the polar world in snow,
Still let thy voice, prevailing over time,
Redress the rigours of th' inclement clime;
Aid slighted truth, with thy persuasive strain
Teach erring man to spurn the rage of gain;
Teach him that states of native strength possessed,
Though very poor, may still be very blest;
That trade's proud empire hastes to swift decay,
As ocean sweeps the laboured mole† away;
While self-dependent power can time defy,
As rocks resist the billows and the sky.

1769 1770

## *From* RETALIATION†

### *[David Garrick]*

Here lies David Garrick, describe me who can,
An abridgement of all that was pleasant in man;
As an actor, confessed without rival to shine,
As a wit, if not first, in the very first line;
Yet with talents like these and an excellent heart,
The man had his failings, a dupe to his art.
Like an ill-judging beauty his colours he spread,
And beplastered with rouge his own natural red.
On the stage he was natural, simple, affecting:
'Twas only that, when he was off, he was acting.
With no reason on earth to go out of his way,
He turned and he varied full ten times a day.

---

*Torno . . . fervours* in icy Sweden; *Pambamarca*, by contrast, is in Ecuador, hence its *fervours* – heats

*laboured mole* man-made breakwater. The last four lines were written by Johnson

*Retaliation* One of several mock-epitaphs on friends in reply to theirs on him: David Garrick had said that Goldsmith 'wrote like an angel, but talked like poor Poll'. Garrick was now the dominant actor of the age

Though secure of our hearts, yet confoundedly sick
If they were not his own by finessing and trick,
He cast off his friends, as a huntsman his pack,
For he knew when he pleased he could whistle them back.
Of praise a mere glutton, he swallowed what came,
And the puff of a dunce, he mistook it for fame;
Till his relish grown callous, almost to disease,
Who peppered the highest was surest to please.
But let us be candid and speak out our mind:
If dunces applauded, he paid them in kind.
Ye Kenricks,† ye Kellys and Woodfalls† so grave,
What a commerce was yours, while you got and you gave!
How did Grub Street† re-echo the shouts that you raised,
While he was be-Rosciused† and you were be-praised!
But peace to his spirit, wherever it flies,
To act as an angel and mix with the skies:
Those poets, who owe their best fame to his skill,
Shall still be his flatterers, go where he will.
Old Shakespeare receive him with praise and with love,
And Beaumonts and Bens† be his Kellys above.

1774

*Kenricks . . . Woodfalls* minor literary men; G. had produced Kelly's sentimental comedy *False Delicacy* in 1768
*Grub Street* the centre of literary drudgery
*be-Rosciused* Roscius, great Roman comic actor of first century BC
*Ben* Jonson (placing Garrick with the great Elizabethan dramatists)

# William Cowper

## 1731–1800

The son of a Hertfordshire clergyman, Cowper attended Westminster School alongside the future satirist-cleric, Charles Churchill. Always mentally delicate, he attempted suicide when involved in a dispute over a public appointment: a religious melancholy which led to belief in his own damnation was stayed by a hope of salvation arising from evangelical Christianity. In 1765, he found protection with a clergyman, Mr Unwin, and his wife, Cowper's spiritual companion until 1796. Further mental attacks and another suicide attempt left him convinced of his own rejection by God. With the evangelical clergyman, John Newton, he had written the *Olney Hymns* (1779), including 'God moves in a mysterious way'. Collections of poems in 1782 and 1785 produced satires and the comic tale *John Gilpin*; he also translated Homer (1791). His long blank verse poem *The Task* (1785) developed from a work of mental relief into tender description and meditation centred on his quiet rural life. In his writings, charm and humanity contrast sadly with images of destruction or isolation associated with his deeper fears ('The Castaway', 1799).

### *From* THE TASK, BOOK I: 'The Sofa'

#### *[Pleasure in Nature]*

Thou[†] knowest my praise of nature most sincere,
And that my raptures are not conjured up
To serve occasions of poetic pomp,
But genuine, and art partner of them all.
How oft upon yon eminence our pace
Has slackened to a pause, and we have borne
The ruffling wind, scarce conscious that it blew,
While admiration, feeding at the eye,
And still unsated, dwelt upon the scene.
Thence with what pleasure have we just discerned

*Thou* Mrs Unwin

The distant plough slow moving, and beside
His labouring team, that swerved not from the track,
The sturdy swain diminished to a boy!
Here Ouse, slow winding through a level plain
Of spacious meads with cattle sprinkled o'er,
Conducts the eye along its sinuous course
Delighted. There, fast rooted in their bank,
Stand, never overlooked, our favourite elms,
That screen the herdsman's solitary hut;
While far beyond, and overthwart the stream
That, as with molten glass, inlays the vale,
The sloping land recedes into the clouds;
Displaying on its varied side the grace
Of hedge-row beauties numberless, square tower,
Tall spire, from which the sound of cheerful bells
Just undulates upon the listening ear,
Groves, heaths, and smoking villages, remote.
Scenes must be beautiful, which, daily viewed,
Please daily, and whose novelty survives
Long knowledge and the scrutiny of years.
Praise justly due to those that I describe.
  Nor rural sights alone, but rural sounds,
Exhilarate the spirit, and restore
The tone of languid Nature. Mighty winds,
That sweep the skirt of some far-spreading wood
Of ancient growth, make music not unlike
The dash of ocean on his winding shore,
And lull the spirit while they fill the mind;
Unnumbered branches waving in the blast,
And all their leaves fast fluttering, all at once.
Nor less composure waits upon the roar
Of distant floods, or on the softer voice
Of neighbouring fountain, or of rills that slip
Through the cleft rock, and, chiming as they fall
Upon loose pebbles, lose themselves at length
In matted grass, that with a livelier green
Betrays the secret of their silent course.
Nature inanimate employs sweet sounds,
But animated nature sweeter still,
To soothe and satisfy the human ear.
Ten thousand warblers cheer the day, and one
The live-long night: nor these alone, whose notes
Nice-fingered art must emulate in vain,
But cawing rooks, and kites that swim sublime

In still-repeated circles, screaming loud,
The jay, the pie, and even the boding owl
That hails the rising moon, have charms for me.
Sounds inharmonious in themselves and harsh,
Yet heard in scenes where peace for ever reigns,
And only there, please highly for their sake. . . .

## *[A Harsher Scene]*

The earth was made so various, that the mind
Of desultory man, studious of change,
And pleased with novelty, might be indulged.
Prospects, however lovely, may be seen
Till half their beauties fade; the weary sight,
Too well acquainted with their smiles, slides off,
Fastidious, seeking less familiar scenes.
Then snug enclosures in the sheltered vale,
Where frequent hedges intercept the eye,
Delight us; happy to renounce awhile,
Not senseless of its charms, what still we love,
That such short absence may endear it more.
Then forests, or the savage rock, may please,
That hides the sea-mew in his hollow clefts
Above the reach of man. His hoary head,
Conspicuous many a league, the mariner
Bound homeward, and in hope already there,
Greets with three cheers exulting. At his waist
A girdle of half-withered shrubs he shows,
And at his feet the baffled billows die.
The common, overgrown with fern, and rough
With prickly gorse, that, shapeless and deformed,
And dangerous to the touch, has yet its bloom,
And decks itself with ornaments of gold,
Yields no unpleasing ramble; there the turf
Smells fresh, and, rich in odoriferous herbs
And fungous fruits of earth, regales the sense
With luxury of unexpected sweets.
There often wanders one, whom better days
Saw better clad, in cloak of satin trimmed
With lace, and hat with splendid ribband bound.
A serving maid was she, and fell in love
With one who left her, went to sea, and died.
Her fancy followed him through foaming waves
To distant shores; and she would sit and weep

At what a sailor suffers; fancy, too,
Delusive most where warmest wishes are,
Would oft anticipate his glad return,
And dream of transports she was not to know.
She heard the doleful tidings of his death –
And never smiled again! And now she roams
The dreary waste; there spends the livelong day,
And there, unless when charity forbids,
The livelong night. A tattered apron hides,
Worn as a cloak, and hardly hides, a gown
More tattered still; and both but ill conceal
A bosom heaved with never-ceasing sighs.
She begs an idle pin of all she meets,
And hoards them in her sleeve; but needful food,
Though pressed with hunger oft, or comelier clothes,
Though pinched with cold, asks never. – Kate is crazed! . . .

## *From* BOOK VI: 'The Winter Walk at Noon'

The night was winter in his roughest mood;
The morning sharp and clear. But now at noon
Upon the southern side of the slant hills,
And where the woods fence off the northern blast,
The season smiles, resigning all its rage,
And has the warmth of May. The vault is blue
Without a cloud, and white without a speck
The dazzling splendour of the scene below.
Again the harmony comes o'er the vale;
And through the trees I view th' embattled tower
Whence all the music. I again perceive
The soothing influence of the wafted strains,
And settle in soft musings as I tread
The walk, still verdant, under oaks and elms,
Whose outspread branches overarch the glade.
The roof, though moveable through all its length
As the wind sways it, has yet well sufficed,
And, intercepting in their silent fall
The frequent flakes, has kept a path for me.
No noise is here, or none that hinders thought.
The redbreast warbles still, but is content
With slender notes, and more than half suppressed:

Pleased with his solitude, and flitting light
From spray to spray, where'er he rests he shakes
From many a twig the pendent drops of ice,
That tinkle in the withered leaves below.
Stillness, accompanied with sounds so soft,
Charms more than silence. Meditation here
May think down hours to moments. Here the heart
May give an useful lesson to the head,
And learning wiser grow without his books.
Knowledge and wisdom, far from being one,
Have oft-times no connection. Knowledge dwells
In heads replete with thoughts of other men;
Wisdom in minds attentive to their own.
Knowledge, a rude unprofitable mass,
The mere materials with which wisdom builds,
Till smoothed and squared and fitted to its place,
Does but encumber whom it seems t' enrich.
Knowledge is proud that he has learned so much;
Wisdom is humble that he knows no more. . .

1785

## THE CASTAWAY†

Obscurest night involved* the sky, — *enwrapped*
Th' Atlantic billows roared,
When such a destined wretch as I,
Washed headlong from on board,
Of friends, of hope, of all bereft,
His floating home for ever left.

No braver chief could Albion boast
Than he with whom he went,
Nor ever ship left Albion's coast
With warmer wishes sent.
He loved them both, but both in vain,
Nor him beheld nor her again.

*The Castaway* Cowper read this incident in Lord Anson's *Voyage round the World* (1748)

Not long beneath the whelming brine,
Expert to swim, he lay;
Nor soon he felt his strength decline,
Or courage die away;
But waged with death a lasting strife,
Supported by despair of life.

He shouted: nor his friends had failed
To check the vessel's course,
But so the furious blast prevailed,
That, pitiless perforce,
They left their outcast mate behind,
And scudded still before the wind.

Some succour yet they could afford;
And, such as storms allow,
The cask, the coop, the floated cord,
Delayed not to bestow.
But he (they knew) nor ship nor shore,
Whate'er they gave, should visit more.

Nor, cruel as it seemed, could he
Their haste himself condemn,
Aware that flight, in such a sea,
Alone could rescue them;
Yet bitter felt it still to die
Deserted, and his friends so nigh.

He long survives, who lives an hour
In ocean, self-upheld;
And so long he, with unspent power,
His destiny repelled;
And ever, as the minutes flew,
Entreated help, or cried – 'Adieu!'

At length, his transient respite past,
His comrades, who before
Had heard his voice in every blast,
Could catch the sound no more.
For then, by toil subdued, he drank
The stifling wave, and then he sank.

No poet wept him: but the page
Of narrative sincere,

That tells his name, his worth, his age,
Is wet with Anson's tear.
And tears by bards or heroes shed
Alike immortalize the dead.

I therefore purpose not, or dream,
Descanting on his fate,
To give the melancholy theme
A more enduring date:
But misery still delights to trace
Its semblance in another's case.

No voice divine the storm allayed,
No light propitious shone,
When, snatched from all effectual aid,
We perished, each alone:
But I beneath a rougher sea,
And whelmed in deeper gulfs than he.

1799 1803

# James Macpherson

## 1736–96

Educated at Aberdeen and Edinburgh Universities, Macpherson had published his own poetry before the *Fragments of Ancient Poetry* (1760) allegedly collected in the Scottish Highlands and translated from Gaelic. In an age whose increasing value on primitive literature saw Bishop Percy's ballad collections, and his and Gray's interest in Norse poetry, it excited the imagination and flattered the Scottish cultural sense that Macpherson should 'find' and translate two Scottish historical epic poems by 'Ossian': *Fingal* (1762) and *Temora* (1763) were admired at home (David Hume and Adam Smith) and abroad (Schiller, Goethe, Napoleon), where they had an extraordinary influence. The hostile camp was led by Johnson, whose Scottish journey confirmed his view (which appears to be near the truth) that the Ossianic poems were a lash-up of Macpherson's inventions and some traditional scraps. The reception of Ossian is a remarkable episode in the history of taste. (See also Johnson's defiant letter to Macpherson on p. 347.)

## *From* FINGAL.† *An Ancient Epic Poem*

### *[Battle is joined]*

'Peace,' said Cuthullin, 'to the souls of the heroes! their deeds were great in fight. Let them ride around me on clouds. Let them show their features of war. My soul shall then be firm in danger; mine arm like the thunder of heaven! But be thou on a moon-beam, O Morna! near the window of my rest; when my thoughts are of peace; when the din of arms is past. Gather the strength of the tribes! Move to the wars of Erin! Attend the car of my battles! Rejoice in the noise of my course! Place three spears by my side: follow the bounding of my steeds! That

*Fingal* Cuthullin, an Irish leader, prepares to do battle with the invader Swaran, King of Lochlin

my soul may be strong in my friends, when battle darkens round the beams of my steel!'

As rushes a stream of foam from the dark shady deep of Cromla; when the thunder is travelling above, and dark-brown night sits on half the hill. Through the breaches of the tempest look forth the dim faces of ghosts. So fierce, so vast, so terrible rushed on the sons of Erin. The chief, like a whale of ocean, whom all his billows pursue, poured valour forth as a stream, rolling his might along the shore. The sons of Lochlin heard the noise, as the sound of a winter-storm. Swaran struck his bossy shield: he called the son of Arno. 'What murmur rolls along the hill, like the gathered flies of the eve? The sons of Erin descend, or rustling winds roar in the distant wood! Such is the noise of Gormal, before the white tops of my waves arise. O Son of Arno, ascend the hill; view the dark face of the heath!'

He went. He, trembling, swift returned. His eyes rolled wildly round. His heart beat high against his side. His words were faltering, broken, slow. 'Arise, son of ocean, arise, chief of the dark-brown shields! I see the dark, the mountain-stream of battle! The deep-moving strength of the sons of Erin! The car, the car of war comes on, like the flame of death! the rapid car of Cuthullin, the noble son of Semo! It bends behind like a wave near a rock; like the sun-streaked mist of the heath. Its sides are embossed with stones, and sparkle like the sea round the boat of night. Of polished yew is its beam; its seat of the smoothest bone. The sides are replenished with spears; the bottom is the footstool of heroes! Before the right side of the car is seen the snorting horse! the high-manned, broad-breasted, proud, wide-leaping, strong steed of the hill. Loud and resounding is his hoof; the spreading of his mane above is like a stream of spray on a ridge of rocks. Bright are the sides of the steed! His name is Sulin-Sifadda!'

'Before the left side of the car is seen the snorting horse! The thin-maned, high-headed, strong-hoofed, fleet, bounding son of the hill: his name is Dufronnal, among the stormy sons of the sword! A thousand thongs bind the car on high. Hard polished bits shine in a wreath of foam. Thin thongs, bright studded with gems, bend on the stately necks of the steeds. The steeds that like wreaths of mist fly over the streamy vales! The wildness of deer is in their course, the strength of eagles descending on their prey. Their noise is like the blast of winter, on the sides of the snow-headed Gormal.

'Within the car is seen the chief; the strong-armed son of the sword. The hero's name is Cuthullin, son of Semo, king of shells. His red cheek is like my polished yew. The look of his blue-rolling eye is wide beneath the dark arch of his brow. His hair flies from his head like a flame, as bending forward he wields the spear. Fly, king of ocean, fly! He comes, like a storm, along the streamy vale!'

'When did I fly?' replied the king. 'When fled Swaran from the battle of spears? When did I shrink from danger, chief of the little soul? I met the storm of Gormal, when the foam of my waves beat high. I met the storm of the clouds; shall Swaran fly from a hero? Were Fingal himself before me, my soul should not darken with fear. Arise to battle, my thousands! pour round me like the echoing main. Gather round the bright steel of your king; strong as the rocks of my land; that meet the storm with joy, and stretch their dark pines to the wind!'

Like autumn's dark storms, pouring from two echoing hills, towards each other approached the heroes. Like two deep streams from high rocks meeting, mixing, roaring on the plain; loud, rough and dark in battle meet Lochlin and Innis-fail. Chief mixes his strokes with chief, and man with man; steel, clanging, sounds on steel. Helmets are cleft on high. Blood bursts and smokes around. Strings murmur on the polished yews. Darts rush along the sky. Spears fall like the circles of light, which gild the face of night. As the noise of the troubled ocean, when roll the waves on high. As the last peal of thunder in heaven, such is the din of war! Though Cormac's hundred bards were there to give the fight to song; feeble was the voice of a hundred bards to send the deaths to future times! For many were the deaths of heroes; wide poured the blood of the brave!

Mourn, ye sons of song, mourn the death of the noble Sithâllin. Let the sighs of Fiona arise, on the lone plains of her lovely Ardan. They fell, like two hinds of the desert, by the hands of the mighty Swaran; when, in the midst of thousands, he roared; like the shrill spirit of a storm. He sits dim, on the clouds of the north, and enjoys the death of the mariner. Nor slept thy hand by thy side, chief of the isle of mist! many were the deaths of thine arm, Cuthullin, thou son of Semo! His sword was like the beam of heaven when it pierces the sons of the vale; when the people are blasted and fall, and all the hills are burning around. Dufronnal snorted over the bodies of heroes. Sifadda bathed his hoof in blood. The battle lay behind them, as groves overturned in the desert of Cromla, when the blast has passed the heath, laden with the spirits of night!

Weep on the rocks of roaring winds, O maid of Inistore![†] Bend thy fair head over the waves, thou lovelier than the ghost of the hills, when it moves, in a sun-beam at noon, over the silence of Morven! He is fallen! thy youth is low! pale beneath the sword of Cuthullin! No more shall valour raise thy love to match the blood of kings. Trenar, graceful Trenar died, O maid of Inistore! His grey dogs are howling at home! they see his passing ghost. His bow is in the hall unstrung. No sound is in the hill of his hinds!

*Inistore* in Swaran's territory

As roll a thousand waves to the rocks, so Swaran's host came on. As meets a rock a thousand waves, so Erin met Swaran of spears. Death raises all his voices around, and mixes with the sounds of shields. Each hero is a pillar of darkness; the sword a beam of fire in his hand. The field echoes from wing to wing, as a hundred hammers that rise, by turns, on the red son of the furnace. Who are these on Lena's heath, these so gloomy and dark? Who are these like two clouds, and their swords like lightning above them? The little hills are troubled around: the rocks tremble with all their moss. Who is it but Ocean's son and the car-borne chief of Erin? Many are the anxious eyes of their friends, as they see them dim on the heath. But night conceals the chiefs in clouds, and ends the dreadful fight!

It was on Cromla's shaggy side that Dorglas had placed the deer; the early fortune of the chase, before the heroes left the hill. A hundred youths collect the heath; ten warriors wake the fire; three hundred choose the polished stones. The feast is smoking wide! Cuthullin, chief of Erin's war, resumed his mighty soul. He stood upon his beamy spear, and spoke to the son of songs, to Carril of other times, the grey-haired son of Kinfena. 'Is this feast spread for me alone and the king of Lochlin on Erin's shore; far from the deer of his hills, and sounding halls of his feasts? Rise, Carril of other times; carry my words to Swaran. Tell him from the roaring of waters, that Cuthullin gives his feast. Here let him listen to the sound of my groves, amidst the clouds of night. For cold and bleak the blustering winds rush over the foam of his seas. Here let him praise the trembling harp, hear the songs of heroes!' . . .

1762

# Edward Gibbon

1737–94

The *Memoirs* or *Autobiography* pieced together from various drafts after Gibbon's death are a major if selective source of information. A learned fourteen-year-old, he went to Magdalen College, Oxford, which he found sunk in indolence and prejudice in his fourteen-month stay. An intellectual convert to Catholicism, he reconverted to Protestantism on being sent to Lausanne, where he formed a romantic attachment which his father persuaded him to break. His study of ancient and modern literature produced a French *Essai* on the topic (1761). Meanwhile he served as captain in the Hampshire Militia. On a visit to Rome in 1764, he decided to write the *History of the Decline and Fall* of the city, later extended to the empire. After years of research, he published his great work in six volumes, 1776–88. During much of this period he was an MP, and for several years a minor official, but he was never a prominent politician; in 1774 he became a member of Johnson's Club; from 1783–93 he lived mainly in Switzerland. Gibbon's vast learning and magisterial prose made the *Decline and Fall* the greatest English history, though its ironic, sceptical manner caused offence to many with its implications that Rome fell as much through Christianity as barbarian attack: his enlightenment belief is in the progress of a rational civilisation. The *Memoirs* too are fascinating partly because of their ironic reticence about his emotional life; he never married.

## *From* MEMOIRS OF MY LIFE

### *[Gibbon at Oxford]*

A traveller who visits Oxford or Cambridge is surprised and edified by the apparent order and tranquillity that prevail in the seats of the English muses. In the most celebrated universities of Holland, Germany and Italy, the students, who swarm from different countries, are loosely dispersed in private lodgings at the houses of the burghers; they dress according to their fancy and fortune; and, in the intemperate quarrels of youth and wine, their swords, though less frequently than of old, are sometimes stained with each other's blood. The use of arms is banished from our English universities; the uniform habit of the academics, the square cap and black gown, is adapted to the civil and even clerical profession; and from the doctor in divinity to the undergraduate, the degrees of learning and age are externally distinguished. Instead of being scattered in a town, the students of Oxford and Cambridge are united in colleges; their maintenance is provided at their own expense, or that of the founders; and the stated hours of the hall and chapel represent the discipline of a regular, and, as it were, a religious community. The eyes of the traveller are attracted by the size or beauty of the public edifices; and the principal colleges appear to be so many palaces which a liberal nation has erected and endowed for the habitation of science.† My own introduction to the University of Oxford forms a new era in my life, and at the distance of forty years I still remember my first emotions of surprise and satisfaction. In my fifteenth year I felt myself suddenly raised from a boy to a man; the persons whom I respected as my superiors in age and academical rank entertained me with every mark of attention and civility; and my vanity was flattered by the velvet cap and silk gown which discriminate a gentleman-commoner from a plebeian student. A decent allowance, more money than a schoolboy had ever seen, was at my own disposal, and I might command among the tradesmen of Oxford an indefinite and dangerous latitude of credit. A key was delivered into my hands which gave me the free use of a numerous and learned library; my apartment consisted of three elegant and well-furnished rooms in the new building, a stately pile, of Magdalen College; and the adjacent walks,† had they been frequented by Plato's† disciples, might have been compared to the Attic shade on the banks of the Ilissus.† Such was the fair prospect of my entrance (April 3 1752) into the University of Oxford. . . . [quotes Bishop Lowth's pleasure in Oxford]

The expression of gratitude is a virtue and a pleasure: a liberal mind will delight to cherish and celebrate the memory of its parents; and the teachers of science are the parents of the mind. I applaud the filial piety which it is impossible for me to imitate; since I must not confess an imaginary debt to assume the merit of a just or generous retribution.

To the University of Oxford *I* acknowledge no obligation, and she will as cheerfully renounce me for a son, as I am willing to disclaim her for a mother. I spent fourteen months at Magdalen College; they

---

*science* learning in general
*walks* Magdalen has beautiful grounds by the river
*Plato* *c.* 428–348 BC: philosopher-teacher in Athens
*Ilissus* river near Athens

proved the fourteen months the most idle and unprofitable of my whole life. The reader will pronounce between the school and the scholar; but I cannot affect to believe that Nature had disqualified me for all literary pursuits. The specious and ready excuse of my tender age, imperfect preparation and hasty departure, may doubtless be alleged; nor do I wish to defraud such excuses of their proper weight. Yet in my sixteenth year I was not devoid of capacity or application; even my childish reading had displayed an early though blind propensity for books; and the shallow flood might have been taught to flow in a deep channel and a clear stream. In the discipline of a well-constituted academy, under the guidance of skilful and vigilant professors, I should gradually have risen from translations to originals, from the Latin to the Greek classics, from dead languages to living science: my hours would have been occupied by useful and agreeable studies; the wanderings of fancy would have been restrained, and I should have escaped the temptations of idleness which finally precipitated my departure from Oxford.

Perhaps, in a separate annotation I may coolly examine the fabulous and real antiquities of our sister universities, a question which has kindled such fierce and foolish disputes among their fanatic sons. In the meanwhile it will be acknowledged that these venerable bodies are sufficiently old to partake of all the prejudices and infirmities of age. The schools of Oxford and Cambridge were founded in a dark age of false and barbarous science; and they are still tainted with the vices of their origin. Their primitive discipline was adapted to the education of priests and monks; and the government still remains in the hands of the clergy, an order of men whose manners are remote from the present world, and whose eyes are dazzled by the light of philosophy. The legal incorporation of these societies by the charters of popes and kings had given them a monopoly of the public instruction; and the spirit of monopolists is narrow, lazy and oppressive: their work is more costly and less productive than that of independent artists; and the new improvements so eagerly grasped by the competition of freedom are admitted with slow and sullen reluctance in those proud corporations, above the fear of a rival, and below the confession of an error. We may scarcely hope that any reformation will be a voluntary act, and so deeply are they rooted in law and prejudice that even the omnipotence of Parliament would shrink from an enquiry into the state and abuses of the two universities. . . .

In all the universities of Europe except our own, the languages and sciences are distributed among a numerous list of effective professors: the students, according to their taste, their calling, and their diligence, apply themselves to the proper masters; and in the annual repetition of public and private lectures, these masters are assiduously employed. Our curiosity may enquire what number of professors has been instituted at Oxford (for I shall now confine myself to my own university); by whom are they appointed, and what may be the probable chances of merit or incapacity? How many are stationed to the three faculties,[†] and how many are left for the liberal arts? What is the form, and what the substance of their lessons? But all these questions are silenced by one short and singular answer. 'That in the University of Oxford, the greater part of the public professors have for these many years given up altogether even the pretence of teaching.' Incredible as the fact may appear, I must rest my belief on the positive and impartial evidence of a philosopher who had himself resided at Oxford. Dr Adam Smith[†] assigns as the cause of their indolence that, instead of being paid by voluntary contributions, which would urge them to increase the number, and to deserve the gratitude of their pupils, the Oxford professors are secure in the enjoyment of a fixed stipend, without the necessity of labour or the apprehension of control. . . .

The College of St Mary Magdalen (it is vulgarly pronounced Maudlin) was founded in the fifteenth century by a Bishop of Winchester; and now consists of a President, forty fellows, and a number of inferior students. It is esteemed one of the largest and most wealthy of our academical corporations, which may be compared to the Benedictine abbeys of Catholic countries; and I have loosely heard that the estates belonging to Magdalen College, which are leased by those indulgent landlords at small quit-rents[†] and occasional fines, might be raised, in the hands of private avarice, to an annual revenue of near thirty thousand pounds. Our colleges are supposed to be schools of science as well as of education; nor is it unreasonable to expect that a body of literary men, addicted to a life of celibacy, exempt from the care of their own subsistence, and amply provided with books, should devote their leisure to the prosecution of study, and that some effects of their studies should be manifested to the world. The shelves of their library groan under the weight of the Benedictine folios, of the editions of the fathers[†] and the collections of the Middle Ages, which have issued from the single Abbey of St Germain des Prés at Paris. A composition of genius must be the offspring of one mind; but such works of industry as may be divided among many hands, and must be continued during many years, are the peculiar province of a laborious community. If I enquire into the manufactures of the monks at Magdalen, if I extend the enquiry to the other colleges of Oxford and Cambridge, a silent blush, or a scornful frown will be the only reply. The fellows or monks of my time were decent easy men who supinely enjoyed the gifts of the

*three faculties* theology, law, medicine
*Smith* 1723–90: Scottish philosopher and economist
*quit-rent* paid in lieu of other services
*fathers* of the church: early Christian writers

founder. Their days were filled by a series of uniform employments: the chapel and the hall, the coffee-house and the common room, till they retired, weary and well-satisfied, to a long slumber. From the toil of reading or thinking or writing they had absolved their conscience; and the first shoots of learning and ingenuity withered on the ground without yielding any fruit to the owners or the public. . . .

As a gentleman-commoner I was admitted to the society of the fellows, and fondly expected that some questions of literature would be the amusing and instructive topics of their discourse. Their conversation stagnated in a round of college business, Tory politics, personal stories and private scandal; their dull and deep potations excused the brisk intemperance of youth; and their constitutional toasts were not expressive of the most lively loyalty† for the House of Hanover. . . .

The silence of the Oxford professors, which deprives the youth of public instruction, is imperfectly supplied by the tutors, as they are styled, of the several colleges. Instead of confining themselves to a single science, which had satisfied the ambition of Burman or Bernouilli,† they teach or promise to teach either history or mathematics, or ancient literature or moral philosophy; and as it is possible that they may be defective in all, it is highly probable that of some they will be ignorant. They are paid indeed by private contributions; but their appointment depends on the head of the house: their diligence is voluntary, and will consequently be languid, while the pupils themselves and their parents are not indulged in the liberty of choice or change. The first tutor into whose hands I was resigned, appears to have been one of the best of the tribe. Dr Waldegrave was a learned and pious man, of a mild disposition, strict morals and abstemious life, who seldom mingled in the politics or the jollity of the college. But his knowledge of the world was confined to the university; his learning was of the last, rather than the present age, his temper was indolent; his faculties, which were not of the first rate, had been relaxed by the climate; and he was satisfied, like his fellows, with the slight and superficial discharge of an important trust. As soon as my tutor had sounded the insufficiency of his disciple in school-learning he proposed that we should read every morning from ten to eleven the comedies of Terence.† The sum of my improvement in the university of Oxford is confined to three or four Latin plays; and even the study of an elegant classic which might have been illustrated by a comparison of ancient and modern theatres was reduced to a dry and literal interpretation of the author's text. . . .

*loyalty* Oxford sympathies were traditionally Jacobite

*Burman . . . Bernouilli* Continental scholars in classics and mathematics

*Terence* Roman comic dramatist (*c.* 190–159 BC)

## *[Gibbon in Love]*

I hesitate from the apprehension of ridicule, when I approach the delicate subject of my early love. By this word I do not mean the polite attention, the gallantry without hope or design, which has originated from the spirit of chivalry, and is interwoven with the texture of French manners. I do not confine myself to the grosser appetite which our pride may affect to disdain, because it has been implanted by Nature in the whole animal creation: *Amor omnibus idem* [Love is the same for all]. The discovery of a sixth sense, the first consciousness of manhood, is a very interesting moment of our lives: but it less properly belongs to the memoirs of an individual, than to the natural history of the species. I understand by this passion the union of desire, friendship and tenderness, which is inflamed by a single female, which prefers her to the rest of her sex, and which seeks her possession as the supreme or the sole happiness of our being. I need not blush at recollecting the object of my choice, and though my love was disappointed of success, I am rather proud that I was once capable of feeling such a pure and exalted sentiment. The personal attractions of Mademoiselle Suzanne Curchod were embellished by the virtues and talents of the mind. Her fortune was humble but her family was respectable: her mother, a native of France, had preferred her religion to her country; the profession of her father did not extinguish the moderation and philosophy of his temper, and he lived content with a small salary and laborious duty in the obscure lot of minister of Crassy, in the mountains that separate the Pays de Vaud from the County of Burgundy. In the solitude of a sequestered village he bestowed a liberal and even learned education on his only daughter; she surpassed his hopes by her proficiency in the sciences and languages; and in her short visits to some relations at Lausanne, the wit and beauty and erudition of Mademoiselle Curchod were the theme of universal applause. The report of such a prodigy awakened my curiosity; I saw and loved. I found her learned without pedantry, lively in conversation, pure in sentiment, and elegant in manners; and the first sudden emotion was fortified by the habits and knowledge of a more familiar acquaintance. She permitted me to make her two or three visits at her father's house: I passed some happy days in the mountains of Burgundy, and her parents honourably encouraged a connection which might raise their daughter above want and dependence. In a calm retirement the gay vanity of youth no longer fluttered in her bosom; she listened to the voice of truth and passion; and I might presume to hope that I had made some impression on a virtuous heart.

At Crassy and Lausanne I indulged my dream of felicity; but on my return to England I soon discovered that my father would not hear of this strange alliance, and that without his consent I was myself destitute and helpless. After a painful struggle I yielded to my fate: I sighed† as a lover, I obeyed as a son; the remedies of absence and time were at length effectual; and my love subsided in friendship and esteem. The minister of Crassy soon afterwards died; his stipend died with him; his daughter retired to Geneva where, by teaching young ladies, she earned a hard subsistence for herself and her mother; but in her lowest distress she maintained a spotless reputation and a dignified behaviour. The Duchess of Grafton (now Lady Ossory) has often told me that she had nearly engaged Mademoiselle Curchod as a governess, and her declining a life of servitude was most probably blamed by the wisdom of her short-sighted friends. A rich banker of Paris, a citizen of Geneva, had the good fortune and good sense to discover and possess this inestimable treasure; and in the capital of taste and luxury she resisted the temptations of wealth as she had sustained the hardships of indigence. The genius of her husband has exalted him to the most conspicuous station in Europe; in every change of prosperity and disgrace he has reclined on the bosom of a faithful friend; and Mademoiselle Curchod is now the wife of M. Necker, the Minister† and perhaps the legislator of the French Monarchy.

1789–93 1796

# THE DECLINE AND FALL OF THE ROMAN EMPIRE *From* Chapter 38

## *General Observations on the Fall of the Roman Empire in the West*

The Greeks, after their country had been reduced into a province, imputed the triumphs of Rome, not to the merit, but to the FORTUNE, of the republic. The inconstant goddess, who so blindly distributes and resumes her favours, had *now* consented (such was the language of envious flattery) to resign her wings, to descend from her globe, and to fix her firm and immutable throne on the banks of the Tiber. A wiser Greek, who has composed, with a philosophic spirit, the memorable history of his own times, deprived his countrymen of this vain and delusive comfort, by opening to their view the deep foundations of the

*I sighed* added from another draft *Minister* of Finance, under Louis XVI

greatness of Rome. The fidelity of the citizens to each other and to the state was confirmed by the habits of education and the prejudices of religion. Honour, as well as virtue, was the principle of the republic; the ambitious citizens laboured to deserve the solemn glories of a triumph; and the ardour of the Roman youth was kindled into active emulation as often as they beheld the domestic images of their ancestors. The temperate struggles of the patricians and plebeians† had finally established the firm and equal balance of the constitution, which united the freedom of popular assemblies with the authority and wisdom of a senate and the executive powers of a real magistrate. When the consul† displayed the standard of the republic, each citizen bound himself, by the obligation of an oath, to draw his sword in the cause of his country till he had discharged the sacred duty by a military service of ten years. This wise institution continually poured into the field the rising generations of freemen and soldiers; and their numbers were reinforced by the warlike and populous states of Italy, who, after a brave resistance, had yielded to the valour and embraced the alliance of the Romans. The sage historian, who excited the virtue of the younger Scipio and beheld the ruin of Carthage, has accurately described their military system; their levies, arms, exercises, subordination, marches, encampments; and the invincible legion, superior in active strength to the Macedonian phalanx of Philip and Alexander. From these institutions of peace and war Polybius† has deduced the spirit and success of a people incapable of fear and impatient of repose. The ambitious design of conquest, which might have been defeated by the seasonable conspiracy of mankind, was attempted and achieved; and the perpetual violation of justice was maintained by the political virtues of prudence and courage. The arms of the republic, sometimes vanquished in battle, always victorious in war, advanced with rapid steps to the Euphrates, the Danube, the Rhine, and the Ocean; and the images of gold, or silver, or brass, that might serve to represent the nations and their kings, were successively broken by the *iron* monarchy of Rome.

The rise of a city, which swelled into an empire, may deserve, as a singular prodigy, the reflection of a philosophic mind. But the decline of Rome was the natural and inevitable effect of immoderate greatness. Prosperity ripened the principle of decay; the causes of destruction multiplied with the extent of conquest; and as soon as time or accident had removed the artificial supports, the stupendous fabric yielded to the pressure of its own weight. The story of its ruin is simple and obvious; and instead of inquiring *why* the Roman empire was destroyed, we should rather be surprised that it had subsisted so long. The

*patricians and plebeians* aristocrats and common people
*consul* joint chief-magistrate
*Polybius* Greek historian of third century BC wars against Carthage

victorious legions, who, in distant wars, acquired the vices of strangers and mercenaries, first oppressed the freedom of the republic, and afterwards violated the majesty of the purple. The emperors, anxious for their personal safety and the public peace, were reduced to the base expedient of corrupting the discipline which rendered them alike formidable to their sovereign and to the enemy; the vigour of the military government was relaxed and finally dissolved by the partial institutions of Constantine,[†] and the Roman world was overwhelmed by a deluge of barbarians.

The decay of Rome has been frequently ascribed to the translation of the seat of empire; but this history has already shown that the powers of government were *divided*, rather than *removed*. The throne of Constantinople was erected in the East; while the West was still possessed by a series of emperors who held their residence in Italy, and claimed their equal inheritance of the legions and provinces. This dangerous novelty impaired the strength and fomented the vices of a double reign: the instruments of an oppressive and arbitrary system were multiplied; and a vain emulation of luxury, not of merit, was introduced and supported between the degenerate successors of Theodosius.[†] Extreme distress, which unites the virtue of a free people, embitters the factions of a declining monarchy. The hostile favourites of Arcadius[†] and Honorius[†] betrayed the republic to its common enemies; and the Byzantine court beheld with indifference, perhaps with pleasure, the disgrace of Rome, the misfortunes of Italy, and the loss of the West. Under the succeeding reigns the alliance of the two empires was restored; but the aid of the Oriental Romans was tardy, doubtful, and ineffectual; and the national schism of the Greeks and Latins was enlarged by the perpetual difference of language and manners, of interests, and even of religion. Yet the salutary event approved in some measure the judgment of Constantine. During a long period of decay his impregnable city repelled the victorious armies of barbarism, protected the wealth of Asia, and commanded, both in peace and war, the important straits which connect the Euxine and Mediterranean seas. The foundation of Constantinople more essentially contributed to the preservation of the East than to the ruin of the West.

As the happiness of a *future* life is the great object of religion, we may hear without surprise or scandal that the introduction, or at least the abuse of Christianity, had some influence on the decline and fall of the Roman empire. The clergy successfully preached the doctrines of patience and pusillanimity; the active virtues of society were discouraged; and the last remains of military spirit were buried in the cloister:

*Constantine* Emperor 311–37; founder of Constantinople; Christian convert

*Theodosius* Emperor 378–95; *Arcadius* and *Honorius*, his sons, reigned in East and West

a large portion of public and private wealth was consecrated to the specious demands of charity and devotion; and the soldiers' pay was lavished on the useless multitudes of both sexes who could only plead the merits of abstinence and chastity. Faith, zeal, curiosity, and the more earthly passions of malice and ambition, kindled the flame of theological discord; the church, and even the state, were distracted by religious factions, whose conflicts were sometimes bloody and always implacable; the attention of the emperors was diverted from camps to synods; the Roman world was oppressed by a new series of tyranny; and the persecuted sects became the secret enemies of their country. Yet party-spirit, however pernicious or absurd, is a principle of union as well as of dissension. The bishops, from eighteen hundred pulpits, inculcated the duty of passive obedience to a lawful and orthodox sovereign; their frequent assemblies and perpetual correspondence maintained the communion of distant churches; and the benevolent temper of the Gospel was strengthened, though confined, by the spiritual alliance of the catholics. The sacred indolence of the monks was devoutly embraced by a servile and effeminate age; but if superstition had not afforded a decent retreat, the same vices would have tempted the unworthy Romans to desert, from baser motives, the standard of the republic. Religious precepts are easily obeyed which indulge and sanctify the natural inclinations of their votaries; but the pure and genuine influence of Christianity may be traced in its beneficial, though imperfect, effects on the barbarian proselytes of the North. If the decline of the Roman empire was hastened by the conversion of Constantine, his victorious religion broke the violence of the fall, and mollified the ferocious temper of the conquerors.

This awful revolution may be usefully applied to the instruction of the present age. It is the duty of a patriot to prefer and promote the exclusive interest and glory of his native country: but a philosopher may be permitted to enlarge his views, and to consider Europe as one great republic, whose various inhabitants have attained almost the same level of politeness and cultivation. The balance of power will continue to fluctuate, and the prosperity of our own or the neighbouring kingdoms may be alternately exalted or depressed; but these partial events cannot essentially injure our general state of happiness, the system of arts, and laws, and manners, which so advantageously distinguish, above the rest of mankind, the Europeans and their colonies. The savage nations of the globe are the common enemies of civilised society; and we may inquire, with anxious curiosity, whether Europe is still threatened with a repetition of those calamities which formerly oppressed the arms and institutions of Rome. Perhaps the same reflections will illustrate the fall of that mighty empire, and explain the probable causes of our actual security.

I. The Romans were ignorant of the extent of their danger and the number of their enemies. Beyond the Rhine and Danube the northern countries of Europe and Asia were filled with innumerable tribes of hunters and shepherds, poor, voracious, and turbulent; bold in arms, and impatient to ravish the fruits of industry. The barbarian world was agitated by the rapid impulse of war; and the peace of Gaul or Italy was shaken by the distant revolutions of China. The Huns, who fled before a victorious enemy, directed their march towards the West; and the torrent was swelled by the gradual accession of captives and allies. The flying tribes who yielded to the Huns assumed in *their* turn the spirit of conquest; the endless column of barbarians pressed on the Roman empire with accumulated weight; and, if the foremost were destroyed, the vacant space was instantly replenished by new assailants. Such formidable emigrations no longer issue from the North; and the long repose, which has been imputed to the decrease of population, is the happy consequence of the progress of arts and agriculture. Instead of some rude villages thinly scattered among its woods and morasses, Germany now produces a list of two thousand three hundred walled towns: the Christian kingdoms of Denmark, Sweden, and Poland have been successively established; and the Hanse merchants, with the Teutonic knights, have extended their colonies along the coast of the Baltic as far as the Gulf of Finland. From the Gulf of Finland to the Eastern Ocean, Russia now assumes the form of a powerful and civilised empire. The plough, the loom, and the forge are introduced on the banks of the Volga, the Oby, and the Lena; and the fiercest of the Tartar hordes have been taught to tremble and obey. The reign of independent barbarism is now contracted to a narrow span; and the remnant of Calmucks or Uzbecks, whose forces may be almost numbered, cannot seriously excite the apprehensions of the great republic of Europe. Yet this apparent security should not tempt us to forget that new enemies and unknown dangers may *possibly* arise from some obscure people, scarcely visible in the map of the world. The Arabs or Saracens, who spread their conquests from India to Spain, had languished in poverty and contempt till Mahomet breathed into those savage bodies the soul of enthusiasm.

II. The empire of Rome was firmly established by the singular and perfect coalition of its members. The subject nations, resigning the hope and even the wish of independence, embraced the character of Roman citizens; and the provinces of the West were reluctantly torn by the barbarians from the bosom of their mother country. But this union was purchased by the loss of national freedom and military spirit; and the servile provinces, destitute of life and motion, expected their safety from the mercenary troops and governors who were directed by the orders of a distant court. The happiness of an hundred millions depended on the personal merit of one or two men, perhaps children, whose minds were corrupted by education, luxury, and despotic power. The deepest wounds were inflicted on the empire during the minorities of the sons and grandsons of Theodosius; and, after those incapable princes seemed to attain the age of manhood, they abandoned the church to the bishops, the state to the eunuchs, and the provinces to the barbarians. Europe is now divided into twelve powerful, though unequal kingdoms, three respectable commonwealths, and a variety of smaller, though independent states: the chances of royal and ministerial talents are multiplied, at least, with the number of its rulers; and a Julian,† or Semiramis,† may reign in the North, while Arcadius and Honorius again slumber on the thrones of the South. The abuses of tyranny are restrained by the mutual influence of fear and shame; republics have acquired order and stability; monarchies have imbibed the principles of freedom, or, at least, of moderation; and some sense of honour and justice is introduced into the most defective constitutions by the general manners of the times. In peace, the progress of knowledge and industry is accelerated by the emulation of so many active rivals: in war, the European forces are exercised by temperate and undecisive contests. If a savage conqueror should issue from the deserts of Tartary, he must repeatedly vanquish the robust peasants of Russia, the numerous armies of Germany, the gallant nobles of France, and the intrepid freemen of Britain; who, perhaps, might confederate for their common defence. Should the victorious barbarians carry slavery and desolation as far as the Atlantic Ocean, ten thousand vessels would transport beyond their pursuit the remains of civilised society; and Europe would revive and flourish in the American world, which is already filled with her colonies and institutions.[1]

III. Cold, poverty, and a life of danger and fatigue fortify the strength and courage of barbarians. In every age they have oppressed the polite and peaceful nations of China, India, and Persia, who neglected, and still neglect, to counterbalance these natural powers by the resources of military art. The warlike states of antiquity, Greece, Macedonia, and Rome, educated a race of soldiers; exercised their bodies, disciplined their courage, multiplied their forces by regular evolutions, and conver-

[1] America now contains about six millions of European blood and descent; and their numbers, at least in the North, are continually increasing. Whatever may be the changes of their political situation, they must preserve the manners of Europe; and we may reflect with some pleasure that the English language will probably be diffused over an immense and populous continent. [Gibbon]

*Julian* Emperor 361–3; administered Gaul from Paris
*Semiramis* mythical Assyrian queen; 'S. of North' was Catherine, Empress of Russia 1762–96

ted the iron which they possessed into strong and serviceable weapons. But this superiority insensibly declined with their laws and manners: and the feeble policy of Constantine and his successors armed and instructed, for the ruin of the empire, the rude valour of the barbarian mercenaries. The military art has been changed by the invention of gunpowder; which enables man to command the two most powerful agents of nature, air and fire. Mathematics, chemistry, mechanics, architecture, have been applied to the service of war; and the adverse parties oppose to each other the most elaborate modes of attack and of defence. Historians may indignantly observe that the preparations of a siege would found and maintain a flourishing colony; yet we cannot be displeased that the subversion of a city should be a work of cost and difficulty; or that an industrious people should be protected by those arts which survive and supply the decay of military virtue. Cannon and fortifications now form an impregnable barrier against the Tartar horse; and Europe is secure from any future irruption of barbarians; since, before they can conquer, they must cease to be barbarous. Their gradual advances in the science of war would always be accompanied, as we may learn from the example of Russia, with a proportionable improvement in the arts of peace and civil policy; and they themselves must deserve a place among the polished nations whom they subdue.

Should these speculations be found doubtful or fallacious, there still remains a more humble source of comfort and hope. The discoveries of ancient and modern navigators, and the domestic history or tradition of the most enlightened nations, represent the *human savage* naked both in mind and body, and destitute of laws, of arts, of ideas, and almost of language. From this abject condition, perhaps the primitive and universal state of man, he has gradually arisen to command the animals, to fertilise the earth, to traverse the ocean, and to measure the heavens. His progress in the improvement and exercise of his mental and corporeal faculties has been irregular and various; infinitely slow in the beginning, and increasing by degrees with redoubled velocity: ages of laborious ascent have been followed by a moment of rapid downfall; and the several climates of the globe have felt the vicissitudes of light and darkness. Yet the experience of four thousand years should enlarge our hopes and diminish our apprehensions: we cannot determine to what height the human species may aspire in their advances towards perfection; but it may safely be presumed that no people, unless the face of nature is changed, will relapse into their original barbarism. The improvements of society may be viewed under a threefold aspect. 1. The poet or philosopher illustrates his age and country by the efforts of a *single* mind; but these superior powers of reason or fancy are rare and spontaneous productions; and the genius of Homer, or Cicero, or Newton, would excite less admiration if they could be created by the will of a prince or the lessons of a preceptor. 2. The benefits of law and policy, of trade and manufactures, of arts and sciences, are more solid and permanent; and *many* individuals may be qualified, by education and discipline, to promote, in their respective stations, the interest of the community. But this general order is the effect of skill and labour; and the complex machinery may be decayed by time, or injured by violence. 3. Fortunately for mankind, the more useful, or, at least, more necessary arts, can be performed without superior talents or national subordination; without the powers of *one*, or the union of *many*. Each village, each family, each individual, must always possess both ability and inclination to perpetuate the use of fire and of metals; the propagation and service of domestic animals; the methods of hunting and fishing; the rudiments of navigation; the imperfect cultivation of corn or other nutritive grain; and the simple practice of the mechanic trades. Private genius and public industry may be extirpated; but these hardy plants survive the tempest and strike an everlasting root into the most unfavourable soil. The splendid days of Augustus† and Trajan† were eclipsed by a cloud of ignorance; and the barbarians subverted the laws and palaces of Rome. But the scythe, the invention or emblem of Saturn, still continued annually to mow the harvests of Italy; and the human feasts of the Læstrigons† have never been renewed on the coast of Campania.

Since the first discovery of the arts, war, commerce, and religious zeal have diffused among the savages of the Old and New World these inestimable gifts: they have been successively propagated; they can never be lost. We may therefore acquiesce in the pleasing conclusion that every age of the world has increased and still increases the real wealth, the happiness, the knowledge, and perhaps the virtue, of the human race.

1781

*Augustus* 63 BC–AD 14; first Emperor
*Trajan* Emperor 98–117; soldier
*Laestrigons* man-eating giants

# James Boswell

## 1740–95

Boswell was the eldest son of the Scottish judge, Lord Auchinleck, a Whig and stern Presbyterian, who opposed his romantic military ambitions and made him follow the family legal tradition. In a period of high life and debauchery in London, Boswell met Samuel Johnson (1763), then left for his Grand Tour on the Continent, during which his pursuit of famous men netted Voltaire and Rousseau. Through Rousseau, he visited Corsica, and attempted to stampede Britain to the cause of its independence: his *Account of Corsica* (1768) won a European reputation. In Scotland, he practised as an advocate, but never attained high office there or in the political career he sought in England. He regularly visited London for its social and intellectual pleasures, and was elected to The Club. His professional career, his drinking, whoring and melancholy, as well as his encounters with Johnson, were recorded for thirty years in journals of great frankness, vividness and dramatic skill in recording conversations. They have only been published in this century; but in them he had found the materials and the method for his two great books, which are innovations in the art of biography: his *Journal of a Tour to the Hebrides* (1785) recorded the clash in 1773 between Johnson and Scotland; his *Life of Samuel Johnson* (1791), a huge work of unprecedented detail, seemed to many a violation of decency and privacy. A worldly failure, Boswell has often been dismissed as a buffoon; but his journals, fascinating human records in themselves, show his ability to select, dramatise and analyse experience.

# *From* LONDON JOURNAL 1762–1763[†]

## *['A Man of Pleasure']*

WEDNESDAY 12 JANUARY 1763. Louisa and I agreed that at eight at night she would meet me in the Piazzas of Covent Garden. I was quite elevated, and felt myself able and undaunted to engage in the wars of the Paphian[†] Queen.

I dined at Sheridan's[†] very heartily. He showed to my conviction that Garrick[†] did not play the great scene in the Second Part of *King Henry* with propriety. 'People,' said he, 'in this age know when particular lines or even speeches are well spoke; but they do not study character, which is a matter of the utmost moment, as people of different characters feel and express their feelings very differently. For want of a knowledge of this, Mr Barry acted the distress of Othello, the Moorish warrior whose stubborn soul was hard to bend, and that of Castalio,[†] the gentle lover who was all tenderness, in the self-same way. Now Mr Garrick in that famous scene whines most piteously when he ought to upbraid. Shakespeare has discovered there a most intimate knowledge of human nature. He shows you the King worn out with sickness and so weak that he faints. He had usurped the crown by the force of arms and was convinced that it must be held with spirit. He saw his son given up to low debauchery. He was anxious and vexed to think of the anarchy that would ensue at his death. Upon discovering that the Prince had taken the crown from his pillow, and concluding him desirous of his death, he is fired with rage. He starts up. He cries, "Go chide him hither!" His anger animates him so much that he throws aside his distemper. Nature furnishes all her strength for one last effort. He is for a moment renewed. He is for a moment the spirited Henry the Fourth. He upbraids him with bitter sarcasm and bold figures. And then what a beautiful variety is there, when, upon young Harry's contrition, he falls on his neck and melts into parental tenderness.'

I yielded this point to Sheridan candidly. But upon his attacking Garrick as a tragedian in his usual way, I opposed him keenly, and declared he was prejudiced; because the world thought him a good tragic actor. 'So do I, Sir,' said he; 'I think him the best I ever saw.' BOSWELL. 'Except yourself, Mr Sheridan. But come, we shall take this for granted. The world then think him near equal or as good as you in what you excel in.' SHERIDAN. 'Sir, I am not a bit prejudiced. I don't

*London Journal* For some weeks, Boswell has been courting an actress at Covent Garden Theatre: his theatrical interests run through the passage

*Paphian* Venus, goddess of love

*Sheridan* actor, father of the dramatist

*Garrick* 1717–79: greatest actor of age

*Castalio* in *The Orphan* (1680) by Thos. Otway

value acting. I shall suppose that I was the greatest actor that ever lived and universally acknowledged so, I would not choose that it should be remembered. I would have it erased out of the anecdotes of my life. Acting is a poor thing in the present state of the stage. For my own part, I engaged in it merely as a step to something greater, a just notion of eloquence.' This was in a good measure true. But he certainly talked too extravagantly.

An old Irish maid, or rather an Irish old maid (O most hideous character!) dined with us. She was indeed a terrible Joy.† She was a woman of knowledge and criticism and correct taste. But there came to tea a Miss Mowat who played once on the stage here for a winter or two, a lovely girl. Many an amorous glance did I exchange with her. I was this day quite flashy with love. We often addressed our discourse to each other. I hope to see her again; and yet what have I to do with anybody but dear Louisa?

At the appointed hour of eight I went to the Piazzas, where I sauntered up and down for a while in a sort of trembling suspense, I knew not why. At last my charming companion appeared, and I immediately conducted her to a hackney-coach which I had ready waiting, pulling up the blinds, and away we drove to the destined scene of delight. We contrived to seem as if we had come off a journey, and carried in a bundle our night-clothes, handkerchiefs, and other little things. We also had with us some almond biscuits, or as they call them in London, macaroons, which looked like provision on the road. On our arrival at Hayward's† we were shown into the parlour, in the same manner that any decent couple would be. I here thought proper to conceal my own name (which the people of the house had never heard), and assumed the name of Mr Digges.† We were shown up to the very room where he slept. I said my cousin, as I called him, was very well. That Ceres and Bacchus† might in moderation lend their assistance to Venus, I ordered a genteel supper and some wine.

Louisa told me she had two aunts who carried her over to France when she was a girl, and that she could once speak French as fluently as English. We talked a little in it, and agreed that we would improve ourselves by reading and speaking it every day. I asked her if we did not just look like man and wife. 'No,' said she, 'we are too fond for married people.' No wonder that she may have a bad idea of that union, considering how bad it was for her. She has contrived a pretty device for a seal. A heart is gently warmed by Cupid's flame, and Hymen† comes with his rude torch and extinguishes it. She said she

*Joy* that is, very Irish
*Hayward* innkeeper (who thinks B. married)
*Digges* actor friend
*Ceres . . . Bacchus* deities of agriculture and wine
*Hymen* god of marriage

found herself quite in a flutter. 'Why, really,' said I, 'reason sometimes has no power. We have no occasion to be frightened, and yet we are both a little so. Indeed, I preserve a tolerable presence of mind.' I rose and kissed her, and conscious that I had no occasion to doubt my qualifications as a gallant, I joked about it: 'How curious would it be if I should be so frightened that we should rise as we lay down.' She reproved my wanton language by a look of modesty. The bells of St Bride's church rung their merry chimes hard by. I said that the bells in Cupid's court would be this night set a-ringing for joy at our union.

We supped cheerfully and agreeably and drank a few glasses, and then the maid came and put the sheets, well aired, upon the bed. I now contemplated my fair prize. Louisa is just twenty-four, of a tall rather than short figure, finely made in person, with a handsome face and an enchanting languish in her eyes. She dresses with taste. She has sense, good humour, and vivacity, and looks quite a woman in genteel life. As I mused on this elevating subject, I could not help being somehow pleasingly confounded to think that so fine a woman was at this moment in my possession, that without any motives of interest† she had come with me to an inn, agreed to be my intimate companion, as to be my bedfellow all night, and to permit me the full enjoyment of her person.

When the servant left the room, I embraced her warmly and begged that she would not now delay my felicity. She declined to undress before me, and begged I would retire and send her one of the maids. I did so, gravely desiring the girl to go up to Mrs Digges. I then took a candle in my hand and walked out to the yard. The night was very dark and very cold. I experienced for some minutes the rigours of the season, and called into my mind many terrible ideas of hardships, that I might make a transition from such dreary thoughts to the most gay and delicious feelings. I then caused make a bowl of negus,† very rich of the fruit, which I caused be set in the room as a reviving cordial.

I came softly into the room, and in a sweet delirium slipped into bed and was immediately clasped in her snowy arms and pressed to her milk-white bosom. Good heavens, what a loose did we give to amorous dalliance! The friendly curtain of darkness concealed our blushes. In a moment I felt myself animated with the strongest powers of love, and, from my dearest creature's kindness, had a most luscious feast. Proud of my godlike vigour, I soon resumed the noble game. I was in full glow of health. Sobriety had preserved me from effeminacy and weakness, and my bounding blood beat quick and high alarms. A more voluptuous night I never enjoyed. Five times was I fairly lost in supreme rapture. Louisa was madly fond of me; she declared I was a prodigy, and asked me if this was not extraordinary for human nature. I said

*interest* worldly advantage

*negus* spiced alcohol

twice as much might be, but this was not, although in my own mind I was somewhat proud of my performance. She said it was what there was no just reason to be proud of. But I told her I could not help it. She said it was what we had in common with the beasts. I said no. For we had it highly improved by the pleasures of sentiment. I asked her what she thought enough. She gently chid me for asking such questions, but said two times. I mentioned the Sunday's assignation, when I was in such bad spirits, told her in what agony of mind I was, and asked her if she would not have despised me for my imbecility. She declared she would not, as it was what people had not in their own power.

She often insisted that we should compose ourselves to sleep before I would consent to it. At last I sunk to rest in her arms and she in mine. I found the negus, which had a fine flavour, very refreshing to me. Louisa had an exquisite mixture of delicacy and wantonness that made me enjoy her with more relish. Indeed I could not help roving in fancy to the embraces of some other ladies which my lively imagination strongly pictured. I don't know if that was altogether fair. However, Louisa had all the advantage. She said she was quite fatigued and could neither stir leg nor arm. She begged I would not despise her, and hoped my love would not be altogether transient. I have painted this night as well as I could. The description is faint; but I surely may be styled a Man of Pleasure.

THURSDAY 13 JANUARY. We awaked from sweet repose after the luscious fatigues of the night. I got up between nine and ten and walked out till Louisa should rise. I patrolled up and down Fleet Street, thinking on London, the seat of Parliament and the seat of pleasure, and seeming to myself as one of the wits in King Charles the Second's time. I then came in and we had an agreeable breakfast, after which we left Hayward's, who said he was sorry he had not more of our company, and calling a hackney-coach, drove to Soho[†] Square, where Louisa had some visits to pay. So we parted. Thus was this conquest completed to my highest satisfaction. I can with pleasure trace the progress of this intrigue to its completion. I am now at ease on that head, having my fair one fixed as my own. As Captain Plume[†] says, the best security for a woman's mind is her body. I really conducted this affair[†] with a manliness and prudence that pleased me very much. The whole expense was just eighteen shillings.

I called at Louisa's and seemed to be surprised that she was abroad. I then went and called at Drury Lane Playhouse for Mr Garrick. I had called for him at his house, but had never found him. He met me with

*Soho* in West End
*Captain Plume* in Farquhar's *The Recruiting Officer* (1706)
*affair* within days, he bitterly finds he has contracted a venereal disease

great civility and even kindness; told me that he had bowed to me in the House of Lords when I had not observed him; said he would be glad to contribute to my happiness, and asked me if I was come to stay. I told him that I hoped to get into the Guards. 'To be sure,' said he, 'it is a most genteel thing, and I think, Sir, you ought to be a soldier. The law requires a sad deal of plodding. But,' said he, 'has your father got over the pangs of your forsaking his scheme?' I told him he was pretty well reconciled. I told him I wanted much to pass some time with him. He said he always breakfasted at nine and would be glad to see me whenever I chose to come and let Mrs Garrick make tea for me. He then carried me to see the paintings of Mr Zoffany in the Piazzas, where Mr Garrick is shown in several different ways. 'Take care, Zoffany,' said he, 'you have made one of these heads for me *longer* than the other, and I would not willingly have it shortened.' In the theatre there was a fine large dog chained. 'This,' said he, 'is Johnston's (the box-keeper's) bear, though I don't know which of 'em is the greatest *bear*.'

I dined nowhere, but drank tea at Love's, and at night went to Covent Garden gallery and saw *The Jovial Crew*.† My frame still thrilled with pleasure, and my want of so much rest last night gave me an agreeable languor. The songs revived in my mind many gay ideas, and recalled in the most lively colours to my imagination the time when I was first in London, when all was new to me, when I felt the warm glow of youthful feeling and was full of curiosity and wonder. I then had at times a degree of ecstasy of feeling that the experience which I have since had has in some measure cooled and abated. But then my ignorance at that time is infinitely excelled by the knowledge and moderation and government of myself which I have now acquired. After the play I came home, eat a Bath cake and a sweet orange, and went comfortably to bed.

1763 1950

## *From* THE LIFE OF JOHNSON

### *[May 1776: A Potential Explosion]*

I am now to record a very curious incident in Dr Johnson's Life, which fell under my own observation; of which *pars magna fui* [I was a great part], and which I am persuaded will, with the liberal-minded, be much to his credit.

*Jovial Crew* operatic version of 1652 play by Rich. Brome

My desire of being acquainted with celebrated men of every description, had made me, much about the same time, obtain an introduction to Dr Samuel Johnson and to John Wilkes,† Esq. Two men more different could perhaps not be selected out of all mankind. They had even attacked one another with some asperity in their writings; yet I lived in habits of friendship with both. I could fully relish the excellence of each; for I have ever delighted in that intellectual chemistry, which can separate good qualities from evil in the same person. . . .

My worthy booksellers and friends, Messieurs Dilly in the Poultry, at whose hospitable and well-covered table I have seen a greater number of literary men, than at any other, except that of Sir Joshua Reynolds, had invited me to meet Mr Wilkes and some more gentlemen on Wednesday, May 15. 'Pray (said I) let us have Dr Johnson.' – 'What, with Mr Wilkes? not for the world (said Mr Edward Dilly): Dr Johnson would never forgive me.' – 'Come (said I), if you'll let me negotiate for you, I will be answerable that all shall go well.' DILLY. 'Nay, if you will take it upon you, I am sure I shall be very happy to see them both here.'

Notwithstanding the high veneration which I entertained for Dr Johnson, I was sensible that he was sometimes a little actuated by the spirit of contradiction, and by means of that I hoped I should gain my point. I was persuaded that if I had come upon him with a direct proposal, 'Sir, will you dine in company with Jack Wilkes?' he would have flown into a passion, and would probably have answered, 'Dine with Jack Wilkes, Sir! I'd as soon dine with Jack Ketch.'† I therefore, while we were sitting quietly by ourselves at his house in an evening, took occasion to open my plan thus: – 'Mr Dilly, Sir, sends his respectful compliments to you, and would be happy if you would do him the honour to dine with him on Wednesday next along with me, as I must soon go to Scotland.' JOHNSON. 'Sir, I am obliged to Mr Dilly. I will wait upon him –' BOSWELL. 'Provided, Sir, I suppose, that the company which he is to have, is agreeable to you.' JOHNSON. 'What do you mean, Sir? What do you take me for? Do you think I am so ignorant of the world, as to imagine that I am to prescribe to a gentleman what company he is to have at his table?' BOSWELL. 'I beg your pardon, Sir, for wishing to prevent you from meeting people whom you might not like. Perhaps he may have some of what he calls his patriotic† friends with him.' JOHNSON. 'Well, Sir, and what then? What care *I* for his *patriotic friends*? Poh!' BOSWELL. 'I should not be surprised to find Jack Wilkes there.' JOHNSON. 'And if Jack Wilkes *should* be there, what is

*Wilkes* 1727–97: rake, wit, and anti-government MP
*Jack Ketch* the hangman
*patriotic* 'factious disturber of the government' (Johnson)

that to *me*, Sir? My dear friend, let us have no more of this. I am sorry to be angry with you; but really it is treating me strangely to talk to me as if I could not meet any company whatever, occasionally.' BOSWELL. 'Pray forgive me, Sir: I meant well. But you shall meet whoever comes, for me.' Thus I secured him, and told Dilly that he would find him very well pleased to be one of his guests on the day appointed.

Upon the much-expected Wednesday, I called on him about half an hour before dinner, as I often did when we were to dine out together, to see that he was ready in time, and to accompany him. I found him buffeting his books, as upon a former occasion, covered with dust, and making no preparation for going abroad. 'How is this, Sir? (said I). Don't you recollect that you are to dine at Mr Dilly's?' JOHNSON. 'Sir, I did not think of going to Dilly's: it went out of my head. I have ordered dinner at home with Mrs Williams.' BOSWELL. 'But, my dear Sir, you know you were engaged to Mr Dilly, and I told him so. He will expect you, and will be much disappointed if you don't come.' JOHNSON. 'You must talk to Mrs Williams about this.'

Here was a sad dilemma. I feared that what I was so confident I had secured would yet be frustrated. He had accustomed himself to shew Mrs Williams such a degree of humane attention, as frequently imposed some restraint upon him; and I knew that if she should be obstinate, he would not stir. I hastened downstairs to the blind lady's room, and told her I was in great uneasiness, for Dr Johnson had engaged to me to dine this day at Mr Dilly's, but that he had told me he had forgotten his engagement, and had ordered dinner at home. 'Yes, Sir (said she, pretty peevishly), Dr Johnson is to dine at home.' – 'Madam (said I), his respect for you is such, that I know he will not leave you unless you absolutely desire it. But as you have so much of his company, I hope you will be good enough to forego it for a day; as Mr Dilly is a very worthy man, has frequently had agreeable parties at his house for Dr Johnson, and will be vexed if the Doctor neglects him today. And then, Madam, be pleased to consider my situation; I carried the message, and I assured Mr Dilly that Dr Johnson was to come, and no doubt he has made a dinner, and invited a company, and boasted of the honour he expected to have. I shall be quite disgraced if the Doctor is not there.' She gradually softened to my solicitations, which were certainly as earnest as most entreaties to ladies upon any occasion, and was graciously pleased to empower me to tell Dr Johnson, 'That all things considered, she thought he should certainly go.' I flew back to him, still in dust, and careless of what should be the event, 'indifferent in his choice to go or stay;' but as soon as I had announced to him Mrs Williams's consent, he roared, 'Frank, a clean shirt,' and was very soon dressed. When I had him fairly seated in a hackney-coach with me, I exulted as much as a fortune-hunter who has got an heiress into a post-chaise with him to set out for Gretna Green.†

When we entered Mr Dilly's drawing room, he found himself in the midst of a company he did not know. I kept myself snug and silent, watching how he would conduct himself. I observed him whispering to Mr Dilly, 'Who is that gentleman, Sir?' – 'Mr. Arthur Lee.' – JOHNSON. 'Too, too, too,' (under his breath) which was one of his habitual mutterings. Mr Arthur Lee could not but be very obnoxious to Johnson, for he was not only a *patriot* but an *American*.† He was afterwards minister from the United States at the court of Madrid. 'And who is the gentleman in lace?' – 'Mr Wilkes, Sir.' This information confounded him still more; he had some difficulty to restrain himself, and taking up a book, sat down upon a window-seat and read, or at least kept his eye upon it intently for some time, till he composed himself. His feelings, I dare say, were awkward enough. But he no doubt recollected his having rated me for supposing that he could be at all disconcerted by any company, and he, therefore, resolutely set himself to behave quite as an easy man of the world, who could adapt himself at once to the disposition and manners of those whom he might chance to meet.

The cheering sound of 'Dinner is upon the table,' dissolved his reverie, and we *all* sat down without any symptom of ill humour. There were present, besides Mr Wilkes, and Mr Arthur Lee, who was an old companion of mine when he studied physick at Edinburgh, Mr (now Sir John) Miller, Dr Lettsom, and Mr Slater the druggist. Mr Wilkes placed himself next to Dr Johnson, and behaved to him with so much attention and politeness, that he gained upon him insensibly. No man eat more heartily than Johnson, or loved better what was nice and delicate. Mr Wilkes was very assiduous in helping him to some fine veal. 'Pray give me leave, Sir: – It is better here – A little of the brown – Some fat, Sir – A little of the stuffing – Some gravy – Let me have the pleasure of giving you some butter – Allow me to recommend a squeeze of this orange; – or the lemon, perhaps, may have more zest.' – 'Sir, Sir, I am obliged to you, Sir,' cried Johnson, bowing, and turning his head to him with a look for some time of 'surly virtue,'† but, in a short while, of complacency.

Foote† being mentioned, Johnson said, 'He is not a good mimic.' One of the company added, 'A merry Andrew, a buffoon.' JOHNSON. 'But he has wit too, and is not deficient in ideas, or in fertility and variety of imagery, and not empty of reading; he has knowledge enough to fill up his part. One species of wit he has in an eminent degree, that of escape.

*Gretna Green* in Scotland, where marriage-laws were laxer

*American* Johnson had written against the colonists' political case

*'surly virtue'* Johnson's poem *London*, l.145

*Foote* Samuel Foote (1720–77), actor-dramatist

You drive him into a corner with both hands; but he's gone, Sir, when you think you have got him – like an animal that jumps over your head. Then he has a great range for his wit; he never lets truth stand between him and a jest, and he is sometimes mighty coarse. Garrick is under many restraints from which Foote is free.' Wilkes. 'Garrick's wit is more like Lord Chesterfield's.' Johnson. 'The first time I was in company with Foote was at Fitzherbert's. Having no good opinion of the fellow, I was resolved not to be pleased; and it is very difficult to please a man against his will. I went on eating my dinner pretty sullenly, affecting not to mind him. But the dog was so very comical, that I was obliged to lay down my knife and fork, throw myself back upon my chair, and fairly laugh it out. No, Sir, he was irresistible. He upon one occasion experienced, in an extraordinary degree, the efficacy of his powers of entertaining. Amongst the many and various modes which he tried of getting money, he became a partner with a small-beer brewer, and he was to have a share of the profits for procuring customers amongst his numerous acquaintance. Fitzherbert was one who took his small-beer; but it was so bad that the servants resolved not to drink it. They were at some loss how to notify their resolution, being afraid of offending their master, who they knew liked Foote much as a companion. At last they fixed upon a little black boy, who was rather a favourite, to be their deputy, and deliver their remonstrance; and having invested him with the whole authority of the kitchen, he was to inform Mr Fitzherbert, in all their names, upon a certain day, that they would drink Foote's small-beer no longer. On that day Foote happened to dine at Fitzherbert's, and this boy served at table; he was so delighted with Foote's stories, and merriment, and grimace, that when he went down stairs, he told them, "This is the finest man I have ever seen. I will not deliver your message. I will drink his small-beer."'

Somebody observed that Garrick could not have done this. Wilkes. 'Garrick would have made the small-beer still smaller. He is now leaving the stage; but he will play *Scrub*[†] all his life.' I knew that Johnson would let nobody attack Garrick[†] but himself, as Garrick once said to me, and I had heard him praise his liberality; so to bring out his commendation of his celebrated pupil, I said, loudly, 'I have heard Garrick is liberal.' Johnson. 'Yes, Sir, I know that Garrick has given away more money than any man in England that I am acquainted with, and that not from ostentatious views. Garrick was very poor when he began life; so when he came to have money, he probably was very unskilful in giving away, and saved when he should not. But Garrick began to be liberal as soon as he could; and I am of opinion, the

*Scrub* servant in Farquhar's *The Beaux' Stratagem* (1707)

*Garrick* formerly Johnson's pupil

reputation of avarice which he has had, has been very lucky for him, and prevented his having many enemies. You despise a man for avarice, but do not hate him. Garrick might have been much better attacked for living with more splendour than is suitable to a player: if they had had the wit to have assaulted him in that quarter, they might have galled him more. But they have kept clamouring about his avarice, which has rescued him from much obloquy and envy.'

Talking of the great difficulty of obtaining authentic information for biography, Johnson told us, 'When I was a young fellow I wanted to write the *Life of Dryden*, and in order to get materials, I applied to the only two persons then alive who had seen him; these were old Swinney, and old Cibber. Swinney's information was no more than this, "That at Will's coffee-house Dryden had a particular chair for himself, which was set by the fire in winter, and was then called his winter-chair; and that it was carried out for him to the balcony in summer, and was then called his summer-chair." Cibber could tell no more but "That he remembered him a decent old man, arbiter of critical disputes at Will's." You are to consider that Cibber was then at a great distance from Dryden, had perhaps one leg only in the room, and durst not draw in the other.' BOSWELL. 'Yet Cibber was a man of observation?' JOHNSON. 'I think not.' BOSWELL. 'You will allow his *Apology*† to be well done.' JOHNSON. 'Very well done, to be sure, Sir. That book is a striking proof of the justice of Pope's remark:

"Each might his several province well command,
Would all but stoop to what they understand."'

BOSWELL. 'And his plays are good.' JOHNSON. 'Yes; but that was his trade; *l'esprit du corps*: he had been all his life among players and play-writers. I wondered that he had so little to say in conversation, for he had kept the best company, and learnt all that can be got by the ear. He abused Pindar to me, and then shewed me an Ode of his own, with an absurd couplet, making a linnet soar on an eagle's wing. I told him that when the ancients made a simile, they always made it like something real.'

Mr Wilkes remarked, that 'among all the bold flights of Shakespeare's imagination, the boldest was making Birnamwood march to Dunsinane; creating a wood where there never was a shrub; a wood in Scotland! ha! ha! ha!' And he also observed, that 'the clannish slavery of the Highlands of Scotland was the single exception to Milton's remark of "The Mountain Nymph, sweet Liberty," being worshipped in all hilly countries.' – 'When I was at Inverary (said he) on a visit to my old friend, Archibald, Duke of Argyle, his dependents congratulated me on

*Apology* see p. 166

being such a favourite of his Grace. I said, "It is then, gentlemen, truly lucky for me; for if I had displeased the Duke, and he had wished it, there is not a Campbell among you but would have been ready to bring John Wilkes's head to him in a charger. It would have been only

"Off with his head! So much for Aylesbury."[†]

I was then member for Aylesbury.'

Dr Johnson and Mr Wilkes talked of the contested passage in Horace's *Art of Poetry*, '*Difficile est propriè communia dicere*.' Mr Wilkes, according to my note, gave the interpretation thus; 'It is difficult to speak with propriety of common things; as, if a poet had to speak of Queen Caroline drinking tea, he must endeavour to avoid the vulgarity of cups and saucers.' . . .

WILKES. 'We have no City-Poet now: that is an office which has gone into disuse. The last was Elkanah Settle.[†] There is something in *names* which one cannot help feeling. Now *Elkanah Settle* sounds so *queer*, who can expect much from that name? We should have no hesitation to give it for John Dryden, in preference to Elkanah Settle, from the names only, without knowing their different merits.' JOHNSON. 'I suppose, Sir, Settle did as well for Aldermen in his time, as John Home[†] could do now. Where did Beckford[†] and Trecothick learn English?'

Mr Arthur Lee mentioned some Scotch who had taken possession of a barren part of America, and wondered why they should choose it. JOHNSON. 'Why, Sir, all barrenness is comparative. The *Scotch* would not know it to be barren.' BOSWELL. 'Come, come, he is flattering the English. You have now been in Scotland, Sir, and say if you did not see meat and drink enough there.' JOHNSON. 'Why yes, Sir; meat and drink enough to give the inhabitants sufficient strength to run away from home.' All these quick and lively sallies were said sportively, quite in jest, and with a smile, which showed that he meant only wit. Upon this topic he and Mr Wilkes could perfectly assimilate; here was a bond of union between them, and I was conscious that as both of them had visited Caledonia, both were fully satisfied of the strange narrow ignorance of those who imagine that it is a land of famine. But they amused themselves with persevering in the old jokes. When I claimed a superiority for Scotland over England in one respect, that no man can be arrested there for a debt merely because another swears it against him; but there must first be the judgement of a court of law ascertaining its justice; and that a seizure of the person, before judgement is obtained, can take place only, if his creditor should swear that he is about to fly

*Off . . . Aylesbury* alters a line from Cibber's adaptation of Shakespeare's *Richard III*

*Elkanah Settle* 1648–1724: antagonist of Dryden

*John Home* 1722–1808: Scottish dramatist (*Douglas*, 1756)

*Beckford* 1709–70: Lord Mayor of London, father of the writer

from the country, or, as it is technically expressed, is *in meditatione fugæ*. WILKES. 'That, I should think, may be safely sworn of all the Scotch nation.' JOHNSON. (to Mr Wilkes) 'You must know, Sir, I lately took my friend Boswell and shewed him genuine civilised life in an English provincial town. I turned him loose at Lichfield, my native city, that he might see for once real civility: for you know he lives among savages in Scotland, and among rakes in London.' WILKES. 'Except when he is with grave, sober, decent people like you and me.' JOHNSON. (smiling) 'And we ashamed of him.'

They were quite frank and easy. Johnson told the story of his asking Mrs Macaulay† to allow her footman to sit down with them, to prove the ridiculousness of the argument for the equality of mankind; and he said to me afterwards, with a nod of satisfaction, 'You saw Mr Wilkes acquiesced.' Wilkes talked with all imaginable freedom of the ludicrous title given to the Attorney-General,† *Diabolus Regis* [King's Devil]; adding, 'I have reason to know something about that officer; for I was prosecuted for a libel.' Johnson, who many people would have supposed must have been furiously angry at hearing this talked of so lightly, said not a word. He was now, *indeed*, 'a good-humoured fellow.'

After dinner we had an accession of Mrs Knowles, the Quaker lady, well known for her various talents, and of Mr Alderman Lee. Amidst some patriotic groans, somebody (I think the Alderman) said, 'Poor old England is lost.' JOHNSON. 'Sir, it is not so much to be lamented that Old England is lost, as that the Scotch have found it.' WILKES. 'Had Lord Bute† governed Scotland only, I should not have taken the trouble to write his eulogy, and dedicate *Mortimer*† to him.'

Mr Wilkes held a candle to shew a fine print of a beautiful female figure which hung in the room, and pointed out the elegant contour of the bosom with the finger of an arch connoisseur. He afterwards, in a conversation with me, waggishly insisted, that all the time Johnson shewed visible signs of a fervent admiration of the corresponding charms of the fair Quaker.

This record, though by no means so perfect as I could wish, will serve to give a notion of a very curious interview, which was not only pleasing at the time, but had the agreeable and benignant effect of reconciling any animosity, and sweetening any acidity, which in the various bustle of political contest, had been produced in the minds of two men, who though widely different, had so many things in common – classical learning, modern literature, wit, and humour, and ready repartee – that

*Mrs Macaulay* 1731–91: republican historian
*Attorney-General* government law-officer
*Lord Bute* 1713–92; Prime Minister of Scots family; procured Johnson's pension
*Mortimer* history play with dedication by Wilkes (1763) ironically criticising the influence of Bute

it would have been much to be regretted if they had been for ever at a distance from each other.

Mr Burke gave me much credit for this successful *negotiation*; and pleasantly said, that 'there was nothing to equal it in the whole history of the *Corps Diplomatique*.'

I attended Dr Johnson home, and had the satisfaction to hear him tell Mrs Williams how much he had been pleased with Mr Wilkes's company, and what an agreeable day he had passed. . . .

1791

# Henry Mackenzie
## 1745–1831

Mackenzie, a Scottish lawyer, was a more robust character than one might deduce from his most successful novel, *The Man of Feeling*, a loosely-structured example of the novel of sensibility, in which Harley, the high-souled hero, cultivates and displays all too publicly deep sympathy for his fellow-man. (The masterpiece of the genre is Sterne's *Sentimental Journey*, where the emotion is tempered by self-knowledge and sexual innuendo.)

## *From* THE MAN OF FEELING

### *[Harley visits a Madhouse]*

Separate from the rest stood one, whose appearance had something of superior dignity. Her face, though pale and wasted, was less squalid than those of the others, and showed a dejection of that decent kind, which moves our pity unmixed with horror: upon her, therefore, the eyes of all were immediately turned. The keeper, who accompanied them, observed it: 'This,' said he, 'is a young lady, who was born to ride in her coach and six. She was beloved, if the story I have heard is true, by a young gentleman, her equal in birth, though by no means her match in fortune: but love, they say, is blind, and so she fancied him as much as he did her. Her father, it seems, would not hear of their marriage, and threatened to turn her out of doors, if ever she saw him again. Upon this the young gentleman took a voyage to the West Indies, in hopes of bettering his fortune, and obtaining his mistress; but he was scarce landed, when he was seized with one of the fevers which are common in those islands, and died in a few days, lamented by every one that knew him. This news soon reached his mistress, who was at the same time pressed by her father to marry a rich miserly fellow, who was old enough to be her grandfather. The death of her lover had no effect on her inhuman parent; he was only the more earnest for her marriage with the man he had provided for her; and what between her despair at the death of the one, and her aversion to the other, the poor young lady was reduced to the condition you see her in. But God would not prosper such cruelty; her father's affairs soon after went to wreck, and he died almost a beggar.'

Though this story was told in very plain language, it had particularly attracted Harley's notice: he had given it the tribute of some tears. The unfortunate young lady had till now seemed entranced in thought, with her eyes fixed on a little garnet-ring she wore on her finger: she turned them now upon Harley. 'My Billy is no more!' said she, 'do you weep for my Billy? Blessings on your tears! I would weep too, but my brain is dry; and it burns, it burns, it burns!' – She drew nearer to Harley. – 'Be comforted, young Lady,' said he, 'your Billy is in heaven.' 'Is he, indeed? and shall we meet again? And shall that frightful man' (pointing to the keeper) 'not be there? – Alas! I am grown naughty of late; I have almost forgotten to think of heaven: yet I pray sometimes; when I can, I pray; and sometimes I sing; when I am saddest, I sing: – You shall hear me, hush!

'Light be the earth on Billy's breast,
And green the sod that wraps his grave!'

There was a plaintive wildness in the air not to be withstood; and, except the keeper's, there was not an unmoistened eye around her.

'Do you weep again?' said she; 'I would not have you weep: you are like my Billy; you are, believe me; just so he looked when he gave me this ring; poor Billy! 'twas the last time ever we met! –

''Twas when the seas were roaring – I love you for resembling my Billy; but I shall never love any man like him.' – She stretched out her hand to Harley; he pressed it between both of his, and bathed it with his tears. – 'Nay, that is Billy's ring,' said she, 'you cannot have it, indeed; but here is another, look here, which I plaited today of some gold-thread from this bit of stuff; will you keep it for my sake? I am a strange girl; – but my heart is harmless: my poor heart! it will burst some day; feel how it beats.' – She pressed his hand to her bosom, then holding her head in the attitude of listening – 'Hark! one, two, three! be quiet, thou little trembler; my Billy's is cold! – but I had forgotten the ring.' She put it on his finger. – 'Farewell! I must leave you now.' – She would have withdrawn her hand; Harley held it to his lips. – 'I dare not stay longer; my head throbs sadly: farewell!' – She walked with a hurried step to a little apartment at some distance. Harley stood fixed in astonishment and pity! his friend gave money to the keeper. – Harley looked on his ring. – He put a couple of guineas into the man's hand: 'Be kind to that unfortunate' – He burst into tears, and left them.

1771

# Robert Fergusson

1750–74

**In a short career which ended in madness, Fergusson wrote poems in English and Scots, and greatly influenced Burns. A fine comic writer, he ridiculed Johnson's visit to St Andrews (where he had studied), and in 'The Sow of Feeling' undercut Henry Mackenzie's sentimentalism. His poems appeared in 1773. His best work shows a critical relish of the Scottish scene.**

## THE DAFT-DAYS†

Now mirk* December's dowie* face — dark gloomy
Glours our* the rigs† wi' sour grimace, — glowers over
While, thro' his *minimum* of space,
The bleer-ey'd sun,
Wi' blinkin light and stealing pace,
His race doth run.

From naked groves nae birdie sings;
To shepherd's pipe nae hillock rings;
The breeze nae od'rous flavour brings
From Borean† cave;
And dwyning* Nature droops her wings, — declining
Wi' visage grave.

Mankind but scanty pleasure glean
Frae snawy hill or barren plain,
Whan Winter, 'midst his nipping train,
Wi' frozen spear,
Sends drift† owr a' his bleak domain,
And guides the weir.* — war

---

*The Daft Days* Time of revelry at New Year
*rigs* field ridges
*Borean* of north wind
*drift* of snow

Auld Reikie![†] thou'rt the canty* hole,   cheerful
A bield* for money caldrife* soul,   shelter   spiritless
Wha snugly at thine ingle* loll,   fireside
Baith warm and couth;*   sociable
While round they gar* the bicker* roll   make   cup
To weet their mouth.

When merry Yule-day comes, I trow,
You'll scantlins* find a hungry mou;   scarcely
Sma' are our cares, our stamacks fou
O' gusty* gear,   tasty
And kickshaws,* strangers to our view,   novelties
Sin fairn-year.*   last year

Ye browster* wives, now busk* ye bra,   ale-seller   dress
And fling your sorrows far awa';
Then, come and gies the tither blaw*   drink
Of reaming ale,
Mair precious than the well of Spa,
Our hearts to heal.

Then, tho' at odds wi' a' the warl',
Amang oursells we'll never quarrel;
Tho' Discord gie a canker'd snarl
To spoil our glee,
As lang's there's pith* into the barrel   strength
We'll drink and 'gree.

Fidlers, your pins in temper fix,
And roset[†] weel your fiddlesticks,
But banish vile Italian tricks
From out your *quorum*,
Nor *fortes* wi' *pianos* mix,
Gie's *Tulloch Gorum*.[†]

For nought can cheer the heart sae weil
As can a canty Highland reel;
It even vivifies the heel
To skip and dance:
Lifeless is he wha canna feel
Its influence.

*Reikie* smoky [Edinburgh]
*roset* rub with rosin
*But banish . . . Gorum* He prefers native music to foreign elaborations

Let mirth abound, let social cheer
Invest the dawning of the year;
Let blithesome innocence appear
To crown our joy;
Nor envy wi' sarcastic sneer,
Our bliss destroy.

And thou, great god of *Aqua Vitæ!*[†]
Wha sways the empire of this city,
When fou we're sometimes capernoity,* crabbed
Be thou prepar'd
To hedge us frae that black banditti,
The City-Guard.

1772

## *From* AULD REIKIE. A POEM[†]

Auld Reikie! wale* o' ilka town best
That Scotland kens beneath the moon;
Whare couthy chiels at e'ening meet
Their bizzing craigs[†] and mou's to weet:
And blythly gar auld Care gae bye
Wi' blinkit and wi' bleering eye:
O'er lang frae thee the Muse has been
Sae frisky on the simmer's green,
Whan flowers and gowans wont to glent* gleam
In bonny blinks* upo' the bent;* of sun field
But now the leaves a yellow die,
Peel'd frae the branches, quickly fly;
And now frae nouther bush nor brier
The spreckl'd mavis* greets your ear; thrush
Nor bonny blackbird skims and roves
To seek his love in yonder groves.
Then, Reikie, welcome! Thou canst charm
Unfleggit* by the year's alarm; unperturbed
Not Boreas, that sae snelly blows,
Dare here pap in his angry nose:
Thanks to our dads,* whase biggin* stands ancestors/predecessors building

*Aqua Vitæ* whisky (Latin: water of life) *bizzing craigs* parched throats
*Auld Reikie* traditional name for Edinburgh

A shelter to surrounding lands.* tenements
  Now morn, with bonny purpie-smiles,
Kisses the air-cock o' St Giles;†
Rakin their ein, the servant lasses
Early begin their lies and clashes;* chats
Ilk tells her friend of saddest distress,
That still she brooks frae scouling mistress;
And wi' her joe* in turnpike stair lover
She'd rather snuff the stinking air,
As be subjected to her tongue,
When justly censur'd in the wrong.
  On stair wi' tub, or pat in hand,
The barefoot housemaids looe to stand,
That antrin* fock may ken how snell* different sharp
Auld Reikie will at morning smell:
Then, with an inundation big as
The burn that 'neath the Nore Loch Brig is,
They kindly shower Edina's roses,†
To quicken and regale our noses.
Now some for this, wi' satyr's leesh,
Ha'e gi'en auld Edinburgh a creesh:* lash
But without souring nocht is sweet;
The morning smells that hail our street,
Prepare, and gently lead the way
To simmer canty, braw and gay;
Edina's sons mair eithly* share easily
Her spices and her dainties rare,
Than he that's never yet been call'd
Aff frae his plaidie or his fauld.
  Now stairhead critics, senseless fools,
Censure their aim, and pride their rules,
In Luckenbooths,† wi' glouring eye,
Their neighbours sma'est faults descry:
If ony loun* should dander* there, boy wander
Of aukward gate, and foreign air,
They trace his steps, till they can tell
His pedigree as weel's himsell.
  When Phœbus blinks wi' warmer ray,
And schools at noonday get the play,
Then bus'ness, weighty bus'ness comes;
The trader glours; he doubts, he hums:

*St Giles* central church
*roses* domestic slops emptied into street
*Luckenbooths* closed stalls

The lawyers eke to Cross repair,
Their wigs to shaw, and toss an air;
While busy agent closely plies,
And a' his kittle* cases tries. hard
  Now Night, that's cunzied* chief for fun, admitted
Is wi' her usual rites begun;
Thro' ilka gate the torches blaze,
And globes send out their blinking rays.
The usefu' cadie* plies in street, messenger
To bide the profits o' his feet;
For by thir lads Auld Reikie's fock
Ken but a sample, o' the stock
O' thieves, that nightly wad oppress,
And make baith goods and gear the less.
Near him the lazy chairman* stands, passenger-carrier
And wats na how to turn his hands,
Till some daft birky,* ranting fu', fellow
Has matters somewhere else to do;
The chairman willing, gi'es his light
To deeds o' darkness and o' night:
  It's never sax pence for a lift
That gars thir lads wi' fu'ness rift;* belch
For they wi' better gear are paid,
And whores and culls* support their trade. fools
  Near some lamp-post, wi' dowy face,
Wi' heavy een, and sour grimace,
Stands she that beauty lang had kend,
Whoredom her trade, and vice her end.
But see wharenow she wuns her bread,
By that which Nature ne'er decreed;
And sings sad music to the lugs,* ears
'Mang burachs* o' damn'd whores and rogues. groups
Whane'er we reputation loss,
Fair chastity's transparent gloss!
Redemption seenil* kens the name seldom
But a's black misery and shame. . . .

1773

# TO THE PRINCIPAL AND PROFESSORS OF THE UNIVERSITY OF ST ANDREWS, ON THEIR SUPERB TREAT TO DR SAMUEL JOHNSON†

St Andrews town may look right gawsy,* — stately
Nae grass will grow upon her cawsey,* — street
Nor wa'-flowers of a yellow dye,
Glour dowy* o'er her ruins high, — gloomy
Sin Samy's head weel pang'd* wi' lear,* — packed learning
Has seen the *Alma Mater* there:
Regents,* my winsome billy* boys! — professors fellow
'Bout him you've made an unco noise;
Nae doubt for him your bells wad clink
To find him upon Eden's* brink, — local river
An' a' things nicely set in order,
Wad kep him on the Fifan border:
I'se warrant now frae France an' Spain,
Baith cooks and scullions mony ane
Wad gar the pats an' kettles tingle
Around the college kitchen ingle,
To fleg* frae a' your craigs* the roup,* — frighten throats hoarseness
Wi' reeking het and crieshy* soup; — oily
And snails and puddocks* mony hunder — frogs
Wad beeking lie the hearth-stane under,
Wi' roast and boild, an' a' kin kind,
To heat the body, cool the mind.
 But hear me lads! gin I'd been there,
How I wad trimm'd the bill o' fare!
For ne'er sic surly wight as he
Had met wi' sic respect frae me.
Mind ye what Sam, the lying loun!* — rogue
Has in his Dictionar laid down?
That aits* in England are a feast — oats
To cow an' horse, an' sican beast,
While in Scots ground this growth was common
To gust* the gab* o' man and woman. — taste mouth
Tak tent,* ye Regents! then, an' hear — heed
My list o' gudely hamel* gear, — homely

---

*To the Principal and Professors of St Andrews* Johnson visited St Andrews in Fife in 1773

Sic as ha'e often rax'd* the wyme* — stretched stomach
O' blyther fallows mony time;
Mair hardy, souple, steive* an' swank,* — firm agile
Than ever stood on Samy's shank.
*Imprimis*, then, a haggis fat,
Weel tottled* in a seything pat, — boiled
Wi' spice and ingans* weel ca'd thro', — onions
Had help'd to gust the stirrah's* mow,* — fellow mouth
And plac'd itsel in truncher clean
Before the gilpy's* glowrin een. — rascal
*Secundo*, then a gude sheep's head
Whase hide was singit, never flead,
And four black trotters cled wi' girsle,
Bedown his throat had learn'd to hirsle.* — rustle
What think ye neist, o' gude fat brose†
To clag* his ribs? a dainty dose! — stick to
And white and bloody puddins routh,* — plenty
To gar the Doctor skirl, O Drouth!* — thirst
Whan he cou'd never houp to merit
A cordial o' reaming claret,
But thraw* his nose, and brize* and pegh* — twist squeeze pant
O'er the contents o' sma' ale quegh:* — shallow cup
Then let his wisdom girn* and snarl — grimace
O'er a weel-tostit girdle farl,* — oatcake
An' learn, that maugre o' his wame,
Ill bairns are ay best heard at hame.
Drummond,† lang syne, o' Hawthornden,
The wyliest an' best o' men,
Has gi'en you dishes ane or mae,
That wad ha' gard his grinders play,
Not to *roast beef*, old England's life,
But to the auld *east nook of Fife*,
Whare Creilian† crafts cou'd weel ha'e gi'en
Scate-rumples* to ha'e clear'd his een; — hind parts
Than neist whan Samy's heart was faintin,
He'd lang'd for scate to mak him wanton.
Ah! willawins,* for Scotland now, — alas
Whan she maun stap ilk birky's mow
Wi' eistacks,* grown as 'tware in pet — dainties
In foreign land, or green-house het,

---

*brose* oatmeal and water
*Drummond* 1585–1649: Scottish poet; ll.65–6 refer to tunes
*Creilian* from Crail, nearby fishing-village

When cog* o' brose an' cutty* spoon — dish, short
Is a' our cottar* childer's boon, — peasant
Wha thro' the week, till Sunday's speal,* — holiday
Toil for pease-clods† an' gude lang kail.* — cabbage
Devall* then, Sirs, and never send — cease
For daintiths to regale a friend,
Or, like a torch at baith ends burning,
Your house 'll soon grow mirk and mourning.

What's this I hear some cynic say?
Robin, ye loun! its nae fair play;
Is there nae ither subject rife
To clap your thumb upon but Fife?
Gi' o'er, young man, you'll meet your corning,* — punishment
Than caption† war,* or charge o' horning; — worse
Some canker'd surly sour-mow'd carline†
Bred near the abbey o' Dumfarline,
Your shoulders yet may gi'e a lounder,* — blow
An' be of verse the mal-confounder.

Come on, ye blades! but 'ere ye tulzie,* — fight
Or hack our flesh wi' sword or gulzie,* — knife
Ne'er shaw your teeth, nor look like stink,
Nor o'er an empty bicker* blink: — cup
What weets the wizen* an' the wyme, — gullet
Will mend your prose and heal my rhyme.

1773

---

*pease-clods* peasemeal rolls
*caption . . .* writs for debt
*carline* old woman

# Richard Brinsley Sheridan

## 1751–1816

The son of an Irish actor, Sheridan was educated in England. His elopement with the singer, Eliza Linley, whom he eventually married, and duels with another suitor, provided hints for *The Rivals*, a great success at Covent Garden in 1775. It was followed by *St Patrick's Day* and *The Duenna*. He bought Garrick's half-share in the Drury Lane Theatre, which he ran, eventually as sole owner. *The School for Scandal* (1777) is one of the century's great comedies, and made a fortune; the burlesque rehearsal-play *The Critic* (1779) shows his awareness of theatrical absurdities. He became a member of Johnson's Club. His later career was mainly devoted to politics: a supporter of Fox and friend of the future George IV, he held various government offices and was a spectacular parliamentary orator, leading the impeachment of Warren Hastings for corruption in India. Financial difficulties followed the demolition of Drury Lane and the burning-down of its successor (1809); his last years were spent mainly in poverty.

## *From* THE SCHOOL FOR SCANDAL†

### Act IV Scene III

### *[Discoveries]*

*A library*

JOSEPH SURFACE *and* SERVANT

JOS. SURF.: No letter from Lady Teazle?

SERV.: No, sir.

† *The School for Scandal* If less coarse and cynical, Sheridan was well aware of Restoration comedy. In the gossipy society of *The School for Scandal*, represented by Lady Sneerwell and Sir Benjamin Backbite (the names suggesting the comic tradition), Sir Peter Teazle comes to doubt the wisdom of his recently taking a young wife. Lady Teazle is being tempted by the calculating hypocrite, Joseph Surface; in contrast (like that between Blifil and Tom Jones in Fielding's novel) his brother Charles is reckless but warm-hearted, and in love with Sir Peter's ward, Maria, whose fortune Joseph covets. Joseph's 'sentiment' consists of moral platitudes. After this climactic 'screen scene', virtue triumphs

JOS. SURF. [*aside*]: I am surprised she hasn't sent if she is prevented from coming! Sir Peter certainly does not suspect me – yet I wish I may not lose the heiress through the scrape I have drawn myself in with the wife. However, Charles's imprudence and bad character are great points in my favour. [*Knocking*]

SERV.: Sir, I believe that must be Lady Teazle.

JOS. SURF.: Hold! see whether it is or not before you go to the door – I have a particular message for you if it should be my brother.

SERV.: 'Tis her ladyship, sir. She always leaves her chair at the milliner's in the next street.

JOS. SURF.: Stay, stay – draw that screen before the window – that will do – my opposite neighbour is a maiden lady of so curious a temper – [*Servant draws the screen and exit.*] I have a difficult hand to play in this affair. Lady Teazle has lately suspected my views on Maria – but she must by no means be let into that secret, at least not till I have her more in my power.

*Enter* LADY TEAZLE

LADY TEAZ.: What sentiment in soliloquy! have you been very impatient now? – O lud! don't pretend to look grave. I vow I couldn't come before.

JOS. SURF.: O madam, punctuality is a species of constancy, a very unfashionable quality in a lady.

LADY TEAZ.: Upon my word you ought to pity me. Do you know that Sir Peter is grown so ill-tempered to me of late! and so jealous of *Charles* too – that's the best of the story, isn't it?

JOS. SURF. [*aside*]: I am glad my scandalous friends keep that up.

LADY TEAZ.: I am sure I wish he would let Maria marry him, and then perhaps he would be convinced, don't you, Mr Surface?

JOS. SURF. [*aside*]: Indeed I do not. – Oh, certainly I do – for then my dear Lady Teazle would also be convinced how wrong her suspicions were of my having any design on the silly girl.

LADY TEAZ.: Well, well, I'm inclined to believe you. But isn't it provoking to have the most ill-natured things said to one? And there's my friend Lady Sneerwell has circulated I don't know how many scandalous tales of me! and all without any foundation too – that's what vexes me.

JOS. SURF.: Aye madam, to be sure that *is* the provoking circumstance – without foundation! yes, yes, there's the mortification, indeed – for when a scandalous story is believed against one, there certainly is no comfort like the consciousness of having deserved it.

LADY TEAZ.: No, to be sure – then I'd forgive their malice – but to attack me, who am really so innocent, and who never say an ill-natured thing of anybody – that is, of any friend – and then Sir Peter too – to have him so peevish, and so suspicious, when I know the integrity of my own heart – indeed 'tis monstrous!

JOS. SURF.: But my dear Lady Teazle, 'tis your own fault if you suffer it – when a husband entertains a groundless suspicion of his wife and withdraws his confidence from her, the original compact is broke and she owes it to the honour of her sex to endeavour to outwit him.

LADY TEAZ.: Indeed! so that if he suspects me without cause, it follows that the best way of curing his jealousy is to give him reason for't.

JOS. SURF.: Undoubtedly – for your husband should never be deceived in you, and in that case it becomes *you* to be frail† in compliment to *his* discernment.

LADY TEAZ.: To be sure what you say is very reasonable, and when the consciousness of my own innocence –

JOS. SURF.: Ah, my dear madam, there is the great mistake – 'tis this very conscious innocence that is of the greatest prejudice to you. What is it makes you negligent of forms and careless of the world's opinion? why, the *consciousness* of your innocence. What makes you thoughtless in your conduct and apt to run into a thousand little imprudences? why, the *consciousness* of your innocence. What makes you impatient of Sir Peter's temper and outrageous at his suspicions? why, the *consciousness* of your own innocence!

LADY TEAZ.: 'Tis very true.

JOS. SURF.: Now my dear Lady Teazle, if you would but once make a trifling *faux pas* [slip], you can't conceive how cautious you would grow – and how ready to humour and agree with your husband.

LADY TEAZ.: Do you think so?

JOS. SURF.: Oh, I'm sure on't – and then you would find all scandal would cease at once, for in short, your character at present is like a person in a plethora† absolutely dying of too much health.

LADY TEAZ.: So, so – then I perceive your prescription is – that I must sin in my own defence – and part with my virtue to preserve my reputation.

JOS. SURF.: Exactly so upon my credit, ma'am.

LADY TEAZ.: Well, certainly this is the oddest doctrine, and the newest receipt for avoiding calumny.

JOS. SURF.: An infallible one, believe me. *Prudence*, like *experience*, must be paid for.

LADY TEAZ.: Why, if my understanding were once convinced –

JOS. SURF.: Oh certainly, Madam, your understanding *should* be convinced – yes, yes – heaven forbid I should persuade you to do anything you *thought* wrong. No, no, I have too much honour to desire it.

---

*frail* unchaste

*plethora* excessive fullness of blood

LADY TEAZ.: Don't you think we may as well leave honour out of the argument?

JOS. SURF.: Ah, the ill effects of your country education I see, still remain with you.

LADY TEAZ.: I doubt they do, indeed – and I will fairly own to you, that if I could be persuaded to do wrong, it would be by Sir Peter's ill-usage sooner than your honourable logic, after all.

JOS. SURF.: Then by this hand which he is unworthy of – [*Taking her hand*]

*Enter* SERVANT

'Sdeath, you blockhead – what do you want?

SERV.: I beg your pardon, sir, but I thought you wouldn't choose Sir Peter to come up without announcing him.

JOS. SURF.: Sir Peter! – Oons and the devil!

LADY TEAZ.: Sir Peter! O lud! I'm ruined! I'm ruined!

SERV.: Sir, 'twasn't I let him in.

LADY TEAZ.: O I'm undone – what will become of me now Mr Logic? – O mercy, he's on the stairs – I'll get behind here – and if ever I'm so imprudent again – [*Goes behind the screen*]

JOS. SURF.: Give me that book.

[*Sits down.* SERVANT *pretends to adjust his hair*]

*Enter* SIR PETER TEAZLE

SIR PET.: Aye, ever improving himself! – Mr Surface, Mr Surface! –

JOS. SURF.: Oh my dear Sir Peter, I beg your pardon. [*Gaping and throws away the book*] I have been dozing over a stupid book! well, I am much obliged to you for this call – you haven't been here I believe since I fitted up this room. Books you know are the only things I am a coxcomb† in.

SIR PET.: 'Tis very neat indeed. Well, well, that's proper – and you make even your screen a source of knowledge – hung, I perceive, with maps.

JOS. SURF.: Oh yes, I find great use in that screen.

SIR PET.: I dare say you must – certainly – when you want to find anything in a hurry.

JOS. SURF. [*aside*]: Aye, or to hide anything in a hurry either.

SIR PET.: Well, I have a little private business –

JOS. SURF.: You needn't stay. [*To* SERVANT]

SERV.: No, Sir, *Exit.*

JOS. SURF.: Here's a chair, Sir Peter – I beg –

JOS. SURF.: No, you must never make it public.

---

*coxcomb* vain, showy person

SIR. PET.: Well, now we are alone, there is a subject, my dear friend, on which I wish to unburden my mind to you – a point of the greatest moment to my peace; in short, my good friend, Lady Teazle's conduct of late has made me extremely unhappy.

JOS. SURF.: Indeed! I am very sorry to hear it.

SIR PET.: Yes, 'tis but too plain she has not the least regard for me – but what's worse, I have pretty good authority to suspect she must have formed an attachment to another.

JOS. SURF.: You astonish me!

SIR PET.: Yes – and, between ourselves – I think I have discovered the person.

JOS. SURF.: How, you alarm me exceedingly!

SIR PET.: Ah! my dear friend, I knew you would sympathise with me.

JOS. SURF.: Yes, believe me, Sir Peter, such a discovery would hurt me just as much as it would you.

SIR PET.: I am convinced of it – ah! it is a happiness to have a friend whom one can trust even with one's family secrets. But have you no guess who I mean?

JOS. SURF.: I haven't the most distant idea – it can't be Sir Benjamin Backbite!

SIR PET.: O no! What say you to Charles?

JOS. SURF.: My brother! impossible! –

SIR PET.: Ah! my dear friend – the goodness of your own heart misleads you – you judge of others by yourself.

JOS. SURF.: Certainly Sir Peter, the heart that is conscious of its own integrity is ever slow to credit another's treachery.

SIR PET.: True – but your brother has no sentiment – you never hear him talk so.

JOS. SURF.: Yet I can't but think Lady Teazle herself has too much principle –

SIR PET.: Aye, but what's her principle against the flattery of a handsome, lively young fellow?

JOS. SURF.: That's very true.

SIR PET.: And then you know the difference of our ages makes it very improbable that she should have a great affection for me – and if she were to be frail and I were to make it public, why the town would only laugh at me, the foolish old bachelor who had married a girl.

JOS. SURF.: That's true, to be sure – they *would* laugh.

SIR PET.: Laugh! aye – and make ballads – and paragraphs – and the devil knows what of me.

SIR PET.: But then again – that the nephew of my old friend, Sir Oliver, should be the person to attempt such a wrong, hurts me more nearly.

JOS. SURF.: Aye there's the point; when ingratitude barbs the dart of injury, the wound has double danger in it.

SIR PET.: Aye, I that was in a manner left his guardian – in whose house he had been so often entertained – who never in my life denied him my advice.

JOS. SURF.: O 'tis not to be credited! There *may* be a man capable of such baseness to be sure, but for my part, till you can give me positive proofs, I cannot but doubt it. – However, if this should be proved on him, he is no longer a brother of mine! I disclaim kindred with him – for the man who can break through the laws of hospitality – and attempt the wife of his friend, deserves to be branded as the pest of society.

SIR PET.: What a difference there is between you! What noble sentiments!

JOS. SURF.: Yet I cannot suspect Lady Teazle's honour.

SIR PET.: I am sure I wish to think well of her – and to remove all ground of quarrel between us. She has lately reproached me more than once, with having made no settlement† on her – and in our last quarrel she almost hinted that she should not break her heart if I was dead. Now as we seem to differ in our ideas of expense, I have resolved she shall be her own mistress in that respect for the future – and if I *were* to die, she shall find that I have not been inattentive to her interest while living. Here my friend, are the drafts of two deeds, which I wish to have your opinion on. By one, she will enjoy eight hundred a year independent while I live, and by the other, the bulk of my fortune after my death.

JOS. SURF.: This conduct, Sir Peter, is indeed truly generous. – [*Aside*] I wish it may not corrupt† my pupil.

SIR PET.: Yes, I am determined she shall have no cause to complain, though I would not have her acquainted with the latter instance of my affection yet awhile.

JOS. SURF.: Nor I, if I could help it. [*Aside*]

SIR PET.: And now my dear friend, if you please we will talk over the situation of your hopes with *Maria*.

JOS. SURF. [*softly*]: No, no, Sir Peter; another time if you please.

SIR PET.: I am sensibly chagrined at the little progress you seem to make in her affection.

JOS. SURF.: I beg you will not mention it – what are my disappointments when your happiness is in debate! [*Softly*] – 'Sdeath, I should be ruined every way! [*Aside*]

SIR PET.: And though you are so averse to my acquainting Lady Teazle with your passion, I am sure she's not your enemy in the affair.

JOS. SURF.: Pray Sir Peter, now oblige me. – I am really too much affected by the subject we have been speaking on to bestow a thought on my

*settlement* formal property arrangement   *corrupt* ruin J's influence over Lady T.

own concerns. The man who is entrusted with his friend's distresses can never –

*Enter* SERVANT

Well, sir?

SERV.: Your brother, sir, is speaking to a gentleman in the street, and says he knows you are within.

JOS. SURF.: 'Sdeath, blockhead – I'm not within – I'm out for the day.

SIR PET.: Stay – hold – a thought has struck me – you shall be at home.

JOS. SURF.: Well, well, let him up. [*Exit* SERVANT] He'll interrupt Sir Peter – however –

SIR PET.: Now my good friend, oblige me I entreat you. Before Charles comes, let me conceal myself somewhere. Then do you tax† him on the point we have been talking on, and his answers may satisfy me at once.

JOS. SURF.: O fie, Sir Peter – would you have me join in so mean a trick – to trepan† my brother to – !

SIR PET.: Nay, you tell me you are *sure* he is innocent – if so, you do him the greatest service by giving him an opportunity to clear himself, and, you will set my heart at rest. Come, you shall not refuse me – here behind the screen will be [*goes to the screen*] – hey! what the devil! there seems to be *one* listener here already – I'll swear I saw a petticoat.

JOS. SURF.: Ha! ha! ha! – well, this is ridiculous enough. I'll tell you, Sir Peter, though I hold a man of intrigue to be a most despicable character, yet you know it doesn't follow that one is to be an absolute Joseph† either! Hark'ee! 'tis a little French milliner, a silly rogue that plagues me – and having some character, on your coming she ran behind the screen.

SIR PET.: Ah, you rogue! – but egad, she has overheard all I have been saying of my wife.

JOS. SURF.: O 'twill never go any further, you may depend on't!

SIR PET.: No! – then efaith, let her hear it out. – Here's a closet will do as well.

JOS. SURF.: Well, go in then.

SIR PET.: Sly rogue! sly rogue! [*Goes into the closet*]

JOS. SURF.: A very narrow escape, indeed! and a curious situation I'm in, to part man and wife in this manner.

LADY TEAZ. [*peeping from the screen*]: Couldn't I steal off?

JOS. SURF.: Keep close, my angel –

SIR PET. [*peeping out*]: Joseph, tax him home! –

*tax* accuse
*trepan* ensnare
*Joseph* in Genesis 39, he resists seduction

JOS. SURF.: Back, my dear friend!

LADY TEAZ. [*peeping*]: Couldn't you lock Sir Peter in?

JOS. SURF.: Be still, my life –

SIR PET. [*peeping*]: You're sure the little milliner won't blab?

JOS. SURF.: In! in! – my good Sir Peter – 'fore gad, I wish I had a key to the door.

*Enter* CHARLES SURFACE

CHAS. SURF.: Hallo! brother, what has been the matter? your fellow would not let me up at first. What, have you had a Jew† or a wench with you?

JOS. SURF.: Neither brother, I assure you.

CHAS. SURF.: But – what has made Sir Peter steal off? I thought he had been with you.

JOS. SURF.: He was, brother – but, hearing *you* were coming he did not choose to stay.

CHAS. SURF.: What, was the old gentleman afraid I wanted to borrow money of him!

JOS. SURF.: No, sir – but I am sorry to find Charles that you have lately given that worthy man grounds for great uneasiness.

CHAS. SURF.: Yes, they tell me I do that to a great many worthy men. But how so, pray?

JOS. SURF.: To be plain with you, brother, he thinks you are endeavouring to gain Lady Teazle's affections from him.

CHAS. SURF.: Who, I! O lud! not I, upon my word. – Ha! ha! ha! so the old fellow has found out that he has got a young wife, has he? – or what's worse, has her ladyship discovered that she has an old husband?

JOS. SURF.: This is no subject to jest on, brother. – He who can laugh –

CHAS. SURF.: True, true, brother, as you were going to say – then seriously, I never had the least idea of what you charge me with, upon my honour.

JOS. SURF.: Well, it will give Sir Peter great satisfaction to hear this. [*Aloud*]

CHAS. SURF.: To be sure I once thought the lady seemed to have taken a fancy to me – but upon my soul, I never gave her the least encouragement. – Besides, you know my attachment to Maria.

JOS. SURF.: But sure, brother, even if Lady Teazle had betrayed the fondest partiality for you –

CHAS. SURF.: Why, look'ee, Joseph, I hope I shall never deliberately do a dishonourable action – but if a pretty woman were purposely to

*Jew* that is, moneylender

throw herself in my way – and that pretty woman married to a man old enough to be her father –

JOS. SURF.: Well! –

CHAS. SURF.: Why, I believe I should be obliged to borrow a little of your morality, that's all. – But brother, do you know now that you surprise me exceedingly, by naming *me* with Lady Teazle – for faith, I always understood *you* were her favourite.

JOS. SURF.: O, for shame, Charles – this retort is foolish.

CHAS. SURF.: Nay, I swear I have seen you exchange such significant glances –

JOS. SURF.: Nay, nay, sir, this is no jest –

CHAS. SURF.: Egad, I'm serious! don't you remember – one day when I called here –

JOS. SURF.: Nay, prithee, Charles –

CHAS. SURF.: And found you together –

JOS. SURF.: Zounds, sir, I insist –

CHAS. SURF.: And another time when your servant –

JOS. SURF.: Brother, brother, a word with you! – [*Aside*] Gad, I must stop him.

CHAS. SURF.: Informed me, I say, that –

JOS. SURF.: Hush! – I beg your pardon, but Sir Peter has overheard all we have been saying – I knew you would clear yourself or I should not have consented.

CHAS. SURF.: How, Sir Peter! – where is he?

JOS. SURF.: Softly, there! [*Points to the closet*]

CHAS. SURF.: Oh, 'fore heaven, I'll have him out. – Sir Peter, come forth –

JOS. SURF.: No, no –

CHAS. SURF.: I say, Sir Peter, come into court. – [*Pulls in* SIR PETER] What, my old guardian! – What – turn inquisitor and take evidence incog.†

SIR PET.: Give me your hand, Charles – I believe I have suspected you wrongfully – but you mustn't be angry with Joseph – 'twas my plan.

CHAS. SURF.: Indeed! –

SIR PET.: But I acquit you. – I promise you I don't think near so ill of you as I did. What I have heard has given me great satisfaction.

CHAS. SURF.: Egad then, 'twas lucky you didn't hear any more – wasn't it, Joseph? [*Half aside*]

SIR PET.: Ah! you would have retorted on him.

CHAS. SURF.: Aye, aye, that was a joke.

SIR PET.: Yes, yes, I know his honour too well.

CHAS. SURF.: But you might as well have suspected him as me in this matter, for all that. Mightn't he, Joseph? [*Half aside*]

---

*incog.* incognito: hidden identity

SIR PET.: Well, well, I believe you.

JOS. SURF.: Would they were both out of the room! [*Aside*]

SIR PET.: And in future, perhaps, we may not be such strangers.

*Enter* SERVANT *who whispers* JOSEPH SURFACE

JOS. SURF.: Lady Sneerwell! – stop her by all means – [*Exit* SERVANT] Gentlemen – I beg pardon – I must wait on you downstairs – here's a person come on particular business.

CHAS. SURF.: Well, you can see him in another room. Sir Peter and I haven't met a long time, and I have something to say to him.

JOS. SURF.: They must not be left together. – I'll send Lady Sneerwell away, and return directly. – [*Aside*] Sir Peter, not a word of the French milliner.

*Exit* JOSEPH SURFACE

SIR PET.: O not for the world! – Ah, Charles, if you associated more with your brother, one might indeed hope for your reformation. He is a man of sentiment – well! there is nothing in the world so noble as a man of sentiment!

CHAS. SURF.: Pshaw! He is too moral by half, and so apprehensive of his good name, as he calls it, that I suppose he would as soon let a priest into his house as a girl.

SIR PET.: No, no – come, come – you wrong him. No, no, Joseph is no rake, but he is not such a saint in that respect either – I have a great mind to tell him – we should have a laugh! [*Aside*]

CHAS. SURF.: Oh, hang him! He's a very anchorite, a young hermit.

SIR PET.: Hark'ee, you must not abuse him. He may chance to hear of it again, I promise you.

CHAS. SURF.: Why, you won't tell him?

SIR PET.: No – but – this way. – [*Aside*] Egad, I'll tell him! – Hark'ee! have you a mind to have a good laugh at Joseph?

CHAS. SURF.: I should like it of all things.

SIR PET.: Then, efaith we will – I'll be quit with him for discovering† me. [*Aside*] – He had a girl with him when I called.

CHAS. SURF.: What, Joseph! you jest.

SIR PET.: Hush! – a little French milliner – [*whispers*] and the best of the jest is – she's in the room now.

CHAS. SURF.: The devil she is!

SIR PET.: Hush – I tell you – [*Points*]

CHAS. SURF.: Behind the screen – 'slife, let's unveil her!

SIR PET.: No, no! He's coming – you shan't, indeed!

CHAS. SURF.: O egad! we'll have a peep at the little milliner.

---

*discovering* revealing

SIR PET.: Not for the world! – Joseph will never forgive me.
CHAS. SURF.: I'll stand by you –
SIR PET. [*struggling with Charles*]: Odds, here he is –

JOSEPH SURFACE *enters just as* CHARLES *throws down the screen*

CHAS. SURF.: Lady Teazle! by all that's wonderful!
SIR PET.: Lady Teazle! by all that's horrible!
CHAS. SURF.: Sir Peter, this is one of the smartest French milliners I ever saw – egad, you seem all to have been diverting yourselves here at hide and seek – and I don't see who is out of the secret! – Shall I beg your ladyship to inform me! – not a word! Brother, will you please to explain this matter? – what! Morality dumb too? – Sir Peter, though I *found* you in the dark, perhaps you are not so now. All mute! Well tho' *I* can make nothing of the affair I suppose you perfectly understand one another – so I'll leave you to yourselves. – [*Going*] Brother, I'm sorry to find you *have given that worthy man so much uneasiness*! – Sir Peter, there's nothing *in the world so noble as a man of sentiment*! *Exit* CHARLES

[*Stand for some time looking at each other*]

JOS. SURF.: Sir Peter – notwithstanding I confess that appearances are against me – if you will afford me your patience – I make no doubt but I shall explain everything to your satisfaction.
SIR PET.: If you please –
JOS. SURF.: The fact is, sir – That Lady Teazle, knowing my pretensions to your ward Maria – I say sir, Lady Teazle being apprehensive of the jealousy of your temper – and knowing my friendship to the family – she, sir, I say – called here – in order that I might explain those pretensions – but on your coming – being apprehensive as I said of your jealousy – she withdrew – and this, you may depend on't is the whole truth of the matter.
SIR PET.: A very clear account upon my word, and I dare swear the lady will vouch for every article of it.
LADY TEAZ. [*coming forward*]: For not one word of it, Sir Peter.
SIR PET.: How! don't you even think it worth while to agree in the lie?
LADY TEAZ.: There is not one syllable of truth in what that gentleman has told you.
SIR PET.: I believe you, upon my soul, Ma'am!
JOS. SURF. [*aside*]: 'Sdeath Madam, will you betray me?
LADY TEAZ.: Good Mr Hypocrite, by your leave I will speak for myself.
SIR PET.: Aye, let her alone, sir – you'll find she'll make out a better story than *you* without prompting.
LADY TEAZ.: Hear me, Sir Peter – I came hither, on no matter relating to

your ward, and even ignorant of this gentleman's pretensions to her – but I came, seduced by his insidious arguments, at least to listen to his pretended passion, if not to sacrifice *your* honour to his baseness.

SIR PET.: Now I believe, the truth *is* coming indeed –

JOS. SURF.: The woman's mad!

LADY TEAZ.: No, sir – she has recovered her senses, and your own arts have furnished her with the means. – Sir Peter, I do not expect you to credit me – but the tenderness you expressed for me when I am sure you could not think I was a witness to it, has penetrated to my heart and had I left the place without the shame of this discovery, my future life should have spoken the sincerity of my gratitude. – As for that smooth-tongue hypocrite, who would have seduced the wife of his too credulous friend while he affected honourable addresses to his ward – I behold him now in a light so truly despicable, that I shall never again respect myself for having listened to him. *Exit*

JOS. SURF.: Notwithstanding all this, Sir Peter, heaven knows –

SIR PET.: That you are a villain! – and so I leave you to your conscience.

JOS. SURF.: You are too rash, Sir Peter – you shall hear me! the man who shuts out conviction by refusing to –

SIR PET.: Oh! –

*They go out,* JOSEPH SURFACE *following and speaking*

1777

# Fanny Burney
## 1752–1840

The daughter of Dr Charles Burney, the historian of music and friend of Johnson, Fanny Burney spent much of her early life mixing with the learned and fashionable. Her epistolary novel *Evelina* (1778) won great fame, and was followed by *Cecilia*, *Camilla* and *The Wanderer*. Her main theme is the exposure of the young heroine to a complex world, in a manner which influenced her admirer, Jane Austen. From 1786 she was Second Keeper of the Robes to Queen Charlotte, acting as deputy to Mrs Schwellenberg, whose behaviour often seemed harsh and tyrannical. In 1793 Fanny Burney married General d'Arblay, a refugee from the French Revolution, and with him was interned by Napoleon in the following decade. Her early diaries describe both the literary world and the milieu of the Royal Family during a period when George III was increasingly suffering from the bouts of mental instability which dogged his later life.

## *From* DIARY

### *[Chased by the King]*

MONDAY, FEBRUARY 2ND 1789. What an adventure had I this morning! one that has occasioned me the severest personal terror I ever experienced in my life.

Sir Lucas Pepys persisting that exercise and air were absolutely necessary to save me from illness, I have continued my walks, varying my gardens from Richmond to Kew, according to the accounts I received of the movements of the King. For this I had her Majesty's permission, on the representation of Sir Lucas.

This morning, when I received my intelligence of the King from Dr John Willis, I begged to know where I might walk in safety? 'In Kew Gardens,' he said, 'as the King would be in Richmond.'

'Should any unfortunate circumstance,' I cried, 'at any time, occasion my being seen by his Majesty, do not mention my name, but let me run off without call or notice.'

This he promised. Everybody, indeed, is ordered to keep out of sight.

Taking, therefore, the time I had most at command, I strolled into the gardens. I had proceeded, in my quick way, nearly half the round, when I suddenly perceived, through some trees, two or three figures. Relying on the instructions of Dr John, I concluded them to be workmen and gardeners; yet tried to look sharp, and in so doing, as they were less shaded, I thought I saw the person of his Majesty!

Alarmed past all possible expression, I waited not to know more, but turning back, ran off with all my might. But what was my terror to hear myself pursued! – to hear the voice of the King himself loudly and hoarsely calling after me: 'Miss Burney! Miss Burney!'

I protest I was ready to die. I knew not in what state he might be at the time; I only knew the orders to keep out of his way were universal; that the Queen would highly disapprove of any unauthorised meeting, and that the very action of my running away might deeply, in his present irritable state, offend him. Nevertheless, on I ran, too terrified to stop, and in search of some short passage, for the garden is full of little labyrinths, by which I might escape.

The steps still pursued me, and still the poor hoarse and altered voice rang in my ears – more and more footsteps resounded frightfully behind me – the attendants all running, to catch their eager master, and the voices of the two Doctor Willises loudly exhorting him not to heat himself so unmercifully.

Heavens, how I ran! I do not think I should have felt the hot lava from Vesuvius – at least not the hot cinders – had I so run during its eruption. My feet were not sensible that they even touched the ground.

Soon after, I heard other voices, shriller, though less nervous, call out: 'Stop! stop! stop!'

I could by no means consent; I knew not what was purposed, but I recollected fully my agreement with Dr John that very morning, that I should decamp if surprised, and not be named.

My own fears and repugnance, also, after a flight and disobedience like this, were doubled in the thought of not escaping: I knew not to what I might be exposed, should the malady be then high, and take the turn of resentment. Still, therefore, on I flew; and such was my speed, so almost incredible to relate or recollect, that I fairly believe no one of the whole party could have overtaken me, if these words, from one of the attendants, had not reached me: 'Doctor Willis begs you to stop!'

'I cannot! I cannot!' I answered, still flying on, when he called out: 'You must, ma'am; it hurts the King to run.'

Then, indeed, I stopped – in a state of fear really amounting to agony. I turned round, I saw the two Doctors had got the King between them, and three attendants of Dr Willis's were hovering about. They all slackened their pace, as they saw me stand still; but such was the excess of my alarm, that I was wholly insensible to the effects of a race which, at any other time, would have required an hour's recruit.†

As they approached, some little presence of mind happily came to my command: it occurred to me that, to appease the wrath of my flight, I must now show some confidence: I therefore faced them as undauntedly as I was able, only charging the nearest of the attendants to stand by my side.

When they were within a few yards of me, the King called out: 'Why did you run away?'

Shocked at a question impossible to answer, yet a little assured by the mild tone of his voice, I instantly forced myself forward, to meet him, though the internal sensation, which satisfied me this was a step the most proper to appease his suspicions and displeasure, was so violently combated by the tremor of my nerves, that I fairly think I may reckon it the greatest effort of personal courage I have ever made.

The effort answered: I looked up, and met all his wonted benignity of countenance, though something still of wildness in his eyes. Think, however, of my surprise, to feel him put both his hands round my two shoulders, and then kiss my cheek!

I wonder I did not really sink, so exquisite was my affright when I saw him spread out his arms! Involuntarily, I concluded he meant to crush me: but the Willises, who have never seen him till this fatal illness, not knowing how very extraordinary an action this was from him, simply smiled and looked pleased, supposing, perhaps, it was his customary salutation!

He now spoke in such terms of his pleasure in seeing me, that I soon lost the whole of my terror; astonishment to find him so nearly well, and gratification to see him so pleased, removed every uneasy feeling, and the joy that succeeded, in my conviction of his recovery, made me ready to throw myself at his feet to express it.

What a conversation followed! When he saw me fearless, he grew more and more alive, and made me walk close by his side, away from the attendants, and even the Willises themselves, who, to indulge him, retreated. I own myself not completely composed, but alarm I could entertain no more.

Everything that came uppermost in his mind he mentioned; he seemed to have just such remains of his flightiness as heated his imagination without deranging his reason, and robbed him of all control over his speech, though nearly in his perfect state of mind as to his opinions.

What did he not say! He opened his whole heart to me – expounded all his sentiments, and acquainted me with all his intentions.

*recruit* recovery

He assured me he was quite well – as well as he had ever been in his life; and then inquired how I did, and how I went on? and whether I was more comfortable?

If these questions, in their implication, surprised me, imagine how that surprise must increase when he proceeded to explain them! He asked after the coadjutrix,† laughing, and saying: 'Never mind her – don't be oppressed – I am your friend! don't let her cast you down! I know you have a hard time of it – but don't mind her!'

Almost thunderstruck with astonishment, I merely curtsied to his kind 'I am your friend,' and said nothing.

Then presently he added: 'Stick to your father – stick to your own family – let them be your objects.'

How readily I assented!

Again he repeated all I have just written, nearly in the same words, but ended it more seriously; he suddenly stopped and held me to stop too, and putting his hand on his breast, in the most solemn manner, he gravely and slowly said: 'I will protect you! – I promise you that – and therefore depend upon me!'

I thanked him; and the Willises, thinking him rather too elevated, came to propose my walking on. 'No, no, no!' he cried, a hundred times in a breath; and their good humour prevailed, and they let him again walk on with his new companion.

He then gave me a history of his pages, animating almost into a rage, as he related his subjects of displeasure with them, particularly with Mr Ernst, who, he told me, had been brought up by himself. I hope his ideas upon these men are the result of the mistakes of his malady.

Then he asked me some questions that very greatly distressed me, relating to information given him in his illness, from various motives, but which he suspected to be false, and which I knew he had reason to suspect: yet was it most dangerous to set anything right, as I was not aware what might be the views of their having been stated wrong. I was as discreet as I knew how to be, and I hope I did no mischief; but this was the worst part of the dialogue.

He next talked to me a great deal of my dear father, and made a thousand inquiries concerning his *History of Music*. This brought him to his favourite theme, Handel;† and he told me innumerable anecdotes of him, and particularly that celebrated tale of Handel's saying of himself, when a boy: 'While that boy lives, my music will never want a

*coadjutrix* Mrs Schwellenberg, Keeper of the Robes

*Handel* George Frideric (1685–1759), German-born composer of opera and oratorio (*Messiah*), spent most of his life in England

protector.' And this, he said, I might relate to my father.

Then he ran over most of his oratorios, attempting to sing the subjects of several airs and choruses, but so dreadfully hoarse that the sound was terrible.

Dr Willis, quite alarmed at this exertion, feared he would do himself harm, and again proposed a separation. 'No! no! no!' he exclaimed, 'not yet; I have something I must just mention first.'

Dr Willis, delighted to comply, even when uneasy at compliance, again gave way.

The good King then greatly affected me. He began upon my revered old friend, Mrs Delany;† and he spoke of her with such warmth – such kindness! 'She was my friend!' he cried, 'and I loved her as a friend! I have made a memorandum when I lost her – I will show it you.'

He pulled out a pocket-book, and rummaged some time, but to no purpose.

The tears stood in his eyes – he wiped them, and Dr Willis again became very anxious. 'Come, sir,' he cried, 'now do you come in and let the lady go on her walk – come, now, you have talked a long while – so we'll go in – if your Majesty pleases.'

'No, no!' he cried, 'I want to ask her a few questions; I have lived so long out of the world, I know nothing!'

He then told me he was very much dissatisfied with several of his state officers, and meant to form an entire new establishment. He took a paper out of his pocket-book, and showed me his new list.

This was the wildest thing that passed; and Dr John Willis now seriously urged our separating; but he would not consent; he had only three more words to say, he declared, and again he conquered.

He now spoke of my father, with still more kindness, and told me he ought to have had the post of Master of the Band, and not that little poor musician Parsons, who was not fit for it: 'But Lord Salisbury,'† he cried, 'used your father very ill in that business, and so he did me! However, I have dashed out his name, and I shall put your father's in – as soon as I get loose again!'

This again – how affecting was this!

'And what,' cried he, 'has your father got, at last? Nothing but that poor thing at Chelsea?† Oh, fie! fie! fie! But never mind! I will take care of him! I will do it myself!'

Then presently he added: 'As to Lord Salisbury, he is out already, as this memorandum will show you, and so are many more. I shall be

*Mrs Delany* (1700–88) had been a friend of Swift and Pope

*Lord Salisbury* Lord Chamberlain; the episode was in 1786

*Chelsea* Burney was organist at Chelsea Hospital

much better served; and when once I get away, I shall rule with a rod of iron!'

This was very unlike himself, and startled the two good doctors, who could not bear to cross him, and were exulting at my seeing his great amendment, but yet grew quite uneasy at his earnestness and volubility.

Finding we now must part, he stopped to take leave, and renewed again his charges about the coadjutrix. 'Never mind her!' he cried, 'depend upon me! I will be your friend as long as I live! – I here pledge myself to be your friend!' And then he saluted me again just as at the meeting, and suffered me to go on.

What a scene! How variously was I affected by it! But upon the whole, how inexpressibly thankful to see him so nearly himself – so little removed from recovery!

I went very soon after to the Queen, to whom I was most eager to avow the meeting, and how little I could help it. Her astonishment, and her earnestness to hear every particular, were very great. I told her almost all. Some few things relating to the distressing questions I could not repeat; nor many things said of Mrs Schwellenberg, which would much, and very needlessly, have hurt her.

FEBRUARY 17TH. The times are now most interesting and critical. Dr Willis confided to me this morning that to-day the King is to see the Chancellor. How important will be the result of his appearance! The whole national fate depends upon it!

WEDNESDAY, 18TH. I had this morning the highest gratification, the purest feeling of delight, I have been regaled with for many months: I saw, from the road, the King and Queen, accompanied by Dr Willis, walking in Richmond Gardens, near the farm, arm in arm! It was a pleasure that quite melted me, after a separation so bitter, scenes so distressful – to witness such harmony and security! Heaven bless and preserve them! was all I could incessantly say while I kept in their sight. . . .

The King I have seen again – in the Queen's dressing-room. On opening the door, there he stood! He smiled at my start, and saying he had waited on purpose to see me, added: 'I am quite well now – I was nearly so when I saw you before – but I could overtake you better now!' And then he left the room.

I was quite melted with joy and thankfulness at this so entire restoration.

1842

# George Crabbe

## 1754–1832

Crabbe was born in the fishing-village of Aldeburgh in Suffolk, about which he often wrote. After practising there as a doctor, he sought a poetic career in London, but was only rescued from destitution by Edmund Burke, who encouraged him to take orders and provide himself with security (he was not a very active clergyman). Burke helped him publish *The Library* (1781), and introduced him to members of The Club, notably Johnson, who gave advice on *The Village* (1783), a grimly realistic antidote to conventional pastoral poetry, which made his name. Following his marriage, he published little for twenty years, although he wrote and burned three novels. *The Parish Register* (1807) was followed by *The Borough* (1810), a descriptive and narrative poem based on Aldeburgh, including the tale of 'Peter Grimes', used for Benjamin Britten's opera. *Tales in Verse* (1812) and *Tales of the Hall* (1819) were further collections of narratives. Although he wrote well into the Romantic period, Crabbe usually persisted with the heroic couplets of an earlier age, and offered unadorned views of nature: his conservatism found sympathetic responses in such admirers of the 'Augustan' manner as Byron and Jane Austen.

### *From* THE VILLAGE

### *[Pastoral?]*

The village life, and every care that reigns
O'er youthful peasants and declining swains;
What labour yields, and what, that labour past,
Age, in its hour of languor, finds at last;
What form the real picture of the poor,
Demand a song – the muse can give no more.
    Fled are those times, when, in harmonious strains,
The rustic poet praised his native plains:
No shepherds now, in smooth alternate verse,
Their country's beauty or their nymphs' rehearse;

Yet still for these we frame the tender strain,
Still in our lays fond Corydons† complain,
And shepherds' boys their amorous pains reveal,
The only pains, alas! they never feel.
On Mincio's† banks, in Cæsar's bounteous reign,
If Tityrus found the Golden Age† again,
Must sleepy bards the flattering dream prolong,
Mechanic echoes of the Mantuan† song?
From truth and nature shall we widely stray,
Where Virgil, not where fancy, leads the way?
Yes, thus the muses sing of happy swains,
Because the muses never knew their pains:
They boast their peasants' pipes;† but peasants now
Resign their pipes and plod behind the plough;
And few, amid the rural-tribe, have time
To number syllables, and play with rhyme;
Save honest Duck,† what son of verse could share
The poet's rapture and the peasant's care?
Or the great labours of the fields degrade,
With the new period of a poorer trade?
From this chief cause these idle praises spring,
That themes so easy few forbear to sing;
For no deep thought the trifling subjects ask;
To sing of shepherds is an easy task:
The happy youth assumes the common strain,
A nymph his mistress, and himself a swain;
With no sad scenes he clouds his tuneful prayer,
But all, to look like her, is painted fair.
I grant indeed that fields and flocks have charms
For him that grazes or for him that farms;
But when amid such pleasing scenes I trace
The poor laborious natives of the place,
And see the mid-day sun, with fervid ray,
On their bare heads and dewy temples play;
While some, with feebler heads and fainter hearts,
Deplore their fortune, yet sustain their parts –
Then shall I dare these real ills to hide
In tinsel trappings of poetic pride?

*Corydon* shepherd in Virgil's *Eclogues*, where *Tityrus* also appears
*Mincio* river near Virgil's birthplace, Mantua; he flourished under Augustus Caesar
*Golden Age* mythical time of harmony, celebrated in pastorals; ll.15–20 are by Johnson
*pipes* for pastoral music
*Duck* Stephen Duck (1705–56), the Thresher Poet, patronised by Queen Caroline

No; cast by fortune on a frowning coast,
Which neither groves nor happy valleys boast;
Where other cares than those the muse relates,
And other shepherds dwell with other mates;
By such examples taught, I paint the cot,* cottage
As truth will paint it, and as bards will not:
Nor you, ye poor, of lettered scorn complain,
To you the smoothest song is smooth in vain;
O'ercome by labour, and bowed down by time,
Feel you the barren flattery of a rhyme?
Can poets soothe you, when you pine for bread,
By winding myrtles round your ruined shed?
Can their light tales your weighty griefs o'erpower,
Or glad with airy mirth the toilsome hour?
Lo! where the heath, with withering brake grown o'er,
Lends the light turf that warms the neighbouring poor;
From thence a length of burning sand appears,
Where the thin harvest waves its withered ears;
Rank weeds, that every art and care defy,
Reign o'er the land, and rob the blighted rye:
There thistles† stretch their prickly arms afar,
And to the ragged infant threaten war;
There poppies nodding mock the hope of toil;
There the blue bugloss paints the sterile soil;
Hardy and high, above the slender sheaf,
The slimy mallow waves her silky leaf;
O'er the young shoot the charlock throws a shade,
And clasping tares cling round the sickly blade;
With mingled tints the rocky coasts abound,
And a sad splendour vainly shines around.
So looks the nymph whom wretched arts adorn,
Betrayed by man, then left for man to scorn;
Whose cheek in vain assumes the mimic rose,
While her sad eyes the troubled breast disclose;
Whose outward splendour is but folly's dress,
Exposing most, when most it gilds distress.
Here joyless roam a wild amphibious race,
With sullen woe displayed in every face;
Who, far from civil arts and social fly,
And scowl at strangers with suspicious eye. . . .

*thistles* first of a series of weeds threatening the crops

## [Rural Life]

Ye gentle souls, who dream of rural ease,
Whom the smooth stream and smoother sonnet please;
Go! if the peaceful cot your praises share,
Go look within, and ask if peace be there;
If peace be his – that drooping weary sire,
Or theirs, that offspring round their feeble fire;
Or hers, that matron pale, whose trembling hand
Turns on the wretched hearth th' expiring brand!
Nor yet can time itself obtain for these
Life's latest comforts, due respect and ease;
For yonder see that hoary swain, whose age
Can with no cares except its own engage;
Who, propt on that rude staff, looks up to see
The bare arms broken from the withering tree,
On which, a boy, he climbed the loftiest bough,
Then his first joy, but his sad emblem now.
He once was chief in all the rustic trade;
His steady hand the straightest furrow made;
Full many a prize he won, and still is proud
To find the triumphs of his youth allowed;
A transient pleasure sparkles in his eyes,
He hears and smiles, then thinks again and sighs:
For now he journeys to his grave in pain;
The rich disdain him; nay, the poor disdain:
Alternate masters now their slave command,
Urge the weak efforts of his feeble hand,
And, when his age attempts its task in vain,
With ruthless taunts, of lazy poor complain.
Oft may you see him, when he tends the sheep,
His winter charge, beneath the hillock weep;
Oft hear him murmur to the winds that blow
O'er his white locks and bury them in snow,
When, roused by rage and muttering in the morn,
He mends the broken edge with icy thorn: –
'Why do I live, when I desire to be
At once from life and life's long labour free?
Like leaves in spring, the young are blown away,
Without the sorrows of a slow decay;
I, like yon withered leaf, remain behind,
Nipt by the frost, and shivering in the wind;
There it abides till younger buds come on,
As I, now all my fellow-swains are gone;

Then, from the rising generation thrust,
It falls, like me, unnoticed to the dust.
'These fruitful fields, these numerous flocks I see,
Are others' gain, but killing cares to me;
To me the children of my youth are lords,
Cool in their looks, but hasty in their words:
Wants of their own demand their care; and who
Feels his own want and succours others too?
A lonely, wretched man, in pain I go,
None need my help, and none relieve my woe;
Then let my bones beneath the turf be laid,
And men forget the wretch they would not aid.'
Thus, groan the old, till, by disease oppressed,
They taste a final woe, and then they rest.
Theirs is yon House that holds the parish poor,
Whose walls of mud scarce bear the broken door;
There, where the putrid vapours, flagging, play,
And the full wheel* hums doleful through the day; spinning-wheel
There children dwell who know no parents' care;
Parents, who know no children's love, dwell there!
Heart-broken matrons on their joyless bed,
Forsaken wives, and mothers never wed;
Dejected widows with unheeded tears,
And crippled age with more than childhood fears;
The lame, the blind, and, far the happiest they!
The moping idiot, and the madman gay.
Here too the sick their final doom receive,
Here brought, amid the scenes of grief, to grieve,
Where the loud groans from some sad chamber flow,
Mixt with the clamours of the crowd below;
Here, sorrowing, they each kindred sorrow scan,
And the cold charities of man to man:
Whose laws indeed for ruined age provide,
And strong compulsion plucks the scrap from pride;
But still that scrap is bought with many a sigh,
And pride embitters what it can't deny. . .

1783

# PETER GRIMES

Old Peter Grimes made fishing his employ,
His wife he cabined with him and his boy,
And seemed that life laborious to enjoy:
To town came quiet Peter with his fish,
And had of all a civil word and wish.
He left his trade upon the Sabbath-day,
And took young Peter in his hand to pray:
But soon the stubborn boy from care broke loose,
At first refused, then added his abuse:
His father's love he scorned, his power defied,
But being drunk, wept sorely when he died.
   Yes! then he wept, and to his mind there came
Much of his conduct, and he felt the shame, –
How he had oft the good old man reviled,
And never paid the duty of a child;
How, when the father in his Bible read,
He in contempt and anger left the shed;
'It is the word of life,' the parent cried;
– 'This is the life itself,' the boy replied;
And while old Peter in amazement stood,
Gave the hot spirit* to his boiling blood: – alcohol
How he, with oath and furious speech, began
To prove his freedom and assert the man;
And when the parent checked his impious rage,
How he had cursed the tyranny of age, –
Nay, once had dealt the sacrilegious blow
On his bare head, and laid his parent low;
The father groaned – 'If thou art old,' said he,
And hast a son – thou wilt remember me:
Thy mother left me in a happy time,
Thou killedst not her – Heaven spares the double crime.'
   On an inn-settle, in his maudlin grief,
This he resolved, and drank for his relief.
   Now lived the youth in freedom, but debarred
From constant pleasure, and he thought it hard;
Hard that he could not every wish obey,
But must awhile relinquish ale and play;
Hard! that he could not to his cards attend,
But must acquire the money he would spend.
   With greedy eye he looked on all he saw,
He knew not justice, and he laughed at law;
On all he marked, he stretched his ready hand;

He fished by water and he filched by land:
Oft in the night has Peter dropped his oar,
Fled from his boat, and sought for prey on shore;
Oft up the hedge-row glided, on his back
Bearing the orchard's produce in a sack,
Or farm-yard load, tugged fiercely from the stack;
And as these wrongs to greater numbers rose,
The more he looked on all men as his foes.
He built a mud-walled hovel, where he kept
His various wealth, and there he oft-times slept;
But no success could please his cruel soul,
He wished for one to trouble and control;
He wanted some obedient boy to stand
And bear the blow of his outrageous hand;
And hoped to find in some propitious hour
A feeling creature subject to his power.
Peter had heard there were in London then, –
Still have they being! – workhouse-clearing men,
Who, undisturbed by feelings just or kind,
Would parish-boys[†] to needy tradesmen bind:
They in their want a trifling sum would take,
And toiling slaves of piteous orphans make.
Such Peter sought, and when a lad was found,
The sum was dealt him, and the slave was bound.
Some few in town observed in Peter's trap
A boy, with jacket blue and woollen cap;
But none enquired how Peter used the rope,
Or what the bruise, that made the stripling stoop;
None could the ridges on his back behold,
None sought him shivering in the winter's cold;
None put the question, – 'Peter, dost thou give
The boy his food? – What, man! the lad must live:
Consider, Peter, let the child have bread,
He'll serve thee better if he's stroked and fed.'
None reasoned thus – and some, on hearing cries,
Said calmly, 'Grimes is at his exercise.'
Pinned, beaten, cold, pinched, threatened, and abused –
His efforts punished and his food refused, –
Awake tormented, – soon aroused from sleep, –
Struck if he wept, and yet compelled to weep,

*parish-boys* parish workhouses apprenticed pauper children to tradesmen (as cheap labour)

The trembling boy dropped down and strove to pray,
Received a blow, and trembling turned away,
Or sobbed and hid his piteous face; – while he,
The savage master, grinned in horrid glee:
He'd now the power he ever loved to show,
A feeling being subject to his blow.
  Thus lived the lad, in hunger, peril, pain,
His tears despised, his supplications vain:
Compelled by fear to lie, by need to steal,
His bed uneasy and unblessed his meal,
For three sad years the boy his tortures bore,
And then his pains and trials were no more.
  'How died he, Peter?' when the people said,
He growled – 'I found him lifeless in his bed;'
Then tried for softer tone, and sighed, 'Poor Sam is dead.'
Yet murmurs were there, and some questions asked –
How he was fed, how punished, and how tasked?
Much they suspected, but they little proved,
And Peter passed untroubled and unmoved.
  Another boy with equal ease was found,
The money granted, and the victim bound;
And what his fate? – One night it chanced he fell
From the boat's mast and perished in her well,
Where fish were living kept, and where the boy
(So reasoned men) could not himself destroy: –
  'Yes! so it was,' said Peter, 'in his play,
(For he was idle both by night and day,)
He climbed the main-mast and then fell below;' –
Then showed his corpse, and pointed to the blow:
'What said the jury?'[†] – they were long in doubt,
But sturdy Peter faced the matter out:
So they dismissed him, saying at the time,
'Keep fast your hatchway when you've boys who climb.'
This hit the conscience, and he coloured more
Than for the closest questions put before.
Thus all his fears the verdict set aside,
And at the slave-shop Peter still applied.
  Then came a boy, of manners soft and mild, –
Our seamen's wives with grief beheld the child;
All thought (the poor themselves) that he was one
Of gentle blood, some noble sinner's son,
Who had, belike, deceived some humble maid,

*jury* at the inquest into the cause of death

Whom he had first seduced and then betrayed: –
However this, he seemed a gracious lad,
In grief submissive and with patience sad.
　Passive he laboured, till his slender frame
Bent with his loads, and he at length was lame:
Strange that a frame so weak could bear so long
The grossest insult and the foulest wrong;
But there were causes – in the town they gave
Fire, food, and comfort, to the gentle slave;
And though stern Peter, with a cruel hand,
And knotted rope, enforced the rude command,
Yet he considered what he'd lately felt,
And his vile blows with selfish pity dealt.
　One day such draughts the cruel fisher made,
He could not vend them in his borough-trade,
But sailed for London-mart: the boy was ill,
But ever humbled to his master's will;
And on the river, where they smoothly sailed,
He strove with terror and awhile prevailed;
But new to danger on the angry sea,
He clung affrightened to his master's knee:
The boat grew leaky and the wind was strong,
Rough was the passage and the time was long;
His liquor failed, and Peter's wrath arose, –
No more is known – the rest we must suppose,
Or learn of Peter: – Peter says, he 'spied
The stripling's danger and for harbour tried;
Meantime the fish, and then th' apprentice died.'
　The pitying women raised a clamour round,
And weeping said, 'Thou hast thy 'prentice drowned.'
　Now the stern man was summoned to the hall,
To tell his tale before the burghers all:
He gave th' account; professed the lad he loved,
And kept his brazen features all unmoved.
　The mayor himself with tone severe replied, –
'Henceforth with thee shall never boy abide;
Hire thee a freeman, whom thou durst not beat,
But who, in thy despite, will sleep and eat:
Free thou art now! – again shouldst thou appear,
Thou'lt find thy sentence, like thy soul, severe.'
　Alas! for Peter not a helping hand,
So was he hated, could he now command;
Alone he rowed his boat, alone he cast
His nets beside, or made his anchor fast;

To hold a rope or hear a curse was none, –
He toiled and railed; he groaned and swore alone.
  Thus by himself compelled to live each day,
To wait for certain hours the tide's delay;
At the same time the same dull views to see,
The bounding marsh-bank and the blighted tree;
The water only, when the tides were high,
When low, the mud half-covered and half-dry;
The sun-burnt tar that blisters on the planks,
And bank-side stakes in their uneven ranks;
Heaps of entangled weeds that slowly float,
As the tide rolls by the impeded boat.
  When tides were neap,† and, in the sultry day,
Through the tall bounding mud-banks made their way,
Which on each side rose swelling, and below
The dark warm flood ran silently and slow;
There anchoring, Peter chose from man to hide,
There hang his head, and view the lazy tide
In its hot slimy channel slowly glide;
Where the small eels that left the deeper way
For the warm shore, within the shallows play;
Where gaping mussels, left upon the mud,
Slope their slow passage to the fallen flood; –
Here dull and hopeless he'd lie down and trace
How sidelong crabs had scrawled their crooked race;
Or sadly listen to the tuneless cry
Of fishing gull or clanging golden-eye;* sea-duck
What time the sea-birds to the marsh would come,
And the loud bittern, from the bull-rush home,
Gave from the salt-ditch side the bellowing boom:
He nursed the feelings these dull scenes produce,
And loved to stop beside the opening sluice;
Where the small stream, confined in narrow bound,
Ran with a dull, unvaried, saddening sound;
Where all, presented to the eye or ear,
Oppressed the soul with misery, grief, and fear.
  Besides these objects, there were places three,
Which Peter seemed with certain dread to see;
When he drew near them he would turn from each,
And loudly whistle till he passed the reach.†
  A change of scene to him brought no relief,
In town, 'twas plain, men took him for a thief:

*neap* having least movement

*reach* stretch of river

The sailors' wives would stop him in the street,
And say, 'Now, Peter, thou'st no boy to beat:'
Infants at play, when they perceived him, ran,
Warning each other – 'That's the wicked man:'
He growled an oath, and in an angry tone
Cursed the whole place and wished to be alone.
  Alone he was, the same dull scenes in view,
And still more gloomy in his sight they grew:
Though man he hated, yet employed alone
At bootless labour, he would swear and groan,
Cursing the shoals that glided by the spot,
And gulls that caught them when his arts could not.
  Cold nervous tremblings shook his sturdy frame,
And strange disease – he couldn't say the name;
Wild were his dreams, and oft he rose in fright,
Waked by his view of horrors in the night, –
Horrors that would the sternest minds amaze,
Horrors that demons might be proud to raise:
And though he felt forsaken, grieved at heart,
To think he lived from all mankind apart;
Yet, if a man approached, in terrors he would start.
  A winter passed since Peter saw the town,
And summer lodgers were again come down;
These, idly curious, with their glasses spied
The ships in bay as anchored for the tide, –
The river's craft, – the bustle of the quay, –
And sea-port views, which landmen love to see.
  One, up the river, had a man and boat
Seen day by day, now anchored, now afloat;
Fisher he seemed, yet used no net nor hook;
Of sea-fowl swimming by no heed he took,
But on the gliding waves still fixed his lazy look:
At certain stations he would view the stream,
As if he stood bewildered in a dream,
Or that some power had chained him for a time,
To feel a curse or meditate on crime.
  This known, some curious, some in pity went,
And others questioned – 'Wretch, dost thou repent?'
He heard, he trembled, and in fear resigned
His boat: new terror filled his restless mind;
Furious* he grew, and up the country ran, mad
And there they seized him – a distempered man: –

Him we received, and to a parish-bed,†
Followed and cursed, the groaning man was led.
Here when they saw him, whom they used to shun,
A lost, lone man, so harassed and undone;
Our gentle females, ever prompt to feel,
Perceived compassion on their anger steal;
His crimes they could not from their memories blot,
But they were grieved, and trembled at his lot.
A Priest too came, to whom his words are told;
And all the signs they shuddered to behold.
'Look! look!' they cried; 'his limbs with horror shake,
And as he grinds his teeth, what noise they make!
How glare his angry eyes, and yet he's not awake:
See! what cold drops upon his forehead stand,
And how he clenches that broad bony hand.'
The Priest attending, found he spoke at times
As one alluding to his fears and crimes;
'It was the fall,' he muttered, 'I can show
The manner how, – I never struck a blow:' –
And then aloud, – 'Unhand me, free my chain;
On oath he fell – it struck him to the brain: –
Why ask my father? – that old man will swear
Against my life; besides, he wasn't there: –
What, all agreed? – Am I to die† to-day? –
My Lord, in mercy give me time to pray.'
Then as they watched him, calmer he became,
And grew so weak he couldn't move his frame,
But murmuring spake – while they could see and hear
The start of terror and the groan of fear;
See the large dew-beads on his forehead rise,
And the cold death-drop glaze his sunken eyes;
Nor yet he died, but with unwonted force
Seemed with some fancied being to discourse;
He knew not us, or with accustomed art
He hid the knowledge, yet exposed his heart;
'Twas part confession and the rest defence,
A madman's tale, with gleams of waking sense.
'I'll tell you all,' he said, 'the very day
When the old man first placed them in my way:
My father's spirit – he who always tried
To give me trouble, when he lived and died –
When he was gone he could not be content

*parish-bed* in the workhouse

*to die* he imagines a death-sentence for murder

To see my days in painful labour spent,
But would appoint his meetings, and he made
Me watch at these, and so neglect my trade.
‘’Twas one hot noon, all silent, still, serene,
No living being had I lately seen;
I paddled up and down and dipped my net,
But (such his pleasure) I could nothing get, –
A father's pleasure, when his toil was done,
To plague and torture thus an only son!
And so I sat and looked upon the stream,
How it ran on, and felt as in a dream:
But dream it was not: No! – I fixed my eyes
On the mid stream and saw the spirits rise:
I saw my father on the water stand,
And hold a thin pale boy in either hand;
And there they glided ghastly on the top
Of the salt flood, and never touched a drop:
I would have struck them, but they knew th' intent,
And smiled upon the oar, and down they went.
‘Now, from that day, whenever I began
To dip my net, there stood the hard old man –
He and those boys: I humbled me and prayed
They would be gone; – they heeded not, but stayed:
Nor could I turn, nor would the boat go by,
But, gazing on the spirits, there was I:
They bade me leap to death, but I was loth to die:
And every day, as sure as day arose,
Would these three spirits meet me ere the close;
To hear and mark them daily was my doom,
And "Come," they said, with weak, sad voices, "come."
To row away, with all my strength I tried,
But there were they, hard by me in the tide,
The three unbodied forms – and "Come," still "come," they cried.
‘Fathers should pity – but this old man shook
His hoary locks, and froze me by a look:
Thrice, when I struck them, through the water came
A hollow groan, that weakened all my frame:
"Father!" said I, "have mercy:" – he replied,
I know not what – the angry spirit lied, –
"Didst thou not draw thy knife?" said he: – 'Twas true,
But I had pity and my arm withdrew:
He cried for mercy, which I kindly gave,
But he has no compassion in his grave.
‘There were three places, where they ever rose, –

The whole long river has not such as those –
Places accursed, where, if a man remain,
He'll see the things which strike him to the brain;
And there they made me on my paddle lean,
And look at them for hours; – accursed scene!
When they would glide to that smooth eddy-space,†
Then bid me leap and join them in the place;
And at my groans each little villain sprite
Enjoyed my pains and vanished in delight.
'In one fierce summer-day, when my poor brain
Was burning hot, and cruel was my pain,
Then came this father-foe, and there he stood
With his two boys again upon the flood:
There was more mischief in their eyes, more glee,
In their pale faces when they glared at me:
Still did they force me on the oar to rest,
And when they saw me fainting and and oppressed,
He, with his hand, the old man, scooped the flood,
And there came flame about him mixed with blood;
He bade me stoop and look upon the place,
Then flung the hot-red liquor in my face;
Burning it blazed, and then I roared for pain,
I thought the demons would have turned my brain.
'Still there they stood, and forced me to behold
A place of horrors – they can not be told –
Where the flood opened, there I heard the shriek
Of tortured guilt – no earthly tongue can speak:
"All days alike! for ever!" did they say,
"And unremitted torments every day" –
Yes, so they said' – But here he ceased, and gazed
On all around, affrightened and amazed;
And still he tried to speak, and looked his dread
Of frightened females gathering round his bed;
Then dropped exhausted, and appeared at rest,
Till the strong foe the vital powers possessed;
Then with an inward, broken voice he cried,
'Again they come,' and muttered as he died.

1810

*eddy-space* circular current

# Robert Burns

## 1759–96

The son of a small farmer from Ayrshire, Burns spent much of his life trying to solve his financial problems by working the land, finally becoming an excise officer in 1789. As a youth, he was well aware of classic English poetry as well as the Scottish vernacular tradition of Ramsay and Fergusson, and in his own work the extent of dialect usage varies greatly. His first collection of *Poems*, which appeared at Kilmarnock in 1786, led to his lionisation by intellectual Edinburgh society, which chose to regard him inaccurately as a 'Heaven-taught ploughman'. (His unorthodox way of life and entanglements with women long distorted views of his career as a whole.) Burns's interest in the native tradition led him to collect and write many poems for *The Scots Musical Museum*, such as 'O my luve's like a red, red rose'. An early supporter of the French Revolution, Burns has remained popular for his pleas for human equality and his celebration of humble worth. More solemn works like *The Cotter's Saturday Night* are complemented by comic narrative in *Tam o'Shanter* and vigorous satire of complacency in 'Holy Willie's Prayer'.

## HOLY WILLIE'S PRAYER –†

And send the Godly in a pet to pray –
Pope.

O Thou that in the heavens does dwell!
Wha, as it pleases best thysel,
Sends ane to heaven and ten to h–ll,
A' for thy glory!
And no for ony gude or ill
They've done before thee. –

*Holy Willie's Prayer* The self-exposure of a stern Calvinist, 'gifted' – chosen to escape damnation. Burns's friend Hamilton was defended by Aiken against the illiberal 'Willie' and Auld

I bless and praise thy matchless might,
When thousands thou has left in night,
That I am here before thy sight,
For gifts and grace,
A burning and a shining light
To a' this place. –

What was I, or my generation,†
That I should get such exaltation?
I, wha deserv'd most just damnation,
For broken laws
Sax thousand years ere my creation,
Thro' Adam's cause!

When from my mother's womb I fell,
Thou might hae plunged me deep in hell,
To gnash my gooms, and weep, and wail,
In burning lakes,
Where damned devils roar and yell
Chain'd to their stakes. –

Yet I am here, a chosen sample,
To shew thy grace is great and ample:
I'm here, a pillar o' thy temple
Strong as a rock,
A guide, a ruler and example
To a' thy flock. –

[O L—d thou kens what zeal I bear,
When drinkers drink, and swearers swear,
And singin' there, and dancin' here,
Wi' great an' sma';
For I am keepet by thy fear,
Free frae them a'. –]

But yet – O L—d – confess I must –
At times I'm fash'd* wi' fleshly lust; troubled
And sometimes too, in warldly trust
Vile Self gets in;
But thou remembers we are dust,
Defil'd wi' sin. –

*generation* birth, by which he inherited the original sin of Adam

O L—d – yestreen – thou kens – wi' Meg –
Thy pardon I sincerely beg!
O may 't ne'er be a living plague,
To my dishonor!
And I'll ne'er lift a lawless leg
Again upon her. –

Besides, I farther maun avow,
Wi' Leezie's lass, three times – I trow –
But L—d, that friday I was fou* drunk
When I cam near her;
O else, thou kens, thy servant true
Wad never steer* her. – rouse

Maybe thou lets this fleshy thorn
Buffet thy servant e'en and morn,
Lest he o'er proud and high should turn,
That he's sae gifted;
If sae, thy hand maun e'en be borne
Untill thou lift it. –

L—d bless thy Chosen in this place,
For here thou has a chosen race:
But G—d, confound their stubborn face,
And blast their name,
Wha bring thy rulers to disgrace
And open shame. –

L—d mind Gaun Hamilton's deserts!
He drinks, and swears, and plays at cartes,
Yet has sae mony taking arts
Wi' Great and Sma',
Frae G—d's ain priest the people's hearts
He steals awa. –

And when we chasten'd him therefore,
Thou kens how he bred sic a splore,* frolic
And set the warld in a roar
O' laughin at us:
Curse thou his basket and his store,
Kail* and potatoes. – cabbage

L—d hear my earnest cry and prayer
Against that Presbytry[†] of Ayr!
Thy strong right hand, L—d, make it bare
Upon their heads!
L—d visit them, and dinna spare,
For their misdeeds!

O L—d my G—d, that glib-tongu'd Aiken!
My very heart and flesh are quaking
To think how I sat, sweating, shaking,
And p-ss'd wi' dread,
While Auld wi' hingin lip gaed sneaking
And hid his head!

L—d, in thy day o' vengeance try him!
L—d visit him that did employ him!
And pass not in thy mercy by them,
Nor hear their prayer;
But for thy people's sake destroy them,
And dinna spare!

But L—d, remember me and mine
Wi' mercies temporal and divine!
That I for grace and gear[†] may shine,
Excell'd by nane!
And a' the glory shall be thine!
AMEN! AMEN!

1785 1789

# TO A LOUSE, ON SEEING ONE ON A LADY'S BONNET AT CHURCH

HA! whare ye gaun, ye crowlan ferlie![†]
Your impudence protects you sairly:
I canna say but ye strunt* rarely, swagger
Owre *gawze* and *lace*;
Tho' faith, I fear ye dine but sparely,
On sic a place.

Presbytry the local church authorities, insufficiently punitive
*gear* worldly possessions
*crowlan ferlie* creeping marvel

Ye ugly, creepan, blastet wonner,
Detested, shunn'd, by saunt an' sinner,
How daur ye set your fit upon her,
Sae fine a *Lady*!
Gae somewhere else and seek your dinner,
On some poor body.

Swith,* in some beggar's haffet† squattle, away nestle
There ye may creep, and sprawl, and sprattle,* scramble
Wi' ither kindred, jumping cattle,* animals
In shoals and nations;
Whare *horn* nor *bane** ne'er daur unsettle, combs
Your thick plantations.

Now haud you there, ye're out o' sight,
Below the fatt'rels,* snug and tight, ribbon-ends
Na faith ye yet! ye'll no be right,
Till ye've got on it,
The vera tapmost, towrin height
O' *Miss's bonnet*.

My sooth! right bauld ye set your nose out,
As plump an' gray as onie grozet:* gooseberry
O for some rank, mercurial rozet,* resin
Or fell, red smeddum* insect-powder
I'd gie you sic a hearty dose o't,
Wad dress your droddum!* backside

I wad na been surpriz'd to spy
You on an auld wife's *flainen toy*;†
Or aiblins* some bit duddie* boy, perhaps ragged
On 's *wylecoat*;†
But Miss's fine *Lunardi*,* fye! bonnet
How daur ye do 't?

O *Jenny* dinna toss your head,
An' set your beauties a' abread!* visibly
Ye little ken what cursed speed
The blastie 's† makin!
Thae *winks* and *finger-ends*, I dread,
Are notice takin!

*haffet* hair on temple
*flainen toy* flannel cap
*wylecoat* flannel vest
*blastie* cursed creature

O wad some Pow'r the giftie gie us
*To see oursels as others see us!*
It wad frae monie a blunder free us
An' foolish notion:
What airs in dress an' gait wad lea'e us,
And ev'n Devotion!

1786

# TAM O'SHANTER. A TALE

Of Brownyis and of Bogillis* full is this buke. goblins

GAWIN DOUGLAS.†

When chapman billies† leave the street,
And drouthy* neebors, neebors meet, thirsty
As market-days are wearing late,
An' folk begin to tak the gate,* road
While we sit bousing at the nappy,* ale
And getting fou and unco* happy, very
We think na on the lang Scots miles,†
The mosses, waters, slaps,† and styles,
That lie between us and our hame,
Whare sits our sulky sullen dame,
Gathering her brows like gathering storm,
Nursing her wrath to keep it warm.

This truth fand honest *Tam o' Shanter*,
As he frae Ayr ae night did canter,
(Auld Ayr, wham ne'er a town surpasses,
For honest men and bonny lasses.)

O *Tam*! hadst thou but been sae wise,
As ta'en thy ain wife *Kate*'s advice!
She tauld thee weel thou was a skellum,* rascal
A blethering,† blustering, drunken blellum;* babbler
That frae November till October,
Ae market-day thou was nae sober;

*Douglas* from a prologue to his Scots translation (1553) of the *Aeneid*
*chapman billies* pedlar fellows
*Scots miles* about one-tenth longer than English
*slaps* gaps in fence
*blethering* foolish-talking

That ilka melder,† wi' the miller,
Thou sat as lang as thou had siller;
That every naig was ca'd a shoe on,
The smith and thee gat roaring fou on;
That at the L—d 's house, even on Sunday,
Thou drank wi' Kirkton Jean till Monday.
She prophesied that late or soon,
Thou would be found deep drown'd in Doon;
Or catch'd wi' warlocks* in the mirk,* — witches, dark
By *Alloway*'s auld haunted kirk.

Ah, gentle dames! it gars me greet,†
To think how mony counsels sweet,
How mony lengthen'd sage advices,
The husband frae the wife despises!

But to our tale: Ae market-night,
*Tam* had got planted unco right;
Fast by an ingle,* bleezing finely, — fire
Wi' reaming swats,† that drank divinely;
And at his elbow, Souter* *Johnny*, — cobbler
His ancient, trusty, drouthy crony;
*Tam* lo'ed him like a vera brither;
They had been fou for weeks thegither.
The night drave on wi' sangs and clatter;
And ay the ale was growing better:
The landlady and *Tam* grew gracious,
Wi' favours, secret, sweet, and precious:
The Souter tauld his queerest stories;
The landlord's laugh was ready chorus:
The storm without might rair and rustle,
*Tam* did na mind the storm a whistle.

Care, mad to see a man sae happy,
E'en drown'd himsel amang the nappy:
As bees flee hame wi' lades o' treasure,
The minutes wing'd their way wi' pleasure:
Kings may be blest, but *Tam* was glorious,
O'er a' the ills o' life victorious!
But pleasures are like poppies spread,
You seize the flower, its bloom is shed;

---

*ilka melder* each meal-grinding
*gars me greet* makes me weep
*reaming swats* foaming new beer

Or like the snow falls in the river,
A moment white – then melts for ever;

Or like the borealis race,†
That flit ere you can point their place;
Or like the rainbow's lovely form
Evanishing amid the storm. –
Nae man can tether time or tide;
The hour approaches *Tam* maun ride;
That hour, o' night's black arch the key-stane,
That dreary hour he mounts his beast in;
And sic a night he taks the road in,
As ne'er poor sinner was abroad in.

The wind blew as 'twad blawn its last;
The rattling showers rose on the blast;
The speedy gleams the darkness swallow'd;
Loud, deep, and lang, the thunder bellow'd:
That night, a child might understand,
The Deil had business on his hand.

Weel mounted on his gray mare, *Meg*,
A better never lifted leg,
*Tam* skelpit* on thro' dub* and mire, rushed puddle
Despising wind, and rain, and fire;
Whiles holding fast his gude blue bonnet;
Whiles crooning o'er some auld Scots sonnet;
Whiles glowring round wi' prudent cares,
Lest bogles catch him unawares:
*Kirk-Alloway* was drawing nigh,
Whare ghaists and houlets* nightly cry. – owls

By this time he was cross the ford,
Whare, in the snaw, the chapman smoor'd;†
And past the birks* and meikle* stane, birches large
Whare drunken *Charlie* brak 's neck-bane;
And thro' the whins, and by the cairn,
Whare hunters fand the murder'd bairn;
And near the thorn, aboon* the well, above
Whare *Mungo*'s mither hang'd hersel. –
Before him *Doon* pours all his floods;
The doubling storm roars thro' the woods;

*borealis race* 'northern lights' in sky *smoor'd* was smothered

The lightnings flash from pole to pole;
Near and more near the thunders roll:
When, glimmering thro' the groaning trees,
*Kirk-Alloway* seem'd in a bleeze;
Thro' ilka bore the beams were glancing;
And loud resounded mirth and dancing. –

Inspiring bold *John Barleycorn*!
What dangers thou canst make us scorn!
Wi' tippeny,† we fear nae evil;
Wi' usquabae,* we'll face the devil! – whisky
The swats sae ream'd in *Tammie* 's noddle,* head
Fair play,† he car'd na deils a boddle.†
But *Maggie* stood right sair astonish'd,
Till, by the heel and hand admonish'd,
She ventured forward on the light;
And, vow! *Tam* saw an unco sight!
Warlocks and witches in a dance;
Nae cotillion brent* new frae *France*, brand
But hornpipes, jigs, strathspeys, and reels,
Put life and mettle in their heels.
A winnock-bunker† in the east,
There sat auld Nick, in shape o' beast;
A towzie tyke,† black, grim, and large,
To gie them music was his charge:
He screw'd the pipes and gart them skirl,†
Till roof and rafters a' did dirl* – shake
Coffins stood round, like open presses,* cupboards
That shaw'd the dead in their last dresses;
And by some devilish cantraip slight†
Each in its cauld hand held a light. –
By which heroic *Tam* was able
To note upon the haly table,
A murderer's banes in gibbet airns;* irons
Twa span-lang,† wee, unchristen'd bairns;
A thief, new-cutted frae a rape,* rope
Wi' his last gasp his gab did gape;
Five tomahawks, wi' blude red-rusted;
Five scymitars, wi' murder crusted;
A garter, which a babe had strangled;

---

*tippeny* twopenny ale
*Fair play* to be fair
*boddle* sixth of a penny
*winnock-bunker* window-seat
*towzie tyke* shaggy dog
*gart them skirl* made them shriek
*cantraip slight* magic skill
*span-lang* hand-span sized

A knife, a father's throat had mangled,
Whom his ain son o' life bereft,
The grey hairs yet stack to the heft;
Wi' mair o' horrible and awefu',
Which even to name wad be unlawfu'.

As *Tammie* glow'rd, amaz'd, and curious,
The mirth and fun grew fast and furious:
The piper loud and louder blew;
The dancers quick and quicker flew;
They reel'd, they set, they cross'd, they cleekit,†
Till ilka carlin* swat and reekit, — witch
And coost† her duddies to the wark,
And linket at it in her sark!†

Now, *Tam*, O *Tam*! had thae been queans,* — girls
A' plump and strapping in their teens,
Their sarks, instead o' creeshie* flannen, — greasy
Been snaw-white seventeen hunder† linnen!
Thir breeks† o' mine, my only pair,
That ance were plush, o' gude blue hair,
I wad hae gi'en them off my hurdies,* — buttocks
For ae blink o' the bonie burdies!* — girls

But wither'd beldams,† auld and droll,
Rigwoodie* hags wad spean* a foal, — coarse wean
Lowping† and flinging on a crummock,†
I wonder didna turn thy stomach.

But *Tam* kend what was what fu' brawlie,* — well
There was ae winsome wench and wawlie,
That night enlisted in the core,
(Lang after kend on *Carrick* shore;
For mony a beast to dead she shot,
And perish'd mony a bony boat,
And shook baith meikle corn and bear,* — barley
And kept the country-side in fear:)
Her cutty sark,† o' Paisley harn,
That while a lassie she had worn,
In longitude tho' sorely scanty,

---

*cleekit* linked arms
*coost . . . sark* threw off her clothes for the business and skipped in her shift
*seventeen hunder* very fine
*Thir breeks* these trousers
*beldams* old women
*Lowping . . . crummock* leaping with a crooked stick
*cutty sark* short shift, of Paisley linen

It was her best, and she was vauntie.* — proud
Ah! little kend thy reverend grannie,
That sark she coft* for her wee Nannie, — bought
Wi' twa pund Scots,[†] ('twas a' her riches),
Wad ever grac'd a dance of witches!

But here my Muse her wing maun cour;* — fold
Sic flights are far beyond her pow'r;
To sing how Nannie lap and flang,[†]
(A souple jade she was, and strang),
And how *Tam* stood, like ane bewitch'd,
And thought his very een enrich'd;
Even Satan glowr'd, and fidg'd fu' fain,[†]
And hotch'd* and blew wi' might and main: — jerked
Till first ae caper, syne* anither, — then
*Tam* tint* his reason a' thegither, — lost
And roars out, 'Weel done, Cutty-sark!'
And in an instant all was dark:
And scarcely had he Maggie rallied,
When out the hellish legion sallied.

As bees bizz out wi' angry fyke,* — fuss
When plundering herds* assail their byke,* — herdsmen, hive
As open pussie's* mortal foes, — hare
When, pop! she starts before their nose;
As eager runs the market-crowd,
When 'Catch the thief!' resounds aloud;
So Maggie runs, the witches follow,
Wi' mony an eldritch* skreech and hollow. — unearthly

Ah, *Tam*! Ah, *Tam*! thou'll get thy fairin!* — deserts
In hell they'll roast thee like a herrin!
In vain thy *Kate* awaits thy comin!
*Kate* soon will be a woefu' woman!
Now, do thy speedy utmost, Meg,
And win the key-stane of the brig* ; — bridge
There at them thou thy tail may toss,
A running stream they dare na cross.
But ere the key-stane she could make,
The fient a[†] tail she had to shake!
For Nannie, far before the rest,

---

*twa pund Scots* several shillings sterling
*lap and flang* leaped and flung herself
*fidg'd fu' fain* twitched eagerly
*The fient a* the devil a; none

Hard upon noble Maggie prest,
And flew at *Tam* wi' furious ettle* ; intent
But little wist she Maggie's mettle –
Ae spring brought off her master hale,
But left behind her ain gray tail:
The carlin claught* her by the rump, clutched
And left poor Maggie scarce a stump.

Now, wha this tale o' truth shall read,
Ilk man and mother's son, take heed:
Whene'er to drink you are inclin'd,
Or cutty-sarks run in your mind,
Think, ye may buy the joys o'er dear,
Remember Tam o' Shanter's mare.

1790 1791

## SONG. AE FOND KISS

Ae fond kiss, and then we sever;
Ae fareweel, and then for ever!
Deep in heart-wrung tears I'll pledge thee,
Warring sighs and groans I'll wage thee. –

Who shall say that Fortune grieves him,
While the star of hope she leaves him:
Me, nae chearful twinkle lights me;
Dark despair around benights me. –

I'll ne'er blame my partial fancy,
Naething could resist my Nancy:
But to see her, was to love her;
Love but her, and love for ever. –

Had we never lov'd sae kindly,
Had we never lov'd sae blindly!
Never met – or never parted,
We had ne'er been broken-hearted. –

Fare-thee-weel, thou first and fairest!
Fare-thee-weel, thou best and dearest!
Thine be ilka joy and treasure,
Peace, Enjoyment, Love and Pleasure! –

Ae fond kiss, and then we sever!
Ae fareweel, Alas, for ever!
Deep in heart-wrung tears I'll pledge thee,
Warring sighs and groans I'll wage thee. –

1791 1792

# SONG. A RED RED ROSE

O my Luve's like a red, red rose,
  That 's newly sprung in June;
O my Luve's like the melodie
  That 's sweetly play'd in tune. –

As fair art thou, my bonie lass,
  So deep in luve am I;
And I will love thee still, my Dear,
  Till a' the seas gang dry. –

Till a' the seas gang dry, my Dear,
  And the rocks melt wi' the sun:
I will love thee still, my Dear,
  While the sands o' life shall run. –

And fare thee weel, my only Luve!
  And fare thee weel, a while!
And I will come again, my Luve,
Tho' it were ten thousand mile!

1794

## SONG. FOR A' THAT AND A' THAT –

Is there, for honest Poverty
That hings his head, and a' that;
The coward-slave, we pass him by,
We dare be poor for a' that!
For a' that, and a' that,
Our toils obscure, and a' that,
The rank is but the guinea's stamp,
The Man 's the gowd* for a' that. – gold

What though on hamely fare we dine,
Wear hoddin† grey, and a' that.
Gie fools their silks, and knaves their wine,
A Man 's a Man for a' that.
For a' that, and a' that,
Their tinsel show, and a' that;
The honest man, though e'er sae poor,
Is king o' men for a' that. –

Ye see yon birkie† ca'd, a lord,
Wha struts, and stares, and a' that,
Though hundreds worship at his word,
He's but a coof* for a' that. fool
For a' that, and a' that,
His ribband, star and a' that,
The man of independant mind,
He looks and laughs at a' that. –

A prince can mak a belted knight,
A marquis, duke, and a' that;
But an honest man's aboon his might,
Gude faith he mauna fa'† that!
For a' that, and a' that,
Their dignities, and a' that,
The pith o' Sense, and pride o' Worth,
Are higher rank than a' that. –

Then let us pray that come it may,
As come it will for a' that,

*hoddin* coarse cloth
*birkie* lively man, with the trappings of high rank (l.22)
*mauna fa'* must not claim

That Sense and Worth, o'er a' the earth
Shall bear the gree,† and a' that.
For a' that, and a' that,
Its comin yet for a' that,
That Man to Man the warld o'er,
Shall brothers be for a' that. –

1795

*gree* highest degree

# William Beckford

1760–1844

A wealthy exotic, MP, and son of a Lord Mayor of London, Beckford spent two of his several periods on the Continent after sexual scandals (the second homosexual). On his return, he spent a fortune on his Gothic mansion, Fonthill Abbey in Wiltshire, whose huge octagonal tower collapsed shortly after its sale in 1822 for £300,000. His tower at the top of Lansdown Road, Bath, still stands. His travel books are overshadowed by *Vathek* (1786), written in French, and translated by Samuel Henley. This oriental tale relates the Caliph's quest for knowledge and sensual experience through acts of barbarism described with a deadpan wit, which finally gives way to a horrific exposure of the price of forbidden knowledge. Here, Vathek's mother Carathis prepares in the tower a sacrifice to the supernatural powers of the cruel Giaour. Morakanabad is his prime vizir, Bababalouk his chief eunuch.

## *From* VATHEK

### *[Sacrifice to the Giaour]*

By secret stairs, contrived within the thickness of the wall, and known only to herself and her son, she first repaired to the mysterious recesses in which were deposited the mummies that had been wrested from the catacombs of the ancient Pharaohs. Of these she ordered several to be taken. From thence, she resorted to a gallery; where, under the guard of fifty female negroes mute and blind of the right eye, were preserved the oil of the most venomous serpents; rhinoceros' horns; and woods of a subtle and penetrating odour, procured from the interior of the Indies, together with a thousand other horrible rarities. This collection had been formed for a purpose like the present, by Carathis herself; from a presentiment, that she might one day enjoy some intercourse with the infernal powers: to whom she had ever been passionately attached, and to whose taste she was no stranger.

To familiarise herself the better with the horrors in view, the Princess remained in the company of her negresses, who squinted in the most amiable manner from the only eye they had; and leered with exquisite delight, at the skulls and skeletons which Carathis had drawn forth from her cabinets; all of them making the most frightful contortions and uttering such shrill chatterings, that the Princess, stunned by them and suffocated by the potency of the exhalations, was forced to quit the gallery, after stripping it of a part of its abominable treasures.

Whilst she was thus occupied, the Caliph, who instead of the visions he expected, had acquired in these unsubstantial regions a voracious appetite, was greatly provoked at the mutes. For having totally forgotten their deafness, he had impatiently asked them for food; and seeing them regardless of his demand, he began to cuff, pinch, and bite them, till Carathis arrived to terminate a scene so indecent, to the great content of these miserable creatures: 'Son! what means all this?' said she, panting for breath. 'I thought I heard as I came up, the shrieks of a thousand bats, torn from their crannies in the recesses of a cavern; and it was the outcry only of these poor mutes, whom you were so unmercifully abusing. In truth, you but ill deserve the admirable provision I have brought you.' – 'Give it me instantly,' exclaimed the Caliph; 'I am perishing for hunger!' – 'As to that,' answered she, 'you must have an excellent stomach if it can digest what I have brought.' – 'Be quick,' replied the Caliph; – 'but oh heavens! what horrors! what do you intend?' 'Come; come;' returned Carathis, 'be not so squeamish; but help me to arrange every thing properly; and you shall see that what you reject with such symptoms of disgust will soon complete your felicity. Let us get ready the pile, for the sacrifice of tonight; and think not of eating, till that is performed: know you not, that all solemn rites ought to be preceded by a rigorous abstinence?'

The Caliph, not daring to object, abandoned himself to grief and the wind that ravaged his entrails, whilst his mother went forward with the requisite operations. Phials of serpents' oil, mummies, and bones, were soon set in order on the balustrade of the tower. The pile began to rise; and in three hours was twenty cubits high. At length darkness approached, and Carathis, having stripped herself to her inmost garment, clapped her hands in an impulse of ecstasy; the mutes followed her example; but Vathek, extenuated[†] with hunger and impatience, was unable to support himself, and fell down in a swoon. The sparks had already kindled the dry wood; the venomous oil burst into a thousand blue flames; the mummies, dissolving, emitted a thick dun vapour; and the rhinoceros' horns, beginning to consume; all together diffused such a stench, that the Caliph, recovering, started from his trance, and gazed wildly on the scene in full blaze around him. The oil gushed forth in a plenitude of streams; and the negresses, who supplied it without intermission, united their cries to those of the Princess. At last, the fire

*extenuated* weakened

became so violent, and the flames reflected from the polished marble so dazzling, that the Caliph, unable to withstand the heat and the blaze, effected his escape; and took shelter under the imperial standard.

In the meantime, the inhabitants of Samarah, scared at the light which shone over the city, arose in haste; ascended their roofs; beheld the tower on fire, and hurried, half-naked to the square. Their love for their sovereign immediately awoke; and, apprehending him in danger of perishing in his tower, their whole thoughts were occupied with the remains of his safety. Morakanabad flew from his retirement, wiped away his tears, and cried out for water like the rest. Bababalouk, whose olfactory nerves were more familiarised to magical odours, readily conjecturing, that Carathis was engaged in her favourite amusements, strenuously exhorted them not to be alarmed. Him, however, they treated as an old poltroon, and styled him a rascally traitor. The camels and dromedaries were advancing with water; but, no one knew by which way to enter the tower. Whilst the populace was obstinate in forcing the doors, a violent north-east wind drove an immense volume of flame against them. At first, they recoiled, but soon came back with redoubled zeal. At the same time, the stench of the horns and mummies increasing, most of the crowd fell backward in a state of suffocation. Those that kept their feet mutually wondered at the cause of the smell; and admonished each other to retire. Morakanabad, more sick than the rest, remained in a piteous condition. Holding his nose with one hand, every one persisted in his efforts with the other to burst open the doors and obtain admission. A hundred and forty of the strongest and most resolute, at length accomplished their purpose. Having gained the staircase, by their violent exertions, they attained a great height in a quarter of an hour.

Carathis, alarmed at the signs of her mutes, advanced to the staircase; went down a few steps, and heard several voices calling out from below: 'You shall, in a moment have water!' Being rather alert, considering her age, she presently regained the top of the tower; and bade her son suspend the sacrifice for some minutes; adding, – 'We shall soon be enabled to render it more grateful. Certain dolts of your subjects, imagining no doubt that we were on fire, have been rash enough to break through those doors, which had hitherto remained inviolate; for the sake of bringing up water. They are very kind, you must allow, so soon to forget the wrongs you have done them; but that is of little moment. Let us offer them to the Giaour – let them come up; our mutes, who neither want strength nor experience, will soon dispatch them; exhausted as they are, with fatigue.' – 'Be it so,' answered the Caliph, 'provided we finish, and I dine.' In fact, these good people, out of breath from ascending fifteen hundred stairs in such haste; and chagrined, at having spilt, by the way, the water they had taken, were no sooner arrived at the top, than the blaze of the flames, and the fumes of the mummies, at once overpowered their senses. It was a pity! for they beheld not the agreeable smile, with which the mutes and negresses adjusted the cord to their necks: these amiable personages rejoiced, however, no less at the scene. Never before had the ceremony of strangling been performed with so much facility. They all fell, without the least resistance or struggle: so that Vathek, in the space of a few moments, found himself surrounded by the dead bodies of the most faithful of his subjects; all which were thrown on the top of the pile. Carathis, whose presence of mind never forsook her, perceiving that she had carcasses sufficient to complete her oblation,† commanded the chains to be stretched across the staircase, and the iron doors barricaded, that no more might come up.

No sooner were these orders obeyed, than the tower shook; the dead bodies vanished in the flames; which, at once, changed from a swarthy crimson, to a bright rose colour: an ambient vapour emitted the most exquisite fragrance; the marble columns rang with harmonious sounds, and the liquified horns diffused a delicious perfume. Carathis, in transports, anticipated the success of her enterprise; whilst her mutes and negresses, to whom these sweets had given the cholic, retired grumbling to their cells.

Scarcely were they gone, when, instead of the pile, horns, mummies and ashes, the Caliph both saw and felt, with a degree of pleasure which he could not express, a table, covered with the most magnificent repast: flaggons of wine, and vases of exquisite sherbet reposing on snow. He availed himself, without scruple, of such an entertainment; and had already laid hands on a lamb stuffed with pistachios, whilst Carathis was privately drawing from a filigree urn, a parchment that seemed to be endless; and which had escaped the notice of her son. Totally occupied in gratifying an importunate appetite, he left her to peruse it without interruption; which having finished, she said to him, in an authoritative tone, 'Put an end to your gluttony, and hear the splendid promises with which you are favoured!' She then read, as follows: 'Vathek, my well-beloved, thou hast surpassed my hopes: my nostrils have been regaled by the savour of thy mummies, thy horns; and, still more by the lives, devoted on the pile. At the full of the moon, cause the bands of thy musicians, and thy tymbals,† to be heard; depart from thy palace, surrounded by all the pageants of majesty; thy most faithful slaves, thy best beloved wives; thy most magnificent litters; thy richest loaden camels; and set forward on thy way to Istakhar.† There, I await thy coming: that is the region of wonders: there shalt thou

*oblation* offering
*tymbals* tambourines
*Istakhar* ruined capital of Persia

receive the diadem of Gian Ben Gian; the talismans† of Soliman; and the treasures of the pre-adamite sultans: there shalt thou be solaced with all kinds of delight. – But, beware how thou enterest any dwelling on thy route; or thou shalt feel the effects of my anger.'

The Caliph, notwithstanding his habitual luxury, had never before dined with so much satisfaction. He gave full scope to the joy of these golden tidings; and betook himself to drinking anew. Carathis, whose antipathy to wine was by no means insuperable, failed not to pledge him at every bumper he ironically† quaffed to the health of Mahomet. This infernal liquor completed their impious temerity, and prompted them to utter a profusion of blasphemies. They gave a loose to their wit, at the expense of the ass of Balaam, the dog of the seven sleepers, and the other animals admitted into the paradise of Mahomet. In this sprightly humour, they descended the fifteen hundred stairs. . . .

1786

*talismans* objects controlling supernatural powers

*ironically* Muslims are forbidden alcohol

# Matthew Gregory Lewis

1775–1818

By the age of twenty-one, Lewis had attended Oxford, visited Weimar and met Goethe, been attached to Britain's embassy in Holland, written *The Monk* (publ. 1796), and become an MP. He knew Scott and, later, Byron and Shelley. His dramas and other tales of terror were overshadowed by his most notorious essay in the 'gothic' novel, which he censored after attacks by Coleridge and others. *The Monk* relates the moral disintegration of a Spanish cleric, who in ignorance rapes his sister and murders her and his mother, and is finally destroyed in his pride by Lucifer.

## *From* THE MONK†

### *[The Invocation of Lucifer]*

She had quitted her religious habit: she was now clothed in a long sable robe, on which was traced in gold embroidery a variety of unknown characters: it was fastened by a girdle of precious stones, in which was fixed a poignard. Her neck and arms were uncovered. In her hand she bore a golden wand. Her hair was loose and flowed wildly upon her shoulders; her eyes sparkled with terrific expression; and her whole demeanour was calculated to inspire the beholder with awe and admiration.

'Follow me!' she said to the Monk in a low and solemn voice; 'all is ready!'

His limbs trembled, while he obeyed her. She led him through various narrow passages; and on every side as they passed along, the beams of the lamp displayed none but the most revolting objects: skulls, bones, graves, and images whose eyes seemed to glare on them with horror and surprise. At length they reached a spacious cavern, whose lofty roof the eye sought in vain to discover. A profound obscurity hovered through the void. Damp vapours struck cold to the Friar's heart; and

---

*The Monk* The protagonist, Ambrosio, has been seduced from his vows by Matilda, disguised as a novice monk. To further his lust for Antonia, who will turn out to be his sister, Matilda invokes demonic powers in the sepulchre

he listened sadly to the blast, while it howled along the lonely vaults. Here Matilda stopped. She turned to Ambrosio. His cheeks and lips were pale with apprehension. By a glance of mingled scorn and anger she reproved his pusillanimity, but she spoke not. She placed the lamp upon the ground, near the basket. She motioned that Ambrosio should be silent, and began the mysterious rites. She drew a circle round him, another round herself, and then taking a small phial from the basket, poured a few drops upon the ground before her. She bent over the place, muttered some indistinct sentences, and immediately a pale sulphurous flame arose from the ground. It increased by degrees, and at length spread its waves over the whole surface, the circles alone excepted in which stood Matilda and the Monk. It then ascended the huge columns of unhewn stone, glided along the roof, and formed the cavern into an immense chamber totally covered with blue trembling fire. It emitted no heat: on the contrary, the extreme chillness of the place seemed to augment with every moment. Matilda continued her incantations: at intervals she took various articles from the basket, the nature and name of most of which were unknown to the Friar: but among the few which he distinguished, he particularly observed three human fingers, and an Agnus Dei† which she broke in pieces. She threw them all into the flames which burned before her, and they were instantly consumed.

The Monk beheld her with anxious curiosity. Suddenly she uttered a loud and piercing shriek. She appeared to be seized with an access of delirium; she tore her hair, beat her bosom, used the most frantic gestures, and drawing the poignard from her girdle plunged it into her left arm. The blood gushed out plentifully, and as she stood on the brink of the circle, she took care that it should fall on the outside. The flames retired from the spot on which the blood was pouring. A volume of dark clouds rose slowly from the ensanguined earth, and ascended gradually, till it reached the vault of the cavern. At the same time a clap of thunder was heard: the echo pealed fearfully along the subterraneous passages, and the ground shook beneath the feet of the enchantress.

It was now that Ambrosio repented of his rashness. The solemn singularity of the charm had prepared him for something strange and horrible. He waited with fear for the Spirit's appearance, whose coming was announced by thunder and earthquakes. He looked wildly round him, expecting that some dreadful apparition would meet his eyes, the sight of which would drive him mad. A cold shivering seized his body, and he sank upon one knee, unable to support himself.

'He comes!' exclaimed Matilda in a joyful accent.

---

*Agnus Dei* image of the Lamb of God

Ambrosio started, and expected the Dæmon with terror. What was his surprise, when the thunder ceasing to roll, a full strain of melodious music sounded in the air. At the same time the cloud dispersed, and he beheld a figure more beautiful, than fancy's pencil ever drew. It was a youth seemingly scarce eighteen, the perfection of whose form and face was unrivalled. He was perfectly naked: a bright star sparkled upon his forehead; two crimson wings extended themselves from his shoulders; and his silken locks were confined by a band of many-coloured fires, which played round his head, formed themselves into a variety of figures, and shone with a brilliance far surpassing that of precious stones. Circlets of diamonds were fastened round his arms and ankles, and in his right hand he bore a silver branch, imitating myrtle. His form shone with dazzling glory: he was surrounded by clouds of rose-coloured light, and at the moment that he appeared, a refreshing air breathed perfumes through the cavern. Enchanted at a vision so contrary to his expectations, Ambrosio gazed upon the Spirit with delight and wonder: yet however beautiful the figure, he could not but remark a wildness in the Dæmon's eyes, and a mysterious melancholy impressed upon his features, betraying the Fallen Angel, and inspiring the spectators with secret awe.

The music ceased. Matilda addressed herself to the Spirit: she spoke in a language unintelligible to the Monk, and was answered in the same. She seemed to insist upon something, which the Dæmon was unwilling to grant. He frequently darted upon Ambrosio angry glances, and at such times the Friar's heart sank within him. Matilda appeared to grow incensed. She spoke in a loud and commanding tone, and her gestures declared, that she was threatening him with her vengeance. Her menaces had the desired effect: the Spirit sank upon his knee, and with a submissive air presented to her the branch of myrtle. No sooner had she received it, than the music was again heard; a thick cloud spread itself over the apparition; the blue flames disappeared, and total obscurity reigned through the cave. The Abbot moved not from his place: his faculties were all bound up in pleasure, anxiety, and surprise. At length the darkness dispersing, he perceived Matilda standing near him in her religious habit, with the myrtle in her hand. No traces of the incantation, and the vaults were only illuminated by the faint rays of the sepulchral lamp.

'I have succeeded,' said Matilda, 'though with more difficulty than I expected. Lucifer, whom I summoned to my assistance, was at first unwilling to obey my commands: to enforce his compliance I was constrained to have recourse to my strongest charms. They have produced the desired effect, but I have engaged never more to invoke his agency in your favour. Beware then, how you employ an opportunity which never will return. My magic arts will now be of no use to you:

in future you can only hope for supernatural aid, by invoking the Dæmons yourself, and accepting the conditions of their service. This you will never do: you want strength of mind to force them to obedience, and unless you pay their established price, they will not be your voluntary servants. In this one instance they consent to obey you: I offer you the means of enjoying your mistress, and be careful not to lose the opportunity. Receive this constellated myrtle: while you bear this in your hand, every door will fly open to you. It will procure you access tomorrow night to Antonia's chamber: then breathe upon it thrice, pronounce her name, and place it upon her pillow. A death-like slumber will immediately seize upon her, and deprive her of the power of resisting your attempts. Sleep will hold her till break of morning. In this state you may satisfy your desires without danger of being discovered; since when day-light shall dispel the effects of the enchantment, Antonia will perceive her dishonour, but be ignorant of the ravisher. Be happy then, my Ambrosio, and let this service convince you, that my friendship is disinterested and pure. The night must be near expiring: let us return to the Abbey, lest our absence should create surprise.'

The Abbot received the talisman with silent gratitude. His ideas were too much bewildered by the adventures of the night, to permit his expressing his thanks audibly, or indeed as yet to feel the whole value of her present. Matilda took up her lamp and basket, and guided her companion from the mysterious cavern. . . .

[In the same sepulchre, unknown to the cavalier Lorenzo, his sister, a nun, has been imprisoned by her Prioress for the disgrace of her baby, now dead. Lorenzo sees a spark of light]

## *[The Prisoner in the Sepulchre]*

It proceeded from a small lamp which was placed upon an heap of stones, and whose faint and melancholy rays served rather to point out, than dispel the horrors of a narrow gloomy dungeon formed in one side of the cavern; it also showed several other recesses of similar construction, but whose depth was buried in obscurity. Coldly played the light upon the damp walls, whose dew-stained surface gave back a feeble reflection. A thick and pestilential fog clouded the height of the vaulted dungeon. As Lorenzo advanced, he felt a piercing chillness spread itself through his veins. The frequent groans still engaged him to move forwards. He turned towards them, and by the lamp's glimmering beams beheld in a corner of this loathsome abode, a creature stretched upon a bed of straw, so wretched, so emaciated, so pale, that he doubted to think her woman. She was half-naked: her long dishevelled hair fell in disorder over her face, and almost entirely concealed it. One wasted arm hung listlessly upon a tattered rug, which covered her convulsed and shivering limbs: the other was wrapped round a small bundle, and held it closely to her bosom. A large rosary lay near her: opposite to her was a crucifix, on which she bent her sunk eyes fixedly, and by her side stood a basket and a small earthen pitcher.

Lorenzo stopped: he was petrified with horror. He gazed upon the miserable object with disgust and pity. He trembled at the spectacle; he grew sick at heart: his strength failed him, and his limbs were unable to support his weight. He was obliged to lean against the low wall which was near him, unable to go forward, or to address the sufferer. She cast her eyes towards the staircase: The wall concealed Lorenzo, and she observed him not.

'No one comes!' she at length murmured.

As she spoke, her voice was hollow, and rattled in her throat: she sighed bitterly.

'No one comes!' she repeated; 'No! They have forgotten me! They will come no more!'

She paused for a moment: then continued mournfully.

'Two days! Two long, long days, and yet no food! And yet no hope, no comfort! Foolish woman! How can I wish to lengthen a life so wretched! Yet such a death! O! God! To perish by such a death! To linger out such ages in torture! Till now, I knew not what it was to hunger! Hark! No. No one comes! They will come no more!'

She was silent. She shivered, and drew the rug over her naked shoulders.

'I am very cold! I am still unused to the damps of this dungeon! 'Tis strange: but no matter. Colder shall I soon be, and yet not feel it – I shall be cold, cold as thou art!'

She looked at the bundle, which lay upon her breast. She bent over it, and kissed it: then drew back hastily, and shuddered with disgust.

'It was once so sweet! It would have been so lovely, so like him! I have lost it for ever! How a few days have changed it! I should not know it again myself! Yet it is dear to me! God! how dear! I will forget what it is: I will only remember what it was, and love it as well, as when it was so sweet! so lovely! so like him! I thought, that I had wept away all my tears, but here is one still lingering.'

She wiped her eyes with a tress of her hair. She put out her hand for the pitcher, and reached it with difficulty. She cast into it a look of hopeless enquiry. She sighed, and replaced it upon the ground.

'Quite a void! Not a drop! Not one drop left to cool my scorched-up burning palate! Now would I give treasures for a draught of water! And they are God's servants, who make me suffer thus! They think themselves holy, while they torture me like fiends! They are cruel and unfeeling; and 'tis they who bid me repent; and 'tis they, who threaten me with eternal perdition! Saviour, Saviour! You think not so!'

She again fixed her eyes upon the crucifix, took her rosary, and while she told her beads, the quick motion of her lips declared her to be praying with fervency.

While he listened to her melancholy accents, Lorenzo's sensibility became yet more violently affected. The first sight of such misery had given a sensible shock to his feelings: but that being past, he now advanced towards the captive. She heard his steps, and uttering a cry of joy, dropped the rosary.

'Hark! Hark! Hark!' She cried: 'Some one comes!'

She strove to raise herself, but her strength was unequal to the attempt: she fell back, and as she sank again upon the bed of straw, Lorenzo heard the rattling of heavy chains. He still approached, while the prisoner thus continued.

'Is it you, Camilla? You are come then at last? Oh! it was time! I thought that you had forsaken me; that I was doomed to perish of hunger. Give me to drink, Camilla, for pity's sake! I am faint with long fasting, and grown so weak that I cannot raise myself from the ground. Good Camilla, give me to drink, lest I expire before you!'

Fearing that surprise in her enfeebled state might be fatal, Lorenzo was at a loss how to address her.

'It is not Camilla,' said he at length, speaking in a slow and gentle voice.

'Who is it then?' replied the sufferer: 'Alix, perhaps, or Violante. My eyes are grown so dim and feeble, that I cannot distinguish your features. But whichever it is, if your breast is sensible of the least compassion, if you are not more cruel than wolves and tigers, take pity on my sufferings. You know, that I am dying for want of sustenance. This is the third day, since these lips have received nourishment. Do you bring me food? Or come you only to announce my death, and learn how long I have yet to exist in agony?'

'You mistake my business,' replied Lorenzo; 'I am no emissary of the cruel Prioress. I pity your sorrows, and come hither to relieve them.'

'To relieve them?' repeated the captive; 'Said you, to relieve them?'

At the same time starting from the ground, and supporting herself upon her hands, She gazed upon the stranger earnestly.

'Great God! It is no illusion! A man! Speak! Who are you? What brings you hither? Come you to save me, to restore me to liberty, to life and light? Oh! speak, speak quickly, lest I encourage an hope whose disappointment will destroy me.'

'Be calm!' replied Lorenzo in a voice soothing and compassionate; 'The Domina of whose cruelty you complain, has already paid the forfeit of her offences: You have nothing more to fear from her. A few minutes will restore you to liberty, and the embraces of your friends from whom you have been secluded. You may rely upon my protection. Give me your hand, and be not fearful. Let me conduct you where you may receive those attentions which your feeble state requires.'

'Oh! Yes! Yes! Yes!' cried the prisoner with an exulting shriek; 'There is a God then, and a just one! Joy! Joy! I shall once more breath the fresh air, and view the light of the glorious sunbeams! I will go with you! Stranger, I will go with you! Oh! Heaven will bless you for pitying an unfortunate! But this too must go with me,' She added pointing to the small bundle, which she still clasped to her bosom; 'I cannot part with this. I will bear it away: It shall convince the world, how dreadful are the abodes so falsely termed religious. Good stranger, lend me your hand to rise: I am faint with want, and sorrow, and sickness, and my forces have quite forsaken me! So, that is well!'

As Lorenzo stooped to raise her, the beams of the lamp struck full upon his face.

'Almighty God!' she exclaimed; 'It is possible! That look! those features! Oh! Yes, it is, it is. . . .'

She extended her arms to throw them round him; But her enfeebled frame was unable to sustain the emotions, which agitated her bosom. She fainted, and again sank upon the bed of straw. . . .

## *[The nun-mother tells of her imprisonment]*

'Thus did I drag on a miserable existence. Far from growing familiar with my prison, I beheld it every moment with new horror. The cold seemed more piercing and bitter, the air more thick and pestilential. My frame became weak, feverish, and emaciated. I was unable to rise from the bed of straw, and exercise my limbs in the narrow limits, to which the length of my chain permitted me to move. Though exhausted, faint, and weary, I trembled to profit by the approach of sleep: my slumbers were constantly interrupted by some obnoxious insect crawling over me. Sometimes I felt the bloated toad, hideous and pampered with the poisonous vapours of the dungeon, dragging his loathsome length along my bosom: sometimes the quick cold lizard roused me leaving his slimy track upon my face, and entangling itself in the tresses of my wild and matted hair: often have I at waking found my fingers ringed with the long worms, which bred in the corrupted flesh of my infant. At such times I shrieked with terror and disgust, and while I shook off the reptile, trembled with all a woman's weakness. . . .'

1796

# Jane Austen

## 1775–1817

Jane Austen's great period belongs to the nineteenth century; but in her early teens she was evidently an avid reader and critic of contemporary fiction, whose absurdities get short shrift in her juvenile writing. In 'Love and Friendship' (written by age 15), the teenage narrator Laura and her friend Sophia ('all Sensibility and Feeling') are staying with Sophia's cousin Macdonald, whose daughter Janetta they encourage to desert her suitor Graham and elope with Captain McKenzie. (The text is partly modernised.)

### *From* LOVE AND FRIENDSHIP

They had been gone nearly a couple of hours, before either Macdonald or Graham had entertained any suspicion of the affair –. And they might not even then have suspected it, but for the following little accident. Sophia happening one day to open a private drawer in Macdonald's library with one of her own keys, discovered that it was the place where he kept his papers of consequence & amongst them some bank notes of considerable amount. This discovery she imparted to me; and having agreed together that it would be a proper treatment of so vile a wretch as Macdonald to deprive him of money, perhaps dishonestly gained, it was determined that the next time we should either of us happen to go that way, we would take one or more of the bank notes from the drawer. This well-meant plan we had often successfully put in execution; but alas! on the very day of Janetta's escape, as Sophia was majestically removing the 5th bank-note from the drawer to her own purse, she was suddenly most impertinently interrupted in her employment by the entrance of Macdonald himself, in a most abrupt & precipitate manner. Sophia (who though naturally all winning sweetness could when occasions demanded it call forth the dignity of her sex) instantly put on a most forbiding look, & darting an angry frown on the undaunted culprit, demanded in a haughty tone of voice 'Wherefore her retirement was thus insolently broken in on?' The unblushing Macdonald, without even endeavouring to exculpate himself from the crime he was charged with, meanly endeavoured to reproach Sophia with ignobly defrauding him of his money. The dignity of Sophia was wounded; 'Wretch (exclaimed she, hastily replacing the bank-note in the drawer) how darest thou to accuse me of an act, of which the bare idea makes me blush?' The base wretch was still unconvinced & continued to upbraid the justly-offended Sophia in such opprobrious language, that at length he so greatly provoked the gentle sweetness of her nature, as to induce her to revenge herself on him by informing him of Janetta's elopement, and of the active part we had both taken in the affair. At this period of their quarrel I entered the library and was as you may imagine equally offended as Sophia at the ill-grounded accusations of the malevolent and contemptible Macdonald. 'Base Miscreant (cried I) how canst thou thus undauntedly endeavour to sully the spotless reputation of such bright excellence? Why dost thou not suspect *my* innocence as soon?' 'Be satisfied Madam (replied he) I *do* suspect it, & therefore must desire that you will both leave this house in less than half an hour.'

'We shall go willingly; (answered Sophia) our hearts have long detested thee, & nothing but our freindship for thy daughter could have induced us to remain so long beneath thy roof.'

'Your freindship for my Daughter has indeed been most powerfully exerted by throwing her into the arms of an unprincipled Fortune-hunter.' (replied he)

'Yes, (exclaimed I) amidst every misfortune, it will afford us some consolation to reflect that by this one act of friendship to Janetta, we have amply discharged every obligation that we have received from her father.'

'It must indeed be a most gratefull reflection, to your exalted minds.' (said he.)

As soon as we had packed up our wardrobe & valuables, we left Macdonald Hall, & after having walked about a mile & a half we sate down by the side of a clear limpid stream to refesh our exhausted limbs. The place was suited to meditation. –. A grove of full-grown elms sheltered us from the East –. A bed of full-grown nettles from the West –. Before us ran the murmuring brook & behind us ran the turn-pike road. We were in a mood for contemplation & in a disposition to enjoy so beautiful a spot. A mutual silence which had for some time reigned between us, was at length broke by my exclaiming –'What a lovely scene! Alas why are not Edward & Augustus here to enjoy its beauties with us?'.

'Ah! my beloved Laura (cried Sophia) for pity's sake forbear recalling to my remembrance the unhappy situation of my imprisoned Husband. Alas, what would I not give to learn the fate of my Augustus! to know if he is still in Newgate,[†] or if he is yet hung. But never shall I be able so far to conquer my tender sensibility as to enquire after him. Oh! do not I beseech you ever let me again hear you repeat his beloved name –. It affects me too deeply –. I cannot bear to hear him mentioned, it wounds my feelings.'

'Excuse me my Sophia for having thus unwillingly offended you –' replied I –and then changing the conversation, desired her to admire the noble grandeur of the elms which sheltered us from the Eastern Zephyr. 'Alas! my Laura (returned she) avoid so melancholy a subject, I intreat you. – Do not again wound my sensibility by observations on those elms. They remind me of Augustus –. He was like them, tall, magestic – he possessed that noble grandeur which you admire in them.'

I was silent, fearfull lest I might any more unwillingly distress her by fixing on any other subject of conversation which might again remind her of Augustus.

'Why do you not speak my Laura?' (said she after a short pause) 'I cannot support this silence – you must not leave me to my own reflections; they ever recur to Augustus.'

'What a beautifull sky! (said I) How charmingly is the azure varied by those delicate streaks of white!'

'Oh! my Laura (replied she hastily withdrawing her eyes from a momentary glance at the sky) do not thus distress me by calling my attention to an object which so cruelly reminds me of my Augustus's blue sattin waistcoat striped with white! In pity to your unhappy friend avoid a subject so distressing.' What could I do? The feelings of Sophia were at that time so exquisite, & the tenderness she felt for Augustus so poignant that I had not the power to start any other topic, justly fearing that it might in some unforseen manner again awaken all her sensibility by directing her thoughts to her Husband. – Yet to be silent would be cruel; She had intreated me to talk.

From this dilemma I was most fortunately releived by an accident truly apropos; it was the lucky overturning of a gentleman's phaeton,[†] on the road which ran murmuring behind us. It was a most fortunate accident as it diverted the attention of Sophia from the melancholy reflections which she had been before indulging. We instantly quitted our seats & ran to the rescue of those who but a few moments before had been in so elevated a situation as a fashionably high phaeton, but who were now laid low and sprawling in the dust –. 'What an ample subject for reflection on the uncertain enjoyments of this world, would not that phaeton & the life of Cardinal Wolsey afford a thinking mind!' said I to Sophia as we were hastening to the field of action.

*Newgate* prison – Augustus has stolen his father's money

*Phaeton* light carriage

She had not time to answer me for every thought was now engaged by the horrid spectacle before us. Two gentlemen most elegantly attired but weltering in their blood was what first struck our eyes – we approached – they were Edward & Augustus – Yes dearest Marianne they were our husbands. Sophia shreiked & fainted on the ground – I screamed and instantly ran mad –. We remained thus mutually deprived of our senses some minutes, & on regaining them were deprived of them again –. For an hour & a quarter did we continue in this unfortunate situation – Sophia fainting every moment & I running mad as often. At length a groan from the hapless Edward (who alone retained any share of life) restored us to ourselves –. Had we indeed before imagined that either of them lived, we should have been more sparing of our greif – but as we had supposed when we first beheld them that they were no more, we knew that nothing could remain to be done but what we were about –. No sooner therefore did we hear my Edward's groan than postponing our lamentations for the present, we hastily ran to the dear Youth and kneeling on each side of him implored him not to die –. 'Laura (said he fixing his now languid eyes on me) I fear I have been overturned.'

I was overjoyed to find him yet sensible –.

'Oh! tell me Edward (said I) tell me I beseech you before you die, what has befallen you since that unhappy day in which Augustus was arrested & we were separated –'

'I will' (said he) and instantly fetching a deep sigh, expired –. Sophia immediately sunk again into a swoon –. *My* greif was more audible, my voice faltered, my eyes assumed a vacant stare, my face became as pale as death, and my senses were considerably impaired –.

'Talk not to me of phaetons (said I, raving in a frantic, incoherent manner) – Give me a violin –. I'll play to him & sooth him in his melancholy hours – Beware ye gentle nymphs of Cupid's thunderbolts, avoid the piercing shafts of Jupiter – look at that grove of firs – I see a leg of mutton – they told me Edward was not dead; but they deceived me – they took him for a cucumber –' Thus I continued wildly exclaiming on my Edward's death –. For two hours did I rave thus madly and should not then have left off, as I was not in the least fatigued, had not Sophia who was just recovered from her swoon, intreated me to consider that night was now approaching and that the damps began to fall. 'And whither shall we go (said I) to shelter us from either'? 'To that white cottage.' (replied she pointing to a neat building which rose up amidst the grove of elms & which I had not before observed –) I agreed & we instantly walked to it – we knocked at the door – it was opened by an old woman; on being requested to afford us a night's lodging, she informed us that her house was but small, that she had only two bed-rooms, but that however we should be wellcome to one of them. We were satisfied & followed the good woman into the house where we were greatly cheered by the sight of a comfortable fire –. She was a widow & had only one daughter, who was then just seventeen – one of the best of ages; but alas! she was very plain & her name was Bridget. . . . Nothing therefore could be expected from her—she could not be supposed to possess either exalted ideas, delicate feelings or refined sensibilities – She was nothing more than a mere good-tempered, civil & obliging young woman; as such we could scarcely dislike her – she was only an object of contempt –.

1790 1922

# Bibliography

References are often given to cheap paperback reprints of standard works which are otherwise only accessible in large libraries.

## *Reference works*

*Annals of English Literature 1745–1950*, 2nd edn (Clarendon Press, Oxford, 1961).
F. W. Bateson and Harrison T. Meserole, *A Guide to English and American Literature*, 3rd edn (Longman, London, 1976).
Samuel Johnson, *Dictionary* (1755); 1 vol. selection by E. L. McAdam and George Milne (Gollancz, London, 1963).
*New Cambridge Bibliography of English Literature*, ed. George Watson, vol. 2, *1660–1800* (Cambridge University Press, 1971).
*Oxford English Dictionary*, 12 vols plus supplements.
*Restoration and 18th-Century Drama*, introd. Arthur H. Scouten (Great Writers Library, Macmillan, London and Basingstoke, 1980).
*Restoration and 18th-Century Prose and Poetry*, introd. Pat Rogers (Great Writers Library, Macmillan, London and Basingstoke, 1983).

## *History*

Maurice Ashley, *England in the Seventeenth Century*, 3rd edn (Penguin, Harmondsworth, 1961).
D. M. George, *England in Transition* (Penguin, Harmondsworth, 1953).
Donald Greene, *The Age of Exuberance: Backgrounds to Eighteenth-Century English Literature* (Random House, New York, 1970).
R. W. Harris, *Reason and Nature in the Eighteenth Century* (Blandford Press, London, 1968).
A. R. Humphreys, *The Augustan World*, revised edn (Methuen, London, 1964).
*New Cambridge Modern History*, relevant volumes.
*Oxford History of England*, relevant volumes.
J. H. Plumb, *England in the Eighteenth Century*, revised edn (Penguin, Harmondsworth, 1963).
Roy Porter, *English Society in the Eighteenth Century* (Penguin, Harmondsworth, 1982).
Pat Rogers, *The Augustan Vision* (Weidenfeld, London, 1974).
Pat Rogers (ed.), *The Context of English Literature: The Eighteenth Century* (Methuen, London, 1978).

James Sambrook, *The Eighteenth Century: The Intellectual and Cultural Context of English Literature, 1700–1789* (Longman, London and New York, 1986).

John Summerson, *Architecture in Britain*, 1530–1830, 5th edn (Pelican History of Art, Penguin, Harmondsworth, 1969).

G. M. Trevelyan, *Illustrated English Social History*, vols 2 and 3, (Penguin, Harmondsworth, 1964).

A. S. Turberville, *English Men and Manners in the Eighteenth Century*, 2nd edn (Clarendon Press, Oxford, 1929).

A. S. Turberville (ed.), *Johnson's England*, 2 vols (Clarendon Press, Oxford, 1933).

Ellis Waterhouse, *Painting in Britain, 1530–1790*, 4th edn (Pelican History of Art, Penguin, Harmondsworth, 1978).

Basil Willey, *The Seventeenth Century Background* (Chatto & Windus, London, 1934).

Basil Willey, *The Eighteenth Century Background* (Chatto & Windus, London, 1940).

Kathleen Williams (ed.), *Backgrounds to Eighteenth-Century Literature* (Chandler, Scranton and London, 1971).

## *Literary History*

John Butt, *The Mid-Eighteenth Century*, ed. Geoffrey Carnall (*Oxford History of English Literature*, Clarendon Press, Oxford, 1979).

*Cambridge History of English Literature*, vols 8–10 (1911–13).

Bonamy Dobrée, *English Literature in the Early Eighteenth Century, 1700–1740* (*Oxford History of English Literature*, Clarendon Press, Oxford, 1959).

Boris Ford (ed.), *From Dryden to Johnson* (New Pelican Guide, Penguin, Harmondsworth, 1982).

Bruce King, *Seventeenth-Century English Literature* (Macmillan History of Literature, London and Basingstoke, 1982).

Roger Lonsdale (ed.), *Dryden to Johnson* (Sphere, London, 1971).

Maximillian E. Novak, *Eighteenth-Century English Literature* (Macmillan History of Literature, London and Basingstoke, 1983).

George Sherburn and Donald F. Bond, *The Restoration and Eighteenth-Century*, 2nd edn (Routledge, London; Meredith, USA, 1967).

James Sutherland, *English Literature of the Late Seventeenth Century* (Oxford History of English Literature, Clarendon Press, Oxford, 1969).

## *Individual Genres*

### Poetry

Donald Davie, *Purity of Diction in English Verse* (Chatto, London, 1952).

Dennis Davison, *The Penguin Book of Eighteenth-Century Verse* (Harmondsworth, 1973).

H. J. C. Grierson and G. Bullough, *The Oxford Book of Seventeenth Century Verse* (Clarendon Press, Oxford, 1934).

Ian Jack, *Augustan Satire* (Clarendon Press, Oxford, 1952).

Samuel Johnson, *Lives of the Poets* (modern selections).

D. W. Lindsay (ed.), *English Poetry 1700–1780* (Dent, London, 1974).

Roger Lonsdale, *The Poems of Gray, Collins, and Goldsmith* (Longman, London, 1969).

Roger Lonsdale, *New Oxford Book of Eighteenth Century Verse* (Oxford University Press, 1984).

*Minor Poets of the Eighteenth Century* (Dent, London, 1930).

Charles Peake (ed.), *Poetry of the Landscape and the Night* (Arnold, London, 1967).

V. de Sola Pinto, *Poetry of the Restoration, 1653–1700* (Heinemann, London, 1966).

Eric Rothstein, *Restoration and Eighteenth-Century Poetry 1660–1780* (Routledge, London, 1981).

James Sutherland, *A Preface to Eighteenth Century Poetry* (Clarendon Press, Oxford, 1948).

There are many authoritative modern texts from Oxford, others include the multi-volume California U. P. Dryden, the Yale *Poems on Affairs of State* and Methuen's Twickenham Pope (1 vol., 1963).

### Fiction

Wayne C. Booth, *The Rhetoric of Fiction* (University of Chicago Press, 1961).

F. W. Bradbrook, *Jane Austen and her Predecessors* (Cambridge University Press, 1966).

A. D. McKillop, *The Early Masters of English Fiction* (University Press of Kansas, Lawrence, 1956).

Ian Watt, *The Rise of the Novel* (Chatto and Windus, London, 1957).

Major series include the Wesleyan Fielding, the Oxford English Novels, Everyman, the Penguin English Library, World's Classics.

### Drama

F. W. Bateson, *English Comic Drama 1700–1750* (Clarendon Press, Oxford, 1929).

F. S. Boas, *An Introduction to Eighteenth Century Drama* (Clarendon Press, Oxford, 1953).

M. R. Booth, *Revels History of Drama in English*, vol. vi, *1750–1880* (1975).

Everyman edition, *The Beggar's Opera and Other Eighteenth-Century Plays* (Dent, London, 1928).

John Loftis, *Comedy and Society from Congreve to Fielding* (Stanford University Press, 1959).

John Loftis, *Revels History of Drama in English*, vol. v, 1660–1750 (1976).

Allardyce Nicoll, *A History of English Drama*, vols 1–3, revised edn (Cambridge University Press, 1952). Covers 1660–1700, 1700–50, 1750–1800.

Simon Trussler (ed.), *Burlesque Plays of the Eighteenth Century* (Oxford University Press, London, 1969).

**Criticism and Other Prose**

J. W. H. Atkins, *English Literary Criticism: 17th & 18th Centuries* (Methuen, London, 1951).

Scott Elledge (ed.), *Eighteenth-Century Critical Essays*, 2 vols (Cornell University Press, Ithaca, 1961).

D. W. Jefferson (ed.), *Pelican Book of English Prose*, vol. 3, *Eighteenth-Century Prose, 1700–1780* (Harmondsworth, 1956).

Arthur Johnston, *Enchanted Ground: The Study of Medieval Romance in the Eighteenth Century* (Athlone Press, London, 1964).

E. D. Jones (ed.), *English Critical Essays* (*Sixteenth, Seventeenth and Eighteenth Centuries*) (Oxford University Press, London, rept. 1963).

Lawrence Lipking, *The Ordering of the Arts in Eighteenth-Century England* (Princeton University Press, 1970).

J. E. Spingarn (ed.), *Critical Essays of the Seventeenth Century*, 3 vols (1908–9; rept. Indiana University Press, Bloomington, 1968).

Peter Ure (ed.), *Pelican Book of English Prose*, vol. 2, *Seventeenth-Century Prose, 1620–1700* (Harmondsworth, 1956).

R. Wellek, *The Rise of English Literary History* (University of North Carolina Press, Chapel Hill, 1941).

R. Wellek, *History of Modern Criticism*, vol. 1, *The Later Eighteenth Century* (Cape, London, 1955).

W. K. Wimsatt and Cleanth Brooks, *Literary Criticism: A Short History*, vol. 2, *Neo-Classical Criticism* (Routledge, London, 1957).

**Readers and Writers**

Alexandre Beljame, *Men of Letters and the English Public in the Eighteenth Century*, 1660–1744 (1881; ed. Bonamy Dobrée, Kegan Paul, London, 1948).

A. S. Collins, *Authorship in the Days of Johnson* (1927).

F. A. Mumby and I. Norrie, *Publishing and Bookselling*, 5th edn (Cape, London, 1974).

Victor E. Neuburg, *Popular Literature: A History and Guide* (Penguin, Harmondsworth, 1977).

Isabel Rivers (ed.), *Books and their Readers in Eighteenth-Century England* (Leicester University Press, 1982).

Pat Rogers, *Grub Street: Studies in a Subculture* (Methuen, London, 1972); (abridged 1980 as *Hacks and Dunces: Pope, Swift and Grub Street*). Also other Rogers works above.

# Index of First Lines

# Index of Authors

# Source List

(Excluding those listed in the Acknowledgements)

**Joseph Addison:** *Critical Essays from 'The Spectator'*, ed. D. F. Bond (Clarendon Press, 1970); **Jane Austen:** *Works, Vol. VI: Minor Works*, ed. R. W. Chapman (OUP, 1954, rev. 1982); **William Beckford:** *Vathek*, ed. R. Lonsdale (OUP, 1970); **James Boswell:** *Life of Johnson* (OUP, rev. 1953); **John Bunyan:** *The Pilgrim's Progress*, ed. R. Sharrock (Clarendon Press, 1960, 2nd edn); **Edmund Burke:** *Philosophical Enquiry into . . . Sublime and Beautiful*, ed. J. T. Boulton (Routledge & Kegan Paul, 1958); **Fanny Burney:** *The Diary of Fanny Burney*, intro, L. Gibbs (J. M. Dent/E. P. Dutton, 1940, rpt 1961); **Robert Burns:** *Poems and Songs*, ed. J. Kingsley (OUP, 1971); **Samuel Butler:** *Hudibras*, ed. J. Wilders (Clarendon Press, 1967); **Lord Chesterfield:** *Letters to his Sons and Daughters* (J. M. Dent/E. P. Dutton, 1929, rpt 1938); **Colley Cibber:** *An Apology for the Life of Colley Cibber*, ed. B. R. S. Fone (University of Michigan Press, 1968); **William Cowper:** *The Poetical Works of William Cowper*, ed. H. S. Milford (OUP, 1934, rpt 1963); **George Crabbe:** *A Selection from George Crabbe*, ed. J. Lucas (Longman, 1967); **Daniel Defoe:** *Robinson Crusoe*, ed. J. D. Crowley (OUP, 1972); **Daniel Defoe:** *Moll Flanders*, ed. G. A. Starr (OUP, 1971); **John Dryden:** *The Poems and Fables of John Dryden*, ed. J. Kinsley (OUP, 1962); **John Dryden:** *Of Dramatic Poesy and Other Critical Essays*, ed. G. Watson (Dent, 1961); **Robert Fergusson:** *Poems by Allan Ramsey and Robert Fergusson*, eds Kinghorn & Law (Scottish Academic Press (Edin), 1974, new edn 1985); **Henry Fielding:** *Joseph Andrews*, ed. M. C. Battestin (Clarendon Press, 1967); **Henry Fielding:** *Tom Jones Vol. 1*, eds M. C. Battestin and F. Bowers (Clarendon Press, 1974); **Henry Fielding:** *Joseph Andrews and Shamela*, ed. A. R. Humphreys (J. M. Dent, 1973); **John Gay:** *The Beggar's Opera*, ed. E. V. Roberts (Edward Arnold, 1969); **Edward Gibbon:** *Decline and Fall of the Roman Empire*, ed. D. M. Low (Chatto & Windus, 1960); **Oliver Goldsmith:** *The Collected Works of Oliver Goldsmith, Vol. 4*, ed. A. Friedman (Clarendon Press, 1966); **Thomas Gray:** *Poetical Works of Gray and Collins*, ed. R. H. Lonsdale (Clarendon Press, 1977); **Thomas Gray:**

*Letters of Thomas Gray*, ed. J. Beresford (OUP, 1925, rpt 1951); **Samuel Johnson:** *Samuel Johnson*, ed. D. Greene (OUP, 1984); **Samuel Johnson:** *Lives of the Poets, Vol. 1* (OUP, 1906, reset 1952); **Samuel Johnson:** From article 'Some Notes on Johnson's Prayers and Meditations' by J. D. Fleeman, *Review of English Studies*, New Series, XIX (OUP, 1968); **Matthew Lewis:** *The Monk*, ed. J. Kinsley and H. Anderson (OUP, 1950); **Henry Mackenzie:** *The Man of Feeling*, ed. B. Vickers (OUP, 1970); **James Macpherson:** *The Poems of Ossian* (Patrick Geddes, 1896); **Lady Mary Wortley Montagu:** *The Selected Letters of Lady Mary Wortley Montagu*, ed. R. Halsband (Longman, 1970); **Lady Mary Wortley Montagu:** *The Complete Letters of Lady Mary Wortley Montagu*, ed. R. Halsband (Clarendon Press, 1965); **Sir Joshua Reynolds:** *Discourses on Art*, ed. R. R. Wark (Yale University Press, 1959, rpt 1975); **Samuel Richardson:** *Pamela* (Penguin, 1980); **Richard B. Sheridan:** *The School for Scandal*, ed. C. J. L. Price (OUP, 1971); **Christopher Smart:** *The Poetical Works of Christopher Smart, Vol. 1*, ed. K. Williamson (Clarendon Press, 1980); **Christopher Smart:** *The Poetical Works of Christopher Smart, Vol. 2*, ed. K. Williamson (Clarendon Press, 1983); **Tobias Smollett:** *Humphry Clinker*, ed. L. M. Knapp (OUP, 1966); **Sir Richard Steele:** *The Spectator*, ed. D. F. Bond (Clarendon Press, 1965); **Laurence Sterne:** *Tristram Shandy*, ed. I. C. Ross (OUP, 1983); **Laurence Sterne:** *A Sentimental Journey*, ed. I. Jack (OUP, 1968); **Jonathan Swift:** *Gulliver's Travels*, ed. A. Ross (Longman, 1972); **Jonathan Swift:** *Jonathan Swift*, eds A. Ross and D. Woolley (OUP, 1984); **James Thomson:** *The Seasons and the Castle of Indolence*, ed. J. Sambrook (Clarendon Press, 1972); **Horace Walpole:** *The Yale Edition of Horace Walpole's Correspondence, Vol. 13*, ed. W. S. Lewis (Yale University Press, 1948, rpt 1970); **Horace Walpole:** *The Yale Edition of Horace Walpole's Correspondence, Vol. 9*, ed. W. S. Lewis (Yale University Press, 1941, rpt 1970); **John Wilmot, Earl of Rochester:** *Poems*, ed. K. Walker (Basil Blackwell, 1984).